The Garland Handbook of Latin American Music

Second Edition

The Garland Handbook of
Latin American Music

Second Edition

Edited by

Dale A. Olsen and Daniel E. Sheehy

Routledge
Taylor & Francis Group

LONDON AND NEW YORK

First published 2000 by Garland Publishing, Inc.
Published 2014 by Routledge
2 Park Square, Milton Park, Abingdon, Oxon OX14 4RN
711 Third Avenue, New York, NY 10017, USA

Routledge is an imprint of the Taylor and Francis Group, an informa business

The Garland Handbook of Latin American Music, second edition, is an abridged paperback edition of
South America, Mexico, Central America, and the Caribbean, volume 2 of *The Garland
Encyclopedia of World Music,* with revised essays

© 2000 Dale A. Olsen and Daniel E. Sheehy; 2008 Taylor & Francis

Typeset in Adobe Garamond and Gill Sans by EvS Communication Networx

Library of Congress Cataloging in Publication Data
A catalog record for this book has been requested

ISBN 978-0-415-96101-1 (pbk)
ISBN 978-0-203-93454-8 (ebk)

1/18 add

TABLE OF CONTENTS

LIST OF AUDIO EXAMPLES ON CD 1 AND CD 2

The following examples are included on the two accompanying audio compact discs packaged with this volume. Track and CD numbers are also indicated on the pages listed below for easy reference to text discussions. Complete notes on each example can be found on pages 537–543.

Compact Disc 1

LIST OF MAPS

LIST OF CONTRIBUTORS

Gage Averill
University of Toronto
Toronto, Canada

Gerard Béhague
University of Texas
Austin, Texas, U.S.A.

Max H. Brandt
University of Pittsburgh
Pittsburgh, Pennsylvania, U.S.A.

John Cohen
Putnam Valley, New York, U.S.A.

Martha Ellen Davis
University of Florida
Gainesville, Florida, U.S.A.

Ercilia Moreno Chá
Instituto Nacional de Antropologia
Buenos Aires, Argentina

J. Richard Haeffer
Arizona State University
Tempe, Arizona, U.S.A.

Linda O'Brien-Rothe
San Pedro School System
San Pedro, California, U.S.A.

Dale A. Olsen
The Florida State University
Tallahassee, Florida, U.S.A.

Suzel Ana Reily
The Queen's University of Belfast
Belfast, Northern Ireland

Carol E. Robertson
Buenos Aires, Argentina

Olavo Alén Rodríguez
Center for Research and Development
    of Cuban Music (CIDMUC)
Havana, Cuba

Raúl R. Romero
Pontifica Universidad Católica del Perú
Lima, Perú

Anthony Seeger
University of California Los Angeles
Los Angeles, California, U.S.A.

Daniel E. Sheehy
Smithsonian Institution
Washington, D.C., U.S.A.

Ronald R. Smith
Indiana University
Bloomington, Indiana, U.S.A.

Sandra Smith
Independent Scholar
California, U.S.A.

Henry Stobart
Cambridge University
Cambridge, England

William David Tompkins
Independent Scholar
Calgary, Alberta, Canada

Héctor Vega Drouet
University of Puerto Rico
San Juan, Puerto Rico

Timothy D. Watkins
Rhodes College
Memphis, Tennessee, U.S.A.

Lois Wilcken
Hunter College
New York, New York, U.S.A.

Holly Wissler
The Florida State University
Tallahassee, Florida, U.S.A.

PREFACE

The many regions that constitute Latin America—that is, the countries and islands in the Western hemisphere that lie south of the United States and use Spanish and/or Portuguese as their major languages—are extremely varied and diverse, as is their musical output. From *tango*, *cuarteto*, and *roc nacional* of Argentina, to *salsa*, *son*, and *merengue* of the Caribbean, from *dakoho*, *huayno*, and *sikuriada* of Amerindian cultures, to the *jarana*, *marimba*, and *chirimía* of Middle Latin America, Latin American music represents a wide range of genres, musical instruments, and styles, and has permeated and influenced civilizations in almost all parts of the globe. *The Garland Handbook of Latin American Music* aims to provide an introduction to these diverse musical sounds and cultures that will be useful for students, scholars, and aficionados of Latin American music. The present Second Edition includes carefully chosen essays from Volume 2 of *The Garland Encyclopedia of World Music*, titled *South America, Mexico, Central America, and the Caribbean*, with articles written by twenty-three scholars who have conducted years of research and fieldwork in their specific areas. Nearly half of the country case study articles were written by scholars from those countries.

HOW THE SECOND EDITION IS ORGANIZED

The Second Edition of *The Garland Handbook of Latin American* Music is organized like the First Edition—that is, into three parts that include introductory chapters in Part 1, essays that focus on issues and processes which have affected the development of music in Latin America in Part 2, and studies of regions, countries, and cultures in Part 3. The Second Edition is, however, greatly expanded and completely revised. The additions are described below.

Each contributing author was encouraged to follow a particular issue-oriented "menu" that includes much of the information generally discussed in Parts 1 and 2, as listed in the

Table of Contents (e.g., geography and demography; indigenous, European, and African heritages; musical instruments; musical genres and contexts; social structure, musicians, and behavior; musical dynamics; learning and music education; governmental policy; and others). Each culture and country entry, therefore, is issue- and process-oriented. In an ethnomusicological way, the essays deal with how music is made by people for themselves, for other people, or for the supernatural. Some entries are naturally more issue- and process-oriented than others, because of the nature of each author's background, training, interests, and knowledge of the total subject matter (each writer carries her/his unique intellectual baggage). Nevertheless, we have aimed for internal consistency in the essays in Part 3.

INTRODUCTION TO THE MUSIC CULTURES OF LATIN AMERICA

Part 1 includes two essays that discuss the diversity of Latin America, its music, and approaches to how Latin American music can be studied. The essay "A Profile of the Lands and People of Latin America" briefly describes the history, geography, demography, and cultural settings of the regions that comprise Latin America. It also includes a list of recent population figures for each of the countries studied (population figures are not included in the country essays). The chapter titled "Studying Latin American Music" discusses some of the basic ways music scholars conduct their research in Latin America, focusing on archaeology, iconography, mythology, history, ethnography, and practice.

ISSUES AND PROCESSES

The first article in Part 2, "The Distribution, Symbolism, and Use of Musical Instruments," reveals the importance of musical material culture in understanding Latin American music. Most music is performed on or accompanied by musical instruments, and because of history, geography, politics, and many other factors, Latin American countries and regions share many music instrument types, but have also developed others that define their uniqueness and individuality.

The following three articles entitled "Musical Genres and Contexts," "Social Structure, Musicians, and Behavior," and "Musical Dynamics" are intended to be both a synthesis of the information in Part 3 and a presentation of new ideas derived from it. The approach of these essays is anthropological, offering students of many backgrounds an opportunity to see how music functions as culture. Part 2 ends with a chapter titled "Music of Immigrant Groups," because Latin America is a land of immigrants, from ancient times to the present.

SELECTED REGIONAL CASE STUDIES

The regions, countries, and cultures discussed in Part 3 are presented in a different order than in the original *Garland Encyclopedia of World Music*, Vol. 2, and there are more countries and cultures included in this Second Edition of the *Handbook* than in the First

Edition. Our rationale is to present them roughly in the way the regions of Latin America were settled, both in antiquity and during the colonial period. This organization also makes it possible to begin with the regions that are possibly best known to readers in the United States because they are the closest in distance and culture (because of immigration) to our country. Thus, both history and geography have influenced the organizational scheme of this volume.

We have chosen to emphasize the information in Part 3 as the main body of *The Garland Handbook of Latin American Music*, and many Latin American countries are included. New to this Second Edition are country chapters on Haiti and Panama. We felt that neither the Dominican Republic nor Cuba should be included without a chapter on Haiti, because of the history, migration, and transculturation in the Greater Antilles, and the important role of Haiti in those processes. Panama is included as the southernmost country of Middle Latin America (or Central America) and because of its unique history as the "crossroads of the world," from ancient times through the present.

Additional chapters have been added on Amerindian musical cultures, including the Tarahumara of Mexico, the Kuna of Panama, and the Mapuche of Argentina (and Chile). Recognizing that Amerindian groups are justifiably nations in their own right, often having their own systems of internal government, religion, and moral codes, we include a total of five essays that provide an overview of several contrasting indigenous cultures from different regions of Latin America (the Warao of Venezuela and Q'eros of Peru are the other two cultures, the latter essay highly revised). Many indigenous cultures are also discussed within the country essays. Another addition is a chapter titled "Afro-Peruvian Musical Traditions," which complements the chapter "Afro-Brazilian Musical Traditions," which, like all the essays, has also been revised and updated.

The South American countries chosen for the *Handbook* are presented more or less geographically from north to south through eastern South America, and from south to north through western South America. Our rationale for this order is to emphasize the commonalities shared by bordering countries. Because of space limitations, it has been impossible to include all the countries of Latin America. It is hoped that interested readers will consult the original *South America, Mexico, Central America, and the Caribbean*, Volume 2 of *The Garland Encyclopedia of World Music* for additional reading.

NEW IN THE SECOND EDITION

The Garland Handbook of Latin American Music has been newly concluded with a "Conclusion" written by Dale Olsen and several of his students from his Music of Latin America class at Florida State University. Incorporating several issue-related ideas, the "Conclusion" includes the following sub headings: "Musical Threads Revisited," "New Wine in Old Bottles," "Cultural Identity vs. Cultural Blurring," and "Looking at the Past, Seeing the Future." These were inspired by critically thinking about the big picture of Latin America, rather than merely enjoying the historical, ethnographic, and sonorous descriptions of particular countries or cultures. It is our major purpose with the *Handbook* to inspire students, scholars, and other readers to think critically about this vitally important region of the world. With that purpose in mind, we have incorporated several "Questions for Critical Thinking" at the ends of the regional sections (Caribbean Latin America, Middle Latin America, South America, and Latin America). The study questions can serve students and teachers alike with thought provoking essay questions, suitable for exams or just mere writing enjoyment.

Also new to the Second Edition is a second CD, which contains audio examples from the Smithsonian-Folkways collection and private collections. See more information below, under the description for the Compact Discs accompanying the book.

Finally, *The Handbook of Latin American Music* now has a companion web site, www.routledge.com/textbooks/9781234567890. This is provided for both teachers and students, and will have several resources: quizzes, sample tests, web links, etc.

ORTHOGRAPHY

Hundreds of languages other than Spanish and Portuguese are spoken in Latin America, and there are many ways to represent them in writing. Often, non-Latin-derived terms are spelled with a modified phonetic alphabet, as in the use of k instead of qu, w rather than gu, gü, or hu, and so forth; the latter forms are derived from Spanish. Nevertheless, certain terms are so fixed in the minds of English readers that we have given spellings in the Spanish style: for example, Inca rather than Inka, *huayno* rather than *wayno*, and *quena* rather than *kena*. We have also chosen to retain the orthography preferred by the authors of particular essays. The large-scale rendering of Amerindian languages, however, is consistent with recent linguistic scholarship. Thus, we have Kechua rather than Quechua and Warao rather than Guarao. Regional varieties will nevertheless occur, as among the Quichua of Ecuador, who speak a dialect of Kechua; the Carib of Venezuela, who speak Karib; and the Guaraní of Paraguay, who speak Tupi-Waraní.

Some authors have chosen to use diacritics to indicate vowel or consonant sounds of particular Native American terms, but none has chosen to use the International Phonetic Alphabet (IPA). Readers can consult an English dictionary to learn how to pronounce vowels that contain diacritic markings. Otherwise, vowel sounds are comparable to Spanish usage. Certain Amerindian languages, however, require additional diacritic markings to represent their sounds properly. Kechua is one of these because of aspirated and explosive consonants. The Kechua-speaking Q'eros, for example, pronounce their name for themselves with an explosive "k" sound not found in English or Spanish. Additionally, some languages have nasal sounds, rendered by the tilde (as in Portuguese): Waiãpi, for example, is pronounced with a nasalized sound on the second "a."

RESEARCH TOOLS

Readers will find research aids throughout the *Handbook*. Maps help locate the places and peoples mentioned in the text; references at the end of each essay specify further readings and recordings to consult. Cross-references to essays in this volume are indicated in small capital letters within brackets. *The Garland Handbook of Latin American Music* provides a wealth of other illustrations, including photographs and song texts.

MUSICAL EXAMPLES

Throughout the *Handbook*, musical examples supplement the verbal representations of musical sound. In all cases, these appear in staff notation or some variation of it. As ethnomusicologists, however, we realize that Western staff notation cannot capture the nuances and subtleties of music sound, although some learning experiences can be gleaned from studying them and even singing them aloud. The majority of them are written in a manner that tries to create a balance between descriptive (what the music is doing) and prescriptive (what you can do with it) music writing. Therefore, they are intended to be singable (depending on how well you read music), and what you sing may give you some idea of what the music sounds like. No musical notation, however, is a substitute for real musical sound. For that reason, two compact discs are included with the *Handbook*, placed inside the back cover.

COMPACT DISCS

The two enclosed compact discs illustrate and supplement many of the essays. Because of the volume's reorganization and the consequent exclusion of essays that pertain to other countries and cultures (e.g., Dutch-, English-, French-, and native-speaking people), the audio examples on the first CD are not always referred to within the main text in the numerical order found on the compact disc. All of the examples on the compact discs, however, are referenced in the margins of the text with a CD icon and track number.

On the first CD we have attempted to incorporate original field recordings by the authors of the essays that represent audio materials not available in commercial stores. The second CD contains audio examples from the Smithsonian-Folkways collection and private collections. We realize that not all countries are equally represented on the enclosed CDs because many excellent commercial recordings are easily accessible (these are listed in "A Guide to Recordings of Latin American Music"). Commercial recordings of Cuban music, for example, are fairly common, while recordings of Bolivian indigenous music are not. Notes on the recordings can be found at the back of the volume, preceding the index.

GLOSSARY

A glossary of over five hundred entries provides definition or identification for ethnic groups and musical concepts, instruments, and genres. Readers will find selected terms and their glosses reproduced on the top of many pages throughout the *Handbook*.

REFERENCES

Following the Glossary and preceding the Index are three sections entitled "A Guide to… Latin American Music." These include listings of reading, listening, and viewing materials. To coincide with the contents in the *Handbook*, these references have been shortened. The list of recordings provides reference to commercially produced sound recordings that reflect the late-twentieth-century proliferation of recordings of Latin American music. Many more recordings, of course, exist in archives and record stores around the world. Likewise, the list of visual materials provides documentation of musical events, dances, and other types of phenomena that include music and dance. These also reflect the recent number of commercially available videocassette tapes and DVDs on the market.

ACKNOWLEDGMENTS

Volume 2 of *The Garland Encyclopedia of World Music*, of which this *Handbook* is but a part, took nearly ten years to complete. During that time we worked steadfastly together to edit, re-edit, and polish the many essays as if we were two ethnomusicological Michelangelos chipping away in an attempt to free "The Captives" from their marble encasements. Michelangelo, it is said, never finished his masterpiece, but we finished ours and have, moreover, repackaged major portions of it into the present Second Edition.

We wish to thank all the contributing authors who have made *The Garland Handbook of Latin American Music* possible. Without their expertise and wonderful work, its publication could never have been completed. We wish to thank the many individuals who have been official and unofficial readers. Jacob Love, the copyeditor of the original volume, deserves our highest praise—he is a true scholar with a breadth of knowledge and love of improvisation that is unsurpassed. Special thanks go to Martha E. Davis, Jane Florine, Katherine J. Hagedorn, T.M. Scruggs, Anthony Seeger, and the late Gerard Béhague, for their many comments and ideas about essays from certain geographic areas. We also appreciate the vision, advice, and support of Constance Ditzel, who represents the publisher for *The Garland Handbook* series.

We thank Karl Barton and Michael O'Connor, respectively, for their assistance with the organization of the glossary and checking reference materials for the First Edition. Thanks also go to Sara Black for her bibliographic assistance with the Second Edition, and especially to Emmanuel Pereira for his breadth of knowledge about Cuba and his persistence that Haiti must be included in the Second Edition. I also thank graduate students Gonzalo Gallardo, Carla Gelabert, and Gregory Mardirosian for their brilliant essays that contributed so much to the composition of the "Conclusion" to this edition. For translations we thank Jane Florine and Timothy Watkins. We have greatly benefited from the photographic contributions of Elena Constatinidou, Arnold Perris, Peter Smith, and many others who are credited in figure captions. On the audio compact disc, certain examples were furnished by Walter Coppens, Charles Sigmund, and Welson Tremura, while John Banks offered considerable assistance in producing the first compact disc. And for their help with many aspects of the CD production, we thank the College of Music of Florida State University and the Smithsonian Folkways Recordings division of the Smithsonian Institution.

Finally, we are grateful to our wives, M. Diane Olsen and Laura Wilmot Sheehy, for their patience, understanding, and encouragement in helping us see this seemingly ongoing project through to its various stages of conclusion.

—DALE A. OLSEN AND DANIEL E. SHEEHY

PART I

Introduction to the Music Cultures of the Region

*Cumbia, salsa, tang*o; Carnival, fiesta, shamanic curing; *mariachi, samba* school, steelband; Rubén Blades, Celia Cruz, Víctor Jara, Antonio Carlos Jobim, Astor Piazzolla—these genres, contexts, bands, and musicians conjure up sinuous rhythms, lyrical melodies, pensive moods, ideological power, and above all, unforgettable musical art. Music, dance, and music-related behavior are of great importance to the people of the countries and cultures south of the Río Grande (the river that separates the United States from Mexico), the island countries and cultures south of Florida, and many Amerindian cultures that thrive within those politically determined regions.

Señor Antonio Sulca,
a blind Quechua
Indian musician from
Ayacucho, Peru, wears a
European-designed suit
as he plays a Spanish-
derived harp. His music
tells of his people from
southern Peru, and his
harp is adorned with
a lute-playing siren,
believed to be an
indigenous protective
and amorous symbol.
Photo by Dale A. Olsen,
1979.

A Profile of the Lands and People of Latin America

Dale A. Olsen

Historical Snapshot
Geography
Demography
Native America in Latin America
Cultural Settings

The essays in this book explore the music of and in the lives of people from a vast region of the Western Hemisphere. They include descriptions of the music of many nations and cultures south and southeast of the continental United States of America. Most of these nations and cultures speak Spanish, Portuguese, English, French, Dutch, Creole, Papamiento, and/or a wide assortment of indigenous languages including (but not limited to) Aymara, Kechua, Kuna, Maya, Nahuatl, Warao, and many more. Many of the native American cultures (Amerindians) studied in this book continue to thrive as autochthonous and somewhat homogeneous entities within many Latin American countries. To call these cultures "Latin American" is admittedly wrong, because that colonialistic term does not represent the area's indigenous heritage or its African heritage. Latin America theoretically refers to people with southern European heritage (i.e., with descendants from Spain, Portugal, France, Italy, although in practice it seems to emphasize only those people of Spanish and Portuguese heritage), and while the majority of the inhabitants of the Hispanic Caribbean, Middle America (i.e., Mexico and Central America), and South America speak either Spanish or Portuguese, many Amerindians and people of African ancestry do not want to be called "latinos." It is with that understanding that we will use the term *Latin America* only as a term of convenience.

History, geography, ecology, demography, economics, and politics have all played an important role in the development, migration, and social categorization of music. For instance, geography influences ecology, ecology influences economics, and economics determines musical events, musical instruments, types of dances, and other aspects of expressive behavior. Geography has also influenced terms for places. For example, while there is no question what comprises South America, Mexico is not usually included within the term *Central America* because tectonically it is a part of North America. In this book we will use the term *Middle America* to include Mexico and the countries of Central America. We will retain the term *Caribbean*, but will include within the term *Caribbean Latin America* the following political entities: Cuba, Puerto Rico, Dominican Republic, and, in deference to its historical and cultural importance to the region, Haiti. These regions basically include the Greater Antilles (Anglophone Jamaica, however, is excluded).

HISTORICAL SNAPSHOT

History helps us to understand settlement patterns that have generated socio-cultural patterns of behavior, including music, dance, and other human expressions. As we consider history, we must look at events both in time and space. Here are some important historical considerations.

After political developments in Europe that primarily involved Portugal and Spain in the late 1400s (the age of exploration, the expulsion of the Moors, the Inquisition, the marriage of King Ferdinand of Aragon to Isabella of Castile), three Spanish ships under the leadership of Cristóbal Colón, known to us as Christopher Columbus, sailed across the Atlantic and made landfall on a small island somewhere in the Caribbean Sea in 1492, perhaps Samana Cay (San Salvador) or Watling's Island, now in the Bahamas. While scholars still argue over the exact spot of the Spaniard's discovery of—or Encounter with—their new world, it is a history known to almost everyone.

On his first voyage, when land was at last sighted, Columbus wrote that his sailors fell to their knees and sang a musical setting of the Salve Regina, a Marian antiphon antedating the eleventh century (from Davis, THE DOMINICAN REPUBLIC, this volume):

> Dios te salve, Reina y Madre de Misericordia;
> Vida, dulzura y esperanza nuestra, Dios te salve.
> A ti llamamos los desterrados hijos de Eva;
> A ti suspiramos, gimiendo y llorando en este valle de lágrimas.
> Ea, pues, Señora, abogada nuestra; vuelve a nosotros esos tus ojos misericordiosos;
> Y después de este destierro, muéstranos a Jesús, Fruto Bendito de tu vientre.
> ¡Oh clemente! ¡Oh piadosa! ¡Oh dulce Virgen María!
> Ruega por nosotros, Santa Madre de Dios,
> Para que seamos dignos de alcanzar las promesas de Nuestro Señor Jesucristo.
> Amen.

> Hail, Queen, mother of pity:
> Life, sweetness, and our hope, hail.
> To you we cry, Eve's exiled children.
> To you we sigh, groaning and weeping in this vale of tears.
> So ah! our Advocate, turn toward us your pitying eyes.
> And after this exile, show us Jesus, blessed fruit of your womb.
> O gentle, O devout, O sweet Virgin Mary.
> Pray for us, holy Mother of God,
> That we may be made worthy of Christ's promises.
> Amen.

The musical activity that occurred in Latin America during the ensuing colonial period included much vocal music. Spanish and Portuguese Catholic musical compositions, such as masses, salves, and *villancicos* (nonliturgical songs), were performed by hundreds of singers and instrumentalists of native American and/or African heritage both at rural Jesuit missions in Bolivia, Brazil, and Paraguay and in elaborate urban cathedrals in Mexico City, Puebla, Guatemala City, Lima, Sucre, Córdoba, and elsewhere. Mutual aid societies and/ or religious brotherhoods known by such names as *cabildos, cofradías, hermandades*, and *irmandades* were formed on plantations and in cities in Cuba, the Dominican Republic, Peru, Brazil, and other places where people of native American, African, and Afro-Latin American heritage performed their music and dances, developing syncretic religious expressions that were mixtures of native American, African, and European beliefs. Spanish and Portuguese renaissance songs and musical instruments were sung and played, and their traditions were preserved in rural Cuba, Brazil, and other countries where there was once an active plantation life.

We also have some idea about what happened during the next several hundred years throughout much of Latin America: after lands were claimed for Spain or Portugal; indigenous people were "converted" to Christianity and forced to work in gold and silver mines or at other hard labor; many native Americans died of disease or committed suicide; African slaves were brought across the Atlantic by the hundreds of thousands to replace the native Americans as slaves to work on plantations; after the abolition of slavery, people of Asian backgrounds (from China, India, Japan, and Java) worked at hard labor in sugar, tobacco, cacao, and coffee fields—and our history books continue with more details that are sometimes hard to accept. These and many more activities led to the musical expressions of today's Latin America.

Independence movements in Latin America ushered in great changes that affected the musical expressions of many countries. Composers wrote songs with topical, nationalistic, and nostalgic content, which were transmitted and remembered in the oral tradition. Military bands influenced regional musical expressions in both rural and urban settings. The emancipation of slaves encouraged European immigration that introduced new musical expressions, such as the accordion and Italian opera. *Mestizo, mulatto*, and *criollo* composers and musicians established national folklore and artistic expressions throughout Latin America. (In South America, *criollo* [creole] generally means born in the New World of European origin, and in the Caribbean it means having some African heritage.)

The twentieth century saw numerous political movements in Latin America that continued to affect the music of particular countries. Partially because of the Mexican Revolution, for example, the *corrido* continued to develop as a song of national expression, and nationalistic composers such as Manuel Ponce, Silvestre Revueltas, and Carlos Chávez immersed themselves in Mexican folklore to find inspiration. The Argentine *tango* was largely an art form inspired by the political climate in Buenos Aires around World War I, and protest music in Brazil, Uruguay, Argentina, and Chile (*nueva canción chilena*) developed as a response to politics in those countries during the 1960s. Musical expressions in Caribbean Latin America, too, have been affected by the politics and social influences of Cuba, the Dominican Republic, Puerto Rico, and the United States. Music in Latin America is a result of these and many more times and places in history.

In the beginning of the twenty-first century, Latin American music continues to play a key role in world music, especially with the growing population of Latin Americans in the United States. Latin American artists like Enrique Iglesias, Marc Anthony, and Gloria Estefan have crossed over from world music to popular music charts. Radio stations, television programs, magazines, and Internet Web sites devoted to Latin American music and culture have proliferated. With such an explosion of interest in all things Latin American, the time is ripe for an overview of not only the popular styles, but, in some ways more importantly, the traditional and folk styles and customs that have influenced Latin American music. While this volume emphasizes the traditional, folk, and native sounds, popular and rock music are also addressed in topical articles and discussed within the articles on individual countries and regions.

GEOGRAPHY

Middle and South America include topographies of extreme contrast. In South America are the world's largest tropical forest (Amazon) and one of its driest deserts (Atacama). There are many lowland basins (Orinoco, La Plata, Amazon) and frigid highlands and glacial peaks (the Andes, including Aconcagua, the highest mountain in the Western Hemisphere). The country of Chile itself is, in reverse, a compressed version of the span from coastal Alaska to Baja California: its land goes from a northern dry desert, fertile central valleys, and lush southern pine forests, to extreme southern, rugged, canyonlike estuaries studded with glaciers, terminating in frigid mountains and waters of the area of the world that is the closest to Antarctica. Within the small country of Ecuador are tropical forests and perpetually snow-capped mountains—both at zero degrees latitude, the equator. Because of such topographies, most of the urban centers of South America are on or near the coasts of the Atlantic, Caribbean, or Pacific. All of these considerations have affected the music of Central and South America.

DEMOGRAPHY

The population figures for the individual countries studied in this book are constantly changing, and official census calculations occur infrequently. The difficulty of counting people in countries where there are teeming cities of migrants, rainforest communities that are difficult to reach and even know about, mountain villages and individual homes that are often inaccessible, and other factors relating to population studies, makes census taking extremely difficult and sometimes impossible. For purposes of presenting a fairly consistent tabulation of population figures for the countries included in this book, the following table is drawn from estimated 2006 population figures as they appear in *The World Factbook*. The countries (and the commonwealth of Puerto Rico) are organized in the order presented in this book.

Map 1.1 Latin America: South America, Mexico, Central America, and the Caribbean

Cuba	11,382,820
Haiti	8,308,504
Dominican Republic	9,183,984
Puerto Rico	3,927,188
Mexico	107,449,525
Guatemala	12,293,545
Panama	3,191,319
Venezuela	25,730,435
Brazil	188,078,227
Argentina	39,921,833
Paraguay	6,506,464
Bolivia	8,989,046
Peru	28,302,603

Demography, the description of human populations, is more than a statistical science, however. When joined with cultural studies, demography becomes more complex than mere calculation of numbers and migration of people. There is probably no place on earth as racially and culturally diverse and complex as the Americas, especially the Americas covered in this volume.

As a way of explaining the complexity of a particular area, George List (1983) has tried to fit certain regions of South America within the framework of a tricultural heritage—native American, African, and Spanish. But within each of these areas there could be dozens of subareas of influence: which native American culture? which African culture? and even which Spanish culture? These are questions that must be asked (Bermúdez 1994). Today we can speak of Latin America as a multicultural heritage and even a transcultural heritage because people representing so many world cultures have immigrated into many South American countries and Mexico especially, globalization has brought many types of music into all regions, and transculturation has allowed for many Latin American musics to flow outward to all parts of the globe.

To attempt to understand the many types of cultural mixing, terms such as *mestizaje* [miscegenation] (a mixing of race and culture usually assumed between native American and Spanish or Portuguese) and *criolismo* [creolism] (usually a mixing of African and European or referring to European descendants born in the New World; usage depends on the country; in Haiti, Creole refers to the language) have been used to categorize people and cultures in Middle America, South America, and the Caribbean. The terms *mestizo* and *criollo* are used throughout these areas by the people themselves; however, they are perhaps less useful today with the amounts of urban migration taking place, the increasing possibilities of upward mobility, and the great influx of immigrants and their descendants from China, England, Germany, India, Indonesia, Italy, Japan, Korea, and elsewhere. Each country has its own ways of using the terms *mestizo* and *criollo* or uses other terms to accommodate its unique demographic mixtures.

Each country also has its native people, many of whom have assimilated and mixed with the foreign dominant cultures in many regions. In other areas, Amerindians have remained the dominant culture. Because of the important contributions American aboriginal people have made to what is today called Latin America, the remainder of this essay discusses their legacies.

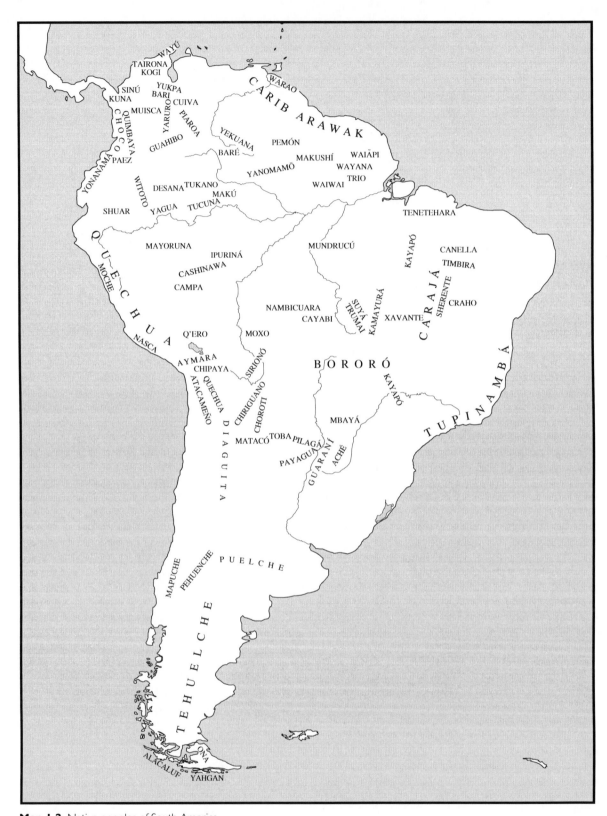

Map 1.2 Native peoples of South America

Introduction to the Music Cultures of the Region

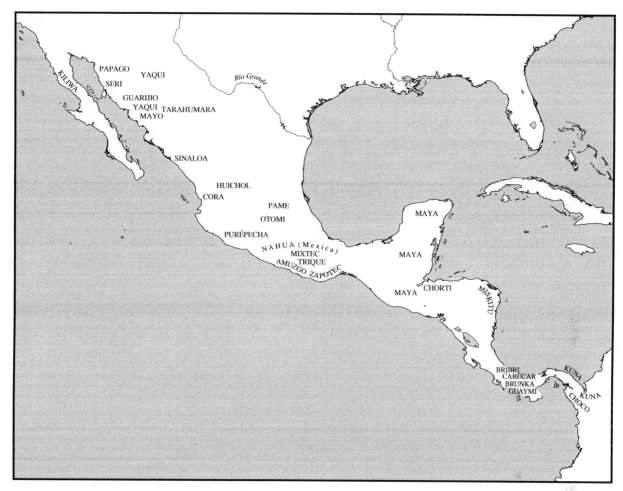

Map 1.3 Native peoples of Mexico and Central America

NATIVE AMERICA IN LATIN AMERICA

On 12 October 1492, the Lucaya, a native people of the Caribbean, discovered Columbus. When he and his crew made landfall on Samana Cay (San Salvador, present Bahamas), they thought they were in the East Indies; therefore they called these people Indians—a term that has caused confusion ever since, especially considering that hundreds of thousands of immigrants from India also live in the Caribbean today. (This volume uses the terms *native American*, *Amerindian*, and *Indian* interchangeably, reflecting particular authors' choices.) In 1492, the islands of the Caribbean and adjacent Atlantic were inhabited by native American peoples, including the peaceful Island Arawak or Taíno (including the Lucaya subgroup) and the warlike Carib. And before them were other groups, including the Yamaye (Jamaica), the Borinquen (Puerto Rico), the Caliponau and Calinago (Lesser Antilles), the Siboney (Dominican Republic), and others (Loukotka 1968).

Columbus had no idea that the islands he encountered were but tiny specks compared to the huge landmasses in the Western Hemisphere, and that millions of people were dwelling in cities larger than many of those in Europe, living and farming in lands higher in altitude than the Italian Alps, and hunting and foraging in tropical forests unimaginable to him.

Native Language Classifications

At the time of the Encounter (a term preferred to the Conquest, because most native Americans were never conquered), it is believed that about 15 million people were living in the South American continent; about 26 million or more were living in Middle America (including present Mexico and Central America) and the Caribbean; and about 5 million were living in North America. These inhabitants of what was to become known as the Americas spoke more than two thousand languages, 1,492 of them in South America alone (Loukotka 1968:17). The South American aboriginal languages can be classified into seven large phyla: Macro-Ge, Macro-Panoan, Macro-Carib, Equatorial, Macro-Tucanoan, Andean, and Chibchan-Paezan; those in Middle America (Central America and Mexico) include three families within the collective group Central Amerind (Kiowa-Tanoan, Uto-Aztecan, and Oto-Mangue) plus Chibchan, Hokan, Penutian, and Equatorial in the Caribbean basin (Greenberg 1987:63, 388–389). Scholars are not in complete agreement with this classification (mostly based on published works), and other systems can be devised. Nevertheless, for the sake of consistency, this system will be followed in this volume.

The native American cultures included in this section of the volume belong to many of those language areas. The map on page 8 shows the approximate locations of the South American native people discussed in this volume. The map on page 9 shows the approximate locations of those from Middle America. Many of these native American cultures are studied in individual essays organized alphabetically by region (for South American regions, see Steward 1949:5, 674). Each is identified according to linguistic affiliation and cultural area and described according to criteria presented in Parts 1 and 2, enabling the reader to make comparisons, observe trends, and so forth.

The Earliest Migrations

The "Indians" in American history books are the native Americans, but even they are descendants of earlier peoples who came from the Old World as discoverers, explorers, invaders, and conquerors. It is widely accepted that, tens of thousands of years ago, hunters followed game across the land bridge between present Siberia and Alaska. During two ice ages, the first one about fifty thousand to thirty thousand years ago and the second one twenty-five thousand to twelve thousand years ago, the oceans receded to create a continuous stretch of tundra between Asia and North America, enabling animals to migrate in search of food, followed by nomadic hunting-gathering cultures (Layrisse and Wilbert 1966:17–18).

For millennia, these early Americans migrated south and southeast, constantly in pursuit of game, being forced farther south by stronger groups of people; some built elaborate cities and ceremonial centers (Chichén Itzá, Mitla, Monte Albán, Tenochtitlán, Teotihuacán, and Tula in Mexico; Iximché, Kaminaljuyú, and Utatlán in Guatemala; Chan Chan and Cuzco in Peru; Tiawanaku in Bolivia; and others), some developed agricultural societies, and others retained hunting-gathering activities. Elaborate priest-god religions developed, while other systems of belief were based on shamanism, whereby a single entranced religious leader communes with the supernatural. In all cases, these peoples developed nations in their own right.

The achievements of many American cultures and nations were distinguished and remarkable. Unfortunately, most of them did not survive the intruders' guns and swords, the enslavement inflicted on them for labor, the diseases unwittingly brought by the Europeans, and the dozens of other wrongs inflicted by one people on others. Hundreds of cultures have survived, however, and some still maintain life-styles and beliefs perhaps similar to those of ancient times while others exist in varying degrees of assimilation. We know little about the present music and musical performance of the native Americans in South America, Mexico, Central America, and the Caribbean, and much study remains to be done.

What remains may be but a mere echo of the past; nevertheless, many musical aspects of today's native Americans still resound and are vital to an understanding of the essence of Mexico, Central America, and South America. Many native American musical forms are being revived while others are being performed with renewed vigor and still others are disappearing. Those that do continue are often important components of revolutionary movements by native Americans (as in Mexico and Guatemala) and non-Indians (as in *nueva canción chilena* "Chilean new song" and the new-song movement throughout Central and South America). In many regions of Mexico, Central America, and South America (Bolivia, Brazil, Peru, and elsewhere), native people themselves make audio and video recordings of their indigenous events for learning and passing on the traditions and/or bringing attention to their way of life, its plights, and its beauties.

CULTURAL SETTINGS

Ethnomusicology is the study of music made by people for themselves, their gods, and/or other people. The people of South America, Mexico, Central America, and the Caribbean are diverse and the countries pluralistic, and their musical styles and other cultural attributes are equally so. When a person is making music for himself or herself, rarely is he or she completely alone: someone—a family member, a friend, a community—is listening, enjoying, crying, or singing along. When music is made for God or the gods, rarely is it done in isolation: people are listening, learning the songs, and perhaps praying or thinking spiritual thoughts. When music is made by a group of people or for a group of people, rarely does the musical event exist without dancing and the participation of members of the family. Music is an affair, an experience, and an event to be shared.

REFERENCES

Bermúdez, Egberto. 1994. "Syncretism, Identity, and Creativity in Afro-Colombian Musical Traditions." In *Music and Black Ethnicity: The Caribbean and South America*, ed. Gerard H. Béhague, 225–238. Miami: North-South Center, University of Miami.

Greenberg, Joseph H. 1987. *Language in the Americas*. Stanford: Stanford University Press.

Layrisse, Miguel, and Johannes Wilbert. 1966. *Indian Societies of Venezuela: Their Blood Group Types*. Caracas: Editorial Sucre.

List, George. 1983. *Music and Poetry in a Colombian Village: A Tri-Cultural Heritage*. Bloomington: Indiana University Press.

Loukotka, Cestmír. 1968. *Classification of South American Indian Languages*. Los Angeles: Latin American Center, University of California.

Steward, Julian H., ed. 1949. *Handbook of South American Indians*. 5 volumes. Washington, D.C.: U.S. Government Printing Office.

The World Factbook (www.cia.gov/cia/publications/factbook/index.html): see individual country entries.

Wauchope, Robert, ed. 1971. *Handbook of Middle American Indians*. Austin: University of Texas Press.

Studying Latin American Music

Dale A. Olsen

The Archaeological Record
The Iconographic Record
The Mythological Record
The Historiographic Record
Ethnology and Practice

Almost everything known about music and musical performance in the Americas comes from archaeology, iconology, mythology, history, ethnology, or current practice. Since antiquity, culture bearers, conquerors, missionaries, Peace Corps volunteers, politicians, grave robbers, scholars, students, travelers, visitors, and many others have contributed to musical knowledge in the Western Hemisphere.

THE ARCHAEOLOGICAL RECORD

Probably all ancient cultures in South America, Middle America (i.e., Mexico and Central America), and the Caribbean—as, indeed, throughout the world—have used music for religious and social reasons. Many have used musical instruments for rhythmic or melodic purposes or as some type of reinforcement of vocal sounds or dancing. Through archaeology it is possible to see (and even to hear) some of the musical instruments of ancient people because many extant musical instruments have been unearthed. Many of these, found in tombs, temples, and other ruins, are available for study in private and public collections. It is possible to see how musical instruments may have been held, which ones may have been played together, and what activities—such as dancing, sacrificing, healing, parading, hunting, and so on—they may have been used for. When musical instruments and performances are depicted in pottery, wood, and any other medium, their study is called music iconology. When such artifacts have been recovered from tombs, temples, and other sites lost in time, music iconology is a branch of archaeomusicology.

Nearly everything said about ancient musical instruments and events has to be qualified with the words *possibly*, *may have*, and other modifiers indicating speculation; people living today can never be certain about artifacts from prehistoric times. The materials of ancient musical instruments can usually be ascertained, and the age of the instruments can be roughly determined—by carbon-14 dating for wood and bone, thermoluminescence (TL) for pottery, and other methods of dating. Instruments can be measured and physically described. Beyond these limits, however, archaeomusicologists must speculate.

The primary drawbacks in the study of ancient musics are the absence of emic points of view (what the bearers of the culture might say about it), observable cultural contexts, and actual sounds. Even if sounds are obtained from ancient musical instruments, it is still the researcher, rather than the bearers of the extinct culture, who causes the sounds to be made. For economic and other reasons, counterfeit artifacts—fakes!—are constructed and circulated, and determining the validity of supposed artifacts can be problematic. Furthermore, carbon-14 dating is not always possible because the procedure destroys part of the artifact, and it may not always be reliable because a buried instrument may receive contamination from seepage, garbage, vegetable matter, the chemical composition of the soil, and other sources, becoming nearly impossible to date by that method. TL dating is rare because few laboratories can do it, and its margin of accuracy is often too wide for it to be useful.

Sometimes, researchers designate as musical instruments ancient objects that may actually have been constructed and used for other purposes: a ceramic water vessel or beaker may be called a drum with its skin missing, a pipe for smoking may be said to be a flute, and so on. At other times, what may be termed an artifact may actually be an ecofact, as when a so-called bone flute is just a bone, or a geofact, as when a so-called polished stone is a naturally polished stone rather than a human-crafted lithophone or stone chime.

Archaeomusicology is the study of music through archaeology, and music archaeology is the study of archaeology through musical instruments. Scholars who study the former are usually trained musicians, while those who study the latter are trained archaeologists (Hickmann 1983–1984). Because no etic conclusions (by an outsider) can be made with certainty since no emic evaluations (by the ancient musician or maker of the instrument) are possible, both fields of study raise more questions than the answers they provide. Musical artifacts can be measured and described, but archaeomusicologists may never know beyond what they can speculate about the use and function of ancient musical instruments, and though the term *scientific speculation* seems like an oxymoron (a self-contradiction), some speculation can be undergirded by the methods of scientific inquiry. New World archaeomusicologists often consult the writings of Spanish chroniclers from the early years of the Encounter, though these writings may not always be accurate and reliable, may contain prejudiced or biased views, and may even transmit misinformation from their native American respondents who may have had some familiarity with their music-making ancestors. There may be difficulties translating the flowery language of early chroniclers—writers who themselves may not have clearly understood what they were describing. Additional scientific speculation can be based on the technique called ethnographic analogy (commonly used in ethnoarchaeology), whereby interpretations of the use and function of ancient culture are made by comparisons with modern cultures. This method can be particularly valuable when the cultures being compared are from the same geographic region, and especially when the living culture claims to be a descendant of the ancient one.

Within the Caribbean, few archaeomusicological studies have been conducted; most come from the Dominican Republic. Within Mexico, Central America, and South America, however, many studies exist; the cultures receiving the most frequent archaeomusicological investigation come from Mexico and Guatemala, including the Aztec, Maya, Nayarit, Olmec, and Toltec; the Central American countries of Costa Rica, Nicaragua, and Panama, including the Chorotega and Nicarao; northwestern Colombia, including the Sinú and the Tairona; the northern Andean countries of Colombia and Ecuador, including the Bahía, Chibcha, Guangala, Jama-Coaque, Manteño, Nariño, Piartal, Tuza, and Valdivia; the central Andean countries of Peru and northern Bolivia, including the Chancay, Chimu, Inca, Moche, Nasca, and Tiawanaku; and the southern Andean countries of Bolivia and Chile, including the Diaguita and San Pedro. Hundreds of ancient cultures thrived in these areas, each with musical activities that were possibly similar, judging by music iconography. This essay describes some extant musical instruments and suggests ideas about ancient musical performance as determined from ancient pottery.

The Caribbean

Archaeological investigations in the Dominican Republic, Cuba, and Puerto Rico have revealed the existence of ancient bone flutes and ceramic vessel flutes with two or three holes for fingering (Boyrie Moya 1971:14–17; Moldes 1975:6–7; Veloz Maggiolo 1972:49). Specific details of their cultural derivations and contexts are unknown, and their use may have been ceremonial, for personal protection, or for diversion. A musical instrument used by the ancient Taíno is the conch trumpet, which may have had a signaling function, as it does today in the Caribbean. It may also have had a ceremonial function, because the protuberances on it resemble those on a Taíno idol (*zemi*), and they may symbolize a volcano or a sacred mountain (Fred Olsen 1974:96).

Middle America

Between 200 B.C. and A.D. 500 along the rugged coast of west-central Mexico, in the present states of Colima, Jalisco, and Nayarit, there lived some of the earliest Mexican cultures to produce musical instruments and depictions of musical performance, both done mostly in fired clay. These artifacts, buried in shaft tombs cut into the volcanic rocks of the highlands, were probably the belongings of a religious elite of shamans and rulers. The instruments include many idiophones (scraped, struck, and rattled); bodies of membranophones; and aerophones, such as ceramic duct globular flutes, duct tubular flutes, panpipes, and conch trumpets. In central Mexico are similar musical instruments plus more elaborate tubular flutes with flared or disk-shaped distal ends that represent flowers or perhaps the sun (Figure 2.1).

distal
The portion of a musical instrument farthest from the mouthpiece

Figure 2.1
A ceramic tubular flute with a long duct mouthpiece, four fingerholes, and an elaborate flared or disk-shaped distal end that perhaps represents flowers or the sun. Perhaps Mexíca (Aztec) culture, central Mexico, about A.D. 1300–1500. Photo by Dale A. Olsen, 1970.

Ancient multiple duct flutes have been discovered in other parts of Mexico and as far south as Guatemala. Their existence suggests that multipart musical textures were used in Mexican and Central American antiquity, though a theory of polyphony is debatable, since no ancient flutists survive to prove or disprove it, and multi-tubed duct flutes are no longer used in the area.

Other types of duct tubular and globular edge aerophones, however, are common in Mexico today, and all have prototypes in ancient times (Crossley-Holland 1980). Robert M. Stevenson (1968) published the most comprehensive study of the ancient instruments and many others. Basing his findings on historical and archaeological records, he showed how native American—mostly Aztec (Nahuatl-speakers) and Maya—musical instruments and performing continued during Mexican colonial times, albeit with changes affected by or as a result of Spanish authority. These changes were structural (instruments made from cane rather than clay, six to seven holes for fingering rather than four, unornamented tubular rather than affixed with a disk at the distal end, a pipe-and-tabor rather than pan-pipe-and-rattle "solo" ensemble) and contextual (instruments no longer used for sacrificial rituals, but for Christian-related ceremonies).

Aztec and Maya influence stretched as far southward as Costa Rica and even Panama, and Chibchan and other South American influences are found in ancient Panama and northward into Costa Rica (Andrews V. 1972; Boggs 1974; Hammond 1972a, 1972b; Rivera y Rivera 1977). Among the former, northern influence is the use of log idiophones similar to Aztec and Maya examples. The latter, southern influence includes ceramic oca-rinas (similar to those of Colombia) in the realistic shapes of animals, birds, fish, humans, and reptiles.

In the southern lowlands of the Nicaraguan Pacific Coast, archaeologists have found small tubular and globular duct flutes and evidence for the existence of a log idiophone (called *teponaztli* by Nahuatl-speaking people further north, whence early Nicaraguans probably came). It is believed that the Chorotega and Nicarao of Costa Rica also migrated from Mexico, and the ancient people from the Diquís region of Costa Rica show possible influences from South America, probably through and as an extension of the Chiriquí of ancient Panama (Acevedo Vargas 1987; Ferrero 1977). Many archaeological sites appear in Panama, though none of them were large ceremonial centers or cities. As found farther north into Mexico and farther south into Colombia, many of the musical instruments excavated by archaeologists in Panama are tubular and globular flutes made from clay.

South America

Hundreds of prehistoric sites are found throughout the northern extension of the Andes and the northern Caribbean littoral of present Colombia. The Spanish conquistadors re-garded this region of South America as most probably the land of the fabled El Dorado (The Golden Man), and they made great efforts to locate his supplies and depositories of precious metal. As a consequence, indigenous nations were quickly destroyed. In the north, the great cities of the Sinú and the villages of the Tairona were sacked and the people were killed, enslaved, or forced into the interior. Musically, the Sinú and Tairona are the most important cultures in the region now known as Colombia because of the numbers of their globular and tubular flutes that have been unearthed (Dale A. Olsen 1986, 1987, 1989, 1990). Colombia, however, is a grave robber's dream (an archaeologist's nightmare), and few excavated artifacts have been properly documented. Many sit today in museums in Bogotá, in private collections, and in stores that specialize in selling antiquities alongside numerous fakes.

The Sinú lived in large cities with elaborate ceremonial centers, situated in the lowlands of northwestern Colombia, along the Sinú River in the present department of Córdoba. Most of their musical instruments are elongated duct flutes made of fired clay. Rather than being tubular, they resemble two cones joined lengthwise at their widest points. Each instrument has four holes for fingering and is in the shape of a fish, or on the proximal cone has the adornment of a long-nosed reptile (Figure 2.2). What these instruments were used for, and what the designs meant, are unknown. There are no living Sinú descendants who can interpret them. It is possible, judging from historical and current cultural attitudes about fish and reptiles, that the instruments had magical power, possibly for protection against supernatural powers (Dale A. Olsen 1989, 2000).

More is known about the Tairona, who lived in villages in the rugged coastal foothills of the Sierra Nevada de Santa Marta in the present department of Magdalena. Most Tairona musical instruments are vessel flutes in the shapes of animals, birds, reptiles, and humans, or anthropomorphic tubular flutes. Because Tairona terrain is higher and drier than the Sinú River basin, archaeologists have been able to excavate houses, ceremonial sites, and tombs, with yields of hundreds of ceramic and gold artifacts. Most ancient aerophones were unearthed in houses or tombs, but not in ceremonial centers, suggesting a personal rather than priestly use for them. To avoid slavery and death at the hands of the Spaniards, the Tairona escaped into the higher elevations of the Santa Marta mountains. Today, the Kogi claim to be their descendants. The Kogi do not play Tairona musical instruments, but they have interpretations for many Tairona artifacts, to which they attribute great power.

The Andean region of Colombia is archaeologically known more for its gold and statuary (as in the San Agustín area) than for its musical instruments. The myth of El Dorado probably began here among the ancient Chibcha, with the legend of the consecration of each new leader, who would have his body coated with gold dust. As an act of rebirth, he would dive from a raft into Lake Guatavita (near present-day Bogotá), to surface reborn as a pure being, free of his golden coating, and filled with the power of the spirit of the lake.

Little is known of the extant musical instruments of the Colombian Andes other than that they were primarily vessel flutes with little decoration. The Nariño (in the southern region of

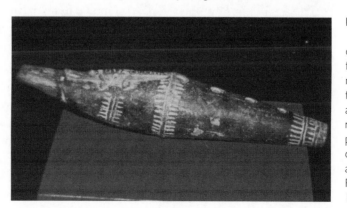

Figure 2.2
A ceramic double-cone-shaped tubular flute with a duct mouthpiece, four fingerholes, and an adornment of a long-nosed reptile on the proximal cone. Sinú culture, Colombia, about A.D. 1300–1500. Photo by Dale A. Olsen, 1974.

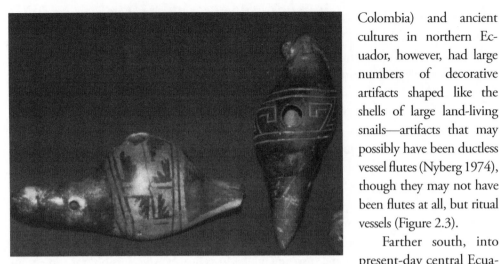

Figure 2.3
Two ceramic figurines (possibly cross-blown globular flutes) in the shape of a snail. Nariño culture, Colombia, about A.D. 1300–1500. Photo by Dale A. Olsen, 1974.

Colombia) and ancient cultures in northern Ecuador, however, had large numbers of decorative artifacts shaped like the shells of large land-living snails—artifacts that may possibly have been ductless vessel flutes (Nyberg 1974), though they may not have been flutes at all, but ritual vessels (Figure 2.3).

Farther south, into present-day central Ecuador, the coastal lowlands have yielded numerous musical artifacts made from clay. Most of them are ductless vessel flutes in the shapes of animals and birds. The culture known as Bahía or Valdivia produced elaborate humanoid-shaped vessel flutes with two chambers and four holes for fingering. These instruments, capable of many multiple pitches, are elaborate in their exterior and interior design (Cubillos Ch. 1958; Hickmann 1990).

Possibly the richest area of the Americas for ancient musical artifacts is coastal Peru, from Lambayeque in the north to Nasca in the south (Bolaños 1981, 1988; Donnan 1982; Jiménez Borja 1951; Dale A. Olsen 1992, 2000; Stevenson 1968). One of the oldest known musical cultures in Peru, however, is Kotosh, high in the Andes in the department of Huánuco. There, what is thought to be a bone flute (with one hole exactly in the middle of its length) was discovered in the Tomb of the Crossed Hands, dating back to about 4500 B.C. (Bolaños 1988:11). Indeed, the precise uses of artifacts are not always clear, and what may seem to be a musical instrument may in fact be something else. In coastal Peru, some artifacts are undoubtedly tubular flutes because of their notched mouthpieces and holes, and numerous ceramic ductless and duct globular flutes have been found (Dale A. Olsen 1992, 2000). It is curious, however, that though cross-blown tubular ceramic flutes existed in ancient Peru, tubular duct flutes did not—at least, none have been discovered.

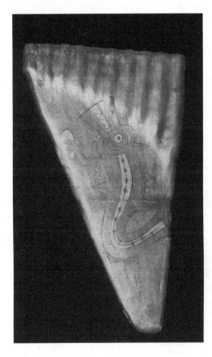

Figure 2.4
A ceramic ten-tubed panpipe with a painted fish deity. Nasca culture, Peru, about 100 B.C.–A.D. 600. Photo by Christopher Donnan, 1972.

Ceramic panpipes from the Nasca culture of southern coastal Peru have been unearthed and studied in detail (Figure 2.4), and precise scientific measurements have been made of their pitches (Stevenson 1960, 1968; Haeberli 1979; Bolaños 1988); the measurements have dispelled the often-believed

Figure 2.5
A ceramic coiled trumpet molded around a ceramic beaker. Recuay culture, Peru, about 200 B.C.–A.D. 550. Photo by Dale A. Olsen, 1974.

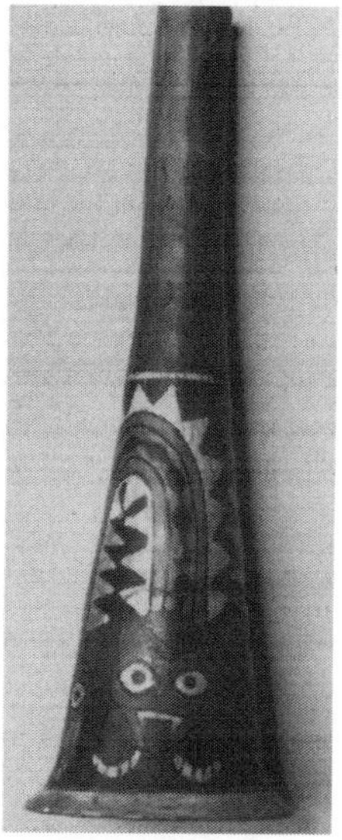

myth that Andean music had pentatonic roots. They have dispelled another belief: that Nasca panpipes were played in pairs using interlocking parts, as they are today in the southern Peruvian Andes. Scholars now believe that those panpipes were played in ensembles, because many instruments with nearly identical tunings have been discovered in common archaeological sites.

Trumpets, aerophones with cupped mouthpieces, were frequent among ancient coastal Peruvians. The Moche made instruments from the shells of conchs and ceramics shaped to resemble such shells. According to music iconography, these musical instruments were used by priests and shamans, or by the fanged deity in the afterlife. The Moche also played ceramic tubular straight and coiled trumpets, the latter depicting open-mouthed jaguars at their distal ends. The inland Recuay used trumpets that sometimes coiled around vases or beakers (Figure 2.5). Farther south, on the southern Peruvian coast, straight trumpets were used by the Nasca and their neighbors in Paracas. These were often painted with motifs of feline, piscine, or solar deities (Figure 2.6).

Figure 2.6
A ceramic straight trumpet. Nasca culture, Peru, about 100 B.C.–A.D. 600. Photo by Christopher Donnan, 1972.

Numerous ceramic membranophones, some with skin intact, have been discovered at Moche, Nasca, and Paracas sites. Those from the Nasca and Paracas civilizations are the largest and most ornate. Some, reaching two meters high, are profusely painted with cat and snake deities (Figure 2.7).

Farther south, in the area of present-day highland Bolivia, musical instruments have been archaeologically discovered from the Tiawanaku culture (1000 B.C.–A.D. 1000), an influential civilization. These artifacts include ceramic vessel flutes and panpipes, bone tubular flutes, and wooden trumpets

Figure 2.7
A ceramic vase drum. Nasca culture, Peru. Photo by Dale A. Olsen, 1979.

Figure 2.8
A wooden straight trumpet. Tiawanaku culture, Bolivia, about A.D. 900–1200. Photo by Christopher Donnan, 1972.

(Figure 2.8). The Tiawanaku culture influenced the Diaguita and San Pedro cultures in the Atacama Desert region of northern Chile, where similar forms and designs among ceramic artifacts can been seen. María Ester Grebe (1974) has done a thorough study of the ancient musical instruments of Chile.

THE ICONOGRAPHIC RECORD

Music iconography is closely related to music archaeology because the source of information is artifactual. Iconography, however, studies the meanings attached, usually pictorially, to artifacts. Music iconography is the description (music iconology, the science) of music through its representation in sculpture, painting, and other plastic arts. Through it, researchers can gain an understanding of events, processes, and performances during the era in which the artifact was authentically used. It is a record of knowledge that is not fully reliable in itself, but when added to archaeological, historiographic, and ethnographic records, can tell much about a culture. Another aspect of music iconography is the study of the designs on musical instruments. One reason for iconography's unreliability is that so much is available only in secondary sources: the originals are difficult to locate because they are rare paintings, drawings, engravings from rare books, or sometimes have disappeared altogether.

In South America, Mexico, and Central America, pre-Encounter musical iconography tells us about the uses of music among the Aztec, Maya, Moche, Nayarit, and other ancient civilizations. In the early post-Encounter period, paintings and drawings from codices and other compilations by chroniclers, missionaries, and others are valuable for their visual commentaries about music. After the Encounter, however, biases appear, and are often represented in art. Flutes, trumpets, and other instruments may be represented larger than life (or smaller), as more complex (or simpler), being played together in unlikely combinations, or in any number of incorrect ways. For this reason, music iconography must be joined with other types of documentation in a check-and-balance manner. As nationalism developed, painting and graphic arts became more detailed and representational. Artists were usually interested in more or less faithfully depicting life in their new countries, and this often included musical life, featuring such activities as playing instruments and dancing. Especially important are paintings of religious festivals, music during work, and music for pleasure. With the growth of tourism since the 1950s, music iconography in the form of items made for sale to tourists (carved gourds, figurines, statues, paintings) has proliferated. Once again, realism is not prevalent, and caricature is common.

The Caribbean

Drawings by chroniclers are somewhat informative about music in the Caribbean during historical times. The chronicler Gonzalo Fernández de Oviedo y Valdés included two drawings of a Taíno idiophonic H-drum, a struck idiophone (which I call an "H-drum" because of the pattern formed by its two prongs cut into the top of a hollow wooden log) closed at both ends (1851, reproduced by Rouse 1963a:plate 90). These drawings are valuable because they suggest a possible connection with the Aztec *teponaztli* or the Maya *tunkul* farther west on the mainland. The Taíno idiophone is called *mayohuacán* by Moldes (1975:6), but Loven (1935:495) writes its name as *maguay*, the term for the century plant (*magüey*), from which it is made. The Taíno H-drum was a large instrument according to René Currasco (former director of a noteworthy folkloric ballet in Santo Domingo, Dominican Republic), who built a reproduction inspired by the historical drawings, and played it while sitting on the floor as his ensemble performed a reconstructed Taíno dance; his instrument stood about 1.2 meters high and measured about one meter in circumference. Loven explains that the Taíno idiophonic H-drum was played by the chief (*cacique*) to accompany the festive song (*areito*) rather than a dance, though this song was possibly danced to. No mention is made of any melodic or linguistic communication on this particular instrument, though it could produce at least two tones. Ferrero (1977:133) reproduced an engraving by Benzoni from 1542, showing a similar instrument of the Gran Nicoya of Costa Rica, having three tongues and played with two sticks.

Rouse (1963b:plate 95) prints a picture by Picard (Fewkes 1907) showing container rattles being used in a Carib war-related dance. The instrument is apparently a large calabash rattle with a long stick handle, on the top of which are numerous vertically extending feathers, in the fashion of each player's headdress. The picture gives evidence of the importance attached to this seemingly sacred rattle, as it is shown being played by priests or shamans—three men of apparently high status, judging from their headdresses and costumes. Each man plays one rattle, while sixteen other men, without headdresses or costumes, dance in a circle around them.

According to music iconography, membranophones (skin drums) may have been used in the ancient Caribbean. A picture (Fewkes 1907, reproduced in Rouse 1963a:plate 92) depicts an Arawak dance to the goddess of the earth, in which two membranophones are played, each with two sticks in the European military-drum fashion. Lewin (1968:53) refers to skin drums among the Arawak during ceremonies of worship, explaining they are "made from the hollow stem of the trumpet tree with manatee skins stretched tightly across." If these portrayals of Arawak ceremonies are accurate, then perhaps European-style membranophones replaced the H-drum idiophones.

Middle America

The figurines of musicians unearthed in west Mexico (Nayarit, Colima) provide many details of instrumental performance, such as what instruments existed, who played them, and which instruments have been continuously used to the present. Some people depicted are musical soloists; others are members of musical ensembles. These were probably ceremonial musical performers, maybe shamans. Container rattles, rasps (Figure 2.9), and tortoise-shell struck idiophones (Figure 2.10) are commonly depicted on figurines as being played by men who often are shown speaking or singing. Single-headed drums and struck conch shells are shown being played in west Mexican iconography (Figure 2.11). Players of aerophones are commonly depicted, giving us valuable information about performance that no longer occurs. Foremost are the player of a three-tubed flute (in Figure 2.12, the

Figure 2.9 (left)
A ceramic figurine of a man playing a rasp. Nayarit culture, Mexico, about 200 B.C.–A.D. 300. Photo by Dale A. Olsen, 1989.

Figure 2.10 (right)
A ceramic figurine of a man playing a tortoise shell as a scraper or percussion instrument. Colima culture, Mexico, about 200 B.C.–A.D. 300. Photo by Dale A. Olsen, 1971.

way the flutist's fingers overlap the holes suggests that multiple sounds were used) and a panpipe-and-rattle "solo" ensemble (Figure 2.13).

Though some musician-depicting artifacts are molded together in clay (Figure 2.14), museums often display individual musician-depicting artifacts together as if to indicate ensemble playing (see Figure 2.11). Grouping such artifacts together is purely speculative. Curators are often influenced by how musical instruments are played in combination today. This technique, called ethnographic analogy (Dale A. Olsen 1990:170), is usually the only way to determine the collectivity of musical instruments unless they are all arranged together in an archaeological site, but even that would not establish the orchestration of specific ensembles or explain how each instrument was used in relation to the others.

Music iconography can reveal information about musical contexts, but it cannot tell us many details about techniques of playing. It can suggest the big picture but not the little picture, the focus of musical detail. For

Figure 2.11
Ceramic figurines: a man plays a single-headed drum with a mallet and a hand (?); another man plays a rattle or strikes a conch. Colima culture, Mexico, about 200 B.C.–A.D. 300. Photo by Miguel Angel Sotelo.

Figure 2.12
A ceramic figurine of a man playing a three-tubed vertical flute. Colima culture, Mexico, about 200 B.C.–A.D. 300. Photo by Dale A. Olsen, 1989.

Figure 2.13
A ceramic figurine of a man playing a four-tubed panpipe with one hand and a rattle with another. West Mexico, about 200 B.C.–A.D. 300. Photo by Dale A. Olsen, 1989.

example, the player of the single-headed drum pictured in Figure 2.11 is probably playing with a mallet, but we cannot tell how he hits the drumhead (in the middle? on the rim of the skin? with his fingers? also with his palm?). Similarly, the player of the three-tubed flute in Figure 2.12 is obviously playing with his fingers, but we cannot tell which parts of the fingers (tips or middle joints), nor can we tell which holes he covers with which fingers (this would be important information to know for the purposes of determining whether or not ancient Mexicans played multipart music on their multi-tubed flutes).

More important, music iconography can show how particular musicians were attired, and from that evidence, scholars can speculate about the performers' social status. For example, the drummer in Figure 2.11 may have been a priest, judging from the elaborate headdress and fancy necklace, and the flutist in Figure 2.12 may have been a commoner, judging from the simple hat and lack of fancy clothing. This is speculation, but scholars have nothing more on which to base their conclusions about musical contexts and musicians' status. Music iconography, at best, offers suggestions about how musical instruments might have been played and what sort of people the players might have been.

Stevenson explains that "at least forty codices record material of interest to the ethnomusicologist. Even late picture books such as the Codex

Figure 2.14
A ceramic figurine of a man and a woman singing together or yelling at each other. West Mexico, about 200 B.C.–A.D. 300. Photo by Dale A. Olsen, 1989.

Figure 2.15

A picture from the
Florentine Codex of
Bernardino Sahagún
(sixteenth century)
showing how Aztec
flutists smashed their
flutes on the steps
of the temple before
being sacrificed.

Azcatitlán (painted ca. 1550 in the northern part of the Valley of Mexico) can yield extremely useful documentation on precontact Aztec music" (1968:10). The Bekker Codex (Martí 1968:83–86) pictures Mixtec musicians playing a variety of instruments in great detail. The Florentine Codex of Bernardino Sahagún shows how Aztec flutists smashed their flutes on the steps of the temple before being sacrificed (Figure 2.15).

Another important source for ancient musical iconography of Middle America is Maya murals, originally painted in temples and tombs. The most famous is from Bonampak, Chiapas, Mexico. It shows numerous Mayan musicians performing together (Martí 1968:facing page 68). Such tomb art is found as far south as Honduras.

In Panama and Costa Rica, several excavated gold artifacts are interpreted as depicting musicians. One of the most famous is from the Coclé culture (about A.D. 1300–1500) in Panama. It is often called the little man flutist (Figure 2.16). The Society for Ethnomusicology (SEM) uses this fig-

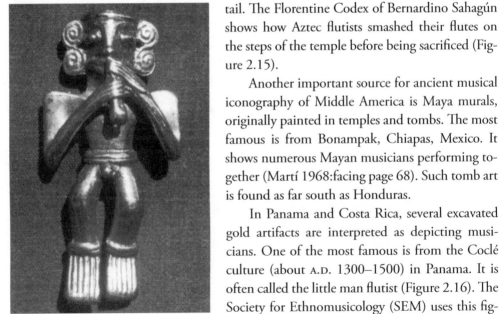

Figure 2.16

A gold figurine of a
man playing what may
be a vertical flute.
Coclé culture, Panama,
about A.D. 1300–1500.
Photo by Dale A.
Olsen, 1989.

ure as its logo (a choice made in 1955 by David P. McAllester), and today its form graces the journal *Ethnomusicology* and other SEM-published items. What is not known is whether the little man is actually playing a flute or a trumpet, smoking a cigar, or chewing sugarcane. Other figurines are clearer. These include a gold biped from the Panamian Veraguas culture (about A.D. 800–1540), who seemingly plays a flute with one hand and a rattle with the other (Figure 2.17). This is a fine example of evidence of the one-man-band personage, who often plays a pipe and tabor in present Middle and South America (Boilès 1966). In this ancient artifact, however, the musician is

Figure 2.17
A gold figurine of a man playing what may be a vertical flute and rattle at the same time. Veraguas culture, Panama, about A.D. 800–1540. Photo by Dale A. Olsen, 1989.

playing a pipe-and-rattle combination. From Palmar Sur, an ancient Costa Rican site, Luis Ferrero (1977:plate 38) reproduces a photograph of a gold figurine of a double-headed flutist: each head plays what may be a flute that resembles the instrument in the Veraguas exemplar; this double-headed flutist is unique in the musical archaeology of the Americas.

South America

Perhaps nowhere in the Americas is music iconography so rich as among the prehistoric Moche of the north Peruvian coast [see Peru], who depicted musical instruments, singing, whistling, instrumental playing, dancing, and costumes on ceramic pots, often in exquisite detail. Some artifacts are difficult to interpret, such as deathlike figures who are playing pan-pipes (Figure 2.18) (Benson 1975; Olsen 2000). Others are quite clear, such as scenes of panpipers where the instruments of two players are connected by a cord, suggesting that panpipes were played by paired musicians—perhaps in an interlocking fashion, as is commonly done today in southern Peru and Bolivia, though this is not known and can never be proven.

In colonial and more recent historic times throughout South America, many paintings, drawings, etchings, and other examples of the plastic arts have depicted musical instruments, singing, instrumental playing, and dancing. These are valuable for learning about colonial music. In colonial paintings of life in Rio de Janeiro, people of African descent are seen playing *mbira*-type plucked idiophones, instruments that have disappeared in modern Brazil.

Figure 2.18
A stirrup-spout ceramic bottle depicts a male deathlike figure playing a panpipe. Moche culture, Peru, about 100 B.C.–A.D. 700. Photo by Dale A. Olsen, 1979.

People in all cultures tell stories. In English, stories passed on orally are called by a variety of names: folklore, folktales, mythology, myths, narratives, oral history, oral literature. Misunderstanding often arises when these terms enter into colloquial speech, because people usually think of a folktale, a myth, a story, and so on, as something that is not true. Actually, mythology is not concerned with proving or disproving truth. It is simply the study of a particular form of discourse. It may be true, or it may be false. Usually it is a little bit true and a little bit false.

Although such communications are often perceived as something other than fact, it is not for persons of one culture to determine whether or not the mythology of another culture is fact or fiction. The mythological record can be an important repository of information from which we can learn something about the meaning and contextualization of another culture's music. Much of what is learned may not exist in current practice (or perhaps it never existed, or exists only for the supernatural), but it may provide a framework on which cultural understanding can be built. This cultural understanding takes place, not usually with details that can be physically measured or scientifically studied, but with emotions, ideas, morals, and beliefs.

A myth is an artifact. Unlike an archaeological artifact, it cannot be dated. Nevertheless, it can often provide data that researchers can use comparatively to help reconstruct cultural history. As a repository of historical fact, a myth is usually unreliable, though ideas about great tragedies (massacres, famines, plagues), large-scale migrations, wars, and other memorable events and situations may be related in narratives or songs. More often, myths may relate ideas about the creation of the universe, taboos on human conduct, and the daily lives of gods, cultural heroes, and ogres. Myths contextualize many musical instruments, and these native (albeit mythological) contexts can be compared with historical or contemporary uses of the same musical instruments. Likewise, myths may contextualize singing and dancing in ways that provide information about cultural continuity, acculturation, and cultural extinction.

Most of what we know from the mythological record of South America, Mexico, Central America, and the Caribbean comes from the twentieth century, the age of ethnographic investigation. Myths, usually transmitted orally, have been collected and written down by historians, travelers, missionaries, anthropologists, ethnomusicologists, and others. Written collections are important for study, but also important are the original rules of preservation (some myths are guarded by shamans, priests, elders, women, and so on) and dissemination, because those processes are essential in maintaining cultural cohesion and continuity. Therefore, mythology has tremendous internal importance for cultures. Scholars can learn much about a culture by studying such internal dynamics (how, when, and why myths are preserved, transmitted, and remembered), and studying the myths themselves (what they mean, inside and outside the culture).

The Caribbean

Much of the folklore of the Caribbean region is Afro-Caribbean in origin. Telling stories, reciting proverbs, and singing songs—possibly African retentions passed on from generation to generation—are commonplace in areas where African slaves and their children lived in great numbers. Many Afro-Caribbean narratives refer to musical performance, musical instruments, dancing, and so forth. The following tale, entitled "Mérisier, Stronger than the Elephants" comes from Haiti, and portions of it tell us important information about local music (Courlander 1976:64–66):

> There was an old man with three sons. One day he fell ill, and he sent a message to his sons, asking them to come to his house. When they arrived, he said to them, "I am an old man, I am sick. If I should die, how will you bury me?"
>
> One son answered, "Father, may you grow strong again. But if you should die, I would have you buried in a mahogany coffin."
>
> Another son answered, "Father, may you live long. But if you should die, I would make you a coffin of brass."
>
> And the third son, named Brisé, replied, "Father, I would bury you in the great drum of the king of the elephants."
>
> "The great drum of the king of the elephants! Who before now has ever been buried so magnificently!" the old man said. "Yes, that is the way it should be." And he asked the son who had suggested it to bring him the drum of the king of the elephants.
>
> Brisé went home. He told his wife: "I said I would do this thing for my father, but it is impossible. Why didn't I say I would make him a coffin of silver? Even that would have been more possible. How shall I ever be able to do what I have promised?"

Thereupon Brisé sets off on a journey, looking for elephants so he can acquire the elephants' great drum. He travels far and visits many people, until he meets Mérisier, a Vodou priest. The story continues:

> Then Brisé understood that the old man was a houngan, a Vodoun priest with magical powers. The old man took out his bead-covered rattle. He shook it and went into a trance and talked with the gods. At last he put the rattle away and said: "Go that way, to the north, across the grassland. There is a great mapou tree, called Mapou Plus Grand Passe Tout. Wait there. The elephants come there with the drum. They dance until they are tired, then they fall asleep. When they sleep, take the drum. Travel fast. Here are four wari nuts for protection. If you are pursued, throw a wari nut behind you and say, 'Mérisier is stronger than the elephants.'"
>
> When day came, Brisé went north across the grasslands. He came to the tree called Mapou Plus Grand Passe Tout. He climbed into the tree and waited. As the sun was going down, he saw a herd of elephants coming, led by their king. They gathered around the mapou tree. The king's drummer began to play on the great drum. The elephants began to dance. The ground shook with their stamping. The dancing went on and on, all night. They danced until the first cocks began to crow. Then they stopped, lay down on the ground, and slept.
>
> Brisé came down from the tree. He was in the middle of a large circle of elephants. He took the great drum and placed it on his head. He climbed first over one sleeping elephant, then another, until he was outside the circle. He traveled as fast as he could with his heavy load.

The story continues to explain how the elephants come after Brisé, and how Brisé stops them each time by throwing a wari nut. The first nut produces a huge forest of pines as a barrier to the elephants, the second a large freshwater lake (which they drink to cross), the third a large saltwater lake (which they drink to cross, but all except the elephant king die). The story continues:

> Brisé came out of the grassland. He followed the trails. He went to his father's house with the drum. When he arrived, his father was not dead; he was not sick; he was working with his hoe in the fields.
>
> "Put the drum away," the father said. "I don't need it yet. I am feeling fine."

Brisé took the drum to his own house. He ate and slept. When he awoke, he heard a loud noise in the courtyard. He saw the king of elephants coming. The elephant ran straight toward the great drum and seized hold of it.

Brisé took the last wari nut that the Vodoun priest had given him and threw it on the ground, saying, "Mérisier is stronger than the elephants!"

Instantly the great drum broke into small pieces, and each piece became a small drum. The king of elephants broke into many pieces, and each piece became a drummer. The drummers went everywhere, each one taking a drum with him.

Thus it is that there are drums everywhere in the country. Thus it is that people have a proverb which says: "Every drum has a drummer."

This tale explains—though with tongue in cheek, of course—why Haiti has so many drums and drummers, but it also explains why Haiti has no elephants. It says the Vodou priest (*houngan*) plays a bead-covered rattle (similar to today's West African and Afro-Cuban instruments), which contrasts with container rattles often found in Haitian Vodou.

Middle America

Much of the mythology of Middle America is native American in origin. Probably all Amerindians have tales that can teach us something about their music. Especially noteworthy are narratives of the Aztec (Nahua), the Huichol, the Maya, and the Kuna. Some are creation myths. Others are everyday stories about animals, life in the forests, and so on. Musical performance, especially singing, is often a part of them.

Peter Furst and Barbara Myerhoff have shown (1966) how an elaborate cycle of myths, which they call an epic prose-poem, provides information about the birth, life, and death of a master sorcerer known as the Tree of the Wind. Also known as the Datura Person, he was responsible for introducing the powerfully dangerous hallucinogen datura to the Huichol of northern Mexico. The cycle provides information about the power of singing and playing the violin by the Huichol, who consider the violin "among their most ancient instruments" (personal conversation, Ramón Medina Silva, a Huichol shaman, 1971). Similarly, Julio Estrada has shown how an Aztec (Nahua) myth explains the creation of the world through the power of the sacred conch trumpet of Quetzalcoatl, the Aztec cultural hero (Estrada 1992:341):

> But his shell horn had no holes: [Quetzalcoatl] then summoned forth the worms, which made the holes; thereupon the male and female bees flew into the shell and it sounded.

Estrada interprets this myth as explaining the "cultivation of the earth. When the shell is played, the wind god and the bees together spread the seed of a new culture" (1992:341). Many cultures (Aztec, Inca, Maya, Moche, and others) venerated conchs and used them as trumpets for sacred purposes; but for native Americans, conch trumpets have power especially when they are sounded, and myths help us understand why.

The sound of the trumpet, significant in prehistoric America, remains an important symbol. A week before Carnaval (Carnival) in Chamulá, Mexico, in 1969, the master of ceremonies gave the following oral proclamation to the village (after Bricker 1973:85–86):

> Chamulas!
> Crazy February!
> Today is the ninth of February, 1969.

The first soldier came to Mexico.
He came to Guatemala;
He came to Tuxtla;
He came to Chiapa;
He came to San Cristóbal.
He came with flags;
He came with drums;
He came with trumpets.
Viva! Viva!

The last cavalier came to Mexico.
He came to Guatemala;
He came to Tuxtla;
He came to Chiapa;
He came to San Cristóbal.
He came with fireworks;
He came with cannons;
He came with fifes;
He came with bugles;
He came with flags;
He came with trumpets.
Mariano Ortega and Juan Gutiérrez came with their young lady, Nana María Cocorina.
They go together into the wood to make love.
They return eating toffee, eating candied squash, eating blood sausage.
Viva Mariano Ortega!

Here we see trumpets, bugles, and other wind instruments as symbols of power, not only of victory in war (the Spanish conquests of Mexico, Guatemala, and Chiapas), but also of spreading the seed—because Nana María Cocorina becomes pregnant (Bricker 1973:118).

South America

The mythology of South American native people is rich. Telling stories is a way of life, and often the distinction between speaking and singing stories is slight. Among South American Amerindians, music is often a part of most myths, and numerous examples portray musical situations that differ from musical situations of the 1990s. Women do not usually play flutes; in myths, however, they are as likely to play flutes as men. An excerpt from a Warao narrative reveals how a woman plays a bamboo flute and sings for magical protection against a jaguar, who is actually a transformed man (Wilbert 1970:164–165):

> He had collected a lot of bamboo and threw it down, "Kerplum." When it became dark he lapped up some water with his tongue, "Beh, beh." After having built up the fire, the boys began to dance. She herself played the flute made of bamboo, "Tea, tea, tea, tail of a jaguar," she said.
>
> The jaguar rushed towards the woman, but she grabbed a piece of firewood and stuck him in the eye. The jaguar stopped. Again, in the dance place, she took the bamboo flute and played, "Tea, tea, tea, tail of a jaguar. Tea, tea, tea, tail of a jaguar." Again the jaguar rushed toward the seated woman. Again, she stuck a piece of firewood into his eye. …
>
> By dawn, he could take no more. He sat with his back to them. The woman's little brother arrived with arrows and spear. "Sister, you all survived the night?"

In anthropology, this is known as a reversal of social order (as when a musical instrument at one time was the domain of one sex, but then switches at some point in history), and often, mythology is the only record of such musical behavior. Furthermore, mythology often elaborates on the processes that produce such cultural changes.

Another trait seen in the above myth, and common in most narratives, is onomatopoeia, as when the jaguar throws the bamboo down and goes "Kerplum." Often such sounds symbolize musical instruments and the noises of everyday life, including the sounds of humans, animals, and spirits. Among the Kalapalo of Brazil, and possibly among most native South American people, spirits have an especially musical language: "Powerful beings are … capable of inventing musical forms, whereas humans are capable only of copying those forms in their performances" (Basso 1985:70). This is one of the main reasons that music has so much power among Amerindians, as shamans and nonshamans alike sing for protection, for curing, and for other types of theurgy (Dale A. Olsen 1996).

THE HISTORIOGRAPHIC RECORD

Musical historiography is essentially musical information written by chroniclers of a culture contemporary with their own. These writings are either emic (insider), such as the Maya writing about the Maya or the descendants of the Inca writing about the Inca (problematic because the notion that descendants have an emic claim on their ancestors can be controversial), Jesuits writing about music at their missions, and so forth, or etic (outsider), such as Spanish chroniclers (cronistas) writing about the music of ancient American civilizations, in which case the information may be biased. Another type of historiographic information is philology, which includes descriptive treatises about musical instruments, musical practices, and language. (Early dictionaries are important sources about music.) Another area is oral history, though oral historians, folklorists, and anthropologists often disagree about whether oral history is history, folklore, or ethnography. Basically, historiographic information consists of ethnographies or travelogs from the past. Such sources can be quite different: some are objective, some are subjective, and some, because of bias or carelessness, may contain misinformation. Sources must always be carefully analyzed and compared with other types of information.

The Caribbean

Early chroniclers (cited in Boyrie Moya 1971:13–14; Loven 1935:492–497; Moldes 1975:6–7) described several musical instruments of the Taíno, even though those Arawak-speakers were nearly extinct. These instruments included what the writers called a skinless drum made from a hollowed-out tree, with an H-shaped incision on the top forming two tongues that players struck; a small gourd or calabash container rattle used during a harvest festival; a large, double-handled gourd or calabash container rattle used by shamans for curing illnesses; snail-shell rattles strung around dancers' legs, arms, and hips; small, metal, castanet-type instruments held between a dancer's fingers; flutes; and conch trumpets. Most of these instruments were used to accompany the singing of religious songs (areito).

J. M. Coopersmith (1949:7–8), describing the Taíno log idiophone, quotes the chronicler Oviedo y Valdés:

They accompany their songs with a drum, which is made from a hollowed trunk of a tree, often as large as a man and sounding like the drums made by the Negroes. There is no parchment on the drum but, rather, holes or slits are made, from which the sound emanates. … The drum … (is cylindrical) in form and made from the trunk of a tree, as large as desired. … It is played with a stick like the tympanum (atabal). One sound-hole in the form of an "H" is cut in the middle of one side of the trunk. The two tongues formed by the "H" are beaten with a stick. On the opposite side of the trunk-section, near the base of the cylinder, a rectangular hole is cut. The drum must be held on the ground, for it does not sound if held elsewhere. … On the mainland, these drums are sometimes lined with the skin of a deer or some other animal. Both types of drum are used on the mainland.

This description is better than those of many other chroniclers, but it is typical because of what is not said. It was apparently uncommon to write about the cultural significance of musical instruments, their origins, or anything else about their seemingly extramusical functions. The obvious question, whether or not the Taíno H-drum was borrowed from the Mexican mainland, was apparently never asked. Few other Taíno instruments are mentioned, and musical occasions are not described at all.

The ancient Carib, by contrast, had more musical instruments, which the chroniclers (unknown writers cited in Petitjean-Roget 1961:51, 67–68 and Rouse 1963b:561; Rochefort 1666, cited by Stevenson 1975:52) described in fuller detail. Among them were container rattles made from gourds; a single-headed drum (membranophone) made from a hollowed tree; bamboo flutes and bone flutes; panpipes; conch trumpets; and even a single-stringed instrument made from a gourd. The chroniclers mentioned that mothers used rattles to soothe their children; men played flutes in the morning while women prepared breakfast and people bathed; panpipes accompanied dancing; and conch trumpets were blown to signal wars and hunting or fishing expeditions.

Middle America

Historical accounts of Amerindian music from Middle America—the area known as the Viceroyalty of New Spain, including the Caribbean islands—date from the early 1500s and were written mainly by Spanish chroniclers. Foremost among them was Bernal Díaz del Castillo, who lived between about 1492 and 1581 (Stevenson 1968:12–14). His accounts vividly describe ritual music for human sacrifices, music for battles, and festival music of the Aztecs.

During the colonial period, religious scholars produced many sources about Amerindian music because they believed that knowing about native music would help missionaries convert the Indians to Christianity. The Franciscan order was dominant in Mexico, where Pedro de Gante was the leading missionary who described Amerindian music during the early years of the conversion process. He wrote in letters to King Charles V of Spain about the Indians' musicality: "I can affirm that there are now trained singers among them who if they were to sing in Your Majesty's Chapel would at this moment do so well that perhaps you would have to see them actually singing in order to believe it possible" (Stevenson 1968:157). The printing of music appeared in Mexico as early as 1556, forty-five years before it appeared in Peru, and elaborate polyphonic scores attest to Amerindian choristers' musical skills.

South America

Spanish and Portuguese conquerors, explorers, religious zealots, and others wrote extensively about the new lands of South America—known as the Viceroyalties of New Granada, Peru, La Plata, and Brazil, the latter under Portuguese rule. One of the most important writers about sixteenth-century Peruvian music was Felipe Guamán Poma de Ayala (1936 [1612–1615/16]), who described Inca music and musical instruments in detail; Guamán Poma's source provides many drawings of Inca musical performance. Another sixteenth-century author, Garcilaso de la Vega (1966 [1609]), the son of a Spanish nobleman and an Incan princess, also wrote extensively about music among the Inca and other Amerindians.

The major religious orders in Spanish South America were the Augustinians, the Dominicans, the Franciscans, and the Jesuits; the last were musically active in Peru and Paraguay until their expulsion in 1767. Their goal was basically the same as that of missionaries in New Spain: spiritual conversion. Like those missionaries, they trained many musicians, chronicled many events involving music, described many musical instruments, and in essence provided some of the first ethnographies of native cultures.

Writings in the historiographic process often become ethnographies when they deal extensively with the behavior of a culture. Likewise, ethnographies become historiographic sources. Indeed, the difference between histories and ethnographies is often slight. Studies about the music of South America that are now important historiographic sources are numerous. Many of them are listed within the particular article references and in the general bibliography of this volume. They include such famous monographs from the first half of the twentieth century as *An Introductory Study of the Arts, Crafts, and Customs of the Guiana Indians* by Walter E. Roth (1924), *La musique des Incas et ses survivances* by Raoul and Marguerite d'Harcourt (1990 [1925]), and *Suriname Folk-Lore* by Melville and Frances Herskovits (1936).

ETHNOLOGY AND PRACTICE

Studies that go beyond the mere description of a culture and include analysis, interpretation, and synthesis based on participant observation, participation, and interaction have moved out of ethnography into ethnology, the science of culture. These include studies in anthropology, ethnobotany, ethnolinguistics, ethnomusicology, folklore, poetics, religion, and so forth, and they number in the thousands of volumes that add to our musical understanding of South America, Mexico, Central America, and the Caribbean.

In the realm of specific musical study, participation in and writing about the music of a culture by its bearers themselves (the emic, or "insider" approach) or by non-culturebearers (the etic, or "outsider" approach) has often resulted in the cultivation of knowledge acquired through practice. Two studies that help describe this approach are *Capoeira—A Brazilian Art Form: History, Philosophy, and Practice* by Bira Almeida, known professionally as Mestre Acordeon (1986), and *Ring of Liberation* by J. Lowell Lewis (1992). Both treat the same musical phenomenon, *capoeira*, a form of Afro-Brazilian music, dance, and martial art, from Salvador de Bahia, Brazil. Because these books differ widely in their approach to this topic, reading them both side by side will provide a better understanding of *capoeira* than reading only one of them. A thorough understanding of a particular musical topic requires the exploration of all the forms of musical scholarship available.

REFERENCES

Acevedo Vargas, Jorge. 1987. *La Música en las Reservas Indígenas de Costa Rica*. San José: Editorial de la Universidad de Costa Rica.

Almeida, Bira (Mestre Acordeon). 1986. *Capoeira—A Brazilian Art Form: History, Philosophy, and Practice*. Berkeley: North Atlantic Books.

Andrews V., and E. Wyllys. 1972. *Flautas precolombinas procedentes de Quelepa, El Salvador*. San Salvador: Ministerio de Educación, Dirección de Cultura, Dirección de Publicaciones.

Basso, Ellen B. 1985. *A Musical View of the Universe*. Philadelphia: University of Pennsylvania Press.

Benson, Elizabeth P. 1975. "Death-Associated Figures on Mochica Pottery." In *Death and the Afterlife in Pre-Columbian America*, ed. Elizabeth P. Benson, 105–144. Washington, D.C.: Dumbarton Oaks Research Library and Collections.

Boilès, Charles L. 1966. "The Pipe and Tabor in Mesoamerica." *Yearbook for Inter-American Musical Research* 2:43–74.

Bolaños, César. 1981. *Música y Danza en el Antiguo Perú*. Lima: Museo Nacional de Antropolog'a y Arqueolog'a, Instituto Nacional de Cultura.

———. 1988. "La Música en el Antiguo Perú." In *La Música en el Perú*, 1–64. Lima: Patronato Popular y Porvenir Pro Música Clásica.

Boggs, Stanley H. 1974. "Notes on Pre-Columbian Wind Instruments from El Salvador." *Baessler-Archiv, Beiträge zur Vŏlkerkunde* (Berlin) 22:23–71.

Boyrie Moya, Emile de. 1971. "Tres flautas-ocarinas de manufactura alfarea de los indígenas de la isla de Santo Domingo." *Revista dominicana de arqueología y antropología* 1(1):13–17.

Bricker, Victoria Reifler. 1973. *Ritual Humor in Highland Chiapas*. Austin: University of Texas Press.

Coopersmith, J. M. 1949. *Music and Musicians of the Dominican Republic*. Washington, D.C.: Pan American Union.

Courlander, Harold. 1976. *A Treasury of Afro-American Folklore*. New York: Crown Publishers.

Crossley-Holland, Peter. 1980. *Musical Artifacts of Pre-Hispanic West Mexico: Towards an Interdisciplinary Approach*. Los Angeles: Program in Ethnomusicology, Department of Music, University of California at Los Angeles.

Cubillos Ch., Julio César. 1958. "Apuntes Sobre Instrumentos Musicales Aborígenes Hallados en Colombia." In *Homenaje al Profesor Paul Rivet*, 169–189. Bogotá: Editorial A B C.

Donnan, Christopher B. 1982. "Dance in Moche Art." *Nawpa Pacha* 20:97–120.

Estrada, Julio. 1992. "The Emergence of Myth as Explanation." In *Musical Repercussions of 1492: Encounters in Text and Performance*, ed. Carol E. Robertson, 337–350. Washington D.C.: Smithsonian Institution Press.

Ferrero, Luis. 1977. *Costa Rica Precolombina: Arqueología, Etnología, Tecnología, Arte*. San José: Editorial Costa Rica.

Fewkes, Jesse. 1907. "The Aborigines of Porto Rico and Neighboring Islands." *Twenty-Fifth Report of the Bureau of American Ethnology*. Washington, D.C.: U.S. Government Printing Office.

Furst, Peter, and Barbara Myerhoff. 1966. "Myth as History: The Jimson Weed Cycle of the Huichols of Mexico." *Antropológica* 17:3–39.

Garcilaso de la Vega, El Inca. 1966 [1609]. *The Incas: The Royal Commentaries of the Inca*. 2nd ed. Edited by Alain Gheerbrant. Translated by Maria Jolas. New York: Avon Books, Orion Press.

Grebe, María Ester. 1974. "Instrumentos musicales precolombinos de Chile." *Revista Musical Chilena* 128:5–55.

Guamán Poma de Ayala, Felipe. 1936 [1612–1615/16]. *Nueva Crónica y Buen Gobierno*. Paris: Institut d'Ethnologie.

Haeberli, Joerg. 1979. "Twelve Nasca Panpipes: A Study." *Ethnomusicology* 23(1):57–74.

Hammond, Norman. 1972a. "Classic Maya Music. Part I: Maya Drums." *Archaeology* 25(2):125–131.

———. 1972b. "Classic Maya Music. Part II: Rattles, Shakers, Raspers, Wind and String Instruments." *Archaeology* 25(3):222–228.

d'Harcourt, Raoul, and Marguerite d'Harcourt. 1990 [1925]. *La musique des Incas et ses survivances.* Paris: Librairie Orientaliste Paul Geuthner.

Herskovits, Melville J., and Frances S. Herskovits. 1936. *Suriname Folk-Lore.* New York: Columbia University Press.

Hickmann, Ellen. 1983–1984. "Terminology, Problems, Goals of Archaeomusicology." *Progress Reports in Ethnomusicology* 1(3):1–9.

———. 1990. *Musik aus dem Altertum der Neuen Welt: Archäologische Dokumente des Musizierens in präkolumbischen Kulturen Perus, Ekuadors und Kolumbiens.* Frankfurt am Main: Peter Lang.

Jiménez Borja, Arturo. 1951. *Instrumentos musicales del Perú.* Lima: Museo de la Cultura.

Lewin, Olive. 1968. "Jamaican Folk Music." *Caribbean Quarterly* 14(1–2):49–56.

Lewis, J. Lowell. 1992. *Ring of Liberation.* Chicago: University of Chicago Press.

Loven, Sven. 1935. *Origins of the Tainan Culture, West Indies.* Gšteborg, Sweden: Elanders Boktryckeri Akfiebolag.

Martí, Samuel. 1968. *Instrumentos Musicales Precortesianos.* México, D.F.: Instituto Nacional de Antropolog'a.

Moldes, Rhyna. 1975. *Música folklórica cubana.* Miami: Ediciones Universal.

Nyberg, John L. 1974. "An Examination of Vessel Flutes from Pre-Hispanic Cultures of Ecuador." Ph.D. dissertation, University of Minnesota.

Olsen, Dale A. 1986. "The Flutes of El Dorado: An Archaeomusicological Investigation of the Tairona Civilization of Colombia." *Journal of the American Musical Instrument Society* 12:107–136.

———. 1987. "The Flutes of El Dorado: Musical Guardian Spirit Effigies of the Tairona." *Imago Musicae: The International Yearbook of Musical Iconography* 3 (1986):79–102.

———. 1989. "The Magic Flutes of El Dorado: A Model for Research in Archaeomusicology as Applied to the Sinú of Ancient Colombia." *In Early Music Cultures, Selected Papers from the Third International Meeting of the ICTM Study Group on Music Archaeology*, ed. Ellen Hickmann and David Hughes, 305–328. Bonn: Verlag für Systematische Musikwissenschaft.

———. 1990. "The Ethnomusicology of Archaeology: A Model for Research in Ethnoarchaeomusicology." *Selected Reports in Ethnomusicology* 8:175–197. *Issues in Organology.*

———. 1992. "Music of the Ancient Americas: Music Technologies and Intellectual Implications in the Andes." In *Musical Repercussions of 1492: Exploration, Encounter, and Identities*, ed. Carol Robertson, 65–88. Washington, D.C.: Smithsonian Institution Press.

———. 1996. *Music of the Warao of Venezuela: Song People of the Rain Forest.* Gainesville: University Press of Florida.

———. 2000. *Music of El Dorado: The Ethnomusicology of Ancient Andean Cultures.* With compact disc materials online. Gainesville: University Press of Florida, 2001 (paperback edition, 2004).

Olsen, Fred. 1974. *On the Trail of the Ancient Arawaks.* Norman: University of Oklahoma Press.

Petitjean-Roget, Jacques. 1961. "The Caribs as seen through the Dictionary of the Rev. Father Breton." *Proceedings of the First International Convention for the Study of Pre-Columbian Culture in the Lesser Antilles (July 3–7, 1961).* Fort-de-France: Société d'Histoire de la Martinique.

Rivera y Rivera, Roberto. 1977. *Los instrumentos musicales de los Mayas.* México, D.F.: Instituto Nacional de Antropología e Historia.

Roth, Walter E. 1924. "An Introductory Study of the Arts, Crafts, and Customs of the Guiana Indians." *Thirty-Eighth Annual Report of the Bureau of American Ethnology to the Secretary of the Smithsonian Institution 1916–1917.* Washington, D.C.: U.S. Government Printing Office.

Rouse, Irving. 1963a. "The Arawak." *Handbook of South American Indians*, vol. 4, ed. Julian H. Steward, 507–546. New York: Cooper Square Publishers.

———. 1963b. "The Carib." *Handbook of South American Indians*, vol. 4, ed. Julian H. Steward, 547–566. New York: Cooper Square Publishers.

Stevenson, Robert M. 1960. *The Music of Peru: Aboriginal and Viceroyal Epochs.* Washington, D.C.: Organization of American States.

———. 1968. *Music in Aztec and Inca Territory.* Berkeley and Los Angeles: University of California Press.

———. 1975. *A Guide to Caribbean Music History.* Lima: Ediciones CULTURA.

Veloz Maggiolo, Marcio. 1972. *Arqueología prehistórica de Santo Domingo.* Singapore: McGraw-Hill Far Eastern Publishers.

Wilbert, Johannes. 1970. *Folk Literature of the Warao Indians.* Los Angeles: Center for Latin American Studies, UCLA.

PART 2

Issues and Processes in the Music of Latin America

Music does not exist without a social context. Even music being recorded "out of context," as in a studio, is within a studio context. Likewise, all music is involved with some kind of social, religious, or economic issue, and a process is always at work. These are often complex phenomena, requiring extensive analysis to be understood.

Musical instruments, for example, do not function by themselves, but are entwined with cultural behavior. It is important to understand not only where musical instruments are found and why certain cultures have the instruments they do, but also what instruments physically and sonically symbolize and what roles they play within that cultural framework. Musical genres too have typical contexts, entwined with social structure and human behavior.

The Americas are diverse for many reasons, especially because they are large-ly populated by immigrants and their descendants, and music often negotiates ethnic and cultural identity among people from different backgrounds, regions, cultures, genders, ages, educational levels, and so forth. Music is also constantly changing because of inside influences (enculturation) and outside contacts (ac-culturation), and new ideas are developed through individual or group creativity, transculturation or cultural exchange, and globalization, especially with regard to popular music genres. Such issues and processes explain how and why music and dance are important, vital, and necessary as vehicles for human understanding.

Dance is a ritual behavior practiced by young and old. This little boy is a *chino* ("humble servant") dancer during the patronal festival of the Virgen de Guadalupe in Ayquina, Chile, 8 September 1968. Photo by Dale A. Olsen.

The Distribution, Symbolism, and Use of Musical Instruments

Dale A. Olsen

The Classification of Musical Instruments
The Distribution of Musical Instruments
Symbolic Interpretations of Musical Instruments
The Influence of Electronics

People make music by playing instruments, singing, or both, often at the same time. Musical instruments tell us much about cultures, not so much as items in themselves, but as tokens of meaning—what they signify to their cultures and how they came to mean what they mean. Musical instruments are artifacts and "ethnofacts"—the former because they are objects created by humans, and the latter because they have meaning, often of a symbolic kind.

The musical instruments found in South America, Mexico, Central America, and the Caribbean are diverse, and their number is large. From the Encounter in 1492 until the present, about two thousand languages have been spoken by native Americans, not including those of North America. If an average of three musical instruments per language group existed, that means that the names of probably six thousand instruments were once being used. The Spanish, Portuguese, Africans, and all the other foreigners who came after the Encounter and up to the present probably introduced another thousand names for musical instruments. Because of the disappearance of native American cultures, assimilation, modernization, and other forces of culture change, a much smaller quantity exists today. Nevertheless, we are still dealing with a vast number, and diversity is still a hallmark of these instruments. A systematic taxonomy of musical instrument classification, therefore, is necessary in order to understand the distribution, symbolism, and use of musical instruments in the area.

This volume classifies musical instruments in two ways. First, whenever possible, they are classified according to the system designed by their culture itself. When an indigenous taxonomy is not known or does not exist, however, they are classified according to an extended set of terms derived from the work of Erich M. von Hornbostel and Curt Sachs: idiophone, membranophone, chordophone, aerophone (Jairazbhoy 1990), electrophone (Bakan et. al 1990), and corpophone (Olsen 1986).

Sounds are transmitted via waves that travel from their sources through air (or water), strike the receiver's eardrum, and register in the receiver's brain. The shape of the wave determines whether what is received is music (and what kind of music), speech, noise, or whatever a culture calls it. The sources that produce what we may call music are what we shall call musical instruments. (These points are important because what we call music or musical instruments may not always be considered music or musical instruments by the people of the cultures themselves.) Given the diversity, large numbers, and complexity (or simplicity) of the sources of sound in the world, an objective system of classification must be employed; this is why the extended Hornbostel-Sachs taxonomy is often used.

An *idiophone* is defined as a "self-sounder"; the entire instrument itself vibrates, sending off waves of sound. This is a huge category because of the cultural diversity of the geographic areas. Because of forced and unforced immigration, idiophones essentially include instruments from Africa, Europe, and Asia, in addition to those of native Americans. Examples of idiophones, using some common and general terms, range from dancers' ankle-tied bells to maracas (*maráka*, from the Tupí language), rhythm sticks, triangles, steel drums, marimbas, gongs, scrapers, and many more.

A *membranophone* is defined as a "skin-sounder" in which a skin (or skins) stretched tightly over a rigid support vibrates, sending off waves of sound. [Listen to "Afro-Martinican street music"] Skin instruments are often called drums, a term otherwise used for the body or chamber. Confusion arises when drum is used for items without a skin, such as oil drums or steel drums—the former not a musical instrument, the latter an idiophone.

DISC ❶ TRACK 38

An *aerophone* is defined as an "air-sounder," a wind instrument in which air within a column vibrates, or in which air acting on the instrument causes it to vibrate, sending off waves of sound. The aerophone category comprises the largest and most complex group of instruments in the Americas, and numerous subgroups can be included within it. Because of diversity, it would perhaps be prudent to refrain from employing terms derived from the classification of Western European orchestral instruments. For example, such terms as *edge aerophone* for *flute*, *lip-concussion aerophone* for *trumpet*, *single-reed-concussion aerophone* for *clarinet*, and *double-reed-concussion aerophone* for *oboe* or *shawm* (a European Renaissance kind of oboe) would be organologically clear. Common sense, however, suggests that for most readers, terms like *flute*, *trumpet*, clarinet, and *oboe* are easier to understand. In all cases, when the common European terms are used in this volume, they will often not mean the European form of the instrument, unless carefully stated so. Other terms such as *ocarina* for *globular flute* (Figure 3.1) and *panpipe* for a multi-tubed flute without

edge aerophone
A flute-type wind instrument
lip-concussion aerophone
A trumpet-type wind instrument
single-reed-concussion
A clarinet-type wind instrument
double-reed-concussion
An oboe-type wind instrument

Figure 3.1
A ceramic dog-shaped ocarina or globular flute with a cross-blown mouthpiece on its stomach (it was photographed upside down to show the mouthpiece) and two fingerholes. Ancient Moche culture, Peru. Photo by Dale A. Olsen, 1996.

holes may be used. In addition, terms *duct* (like the mouthpiece of a recorder) and *ductless* (like the mouthpiece of a Western flute, a single tube of a panpipe, or the Andean notched flute, Figure 3.2) here serve to clarify the subcategory of flute-type instrument. Indeed, the literature on the subject of aerophones can be confusing because styles of writing are often unclear, and descriptions are often incomplete.

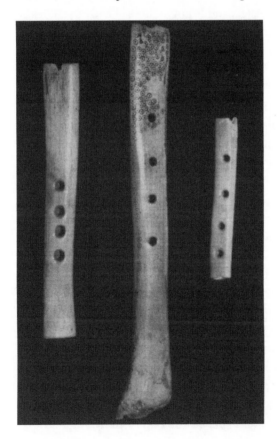

Figure 3.2
Three bone flutes with notched mouthpieces and four fingerholes: left and right, the ancient Nasca culture; middle, the Chancay culture, Peru. Photo by Dale A. Olsen, 1973.

A *chordophone* is defined as a "string-sounder" in which a string (or strings) stretched tightly over a rigid support vibrates, sending off waves of sound. Most musical instruments in this category derive from Iberian prototypes, and their names are most often given in their English forms, rather than Spanish or Portuguese (guitar for *guitarra*, harp for *arpa*, mandolin for *mandolina*, and violin for *violín*, for example). Sometimes "guitar type" or "small guitar" are used in scholarship, but that usage tends to confuse rather than clarify because there are so many variants. Several instruments derive their names from their number of strings or string courses, such as the *tres* (Figure 3.3) and the *cuatro*, whose names are determined by numbers of strings or string courses, except for the Puerto Rican *cuatro*, which has ten strings. Terminology often means different things from one country to the next. The term *guitarrón* "big guitar," for example, is used in Mexico, Peru, and Chile, where each instruments differs. In Mexico it is a large pot-bellied bass instrument (see MEXICO); in Peru it is a large normal-looking guitar; and in Chile it is a large rustic guitar with twenty-five strings, including several resonating or sympathetic strings called "little devils." [Listen to "Canto a lo pueta"] DISC ❶ TRACK 17

An *electrophone* is defined as an "electronic sounder" in which a vibration or action is produced by electronic means, sending off waves of sound. This category serves for several instruments used in contemporary or pop music and includes the synthesizer and computer-generated devices. An electric guitar, however, may be a chordophone with an electronic attachment, a pickup, connected to an amplifier.

A *corpophone* is defined as a "body sounder" in which a vibration or action is produced by a body part (or parts), sending off sound waves. This category includes handclaps, slaps of the buttocks, snaps of the fingers, and so forth, but does not include vocalizations. Musical vocal sounds are songs; the word chant is not used unless it is specifically defined within particular entries.

Karl Gustav Izikowitz attempted to list and analyze all the musical instruments of native South America (Izikowitz 1970 [1935]). Other scholars have made similar attempts for particular countries, including Argentina (Vega 1946), Bolivia (Díaz Gainza 1962), Colombia (Bermúdez 1985), Ecuador (Coba Andrade 1981), Guyana (Roth 1924), Peru (Bolaños et al. 1978), and Venezuela (Aretz 1967). Izikowitz's book is a bibliographic study based on the descriptions of musical instruments published by anthropologists and other researchers; the other publications are primarily based on fieldwork by the authors. The above-listed country studies include more instruments than those of native peoples.

Figure 3.3
The *tres*, a guitar-type instrument with six strings strung into three courses, common in Cuba and Dominican Republic. This man plays with a Dominican *merengue* quartet. Photo by Dale A. Olsen, 1977.

THE DISTRIBUTION OF MUSICAL INSTRUMENTS

A topic of scholars' concern is the distribution of musical instruments. At a general level, this distribution in the southern Americas is determined by one or more of these factors: the locations of the cultures that use them at present, the locations of the cultures that used them at one time, and the locations of their use in popular music.

The first factor is a logical truism, something to be expected. General examples are the distribution of African-derived membranophones around the coast of South America from Rio de Janeiro, Brazil, northward to the Caribbean coast of Colombia, northward from Colombia through Belize, southward from Colombia to coastal Ecuador, and into the cultures of the Caribbean basin—areas where the largest numbers of African slaves were concentrated. Particular examples are the use of *rum* membranophones in the Candomblé rituals of Bahia, Brazil, and *batá* drums in the Santería rituals of Cuba. Another example is the use of guitars or guitar-type instruments wherever Spanish or Portuguese heritage is strong.

The second factor relates to the use of instruments by people who were not the original users, but because the original users lived in the area in times past, they influenced the present users. An example of this is the use of *marimba* xylophones by Maya people in Guatemala, who learned the instruments from African former slaves or runaway slaves whose descendants no longer inhabit the area.

The third factor is determined by the importation of certain instruments because of popular music. An example is the use of the *charango* in Santiago, Chile, by performers of *nueva canción* in the 1960s and 1970s, such as Inti Illimani and Quilapayún, and its continued use in certain Chilean rock groups of the 1990s, such as Los Jaivas.

SYMBOLIC INTERPRETATION OF MUSICAL INSTRUMENTS

The distribution of musical instruments can be affected by culturally determined factors, most of them imbued with interpretations of symbolism or iconicity: concepts of ideal qualities of sound, concepts of physical duality, ideas about extramusical power, the need for giving signals, and the introduction of instruments by agents of foreign powers (such as Jesuit missionaries in 1700s and military bands in the 1800s).

Concepts of ideal qualities of sound

During pre-Columbian times, the predominant melodic musical instrument type was probably the edge aerophone, or flute. This conclusion is based on archaeology and is therefore verified only in areas where archaeological studies have been possible, namely the western third of South America and nearly all of Mexico and Central America. Because of humidity, tropical-forest terrain does not preserve items of material culture made from cane, clay, and bone, whereas dry climates do. The study of living tropical-forest cultures, however, reveals a high use of edge aerophones that are not related to European or African types (bone or cane tubular flutes played vertically, for example), suggesting that the tradition has probably continued from ancient times (see Okada 1995:video examples 26 and

27). Other edge aerophones, however, are found in archaeology but have not survived in living cultures. Globular flutes, for example, were common in ancient Mexico, Colombia, Peru, and elsewhere, but have disappeared from common use. Likewise, multiple tubular flutes with holes for fingering were prevalent among the Maya and Aztec but have since disappeared. In some regions of the Andes, such as the Mantaro Valley of Peru, many edge aerophones have been replaced by European clarinets and saxophones. Nevertheless, the ancient exemplars and the current usage (including the substitutions) suggest an edge-aerophone distribution wherever native Americans and their descendants (*mestizos*, or people of mixed race and/or culture) are located today. The distribution is, in fact, so prevalent that native Central America and western South America can be considered edge-aerophone (flute) cultures.

Evidence suggests that lip-concussion aerophones, or trumpets, have continued since antiquity in the Andes, though the materials have often changed from ceramic and wood to cow horn and sheet metal, while the shells of conchs remain fairly constant in certain areas, including Central America and Peru. Although evidence does not exist for single-reed-concussion aerophones in the ancient Americas, idioglot and heteroglot clarinets are common today in tropical-forest cultures (Waiãpi, Warao, and Yekuana, for example) and elsewhere (Aymara and Guajiro). They may have existed in pre-Columbian times, and perhaps only their reeds disappeared; for example, tubes interpreted as bone, ceramic, or wooden "flutes" or "trumpets" in Mexican, Guatemalan, and Peruvian musical archaeology may have been single- or double-reed-concussion aerophones whose vegetable-matter reeds perished. Today's use of shawms (*chirisuya* and *chirimía*) in Peru and Guatemala, possibly introduced by Spanish missionaries, may actually suggest continuity rather than cultural borrowing, a sort of new wine in old bottles. The prevalence of lip- and reed-concussion aerophones among native Americans suggests a pairing or dualistic usage with the use of edge aerophones. Though the "flutes" are whistle-tone instruments, the "trumpets," "clarinets," and shawms are buzz-tone instruments.

Such dualism can be seen as a relationship of opposites, a common phenomenon with regard to the physical use of instruments, such as male and female pairs of instruments, especially in the siku "panpipe" traditions of Bolivia and Peru. Dualism of sounds or tones exists in the Amazon tropical forest among the Tukano of Colombia, who attach sexual symbolism to the sounds of their instruments (Reichel-Dolmatoff 1971:115–116). The whistling tone of edge aerophones, for example, symbolizes sexual invitation, while the buzz of lip- and/or single-reed-concussion aerophones symbolizes male aggressiveness. These opposites are joined, and their union is supported by percussion sounds of membranophones and idiophones, which symbolize "a synthesis of opposites ... an act of creation in which male and female energy have united" (Reichel-Dolmatoff 1971:116). This native tripartite theory of music explains the Tukano use of musical instruments and can possibly explain similar usage throughout native South America, especially in parts of the tropical forest, the Andes, and the circum-Caribbean area, where whistle-tone, buzz-tone, and staccato-tone sounds are common.

Throughout most of the central Andes of South America, the area at one time dominated by the Inca, there exists a preference for high-pitched sounds as exemplified by the whistle tones of flutes. This high-pitched aesthetic, favored by the Quechua (also Kechua) and the Aymara, is also found in their choice of the tightly strung *charango*, a small, guitar-type chordophone, as an accompanying instrument, and their style of singing, most often performed by women. The distribution of flutes throughout this region, from panpipes to duct and ductless edge aerophones, is related to the preference for high-pitched tones.

Concepts of physical duality

We have already seen how dualism is expressed in the sounds musical instruments make; the concepts of the whistle tone and buzz tone combine to create power, according to the Tukano. Many other native American cultures employ the concept of duality, but in a physical way: two instruments, or two halves of one instrument, symbolic of male and female, unite to create a whole. The distribution of symbolically male and female musical instruments coincides with cultures that interpret power as the union of opposites. Nowhere is this belief stronger than in the Andes of South America.

The *siku* panpipe set of the Peruvian and Bolivian Aymara requires two people to play each half of the instrument in an interlocking fashion. Called *ira* and *arca*, the halves are respectively male (the leader) and female (the follower). To play a melody together by joining individual notes in alternation is called in Aymara *jjaktasina irampi arcampi* "to be in agreement between the *ira* and the *arca*" (Valencia Chacón 1989:34, English version). This technique is related to the dualistic symbolism common among Andean native people, for whom the sun and the moon are dichotomous creator beings, associated respectively with male and female. But not all dualistic symbolism is mythological or cosmological; it can be sociological when each half of a panpipe ensemble known as *chiriwano* represents a particular community. Two metaphorical neighboring communities—each half of the panpipe ensemble—"play their particular melodies simultaneously in a type of counterpoint," like a musical duel, "in which each community unit tries to play its melody at a louder volume than the other, in order to dominate." This musical and physical dualism ("duelism") is a metaphor of the Andean society, in which two halves, the leaders of each community, "are structurally necessary to complete the whole" (Turino 1987:20, translated by Dale A. Olsen). This aspect of two parts working together to make a whole is related to the pre-Spanish concept called *mita* (*minga*), a communal work effort, in which the whistle tone of a *pinkullo* (*pingullo*) duct edge aerophone is coupled with the buzz tone of the bass snare drum as it produces its staccato synthesis of opposites to accompany work.

Panpipes of the Aymara and Chiriwano are not the only instruments played in a dualistic manner symbolizing male and female. Among the Yekuana of the southern Venezuelan tropical forest, *tekeya* single-reed-concussion aerophones are always played in pairs, one male and the other female. Their music is symbolic of "the movements and songs of a mythological animal pair" (Coppens 1975:1). Among the descendants of African slaves in the Pacific coast of Colombia (the Chocó region), two one-headed membranophones known as *cununo mayor* and *cununo menor* are designated as male and female, respectively (Whitten 1974:109).

Ideas about extramusical power

Many of the Andean *siku* traditions, though imbued with dualistic symbolism, are symbolic in other ways as expressed in particular musical occasions replete with elaborate costumes for the musician-dancers. One of the most symbolic is the Kechua *ayarachi* panpipe ensemble, "related to the cult of the condor, considered a totemic bird among Andean cultures. The garments of *ayarachis* and a ceremony alluding to this bird are indications of this character" (Valencia Chacón 1989:69, English version).

The allusion to animals is an important use of symbol with regard to musical instruments. The animal for which an instrument has symbolic significance is usually a living animal. The Quechua *antara*, a single-unit (having one part only) panpipe and an important instrument of the Inca, was often made from human bones. Human body parts imbued musical instruments with power, and *antara* panpipes made from human bones, "just like the drums from human skin, were not meant to be ordinary musical instruments. Instead, considering the joining of the parts: bones, skin, etc. for their essences, their voices should have been something alive" (Jiménez Borja 1951:39, translated by Dale A. Olsen). Indeed, life—its creation and continuation—is assured by fertility, by the joining of male and female, by the planting and harvesting of crops, by the abundance of rain.

In many regions of the Andes, the *pinkullo* duct aerophone (the term and the "flute" are used by the Aymara and the Kechua) is seasonal, played only during particular calendrical periods, such as the rainy season from October through March:

> This flute is played during the season when the great rains begin. ... Before playing the instrument it is moistened in chicha [beer], alcohol, or water. The coincidence of ... festivals with the arrival of the rains, the moistening of the wood before making the flutes, and the moistening of the instruments before playing them, is quite significant. (Jiménez Borja 1951:45, translated by Dale A. Olsen)

The *pinkullo* is associated with fertility, as the symbolism suggested above would indicate.

Flutes are obvious symbols of fertility because of their phallic shape, and they often have the role of a charm, endowed with power to entice a female lover to a male (they were played only by men in the Andes). So powerful was the sound of the *kena* ductless edge aerophone to the Inca in ancient Cuzco, Peru, that women could not resist it: "The flute ... is calling me with such tenderness and passion that I can't resist it. ... My love is calling me and I must answer him, that he may be my husband and I his wife" (Garcilaso de la Vega 1966 [1609]:87). One ancient technique was to play the *kena* within a clay pot—an obvious symbol of the sexual act, its musical imitation forbidden by the Roman Catholic Church. Nevertheless, the tradition persisted into the colonial period, and Borja describes such a jar found in Huamanga, department of Ayacucho, Peru. It has a small opening at the top for inserting the flute, two larger openings in the sides for the player's hands, and two eyelets on the sides so it can be suspended around the *kena* player's neck (Jiménez Borja 1951:37). He explains that to play the *kena* into such a specially designed clay vessel creates a magical voice that "defeats death and promotes life" (Jiménez Borja 1951:36). To further support the fertility symbolism of the Andean flute, especially as an instrument used during planting-related festivals, the term *pingullo* combines the Kechua *pinga* and *ullu*, words glossable as "penis" (Carvalho-Neto 1964:342).

MUSICAL INSTRUMENTS FOR SIGNALING AND WORKING

Musical iconicity (relationship between form and meaning) is another criterion for the use of musical instruments in Peru. The *clarín* is a long, side-blown, lip-concussion aerophone made from bamboo and cow horn, played outdoors by men during Roman Catholic patronal festivals and *mingas*, traditional communal working parties. In the latter usage, the *clarinero* (player of the clarín) directs the work and sets the rhythms. Gisela Cánepa (cited in Romero 1987) delineates four sections in the *minga*, all determined by the music of the *clarinero* music: the *alabado*, or announcement; the *llamada*, which tells the workers to begin laboring; the *trabajo*, or working period; and the *despedida*, after the workers have returned home. During the *trabajo*, the musician plays melodies that announce and set the paces of the jobs to be accomplished; he even plays throughout the periods of rest.

The Ecuadorian *rondador* ("one who makes the rounds") is a single-unit panpipe that derived its name from its use by night watchmen who played it while making their rounds to ease their boredom. Similar panpipes were used in other regions by knife sharpeners (and pig castrators) as signals that they were in the vicinity looking for work. Today the *rondador* is often played by blind beggars in the streets of Quito and elsewhere. [Listen to "Song by blind *rondador* (panpipe) player"]

DISC❶TRACK19

THE INTRODUCTION OF EUROPEAN MUSICAL INSTRUMENTS

Spanish Catholic missionary influence

When the Spanish Catholic missionaries came to Latin America in the mid-1500s to convert and teach the Amerindians, they employed musical instruments that they thought would assist in the conversion because of their heavenliness. These instruments, often used to play bass, harmony, and melody in the absence of an organ, were the harp and the violin (Figure 3.4). The introduction of Western musical instruments by the Catholic missionaries was new to the Amerindians, but the idea of using musical instruments for religion and supernatural power was not—since ancient times, musical instruments have been tools for supernatural communication and power. This may be one of the major reasons that native Americans found the new musical tools acceptable. Today the harp is no longer used for religious purposes in churches, although it is used in religious processions with other instruments; it is more commonly used as an accompanying instrument for songs about love and other aspects of daily life. [Listen to "Song in Quechua about a young man, alone in the world, looking for a wife"]

DISC❶TRACK20

The guitar was considered by the missionaries too secular for converting the Amerindians to Christianity. Rather, it was the preferred musical instrument of minstrels, used to accompany all types of songs of loneliness and dances of joy. After the expulsion of the Jesuits (in 1767), the harp, violin, and the guitar (and its many variants) continued to be played by

Amerindians and *mestizos* until their European origin was all but forgotten. José María Arguedas (1977:16) wrote: "Harp, violin, transverse flute, and *chirimía* are Indian instruments in the Peruvian mountains. … I remember with special … sentiment the expression of amazement of some of my friends, well known *mistis* or men of the village, upon finding that the harp, violin and flute are not Indian instruments, but European ones."

The shawm, known as *chirimía* in Colombia, Ecuador, Guatemala, and Mexico and *chirimía* and *chirisuya* in Peru, was brought, in its European form, by the Spanish colonists. It was used at Jesuit and other Roman Catholic

Figure 3.4
During the St. John the Baptist patronal festival in Acolla, Peru, a violinist and a harpist, members of an *orquesta típica del centro*, perform for a private party. Photo by Dale A. Olsen, 1979.

missions as an outdoor instrument in processions, festivals, funerals, and other church-sponsored events. Additionally, it heralded the conquistadors' entrances into indigenous cities and was later played for social and political events of the Spanish aristocracy (Stevenson 1968:289). When many native peoples in the viceroyalties of New Spain, New Granada, and Peru learned how to play the *chirimía*, it took on indigenous characteristics (use of a split condor quill for a double reed, for example) and became considered one of their own.

The pipe and tabor—one person playing a vertical duct flute and drum at the same time—was probably introduced by the Spanish, though there is evidence for one-person flute-and-drum or flute-and-rattle ensembles from ancient times in Mexico, Central America, and the Andes. In the Andes, the uniqueness of the ensemble is the use of the duct flute with drum, because duct vertical flutes were not known before the Spanish encounter (Figure 3.5). Today in northern Peru, people not uncommonly make them from plastic tubing.

Military-band influences of the 1900s

Indigenous people, especially the Inca, had their own ensembles of military musical instruments, including the *kepu* (conch trumpet) and *wancar* (membranophone), as Garcilaso de la Vega wrote in 1609: "All night long, the two armies remained facing each other, on the alert. When day broke, the conch horns, timpani, and trumpets began to sound, and they marched toward each other, with loud shouting. Leading his troops, the Inca Viracocha struck the first blow and, in no time, there was a terrible struggle" (1966 [1609]:167). These musical instruments evoked fear in their enemies because the drums were of-

Figure 3.5
Two pipe-and-tabor musicians (*cajeros*) perform at the Huanchaco patronal festival in Los Baños del Inca, Peru. Photo by Dale A. Olsen, 1979.

ten made from the skins of their families, killed in battle. Bernabé Cobo wrote in about 1650 that Tupac Inca Yupanqui, the tenth Inca king, "had the two main *caciques* [chiefs] skinned, and he ordered two drums to be made from their hides. With these drums and with the heads of the executed *caciques* placed on pikes, and with many prisoners to be sacrificed to the Sun, the Inca returned in triumph to his court, where he celebrated his victories with great sacrifices and *fiestas*" (1979:143). Therefore, the introduction by the Portuguese, Spanish, and *criollos* (Spanish-descended people) of "trumpets" and "drums" as military instruments into formerly Portuguese- and Spanish-held lands was modernization rather than innovation.

European-derived wind ensembles or bands (mainly German-influenced) were the result of the late-nineteenth- and early-twentieth-century introduction of the military-band concept into the recently independent countries of the Americas. The appearance of such instruments as trumpets, trombones, baritones, tubas, clarinets, saxophones, snare drums, and bass drums coincided with the development of modern armies. While the context was no longer to intimidate the enemy, bands played for processions and parades during religious festivals and military rituals, and provided music for dancing.

German immigrant influence of the 1900s

Besides the influence in the development of military bands, the German-manufactured accordion (*acordeón*) was introduced by German immigrants in the early 1900s. The accordion and its variants (*bandoneón*, *concertina*, and others) are aerophones, even though the multiple single reeds within the instrument do not come in contact with the player's mouth (unlike the harmonica, which is also an aerophone). [Listen to "Tengo que hacer un barquito," a Chilean *cueca* dance-song accompanied by a button accordion] In Colombia, the accordion replaced the locally fabricated *caña de millo*, a single-reed concussion aerophone used

DISC ❶ TRACK 18

Figure 3.6
In a Colombian *vallenato* ensemble in Miami, Florida, a musician plays a button accordion. Photo by Dale A. Olsen, 1988.

in popular ensembles to perform *vallenato*, a rural form of *cumbia* from the region of Vallenata. Today's *vallenato* groups use the button accordion (Figure 3.6), several membranophones, a *guacharaca* (a scraper made from wood or bamboo), and an electric bass (Bermúdez 1985:74; see Marre 1983). In the cities of Colombia, Peru, and elsewhere, accordions are often used in *tunas* or *estudiantinas*, ensembles usually of student musicians who play Spanish-derived and other folkloric music on guitars, mandolins, violins, and other European instruments.

Related to the accordion because it has multiple single reeds is the harmonica (*rondín*) from Ecuador, Peru, and Colombia, where it is called *armónica*, *dulzaina*, and *sinfonía*. It was introduced by German immigrants in the late 1800s and early 1900s; today it is still manufactured in Germany by the Höhner company and imported to the Americas.

THE INFLUENCE OF ELECTRONICS

Electronics has been one of the most important influences in the producing and receiving, the preservation and learning, and the dissemination and commodification of music in South America, Mexico, Central America, and the Caribbean. Amplifiers for *charangos*, guitars, harps, flutes, panpipes, and other acoustic instruments are common in urban areas, but so are electrophones such as synthesizers. Equally important as musical instruments are the numerous devices for musical—and audiovisual, as in video cameras—recording and playback, such as boom boxes, radios, television sets, phonographs, and tape recorders. Also important are electronic-enhancement devices such as microphones, soundboards, speakers, and other elements of public-address systems and amplifiers. These, like the aerophones, chordophones, idiophones, and membranophones that they amplify, often require skilled technicians who function as performers in their own right.

ELECTRONIC PRODUCTION AND RECEPTION OF MUSIC

Just as brass bands have replaced weaker-volume panpipe ensembles in some regions of the Andes, so have electronically enhanced guitars and keyboards replaced weaker-volume samba bands in some regions of urban Brazil, and electronically enhanced horns and keyboards have replaced steel drums for some musical events in Trinidad. Stages in Córdoba, Argentina, are packed with speakers and electronic equipment during performances of *cuarteto* music; stages in Santiago and Viña del Mar, Chile, are likewise filled with sound-enhancement devices during rock concerts and performances by groups such as Los Jaivas and Inti Illimani.

Many countries, such as Brazil, Jamaica, and Mexico, have thriving music industries based on the electronic production of recordings. Since the 1980s, many urban centers have competed with the United States in producing *música latina*. The 45-rpm recording was the important medium of the 1970s, but the 1980s and 1990s were the decades of the cassette tape. By the mid-1990s, compact discs had become popular in large urban areas, and many musical stars were re-releasing on CDs and cassettes their recordings previously released on vinyl.

The reception of music, too, has become dependent on electronic devices. Probably every home in urban areas has a cassette recorder on which tapes of recent and nostalgic music can be played. Likewise, radios and television sets are important musical receivers found in most urban homes, delivering the latest songs by crooners and sexy stars such as Caetano Veloso and Xuxa.

ELECTRONIC PRESERVATION AND LEARNING OF MUSIC

It is not unusual in the 1990s to see native Americans, *mestizos*, or even tourists recording music on boom boxes during patronal and other religious festivals in the Amazon of

Brazil, the Andes of Peru and Bolivia, or other locations that normally do not have electricity. The effects of battery-operated recording devices are overwhelming, and often musical preservation on tape and dance preservation on video is a vital technique for the process of learning.

Musicians from many countries in the Caribbean, Central America, Mexico, and South America have interest in preserving music and dance for the purpose of learning and passing on traditions. In Brazil, the phenomenon known as *parafolclore* is based on the staging of folkloric events, and the learning process is often derived from the electronic preservation of traditional *folclore* events that have been recorded by amateurs with their boom boxes. In more sophisticated circles, recordings are made with Nagra and other professionally designed tape recorders, or on videotape, for preservation in institutes and other academic archives.

ELECTRONIC DISSEMINATION AND COMMODIFICATION OF MUSIC

Electronic dissemination of music is usually done for purposes of commodification. Money is usually the bottom line, though cultural patrimony and ethnic identity may be reasons for the popularity of karaoke among people of Asian descent in South America during the 1980s and 1990s. In São Paulo, Buenos Aires, and other cities where people of Chinese and Japanese descent live, karaoke bars feature the latest musical hits from Japan and the most recent audio, video, and laser-disc technologies. Karaoke in Spanish and Portuguese, featuring regional popular songs, is common in urban bars, where commodification—sales of food and liquor—is more important than the ideals of patrimony and ethnicity.

Sales of cassettes and CDs, however, are the most important means for making money by producers, whereas live concerts are probably the most lucrative means for the performers themselves. Both depend on musical dissemination via electronic sound-producing devices, the latest musical-instrument technologies.

REFERENCES

Arguedas, José María. 1977. *Nuestra Música Popular y sus Intérpretes*. Lima: Mosca Azul & Horizonte.
Aretz, Isabel. 1967. *Instrumentos Musicales de Venezuela*. Caracas: Universidad de Oriente.
Bakan, Michael, Wanda Bryant, Guangming Li, David Martinelli, and Kathryn Vaughn. 1990. "Demystifying and Classifying Electronic Music Instruments." *Selected Reports in Ethnomusicology* 8:37–65.
Bermúdez, Egberto. 1985. *Los Instrumentos Musicales en Colombia*. Bogotá: Universidad Nacional de Colombia.
Bolaños, César, Fernando García, Josafat Roel Pineda, and Alida Salazar. 1978. *Mapa de los Instrumentos Musicales de Uso Popular en el Perú*. Lima: Oficina de Música y Danza.
Carvalho-Neto, Paulo de. 1964. *Diccionario del Folklore Ecuatoriano*. Quito: Editorial Casa de la Cultura Ecuatoriana.
Coba Andrade, Carlos Alberto G. 1981. *Instrumentos Musicales Populares Registrados en el Ecuador*. Otavalo: Instituto Otavaleño de Antropología.
Cobo, Father Bernabé. 1979. *History of the Inca Empire*. Edited and translated by Roland Hamilton. Austin: University of Texas Press.
Coppens, Walter. 1975. *Music of the Venezuelan Yekuana Indians*. Liner notes. Folkways Records FE 4104. LP disk.

Díaz Gainza, José. 1962. *Historia Musical de Bolivia*. Potosí: Universidad Tomás Frias.

Garcilaso de la Vega, El Inca. 1966 [1609]. *The Incas: The Royal Commentaries of the Inca*. 2nd ed. Edited by Alain Gheerbrant. Translated by Maria Jolas. New York: Avon Books, Orion Press.

Izikowitz, Karl Gustav. 1970 [1935]. *Musical Instruments of the South American Indians*. East Ardsley, Wakefield, Yorkshire: S. R. Publishers.

Jairazbhoy, Nazir Ali. 1990. "An Explication of the Sachs-Hornbostel Instrument Classification System." *Selected Reports in Ethnomusicology* 8:81–104.

Jiménez Borja, Arturo. 1951. *Instrumentos Musicales del Perú*. Lima: Museo de la Cultura.

Marre, Jeremy. 1983. *Shotguns and Accordions: Music of the Marijuana Growing Regions of Colombia*. Beats of the Heart series. Harcourt Films. Video.

Okada, Yuki. 1995. *Central and South America. The JVC / Smithsonian Folkways Video Anthology of Music and Dance of the Americas*, 6. Multicultural Media VTMV 230. Video.

Olsen, Dale A. 1986. "It Is Time for Another -Phone." *SEM Newsletter* 20(September):4.

———. 2004. "Aerophones of Traditional Use in South America, with References to Central America and Mexico." In, *Music in Latin America and the Caribbean, An Encyclopedic History, Vol. 1, Performing Beliefs: Indigenous Peoples of South America, Central America, and Mexico*, ed. Malena Kuss 261-326. Austin: University Press of Texas.

Reichel-Dolmatoff, Gerardo. 1971. *Amazonian Cosmos: The Sexual and Religious Symbolism of the Tukano Indians*. Chicago: University of Chicago Press.

Romero, Raúl. 1987. *Música Andina del Perú. Liner notes. Lima: Archivo de Música Tradicional*, Pontificia Universidad Católica del Perú, Instituto Riva Agüero. LP disk.

Roth, Walter E. 1924. *An Introductory Study of the Arts, Crafts, and Customs of the Guiana Indians*. Annual Report 38, 1916–1917. Washington, D.C.: Bureau of American Ethnology.

Stevenson, Robert. 1968. *Music in Aztec and Inca Territory*. Berkeley: University of California Press.

Turino, Thomas. 1987. "Los Chiriguanos." In *Música Andina del Perú. Liner notes. Lima: Archivo de Música Tradicional*, Pontificia Universidad Católica del Perú, Instituto Riva Agüero. LP disk.

Valencia Chacón, Américo. 1989. *El Siku o Zampoña. The Altipano Bipolar Siku: Study and Projection of Peruvian Panpipe Orchestras*. Lima: Artex Editores.

Vega, Carlos. 1946. *Los Instrumentos Musicales Aborígenes y Criollos de la Argentina*. Buenos Aires: Ediciones Centurión.

Whitten, Norman E., Jr. 1974. *Black Frontiersmen. Afro-Hispanic Culture of Ecuador and Colombia*. Prospect Heights, Ill.: Waveland Press.

Musical Genres and Contexts

Anthony Seeger

Dance, Sounds, and Movements
Religious Music
Secular Music
Tourism
The Music Industry

Music is being played or listened to almost everywhere and most of the time in Mexico, Central America, South America, and the Caribbean. Ranging from the sound of a single flute played by a lonely shepherd in a high mountain valley, to privately performed curing ceremonies witnessed only by the curers and the ill, to radios or computer files playing in thousands of homes, to massive celebrations mobilizing hundreds of thousands of participants packed into the broad avenues and civic squares of densely populated cities, the richness and diversity of the musical traditions seem almost to defy description.

Yet this musical diversity has underlying patterns that enable observers to speak about the music of the entire region. This article presents some of the significant general features of the musical genres performed and the contexts in which music is played, drawing on the material from the entries on specific societies and nations, where these processes are described with more attention to local histories and the specifics of social processes, cultures, and styles.

The principal contexts of which music is a part in the Americas include religious activities, life-cycle celebrations, leisure, tourism, and, to a lesser degree, work. Some of these categories are general throughout the lands covered by this volume, but in other cases (such as tourism) music is more heavily involved in some places than in others.

Many are the contexts for musical performance in the Americas. Although some new contexts replace older ones, what appears to happen more often is that new contexts are added to older ones, which after a generation may eventually be replaced. The music changes, but the contexts often remain, and music itself goes on: work, life-cycle rituals, religious events, urban entertainment, tourism, and mass media all include musical performances of significance to their participants.

DANCE, SOUNDS, AND MOVEMENTS

Music and movement are closely intertwined in South America, Mexico, Central America, and the Caribbean. Some native South American communities use the same word for both, arguing that appropriate movements are as much a part of a performance as the sounds themselves. Stylized movements are often an important part of musicians' performances; dancing has been an important part of secular music for centuries, and the name of a rhythm or a dance may define a genre—such as the waltz, the *tango* (Figure 4.1), and the *samba*. Also found throughout the region are dance-dramas, in which music, speech, and movement combine to depict a story (such as a battle between Moors and Christians or the crucifixion of Jesus), often performed in association with the religious calendar, and occasionally with civic and national holidays. Body movements, like the sounds with which they may be associated, are endowed with meaning and convey attitudes, values, and individual and shared emotions.

Ritualized movements throughout the region include children's games; musicians' movements while performing; processions; and solo, couple, and group dances. Though some common features can be discerned, dances of Amerindian, African, and European origins have distinctive features, often combined today in popular traditions. Traditional Amerindian dances tend to involve stamping or moving the legs and arms to a fairly regular rhythm, with the rest of the trunk and head fairly straight and rigid. Dances in circles and lines are common, usually with the genders separated; dancing in couples was extremely rare, if found at all. In European dance traditions, the trunk and head are fairly motionless, the legs usually move to a simple rhythm, and dancing in couples (and combinations of couples) is often a defining feature. Dances that originated in Africa frequently involve moving different parts of the body to different rhythms—resembling the polyrhythmic patterns of the music itself. Formations by individuals and in lines and circles are more common than dances in couples.

Figure 4.1
Two of the most outstanding tango dancers—Milena Plebs and Miguel Ángel Zotto—in their show *Perfume do Tango* at the Sadler's Wells Theatre, London, 1993. Photo courtesy of Ercilia Moreno Chá.

During the past five hundred years, whatever distinctness the dances of different ethnic groups once had has been blurred by adaptations of existing styles and creations of new ones. This situation is especially true of twentieth-century popular dances, which have often drawn heavily on African-descended traditions. Amerindian and African religious traditions reveal their origins with greater clarity than secular dances. European religions have had an ambivalent attitude toward music and dance altogether—often banning the performance of secular music and dance and discouraging dancing in religious services. Whereas music and dance open communication with spirits in many Amerindian and African-based religions, silent prayer is considered the most effective communication with the deity in many Christian churches.

Dance halls, nightclubs, and life-cycle celebrations of which dancing in couples is a part (birthday parties and weddings, for example) are important performance locations that provide the livelihood for many musicians. The importance of these locations may have influenced the development of musical technology (in favor of louder instruments that can be played for many hours), and technology has influenced the development of these venues. Many articles in this volume touch on the importance of secular social dancing in the musical environments of the different areas and describe specific dances that were, and are, popular. It is important to remember that rhythms for dancing usually involve distinctive body movements, and that the challenge, pleasure, exhilaration, and meaning of moving the body are an important part of musical events almost everywhere.

RELIGIOUS MUSIC

Amerindian belief systems

Before the colonization of the Americas by Europe beginning in 1492, it is quite likely that most musical events were in some form or another part of religious or state-sponsored events. Where states were based on religion, it is difficult to separate the concepts of religion and politics. The elaborate ceremonies described by the Maya and the Inca for their Spanish conquerors included musical performances by specialists. The religious rituals of the coastal Tupi-Guaraní in Brazil and the island-dwelling Arawak and Carib communities in the Caribbean featured unison singing, shouts, dancing, and the sound of flutes and rattles. The archaeological record is replete with examples of clay wind instruments; in the humid areas, little else has survived.

Intensive investigation of Amerindian music in the twentieth century has necessarily been restricted to areas where such groups survive and continue to practice what appear to be traditional religions and musical forms. They are often found living in "refuge areas"— remote locations, away from non-Indian settlements, in areas of relatively little economic importance to the national society, and where missionization is recent, tolerant, or ineffective. With small populations and facing the effects of new diseases and economic changes, these groups cannot serve for generalizing about the musical situation in the pre-Columbian empires. Their music, however, reveals striking similarities to descriptions written in the 1500s and 1600s of performances in the nonstate societies. In these refuge areas, music continues to be closely related to religious events, and to direct communications with spirits and interactions with spirits of animals (such as jaguars, deer, and vultures) or ancestors. In some cases, musical sounds are themselves the voices of spirits; the performers may or may not be hybrid humans or spirits, and the instruments themselves spirits. Dale Olsen, in his discussion of communication with spirits among the Warao, describes a feature that reappears throughout South America [see WARAO].

Shamanism and music

Shamanism is a widespread form of communication with spirits. It was found from the extreme southern tip of Argentina and Chile through northern Mexico and right up into the arctic. At one level, shamanism is communication with spirits for the purpose of healing or sickening an individual or a community. At another level, shamanism is a practice that demonstrates to onlookers the continued presence and power of spirits. It makes the sacred visible and experienced directly by the population. Shamans may use tobacco and other narcotics and hallucinogens in conjunction with singing, or they may rely on singing alone. In a few cases, they do not employ music at all. When music is part of shamanism, it can simultaneously structure the shaman's experiences and communicate them to the community as it teaches children how to be shamans and what the supernatural world is like. Like many aspects of community life, it is at once a religious, social, and instructional event.

Shamanism is often a domestic or community practice, but many communities perform larger ceremonies to which they invite neighboring communities. These may involve feasting, drinking homemade beer or ingesting narcotics or hallucinogens, and making music and dancing (as in the upper Rio Negro). Metamorphosis, a transformation into an animal or spirit, is characteristic of a great deal of native South American religion. Shamans transform themselves into animals for their journeys. Through music, dance, and ritual structures, groups of performers are transformed into groups of animals and spirits. Amerindian religious experience is frequently achieved through altering perception by means that include deprivation, narcotics, hallucinogens, and long periods of activity, such as singing and dancing. Altered states are interpreted as the transformation of humans into more powerful beings. The transformation is achieved, in many cases, through music itself. The music is thought to originate in the natural or ancestral world and is taught to the performers by religious or musical specialists. Humans sing songs of the natural world and become themselves somewhat like the originators—ancestors, animals, or spirits. Rituals often involve some kind of terminating event in which the transformed beings are turned back into humans again.

The music in such events often appears repetitive and is frequently "interrupted" by "nonmusical" sounds, such as animal cries and shouts. Repetition is part of the efficacy of the music—it can provide the underlying structures on which the events develop. The development or drama may not be in melody and timbre, but in the texts and experiences recounted. Often, the music continues for the duration of the event—which may last hours, or even days and weeks. Where animal spirits are powerful and sometimes sacred, it should be no wonder that animal cries appear in the performances. They should not be considered extramusical, however, since their absence may result in a performance considered unsatisfactory or without effect. They may be nonmelodic, but they are not extramusical.

Syncretism and music

In Amerindian communities where missionaries have been active and there is a long history of contact with the colonizers, musical traditions developed that in many places combine aspects of native and colonizer religious events and similarly combine their musical forms and performances. The merging of styles and events through a colonial encounter is much more common than isolation in Mexico and Central and South America. Saint's-day celebrations in the Andes and the highlands of Mexico and Guatemala often combine public inebriation, shouts and cries rarely heard in European performances, and traditional Amerindian instruments with Roman Catholic holidays. In Andean communities in some areas of Peru, Christian holidays are the most important "traditional" musical events that survive.

In some Amerindian communities, especially those influenced by Protestant missionaries, the singing of hymns has replaced all traditional musical forms. In some places, this change has led to unusual new musical events, such as hymn-writing competitions and writing hymns in indigenous languages. In others, the singing of hymns and national and international popular music are the only genres performed today.

European-introduced Christianity

Most countries in Mexico, Central America, South America, and the Caribbean are nominally Christian, and most of their people are Roman Catholic. This situation is the result of extensive colonization by Spain and Portugal. Amerindians and enslaved African populations were converted to Christianity, and under colonial rule, the Roman Catholic Church influenced their beliefs and social institutions tremendously. The mass itself was seldom elaborated musically, and then for special occasions only, and the singing of hymns has only recently been introduced; but Roman Catholic missionaries were quite concerned with the musical development of the Amerindians they encountered. They set up music schools in several countries, and introduced their own music in part to replace the "diabolical" traditions they encountered. Some enslaved Africans were similarly taught to play European instruments and participated in many kinds of musical events.

The church supported the establishment of social groups called brotherhoods (Portuguese *irmandades*, Spanish *cofradías*), which had been organized in Europe but in the New World came to be one of the few organizations available to enslaved Africans and their descendants. These institutions had both social and religious features and often included the performance of music and dancing on religious occasions. Voluntary religious organizations, continued by the descendants of these brotherhoods, survive in many parts of Mexico, Central America, South America, and the Caribbean, where they perform on saints' days and around Christmas.

For many communities of Amerindian, African, and European descent alike, the Christian religious calendar has structured the most important public musical events of the year. The birth of Jesus is celebrated in the end of December, at Christmas. Local community celebrations frequently extend to 6 January, with pageantlike wanderings of kings bearing gifts. Jesus' crucifixion and resurrection, celebrated during Holy Week (culminating in Easter), are preceded by a penitential period called Lent, which itself is preceded by enthusiastic celebrations of Carnaval (Carnival) during the final days before Ash Wednesday and the beginning of Lent. Carnival celebrations, not always welcomed by the church, are considered to be a kind of last chance for fleshly excesses before Lent, and music often plays an important role in the events. The most famous of these may be in the Caribbean, in Rio de Janeiro, and in New Orleans, but Carnival celebrations and restrictions on musical performances during Lent are found in many communities throughout the area.

In addition to these religious events, the days of many different saints are celebrated in different areas. In some cases, a country may celebrate a saint (as Mexico does the Virgin of Guadalupe); in others, a certain saint may be celebrated as the patron of a particular city, a particular trade, or a particular ethnic group. Often saints' days are occasions for competitions in music and dance. Communities with populations of African and Amerindian descent have often combined elements of previous beliefs with Roman Catholic ones—which has led to a multiplicity of traditions throughout the region.

In the twentieth century, evangelical Protestant groups have made considerable inroads into Roman Catholicism and African spirit-based religions. Hymns, sung in Spanish, Portuguese, English, and Amerindian languages, are a common musical form. Among the Protestant sects are Hallelujah groups, in which possession by spirits is common, often to the accompaniment of some form of participatory music. In some communities, considerable conflict occurs between religious groups, expressed in musical events, theology, and church rituals.

African-introduced religions

Africans were enslaved and brought to the Americas from widely variant societies and regions. They therefore had no unifying language, religion, or musical tradition. Many, however, shared general musical traits that transcended particular African communities—among them collective participation in making music, call-and-response singing, and dense and often interlocking rhythms played on drums.

Enslaved peoples of African descent turned to, and were in some cases encouraged to turn to, Christian churches for worship. They brought to these churches a musical tradition that persisted despite systematic efforts to suppress some of its African elements, such as the playing of drums (repeatedly outlawed in different countries). Important, too, were brotherhoods where slaves and free people of African descent could meet to socialize and to prepare ritual events. These have continued in such places as St. Lucia, Brazil, and Panama (Figure 4.2), where their members perform on certain religious occasions. Important among the performances are *congos*, dramatic presentations of stories, combining special forms of speech, music, and highly coordinated dancing.

Among the later waves of peoples brought to the New World were Yoruba-speaking populations from West Africa, whose religion included the worship of divine beings that would possess adepts and speak through them. These religions have persisted throughout the Caribbean and along Brazil's east coast right into Argentina, under various names and using various musical forms. Called Santería in Cuba, Vodou in Haiti, Candomblé in northeastern Brazil, and other names in other countries, they usually employ a set of three sacred drums and other instruments whose rhythms are specific to specific divine beings. Called by the rhythms, the gods descend and "ride" the bodies of specific worshipers. Though formerly persecuted in some countries, these religions are expanding to new audiences.

Figure 4.2
Cristo Negro (Black Christ); Christ's crucifixion celebrated by a *cofradía* (brotherhood) in Portobelo, Panama. Photo by Ronald R. Smith.

Other religious communities

Significant populations of peoples of South Asian and Indonesian descent live in the Caribbean and the Guianas (Guyana, Surinam, French Guiana), and their celebrations are often related to ritual observances of their own. Some European immigrant groups have brought with them their own religious organizations, and these influence different countries to different degrees. Since 1898, Japanese immigrants have introduced their religions into South America [see Music of Immigrant Groups].

SECULAR MUSIC

A great deal of musical performance may be characterized as nonreligious, or secular. There is no attempt in such music to address divinities or to call spirits to inhabit a space or a body. Some apparently secular events, such as saints' days, are intimately tied to the sacred calendar; some are tied to an agricultural calendar; some are related to life-cycle events; some are tied to national holidays and music festivals.

Music for work

A few kinds of music were developed to accompany collective labor. Before steam and electricity came to the aid of human muscles, coordinated labor was the most effective way to move heavy loads and raise heavy sails. In some situations, a fixed rhythm allowed laborers to work at a steady, slow pace, and served to while away the hours.

With the predominance of steam, gasoline, and electric energy, work-related songs are rarely performed. In many parts of the region, however, music continues to be part of the workplace. In Peru, certain collective agricultural work is accompanied by music played on flutes and drums or on other instruments. In many parts of the region, agricultural workers take battery-operated radios to listen to popular music as they labor in the sun. The productivity of workers in offices may be carefully manipulated by local forms of Muzak in air-conditioned office buildings in the capital cities, and shoppers may be guided by music played in malls.

More frequently than actually creating the pace at which people work, music marks the beginning and ending of seasons: to begin the planting, to celebrate the harvest, to commemorate a particularly good manufacturing year. Agricultural rituals occur in most countries with large Amerindian populations and in Amerindian communities, but they also occur in communities of European immigrants and populations of African descent.

Life-cycle celebrations

A great deal of music is performed around events in human lives. These range from Amerindian initiations to European-influenced birthdays, weddings, anniversaries, and funerals. Many of these events include social dancing, drinking, and eating, and some are highly elaborate. In many countries, weddings are festive events, and performing at them is an important source of income for musicians. Fifteenth-birthday celebrations are major social occasions for young women and their families in much of Mexico and Central and South America. Courting, making new acquaintances, and renewing acquaintances are often part of life-cycle celebrations. They typically include a group of invited celebrants of both sexes and various ages and professional or semiprofessional musicians. Recorded music, occasionally with a disc jockey, may animate the events. Although birth and christening ceremonies are important in some communities, in others death is ritually elaborated. Funerals are usually occasions for sadness, but this does not detract from their musical elaboration. Two good examples of funeral music are the *koutoumba* wake in St. Lucia [Listen to "Koumen non K'alé fè"] and the wake for a child in Ecuador. These celebrations typically include a group of invited celebrants and a professional drummer for the former (Guilbault 1998:948) and a semiprofessional harpist- or violinist-singer for the latter (Schechter 1998:423). The parties often begin in the afternoon and extend into the evening, or where rural roads and a large distance between neighbors make travel difficult, into the next day.

DISC ❶ TRACK 39

Nightclubs, bars, brothels, dance halls, clubs, streets

The urban-music scene includes a number of institutions where musicians are employed, music is performed, and people watch, listen, and dance. The audiences are mostly fairly young, attendees are not related to one another, and the musicians are professional and paid or receive contributions.

Bars and brothels are the legendary birthplaces of new forms of popular music, and are one of the reasons many musicians have often been associated with immorality and sexuality. For most of the twentieth century, bars and brothels have been important employers of musicians, and many genres of popular music have evolved from the urban Bohemia:

the Cuban *habanera*, the Argentinean *tango*, the Brazilian *choro*, Dixieland jazz, and other forms have been associated with these urban institutions.

Nightclubs are a somewhat different institution. They run the gamut from bars with shows to tourist-oriented theaters where specially produced shows are presented to largely foreign audiences. In some cases, touristic nightclubs build on the foundations of earlier, less high-class institutions—as in the *tango* nightclubs of Buenos Aires; the jazz clubs of New Orleans; folkloric *peñas* in Santiago, La Paz, and Lima; steakhouses in Asunción; and others.

Dance halls are places where, for a small fee, singles or couples can enter to dance, mingle with others, and buy drinks and food. Many of these businesses specialize in a certain kind of music, frequently a genre of popular music or the music of a group of immigrants who have moved to the city. Immigrant clubs are legion in Peru, in Brazil, and in some other countries. Dance halls specializing in disco music (in the 1970s) and more recently hip-hop, house music, and other contemporary genres are outgrowths of these institutions. These are mostly frequented by young adults, though some clubs cater to an older clientele and usually play older forms of popular music.

Athletic competitions, political rallies, and other large, voluntary, public events often have musical components in Mexico, Central America, South America, and the Caribbean. Brazilian soccer games are noteworthy for the percussion bands that encourage the players with throbbing rhythms. Political rallies may be animated by protest songs, or by bands playing anthems. Civic holidays are often marked with parades and bands. When large groups of people meet, organizers may arrange for music that represents the event itself, or the participants may bring their own. The kind of music performed, and the interpretation of that music, is a significant part of the events.

The street is an open-air stage for arranged or spontaneous performances. Some musicians are the musical equivalents of hawkers and vendors. Others are beggars or simply entertainers. Often street musicians play homemade instruments (Figure 4.3).

Figure 4.3
The Port-au-Prince street musicians Jean and Narat Nicola, who call themselves the Beggar's Band. The two sing and play a variety of domestic utensils recycled as percussion instruments. Photo by Steve Winter, 1989.

Tourism is an important feature of the economies of Mexico and many Central and South American and Caribbean nations. Drawing visitors from the United States, Canada, Europe, and Asia through their natural attractions (beaches, climates) and cultural attractions (coffee houses, concerts, festivals, nightclubs) is essential to the economic health of most Caribbean nations, and it is important to most of the rest (Figure 4.4). Artistically, the tourist industry is a double-edged sword: it supports local musicians but imposes changes on their art in the interest of pleasing a foreign audience that is largely ignorant of local traditions.

In large countries such as Brazil and Argentina, internal tourism is a significant feature of the economy. States in the northeast of Brazil are visited by wealthy residents of the south in much the same way that some Caribbean islands are visited by people from other countries. These visitors are looking for a rural life-style and often want to have the opportunity to see local traditions.

The traditional arts in many countries are supported to a greater or lesser degree by tourism. In some cases, the tourist office pays for the performers' costumes and expenses; in other cases, it organizes events and controls who performs and who attends. Tourists, however, do not usually understand the traditions, and as they are on a holiday schedule, events are often shortened for their convenience. In the end, tourism may create venues and performances that differ distinctly from those of the community, and in some cases these can destroy the older, community-oriented traditions altogether.

Figure 4.4
A masquerade being performed for tourists from a cruise ship on the beach in Soufrière, St. Lucia. The instruments are a bamboo flute, a bass drum, and a snare drum. The masquerader reaches out his left hand as he asks for money. Photo by Dale A. Olsen, 1977.

Mass media—radio, television, computers, cassettes, CDs, videotapes, digital file trans-fers—have transformed the musical environment at an ever-increasing rate during the twentieth century. The entertainment industry creates an important venue for perfor-mance and an influential conduit for new styles. Musical performance is no longer a face-to-face event, and new genres, new styles, and new audiences have been created through this transformation.

Technology has at times influenced musical performances in concrete ways. The stan-dard three-minute length for recorded songs was determined in part by the playing time of a wax cylinder, and later by that of a ten-inch 78-rpm record. The difficulty of controlling radio emissions across national boundaries has led to exchange of musical ideas despite local laws and import restrictions. The possibility of creating certain sounds in a studio af-fects the way live performances are evaluated. The impact of these media is so widespread that it is difficult to imagine musical life without them.

Radio, television, and computers

Satellite dishes are popular over much of the region. Music Television (MTV, VH1, and so on) has had a tremendous impact on musical performance in areas where its channels are received. So have local soap operas and other shows. The arrival of electricity, and with it radio and television, appears to result in a quick decline of domestic musical genres: the time that people used to spend singing to each other is now spent listening to or watching others perform.

One result of the impact of mass media on large populations has been the systematic attempts of national governments to control what is transmitted and to place various kinds of censorship on the media. Many countries have imposed some kind of control on radio networks and require a certain percentage of the transmissions to be music from their own country or region. The rest of the time, stations mostly feature popular music from several sources, especially North America. Television programs, being more expensive to produce, are often purchased directly from other countries.

Live performances often include topical songs and local references, but broadcast re-strictions in many countries have limited which kinds of ideas can be expressed in music or image. This control has operated with varying degrees of success and has often been opposed by artists—many of whom have been imprisoned or even killed under military regimes as in Argentina, Brazil, and Chile. When music becomes associated with a lower-class or marginal life-style, its practitioners are likely to suffer various kinds of police and political repression.

Audio and video recordings

Many countries have a small recording industry that focuses on inexpensive media, such as audiocassettes, that feature local artists. A locally clandestine industry often produces pirated versions of international hits. Larger countries have subsidiaries of the large multi-national recording companies, which publish local music and international popular music. Often local musical styles have been adapted, recorded, and popularized by musicians in North America. In some cases, however, local styles became international ones: one need only think of calypso, reggae, *samba*, and *tango*. In most cases, the more popular singers are signed by transnational recording companies.

Recordings involve more than a performer and a machine that records sounds: producers, record-company executives, recording engineers, marketing specialists, and many others play important roles in determining the sound of a performance and its diffusion through mass media. Some artists feel they are losing control over their art; others welcome advice from those who know how to make them fit into a pattern that brings success. The relationship among artists, their record companies, and their music is quite complex and varies from genre to genre and place to place.

Widely separated communities within the same country, or communities whose members span several different countries, often create informal networks of audio and videotape exchanges. The Indian and Javanese communities in Trinidad and Surinam exchange recordings with relatives in the home countries. Small shops in Miami, New York, and other North American cities feature local recordings from Mexico, Central America, and the Caribbean. Some record stores in the United States specialize in importing music from one area or another.

REFERENCES

Guilbault, Jocelyne. 1998. "St. Lucia," in *South America, Mexico, Central America, and the Caribbean*, Vol. 2, *The Garland Encyclopedia of World Music*, eds. Dale A. Olsen and Daniel E. Sheehy, 942–951. New York: Garland Publishing.

Schechter, John M. 1998. "Ecuador," in *South America, Mexico, Central America, and the Caribbean*, Vol. 2, *The Garland Encyclopedia of World Music*, eds. Dale A. Olsen and Daniel E. Sheehy, 413–433. New York: Garland Publishing.

Social Structure, Musicians, and Behavior

Anthony Seeger

Defining Social Features of Musical Performance
Social Groups and Musical Performance
Musical Performance and Musical Events
Mediated Music
Ownership and Rights

Music is firmly embedded in social life and contributes to the ways in which people in most societies work, play, worship, and reproduce themselves, socially and biologically. Music is part of social life because musicians and their audiences are part of larger groups and processes. Composers, performers, and audience members have families, participate in social life, have some attitude toward religious beliefs, and have been brought up under unique historical conditions. Musicians and their audiences use music as a resource for a variety of religious and social purposes. Small Amerindian villages and large nation-states may be seen as comprising social groups, each with its own kinds of music, performing together or apart. As they perform, they express, re-create, or transform the social fabric of the communities themselves in a constant musical process of reformulation and renewal.

In Mexico, Central America, South America, and the Caribbean, people have performed to attract lovers and to make fun of them, to support governments and to criticize them, to march to war and to oppose it, to worship gods and to be possessed by them. Some music has been taught in schools, supported by government funds, or sold through commerce. Other music has been prohibited or censored—by parents, slaveholders, governments, and religious leaders. Musical performances are among the ways people express personal, political, and religious beliefs. In so doing, they create and express attitudes about people, social groups, and various experiences.

It is easy to see that music is part of social life; it is more difficult to determine how. Simply looking at an event and asking straightforward, journalistic questions about it is a good start. Performances usually involve certain types of individuals and groups, to the exclusion of others. Different audiences express allegiances to different genres, attend at different times of day or night, and associate music with different goals and values.

The social contexts of many particular genres may be discovered in the individual entries of this volume, in which musical differences by gender, age, social class, ethnocultural group, and religion frequently appear. What needs to be stressed as a general principle is that most social identities—an individual's membership in a particular group—are partly constructed through music. Gender and age are relatively fixed, but an individual's membership in many ethnocultural and social-class groups depends on demonstrating certain cultural preferences and styles, often including performance of or admiration for particular types of music, dress, bodily ornamentation, and cuisine. Different identities can be expressed with different musical forms: we can sing a national anthem as members of a nation and a regional song as a member of a region, or we can perform music that identifies us as an ethnic minority. People may activate different identities through the music they choose to perform or listen to. Or they may consciously introduce certain styles into their music to indicate specific cultural relationships, as when Peruvians or Brazilians of African descent introduce musical features learned in contemporary Africa to indicate the relationship of a genre to the African diaspora, or when a Paraguayan community of German descent adopts new German genres and styles.

Music is part of social life because musicians and their audiences are part of a larger society. In moments of ethnic or political crisis, music is a form of cultural expression that becomes an area of attention and conflict. Groups that earlier played various styles may begin to define themselves by a single genre; rallies of different political parties may feature different kinds of music, and arguments over what kind of music to play at a dance may express fundamental political and cultural differences. Music, and the performing arts more generally, can become the focus of intense interest (and violent repression), because art can be used to express complex social and political ideas.

Partly because societies are such large, complex subjects, the entries in this volume describe extremely different kinds of relationships between music and society. Taken as a whole, however, they reveal some regularities. One way to define the social features of musical performances is to look for answers to a few simple questions about a performance or genre: who is performing? for whom are they performing? what are they performing? where are they performing? when is it performed? why are people performing that music in that way? The first two questions direct our attention to the people involved; the fourth and fifth, to the specifics of the event itself; the third is about the music itself; and the sixth raises the issue of motivation. The answers to these questions are an introduction to the social contexts of musical performance.

DEFINING SOCIAL FEATURES OF MUSICAL PERFORMANCE

Who is performing?

The answer is usually simple: a group of children, a military band, an all-male chorus of retired truckers, an all-female unaccompanied group, a foreign rock band. The performers may be identified with an ethnocultural group (Amerindian, African, or European descent, or more specifically German, Prussian, and so on). Yet the implications of who is performing begin to indicate the significance of the music. Individuals affiliate themselves with groups, and every group has relationships with other groups—relationships that usually change over time. Thus age, gender, occupation, and nationality can all be significant aspects of musical performance, especially since conflict often occurs between different ages, genders, occupations, and nationalities.

For whom are they performing?

For an analysis of the relationship of music to social behavior, the audience is just as important as the performers. Ethnomusicologists are not the only ones curious about who listens to a certain genre of music: record-company executives, radio stations, and professional musicians all want to know about their audiences. The musicians may be performing for children (Figure 5.1) or adults, for politicians or their critics, or for members of their own ethnocultural group or of another one. Each context usually holds different meanings for the participants.

Figure 5.1
A young girl of Japanese descent (*sansei*, third generation) is spellbound at seeing and hearing a trombone being played in a *caipira* band during the 1981 *festa junina* (June Festival) in São Paulo, Brazil. Photo by Dale A. Olsen.

What are they performing?

Musical sounds are quite variable: they all have tone (pitch), timbre (quality), and amplitude (loudness), and are usually arranged into pulsing series (rhythms) that unfold in larger overall structures (strophic, binary, variational, and so on). At any given time, certain sounds are associated with certain groups (age, gender, occupation, ethnicity, cultural roots) and certain situations. These features may change over time; they are not fixed. The performance of a certain musical style, or attendance at the performance, often indicates some kind of statement about allegiance with a group or its goals. The exclusion of a musical genre or style may indicate opposition to the group with which it is identified. What kinds of music are not performed can be as important as what kinds of music are performed.

Where are they performing?

Music takes some of its meaning from the place in which it is performed. A song performed in a military parade in the civic center, surrounded by the president's palace, the ministry of justice, and large bank buildings, has different implications from the same song performed on a protest march, in a bar or a brothel, or in a church. Musical repertoire may move from context to context, but it often changes meaning as it does. It may bring some of its earlier meaning to its new context, permitting people to use music ironically, angrily, adoringly, and in many other ways. This ability is partly created by the contexts it is performed in, and by the way it is performed.

When is the music performed?

Different times can have different meanings. The dawn has tremendous significance for many Amerindian groups, and a great deal of music is performed at dawn. Many performances coincide with the agricultural cycle of planting, irrigating, and harvesting crops. Others are part of the Christian calendar of Christ's life (Christmas, Easter, saints' days), or Jewish, Hindu, or other religious calendars. Music associated with leisure, however, will be performed when people are not required to work: on weekends, in the evenings, on holidays and festivals. Some forms, such as Muzak, are designed to be played during working hours; but no one would confuse a quiet Muzak performance of a rock song in an air-conditioned office building with a late-night concert of the "same" song in a stadium where thousands of people are dancing to deafening sounds from huge speakers. Like space, the time of a performance can indicate something about its significance.

Why are people performing that music in that way?

The question why has many answers that can come from many different positions. The musicians may say, "We perform to eat." The audience may say, "We listen because we like them." But that is only part of the answer. Why perform a given piece for a certain audience in a certain place at a certain time? The more specific the question, the more significant the answer may be. It might be: "We performed Mozart because the audience is so uneducated they wouldn't appreciate John Cage," or "We sang the national anthem as our protest march passed the police station so they wouldn't come out and beat us up," or "We had to play something loud to get the audience dancing," or "We thought it would be funny to play the brass-band piece on these instruments." All musicians have to eat, and most audiences have the option of being somewhere else, military and civic events excepted. But those alone do not explain an event. Instead, the specifics of each situation and the decisions made in it can be far more revealing than the generalities.

SOCIAL GROUPS AND MUSICAL PERFORMANCE

Small Amerindian communities and nation-states alike reveal musical distinctions based on gender, age, and other social groups.

Gender

Gender identity is distinct from sexual identity. A person has a sexual identity based on physiological traits; a person's gender identity is a social construction. Male humans are physiologically the same, and distinct from female humans. Different societies, however, define gender identities differently. This distinction is important because gender identity can change during an individual's lifetime, while biological identity does not (without surgical intervention). In some communities and some contexts, the musical roles of men and women may be rigidly separated when they are young, and then become more alike after a woman's menopause. In other communities and other contexts, men and women may exchange roles, sing in one another's styles, and use gender definition (and ambiguity) as part of their musical performance.

Music is also one of the ways gender and its meaning are established and perpetuated. The relationship of gender to musical performances is complex, varies considerably among different groups and at different times, and is changing rapidly as the relative positions of men and women change throughout Mexico, Central America, South America, and the Caribbean. The ambiguity of gay, lesbian, and bisexual gender roles receives musical and ritual expression in certain secular and religious music, among them transvestite performances in nightclubs (secular) and Brazilian Candomblé (religious). In most Amerindian communities, men play a greater number of musical instruments and are more deeply involved in public rituals than women. Women traditionally sang but rarely played wind instruments, drums, or rattles. Sometimes women were prohibited from even seeing sacred instruments. But distinctions of gender are not restricted to Amerindian communities: worldwide, few orchestra conductors are women, and the Roman Catholic Church bars women from the priesthood; most members of *salsa* or *mariachi* ensembles are men.

Amerindian women sometimes have entirely separate ceremonies in which they are full participants, ceremonies like *iamuricuma*, a ceremony in the Xingú region of Brazil, and *machitún*, a shamanistic role among the Mapuche of Argentina and Chile. In Amerindian and rural communities, where women's life-styles may remain more traditional than those of their husbands and sons, women often preserve traditions that once were performed by men: the last singers of the Selk'nam men's chants in Tierra del Fuego were women, as are most remaining singers of Spanish and Portuguese ballads (romances). With changes in gender roles can come changes in musical participation.

Age

Age may or may not be a significant factor in different musical performances, and it is hard to generalize across the region. Different societies define age somewhat differently: in some, age or status is determined, not by years alone, but also by a person's perceived stage in life—whether he or she is dependent on parents, married with children, a grandparent, and so on. Nevertheless, in almost every society, people of different ages perform or listen to different genres of music in groups to some degree differentiated by age. In some cases, they may perform the same genre in different ways. Children are sometimes included in musical events (Figure 5.2), and at other times they are excluded; yet children often have their own musical genres, passed on intact from older child to younger child, quite outside the formal adult-to-child instructional hierarchy. This situation is true of many children's games and dances. Children learn a great deal about adult genres just by listening—things they may perform only many years later. Unmarried men and women are active participants in many social dances and music-related courting activities. Married adults have been the most frequent public performers, but many popular musicians are young adults. The elderly may participate less in public rituals, or they may be revered as a source of wisdom and knowledge, and be deeply involved in teaching younger generations.

Figure 5.2
A boy playing a *güiro* in a *conjunto típico* (typical ensemble) in Panama. A button accordion is to his right. Photo by Ronald R. Smith.

A few societies of the region have genres restricted to grandparents.

The most common form of age-related musical preference is the way different generations view different forms of popular music, often admiring most the forms that were popular when they were adolescents. In urban communities, people seem to be attracted to new forms of popular music during their adolescence, and then to continue to be fans of that music for the ensuing decades, while new generations of youth find new types of music to identify with. Dance-oriented clubs in such cities as Rio de Janeiro seem to have an almost age-grade quality to them. In popular music, musical preference is one of the classic conflicts between parents and children, and between schoolteachers and schoolchildren. The older generation almost always laments the passing of some form, the middle generation is letting it pass, and the younger generation has new interests. This succession, however, is not automatic: the younger generation sometimes becomes more interested in traditional forms as it ages, and eventually they become elders who lament the disappearance of the same traditions their parents and grandparents lamented—and yet the tradition survives.

Kinship

Kinship roles may be important in certain genres. Birthday parties, with their English, Spanish, or Portuguese versions of "The Birthday Song" ("Happy birthday to you") are typically attended by people of various ages and both sexes, many of whom are related by kinship or age to the celebrant. Many local bands include family members. Sometimes the significant groups are not the immediate family, but other kinship-based groups. Among the Gê-speaking Indians of Brazil, various social groups are identified by a musical genre, a style of performance, or even a musical text.

Occupation

Occupations often have traditions of their own, and some of these may be musical. Clearly the occupation of "musician" has musical features, but shamans and ritual specialists in tribal societies know more about musical performances than most other adults. Other occupations may have their own musical forms: seamen coordinated their labor through chanties, and itinerant traders, with their packs filled with merchandise, carried musical traditions and stories to isolated settlements. In some places, different occupations have their own social clubs, with their own performances at leisure times or holiday festivals. Today, travelers often bring cassettes and videos with them when they visit friends or relatives in distant places. Airline pilots are sometimes couriers in networks that bring recently released recordings of popular music directly to clubs and dance halls in Mexico, Central and South America, and the Caribbean. Taxi drivers may double as distributors of records.

Social class

Social class is often a factor in the performance in or attendance at musical events: just as people of different ages express their solidarity through participating in different musical traditions, so may people of different social classes choose to identify themselves with different genres or styles of performance. Social class is defined in a number of ways and can be quite complex in Mexico, Central and South America, and the Caribbean. Clearest of all are contrasts between urban elite and rural poor. The culture of the elites has traditionally been oriented toward Europe and the United States, including classical, popular, and avant-garde musical styles of performance. Urban workers may identify with a national form of popular music, whereas rural workers and recent immigrants to the large cities often prefer a rural-based country music such as the Brazilian *música caipira* (Figure 5.3) or Amerindian-based popular music such as the Peruvian *huayno* (*wayno*). In some cases members of the working

class will prefer international music, such as funk, hip-hop, and urban genres from Europe and North America.

How important these distinctions are will vary over time and by circumstance. Special cases contradict easy generalities, such as communities of Italian laborers who are enthusiastic fans of nineteenth-century Italian opera, a genre otherwise appreciated largely by an urban elite. When class conflicts are strong, the identification of a group with a particular type of music often has political implications. Then men and women of different social classes may identify themselves with the music of one of the classes as an expression of ethnic, cultural, or political unity, and governments may institute censorship or harassment.

Figure 5.3
A *caipira* band performs during the 1981 *festa junina* (June Festival) in São Paulo, Brazil. From left are a bass drum, an alto saxophone, and a snare drum. Photo by Dale A. Olsen.

Religion

Religions influence musical performances and audience participation. Many religions employ distinctive musical forms, and some forbid other kinds of musical performances or condemn music and dance. Amerindians under missionary influence sometimes saw their sacred instruments exposed and burned, and at other times were dissuaded from performing traditional genres by threats and coercion. Overall, European religious music has been a powerful influence on musical performances throughout the entire region. Sometimes religious genres appear in secular situations, and sometimes religions limit musical performances. Islam and some Christian Protestant fundamentalists prohibit drinking and mixed-sex dancing, and frown on participation in musical events in bars, brothels, and nightclubs. Different religious groups may have their own genres and their own professional musicians, as with Christian rock and Christian country, with which members of the religious group identify.

Politics

Politics and music have a long history of association throughout the region—military bands, national anthems, warm-up groups at political rallies, composers of topical songs performing on street corners and in nightclubs. Music must be considered a potent political tool. Over the centuries, governments have harassed, censored, banned, exiled, jailed, tortured, and killed composers and performers from widely different social classes. In addition to the religious repression of musical styles, political persecutions have occurred repeatedly. In different countries, descendants of African slaves were forbidden to play drums and were pressured to abandon certain musical genres. In the 1940s, Brazilian country musicians were censored and jailed for their topical verses. In the 1960s and 1970s, many performers of new song (*nueva canción*), a genre that began in Chile and transformed topical singing over a wide region, were severely punished. The Chilean composer and performer Víctor Jara was tortured and killed in reprisals against his songs. Sometimes just performing a certain genre of music is understood by all parties to be a protest. Not all music is political all of the time; but when other aspects of public life become intensely politicized, music tends to become so too.

Ethnicity

Throughout the twentieth century, ethnicity has been one of the most important mechanisms through which mass movements have been created on the basis of perceived and created differences in ethnicity. The musical implications appear in movements based on identification with ancestors brought to the Americas from Africa. Musical styles clearly descended from musical traditions brought to the Americas and the Caribbean by enslaved Africans have been perpetuated and widely used by people of African descent as a means of affirming a collective identity, from which elements traceable to other ethnic groups have been removed. Frequently, musicians emulate contemporary African styles as they perpetuate older local styles. Certain Amerindian genres, and the practice of performing in unison ornamented with paint and feathers, or playing the flute, are means through which local groups affirm a native identity in many locations. Especially in places where

Amerindian identity can confer a legal or social advantage, earlier traditions were revived or recreated. European identity is often fragmented: German dance bands, Italian *arias*, Portuguese *fados* and romances, and Spanish lullabies survive in ethnic communities. Conflicts sometimes arise when the members of one ethnic group prohibit members of others from participating in their performances.

An ethnocultural group may formally identify itself with a particular musical genre, but its members may practice other genres, sometimes bringing to the other genres some of the musical styles of the formally adopted one. Muslim and Jewish communities do not celebrate Christmas or Easter but often participate in national civic rituals and music festivals. Japanese immigrants in Brazil perform and appreciate a number of Japanese musical genres, but a large part of the local Japanese population enjoys Brazilian popular music. The descendants of Italian immigrants may listen to more opera than other members of their social class because of their pride in the genre itself.

Sometimes a reevaluation of an ethnocultural group will involve creating a new meaning for its music. This is the case of music performed by Brazilians of African descent in the late twentieth century: the musical relationships of their music to the musical traditions of Africa are not only recognized, but encouraged, through visits to Africa and a reevaluation of the history of the music of the Brazilian northeast.

Music is a social resource that can communicate statements of identity and attitudes. Musical performance has been shown to be a resource for expressing identity of and differences of gender, age, kinship, social class, ethnicity, religion, political persuasion, and nationality. The examination of almost any performance reveals how the practitioners and audiences are using these criteria to create meaningful events.

MUSICAL PERFORMANCE AND MUSICAL EVENTS

Music is not simply a sound in the air. Musical performance includes the intention of making sounds; the preparation for making them; the making of them; the sounds themselves; their reception, interpretation, and evaluation by an audience; and their perpetuation through new performances. An ethnomusicologist approaches musical performance by looking at many of those features: the goals, the rehearsals, the construction of the instruments and their use, the public performance, and its evaluation. An examination of these can assist in the understanding of the sounds themselves.

The structure of musical events varies considerably in Mexico, Central and South America, and the Caribbean. Some musical events are domestic and informal and do not require special organization or written rules. Others are national events—wars, athletic competitions, and national holidays—where different types of music are often rigidly prescribed. Forms that require the cooperation of a group of musicians usually entail defined obligations. Most groups must meet on a regular basis to practice, to learn a new repertoire, and to socialize. The organizations through which this may be done can be occupational (in one Peruvian town, truck owners founded one dance group and truck drivers another), religious (as in the brotherhoods already described), regional (as in the neighborhood organization of the early *samba* schools in Rio de Janeiro), or based on age or kinship. Rehearsals, if any occur, are usually private and have rarely been studied. Yet many decisions central to the public performances of music are made in them. In some rural areas, practice sessions may often have formal and informal components, with dancing and parties lasting late into the night and many participants returning home only the next day. As the date set for the performance approaches, practices intensify and often become more frequent. In some cases, as in the *samba* schools (*escolas de samba*) of Rio de Janeiro, rehearsals become public events, with large numbers of tourists participating in the preparations for Carnaval (Carnival). The final, public performances vary widely. Processional forms are common, as in parades during Carnaval in Rio, or in saint's-day processions in the Andes and elsewhere, when an image of a saint is paraded around a community (Figure 5.4). So, too, are social dances common, where large numbers of people gather in a confined space—to eat, drink, and dance.

DISC ❶ TRACK 32 Another typical event in Mexico, Central and South America, and the Caribbean is the competition, such as the *Chinegros* dance duel in Nicaragua. [Listen to "El Corredizo"] Many national, civic, and sometimes even religious events are staged in the form of competitions among bands, for awards that may be monetary or purely symbolic. Brass bands, steel bands, troupes of dancers, songwriters, and many other musical performers are judged, and winners are announced. The rules are elaborately laid out, and what seems like a spontaneous performance may well be defined as much by the rules of the competition as by the performers' creativity. Judged-performance formats reappear throughout the individual articles of this volume, but Rio de Janeiro's Carnaval is one of the best examples. The neighborhood-based *samba* schools compete on several fixed criteria for prestige, civic funds, and participation in three different levels of competition. Each year, the two lowest-ranked groups in the top group go down to a lower level, whereas the two highest-ranked ones in the lower level move up. Rio de Janeiro's Carnaval is extremely structured: only percussion and friction instruments can be used, no motorized floats are allowed, and a

Figure 5.4
During the procession of the faithful who carry the statue of the Virgin in the patronal festival of the Virgen del Carmen in Alto Otuzco, Cajamarca, Peru, music is performed by female singers, a pipe-and-tabor player, and a *clarinero* who plays a twelve-foot-long *clarín* trumpet. Photo 1979 by Dale A. Olsen.

Figure 5.5
In Capachica, Department of Puno, Peru, a band consisting of brass instruments, clarinets, cymbals, and drums plays in celebration and informal competition with other bands during the patronal festival of San Salvador. Photo by Dale A. Olsen, 1979.

rigid timetable must be followed. Elsewhere, competitions are more informal, as in patronal festivals in the Andes, where one band tries to outdo the other, but there are no judges other than the participants, the dancers, and the crowd (Figure 5.5).

MEDIATED MUSIC

When performers and audiences are separated by time and space, they may be called mediated. Performances are preserved and transmitted over media, preserved on wax cylinders, tapes, compact discs, or videotapes, and transmitted by radio, commercial recordings, television, videotape, or the Internet.

Mediated performances differ from the events described above because there is much more variety in the use of the performances. A person can listen to a recording of religious music anytime, not only in church. A television can transmit the sounds of deceased artists, whose contributions have long been adopted by different groups. And the commercial nature of the popular music recording and concert industry influences the social organization of its production and reproduction.

Live performances of large popular-music bands often involve managers, roadies, and promoters. Performance venues need to employ booking agents and all the employees of the location: ushers, ticket collectors, bartenders, security, stage crews, lighting-and-sound technicians, and so forth. Both sides may employ lawyers, insurance companies, and the services of innumerable specialists, though the specifics may vary from group to group and genre to genre. The tour of a large group is as much like a military campaign as anything else: it requires that a large number of people and heavy equipment arrive in a location that is prepared for them at a fixed time, and move out quickly afterward. Expectations vary considerably, however, and attitudes toward late arrivals and no-shows vary from genre to genre, from site to site. As the scope of the event increases, the amount of money that must be collected and paid out increases, and the number of positions and requirements increases proportionally.

The recording industry adds new roles to musical performance. Regardless of the type of group (whether it be a small community band with a homemade cassette recording, or a large popular group recording for a multinational recording company), some new roles are involved in the structure, the timbre, and the performance of the sounds. The industry itself applies some restrictions: the music on a CD cannot be more than seventy-five minutes long; a single song often will not receive airplay if it is more than four or five minutes long—a holdover from when 78-rpm records could hold no more than about five minutes of music.

Producers of records are a specialized group: their job is to help the band create a sound in the studio that will meet their needs, usually the need to sell as many copies as possible. Producers may have tremendous artistic control: they may insist that an electric bass be added to a genre where there has never been one before, or they may recommend that a full orchestra be added to a folk song. Depending on the power the group has with the record company itself, the producer may have final authority. Record companies themselves can be extremely bureaucratic. They tend to be uninterested in groups that will not quickly recoup the financial investment made in them. Record companies, too, have marketing departments, people who specialize in getting music played on radio, and sales forces that go to record stores. Record stores have their rents, their employees, their losses to theft, and payments to make on their stock.

Touring groups of musicians who make recordings attract a fairly large industry of specialists who are not themselves performers, but make their living from music. In large countries such as Brazil, Peru, and Mexico, the industry is quite complex and developed. In some smaller countries, more of the recorded music is imported, and there is a far less developed social organization of distribution, mass-media performance, and airplay.

OWNERSHIP AND RIGHTS

Another feature of musical performance that has grown alongside commercialization and a popular-music industry that emphasizes novelty is the industry of intellectual property. In many Amerindian and rural traditions, the actual ownership of a musical idea is considered unimportant, especially after the live performance at which it is introduced. European-modeled copyright laws, however, emphasize individual creativity and allow an author to copyright, or to keep other people from performing, a song or a musical idea unless they pay a royalty to the composer. A famous example was "The Birthday Song," composed in the 1920s. Anyone who records it was expected to pay a royalty to the songwriter for each unit sold—anywhere in the world. Anyone who performs it in a film, on a stage, or on television is similarly expected to pay a music-publishing company for the use of the song.

The objective of copyright is to enable writers (including composers and songwriters) to earn income by giving them, or their music-publishing company, the exclusive right to record their composition. Anyone else who does so must request a license and pay a fee.

For this reason, under international law, all "traditional" folk songs, and all Amerindian traditions without a single author and more than seventy-five years old, cannot be copyrighted. The law, therefore, rewards novelty and discourages tradition. It does more: a composer can base a composition on a traditional song and then copyright the new version in his or her name. This practice can lead to a kind of intellectual colonial exploitation: the musical ideas of a community that can be deemed "traditional" can be effectively taken, individualized, and profited from. There are cases, especially in the Caribbean (whence have come elements of some popular North American genres), where fortunes have been made through musical copyright of previously traditional materials.

In many subtle ways, copyright laws influence the music performed and the music an audience hears. First, performers are encouraged to create their own material to make money from the royalties; second, record companies try to obtain the music-publishing rights on those songs to profit from them; third, certain performance locations, in an effort to avoid paying copyright fees, ask that groups restrict themselves to their own compositions or songs in the public domain (not under copyright); and fourth, it can be less expensive for radio stations to play music by long-dead composers of classical music—safely beyond copyright concerns—than contemporary music.

To combat perceived inequities in the copyright law, some South American countries have taken steps to protect traditional music. Bolivia enacted a public-domain law that requires royalties to be paid to the state on all traditional songs. Brazil proposed a law that would give Brazilian indigenous communities perpetual rights to their intellectual property (with the objective of protecting their shamans' pharmaceutical knowledge, and incidentally their music, dance, and other collective creations). The Brazilian law gives indigenous communities far more protection than it gives non-Indians, but it is consistent with a tendency toward longer-lasting terms and a broader extension of laws concerning intellectual property into all areas of life, among them music.

While indigenous groups wish to protect their intangible cultural heritage indefinitely, on the other side many members of the general public want free access to musical forms of all kinds. In the first years of the twenty-first century, a major confrontation between computer users able to download music and video files and the companies that claimed the copyright on those files led to a number of court cases and lawsuits. The technology of digital music will certainly transform the music industry as it developed in the twentieth century. It may also have a profound impact on the observance of copyright laws and the ability of individuals, communities, and corporations to restrict access to ideas and performances.

The ways musicians and their audiences define themselves and their music are part of the social processes of the communities in which they claim membership. How they use age, gender, social class, ethnocultural affiliation, space, and time are important for understanding the musical performances themselves and the societies in general. The ethnomusicological approach to music is to examine the sounds of musical performances within the context of the social processes of which they are a part. As is repeatedly demonstrated in the articles of this volume, the relationship of the sounds of music to the social features of their performance is an intimate one.

Musical Dynamics

Anthony Seeger

Musical Enculturation or Socialization
Acculturation and Stylistic Change
Transnational and Transcultural Musical Influences

Most musical traditions are always changing, if at varying rates, through innovation by creators and performers, influences from other traditions, revivals of almost forgotten styles, changes in other features of social and cultural life, and many other causes. Yet outside of studies of popular music, we have little idea of how these changes occur. When a ceramic pot breaks and is discarded, its pieces are eventually covered by earth and preserved virtually unchanged for centuries. When a community is abandoned, the structures of its houses, the location of its hearths, trash from its residents, pollen from its gardens, and some remnants of its food often endure and give mute testimony to details of the life those residents led thousands of years ago. But the operative word is mute: there is no sound.

Music could be preserved only in the minds of living practitioners until 1877, when Thomas Edison invented the phonograph using a tin-foil cylinder and an amplifying horn. Before then, people had no way to capture musical sounds. Various methods of musical notation had been developed, but these typically focused on only a few features of musical performances. The rest were transmitted through oral traditions (through teaching) and aural traditions (through hearing) and usually changed, in often unconscious ways, over time. Edison's invention of the phonograph spurred the emergence of ethnomusicology as a discipline because at last it was possible to record sounds in distant places and to listen to them repeatedly for analysis. Researchers eventually took advantage of the phonograph for capturing the sounds of speech and music, and research centers soon appeared. In 1899, the first audio archive was founded in Vienna; in 1901, one was founded in Berlin. Later, archives were founded in the United States. The music industry grew up around audio recording and playback using three-minute wax cylinders or flat discs, and for many traditions, the relationship of tradition and change can be documented from then on.

In the twenty-first century, when audio- and video-recording devices are easy to use and virtually ubiquitous (they are even found in isolated Amazonian communities), it is hard to imagine musical traditions without any recording, playback, or radio. Until the twentieth century, however, the worldwide musical record is based on written descriptions, transcriptions, and manuscripts. For the Americas, the record is even poorer: Amerindians did not transcribe the details of their musical sounds, and the documents produced after Columbus's voyage, though better than nothing, are far less detailed than the manuscript materials available in Europe and parts of Asia.

Despite the sparseness of the records, we know that two associated waves of music were carried from Europe to the rest of the world, often transforming musical traditions and sometimes providing the basis for the creation of new local traditions. These were religious hymns and other church music, carried by missionaries, and brass bands, carried by soldiers, as the European powers explored and conquered. These became the first worldwide influences, eventually to be followed by certain dances and twentieth-century popular music. Mexico, Central and South America, and the Caribbean are filled with examples of religious and band-produced music—examples that have received local forms and are used in ways quite different from their original intentions. Musical changes, though somewhat difficult to document for earlier periods but dramatically represented today by satellite transmissions of popular music, are hundreds of years old in the Western Hemisphere.

Musical change has traditionally been discussed using concepts developed by anthropologists in the 1930s to describe the continuity and change of cultures. These concepts include music *enculturation* (the acquisition of musical knowledge, or music learning), *acculturation* (the changes that occur when members of different cultures come into continuous contact), and *transculturation* (what happens when distant cultural groups influence one another). Musical *deculturation* (the loss of culture without the implication of the replacement of it by another) is also described for some communities.

The trouble with these concepts is that they are inherited from a cultural anthropology that described cultures as unitary. In that view, a group has a single culture; two groups have two cultures, and when they are face to face, they interact and something happens. Today, researchers are likelier to view communities as comprising various groups with different sets of values that are often in conflict in specific social processes. Musical performance is one of the domains through which ideas and values are expressed, in which they may be contested, or in which they may be repressed and their participants eliminated. Similarly, individual members of communities may be masters of more than a single musical tradition—they may be bimusical or trimusical, able to shift from style to style with changes in contexts. The decision of which style to learn, which to perform on a given occasion, and which to pass on to one's children or disciples is shaped by many considerations that may have to do with ethnocultural affiliation, social class, political conjunctures, or economic or spiritual rewards. Unfortunately, ethnomusicologists lack a coherent analytic terminology with which to discuss these processes.

Thus, though the words are used in this volume, enculturation and acculturation and the other such terms must be understood to represent complex interrelationships of groups of people, individual choices, and musical contexts. Unlike milk, culture is not something with which a person is filled like a jug, or with which various flavors can be mixed to create flavored milkshakes. Enculturation, or musical socialization, is in many communities a complex and many-layered process. Acculturation, or the combination of traits from two or more musical traditions, is often a representation of relationships of political and symbolic power whose musical expression is a conscious commentary on those relationships. Behind the words lie the complex situations described in the entries to this volume, filled with conflict, choice, and creativity.

MUSICAL ENCULTURATION OR SOCIALIZATION

Enculturation literally means "giving culture" or "endowing with culture." In music, it usually refers to the ways members of a community become practitioners of their community's music. Music education is one form of musical enculturation; growing up in a family band is another.

Different musical traditions use sounds in different ways. Rhythms, pitches, timbres, and texts may all be employed differently within a certain community and among different groups. Children, born with the potential for all languages and all musical systems, are socialized into only a few of them—sometimes one, sometimes several. In most communities, every member is expected to be able at least to sing a few songs; in some, to perform on instruments and dance. Musical socialization also includes attitudes toward certain sounds and aural structures, and toward those who produce or enjoy them.

If all members of a community learn a few skills, attitudes, and values, a small number of community members usually learns how to innovate, often within fairly fixed, but constantly changing, limitations. These skills may be acquired through informal exposure, formal training, or years of apprenticeship. Musical knowledge may be voluntarily acquired or forced, but in most communities in Mexico, Central and South America, and the Caribbean, musical expertise is learned voluntarily by a self-selected group of individuals. It may be acquired from relatives, from friends and peers, in institutions such as schools and churches, from specialized teachers, from books, and more recently from audio and multimedia recordings. Family and peers appear to be important everywhere; institutions, specialized teachers, and recordings are found in widely different relationships and interact in complex ways to influence a community's musical traditions.

Musical enculturation probably begins before birth, with patterns of sounds transmitted to the fetus with the sound of the pregnant woman's heartbeat. So far, we know little about what, if any, information a child retains from its prenatal musical experiences. After birth, throughout much of the region, infants are carried almost everywhere by their mothers or another female relative during the initial months, and they hear whatever music is being performed around them. It could be argued that children learn to sing before they learn to talk, in that systematic patterns of pitch, rhythm, and timbre appear in their vocalizations before referential language. Yet again, we have little information about cross-cultural parallels, or relationships of infant babbling to musical traditions, at that age.

By the time children are about three and begin to play together, a whole system of musical sounds and structures has probably been learned; and during later childhood, it is increasingly fixed. In some communities, adults sing special songs to children—often containing simplified melodies, rhythms, and words. In other communities (particularly Amerindian communities), there may be no lullabies and no special children's songs: the children fall asleep or stay awake to the sounds of adult music.

A child's first music teacher is often another child. Children in most communities learn to perform songs and games by playing with other children. These may be passed on for generations from one child to another, without involving adults. Collections of children's genres have been made in African-American and European-American communities; we know much less about children's music in Amerindian communities. The examples we have show that children often perform shortened and simple versions of adult genres.

Religious institutions and practices are important in musical education throughout South America, Mexico, Central America, and the Caribbean. Religious events (saints' days, Christmas, Easter, and so forth), most shamanism, and African-derived possession religions—all include music. Children and young adults of the region probably learn more music by participating in religious events than they do in schools. In areas where there are no schools at all, children may still be exposed to religious music. In the 1500s, the Jesuits taught Amerindians how to play European instruments and how to compose music in the European style of the period. Today, various choral settings of the Mass are available, as are musical performances around saints' days. Protestant services are punctuated by hymns, and many churches have children's choirs and adult choruses. The African-derived religions that invoke direct contact with saints and spirits—Santería in Cuba, Vodou in Haiti, Candomblé in Brazil—teach children other musical skills: multiple rhythms, forms of vocal interrelationships, postures, movements, and styles of performance. Before missionary repression, a great deal of Amerindian music was religious, and music and contact with powerful beings were closely related. In all these cases, children observe performances, and are exposed to musical styles that influence them throughout their lives.

Though religious institutions are found in almost every part of Mexico, Central and South America, and the Caribbean, formal education in schools and conservatories varies widely from place to place. Formal education is usually available only to part of the population, often differentiated from the rest by social class and geographic area, financial status, degree of urbanization, and other factors. In many rural areas, there is little formal education, and children acquire musical training by listening to their families, to other adults, to neighborhood performances, radio and recordings, and eventually performing themselves.

The availability of elementary and secondary schools does not mean that children learn much music there. Music is not usually a high-priority pedagogical subject. The music usually taught in most schools bears little resemblance to the music of the child's community or the genres favored by the child's peers. Musical curricula have usually been designed by educators and musicians of a different social class, ethnic group, part of the country, or (in colonial periods) by specialists completely removed from the local culture. The distance between the curriculum and the local community culture is being reduced in some countries in the region, but in others continues to grow, as forms of popular music continue to be ignored in schools in favor of exclusively European-influenced forms. Schoolchildren often learn choral singing; in urban areas, orchestras and bands are found occasionally. Children learn something in music lessons at school, but its relationship to the traditions into which they were born and that they may perform in the future is quite variable.

For children who are particularly interested in music, or whose families want to encourage them to be musicians, the methods through which they acquire advanced training vary according to some of the same factors that determine opportunities for formal education. Motivated children in most areas attach themselves formally or informally to local performers, and they learn through watching, performing, and eventually becoming part of the performing group. In large urban areas, an extracurricular network of music teachers may provide lessons in various instruments for a fee. Members of the elites of most Mexican, Central and South American, and Caribbean countries pay for formal music lessons. Children perceived as being more talented or gifted or devoted to the subject may take further lessons with specialists of increasing ability, eventually entering music conservatories, in their own countries or abroad. The process is rather similar in every case: a child is motivated by outside encouragement, and this motivation is reinforced if he or she can master the required musical skills. Most music conservatories in the region specialize in advanced training in the performance, composition, and instruction of European classical music, though there are exceptions. Many countries have undergraduate and graduate programs in Historical Musicology and Ethnomusicology. Particularly in ethnomusicology the number of students, university centers, and publications is increasing rapidly throughout much of the region.

In addition to face-to-face means of learning skills, a large amount of music is learned today from recorded music, radio, and television. In most communities, children are exposed to recorded music from the womb on. In addition to passive listening, many children pay careful attention to recordings or broadcasts, and they actively learn styles of songs, music, and dance that they practice and teach to one another. Children also learn attitudes toward different musical styles and performance practices from media sources. Since media can reach far from the source of performance, children can be influenced by forms entirely foreign to their area, by performers and styles they may never see in person. The increasingly extensive reach of media is having greater and greater impact on musical traditions throughout the Americas.

Parents, religious groups, and nations have all, at some time in the past few decades, tried to restrict the kinds of music to which children are exposed through the media. (Before electronic media had any important influence, people in the same roles regulated face-to-face musical performances.) Parents may forbid certain kinds of music in the home; churches may restrict their members' music or dance; and nations, to control the international, capital-intensive, market-oriented musical performances that predominate on public media, have offered incentives for certain kinds of music and censored others. These restrictions have met with varied success, pitting children against parents, religious leaders against nonbelievers, and nations against one other in such a way that some kinds of music are divisive rather than unifying. Forms of expression become domains for moral and political contention.

In general, repression seems to have only intermittent success. More successful are the encouragement of individuals and institutions to foster children's active participation in alternative musical events, and efforts to endow those events with positive value and status.

ACCULTURATION AND STYLISTIC CHANGE

The term *acculturation* was defined by anthropologists Robert Redfield, Ralph Linton, and Melville Herskovits in an important paper: "Acculturation comprehends those phenomena which result when groups of individuals having different cultures come into continuous first-hand contact, with subsequent changes in the original cultural patterns of either or both groups" (1936:149). The term is often used to describe a process whereby individuals adopt the values, performance styles, and repertoire of another community. The advantage of the term is its vagueness; the problem is that it gives no indication of the relationship between the influencing and influenced culture(s). In music the term was used extensively by Melville Herskovits and others and continues in use precisely because its generality allows for further definition through examples.

In South America, Mexico, Central America, and the Caribbean, a great deal of observed acculturation has involved relationships of cultural, economic, and political dominance of one group over another. Music becomes one of the domains that expresses the relation of the groups to one another. This is not true everywhere. Scholars are still trying to discover a suitable language to express the processes through which communities produce cultural forms that combine features of different communities into new forms. Until such a language is developed, it is best to pay close attention to the details of the interaction of groups, and not simply to the musical results obtained by their members.

Amerindian communities in the Amazon have been learning one another's songs for hundreds of years. The mechanisms through which songs have been learned vary: sometimes they were learned from captured enemies, sometimes from peaceful trading partners, sometimes through marriage exchanges, and now through radio and recordings; but the result has been that part of the community's music has come from outside that culture. Amerindian communities often perform songs in a language they do not understand. They usually adopt other Amerindian styles selectively and continue to practice many of their own music and dance forms. Learning another community's musical style is not always, in these cases, a sign of cultural or political exploitation.

Members of different European communities also learned one another's styles. Examples are legion in classical concert music, where composers of one country were hired by patrons of another country to introduce prestigious forms to their courts. The combination of forms is obvious in communal dances in South America, where polkas (originally from Poland) are played between dances associated with other countries: a Viennese waltz (Austria), a schottische (Scotland), a *fandango* (Spain), a *tango* (Argentina), or a *samba* (Brazil). Here, too, the band's decision to play a given dance may be less a reflection of cultural dominance than of the dancers' interests in variety.

Most relationships between European colonists and Amerindians, and between European colonists and the Africans they used for labor, were dominating and exploitative.

Amerindians were usually discouraged or prohibited from performing some or all of their traditional music, and new forms were imposed on them. Similarly, enslaved Africans were often prohibited from performing most genres, and in some cases European church music was offered as an exclusive replacement for their earlier traditions. Though the region reveals a complex variety of restrictions and alternatives, the relationships among communities from Europe, Africa, and the Americas differed from most of those among Amerindian groups.

An important thing to remember about South America, Mexico, Central America, and the Caribbean is that the large ethnocultural groups are not monolithic blocks. There are many different Amerindian societies, each with its own set of values, its own specific experience with other societies, and its own specific use of music in determining its future. There are many different groups of Europeans, each with its own musical traditions, some of which have tenaciously been preserved in the Americas long after they have disappeared in their homelands. Members of many different African communities were enslaved. Except for a few, such as the Yoruba, a large amount of the individual cultures has not survived. But in their place a general African-derived culture developed—in workplaces and the Maroon communities that coalesced in many countries. Significant populations of South Asians, Indonesians, and Japanese live in some countries. Important local differences occur in the cultural attributes found and community members' values and intentions, and it is unproductive to generalize without reviewing the data found in this volume.

Members of communities that are largely dominated by another community react in different ways to the forceful suppression of earlier traditions and the imposition of new ones. In some cases, they will actively embrace the new form and become creative within the new genre. The Waiwai of Brazil and the Guianas today sing little besides hymns, but they have adapted Protestant hymns to their intercommunal relationships; their villages engage in hymn-writing competitions, and the composition of hymns has become a culturally accepted creative activity. In other cases, stylistic features from some genres carry over into new musical forms. Some older traditions may be maintained as a form of protest, a means of transmitting knowledge and perpetuating other aspects of social and cultural life. African traditions have influenced a great deal of the music in the Caribbean, northeastern Brazil, and some areas on the Pacific coast, especially celebrations of Carnival and popular music.

In some cases we can trace a trend called *deculturation*. This happens when the members of a community cease to practice their earlier culture but do not replace it with anything else. Deculturation may simply be a phase in the longer process by which some traditions are replaced by others, but it is often distressing to community elders and ethnomusicologists when a community abandons a long-established musical tradition and does not become proficient at another one. An Amerindian community, for example, might cease to perform its own traditions and simply stop making music, merely listening to recorded music on radio and cassettes.

More frequent, probably, are communities in which a few genres and some aspects of the former musical traditions are maintained somewhat unchanged, while others are adapted to new musical forms and contexts dictated by the dominating culture. European

Christian music has been transformed by the musical contribution of African American performers and composers. The celebration of saints' days in the Andes has been transformed by the use of Amerindian instruments and styles of performance. When used in these situations, acculturation usually means the combination, or fusion, of two or more styles. Other words often used for this are *creolization* and *hybridization*. Once again, the terms are shifting, as scholars try to fit their concepts better to the complexity of the processes they see occurring.

Creolization takes its definition from linguistics, which describes a creole language as a complete language based on one or more other languages but distinct from any of them. Thus, in Haiti and elsewhere, French creole languages are unlike French and English and have proved relatively stable through time. Similarly, one could point to some musical styles that are neither European nor African in form but represent a fairly stable combination of traits. The important thing to remember here, though, is that musical fusion does not take place in a vacuum and is not free of values. It is a factor in the social situation of which it is a part.

When the word *creolization* is applied to music, it is a vague term, as it is more difficult to tell when a musical tradition is "independent" of its parent traditions. At one time, a group will point to certain fusion traditions with pride and say, "That's our music." At another time, they may denounce the same tradition with disdain and complain, "That's a terrible mixture of our beautiful tradition with their ugly one." Traditions that are seen as mixed are often the subject of considerable conflict. Over time, however, one can often trace how these adaptations of parts of other community's styles begin as criticized hybrids and become an integral part of a community's music. In other cases, one can trace how a shared musical tradition is eventually "purified" and becomes the symbolic property of only one of the contributing communities. Different countries reveal different dynamics, as the entries in this volume demonstrate.

The creative mixing of aspects of musical traditions is achieved in many ways: through instrumentation; musical texture, structure, and performance style; musical appropriation; and the creation of genres for new audiences. These features appear frequently throughout the entries.

Instrumentation

Musical instruments are at once sound-producing objects and highly significant representations of a community's history. Thus, a nationalist composer or regional folk-rock group might use traditional Amerindian instruments to give their otherwise European compositions a national flavor; or, moving in the other direction, an Amerindian group might adopt an electric bass or rhythm section to make its music louder, more "modern," or commercially successful. The introduction of new musical instruments into a tradition does not, by itself, indicate whether the resulting change is considered to be highly significant. For example, the timbres of certain instruments have replaced others for practical or economic reasons. In the 1800s, the German accordion, with its loudness and versatility, replaced other instruments in dance-oriented bands throughout the region (Figure 6.1). Many musical genres, however, continued to be performed on the new instrument. Musical

Figure 6.1
In Santo Domingo, Dominican Republic, three musicians in a small *merengue* group play in front of a restaurant. Left to right: a *tambora*, a *güira* or metal scraper, and a button accordion. Photo by Martha Ellen Davis, 1991.

instruments are sometimes identified with the communities in which they originated: rattles and flutes with Amerindians; percussion instruments, musical bows, and *xekeres* (*shekeres*) with Africans; and stringed and brass instruments with Europeans. New instruments, such as the electronic keyboard, have often been adapted to older forms. Sometimes old instruments are revived in new forms. South America has seen a great deal of creative use of musical instruments in traditions quite unlike those in which they originated.

Musical texture, structure, and performance

Chordal texture (harmony) was one of the defining features of sixteenth-century European music, and it continues to define much of the music of the region. The multipart, chordal approach to music was distinct from that of the Amerindians, whose polyphony did not work like harmony in the Western sense. Some African traditions employed multipart harmony; others did not. Amerindian communities and descendants of African slaves learned to perform harmonic structures, often in churches, and many of them carried this form into secular genres. The use of harmonies and the harmonic structures of pieces can be quite variable and are often defining features of genres.

Most Amerindian music featured a single, fairly steady, rhythmic pulse, with melodic syncopation in the vocal parts. A great deal of African music had complex, interlocking rhythms, played on membranophones or idiophones, or by slapping the body. European rhythms could be complex, but most dances were arranged in simple 2/4, 3/4, 4/4, or 6/8 time, and lacked the rhythmic complexity of West African drumming. The rhythmic structures of African music have been greatly admired by people from many communities, and they have been widely adapted in some modified form to create new musical genres.

Call-and-response forms, improvisation, and broad community participation in making music have all been identified as having African origins. Certainly these performance processes appear in traditions bearing other obvious African influences. But not all examples of these features should be unquestionably traced to African influences, as they also appear in European and Amerindian traditions.

Musical appropriation

In Mexico, Central and South America, and the Caribbean, different groups have often adapted one another's styles, consciously or unconsciously, with the variety of results described in the individual entries. Powerful communities, often European and Christian, have sometimes forced their musical traditions on Amerindians and communities of African descent. Simultaneously, the same wealthy, European-influenced populations in many countries have admired and appropriated, often for their material benefit, the music of the poor and often African or Amerindian peoples in their countries. It has been argued that the poorer parts of the societies throughout Mexico, Central and South America, and the Caribbean have produced many of the musical styles that have subsequently become national styles or popular forms of music. There are different ways to interpret this phenomenon. It may be seen as cultural exploitation or as a musical parallel to classic colonialism (one group provides the raw materials; the other group packages it and sells it back) or simply an uncomplicated case of admiration and borrowing. In many cases, the evidence apparently supports the first two interpretations more than the last.

The patterns of cultural appropriation found in Central and South America and the Caribbean raise important issues of intellectual property and ethics. Most copyright laws exclude traditional music from their purview and give little protection to rural and less wealthy composers and performers. Popularizers have often shown little interest in crediting their sources, to say nothing of paying them a share of royalties (Wallis and Malm 1984). Although these attitudes are changing in a few countries, abuses have made many local musicians suspicious of outsiders carrying tape recorders or video cameras and may impede even legitimate and ethically aware investigations of musical performances in some communities and some countries. Some efforts are underway in various countries to modify the cultural and class biases of existing copyright laws, but most actual modifications apparently perpetuate and accentuate the rights of literate professional musicians with legal assistance over those of nonliterate but highly creative musicians whose work grows out of a strong vernacular tradition.

The creation of genres for new audiences

The most important face-to-face musical genre developed for specialized audiences, and one that often combines unusual mixtures of the above features, is music for tourists. Tourism is a major influence on the creation of musical styles considered appropriate to new audiences, especially those from outside the community (Lewin 1988). Throughout Mexico, Central and South America, and the Caribbean, tourism is an important part of national economies, and many aspects of culture have adapted to the new audiences tourism provides.

Touristic audiences are not neutral, however. They bring with them expectations of diversion, a short attention span, a lack of understanding of local languages and traditions, and often an ignorance of religious matters. Most performers voluntarily, often at organizers' request, adjust their performances to present them within times and in locations set by tourists' schedules. As surely as other economic systems have created or discouraged certain kinds of musical performance, so does tourism.

TRANSNATIONAL AND TRANSCULTURAL MUSICAL INFLUENCES

Since before Columbus, musical, economic, and other cultural influences have flowed back and forth between the highlands and the lowlands, between North and South America, and around the Caribbean. The arrival of Europeans and Africans stepped up the pace of interaction. Music probably followed the trade routes, with seaports and riverine ports becoming centers of creativity and patronage for the arts, and the trade routes carrying the new creations to other cities and other patrons. In the Atlantic, New Orleans, Havana, Rio de Janeiro, Buenos Aires, and other ports were the originators of distinctive styles of music whose popularity spread far beyond the country's borders. In the Pacific, similar processes certainly occurred among the former Spanish colonies.

Few records of this transnational musical cross-fertilization existed until the era of sheet music, when popular music in its current form emerges in historical documents. The utilization of early recording devices at the start of the twentieth century escalated the trend, and a transnational popular-music industry began to flourish. At first, most recordings were produced in North America or Europe, but by the 1920s several countries had flourishing music industries, often owned or licensed by multinational corporations. The popular musical forms of Mexico, Central and South America, and the Caribbean have had a tremendous impact on the popular music of Europe, Africa, and other parts of the world.

Tango, for example, has had a tremendous impact on France and other parts of Europe, Japan, and the United States. Today, there are hundreds of *tango* clubs in Finland, where *tango* has become almost a national dance. As the *tango* retreats into the realm of tourist art in Argentina, it flourishes as a creative form in northern Europe.

Another example of transnational music is the spread of Andean music to other parts of the world, beginning with the popular recording of "El Cóndor Pasa" in the 1960s by Simon and Garfunkel. Moreover, since the residence of Andean musical ensembles such as Inti Illimani and Quilapayún in Europe following the 1973 military coup in Chile, Andean (or "pan-Andean") folkloric music has been popular outside of its homelands. Andean music groups performing at American universities (Figure 6.2) or on the streets of European cities (Figure 6.3) are commonplace.

Popular music from the Caribbean probably had a large influence on African highlife and other African genres of popular music that later swept back across the Atlantic to the Americas, and returned some of the influences with new features. Subsequently, *merengue*, reggae, *salsa*, *soca*, and other Caribbean musical genres have had a tremendous impact on the Americas and far beyond. The traditions from this region are influencing the development of musical traditions around the world.

What is the source of the impact of Caribbean music on the rest of the world? Part of it can be traced to the widespread adoption of a context common in many countries: the dance hall. Most widespread genres have been danceable genres. If any of them had religious aspects, such as reggae's relationship with Rastafarian beliefs, these aspects are largely shed by the time the form enters the hall. For some genres, socially and politically conscious vocals are

Figure 6.2
The San Francisco–based Andean music ensemble Sukay performs on the campus of the University of Florida. Left to right: a guitar, a panpipe set, and a *charango*. Photo by Dale A. Olsen, 1986.

attractive to audiences far from the political events in which the song originated. Not to be discounted either is the combination of musical familiarity with musical difference that the various mixtures of styles have brought about in the Americas. Record companies, tourism bureaus, music television, and the other parts of the music business also support the spread of music around the world. And

Figure 6.3
A South American Andean music group plays on the streets of Helsinki, Finland. Left to right: a *bombo* (with *kena* and *siku* around the musician's neck), a *kena* (with *siku* around the musician's neck), and a *charango*. Photo by Arnold Perris, 1985.

new composer-musicians, hearing the music, will take it and create new forms, which will themselves come resounding back to the Americas from places such as Bombay, Hong Kong, Jakarta, Kinshasa, Paris, and Tokyo. This process shows every sign of speeding up as the Internet eases the sending of large and digitized music files and home studios become more widespread.

Some of the music of Mexico, Central and South America, and the Caribbean continues to be heard only within its community. Others of its musical traditions have become part of the world's repertoire. The relationship between local and transnational musics is a theme that reappears again and again in these entries. It remains a challenge for all musicians and communities in the twenty-first century, when current trends will probably continue at an increasing rate.

Though the means by which musical traditions are learned, preserved, transformed, and even performed are constantly changing, the overall use of music in social life is probably increasing. The ways individuals and groups use music, the ways it is taught, the genres deemed significant, the genres that are transformed, the genres that spread across the globe, and the relationships among groups of people given expression through music will continue to be a significant part of musical performances in this hemisphere.

REFERENCES

Lewin, Olive. 1988. "Banana Boat Song Forever?" In *Come Mek Me Hol' Yu Han': The Impact of Tourism on Traditional Music*, ed. Adrienne L. Kaeppler, 1–5. Kingston: Jamaica Memory Bank.

Redfield, Robert, Ralph Linton, and Melville Herskovits. 1936. "Memorandum for the Study of Acculturation." *American Anthropologist* 38:149–152.

Wallis, Roger, and Krister Malm. 1984. *Big Sounds from Small Peoples: The Music Industry in Small Countries.* London: Constable; New York: Pendragon Press.

Music of Immigrant Groups

Dale A. Olsen

China
India
Japan
Germany
Italy
Spain
Chile
Out-Migration

By immigrants we mean people, other than Amerindians, who entered the Americas of their own free will. All people in the Americas are the result of some type of in migration (i.e., immigration)—human beings did not originate in the Western Hemisphere, as far as archaeologists can tell. Normally, however, Amerindians (i.e., native Americans) are not considered immigrants, even though their ancestral homes were not in the Americas (the original Amerindians came from Asia). Likewise, African slaves were brought to the Americas against their will, and such forced immigration will not be included within this essay on immigration. This is not meant to exclude people of African ancestry who were brought to the Americas against their will. Their forced migration can be included under another term: *diaspora* or "scattering." Individual country chapters in this book discuss both the music of Amerindians and African descendants.

People belonging to the New World colonial powers who migrated are generally considered immigrants because they migrated (immigrated) to seek a better life, escape persecution, find religious freedom, strike it rich; some can be considered economic immigrants, others refugees, and still others, soldiers of fortune. For the purposes of this essay, colonial immigrants before the independence period (roughly before 1850) are not included in this discussion because of a lack of space. The cultural achievements of the colonial or pre-independence immigrants were part of the national development of the countries to which they settled, and their musical achievements in the Americas are fundamental to each country where they settled.

Immigrants, then, in the context of this particular overview, will only include those people who left their homelands to go to a new country in the Americas to work and hopefully settle as a member of that country, rather than go to a colonial outpost belonging to their motherland. By "country" then, we mean after independence.

Immigration basically began after 1850, flourished until World War II, and continues today to a lesser degree. Its primary cause was the need for cheap labor in agricultural areas of South America, Central America, Mexico, and the Caribbean after the abolition of slavery, when immigration contracts were drawn up between particular countries to receive indentured workers and others for labor. Even before emancipation, many countries had begun to import persons from several parts of Asia as indentured workers, drawing many from their colonies on the opposite side of the globe. The British in Trinidad and Guyana (then British Guiana) sought out workers from India; the Dutch in Surinam (then Dutch Guiana, sometimes spelled Suriname) brought laborers from Indonesia. Policies of immigration were contracted with governments of other Asian countries, resulting in the importation of workers from China and Japan (including Okinawa). Later, huge numbers of immigrants, including many Jews, came from Europe, especially Croatia, Germany, Greece, Italy, Lithuania, Poland, Russia, Serbia, and Spain; and sizable numbers came from West Asia, mostly from Lebanon, Syria, and Turkey. The incentive for these people to emigrate (i.e., out migration, or leave their homelands) was also economic. Most of them came from the lower classes of their societies, and they wanted to elevate their status by making quick money and returning home. Others chose to emigrate because their own countries were overcrowded—another trait that affected personal economic welfare. These latter immigrants tended to stay in the new lands of opportunity. Many of the former stayed because their dreams had not always been based on reality—money was scant, disease caused problems that made returning impossible, marriage to locals created new family obligations, ships were rare, and fares were expensive.

In addition to the immigrants from across the Atlantic and Pacific Oceans, much internal immigration within the Western Hemisphere has occurred because of political turmoil or economic hardship. Many Chileans have immigrated to Mexico and Venezuela, Bolivians to Chile, Argentines to Brazil, Cubans to Panama—and, of course, multitudes to the United States of America.

Thus, ethnic groups and individuals of diverse national origins in the Caribbean, Central America, Mexico, and especially South America, are many. Overall, they have retained many cultural ways, including music, which often serves as a tool for retaining or teaching cultural identity. When people immigrate in large numbers, they usually do at least three things to preserve their cultural identity: they organize schools for their children, with qualified teachers to continue instruction of their native languages (children's songs often serve for teaching language and culture); they organize religious organizations and build houses of worship (music is part of traditional worship in most religions); and they organize cultural associations that sponsor sports, music, dancing, eating, handicrafts, and other socializing activities.

Below, several of these immigrant groups are discussed by national (rather than ethnic or religious) origin, in the order in which they first arrived in noteworthy numbers. Many cultures are not included only because ethnomusicological research on them is lacking.

CHINA

The importation of indentured workers from China began as early as 1849 in Peru and 1853 in Surinam. By 1872, thousands of Chinese had entered Peru as laborers (Gardiner 1975:6), and about twenty-five hundred Chinese had come to the Dutch colony of present Surinam to work (de Waal Malefijt 1963:22). Roughly 150,000 Chinese, mostly from Canton, immigrated to the Spanish colony of Cuba. After Peru won its independence, Chinese came to the islands off the Peruvian coast to mine their deposits of *guano* (accumulated droppings from birds, used for fertilizer); they also came to work on the sugar plantations in coastal river oases, and in nitrate mines on the south coast. After 1930, thousands of Chinese workers immigrated to Argentina and Brazil, many from Peru.

After fulfilling their contracts as agricultural laborers, most Chinese moved to urban areas, where they opened laundries, restaurants, and grocery stores. Living near each other and relying on one another to survive persecutions resulting from the "yellow peril" (negative attitudes and oppression of Asians by non-Asians), they created Chinatowns. These became the locales of musical activities, mostly including theatrical presentations of Chinese operas and other forms of entertainment. The main purpose of such musical activities was socialization.

In the 1990s, Chinese musical activities in such urban areas as Buenos Aires, Lima, and São Paulo consist mostly of talent shows and karaoke contests. In number and variety, musical activities have never equaled those of the Chinese living in San Francisco or New York, most probably because of ethnic assimilation and the smaller numbers of Chinese in South America. Both factors resulted from the fact that Chinese immigration to South America and the Caribbean peaked early, leading to assimilation, and never reached the tidal-wave proportions that it did in the United States. Similarly, musical syncretism with European and African forms never materialized for the same reasons. Nevertheless, important musicians—notable not because they are Chinese, but because they are talented—have been of Chinese heritage. In Trinidad, for example, Kim Loy was a famous *panman* (steel drummer), and Selwyn Ahyoung, whose grandfather was Chinese and grandmother African, had a great future as an ethnomusicologist until his untimely death in 1987.

INDIA

The second immigrant culture to arrive in the New World as agricultural workers came from Calcutta to Surinam in 1873. Urban people, these Indians went straight to plantations to do labor at which they had no experience. Soon, rural people were brought over, and by 1916 more than thirty-four thousand lower-caste Indians had immigrated to Surinam (de Waal Malefijt 1963:23). Similarly, the British sent Hindu indentured servants for work in Trinidad and Guyana. In 1987, roughly 41 percent of the population of Trinidad was of East Indian descent.

Asian Indian influence in the musics of Guyana, Surinam, and Trinidad has been extensive. These immigrants introduced two religions, Hinduism and Islam, and freedom of worship and musical expression has always been possible in the new lands. Singing is the most important medium of Asian Indian musical expression, including songs for festivals, ritual songs for childbirth, marriage, and death, work-related songs, and Hindu *bhajan*, devotional songs (Arya 1968:19–31; Manuel 1995:212).

Musical instruments used by the people of Asian Indian descent include numerous idiophones, membranophones, two chordophones, and an aerophone with a keyboard. The main instruments in the first category are two metal rods (*dantal*), two brass cymbals (*jhanjh*), and two brass cups (*majira*); each set of instruments is concussed (clashed together) to provide rhythmic accompaniment to membranophones. The most common membranophones include two single-headed and closed drums (in the shape of a kettle), one double-headed drum (in the shape of a barrel), and a tambourine. These are the *tassa* and the *nagara* (the kettle-shaped drums) and the *dholak* (the barrel-shaped drum). The *tassa*, played for Islamic festivals, is struck with a stick by men for the Muharram festival and by women for the Matkor procession (Arya 1968:8). The *nagara* is played with two sticks for weddings and other festivities. The *dholak* is played during weddings. The chordophones include a bowed lute (*sarangi*) and a plucked lute (*tanpura*); as in India, the former is a melodic instrument for classical music, and the latter provides a drone. The most common melodic instrument is the harmonium, a reed organ or multiple single-reed aerophone with keyboard. This is the universal instrument for accompanying *bhajan* songs.

The singing of *bhajans*, Hindu religious songs of praise to God in any of his manifestations or incarnations, is quite common among people of Asian Indian heritage in Guyana, Surinam, and Trinidad. Performances, to the accompaniment of a harmonium, are often social in context.

Muharram or Hosay, a Muslim festival, is celebrated by Hindus in Guyana, Surinam, and Trinidad. It commemorates the martyrdom of the brothers Hasan and Husain in A.D. 680. Matkor, a festival celebrated in Surinam, celebrates the mother-goddess's embodiment as the earth and other forms (Arya 1968:13).

Classical singing (*tan*) is performed by Asian Indians in Trinidad during their celebrations after wedding rituals, especially the dinner, when hired musicians with beaters (*dantal*), a *dholak*, and a harmonium accompany the singing of *tan* (Manuel 1995:215). This singing is followed by song duels (*picong*-style) and so-called chutney songs, which are danceable and easy to sing.

Asian Indians in the 1990s often maintain cultural contact with India by traveling to the motherland, reading India-oriented books and magazines, watching Indian films, and listening to Indian cassette tapes. At weekend public dances in Trinidad, they first listen to Indian film music, and then begin performing chutney dances, marked by special movements of the pelvis and gestures of the hands and accompanied by beer drinking. In the 1980s, chutney combined with *soca* (soul calypso) to become chutney-soca, a mixture of Trinidadian modern calypso, sung in Hindi with Indian vocal ornamentations and *dholak* accompaniment. Noted singers of this tradition are Anand Yankaran of Trinidad and Kries Ramkhelawan of Surinam. Rikki Jai and Drupatee Ramgoonai, Trinidadian Indian calypsonians, write popular calypsos with racial and cultural-unity themes. Also in Trinidad, the leader of the famous band known as Amoco Renegades is the Indian-Trinidadian Jit Samaroo (Manuel 1995:219–220). Even before the rise of these musical leaders of Indian heritage, the playing of *tassa* was an important influence in the development of steelband and *soca*.

JAPAN

Japanese indentured workers first reached Peru in 1899. Many came from Okinawa via Hawaii, where they had gone about thirty years before. The first Japanese workers to enter Peru (including people from Okinawa, politically but not ethnically Japanese) were 790 men who came to work in coastal sugarcane plantations (Morimoto 1979:13–14). Japanese immigration next included Brazil, beginning in June 1908, when 781 people (324 from Okinawa), including 158 families, arrived at the port of Santos to work in the coffee plantations (Ando 1976:138; Fujii and Smith 1959:3). By 1940, people of Japanese ancestry in Peru totaled 17,638, and in Brazil there were about 188,500 Japanese; more than 75 percent of those in rural areas were landowners (Cowles 1971:87). In the 1990s, the largest population of people of Japanese ancestry outside Japan is in Brazil; the second-largest is in the United States (including Hawaii), the third in Peru, the fourth in Canada, and the fifth in Argentina (Gardiner 1975:133). Sizable numbers of Japanese live in Bolivia, Colombia, Ecuador, Mexico, Paraguay, and other countries of the Americas.

The Japanese, like the Chinese, Indians, and Indonesians before them, chose to emigrate from their homelands to become wealthy—a promise usually made by immigration officials. However, wages were low, working conditions difficult, living conditions crowded, diseases rampant, persecution common, and loneliness almost unbearable. An added difficulty in Peru for the Japanese male workers was the initial lack of Japanese women; married men later had their families sent over, and single men married female immigrants, who were often "picture brides" (arranged marriages based on photos).

In contrast, most Japanese in Brazil were admitted in family groups as colonists and drew strength from family socializing as a means of easing the pressures of being in a new country. Making music and drinking rice wine were two of these social activities. Their music consisted of singing popular songs or folk songs of the day, usually unaccompanied because musical instruments from Japan were rare (Handa 1971:220). The Japanese New Year's festival (O-Bon) and the Japanese emperor's birthday were two celebrations that always included music and dance.

After 1930, Japanese immigration included Argentina and Paraguay (in addition to Brazil and Peru), where colonists introduced new methods of horticulture—growing flowers and citrus. Most immigrants were peasant farmers from Okinawa, whose only musical performances had included singing folk and popular songs; by then, however, *shamisen* (Japanese orthography) and *sanshin* (Okinawan orthography) were available. These were lutes often made locally from South American wood and local dogskin or imported snakeskin; sometimes they were made from lard tins in Brazil (Olsen 2004).

In all South American countries, Japanese immigration stopped during World War II. After the war, it remained closed in Peru but resumed in Brazil in 1951. Additionally, in a program initiated by the U.S. Army, Okinawan immigrants came to Bolivia to establish farms in the Chaco region, east of the Andes; larger numbers came to Argentina and Paraguay. From 1951 to 1970, more than fifty-six thousand Japanese immigrated to Brazil, including many white-collar workers, intellectuals, and trained musicians who had lost their homes to the fires and bombs of the war. These new waves of Japanese immigration led to the performing and teaching of music in urban regions of Brazil and Argentina, most notably in São Paulo, Curitiba, and Londrina in Brazil, and Buenos Aires in Argentina. Japanese musical activity has not developed so strongly in Bolivia, Paraguay, and Peru (Olsen 1980), though acculturated forms such as karaoke "empty orchestra"—recordings of pop and folk songs minus the singer, a type of sing-along to cassette tapes and videos—is extremely popular there, as they are in Argentina and Brazil.

Today, most people of Japanese descent live in urban areas of South America, where musical performance is often a means of socializing and maintaining ethnic identity (Olsen 1983). Many Japanese folk song (*minyō*) clubs have sprung up in the Japanese quarter of São Paulo (Liberdade), in Curitiba, and in Londrina in Brazil; and in Lima, Peru. Clubs dedicated to Okinawan *minyō* and *koten* (classical music) flourish in Buenos Aires, Lima (Figure 7.1), and São Paulo. These organizations hold rehearsals weekly (when their members gather to drink tea or beer and eat cookies), present concerts, and often compete with each other in contests. Such activities are so well-organized in São Paulo that each year's winner receives a trip to Japan and the opportunity to perform in Tokyo and make a recording with a famous Japanese singer. The singing of Japanese folk songs is usually promoted by Japanese cultural centers (São Paulo has two centers, one for Okinawan-Japanese and another for Naichi-Japanese, or ethnic Japanese), where yearly talent shows feature traditional musical, dance, and cultural genres.

The *koto* (Japanese orthography) and *kutu* (Okinawan orthography, a thirteen-stringed zither), the *shamisen* and *sanshin* (three-stringed plucked lutes, respectively from Japan and Okinawa), and the *shakuhachi* (a Japanese notched vertical bamboo flute) are the most popular Japanese classical musical instruments in São Paulo, Brazil, the capital of Japanese musical performance in all of South America, Mexico, Central America, and the Caribbean. These instruments are usually imported from Japan, since classically trained Japanese-Brazilian musicians desire the finest available instruments.

Figure 7.1
In the Japanese-Peruvian Cultural Center in Lima, Okinawan-Peruvian women play zithers (*kutu*), and men play lutes (*sanshin*). Photo by Dale A. Olsen, 1979.

Brazil has several Japanese court-music orchestras (*gagaku* "elegant music"), all associated with the Tenrikyō religious centers in São Paulo and Baurú, Brazil, where they serve ritual purposes. Tenrikyō, a Japanese religion that developed in the late 1800s, features dance as part of its daily ritual, usually to the accompaniment of *koto* and bowed *shamisen* (*kokyu*). Both instruments were manufactured in Brazil in the 1980s (Olsen 1982, 2004), but in the 1990s they are imported from Japan. The *koto* was made from Brazilian woods (especially cedar), and the *kokyu* was constructed from lard cans. Tenrikyō centers in Asunción and Piriapó, Paraguay, have *kotos* and *shamisens* donated by the main church in Tenri, Japan.

In São Paulo, Brazil, in the 1990s, classical Japanese music includes *nagauta*, *katarimono*, and *jiuta* (*shamisen* or *sangen* traditions); *sōkyoku* (*koto* tradition); *shakuhachi honkyoku*; *gagaku*; and *nō*. The Ikuta-ryū (school or cult founded by Mr. Ikuta) and Yamada-ryū styles of playing the *koto* are represented by teachers who are *nisei*, second-generation residents born overseas to Japanese-born parents. Likewise, both *shakuhachi* schools, Tozan-ryū and Kinko-ryū, are taught and performed in São Paulo by *issei*, first-generation residents born in Japan. Students of *koto* and *shakuhachi* often include non-Japanese people and adult Japanese of all generations who desire to learn more about their Japanese heritage. Tsuna Iwami (born 21 March 1923 in Tokyo; immigrated to Brazil in 1956) is the most important leader of classical Japanese chamber music in the southern hemisphere of the Americas. He is a master (*iemoto*) in the Kinko-ryū *shakuhachi* tradition, with the professional name of Baikyoku V, awarded to him by *iemoto* Araki Kodō IV in 1941 (Olsen 1986:2–4). In addition, Tsuna Iwami studied composition in Japan with Kishio Hirao, graduated from the University of Kyōtō in chemical engineering and industrial administration, and retired in the early 1990s to continue composing music and making pottery. He has composed in a European postimpressionist idiom, and in the 1990s he has modernized his style, usually fusing *shakuhachi* and contemporary sounds. He performs widely in Brazil, where he is sought out as a teacher and lecturer.

Most young people of Japanese ancestry in South America have little knowledge of Japanese traditional music, but they are interested in learning about the heritage of their ancestors, especially the language, baseball (*béisbol*, which they claim the Japanese invented, and which they regard as a warrior attribute, *bushidō*), and karaoke. The last is popular and is used to teach and maintain Japanese philosophy, morals, and culture. Youths who cannot speak Japanese learn to read and sing in the language by becoming temporary pop singers in the company of their friends. In the late 1990s, karaoke singing is the most important medium for maintaining a Japanese identity among the South American people of Japanese ancestry.

GERMANY

German communities arose especially in Argentina, Brazil, Chile, and Paraguay. Germans immigrated to the first three countries as colonists during open-immigration periods of the late 1800s and early 1900s; in Paraguay, many Germans are Mennonite farmers who received homesteading rights in the Chaco region; and in the 1930s, many German Jews emigrated to escape Nazi-sponsored persecution, and many *Volksdeutsche* (German-speaking Protestants living in Russia) immigrated into Argentina.

The obvious musical-instrument legacy of the immigrant German people is the accordion, of which two forms are found in the southern Americas: the button accordion (*acordeón de botones*) and the piano accordion (*acordeón de teclas*). In Argentina, a variant of the first type is known as *bandoneón*, invented in 1854 by Heinrich Band, after whom it is named. Most of today's accordions are German instruments made by Höhner, a company that manufactures musical instruments in Germany. Sometimes folkloric ensembles use both types, as seen among the German-derived groups on the island of Chiloé, in southern Chile (Yévenez 1980:57). The accordion has found its place in folk and popular music from the *tonada* in Chile to the *tango* in Argentina.

Additionally, German immigrants introduced dances, including the polka, the schottische, and the waltz. These dances have fused with national types to become the *gato polqueado* in Argentina, the *polca* in Paraguay, and the *vals criollo* in Peru.

Germans first immigrated to Chile in the 1840s, when land was granted to them. Today in the southern lake district of Chile, several towns and cities (Valdivia, Osorno, Puerto Varas, and others) have large German-speaking populations. German architecture, breweries, and Lutheran churches abound in this area. Throughout central and southern Chile, the Chilean folklorist and singer Violeta Parra collected many German-influenced songs, especially waltzes.

In the German community of Alto Sampaio in southern Brazil, a singing society (*sociedad de canto*) was the most important cultural organization of the immigrants, "because the German loves to sing, and by singing he or she thematically reproduces German culture" (Flores 1983:256, translated by Dale A. Olsen).

ITALY

Italians constitute the largest immigrant culture in Argentina and make up large numbers of the immigrant population in southern and central Brazil and southern Chile. Although most Italian immigrants to the United States were from southern Italy and Sicily, most Italians who moved to Argentina were from northern Italy, including the border regions between Italy and Austria. For that reason, "the accordion … has challenged the guitar as the Argentine's favorite instrument" (Solberg 1966:19), signifying that Germany alone cannot take credit for the introduction of the accordion into Argentina.

Perhaps the most important Italian trait brought to South America is the singing of, and love for Italian opera and art songs. The popularity of Italian opera in Buenos Aires was influential in the opening of the famous Teatro Colón in 1857. Bellini's Norma was first performed in Rio de Janeiro in 1844 (thirteen years after its premiere), and for the next twelve years, that city was the focal point of the Italian "prima donna personality cult" in Brazil (Béhague 1979:112). The popularity of opera among the rubber barons of the Brazilian Amazon led to the construction of an opera house in the city of Manaus; it was completed in 1910, at the end of the rubber boom.

SPAIN

After the Italians, Spaniards (mostly from Galicia) were the second-largest immigrant group in Argentina. Because the national origin of most Argentines is Spanish, the Spanish immigrants had only slight adjustments to make, and upward mobility came quite easily. Many began as common laborers in Buenos Aires (garbage collectors, dock workers, street sweepers), but soon became retailers (Solberg 1966:20). The Spanish have retained their cultural identity, especially in Buenos Aires, where one of the main streets, the Avenida de Mayo, features Spanish cantinas (combination bars and coffeehouses) frequented by people who think of themselves as Spanish rather than Argentine.

The music of Argentina owes much to Spanish culture, but in this most European of the South American countries, this debt stems as much from the Spanish of the colonial period as it does from Spanish immigrants. It is not possible, for example, to slice the *tango*—the national music and dance of Argentina, especially Buenos Aires—into parts and claim that a certain percentage of it is musically a result of Spanish (or Italian) immigration. Perhaps it is wiser to view the *tango* as a musical product of common Spanish laborers who worked the docks of Buenos Aires. In any event, the concept of cultural identity through music, where the immigrants are of the same heritage as the colonists, is not so easily defined as that of persons who look and speak differently from those of the dominant culture.

CHILE

During the early years of the Chilean *coup d'état* (September 11, 1973), when President Allende was murdered and General Pinochet became the military dictator, many supporters of the deposed government—including musicians and artists—fled, fearing persecution and death. Because panpipes (*siku*), notch flutes (*quena*), and small guitars (*charango*) were featured in the protest movement called *nueva canción* ("new song"), Pinochet made their playing unlawful. Other acts of oppression followed. The folksinger-guitarist-composer-poet Víctor Jara was tortured and murdered. Jorge Peña, conductor of the children's orchestra in La Serena, was murdered because he had taken his orchestra on a tour to Cuba. In response, many Chilean musicians left for Brazil, Mexico, Venezuela, and elsewhere, especially Europe and the United States. Symphonic musicians left Santiago and joined orchestras in other cities outside Chile, such as Mexico City and San José, Costa Rica. Musicians such as Ángel and Isabel Parra fled to Mexico, where they continued to perform, compose, and record their music. The musical impact of Chilean immigrants since 1973 has been felt as far away as Paris, Rome, San Francisco, and Tokyo.

OUT-MIGRATION

The migration of people out of their homelands to other areas is emigration, or out-migration. It is caused by overt political oppression, as experienced in Chile in the 1970s, or by covert political oppression (when people are not recognized as political refugees), as experienced by thousands of Mayan people who fled political and economic oppression and death in Guatemala during the 1980s and 1990s, and have established new communities in Indiantown, Florida, and parts of southern California. In Indiantown, the Maya have continued their religious beliefs and life-styles, replete with *marimba* music and song, in country settings reminiscent of their rural habitats in Guatemala. Although these out-migrations are recent, others happened shortly after independence and the abolition of slavery in the Americas and included Afro-Brazilians returning to Angola and African Americans returning to Liberia. The out-migration of Cubans to Miami, New York, and elsewhere in the United States is another example of politically motivated movement, whereas the out-migration of Puerto Ricans to New York and Hawaii and of Haitians to Miami and New York are examples of economically motivated movement. The out-migration of people from Mexico and every country in South America, Central America, and the Caribbean has deeply affected the music of the United States and, to a lesser degree, other wealthy countries of the world where policies on immigration have been open.

REFERENCES

Ando, Zenpati. 1976. *Estudos Socio-Históricos da Imigração Japonesa*. São Paulo: Centro de Estudos Nipo-Brasileiros.

Arya, Usharbudh. 1968. *Ritual Songs and Folksongs of the Hindus of Surinam*. Leiden: E. J. Brill.

Béhague, Gerard. 1979. *Music in Latin America, an Introduction*. Englewood Cliffs, N. J.: Prentice-Hall.

Cowles, Maria Antonia Lopes. 1971. "Panorama Geral da População Japonesa e seus Descendentes bo Brasil." In *O Japonés em São Paulo e no Brasil*, 87–91. São Paulo: Centro de Estidos Nipo-Brasileiros.

de Waal Malefijt, Annemarie. 1963. *The Javanese of Surinam: Segment of a Plural Society*. Amsterdam: Royal Van Gorcum.

Flores, Hilda Agnes Hübner. 1983. *Canção dos Imigrantes*. Porto Alegre, Brazil: Escola Superior de Teologia São Lourenço de Brindes/Universidade de Caxias do Sul.

Fujii, Yukio, and T. Lynn Smith. 1959. *The Acculturation of the Japanese Immigrants in Brazil*. Gainesville: University of Florida Press.

Gardiner, C. Harvey. 1975. *The Japanese and Peru, 1873–1973*. Albuquerque: University of New Mexico Press.

Handa, Tomoo. 1971. "Senso Estético na Vida dos Imigrantes Japoneses." In *O Japonês em São Paulo e no Brasil*, 220–236. São Paulo: Centro de Estudos Nipo-Brasileiros.

———. 1980. *Memorias de un Imigrante Japonês no Brasil*. São Paulo: Centro de Estudos Nipo-Brasileiros.

Manuel, Peter. 1995. *Caribbean Currents*. Philadelphia: Temple University Press.

Morimoto, Amelia. 1979. *Los Jamones y sus Descendientes en le Peru*. Lima: Fordo Editorial del Congress del Peru.

Olsen, Dale A. 1980. "Japanese Music in Peru." *Asian Music* 11(2):41–51.

———. 1982. "Japanese Music in Brazil." *Asian Music* 14(1):111–131.

———. 1983. "The Social Determinants of Japanese Musical Life in Peru and Brazil." *Ethnomusicology* 27(1):49–70.

———. 1986. "A Japanese Master Musician in a Brazilian Context." *Hôgaku* 2(2):19–30.

———. 2004. *The Chrysanthemum and the Song: Music, Memory, and Identity in the Japanese Diaspora to South America*. Gainesville: University Press of Florida.

Solberg, Carl Edward. 1966. "The Response to Immigration in Argentina and Chile, 1890–1914." Ph.D. dissertation, Stanford University.

Yévenez S., Enrique. 1980. *Chile—Proyección Folklórica*. Santiago: Edward W. Leonard.

PART 3

Nations and Musical Traditions

Excluding native or Amerindian cultures, the politically determined nations in South America, Middle America, and the Caribbean number less than fifty, but the names for their musical traditions—including dances, festivals, genres, musical instruments, and songs—number into the thousands. The people and their musical traditions are of Native American, African, European, Asian, and other derivations. Most are a mixture of many heritages.

None of the nations, countries, or subcultures in South America, Middle America, and the Caribbean has developed or exists in isolation, and each has experienced musical and cultural growth. This photograph of a procession in northern Peru reveals one of the most important aspects of a culture: musical syncretism, possibly better described as cultural layering because Amerindian and Spanish elements often exist side by side.

A procession with the statue of the Virgen del Carmen during a patronal festival in Los Baños del Inca, Cajamarca, Peru, 16 July 1979. A *clarín* trumpeter precedes the religious statue while singers and dancers follow. Photograph by Dale A. Olsen.

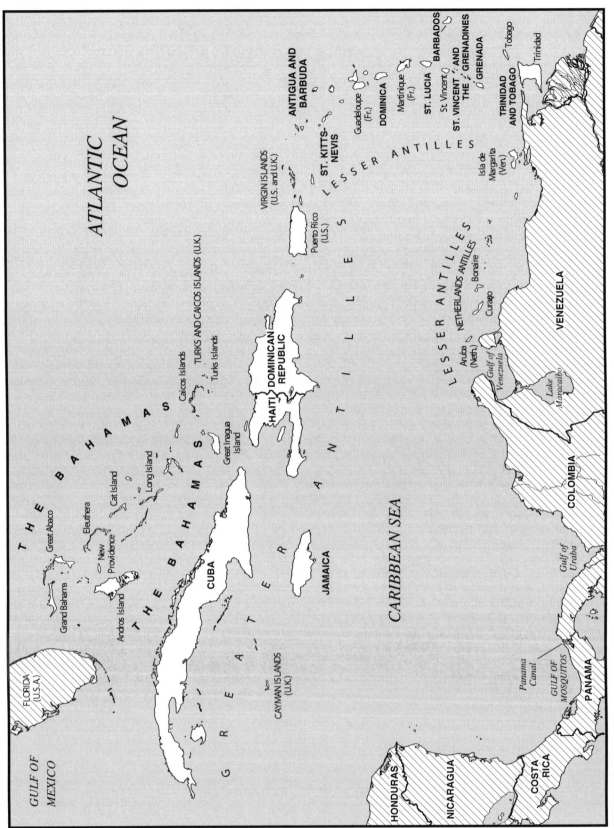

Map 8.1 The Caribbean region

Caribbean Latin America

The term *Caribbean* creates many images. It is familiar to all as an exotic place, a tourist haven, the setting for "fun in the sun," the home of "island music," mostly stereotypes created by the tourist industry. What we term *Caribbean Latin America*, however, is the Spanish-speaking area of the Greater Antilles that includes the mountainous islands of Hispaniola (the Dominican Republic occupying the eastern two-thirds of the island), Cuba, and Puerto Rico; additionally, we include Haiti because its history and culture were (and are still) closely aligned with the Dominican Republic and Cuba and because French (like Spanish) is a Latin-derived or romance language. While this area has certainly caused stereotypes of its own, it is culturally a different region than the Lesser Antilles that inspired calypso, *soca*, steelband, reggae, *zouk*, and other musical styles that have been such a part of the "island music" scene. Of course, one of the most important elements of what could be viewed as a musical "Latin explosion" in the United States is also a type of "island music": *salsa*. This is music from Caribbean Latin America, which, as many people realize, also owes much of its development to New York and Miami. Many other types of Caribbean Latin American musical expressions, however, have also been a part of the "Latin music" scene in the United States, including *bolero, cha-cha-chá, mambo, merengue, plena, rumba*, Santería, and much more.

The Spanish exploration of their "new world" began in this region of the Caribbean Basin, a region named after some of the native inhabitants whom they considered unfriendly: Carib, a term that also came to mean "cannibal." But the first inhabitants encountered by the Spanish were the Taíno, Arawak speakers, whom they found to be friendly. Many of the original names for these islands are Taíno names, such as *Cubanacán* for Cuba, *Haiti* ("mountainous land"), *Quisqueya* for the Dominican Republic, and *Borinquen* for Puerto Rico. By the mid 1500s, vast numbers of the original population of several million Arawak and Carib had been exterminated by disease, warfare, and suicide, although recent studies suggest that the Taíno presence continued longer than earlier believed (Guitar 2006:48).

Besides the shared Taíno background and the Spanish language, there are other threads that bind together the major islands of Caribbean Latin America. The plantation economy based on sugar is perhaps the most important, for it led to the importation of hundreds of thousands of African slaves whose music and culture have blended with Amerindian and Spanish music and culture for centuries. The African presence, in fact, is probably the most obvious thread that pervades the Caribbean. African slave influences, and those of the *cimarrones* ("runaway slaves," also Maroon and Seminole, the latter word an Anglicized form of the Spanish *cimarrón*), resulted in runaway Taíno and African slaves living and fighting side by side, leading to slave rebellions that ultimately resulted in Haiti's independence. Shared similarities between Taíno and Africans led anthropologist Maya Deren (1953) to call this concept "cultural convergence," which she argues can be seen today in Haiti and possibly other islands of the Greater Antilles.

Another common thread is geography, as the Greater Antilles are equally mountainous or hilly, lush, and susceptible to hurricanes and other storms. Another is flora and fauna, as a bounty of tropical plants and birds have created a virtual "Garden of Eden." Another is religion, as Roman Catholicism became the official religion, if not the dominant one. The proliferation of African slaves from a variety of African nations led to a diversity of belief systems among the African-derived communities, some blending with Roman Catholicism more than others, and some even blending with Amerindian cultural characteristics. Musically, most of the Caribbean shares in the celebration of Carnival (called *Carnaval* in Spanish), the pre-Lenten festival common in so many Catholic countries and/or regions, from Italy to New Orleans and Brazil to Cuba. Parading and dancing during each country's carnival are also shared characteristics. In spite of such historical, language, geographic, and cultural commonalities, however, each of the islands in Caribbean Latin America is profoundly unique in many ways. Just how and why different regional expressions of music and dance developed and evolved is one of the most fascinating studies in ethnomusicology.

Surprisingly, perhaps, twenty-first-century politics have not affected the traditional musics of Caribbean Latin America as much as might be expected, and this is because of the common historical foundation of Cuba, Haiti, Dominican Republic, and Puerto Rico. All four countries, of course, have African-derived and Spanish-derived (or French-derived in Haiti) expressions of music and dance, plus a variety of blends among them. For example, African-derived drums can be found in a variety of contexts, as well as Spanish-derived singing styles and construction of lyrics. Into the twenty-first century those and many more traditional elements continue, along with the addition of new elements that may owe their existence to political ideologies, commercialism, globalization, and other modern and postmodern trends. The four countries of Caribbean Latin America are tremendously interesting to many scholars from the point of view of how they have uniquely developed in the past hundred years: Haiti and the Dominican Republic as totalling independent republics of about eighteen million people, Cuba as a Communist regime with approximately eleven million people, and Puerto Rico as a Commonwealth of the United States with less than four million people. Music is one of the important measures of their identities.

REFERENCES

Deren, Maya. 1991 (1953). *Divine Horsemen: The Living Gods of Haiti*. New York: McPherson.
Guitar, Lynne. 2006. "Boiling It Down." In *Slaves, Subjects, and Subversives: Blacks in Colonial Latin America*, eds. Jane G. Landers and Barry M. Robinson, 39–82. Albuquerque: University of New Mexico Press.

Cuba

Olavo Alén Rodríguez

The Indigenous Heritage
The European Heritage
The African Heritage
The Emergence of Cuban Music
Musical Genres and Contexts
Vocal and Instrumental Ensembles
European-derived Art Music and Music Education
Administrative Structures and Institutions of Music

The Republic of Cuba is a nation of more than sixteen hundred keys and islands located in the northwestern Antilles. The main island, Cuba, with a surface area of 105,007 square kilometers, is the largest of the Antilles. Most of the national population is descended from Spaniards (mostly from Andalucía and the Canary Islands) and Africans (mostly Bantu and Yoruba). Small populations derive from Caribbean people from other islands, French, and Chinese. Spanish is the official language, but some Cubans still speak several African-derived languages. Local religions include several derived from African religions, but the largest in membership is Roman Catholicism.

THE INDIGENOUS HERITAGE

Before Europeans arrived, aboriginal groups occupied the archipelago known today as the Greater Antilles, calling the largest island "Cuba." Economically and socially, the most developed Amerindians were an Arawak people, known to later scholars as Taíno. According to accounts by early European chroniclers and travelers, the most important cultural activity of the Taíno was the feast known as *areito* (also *areyto*), the main social event for the practice of music and dance. We know only a few specifics about Taíno music, including the fact that performers used idiophonic soundmakers like jingles and maracas and an aerophone they called *guamo*, made from a snail shell opened at its pointed end. Little to none of the artistic elements of Taíno culture became a part of what centuries later was to be known as Cuban music, though some other cultural traits (such as foods and domestic architecture) survived in latter-day Cuban culture.

Beginning at the period of conquest (1492) and during the colonization of the island by Spain, Cuba's autochthonous population died out as a result of imported diseases (such as the common cold and influenza, for which the Amerindians had no natural antibodies), the forced labor to which they were subjected (in the Spanish quest for nonexistent gold and silver), and mass suicide in response to this forced labor. About a hundred thousand Amerindians were living in Cuba at the time of its discovery by the Spanish. Information from fifty to seventy-five years later places the indigenous population of the island at no more than two thousand.

THE EUROPEAN HERITAGE

After Columbus' first landfall on a small island in the Bahamas on October 12, 1492 (Rouse 1992:142), he and his three ships explored the northern coast of Cuba. In that first voyage by Columbus, the European explorers made landfall on October 28 of the same year (ibid.:142), slowly exploring the northern coastline, heading east and crossing open water to the north shore of Haiti where they built a fort called *La Navidad* (143). After exploring the northern coast of Hispaniola, Columbus and his remaining two ships returned to Spain.

The convenience of Cuba's geographical position made it an important port of call for Spanish ships traveling to Mexico and South America. Cuba (especially the ports of Havana and Santiago) provided facilities for repairing ships and supplies of food and water. Beyond that, however, there was little to attract Spanish settlers—the gold laden mainland of Mexico was far more attractive to them. Nevertheless, the need for provisions fostered the local development of agriculture, based on an enslaved labor force of local Amerindians. It also led to the establishment of the first Cuban bishopric in 1518 in Baracoa, which was moved in 1522 to Santiago where it became Cuba's first cathedral (Carpentier 1979:68–69). Few Spanish musicians settled in Cuba during the early sixteenth century, not until the development of sugar plantations in the 1570s, which also contributed to the growth of urban areas. Eventually military bands were brought to Cuba from Spain to perform for the Spanish troops, and their musicians played an important role in Cuba's colonial musical life, as did Spanish musicians who came to settle, bringing their musical instruments—*laúd*, *bandurria*, and guitar—with them. Performances of Spanish poetry in meter, such as the *cuarteta* and the *décima*, took place, and Spanish balladry (*el romancero español*) played an important role in the development of Cuba's song traditions.

THE AFRICAN HERITAGE

With the development of sugar plantations and other types of agriculture in Cuba, Amerindian (Taíno) workers rapidly declined in numbers, necessitating new sources of labor:

slaves, imported from Africa. By about 1550, African slaves had begun to replace indigenous laborers to become a major factor in the colony's economic development. The importation of Africans reached its peak between 1761 through 1870, when approximately seven hundred thousand slaves were brought to Cuba (Rogoziński 1999:141).

There is little documentation of early African music in Cuba. During Cuba's lengthy colonial era, however, African slaves remembered and performed their musical traditions, mixed with and/or developing new forms. The music of African people and their descendants in Cuba was played on instruments fashioned after African prototypes, because slaves were not allowed to bring any musical instruments from their African homelands. Nevertheless, African music found fertile soil for development in Cuba, particularly as part of the slaves' reorganization of their religions and beliefs. Because all African religions have their own music, the religions brought by African groups to Cuba enriched the musical arts of the entire region. Even today, we often find musical instruments, characteristic ways of playing them, songs, rhythms, dances, and even the use of music for magical functions—all practiced in a way resembling their New World beginnings, much as they must have been when Africans brought their music to Cuba, hundreds of years ago. Over the years, African and Spanish music blended, resulting in a variety of Cuban musical and dance genres.

The most important African ethnic groups that participated in the development and cultural blending of the Cuban population were the Yoruba, different groups of Bantu linguistic stock, and some groups from the former area of Calabar (Dahomey). Because of the dehumanizing nature of the African slave trade, however, and the fact that precise records of slave origins were not kept, it is not known to which ethnic group the early slaves (in the sixteen–seventeenth centuries) pertained. Therefore, the following categories are arranged arbitrarily, beginning, however, with the Yoruba, about whom most is known.

Yoruba heritage and Santería religion

An agreement in 1817 between Spain and the United Kingdom gave the slave trade to the British, allowing for the importation of four hundred thousand Africans, mostly Yoruba people who came to be known in Cuba as Lucumí. After 1836, mostly Yoruba slaves continued to be brought in at the rate of 1,150 per month. Most Yoruba slaves (including Egbado, Ijesha, Ketu, Nago, Oyo, and other Yoruba-speakers) disembarked on Cuba's western coast, mainly in Matanzas, Havana Province, and the city of Havana. Therefore, Yoruba music has remained, as a rule, more authentically preserved in western Cuba than in eastern Cuba. The survival of Yoruba music and dance in Cuba can be partially attributed to the fact that the Yoruba arrived late in the slave trade, between 1820 and 1840 (Marks 1994).

Many African traditions were preserved in Cuba because the Spanish masters allowed slaves to use their traditions of drumming and dance to worship as they had in Africa. The Spanish also allowed the slaves to organize mutual-aid societies (*cabildos*) so they could better handle their new way of life. These societies often had a king, a queen, and a complex social hierarchy with different levels, conferring prestige on the members of the group who held offices. This relative leniency, combined with compulsory baptism into Roman Catholicism, resulted in the syncretism of West African deities with Christian saints. In this sense, the Yoruba-Cubans went so far as to name their religion Santería, in

Figure 9.1
A famous *babalawo* adjusts the *chaworó* bells on his sacred *batá* drum. Photo courtesy of the Archives of CIDMUC (Center for the Research and Development of Cuban Music), Havana.

a frank allusion to the Christian saints. Other Cuban names for this religion are Regla de Ocha (Doctrine of the Ocha [Osha, *orishas* "deities"]) and Lucumí (González-Wippler 1973:1).

Many Yoruba and their descendants congregated around temple-homes (*ile-ocha*), headed by a religious godfather (*tata-nganga*) or godmother. These buildings usually had a room (*igbodu*) that held the magical objects devoted to *orishas*. It is in these rooms that believers still perform the rhythmic patterns that invoke *orishas*. These patterns follow a preestablished order (*oru*, or *oru* de Igbadú). Female priests are known as *iyalochas*; male priests, as *babalochas*. The highest rank, *babalawo*, it is reserved for men, as it was in Africa (Figure 9.1).

Musical instruments

The most important musical instruments used in Santería rituals are two-headed *batá* drums (Figure 9.1), always played in sets of three. These drums, rebuilt from the collective memory people of African heritage, have retained the original hourglass shape of their African prototypes, but a clearer differentiation has been established in the diameter of the skins. The drum with the lowest pitch is the *iyá*, the middle drum is the *itótele*, and the smallest one is the *okónkolo* (Cornelius 1990:134). The tensions of the *batá's* skins are fixed with tensor straps, usually made of rawhide. Sometimes bronze jingle bells (*chaworó*) are fastened around the heads of the *iyá*. The *batá* performer sits and holds his drum horizontally on his lap so he can strike both drumheads with his hands (one at a time). The total of six different pitches produced by the collective six hands of three *batá* drummers are interlocked to form pitched rhythmical patterns (*toques*) that correspond to the three tonal levels of the Yoruba language. Each *toque* is a type of communicative statement with a particular *orisha*, which includes over twelve deities in Cuba. [Listen to "Ibarabo Ago Mo Juba"]

DISC ❷ TRACK 1

Also rebuilt by the Yoruba in Cuba were the *iyesá*, a set of four cylindrical, different-sized double-headed drums. The tension of the skins is maintained with tensor thongs that stretch from one skin to the other. Other Yoruba drums in Cuba are the *bembé*, made in differing sizes from hollowed tree trunks. The skins are nailed on and tightened by heat from a fire. *Bembé* are not used for religious purposes (Ortiz 1954).

Another group of instruments used by the Yoruba in Cuba is a set of shaken idiophones, known by several terms: *abwe*, *güiro*, or *shekere* (also spelled *chéquere* in Spanish). These instruments are made from three large gourds covered with bead-studded nets. Each net fits loosely around a gourd, and when the instrument is shaken, the beads (made from seeds) strike the gourd's exterior. This set of gourds is usually accompanied by a steel hoe blade (*hierro*), struck with an iron bar. In this polyrhythmic music, the blade sets and maintains the beat (see Okada 1995: example 2).

Bantu heritage and Congo (Kongo) secret societies

Slaves from the geographical areas of Africa where the Bantu-speaking nations lived contributed heavily to Cuban musical culture. The zone from which most Bantu-speaking slaves were taken is the Congo Basin and both sides of the Congo River. In Cuba, these slaves were generically known as Congos, and they were the groups to arrive to Cuba illegally after slavery was abolished in 1886. It would be hard today to identify traits that would distinguish the ethnic groups of this linguistic complex, but the Loango, the Bavili, the Bacongo, the Mayombe, and the Ndongo have provided the greatest contribution to Cuban culture. The Congos also organized mutual-aid societies (*cabildos*) like those of the Yoruba. Like the Yoruba, they congregated around godfathers' temple-homes, creating nuclei of godchildren.

Musical instruments

The Congos brought not only their religion but also the feasts, dances, and music with which they were familiar. They reconstructed many instruments in Cuba. Among these were several wooden idiophonic percussion instruments, of which the *guagua* (or *catá*) is the only survivor. It is a hollowed trunk, struck with two sticks. Membranophonic drums introduced in Cuba by the Congo constituted the *ngoma* ensemble (Ortiz 1954). *Ngoma* drums, made of wooden staves, are single headed and barrel shaped. The drums are usually played alone, but sometimes they are accompanied by the *kinfuiti*, another drum introduced in Cuba by the Congo. The Congo also introduced *makuta* beats and dances, employed in a celebration that is no longer observed. The last record of that festivity is in the early twentieth century, around Sagua la Grande. The Congo instruments that had the greatest cultural impact were *yuka*, drums made from hollowed fruit-tree trunks, with a skin tacked to one end and usually played in a set of three. The largest drum is the *caja*, the middle drum is the *mula*, and the smallest is the *cachimbo*. These names seem to have come from the *ngoma* ensemble.

Carabalí heritage and Abakuá secret society

The Calabar area of the western coast of Africa, between the Niger and Cross rivers along the Nigeria-Cameroon border (southeastern Nigeria and southwestern Cameroon), is the place of origin of slaves known as Carabalí. Their *cabildos* were known as Carabalí *cabildos*, and their mutual-aid societies came to be known in Cuba as Abakuá secret societies or Abakuá powers. These organizations were strong among harbor workers, especially in Havana, Matanzas, and Cárdenas, and they greatly influenced the development of Cuban music. The first of these societies, the Potencia Efik-Buton, consolidated an Apapa Carabalí cabildo founded in the township of Regla in 1836. The members of these societies were called *ñáñigos* in Cuba.

For feasts and ceremonies, the Abakuá followers use two sets of instruments. One set consists of four drums that make a series of isolated sounds having symbolic importance. The other set, the *biankomeko* ensemble, is made up of four drums, each with a single head of goatskin, played only with hands (Courlander 1942:233): *bonkó-enchemiyá, biankomé, obi-apá,* and *kuchí-yeremá.* These drums are accompanied by a cowbell (*ekón*), sticks (*itones*), and two rattles (*erikúndi*).

Ewe and Fon heritages and Arará secret society

From the ancient kingdom of Dahomey (the present-day Republic of Benin) came slaves who founded the Arará *cabildos* in Cuba. They were representatives of several peoples, the most important of which were the Ewe and the Fon. Many Africans enslaved in Dahomey were taken by the French, so French colonies—mainly Haiti and Louisiana—received a large number of Ewe and Fon slaves. The slave rebellion headed by Toussaint L'Ouverture in Haiti forced many people to flee Cuba's nearest neighbor to the east, and from 1789 to 1804, large numbers of French planters and their faithful slaves migrated to Cuba. A resulting musical form of this time was the *tumba francesa* or "French drum," referring to Haitian music and dance (Alén Rodríguez 1986). Today, this survives only in performances by national dance troupes (see Okada 1995: example 4).

The most direct transposition from Africa to Cuba, however, was achieved by the Arará, who transferred their festive and religious activities just as they had been performed in Africa. The Arará *cabildos* preserved an ensemble made up of four drums. Their names vary greatly from community to community, but the most frequent names are *hunguedde, huncito, hun,* and *hunga* (see also Courlander 1942:236). In addition, Haitian *rada* drums are usually used in Afro-Cuban-Haitian ensembles (Figure 9.2) when they perform during Vodú rituals (Emmanuel Pereira, personal communication with Dale Olsen, 2007).

Other West African heritages

The Mina, Manding, and Gange *cabildos* had a much smaller impact on the development of Afro-Cuban music. The Mina *cabildos* let in Ashantis, Fantis, Guaguis, Musinas, and others

Figure 9.2
An Afro-Cuban-Haitian ensemble, Petit Dancé from Las Tuna (1983) plays *rada* drums. Left to right: *segón, gwo tanbou* (also called *tambor radá*), and *leguedé*. Photo courtesy of the Archives of CIDMUC, Havana (thanks to Emmanuel Pereira for drum identification).

taken from the former Gold Coast, now the Republic of Ghana. The Manding *cabildos* took in slaves that had come from present-day Sierra Leone and parts of Guinea, representing the Alogasapi, the Bambara, the Lomba, the Sesere, and the Soso. The Gange are of Manding stock, and the Azziero, the Bay, the Gola, the Longoba, the Mani, and the Quisi are among them.

In social and economic spheres and the forms of artistic expression, a distinctively Cuban nationality is thought to have emerged between 1790 and 1868, when there appeared musical genres that, despite having their roots in Spain and Africa, displayed elements of Cuban origin. There occurred a great surge of music played by academically-trained Spanish musicians who had solid technical foundations in composition and performance. Musical ensembles were organized around the churches, particularly in Havana and Santiago de Cuba. This period also witnessed the immigration of people of French descent from Haiti, and later from Louisiana.

Another important influence during this period was the introduction of opera and *zarzuela* companies that came from Italy and Spain. In urban areas, genres such as the Cuban *contradanza* and later the *habanera* were born. Traditional Cuban song took shape, as did the *orquestas típicas* that played dances. In rural areas, the musical genres that were later to be known as the *punto campesino* (in central and western Cuba) and the *son* (in eastern Cuba) also emerged. In the chapels of Santiago de Cuba and Havana, musicians such as Esteban Salas y Castro (1725–1803) and Juan París (1759–1845) modernized the compositional techniques of Cuban ecclesiastical music.

The period 1868–1898 was marked by rebellions against Spanish rule. The Spanish government abolished slavery gradually beginning in 1880 and definitively in 1886, freeing about a quarter of a million landless blacks, many of whom migrated to urban outskirts. Before 1871, an estimated 150,000 Chinese laborers were brought to Cuba, mainly from Canton; though they eventually organized their own Chinatown in Havana and spread throughout the country, their tendency to stick together in closed groups limited their contribution to the common musical culture.

Important Cuban folkloric genres appeared in the urban peripheries during this period. Notable among these were *rumba* and *comparsas* (see below). A vast migration from rural to urban areas, especially to Havana, contributed to the integration of many local traditions that had developed in different areas of the country. The effects of this migration were complemented by the movement of troops resulting from the wars for independence. Concert music changed considerably, particularly piano music in the city of Havana. Outstanding musicians appeared, such as Manuel Saumell (1817–1870), whose *contradanzas* for piano gave rise to Cuba's own concert music.

In 1898, in the last of the three wars for independence, U.S. intervention on behalf of the rebels helped free Cuba from Spanish rule. But U.S. military occupation (1 January 1899 to 20 May 1902) brought North American capital investments in Cuba, and with them came the influence of North American lifeways on Cuban cultural expressions.

The republican period, 1902–1959

Under the republic, a national consciousness based on Cuba's position as a politically independent nation began to arise. People became increasingly aware of the need to develop a Cuban musical culture, and simultaneously the music of Cuba began to have influence outside Cuba. The early contacts of Cuban musical genres—particularly the *son*—with

American jazz left marked effects on Cuban genres and jazz, and on the popular music of the United States. In turn, the *rumba* and the *son*, and later the *cha-cha-chá* and the *mambo*, had impact on Europe during this period. Cuban musical instruments such as the *tumbadora* and *bongos* began to be used in diverse instrumental ensembles in cultures outside Cuba.

Concert music, particularly symphonic music, also developed. With the emergence of a strong nationalistic awareness came musicians such as Alejandro García Caturla (1906–1940) and Amadeo Roldán (1900–1939), who used the most up-to-date compositional techniques of the times to create works of a marked national character. The most important contribution to this musical nationalism was through folkloric music.

Professional popular music, with deep roots among the population and intimate links to dance, left its mark too. Professional popular music differed from folk music by the use of technical elements in composition and interpretation that were taken from the music of Europe. This music became easily commercialized because of its ready adaptation to radio and television, the media of mass communication. These media, in turn, affected the development of the Cuban folkloric ensembles of the times. Dance music was by far the most popular, with roots deep in tradition.

Cuban music was nourished by waves of immigrants from the Caribbean, mainly from Haiti and Jamaica. These immigrants were brought to remedy the shortage of manpower in the sugar industry and in the growth of the railroads. Emmanuel Pereira (n.d.) explains the following about Haitian influences in Cuba during the early twentieth century:

> Between roughly a twenty year period (1915–1934 in Haiti and 1916–1930 in the Dominican Republic), as a result of the Monroe Doctrine, Haiti and the Dominican Republic were under American occupation. This prompted many blacks to leave both sides of the island for Cuba, although the largest number of people that went to Cuba to cut sugarcane were Haitians, in particular from the southern part of Haiti, Aux Cayes, Aquin, to as far as Jeremie. Unlike the descendents of the eighteenth century Haitian immigrants who introduced *tumba francesa*, children of the later immigrants see themselves as descendants of Haitians. Therefore, their culture can be identified with present day Haitians: they speak southern Haitian Creole, and their rituals, music, and lyrics are similar to Vodú, *rara*, *meringue*, and *kompa* from southern Haiti. Migrations of Haitians to Cuba eventually stopped, however, as a result of Fidel Castro's revolution that restructured Cuba's plantation system, making the highly reputed and legendary machete-wielding Haitian immigrant farmer a historical phenomenon. There are stories of machete wielding sugarcane cutters who worked with *lwas* [see HAITI] at their sides, from sun up to sun down. The folkloric machete dance depicting the Haitian immigrant farmer is still widely seen in Cuba. It is a dangerous dance because the dancers use real metal machetes. They stand on them with their bare feet, run the blades across their tongues, and stab their bare bellies with the sharp points of the blade.

In the 1940s and 1950s, the increased importance of radio, the introduction of television (in 1950), the appearance of several small record companies, and the construction of important musical theaters all fostered a boom in Cuban music, mostly limited to Havana. By about 1950, the nationalistic movement in musical composition was replaced by a neoclassical trend that centered on the Grupo de Renovación, headed by a composer of Catalonian origin, José Ardévol (1911–1981).

After 1959

The revolution of 1959 began the transition to a socialist society. The government instituted a free educational system whose curriculum included the arts. The National Council of

Culture was founded under the Ministry of Education, and in 1976, the council was elevated to the rank of Ministry of Culture. The National Council of Culture aimed to rescue Cuba's folklore. It allocated significant resources to the development of professional music and the Amateur Movement, which eventually produced many professional musicians.

Musicological research was organized, and a cultural policy was designed to find and preserve, in every municipality, the country's musical culture. A national system of music schools was organized, and elementary music schools were opened in practically every important city. A system of enterprises was organized to include all the country's soloists and musical ensembles. These enterprises saw to the contracting and programming of musicians, who were guaranteed steady employment and stable salaries.

The Musical Publications and Recording Studios (EGREM), Cuba's musical publications and recording enterprise, was organized and given the responsibility of producing recordings and publishing scores of Cuban music. One of the spinoffs of EGREM was the National Music Publishing House (Editora Nacional de Música).

A factory was established to mass-produce autochthonous musical instruments that until then had been produced only by individual craftsmen. Consequently, there was an increased availability of *bongos*, rattles (*chéqueres*), drums of the Abakuá secret society, and other African-Cuban musical instruments. Instruments such as *bongos*, *tumbadoras*, guitar, and *tres*, which had been produced on a limited scale, were turned out in greater numbers.

The Ministry of Culture fostered the development of institutions that were already doing musicological research. One was the Seminario de Música Popular (Popular Music Seminar). Other, more comprehensive, institutions—the National Museum of Cuban Music and the Center for the Research and Development of Cuban Music (CIDMUC) —were also founded.

From its inception, the National Council of Culture and later the Ministry of Culture organized festivals dedicated to music. They included the National *Son* Festival, the Rumba Festival, the Electro-Acoustic Music Festival in Varadero, the Chamber Music Festival in Camagüey, the National Choral Festival in Santiago de Cuba, and others. Based on the Amateur Movement, a system of *casas de cultura* ("houses of culture") was developed in all the country's municipalities. These institutions not only foster the organization of musical groups of all kinds but also teach music and follow up on amateurs' musical education.

During this period, contemporary music took shape. It accommodated a broad range of aesthetic perspectives, including conventional neoromantic techniques for orchestral work and bold experiments in electroacoustic music. The tendencies that most contributed to the contemporary music of the period were aleatorism and neoserialism.

Professional popular music saw a marked development of the *son*, particularly in connection with *nueva trova*, a nationalistic movement, founded in 1962. The *son*, particularly its urban variants, became practically synonymous with Cuban popular dance music and had a far-reaching impact on the music later known as *salsa*. The influence of the *son* on the creation of *salsa* has been so far reaching that many specialists have mistaken one for the other.

Folkloric music became stronger in urban areas. People of central and western Cuba continued singing songs of the *punto cubano* complex (see below), and the variants of the *son* (including the *son* subgenre called *changüí* from eastern Cuba) retained their predominance in the rural areas of the eastern provinces. The *rumba* remains a broadly practiced genre, particularly in Havana and in Matanzas Province. Cuban musicians still compose *boleros*, *cha-cha-chás*, *contradanzas*, *danzones*, and *guarachas*, but none of these is as popular as the *son*.

MUSICAL GENRES AND CONTEXTS

The history of Cuba's musical culture reflects a complex pattern of migrations and cultural confluences, leading to the emergence of widely differing musical traditions in remote areas of the country. These factors contributed to the development of a variegated national musical culture with local musical types. Communication between these areas and among the strata of the population has helped some local traditions gain national popularity and become typical expressions of a Cuban national identity.

The genres of Cuban traditional music can be grouped into five complexes (*punto cubano*, *rumba*, *son*, *canción*, and *danzón*), each comprising related musical genres based on common musical aptitudes and behaviors. These complexes are determined by style, instrumentation, and the makeup of traditional ensembles.

The **punto cubano** complex

Punto cubano (also called *punto guajiro* and *punto campesino*) and the entire complex of rural musical genres it embraces make up this generic complex of Cuban music. It has developed largely within the framework of rural music in central and western Cuba, where country *tonadas*, *puntos fijos*, *puntos libres*, *seguidillas*, and other forms remain common. *Tonadas* are tunes or melodies sung to recite *décimas*. The *punto* can be *fijo* ("fixed") or *libre* ("free"): if the accompaniment of the *laúd* and guitar is always present, then the *punto* is *fijo*; if the accompaniment stops to let the singer sing his melody and *décima* alone, the *punto* is *libre*. In the *seguidilla*, the singer uses versification that gives the impression of a never-ending strophe. When sung as a duel, the genre is called *controversia* (see *The Americas II* 1990: example 28–4). *Guateques campesinos* was the name given to the typical parties of the farmers where the *puntos* were sung.

Dances for these genres, called *zapateos*, developed during the 1800s. The *zapateo* is no longer danced. It has been replaced by dance forms borrowed from the *son* and other country dances of the eastern end of the island. The transformation and modernization of the genres of this complex have been slower than in the other complexes of Cuban music, perhaps because the genres are limited to the rural population. Professional musicians have adopted some of these genres, though usually when combining them with elements of other generic complexes, such as the *son* and the *canción*.

The **rumba** complex

Another important generic complex in Cuba is *rumba*, whose name probably derives from African-Caribbean words (such as *tumba*, *macumba*, and *tambo*) referring to a collective secular festivity. Originally, in the marginal suburbs of Havana and Matanzas, the word meant simply "feast." In time, it took the meaning of a Cuban musical genre and acquired a specific instrumental format for its performance (see Okada 1995: example 3). It even gave rise to its own instruments: *tumbadoras* (often called *congas*), which have spread throughout the world.

Rumba is said to have originated in the ports of Matanzas, performed by Afro-Cuban dock workers. In the beginning, the instruments that played rumbas were different-sized wooden boxes (*cajones*), shipping crates common at the docks. Eventually, they evolved into three barrel-shaped drums, first called *hembra* ("female"), *macho* ("male"), and *quinto* ("fifth"), and later called *salidor* ("starter") or *tumbadora*, *tres-dos* ("three-two") or *tres golpes* ("three beats"), and *quinto*. In African musical cultures, female drums, also called mother drums, are tuned in the lowest registers. Male drums are in the mid-registers, and *quintos* are tuned in the upper registers. The *salidor* is the first drum that plays. *Tres-dos* indicates that the drum will normally be beaten in a combination of three and two beats. These drums were generically called *tumbadoras*. With their appearance, the instrumental format of the *rumba* was fixed. This ensemble is often complemented by a small *catá*, a hollowed tree trunk, struck with two sticks.

All genres of the *rumba* have the same structure. The lead singer starts with a section that *rumberos* (*rumba* players) call the *diana*. The singer then goes into a section of text that introduces the theme (the *décima*), and only after this does the *rumba* proper begin, with more active instrumental playing and a section (*montuno*) alternating between the soloist and the small choir, in call-and-response fashion.

Of the genres that make up the *rumba* complex, the *guaguancó*, the *columbia*, and the *yambú* are the most popular in Cuba. The *guaguancó* has most deeply penetrated into other functional spheres of Cuban music, and is most generally identified with the concept of the *rumba*. [Listen to "Las Leyendas de Grecia"] The performance of *guaguancó* may include DISC❷TRACK2 couple dancing, and the music and the dance have elements that reflect Bantu traits. The *columbia* is a solo male exhibition dance that features flashy dancing. By contrast, the *yambú* is designated for older people, and is a couple dance. Generally *cajón* box drums accompany the *yambú* (see Okada 1995: example 3).

The **son** complex

The combination of plucked strings and African-derived percussion instruments gave birth to a musical genre called *son*, first popular among peasants of eastern Cuba. During the twentieth century, the *son* complex, because of its influence on dance music and its projection into practically all social and functional spheres of musical activity in the country, has been the most important musical genre in Cuba. Its earliest manifestations, perhaps dating as far back as about 1750, were among the first Cuban musical genres or styles about which information survives.

The *son* took shape in rural easternmost Cuba. Its oldest genres include the *son montuno* (from the Sierra Maestra range) and the *changüí* (from the area of Guantánamo). [Listen to "Así es el Changüí"] The formal structure of the oldest *sones* is the constant alternation of a DISC❷TRACK3 soloist with a refrain, typically sung by a small group. When the *son* emerged from rural areas, it acquired another important structural element: the inclusion of an initial closed structure

in binary form, followed by a *montuno*, a section in which a soloist alternates with a small choir in responsorial fashion.

The instrumental ensembles (Figure 9.3) that played *sones* always combined plucked string instruments—guitar, *laúd* (a type of guitar, from the Arabic *'ud*), *tres* (a guitar with three courses of double strings), and later the string bass—with percussive instruments such as *bongos*, *tumbadoras* (*congas*), *claves*, *maracas*, and the *güiro* (here a gourd scraper). The vocal soloist is often the one who plays the claves, and the singers of the responsorial refrain are the other instrumentalists in the ensemble.

Within the context of the *son*, musicians exploited two important instruments for Cuban music—the *tres* and *bongos* (Figure 9.4). The *tres* is a Cuban plucked stringed instrument that differs from the guitar mainly because of the way the strings are tuned. Three pairs of strings (each with a pitch and its octave) are plucked to build melodies as counterpoints to the main melodies of the singer.

Figure 9.3
A son ensemble in the mountain area of Oriente. Left to right: *tres, tumbadoras, laúd, contrabajo, tres,* and *tres.* Photo courtesy of the Archives of CIDMUC, Havana.

The *canción* complex

Another generic complex is the *canción* ("song"), embodied in Afro-Cuban forms and styles of singing. References to songs written by Cuban composers appear as early as about 1800. These songs, written in the Italian style of the day, had no features that could identify them as Cuban, but they gave rise to Cuban lyrical songs. The earliest appearance of Cuban elements took place in the texts. By about 1850, many songs of this type (such as "La Bayamesa" by Carlos M. de Céspedes) were in circulation.

The development of lyrical songs in Cuba led to a new genre, the *habanera*, which became an important generic prototype after Eduardo Sánchez de Fuentes composed his *habanera* "Tú." A well-known *habanera* occurs in Georges Bizet's *Carmen*, premiered in Paris in 1875.

Songs for two voices in parallel thirds and sixths and using the guitar as the instrument of preference have been in frequent use since the 1800s. They laid the foundation for the emergence of another genre of the Cuban song, the *canción trovadoresca*, a genre that takes its name from the name its most important interpreters

Figure 9.4
A man plays *bongos.* Photo courtesy of the Archives of CIDMUC, Havana.

gave themselves: *trovadores* ("troubadours"). Personalities such as José "Pepe" Sánchez, Sindo Garay, Manuel Corona, and Alberto Villalón decisively shaped the musical genre that has come to be known as the traditional *trova*.

The distinguishing feature of this genre in Cuba is the way the song became closely associated with the singer, who moved around accompanying himself on the guitar, singing about things he knew or whatever struck his fancy. The word *trovador* was probably an attempt by these artists to establish a relation between what they did and the functions they attributed to the troubadours of medieval Europe. This genre developed greatly in Cuba after the 1960s, giving rise to a new movement, *nuevatrova* ("new song"), that developed its own administrative structure and gained throughout the country hundreds of members. Today, the movement has become weak and has given way to *boleros* and other forms of romantic songs within salsa music.

Before the 1850s, this tradition was intended primarily for listening, not dancing. The situation changed with the rise of the important musical genre known as *bolero*, born in Cuba from antecedents in the Spanish *bolero*. Rhythms taken from those played by the Cuban percussive instruments of African origin were added to the traditional forms of the Spanish dance and melody. The creators of the new genre were a group of *trovadores* from Santiago de Cuba who performed the *canción trovadoresca*. They gave the *bolero* stylistic elements and rhythms from the *son*, then popular only in rural eastern Cuba. José "Pepe" Sánchez is considered the composer of the first Cuban *bolero*, a genre cultivated by many songwriters and musicians abroad. In some Caribbean countries, it is one of the most important genres of popular music (see PUERTO RICO).

During the 1800s, societies whose only objective was to make music came into being. This is the case with *clave* choirs (*coros de clave*), which originated in Matanzas and Havana. These organizations had repertoires of songs called *claves*, composed by its members. They lost favor and disappeared early in the 1900s, but they contributed to the Cuban musical heritage a genre that preserves the original name.

Another musical genre of the *canción* complex is the *criolla*. It resulted from the continued development of the *clave*. The composer of the first *criolla* was Luís Casas Romero, who wrote his "Carmela" in 1908. *Criollas* are songs written in urban forms and style, with texts referring to rural themes. The tempo is slower than in the *clave*, and the meter is 6/8. The form is binary, and the harmonies are often modal.

With the *clave* appeared another genre, the *guajira*. It is written in 6/8 meter alternating with 3/4 (this rhythm is called *sesquiáltera* in Spanish), and often includes musical affectations evocative of the rural peoples' plucked stringed instruments. The texts of the *guajira* centered on the beauty of the countryside and pastoral life (see *The Americas II* 1990: example 28-3).

Cuban songs in general, but particularly the *bolero* and the *canción trovadoresca*, have joined with other Cuban musical genres, such as the *son*, to produce mixed genres that have influenced Cuban dance music.

The *danzón* complex

A large migration of French people and Haitians with French customs arrived in Cuba at the end of the 1700s, when the character of the Cuban nation was taking shape. This migration gave rise to the fourth generic complex, the *danzón*, which had its origins in the early Cuban *contradanzas*, and projects forward in time to the *cha-cha-chá*.

The interpretation in Cuba of French *contredanses*—especially with the violin-piano-flute format—led to the development of a *contradanza* that may be considered Cuban, especially with the later introduction of percussive instruments taken from Afro-Cuban music. The earliest *contradanzas* were played by two different musical ensembles: the *charanga* (a Cuban popular music orchestra consisting of two flutes, piano, *pailas*, *claves*, *güiro*, two *tumbadoras*, four violins, and eventually a cello) and the *orquesta típica* ("typical orchestra" or folkloric orchestra). The development of these orchestras, and the evolution and change experienced by the French and local *contredanses* in Cuba, gave rise to musical genres such as the *danza*, the *danzón*, the *danzonete*, the *mambo*, and the *cha-cha-chá*.

The *contradanza* acquired its distinctive profile during the 1800s and became the first genre of Cuban music to gain popularity abroad. It had four well-defined routines: *paseo* ("walk"), *cadena* ("chain," with the taking of hands to make a chain), *sostenido* ("holding of partners"), and *cedazo* ("passing through," as some couples make arches with their arms while others pass under them). Its structure is binary, and each section usually has eight measures. In the mid-1800s, the composer and pianist Manuel Saumell transformed it into a vehicle for concert music; thus, it became the first autochthonous genre included in the concert-hall repertoire.

Danzas cubanas were the result of the evolution of the older *contradanzas*. Played by ensembles known as French *charangas* (*charangas francesas*), they evidenced greater contrast between the first and second parts of the overall binary structure. These pieces gave rise to the most important member of the complex, the *danzón*, of which Miguel Failde composed and premiered the first example, "Las Alturas de Simpson," in Matanzas in 1879.

Like the *contradanza*, the *danzón* was a square dance, but its figurations were more complex. The transformations brought about in it, particularly through the addition of new parts, gave it the structure of a five-part *rondo*. This might have been the origin of its name, since the addition of parts enlarged the piece, making it a "big danza" (the -ón suffix in Spanish is augmentative). The *danzón* is an instrumental genre usually written in 2/4 meter. Once considered the national dance of Cuba, it enjoyed enormous popularity during the late 1800s and early 1900s.

In 1929, another musician from Matanzas, Aniceto Díaz, combined elements from the *son* and the *danzón*, added a vocal part, and created a new style of *danzón* called the *danzonete*. His first composition in this style, "Rompiendo la rutina" ("Breaking the Routine"), established the *danzonete* as a new musical genre. During the 1950s, further transformations of vocal *danzones* and the *danzonetes*, with the addition of new instruments to typical *charangas*, paved the way for Damaso Pérez Prado and Enrique Jorrín to create two new musical genres: the *mambo* and the *cha-cha-chá*.

Vocal and instrumental ensembles

The accompanimental requirements of certain musical genres fostered the creation of distinct types of musical ensemble. Plucked stringed instruments, with the guitar and the *tres* as the most central ones, produced the typical sound of most Cuban music. Also important were rhythmic patterns borrowed from the music of the Spanish *bandurria* and played by Cuban rural people on the *laúd*. The *bandurria* and the *laúd* are plucked stringed instruments brought by the Spanish settlers.

To the sound of the plucked strings was added that of African-derived percussion instruments. Ensembles took in *bongos*, *claves*, the *güiro* (and the *guayo*, its metallic counterpart), *maracas*, and the mule jawbone rattle (*quijada*), the *botija* ("jug"), and the *marímbula* made from a large wooden box with metal tongues. Two metal bars are fixed to the side of the box so that metal strips can be inserted and held fast to serve as tongues (*languettes*), which the performer plucks with his fingers. The tuning of the tongues is done by loosening the bars and adjusting the length of the tongues. The performer usually sits on the box with his legs on either side of the *languettes* [see DOMINICAN REPUBLIC]. The acoustic principle of the *marímbula* has antecedents in the plucked idiophone known as *mbira*, which belongs to many peoples of Africa; and a nearly identical large plucked idiophone is found in Nigeria.

The most important percussive membranophones that developed included the *tumbadoras* (*congas*), *timbales* (big hemispheric drums played with two sticks covered with cloth or leather), and *pailas* (cylindrical metal drums played with two wooden sticks). Many variants of the cowbell (*cencerro*) also developed. In performance, these instruments were often combined with instruments brought from Europe and assimilated into Cuban music in their original organological forms, as happened with the piano, the flute, the violin, the guitar, and other instruments.

This blend of instruments created the instrumental formats that give Cuban music a distinctive character. The most important among them are the following: *dúo*, *trío*, *cuarteto*, *septeto*, *conjunto*, *charanga típica*, *orquesta típica*, *piquete típico*, *órgano oriental*, *estudiantina*, *coro de clave*, *guaguancó* group, *comparsa*, and *gran combo* or *gran orquesta*.

The *dúo* consists of two guitars or a guitar and a *tres*. The artists sing two parts or melodic lines, called *primo* ("first") and *segundo* ("second"). This combination often serves for *boleros*, *canciones trovadorescas*, *claves*, *criollas*, and *guajiras*. In the eastern provinces, the *dúo* serves frequently for performances of *sones montunos*.

The *trío* retains the two vocal melodic lines. The third performer often sings the *primo* while playing *claves* or *maracas*. The repertoire of the *trío* resembles that of the *dúo* because both are closely related to the *canción trovadoresca*. When this type of ensemble reached the cities, it took the *son* into its repertoire. Today, *tríos* appear throughout the nation. One of their most outstanding representatives was the Trío Matamoros, famous during the 1940s.

The *cuarteto* format includes two guitars (or guitar and *tres*), *claves*, and *maracas*. Sometimes, rather than *claves* or *maracas*, the fourth instrument is a muted trumpet. These groups retain the two melodic lines (*primo* and *segundo*), and base their repertoire on mixed genres such as the *guaracha-son*, the *bolero-son*, and the *guajira-son*. This ensemble was popular during the 1930s. [Listen to "Yo Canto en el Llano"] DISC ❷ TRACK 4

The instruments of the *septeto de son* are guitar, *tres*, trumpet (usually with mute), *maracas*, *claves* (played by the vocalist), *bongos*, and *marímbula* or *botija*. In its most recent version, a string bass replaces the *marímbula*. The *septeto* resulted from adding a muted trumpet to the *sexteto de son*. This combination crystallized in the 1920s, when the *son* was gaining popularity in the cities. One of the most important *septetos* in the history of Cuban music is Ignacio Piñeiro's Septeto Nacional, a paramount example of a traditional Cuban musical ensemble.

The *conjunto*, another type of ensemble, consists of piano, *tres*, guitar, three or four trumpets, *bongos*, bass, and singers. The singers often play *maracas* and *claves*, or *quijada* and *güiro*. The repertoire of the *conjunto* includes *boleros*, *guarachas*, and *cha-cha-chás*, and it sometimes plays mixed genres such as *guajira-son* and *bolero-son*. The Cuban *conjunto* enjoyed its greatest popularity in the 1950s, especially after the introduction of television in Cuba. Among the most outstanding representatives are the *conjuntos* of Chappotín, Pacho Alonso, Roberto Faz, and Conjunto Casino.

The *charanga típica* includes a five-key transverse flute, a piano, a string bass, *pailas*, two violins, and a *güiro*. It emerged during the first decade of the twentieth century; after 1940, it doubled the number of violins, and added a *tumbadora* and (later, sometimes) a cello. Some *charangas* have replaced the *pailas* with a complete set of drums and have included electric instruments such as electric bass, electric piano, and synthesizer. The term *orquesta* ("orchestra") has been commonly used since about the 1960s. Foremost in the repertoires of these orchestras was the *danzón*, but now the *son* is the most frequently played genre. During its popularity, these ensembles had no vocalists, but with the creation of the *cha-cha-chá* in the 1950s, they began to feature singers or a small choir. Arcaño y sus Maravillas and the Orquesta Gris are among the most important representatives of the instrumental phase of the *charanga*, and Orquesta Aragón and Enrique Jorrín's orchestra are probably the most important of the phase that included vocalists. One of the most successful *charangas* with electric instruments is Los Van Van.

The *orquesta típica*, a nineteenth-century ensemble no longer popular, consisted of two clarinets, two violins, a string bass, a cornet or a trumpet, a valve or slide trombone, an ophicleide (*bombardino*), *pailas*, and a *güiro*. The oldest European-derived instrumental ensemble in Cuba, it has fallen into disuse. Its repertoire included *contradanzas*, *habaneras*, rigadoons (*rigodones*), lancers, *danzas*, and *danzones*. In 1879, Miguel Failde, a musician from Matanzas, composed and played the first *danzón* with one of these orchestras, which he directed.

Also during the 1800s, wandering musicians organized *piquetes típicos* to play in amusement parks and circuses throughout the country. These ensembles were made up of a cornet or a trumpet, a trombone, a clarinet, an ophicleide, two *pailas*, and a *güiro* (or *guayo*). These groups may have been born of the *orquesta típica* when economic adjustments reduced the number of employed musicians. Their usual repertoire included *danzas*, *pasodobles*, *danzones*, *rumbitas*, and other genres that proved difficult to adapt to other types of ensembles. The *órgano oriental* is the type of large crank organ imported from Europe to the areas of Manzanillo and Holguín in eastern Cuba beginning around the mid-1800s. Later manufactured in those locations, it served for public dances. The organs were accompanied by *pailas*, a *guayo*, and, at a later stage, *tumbadoras*. Their repertoire included the *danza*, the *danzón*, the polka, and the *son*. The building of such organs became a family tradition in the east of the country. The Borgollas were the most important builders in Manzanillo, and the Ajo de Buenaventura family was the most outstanding in Holguín.

In the late 1700s and early 1800s, the *estudiantina* was made up of two singers who sang *primo* and *segundo* while playing *maracas* and *claves* plus others performing on a trumpet, two *treses*, a guitar, *pailas*, and a string bass. Some *estudiantinas* also included a *marímbula*. Their repertoire was based mainly on the *son*, but they also played *danzones*. Their tradition centered in Santiago de Cuba.

The *coro de clave* was a choral ensemble with a repertoire based on a musical genre known as *clave*. Each ensemble had a hierarchy in which some members played a featured role. Some were the *clarina*, a powerful-voiced woman who stood out from the choir; the *decimista*, who composed the texts for the songs; the *tonista*, who kept the group in tune and signaled the choir to begin the singing; the *censor*, responsible for the quality of the song texts and the beauty of the melodies; and the *director*, the most experienced member. These choirs were accompanied by *claves* and a small drum, later replaced by a stringless banjo struck on the resonator box. Some groups included a *botija* and a small diatonic harp. The *coros de clave* disappeared early in the twentieth century.

The *guaguancó* group has a soloist and a small choir, three *tumbadoras*, *claves*, and occasionally a small *catá*. Its repertoire includes the genres that make up the *rumba*: *guaguancó*, *columbia*, and *yambú*. One of the most important groups is Los Muñequitos, in Matanzas (see Okada 1995: example 3).

The instrumentation of *comparsas* has never been stable. They usually require instruments that can be carried and played at the same time. The most frequently used are *tumbadoras*, *congas*, bass drums, *galletas* ("cookies," big drums in the shape of a cookie, played with a stick covered with cloth or leather), *bocus* (long, conical drums hung from the player's neck and shoulder and beaten with bare hands), cowbells, plowshares, steel rings, and other improvising instruments. In later phases, *comparsas* have included a trumpet as a solo instrument.

Comparsas accompany dancers who parade through the streets during Carnaval (Carnival). They had their origins in the celebration of Epiphany, 6 January, during the colonial period. (The slaves were treated like children in many ways, and 6 January was Children's Day in the Spanish colonies.) Carrying lanterns and flags, slaves would take to the streets in the typical attire of their homelands. They would dance and parade to the governor's palace, where they would revel in African-derived dramatic presentations, songs, and dances.

Finally, the *gran combo* or *gran orquesta* is another important type of ensemble, influenced by jazz bands in the United States. Particularly after the 1950s, jazz bands began to be organized in Cuba with repertoires that included *guarachas*, *boleros*, and *sones montunos*. The instrumentation of these bands consisted of trumpets; trombones; alto, tenor, and baritone saxophones; piano; bass; drums; and Cuban percussion. They occasionally included a flute and a clarinet. It was with these bands that the *mambo*, an important musical genre, was born. One of the most important jazz bands was the Benny Moré Band, which became popular in the 1950s.

National anthem

Cuba's national anthem, titled "La Bayamesa" ("The Bayamo Song"), has been in existence since 1868 when it was first performed during the battle of Bayamo in the Ten Year's War with the Spanish (1868-78). The songwriter (music and words, http://david.national-anthems.net/cu.txt) was Pedro Figueredo, who was captured by the Spanish during the war and executed by firing squad in 1870. The song, with its first two verses only, was adopted in 1940 as Cuba's national anthem and has continued as such throughout the communist regime.

LEARNING, DISSEMINATION, AND PUBLIC POLICY

Music was taught in Cuba by settlers who arrived in the 1500s. Historical documents say a musician named Ortiz, living in the town of Trinidad in the 1500s, opened a school to teach dancing and the playing of musical instruments. Manuel Velásquez, the first organist of the cathedral of Santiago de Cuba, taught singing to children who participated in the religious services. Havana's first professor of music was Gonzalo de Silva, who taught singing and organ around 1605.

During the 1700s, the teaching of music was centered in the chapels of the Cathedral of Santiago de Cuba and in the Parroquia Mayor of Havana. Near the end of the 1700s, Esteban Salas y Castro, an important Cuban composer of ecclesiastical music, founded and headed a music chapel at the Cathedral of Havana. *Capilla de música* ("music chapel") was the name given to groups of musicians who performed for Roman Catholic services. They composed church-oriented pieces, including *cantatas*, *villancicos*, and *pastorelas*, and taught music within the church. Salas y Castro's patience and dedication turned his chapel into Cuba's first real school of music. The wave of French immigrants from Haiti and the Dominican Republic late in the 1700s also had a salutary influence on musical pedagogy.

In a steady flow throughout the 1800s, Spanish musicians came to Havana to play and teach. One of the earliest was José M. Trespuentes, who from the 1830s taught violin, harmony, counterpoint, and composition. The second half of the century saw considerable growth in piano instruction. Piano virtuosos sojourned in Havana and taught talented pupils. Visiting from North America, Louis Moreau Gottschalk (1829–1869) organized spectacular concerts in Havana and Santiago de Cuba and gave piano lessons to Nicolás Ruiz Espadero and others, but eventually left Cuba. Espadero, a great maestro himself, taught the distinguished virtuosos Cecilia Aristi, Gaspar Villate, and Ignacio Cervantes. The last taught the ensuing generation of pianists, represented by his daughter, María Cervantes, and Eduardo Sánchez de Fuentes. In 1885, the Dutch master Hubert de Blanck settled in Cuba and founded the conservatory that bears his name. He designed its curriculum to include the most advanced techniques of the times.

Early in the 1900s, private conservatories were founded in Havana and other important cities. Changes taking place in the teaching of music in the United States spurred changes in Cuba. Eminent musicians such as Amadeo Roldán taught at these conservatories, where many musicians of the period were trained, particularly those who played in the country's chamber-music ensembles and symphony orchestras.

Military bands played an important role in the teaching of music from the late 1800s. Apprentices trained in them later replaced their teachers or joined the bands. This system was particularly important in the larger cities of central Cuba: Remedios, Sancti Spiritus, Cienfuegos, and Caibarién became important musician-training centers.

Under the direction of Guillermo Tomás, the Municipal Conservatory of Music was founded in coordination with the Municipal Band of Havana. This institution has trained several generations of important musicians. It is named after Amadeo Roldán, its director in the middle of the century, who guided the introduction of important changes in the programs and curricula.

Until 1959, the Municipal Conservatory of Havana was the only government-sponsored center for the teaching of music. Since then, provincial schools have been opened in Pinar del Río, Matanzas, Santa Clara, and Camagüey provinces. Two other municipal conservatories were opened in the city of Havana: one in Marianao, named after Alejandro García Caturla, and another in Guanabacoa, named after Guillermo Tomás.

The need for instructors to satisfy the major demand created by the Amateur Movement led to the founding of the School of Arts Instructors in 1961. The National School of Art, with its School of Music, was founded in May 1962; it has trained the most important performers, composers, and musicologists of the late twentieth century. The Higher Institute of Art, founded in 1976, immediately opened its School of Music, Cuba's first university-level school of music. In 1978, to provide facilities for working musicians to take their degree, the National Center for Higher Professional Education was opened. In the 1990s, the progress made in Cuban musical education has led to important results in piano and guitar performance and in musicology.

The Musical Institute for Folk Music Research, founded in 1949 in Havana under the direction of the eminent musicologist Odilio Urfé, was later renamed the Popular Music Seminar. In 1989 it became the Odilio Urfé Center for Promotion and Information on Cuban Music. It has a huge store of information on the *danzón*, the *teatro bufo*, the *teatro lírico*, and Cuban vaudeville.

The Ignacio Cervantes Professional Music Upgrading Center, a teaching institution for professional musicians who want to complete their academic training, was founded in Havana in 1964. It has branches in every province.

Administrative structures

Between 1959 and 1976, musical activity in Cuba was the responsibility of councils, departments, or divisions of the Ministry of Education. In 1976, the Ministry of Culture was organized and took responsibility for musical activity. In 1989, the Cuban Institute of Music was organized to administer all musical activity within the Ministry of Culture. All existing government institutions that had to do with music were subordinated to it.

The National Center for Concert Music concerns itself with concert musicians and chamber-music groups. It attends to the programming and promotion of these artists within the country and abroad. The Philharmonic Organization of Havana oversees programming and promotion for the symphony orchestra, other important chamber-music groups, and the country's most important conductors. The National Center for Popular Music, taking responsibility for soloists and ensembles that play popular Cuban music, programs and promotes these artists nationally and internationally.

The Center for the Research and Development of Cuban Music (CIDMUC) was founded on 26 December 1978 in Havana with the primary objective of fostering knowledge, research, and general information on Cuban music. It has two musicological-research departments and an information department. Its Basic Research Department oversees historical and ethnomusicological research, including organological studies and the transcription of Cuban music. Its Department of Development does research in the fields of the psychology and sociology of music. It also does statistical studies related to professional music activities in Cuba.

The National Museum of Cuban Music, founded in 1971, has a collection that includes valuable musical instruments, old scores of Cuban music, and other documents of historical value. It has hosted research in the field of restoration and has organized lectures, exhibits, concerts, and lecture-recitals based on the documents in its collection.

The Musical Publications and Recording Studios (EGREM) has the responsibility of producing recordings, Cuban musical instruments, and musical scores. It has several recording studios, a disc pressing factory, a musical instrument factory, and the National Music Publishing House. In 1986, in cooperation with the last, it founded a quarterly musical magazine, *Clave*.

FURTHER STUDY

Major studies of Cuban music before 1960 include those by Alejo Carpentier (1979 [1946]), Emilio Grenet (1939), and Fernando Ortiz (1981 [1951]). Musical instruments have been documented by Harold Courlander (1942), Fernando Ortiz (1954), and others. The most recent publication about musical instruments written by Cuban scholars is the two volume set titled *Instrumentos de la música folclórico-popular de Cuba*, published by the Centro de investigación y Desarrollo de la Música Cubana (Eli Rodríguez, et al. 1997).

Cuban scholars have written many accounts about their own music, especially since the 1970s. One of the most important compendiums about Latin American music is *Ensayos de Música Latinoamericana*, edited by Clara Hernández (1982). It includes eight essays on Cuban music. Studies about socialization and music in Cuba are by Ageliers León (1984) and María Teresa Linares (1974). Odilio Urfé (1984) published a valuable chapter on Cuban music and dance in the book *Africa in Latin America*. Olavo Alén Rodríguez (1986, 1994) has written books on Afro-Cuban music, specifically on *tumba francesa* and *salsa*, respectively. The most widely distributed journal devoted to Cuban music is *Clave*, published in Havana. Its issues contain essays and news about Cuban folk and art music and musicians.

Since the 1980s, North Americans have written numerous studies of Cuban music, including *salsa* and its precursors in Cuba and development in New York City. Vernon W. Boggs (1992b) compiled a book entitled *Salsiology*, which includes chapters by Larry Crook (1992) and Vernon W. Boggs (1992a) about particular aspects of Cuban music. Important studies about Cuban music are by Steve Cornelius and John Amira (1992), Katherine Hagedorn (2001), Peter Manuel (1990), Robin D. Moore (1997), James Robbins (1990), Roberta Singer (1983), and David F. García (2006).

REFERENCES

Alén Rodríguez, Olavo. 1986. *La música de las sociedades de tumba francesa en Cuba*. Havana: Casa de La Américas.

———. 1994. *De los afrocubano a la salsa*, 2nd ed. Havana: Artex S. A. Editions.

The Americas II. 1990. Tomoaki Fujii, ed. Produced by Katsumori Ichikawa. JVC Video *Anthology of World Music and Dance*, vol. 28 (VTMV-230). Videocassette.

Boggs, Vernon W. 1992a. "Founding Fathers and Changes in Cuban Music Called Salsa." In *Salsiology*, ed. Vernon W. Boggs, 97–105. New York: Excelsior Music Publishing Company.

———, ed. 1992b. *Salsiology*. New York: Excelsior Music Publishing Company.

Carpentier, Alejo. 1979 [1946]. *La música en Cuba*. Havana: Editorial Letras Cubanas. English translation, *Music in Cuba*.

Clave: Revista Cubana de Música. Havana: Dirección de Música, Ministerio de Cultura.

Cornelius, Steven. 1990. "Encapsulating Power: Meaning and Taxonomy of the Musical Instruments of Santería in New York City." In *Selected Reports in Ethnomusicology* 8:125–141.

Cornelius, Steve, and John Amira. 1992. *The Music of Santería: Traditional Rhythms of the Batá Drums*. Crown Point, Ind.: White Cliffs Media.

Courlander, Harold. 1942. "Musical Instruments of Cuba." *Musical Quarterly* 28(2):227–240.

Crook, Larry. 1992. "The Form and Formation of the Rumba in Cuba." In *Salsiology*, ed. Vernon W. Boggs, 31–42. New York: Excelsior Music Publishing Company.

Eli Rodríguez, Victoria, et al. 1997. *Instrumentos de la música folclórico-popular de Cuba*, Vol. 1 and 2. Havana: Centro de Investigación y Desarrollo de la Música Cubana

González-Wippler, Migene. 1973. *Santería: African Magic in Latin America*. Bronx, N.Y.: Original Products.

García, David F. 2006. *Arsenio Rodríguez and the Transnational Flows of Latin Popular Music*. Philadelphia: Temple University Press.

Grenet, Emilio. 1939. *Popular Cuban Music*. Havana: Ministerio de Educación, Dirección de Cultura.

Hagedorn, Katherine. 2001. *Divine Utterances: The Performance of Afro-Cuban Santería*. Washington, D.C.: Smithsonian Institution Press.

Hernández, Clara, ed. 1982. *Ensayos de Música Latinoamericana*. Havana: Casa de las Américas.

León, Ageliers. 1984. *Del canto y el tiempo*. 2nd ed. Havana: Editorial Letras Cubanas.

Linares, María Teresa. 1974. *La música y el pueblo*. Havana: Editorial Pueblo y Educación.

Manuel, Peter. 1990. *Essays on Cuban Music: Cuban and North American Perspectives*. Lanham, Md.: University Press of America.

Marks, Morton. 1994. *Afro-Cuba: A Musical Anthology*. Rounder CD 1088. Compact disc and notes.

Moore, Robin D. 1997. *Nationalizing Blackness. Afrocubanismo and Artistic Revolution in Havana, 1920–1940*. Pittsburgh: University of Pittsburgh Press.

Okada, Yuki. 1995. *The Caribbean. The JVC Smithsonian Folkways Video Anthology of Music and Dance of the Americas,* 4. Montpelier, Vt.: Multicultural Media VTMV-228. Video.

Ortiz, Fernando. 1954. *Los Instrumentos de la Música Afrocubana*. Havana: Cárdenas and Compañía.

———. 1981 [1951]. *Los Bailes y el Teatro de los Negros en el Folklore de Cuba*. Havana: Editorial Letras Cubanas.

Pereira, Emmanuel. n.d. "Haitian Musical Influences in Cuba." Unpublished paper in ethnomusicology, Florida State University, January 18, 2007.

Robbins, James. 1990. "The Cuban Son as Form, Genre, and Symbol." *Latin American Music Review* 11(2):182–200.

Rogoziński, Jan. 1999. *A Brief History of the Caribbean: From the Arawak and the Carib to the Present*. New York: Penguin Putman.

Rouse, Irving. 1992. *The Tainos: Rise and Decline of the People who Greeted Columbus*. New Haven: Yale University Press.

Singer, Roberta L. 1983. "Tradition and Innovation in Contemporary Latin Popular Music in New York City." *Latin American Music Review* 4(2):183–202.

Urfé, Odilio. 1984 [1977]. "Music and Dance in Cuba." In *Africa in Latin America: Essays on History, Culture, and Socialization*, ed. Manuel Moreno Fraginals, 170–188. Translated by Leonor Blum. New York: Holms and Meier.

Haiti

Gage Averill and Lois Wilcken

The Indigenous Heritage
The African Heritage
Music Genres and Contexts
Traditional Music and Migration
Urban Popular Musics
Musical Style
Learning, Dissemination, Tourism, and Public Policy

Haiti ("mountainous land") is the Arawak name for the second largest island in the Caribbean that the Spanish named Hispaniola. Situated between Cuba to the west and Puerto Rico to the East, Hispaniola was first controlled by Spain, then France, then independent Haiti, and today it includes the modern nation of Haiti in the western third and Dominican Republic in the remaining two-thirds of the island. A Francophone country, Haiti is included in Caribbean Latin America because French is a romance language, Haiti's history is a part of the Dominican Republic's history, and Columbus' first settlement in the New World was La Navidad, on the north coast of present Haiti. The official language of Haiti is French, but the real language is Creole; the majority of Haitians are Roman Catholic, but they may be practitioners of Vodou at the same time.

THE INDIGENOUS HERITAGE

The earliest known inhabitants of Haiti were the Ciboney (a culture that predated the Arawak-speaking Taíno), but by 1492, when Columbus explored the north coast of the island, the Arawak had driven them into the southwestern peninsula. Spanish settlers rarely visited the Ciboney, and their fate is unknown. The tools they left say little of their social life and religion, and no musical instruments of their manufacture are known.

Of the Arawak (the first group the Europeans met in Hispaniola), the Taíno subgroup was predominant. The Taíno used songs to record myths and history, to commemorate the chiefs' marriages and funerals, to tout military victories, and to accompany dancing (Rouse 1948:522–539). Chiefs presided over dances, leading movement and song. Corn beer and snuff fueled Taíno *areito* (music and dance events featuring songs that lasted from three to four hours each—or until participants collapsed in exhaustion). Chiefs and their assistants played drums, stone-filled gourd rattles, and castanets made of metal plates, while dancers' kinetic energy generated percussive clattering from strings of snail shells encircling their arms and legs. Songs, drumming, and dances marked an annual procession to the temple to feed the chiefs' sacred stones, and shamans utilized song and sacred rattles in healing.

The Spanish system of exploitation (*repartimiento*) put all male Taíno to work in gold mines and on plantations. Many died from overwork and malnutrition, some committed suicide, and others died of smallpox. Fifty years after the Spanish arrived, only a few thousand Taíno survived; secure in mountainous retreats, they intermarried with African Maroons (runaway slaves).

Did Taíno culture have an impact on that of later Haiti? Linguistic and mythical data may support the argument that some traits of Haitian religion are more readily explained in Arawak than in African terms (Deren 1984:271–286). Early reports of contact between Africans and Taíno invite speculation about shared musical concepts and practices. The sacred rattle (*tchatcha*, like a maraca) of the Petro rite of Haitian Vodou probably descended from its Amerindian counterpart. But aside from these traces, Taíno culture essentially vanished with its people.

THE EUROPEAN HERITAGE

The French had long desired a foothold in the colonial Caribbean, and in 1697 they had their opportunity when Spain ceded the westernmost third of the island of Hispaniola to them (see DOMINICAN REPUBLIC). As their "jewel in its colonial crown" (Davis, this volume), the French, numbering thirty thousand strong, and with five hundred thousand African slaves, produced coffee, cotton, indigo, and especially sugar. This life of luxury for the French, however, ended in the 1790s.

AFRICAN HERITAGE

As the Taíno population waned, the Roman emperor, Charles V, authorized the importation of African slaves to Hispaniola and elsewhere in the Spanish Caribbean. In the late 1600s, with the consolidation of French rule, a period of intense cultivation of sugar ensued, accompanied by a rapid increase in the number of slaves, free blacks, and mulattoes. Neo-African religious groups, particularly in Maroon settlements, raised the political consciousness of the slaves, whose movement led to an uprising in 1791 by ex-slave Toussaint L'Ouverture. This was followed by the abolition of slavery, the flight or death of most

Frenchmen and their families, and Haitian independence in 1804. Music and dance were focal points in the religious-political complex that made up the new Haiti.

Despite the role of African belief systems in the Haitian revolution of 1791, Roman Catholicism became the state religion. The bourgeoisie's eagerness to appear civilized (à la France), negative international press vis-á-vis Vodou (as the religion came to be called in Haiti, after a Fon word for "spirit"; it is spelled Vodú in Spanish), and the proselytizing activity of Rome explain the outlawing of neo-African worship in the 1800s. Politico-religious Maroon societies (Sanpwél, Bizango) trained guerrillas to protect land from seizure by the elite—and, in the 1900s, by U.S. marines. Nevertheless, the latter occupied Haiti for nineteen years, from 1915 to 1934, supporting mulatto rule. Black Haitian governance did not occur again until 1946, when several coups d'etat provided several inefficient leaders, culminating in the installation of president-for-life Francois "Papa Doc" Duvalier (1907–1971) in 1957. Duvalier manipulated the ideologies of negritude and Vodou to secure power over the masses. In 1986, when his son and successor, Jean-Claude "Baby Doc" Duvalier, fled the country, Vodou priests and priestesses who had openly participated in Duvalierist politics became targets of popular vengeance, and a vitriolic debate between followers of Vodou and Christian leaders ensued. In that climate, the constitution of 1987 became the first to legalize Vodou cults.

MUSICAL GENRES AND CONTEXTS

The following discussion examines Haiti's neo-African music and dances with particular attention to Vodou. Because specific African nations (Dahomean, Congolese) became associated with particular geographic niches within colonial Haiti, the regionality of Vodou should be uppermost in the reader's mind. The variety of Vodou discussed below prevails in western Haiti, including Port-au-Prince. Many Haitians maintain that "the real Vodou" is exclusive to rural Haiti, and some believe that Vodou in Port-au-Prince has been commercialized for tourists. The persistence of Vodou in urban Haiti, despite the collapse of the tourist industry in the early 1980s, casts doubt on this claim. In the city, as in the country and in the Haitian diaspora, the structures necessary to Vodou are in place, and Vodou is thus a "vehicle of spiritual, cultural, socioeconomic, and political exchange between urban and rural sectors" (Dauphin 1986:23).

Vodou

Theories and practices of neo-African religion in Haiti (Deren 1984; Métraux 1972) place emphasis on serving the *lwa* (*loa*), a term that comes from a Bantu word for "spirit" (Courlander 1973:19). Devotees acknowledge a supreme being, but only spirits play an active role in human life.

The Vodou *lwa* are organized into nations (*nasyon* in Kwéyòl "Creole," the dominant language of rural Haiti), corresponding loosely to ethnic groups (of West African and Congolese origin) from which the slaves of colonial Haiti came. Ritual practice evolved in the context of prerevolutionary Haiti, when, for the purpose of resistance, slaves organized into confederations of nations. The confederative concept is apparent in Vodou rites that salute the national *lwa*. The *lwa* are also associated with natural elements and aspects of human personality: Nagos are known for militancy, Ibos for arrogance, and Kongos for grace and sociability.

The national *lwa* are grouped under two major branches, Rada and Petro (Petwo in Creole). The *lwa* of the Rada branch are cool, beneficent, hierarchical, and formal, and relations between these spirits and their servants are balanced and mutually beneficial (Fleurant 1996). The *lwa* of the Petro branch are hot, aggressive, decentralized, and informal, and they often demand more of their servants than they give.

Music and dance are part of the symbolic web that represents the spirits and calls on them to possess devotees (Wilcken 1992). Dances, songs, percussive patterns, instruments, and performance practices distinguish the nations. Music is most prominent in the evening ceremony (*seremoni* or *dans*), in which a *lwa* may be fed or an individual initiated.

Deren (1984) and Métraux (1972) give details of ritual forms and occasions, personnel, and temples. A priest (*oungan*) or a priestess (*manbo*) officiates over a ceremony, assisted by initiates (*ounsis*) who sing and dance to the accompaniment of a battery of three drums (*manman, segon, boula*, all led by a master drummer) plus a struck iron idiophone (*ogan*). The battery is sometimes embellished by a *bas* or *tanbourin*, a frame drum of low pitch, which keeps a slow pulse. In Rada rites, the priest or priestess keeps time with one type of rattle (*ason*), and then for Petro rites changes to another type (the *tchatcha*). The *poto mitan*, a column in the center of the temple, is a focal point for dancing. The battery is positioned where the master drummer can keep watch over the event.

Vodou percussive instruments intimately interweave to fashion cyclical patterns, in which rhythm and sonority are salient features. A slow pulse, usually defined by the frame drum or the rattle, underlies the patterns, whereas the interrelationships of individual instruments generate a fast pulse. The drums are capable of a range of sonority, colored by the material and construction of the instruments (Figures 10.1 and Figure 10.2) and controlled by players' techniques. The patterns *of ogan, boula, segon,* and *manman* range from simple to complex, respectively.

Music expresses relationships among the nations, and between the Rada and Petro branches. Figure 10.3 shows how features of construction, performance, and rhythm are used in accompanying the dances of the major nations. Rada and Nago drums stand out from the others in construction and mode of playing. In Petro dances, the *ogan* plays a 3+3+2 pattern or is embedded in the pattern of the master drum. In a transitional position between Rada and Petro in the ritual order, variously classified

Figure 10.1
A *manman* drum (the mother drum) used in Rada ceremonies sits in a doorway. Its single cowhide head is fastened into the wooden body with pegs and is struck with a special stick called *agida*. The drum is decorated with the ritual diagram (*vèvè*) for the *lwa* Ezili. Photo by Lois Vicken.

Figure 10.2
A *baka* drum used in Petro ceremonies leans against the wall of an *ounfò* (inner sanctuary in Carrefour du Fort, Haiti. Unlike the Rada drum, the Petro goatskin drum has a single head laced to the wooden body and is struck with the hands. The spots painted on this drum serve as protective markings and can also be seen on the wall of the *ounfò*. Photo by Elizabeth McAlister, 1991.

by informants, *djouba* (the Vodou dance of the earth *lwa*) shares features of both branches. For playing *djouba*, the drum is laid on the ground and played with hands and feet, because *djouba* spirits live in the earth.

The break (*kase*) of Vodou drumming, a pattern played by the master drummer, cues the dancer to execute a movement also known as a *kase*. Drummers and adepts claim it is an agent of spirit possession. A master drummer is attuned to the kinetics of the ritual. When he sees the onset of possession in an adept, he plays a *kase* to bring the spirit fully to the adept's head. The structure of the master drummer's *kase* is oppositional to the structure of the main pattern. The effect is one of displacement within a continuously cycling pattern.

Haitians group Vodou songs according to the spirits whom they address, and the songs in a given group may share melodic features, such as scale, contour, and intervallic content. A common triadic motif may typify songs for the Rada spirit Ezili Freda (Dauphin 1986:82–83), but more evidence is needed to confirm what the experienced listener suspects. The typical scale is anhemitonic pentatonic, but some songs are based on diatonic scales.

Singing is customized to events. To accompany a specific ritual activity, singers exploit the brevity of phrases, the flexibility of responsorial singing, and the possibility of concatenating more than one song. Phrases tend to be two or four *ogan* patterns in length. A priest, a priestess, or a musical specialist (*onjènikon*) sings several phrases, repeated by the chorus of initiates. Before singers change to a new song, they usually alternate the final phrase between soloist and chorus. The number of calls and responses depends on the time necessary to complete whatever ritual action the song accompanies. Many drummers mark with a *kase* the transition from one song to the next.

Figure 10.3
The major nations of the Haitian pantheon, with the types of drumheads, performance techniques, and timeline patterns used for each. Nations are listed from left to right, in ritual order. *Djouba* shares features of Rada and Petro.

Vodou Branches	Rada			Petro			
The major nations	Rada	Nago	Djouba	Petro	Ibo	Kongo	Gede
Drums with cowskin heads	X	X					
Drums with goatskin heads			X	X	X	X	X
Drums played with sticks/hands	X	X					
Drums played with hands only			X	X	X	X	X
Drums have pegged-on heads	X	X					
Drums have laced-on heads			X	X	X	X	X
Drums play 6/12 pulses	X	X	X				
Drums play 8/16 pulses				X	X	X	X
Drums play 3+3+2 patterns				X	X	X	X

Vodou and Christianity

Servants of the *lwa* incorporate Christian elements into their practice, not to deceive church authorities but because they believe in the efficacy of these elements (Métraux 1972:358). The Christian constituents of Vodou range from superficial to substantial. Chromoliths of saints (*imaj*) representing *lwa* by virtue of superficial resemblances, synchronize the Christian and the Vodou calendars. The practice of baptism has been incorporated wholesale into Vodou, which baptizes not only servants but all ritual objects as well.

The most striking Christian component of Vodou ceremonies is an opening litany, or *priyè ginen* "African prayer." It begins with several Christian songs in French, followed by a long, chanted litany in Creole of saints, and then of Vodou spirits. Steadily intensifying drumrolls accompany it. The officiating priest or priestess leads a prayer and adds a shimmer to the drumrolls by shaking a rattle. The repetition of the chant and the uninterrupted, random percussion keep the congregation in a state of suspense and anticipation, so when the drums break into *yanvalou* (rhythm and dance used in Rada rites) for Legba, the *lwa* who opens the gate to the spirit world, the sense of having arrived is powerful. [Listen to "Song for Legba, dance for Ogoun"]

DISC ❶ TRACK 36

Since the 1930s, Roman Catholic composers have spearheaded a movement to incorporate elements of African-Haitian folklore into their liturgy. In the late 1940s, they began using drums in it, and they worked with Vodou drummers to determine which rhythms were most appropriate to accompany singing in church. In the 1960s, the Second Vatican Council nourished the ideals of their movement. Many folkloric dance companies have been formed under the aegis of local parishes.

Music and collective labor

Haitians have applied the traditions of collective labor in various contexts but most notably in agriculture. About 80 percent of the population is rural. Local collective-labor associations have parallels in West Africa (Paul 1962:213–220), and the lack of technological sophistication in the Haitian countryside has fostered the continuity of the associations.

The term *konbit* (possibly deriving from the Spanish *convidar* "to invite") refers equally to a collective-labor association and to the event it organizes. In some regions, the association is called *sosyete kongo* (Herskovits 1975:70). Most often, the *konbit* meets to till the fields, but it may gather for other activities that benefit from cooperative effort, such as building houses and sorting coffee.

A *konbit* emphasizes music as a propelling force (Courlander 1973:117–118). In the early morning hours, song leaders (*sanba*) and musicians with drums, trumpets, bamboo trumpets (*vaksin*), conch trumpets (*lanbi*), and hoe blades struck with stones signal the *konbit*; they continue to accompany the labor of the day. The leaders and workers sing responsorially. Some songs are old, but newly invented texts use topical material. The rhythms derive from rural dances, including *djouba*. The traditional *konbit* culminates in singing, dancing, and drinking—a party centered on a meal prepared by women. Regional variations of collective-labor parties exist (Paul 1962:205–213).

Secular Songs

Secular songs constitute a major part of Haiti's musical traditions. The composer of the folkloric song is a *sanba* (the same term applied to the song leader of the *konbit*). Haitians classify folkloric songs by social rather than aural criteria. One collector (Dauphin 1981) classifies children's songs by scalar structure, using the Kodály method. Haitian children who grow up with this repertoire identify everyday, calendrical, and occasional songs. A French influence is more pronounced in children's songs than in other categories of folkloric song, possibly because they are diffused by schools in urban and suburban areas (Paul 1962:42).

Songs of social sanction complain of adultery, abuse, duplicity, and so on. Others feature gossip. Many, utilizing Vodou rhythms and melodies, may stem from possession in the Vodou temple (Paul 1962:42–43). This category also incorporates political commentary (Courlander 1973:148–162) typical of *rara* processionals.

Rara

Rara is a seasonal ritual of the countryside (and of lower-class urban neighborhoods). It begins after Carnival and builds to its conclusion on Easter weekend (*Caribbean Revels* 1991). Membership in the processional bands (*bann rara*) may be coterminous with membership in a Vodou temple, a secret society, or residence in a particular neighborhood or extended-family compound (*lakou*). The bands demonstrate a widespread African American predilection for intricate social hierarchies in carnivalesque celebrations that mimic military, governmental, and royal hierarchies. A typical roster might include:

1. A *mèt* or *pwezidan:* the "owner" (sometimes a Vodou priest), who made a "promise" to the *lwa* to organize a *rara.*
2. A *kòlonèl:* the director, who carries a whip and a whistle (ritual media, also used by the second in command—the *laplas*—in a Petro ceremony; Figure 10.4). Both items are rich in symbolic content. Under slavery, the whip was a symbol of power; in *rara*, it has spiritual significance. As in some Petro ceremonies, it dispels malevolent *lwa* and purifies the secular space through which the band will pass. The *kolonèl* must disperse spiritual charms (*zanm kongo*) or powders (*poud*), left by other groups to *kraze* "break, disorganize" the *rara.*
3. *Majò jòn* twirlers who handle and throw batons, dance, and honor important members of the group and onlookers (Figure 10.4). In the south, they typically wear sequined vests, aprons, short pants with scarves tucked into their belts, sun glasses, baseball caps, and tennis shoes. In the north, the hats tend to be more decorative, and other aspects of the costuming differ. Colors, designs, and banners can represent the group's patron *lwa*. Many groups annually make these outfits and banners anew, only to destroy them after the *rara* season.
4. *Renn:* "queens" who wear fancy dresses (often red), parade, dance, and collect money for the band.

Rara also has secular features, including an exuberant and sensual celebratory ethos, plus usually topical, bawdy, critical, and allusive musical texts. However, the ritual fulfills an important sacred duty and is connected to issues of life, death, and rebirth. *Rara* bands are dedicated to *lwa* such as those from the Petro or the Gede families. Bands "incorporate" during Gede days (around Halloween and All Souls Day) or just after Carnival and hold ceremonies to consecrate the band and its instruments. For the *lwa*, they draw maize symbols (*vèvès*) on the ground; they sing and pray for the band's protection. In the *peristil* (an open area for dance in a temple), a band will put to sleep (*kouche*) its musical instruments and batons—a ritual also performed for Vodou drums. Most processional activity occurs at night, with the temple as a point of origin. Because the *rara* traverses public roads and cemeteries, bands invoke *lwa* such as Baron Samdi, Papa Gede (ruler of cemeteries), or Legba (guardian of gateways and crossroads).

The musical ensembles that accompany *rara* feature *vaksin* ("bamboo trumpets"; Figure 10.5) and flared *kònè* ("tin horns"; Figure 10.6). Individual pitches on different trumpets interlock in short melodic-rhythmic ostinati. As they are blown, these instruments are struck on their sides with sticks to produce a timeline (*kata*). They are accompanied by *tanbou petro* and *kongo* (single-headed, hand-beaten drums), *kès* (double-headed, stick-beaten drums), frame drums, *graj* (metal scrapers), metal trum-

Figure 10.4
In Léogane, Haiti, *majò jòn* (center, a twirler) and a *kòlonèl* (left of center), the director, with a whip around his neck), lead a *rara* procession. Photo by Elizabeth McAlister, 1991.

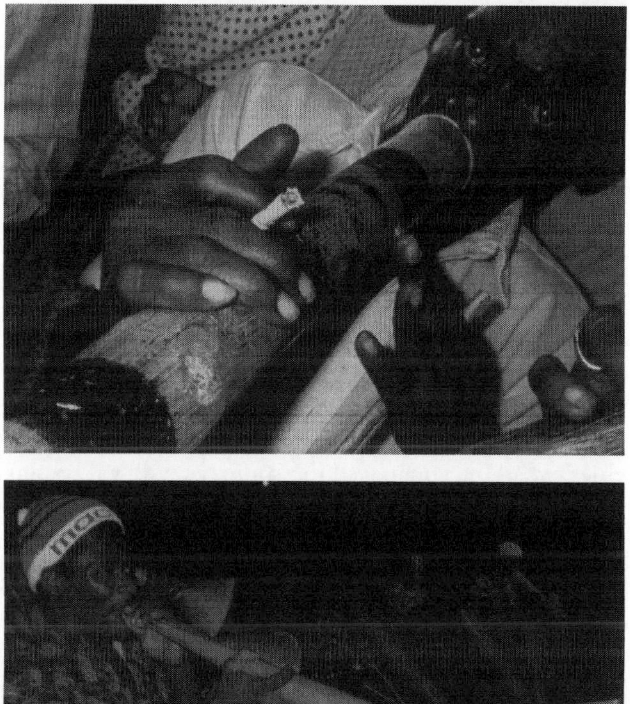

Figure 10.5
A *vaksin* (single-note bamboo trumpet) player in the *rara* band Modèle d'Haïti in Léogane, Haiti. Photo by Elizabeth McAlister, 1991.

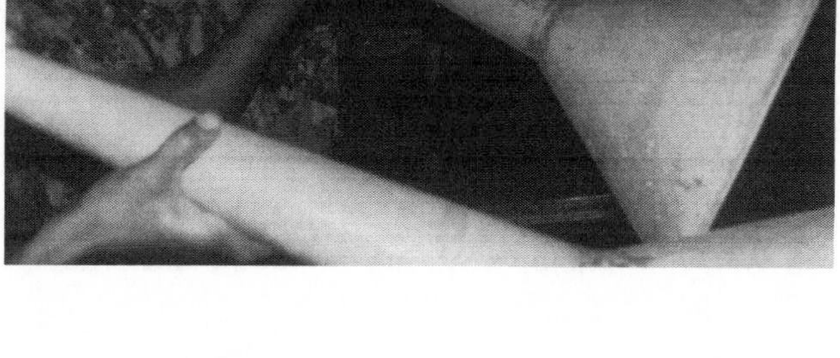

Figure 10.6
Kònè ("tin horn") players in the *rara* band Vodoule of Port-au-Prince, Haiti, with several *vaksin* in the background. Photo by Gage Averill, 1995.

pets, *tchatchas*, tin rattles, and other instruments (see Okada 1995: example 11). [Listen to "*Rara* instrumental music"]

TRADITIONAL MUSIC AND MIGRATION

Since the Duvaliers came into power, about one million Haitians have left Haiti and migrated to Cuba, the Dominican Republic, the United States, and elsewhere. Haitians in the diaspora (especially in the United States) tend to cluster in urban neighborhoods, where they seek mutual support. Music and dance can be a means of recreating the familiar and strengthening the support system.

Haitian immigrants include Vodou priests, priestesses, initiates, and drummers. Some have established societies with stable memberships; others fulfill their obligations to the *lwa* as they wait to accumulate the capital to return to Haiti and build temples there. To insure privacy, practitioners often conduct their rituals in basements. Because space is limited, they can only rarely dance around a *potomitan*. In such enclosed spaces, the drumming sometimes overwhelms the singing. Despite these limitations, spirit possession occurs, servants find joy in the rituals, and they pass the repertoire on to their diaspora-born children.

Throughout the 1970s, folk-dance companies appeared regularly in Haitian festivals in New York; but in the 1980s, performances for Haitian audiences declined. Haitian folklore found a more receptive audience among outsiders. Meanwhile, a popular music that incorporated folkloric elements into a commercial framework won Haitian listeners. Both phenomena suggest that the cultural isolation of Haitians in the diaspora was diminishing.

URBAN POPULAR MUSICS

In the early 1800s, peasants fled plantations and established homesteads in inaccessible rural hinterlands, escaping federal oppression and reestablishing neo-African practices of settlement and agriculture. The elite settled in Port-au-Prince and a few small provincial cities, where they managed the country's political system and dominated its economy.

Like *rara*, many ostensibly rural genres made the transition to urban Haiti. Parties (*bambòch*) held in makeshift thatched huts (*tonèls*) in poorer neighborhoods, Vodou ceremonies in family compounds, *rara* bands in Carnival, and Christian religious music—all resemble their rural counterparts. As in most of the world (including countries without highly developed industrial sectors), a particularly urban music of syncretic origins depends, for form and coherence, on urban dance contexts, middle- and upper-class patronage, foreign influences, the recording industry, and broadcast media.

Poverty, the gulf between the social classes, and the separation of city and countryside have had important consequences for Haitian urban popular music. Low incomes (in 1997, about U.S. $300 per capita annually) have made the development of a highly capitalized music industry impossible. Instead, small businessmen predominate; there is little in the way of development or promotion, and producers focus on short-term gain. For sales, musicians rely on markets in the French Antilles, the American diaspora, and France (Averill 1993). Despite undercapitalization and a depressed market, hundreds of aspiring commercial bands struggle for success. The economics of Haitian music have worked against widespread penetration of foreign-music markets and have kept the technology and standards of recording and performance lagging behind international pop.

Though urban musics are produced in urban areas and disseminated through urban-based media, their impact is felt nationwide. Radio blankets all areas of Haiti, and most Haitians have access to it in some form or another. Because the majority of Haitians are illiterate and more than sixty stations broadcast within the country, radio is critical as a source of news and cultural information. As Haiti urbanizes and children of peasants move to the cities, more and more families have personal connections to the urban environment.

In the early 1900s, urban Haitians gathered at public dances, *douz edmi* ("twelve and a half," the name taken from the men's price of admission in centimes). The standard ensemble for these events was *òkès bastreng*, a French-style string and wind ensemble. After 1945, Port-au-Prince had a lively calendar of *gran bals* for elite classes in hotels, restaurants, and private clubs (such as the Cercle Bellevue and Portauprincienne). Many hotels and restaurants sponsored orchestras such as the Ensemble Riviera, the Ensemble Ibo Lèlè, and the Ensemble Aux Calabasses. Nighttime dances (*sware*) took place in *boîtes de unit* and clubs. At prostitutes' balls (*bal' bouzen*) in the brothels of Carrefour, patrons danced with prostitutes to live or recorded music. A type of dance known as *kèmès* grew out of the bazaars and family socials that followed religious services in church on Sunday afternoons; eventually, the word *kèmès* came to mean any early afternoon or early evening concert.

For excitement and impact on commercial music, no single urban event in Haiti can compete with Carnival. An informal Carnival had taken place since colonial times. In addition to commercial and governmental floats, there are always large, popular masques, including *batonyè* ("stick dancers"), *trese riban* ("maypole dancers"), *chaloska* ("a spoof of military officers", named after General Charles Oscar), *gwo tèt* ("large heads" fashioned after famous politicians), *djab* ("devils"), *Endyèn Madigra* ("Mardi Gras Indians"), and many others.

At Carnival, percussion and vocal bands (and many *rara* bands) provided acoustic processional music; but since the 1950s, electrified *konpa* bands on floats with massive speakers have dominated the event. *Mereng koudyay* (or *mereng kanaval*), a genre of fast, marchlike *konpa* similar to the *biguine vidé* of Martinique and the *samba enredo* (theme *samba*) of Brazil, has developed as the typical Carnival rhythm, the basis for the annual competition for best song at Carnival.

In 1949, on the waterfront, as part of a bicentennial celebration of the capital, the Théâtre Verdure was built. It was home to weekly concerts of the orchestra Jazz des Jeunes, which accompanied the Troupe Folklorique Nationale. Rebuilt and renamed (Théâtre National), it is used for large concerts. Other concerts take place in movie theaters. In the 1960s, Sunday concerts at movie theaters in Port-au-Prince became a major venue for emerging student *mini-djaz* groups. Gala concerts, featuring a mix of folk-dance troupes, romantic singers, dance bands, and comedians, are held there. In the diaspora, this type of concert (*spèktak*, or *gala*) is popular with well-to-do Haitians.

In the summer, a period of many patronal festivals (*fèt patwonal*), urban bands tour the countryside. The festivals feature ceremonies in church, roving troubadour groups (*twoubadou*), dances under the arbor (*anba tonèl*), and food and drink sold on the street.

Media and the recording industry

The first radio station in Haiti, Radio HHK, went on the air in 1927 as a project of the U.S. Marines. In general, however, radio remained a toy of the wealthy until after 1945. A private station, Radio HH3W (later 4VRW, Radio d'Haïti), was launched in 1935; after 1945, it began a series of live *radio-théâtres* from the Ciné Paramount, and eventually from its broadcast-studio auditorium. Radio d'Haïti, owned by Ricardo Widmaier, was the site of the first recordings made in Haiti. In 1937, Widmaier issued a limited-edition recording of "Jazz Duvergé," but Joe Anson's label, called Ibo Records, made the first commercial Haitian recordings, beginning with the Ensemble Aux Calabasses in the mid-1950s.

The most active Haitian labels have been a series of four companies based in the diaspora but recording and marketing in Haiti and the diaspora, starting with Ibo Records. In the mid-1960s, Marc Duverger's Marc Records produced recordings of many *mini-djaz* and larger orchestras. In the 1970s, Fred Paul's Mini Records became the largest producer of Haitian records and sponsored an ensemble, Mini All Stars. Others have produced recordings but mostly as a sideline.

In Haiti, sales of five thousand are considered respectable. Outside the country, especially in the diaspora and in the French Antilles, Haitian artists have done much better. By exploiting the global market through tours and agreements with French labels, some have sold more than fifty thousand albums.

In the 1970s, the pirate-cassette industry dominated the production of music within the country. Record stores marketed copies of legitimate recordings and unauthorized recordings of live concerts. Similar cassettes were sold on the streets. By all estimates, the cheap cassettes (U.S. $2 to $5 typically) vastly outsold the approved ones. In the 1980s, the Haitian music industry typically produced fifty to eighty albums a year.

In 1989, Haitian producers began to market compact discs of current releases and selected previous releases. Few in Haiti itself own CD players, and the Haitian industry is converting only slowly and cautiously to the CD format. Since 1988, many artists with hit records have released videos for Haitian television programs, Creole-language programs in the United States, and programs on French and French-language stations in West Africa and the French Antilles. In the 1990s, musicians such as Emeline Michel and the *mizik rasin* group Boukman Eksperyans have secured international recording contracts.

Many Haitian performers belong to SACEM, the French society of musicians and composers. In 1995 Haiti became a signatory nation of the Berne Convention governing intellectual property.

Commercial genres and ensembles

The Haitian elite traditionally patronized the *mereng-lant* ("slow *méringues*") played by pianists or chamber ensembles (Fouchard 1988). After the popularity of North American jazz in urban Haiti in the 1930s, jazz bands began to arrange *méringues* too. The *méringue* was also performed by troubadour (*twoubadou*) groups—small guitar and percussion bands, patterned after the Cuban *son* trios and quartets (Figure 10.7).

Figure 10.7
A hotel-style *grenn siwèl* or *twoubadou* ensemble performs *méringues* with *baka* drum, *malinba*, guitars, and maracas. Photo by Steve Winter, 1989.

In Port-au-Prince and Cap Haïtien, an influx of tourists after World War II helped support hotel- and casino-based *méringue* orchestras, such as the Orchestre Casino Internationale. In response to the *négritude* movement and its mandate to develop indigenous forms of popular culture, bands experimented with Vodou rhythms. The most famous of these bands was Jazz des Jeunes, pioneers (after 1943) of the genre *mereng-vodou* or *vodou-jazz*. In this fusion, the instrumentation resembles that of Cuban big bands with the addition of Vodou drums, but the melodic contours, rhythms, and texts come from Vodou and peasant dances. *Négritude* also influenced the composition of art music (*mizik savant*) by Haitian composers, resulting in the production of a corpus of nationalist, Vodou, and *mérengue*-inspired concert pieces, such as Justin Elie's *Fantasie Tropicale* and Werner A. Jaegerhubers *Complaintes Haïtiennes* (Dumervé 1968; Largey 1991).

In the mid-1950s, the saxophonist Nemours Jean-Baptiste and his ensemble began to restructure the popular Dominican *merengue perico ripiao* or *merengue cibaeño* to produce the *konpa-dirèk* (French *compas direct*), or simply *konpa*. Within a few years, they had established it as Haiti's first commercially successful dance music. The saxophonist and bandleader Wébert Sicot had created a nearly identical dance called *kadans ranpa* (French *cadence remparts*, originally creolized as *rempas*). The contest between these genres and bands enlivened Haitian music for a decade; theirs was the first music to be widely distributed in Haiti on records (78-rpm disks; later, long-playing disks). From their positions on floats, these bands dominated Carnival with amplified music.

A younger generation of middle-class boys who played imported rock and roll, locally called *yeye* (from "yeah, yeah, yeah," a refrain by the Beatles), picked up *konpa* and *kadans*. Their *konpa-yeye* hybrid ensembles became known as *mini-djaz*, a term that distinguished them from big bands—and made an analogy with an English term first used in 1965: "miniskirt," the name of a women's fashion style. Instrumentation consisted of two electric guitars, electric bass, *conga*, bell-and-tom, and tenor saxophone; keyboards and accordions were occasionally added. Groups like Shleu-Shleu, Les Ambassadeurs, Les Fantaisistes de Carrefour, and Les Loups Noirs played in the mid-to-late 1960s at movie theaters for Sunday concerts, student parties, and the like. The most popular bands began to record after 1967. Within a few years, many had immigrated to the United States to perform for Haitian audiences in the diaspora. By 1974, Shleu-Shleu, Tabou Combo, Skah Shah, Volo Volo, Magnum Band (Figure 10.8), and others had become established abroad; they entertained nostalgic émigrés and provided a social context for community gatherings.

Figure 10.8
The *kompa* guitarist Alex "Dadou" Pasquet peforms with his Magnum Band at Le Chateau nightclub in the Carrefour District. Photo by Gage Averill, 1989.

This was also a period in which Haitian groups became popular in the French Antilles, where they helped spark a *kadans* movement.

In the 1970s, *mini-djaz* borrowed instrumental resources from Caribbean dance bands of Trinidad, Dominica, and Martinique, adding drum sets, extra wind instruments, and finally synthesizers. By the late 1970s, they were no longer so mini: an average band had about twelve or thirteen members.

In the late 1970s and 1980s, more and more Haitian bands and performers—such as Manno Charlemagne, Les Frères Parent, Ti-Manno (Roselin Antoine Jean-Baptiste), and Farah Juste—took part in opposing the Duvalier dictatorship; they produced *mizik angaje* ("politically committed music"). Frustration with a perceived stagnation in popular musics and the search for post-Duvalier cultural forms resulted in new musical directions. A youthful technological-music movement (the *nouvèl jenerasyon,* or "new generation") and *mizik rasin*, a neotraditonal music (mixing Vodou, *rara*, and electrified commercial pop), emerged (Averill 1997).

Gender, age, and class in Haitian popular music

In the production of urban and commercial musics, men are much more involved than women, and the contexts for the urban consumption of music—bars, clubs, even *tonèls*—are frequented more by men than by women. Partly because many Haitians consider unattached women who frequent such establishments disreputable, the number of women who play or sing in commercial bands is negligible. Women have, however, achieved success as patriotic, political, and romantic singers.

Mini-djaz emerged as a phenomenon of youth: an expression of school-age, middle-class boys in Port-au-Prince and a handful of cities in Haiti. The most fervent fans aged with the musicians who invented the genre; by 1995, the bulk of them had reached their forties. The *nouvel jenerasyon* was a reaction to this situation by a younger audience. Musical hits serve as markers of personal and collective history, and older audiences in Haiti and in the diaspora tend to be conservative about the musics that accompanied and helped define their adolescence. A striking change is evident among Haitian teenagers in the diaspora, who readily adopt African-American subcultural norms, disparaging less-acculturated Haitian immigrants as newcomers. Rap and Jamaican-style *ragga* (dance-ball style of chanting) have become popular among immigrants of this age.

Haitian urban genres carry associations of class, but few genres are exclusive in this way. Most genres appeal to more than one social class, and genres can be subdivided by differences in style that subtly articulate class origins and affiliations. Mediating against a mechanical linkage between style and class is the potential for symbolic upward and downward social mobility through music. Indigenous movements in popular music (*vodou-jazz* and *mizik rasin*) effectively reach downward in class symbolism, aligning musicians and audiences with aspects of peasant or lower-class culture. Music also serves as a means for musicians to socialize with members of elite classes, though this socialization usually occurs within the context of musical employment.

Popular musical style

Haitian popular music is structured along principles common to many African-Caribbean urban musics. Multiple percussive instruments of different sonorities and pitch levels interact to form a cyclical pattern. In *konpa*, certain melodic instruments play *ostinati* that articulate changes of chords, and others serve as solo instruments. Harmonic progressions are variable, but most dance sections settle down to a two-chord pattern, often V—I (the tonic is often minor). Most songs begin with an instrumental introduction, progress to a lyrical song section, and end with an ostinato-dominated "groove section," featuring short, responsorial vocals.

Haitians base aesthetic judgments on the singers' vocal quality, the "sweetness" of the overall sound, the subtlety of timing in the rhythm section, but more than any single feature, the degree to which the band moves an audience and creates the proper ambience: *cho* ("hot") for certain occasions, *tèt kole* ("cheek-to-cheek") for others. At large, outdoor events, audiences prefer music that is lively, that gets an audience *antyoutyout* ("carried away" or *anraje* "worked up")—music with which to *mete de men nan lè* ("put one's hands in the air"). At clubs, the music accompanies close *konpa* dancing, often *kole-kole* ("glued together" or *ploge* "plugged" together).

Urban commercial music has become nearly ubiquitous in the soundscape of Haitian cities. On cassette and on radio, it provides background music in stores, in restaurants, and on public transportation. On radio and television, it sells commercial products and candidates for public office. Because most Haitians cannot read, urban popular musics serve as part of the technology of advertising, promotion, education, and information.

NATIONAL ANTHEM

In commemoration of Haiti's centennial celebration, the government held a contest for a national anthem in 1903. The winner was a song titled "La Dessalinienne," written in honor of Haiti's revolutionary hero and first ruler, Jean-Jacques Dessalines. Composed by Nicolas Geffard to lyrics by Justin Lhérisson, "La Dessalinienne" in French or "Ladesalinyén in Kreyól ("The Dessalines Song" in English) was adopted as the national anthem of Haiti in 1904. The song begins by honoring the past: "Pour le Pays, pour les Ancêtres, Marchons unis…" in French or "Pou Ayiti, Peyi Zansèt yo, Se pour n mache…" in Kreyól ("For our country, for our forebearers, united let us march…" or "For the country, for the ancestors, we walk united…" in English). Followers of Vodou see this opening lyric as a veneration of their belief as well as a veneration of their country and its founder.

LEARNING, DISSEMINATION, TOURISM, AND PUBLIC POLICY

Formal musical training in Haiti was hard to get. Schooling was reserved for children of the elite, some of whom continued their studies in France or the United States. As part of a French-influenced upbringing, trained musicians provided private lessons for upper-class children. Training was also provided to immediate members of families; and for this reason (until about 1950), parlor, orchestral, and dance-band music was the primarily the province of a limited number of families. Members of other classes could develop musicianship in military brass bands (*fanfa* or "fanfares"), and could parlay their skills into a position with a *méringue* band when they left the armed services. Bandleaders disproportionately came from musical families and brass bands, because it was they who had mastered *solfège*, a mark of literate musicians. With expansion of religious and public education for the middle classes, musical education became somewhat democratized, though the lack of money, teachers, and instruments marginalized the process. A few *lycées* (equivalent to high schools), such as the Lycée Pétion and the Lycée Saint Louis de Gonzague have brass bands, and the Episcopal school L'Ecole Ste. Trinite has a full orchestra. The main fare for these programs consists of European-American classical music, supplemented by Haitian "autochthonous-school compositions," but some students play jazz or Haitian popular music on their own.

Schools and churches typically have choirs, which serve as another training center for musicians, especially female vocalists. Most women in commercial folk music and popular music received training in religious choirs. Little instruction in anything resembling Haitian traditional music takes place outside of the ethnology program at the Université de l'État (State University).

Tourism and staged folklore

The issue of Haitian cultural identity has been strongly contested since early in the U.S. occupation (1915–1934). During the 1940s, the government institutionalized *négritude* and created the Bureau of Ethnology. New possibilities for the expression of Haitian identity precipitated a folkloric movement. The tourist market also stimulated the development of folkloric companies and their repertoire. In 1949, the intersection of these internal and external forces led to the creation of a government-backed ensemble, La Troupe Folklorique Nationale.

Folkloric companies spotlight dancers, a drum ensemble modeled after the Vodou battery, and a chorus. In choreographies based on Carnival and *rara* dances, extra players provide the requisite winds and percussion. Folkloric costumes are stylized imitations of peasant clothing. Dances are associated with Vodou, Carnival, *rara* festivals, and *konbit*. Dances of European origin (waltz, lancers, polka) are sometimes choreographed as part of an *afranchi* ("freed slave") segment, but staged folklore emphasizes the Africanness of Haiti's past.

The choreography elaborates and varies the basic movements of a given dance and utilizes *vèvè* designs on the floor. Dancers and choreographers continually spin out variations of source material. The master drummer creates accompanying patterns that bind sound and movement. The music on stage is further distinguished from its sources in its use of the *kase*. During a Vodou ritual, the drummer decides when to play a *kase*, and he bases his decision on the psychosocial dynamics in progress. In staged folklore, the points of *kase* are fixed during rehearsal.

Staged folklore replaces the open-ended structures and religious function of Vodou drumming with predetermined forms that function as entertainment. It introduces the notion of *vèvè*; however, it maintains the instrumentation and the songs of its sources. Though the function of the *kase* changes, its form stays intact. Dance, though elaborated, maintains its centrality and—with music and costuming—projects a selected cultural identity.

In 1949, Haiti's first major tourist-oriented extravaganza, the bicentennial of Port-au-Prince, employed folkloric music-and-dance groups. It began a long tradition of government-sponsored performances of these groups, under administrations of varying political ideologies. Many *négritude*-influenced musicians supported "Papa Doc" Duvalier's quest for the presidency and composed folkloric songs in his praise. But the bulk of Duvalier patronage and promotion went to the *konpa* groups, whose popularity was more or less coterminous with his. His government and his private militia (Tonton Macoutes) commissioned pieces from *konpa* bands and *mini-djaz*, promoted the groups at Carnival, and hired them for private parties. In addition, local political rallies were considered incomplete without local *konpa* bands or *rara* groups to enliven the occasion and to create an effervescent, *koudyay* "carnival-!ike" ambience.

Public policy

Duvalier's son, "Baby Doc," ardently admired *mini-djaz*; under his rule, as part of an effort to promote a new, more modern, middle-class image of Haiti, these groups received government patronage and commissions. In post-Duvalier Haiti, political instability precluded an active governmental policy toward music, though in 1988 there was a brief appointment of a minister of culture.

The years under de facto military rule (1991–1994) produced a deepening of the gulf between musicians who supported President Jean-Bertrand Aristide (a Roman Catholic priest and proponent of liberation theology, himself a guitarist and songwriter) and those who favored the military and its supporters. Aristide's election (1990) and the restitution of civilian government (1994) inspired some *angaje* ("politically engaged musicians") to participate in the political process as candidates for elected office and advisers to the government—one of whom, Manno Charlemagne, was elected mayor of Port-au-Prince in 1995.

FURTHER STUDY

Rara, in addition to Vodou, has been one of the most recently studied genres from Haiti's rich musical palette. Religion scholar Elizabeth McAlister's book *Rara! Vodou, Power, and*

Performance in Haiti and Its Diaspora (2002) includes a CD and her CD/63-page book compilation *Angels in the Mirror* contains extensive cultural information about Vodou and Haitian music. Now over ten years old, the excellent video footage of *rara* in *The JVCV/ Smithsonian Folkways Video Anthology of Music and Dance of the Americas* (Okada 1995), Vol. 4 (example 11), is valuable for teaching purposes. The latest of *Caribbean Currents: Caribbean Music from Rumba to Reggae*, by Peter Manuel, with Kenneth Bilby and Michael D. Largey, includes the "Haiti and the French Caribbean," by Largey. Largey's dissertation, "Musical Ethnography In Haiti: A Study of Elite Hegemony and Musical Composition (Ethnography)," has recently been revised and published in the Chicago Studies in Ethnomusicology Series ase *Vodou Nation: Haitian Art Music and Cultural Nationalism* (2006).

REFERENCES

Averill, Gage. 1993. "Toujou Sou Konpa': Issues of Change and Interchange in Haitian Popular Dance Music." In *Zouk: World Musk in the West Indies*, ed. Jocelyne Guilbault with Gage Averill, et al., 68–89. Chicago: University of Chicago Press.

———. 1997. *A Day for the Hunter, a Day far the Prey: Popular Music and Power in Haiti*. Chicago: University of Chicago Press.

———. 2003. Review of *Rara!: Vodiu, Power, and Performance in Haiti and Its Diaspora* by Elizabeth McAlister. Latin American Music Review 24/1 (Spring/Summer): 136–139.

Caribbean Revels: Haitian Rara and Dominican Gaga. 1991. Recordings by Verna Gillis. Notes by Gage Averill and Verna Gillis. Smithsonian Folkways SF-40402. LP disk.

Courlander, Harold. 1973. *The Drum and the Hoe: Life and Lore of the Haitian People*. Berkeley: University of California Press.

Dauphin, Claude. 1981. *Brit kolobrit: Introduction Méthodologique Suivie de 30 Chansons Enfantiles Haïtiennes*. Québec: Editions Naaman de Sherbrooke.

———. 1986. *Musique du Vaudou: Fonctions, Structures, et Styles*. Sherbrooke: Editions Naaman.

Deren, Maya. 1984 (1953). *Divine Horsemen: The Living Gods of Haiti*. New Paltz, N.Y.: McPherson & Co.

Dumervé, Etienne Constantin Eugene Moise. 1968. *Histoire de la Musique en Haïti*, Port-au-Princec: Imprimerie des Antilles.

Fleurant, Gèrdis. 1996. *Dancing Spirits: Rhythms and Rituals of Haitian Vodun*. *The Rada Rite*. Westport, Conn.: Greenwood Press.

Fouchard, Jean. 1988. *La Méringue. Danse Nationale d'Haïti*. Port-au-Prince: Editions Henri Deschamps.

Herskovits, Melville. 1975. *Life in a Haitian Valley*. New York: Octagon Books.

Largey, Michael. 1991. "Musical Ethnography in Haiti: A Study of Elite Hegemony and Musical Composition." Ph.D. dissertation, Indiana University.

———. 2006. *Vodou Nation: Haitian Art Music and Cultural Nationalism*. Chicago: University of Chicago Press (Chicago Studies in Ethnomusicology).

Manuel, Peter, with Kenneth Bilby and Michael Largey. 2006. *Caribbean Currents: Caribbean Music from Rumba to Reggae* (2nd ed.). Philadelphia: Temple University Press.

McAlister, Elizabeth. 2002. *Angels in the Mirror*. Berkeley, Calif.: University of California Press.

———. 2002. *Rara! Vodou, Power, and Performances in Haiti and Its Diaspora*. Berkeley, Los Angeles, and London: University of California Press.

Métraux, Alfred. 1972. *Voodoo in Haiti*. New York: Schocken Books.

Okada, Yuki. 1995. *The Caribbean. The JVC Smithsonian Folkways Video Anthology of Music and Dance of the Americas*, 4. Montpelier, Vt.: Multicultural Media. VTMV-228. Video.

Paul, Emmanuel. 1962. *Panorama du Folklore Haitien: Présence africaine en Haïti*. Port-au-Prince: Imprimerie de l'Etat.

Rouse, Irving. 1948. "The Arawak." In *Handbook of South American Indians, 4. The Circum-Caribbean Tribes*, ed. Julian H. Steward, 507–546. Washington, D.C.: U.S. Government Printing Office.

Wilcken. Lois E., featuring Frisner Augustin. 1992. *The Drums of Vodou*. Tempe, Ariz.: White Cities Media.

The Dominican Republic

Martha Ellen Davis

The Indigenous Heritage
The European Heritage
The African Heritage
Musical Genres and Contexts
Music Learning, Dissemination, Tourism, and Public Policy
Further Study

The Dominican Republic constitutes about two-thirds of the second largest island (after Cuba) in the Caribbean, known as Hispaniola (from La Isla Española, as named by Columbus) since colonial times. It has a surface area of 48,400 square kilometers and a land that includes low mountains through its central area, culminating in higher and more rugged terrain near the border with Haiti to the west, with whom the Dominican Republic has politically shared the island since 1844.

THE INDIGENOUS HERITAGE

As elsewhere in the Americas and the world, three principal sources help piece together Dominican musical history: archaeology, the written record, and ethnography (using the living tradition as a key to an unwritten past). The Taíno were a subgroup of the Arawak, one of the four huge language families of tropical South America. Seafaring Arawak from the Amazon and the Orinoco populated the Antilles one by one, arriving at Hispaniola, which they called *Quisqueya* or *Haiti* ("mountainous land"), more than four thousand years ago. When Europeans arrived, the Taíno of Borinquen (Puerto Rico) and Quisqueya were being conquered by the bellicose Caribs, another of the four main tropical South American language families.

Taíno musical culture is represented by little material evidence, since much of it was vocal. The Spanish chronicler Las Casas (1958) describes the singing of large groups of

Taíno women when they gathered to grate manioc for toasted cassava cakes (*casabe*). They had neither skin-covered drums nor stringed instruments. Flutes made of clay, bone, and perhaps cane, were described, yet few specimens survive. The most important instrument was a hollowed log idiophone with an H-shaped slit on its top (*mayohuacán*), played during the *areito* (also *areyto*), a ritual in which dancers played *maracas* and may have worn rattles tied to their ankles. The Taíno used conch trumpets (*fotutos*) for signaling, as they are still used in some rural areas to announce meat for sale, danger, or death.

The *areito* was the main musical event of Quisqueya, Cuba, and Borinquen. Despite variations based on region and social occasion, it was a large-scale sung dance ritual that could last for hours or days, with a vocal or dance leader and a chorus or dance group of as many as three hundred men or women or both, accompanied by a struck log idiophone. It could be performed for various occasions: to make a petition (as for the fertility of a crop or protection from hurricanes), to render homage (as in Princess Anacaona's *areito* for the governor of Hispaniola, with her three hundred maidservants as dancers), to celebrate an important marriage or a victory in war, to solemnize a funerary memorial, or to foster recreation. The text of the *areito* conserved, reiterated, and commemorated the past and the ancestors and their deeds, sometimes mentioning how each had died. There were also lighthearted, seemingly silly texts. Some celebratory occasions included such prodigious consumption of alcohol that the revels ended in drunkenness.

The vocal chorus and dancers were positioned in a linear, circular, or arch formation, maintaining close contact with one another by holding hands or linking arms. The soloist and chorus moved forward and backward in rhythm with impeccable precision, the dancers playing maracas and perhaps wearing ankle-tied rattles. The leader (*tequina*), a man or a woman (and probably a shaman), sang responsorially with the chorus, who repeated the leader's every line, but at a lower or higher pitch, while the leader kept dancing in silence. A soloist could be replaced but no break would occur until the narrative song was finished; this could take three or four hours, or even from one day to the next. The tune and movements could alter when a new soloist took over, but the narrative had to continue; yet the tune for a new sung story could be the same as the former one.

THE EUROPEAN HERITAGE

At the time of the Spanish Encounter with the New World, Spanish culture represented the fusion of Sephardic Jewish, Moorish, and Celtic-Iberian elements. The Reconquest of Spain, known as the Spanish Inquisition, with its final and definitive expulsion of Jews and Moors from Spain in 1492, occurred only about a month before Columbus began his first voyage; one destination of the Jewish and Moorish flight from Spain was the New World. The first settlement of the Spanish in the Americas was La Navidad on the northwestern shore of Hispaniola; destroyed by the native Americans, today the archaeological site is a part of Haiti (see HAITI). The later Spanish colony further east was called Santo Domingo and was first settled by Spanish peasants from Extremadura and Andalucía and Jews and Moors who fled Spain during the Spanish Inquisition; evidence of Jewish and Moorish influence in Hispaniola appears in architecture, dialect, and the oldest musical styles and genres. In the late 1600s, an important wave of immigrants arrived from the Canary Islands.

When Spain discovered the high cultures and treasures of Mexico (1519) and Peru (1532), it left its colony in Hispaniola to languish as a colonial backwater. This policy allowed France to gain a foothold in the island, leading to the 1697 treaty that ceded to France the western third of Hispaniola, called Saint-Domingue (a translation of Santo Domingo, the name of the Spanish colony), which once again became Haïti on achieving independence (1804). France commenced to develop Saint-Domingue as the jewel in its colonial crown. By about 1530, with the island's exploitable gold exhausted and the indigenous population drastically reduced, the basis of the accrual of wealth shifted to agriculture, primarily sugarcane cultivation, carried out by African slaves. The millions of Africans brought by the French into Saint-Domingue and their ethnic origins led to the development of a society more densely populated than and culturally different from neighboring Santo Domingo. Through slave rebellions Haiti achieved its independence from the French in 1804. Less than two decades later, Haiti invaded and occupied Santo Domingo in 1822, freeing it from the Spanish yoke, but occupying it with brutal force until 1844, when Santo Domingo liberated itself from the Haitian yoke, declared its independence, and changed its name to the Dominican Republic. For a short time, from 1861–1865, the country again became a Spanish colony, then a portion was sold to the United States, followed by several corrupt dictatorships, and so on until American intervention in 1916 (lasting until 1930), followed by the dictatorial regime of the Generalissimo Rafael Trujillo, until his assassination in 1961.

European-derived musical genres and contexts

Recalling the *Salve* sung by Columbus and his crew upon their first landfall (see text by Davis in A PROFILE OF THE LANDS AND PEOPLE OF LATIN AMERICA), a similar Catholic praise genre developed in Santo Domingo, known as the Dominican *Salve Regina* (Davis 1981b). Today this includes the sung rosary and other pious prayers, music, iconography, and ritual procedures that were introduced by the clergy and then perpetuated by folk priests (*rezadores*) and other devotees in remote rural areas. The conservation of archaic liturgical practices in folk ritual demonstrates the importance of the oral tradition as a source of historical documentation.

The Dominican *Salve* (short for *Salve Regina*) is the musical cornerstone of the Spanish-derived saint's festival (*velación, noche de vela, velorio de santo*; *vela* is Spanish for "vigil"), the most frequent and ubiquitous event of Dominican folk Christianity (Figure 11.1). Rural based and individually sponsored, the saint's festival is undertaken initially in payment of a vow for divine healing, but it usually recurs annually as an inherited obligation. Its celebration lasts all night. After each of three rosaries (*tercios*), three sacred "*Salves de la Virgen*" ("Hails of the Virgin") are sung at the altar. In the east, the liturgical *Salves* are followed by others in a style representing an African-influenced (see below) evolution of the genre (Figure 11. 2 and Figure 11.3); but in the southwest and north, the three sacred *Salves* are followed by further *Salves* of similar style, sung antiphonally to an infinite number of melodies, until the next of the three rosaries in the event (Figure 11.1).

Figure 11.1
At San Juan de la Maguana, people perform the "*Salve de la Virgen*." At a saint's festival in the southwest region, men and women may participate in antiphonal performance of the unaccompanied *Salve*. The performers often try to out-sing each other in the style of the Hispanic *desafío*. Photo by Martha Ellen Davis, 1978.

Other Spanish influences on Dominican traditional music are unaccompanied, unmetered, melismatic, and antiphonal vocal styles. Sung high in male and female registers with tense vocal production, they are often in the minor mode or use a neutral third, but are unornamented. The genres include other types of ritual song of folk Christianity for saints' or death ceremonies—the (partially) sung rosary, altar and procession songs other than *Salves* (generically called *versos*), songs for children's wakes (*baquiné*) such as the almost extinct *mediatuna* of Cibao, the northern region; romances or Spanish ballads (Garrido Boggs 1946); children's songs and games (Garrido Boggs 1980 [1955]); antiphonal, unmetered work songs (*plenas*, not to be confused with Puerto Rican *plenas*); and various improvisatory sung conversations or debates (*desafíos* 'challenges'), performed within the context of agricultural labor (such as the *chuin* of Baní), for social commentary, expression of devotion, or courtship in a festive context, even at the periphery of a wake (such as the *décima*), or as ritual (such as the *tonadas de toros* of the east).

Figure 11.2
At the chapel of an Afro-Dominican religious brotherhood, Santa María, San Cristóbal, women perform the "*Salve con versos*" with percussive accompaniment by polyrhythmic clapping. Photo by Martha Ellen Davis, 1982.

Figure 11.3
Performance of the "*Salve de pandero*," an African-influenced extreme of the "*Salve con versos*" in the central-south region, entails various small membranophones including the round *pandero* hand drum and the absence of liturgical text. Performed in San Cristóbal at a saint's festival for St. James (pictured on altar, seen under woman's chin on far left). Photo by Martha Ellen Davis, 1976.

The improvisatory sung conversation or debate (*desafío*), a Mediterranean phenomenon, is a mode of male expression, but in courtship, a woman may use it wittily to evade or metaphorically to accept a man's advances. On the whole, in the Dominican repertoire, improvisatory verbal dexterity in song and the poetic genre of the *décima* are not nearly so important as elsewhere in the Hispanic Caribbean, though their social function is the same. The Dominican *décima* is usually spoken, rather than sung, and when sung is never instrumentally accompanied.

European-derived musical instruments and ensembles

Instrumental music of Spanish influence formerly accompanied largely creole social-dance genres with Spanish-derived stringed instruments: the now extinct treble guitar (*tiple*); the *cuatro* with four double courses of strings (not to be confused with Puerto Rican and Venezuelan *cuatros*); the *tres*, traditionally triangular or guitar-shaped, now only the latter, with six strings in three double courses, tuned E–G–c with the G strings of different thick-

Figure 11.4
A small social-dance ensemble, performing for tourists at the Boca Chica beach (Distrito Nacional). It features the *tres* (here a guitar strung with three double courses of strings), typical of dance ensembles of the south before the introduction of the accordion from the Cibao region (north). The drum is an upended *tambora* played like a southern *balsié* or Cuban conga (see Figure 11.8 and compare the *tambora* of the *merengue típico* in Figure 11.6). The ensemble also includes the *güira* metal scraper and the *marimba*. Photo by Dale A. Olsen, 1977.

nesses (Coopersmith 1976 [1949]) (Figure 11.4); and the *guitarra*, the six-stringed Spanish guitar. All these were largely replaced about 1880 by the Höhner button accordion, introduced through trade with Germany, though the *tres-* and guitar-based *merengue* has been regaining popularity since the 1970s.

Brass bands and dance bands (see below) represent another kind of European-derived ensemble; the former play marches, arrangements of art music, and creole dance music, bridging nonliterate and literate musical domains.

THE AFRICAN HERITAGE

The Amerindian population of Hispaniola—at least one million persons—was so rapidly reduced by warfare, disease, and suicide that its replacement by an African workforce began as early as 1502. The first Africans (*ladinos*) were Spanish-speaking Christians from Spain, present there in servitude for a century before 1492. They were soon joined in Hispaniola by *bozales*, direct imports from the African continent, starting with Wolof (*golofes*) from the Senegambian region. Later shipments embarked from increasingly southerly points on the West African coast until they were coming from the Congo-Angolan region. In 1822, the Haitian occupation ended the local slave trade. Before the 1540s, notable contact occurred between Taínos and Africans in their flight from bondage. In contemporary rural society, Afro-Dominican enclaves are important conservators of Taíno material culture.

The black population of the Dominican Republic was enriched in the nineteenth and twentieth centuries by three immigrations: in 1824–1825, when the whole island was the Republic of Haiti, six thousand Afro-North-American freemen arrived as part of the same initiative that founded Liberia (Davis 1980b, 1980c, 1981a, 1983); in the late 1800s, laborers, stevedores, teachers, and pastors were attracted from the anglophone Lesser Antilles to the booming sugar industry in the Dominican southeast around San Pedro de Macorís (where they are pejoratively called *cocolos*); in the mid-twentieth century, the sugarcane business in many areas required the seasonal importation of thousands of Haitian seasonal workers (*braceros*) under conditions described as neoslavery. Many, estimated up to a million, have stayed and sometimes have intermarried, their children becoming bicultural Dominicans. These components of the population have contributed to the fabric of contemporary national culture, especially nonliterate musical culture.

Afro-Dominican musical genres and contexts

Dominican genres of notably African heritage (Davis 1980a) include metered, responsorial work songs (*plenas*), such as wood-chopping songs (*plenas de hacha*); stories about animals, with their characteristic little sung responses (Andrade 1976 [1930[); the semi-sacred music of longdrums (*palos, atabales*) associated with Afro-Dominican brotherhoods (Davis 1976) and used in saints' festivals and sometimes *Vodú* ceremonies (Davis 1987a) (Figure 11.5); influence on Dominican creole social-dance music (Figure 11.6, Figure 11.7, Figure 11.8) and nonliturgical *salves*; and the "*cocolo*" fife-and-drum ensemble (Figure 11.9) and the Haitian-Dominican *gagá* society and ensemble (Figure 11.10), each associated with a different sugarcane settlement (Rosenberg 1979).

Figure 11.5
The longdrum dance, *baile de palos*, representing ritual pursuit, a possible descendant of the colonial *calenda*. The women at the left, singing the response, also play single maracas, reflecting influence from the *congo* ensemble of the Villa Mella region, of which Los Morenos is an enclave. Photo by Martha Ellen Davis, 1980.

Musical societies, events, and activities of African influence represent a New World continuity of elements of African political or religious societies, a pan-African polytheism, the attribution to divine forces of luck and the causes and cures of disease, the concept of ancestors as elders, systems of collective agricultural labor, and some forms of recreation. Political or religious societies under slavery in the New World were cast in nonthreatening or Christianized contexts, such as the confraternity or religious brotherhood (*cofradía*, *hermandad*), or in a playful context, such as Carnival (*Carnaval*). The elite of colonial slave society is represented in the hierarchy of the Haitian and Haitian-Dominican *gagá* societies.

African polytheism, which syncretized with the polytheism of the Roman Catholic Church, is represented in the configuration of saints served by folk-religious ritual activities, mainly saints' festivals, processions, and pilgrimages. Devotion to ancestors is represented in rituals at the deathbed, the wake, the nine-night *novena* prayer cycle, the final *novena* (like a second wake), and the anniversary of death (sung rosary for adults, *Salves* or the Hispanic *mediatuna* in the north for young children); when the deceased was a member of a religious brotherhood, longdrums are played.

These rituals are related to folk medicine, for they can be performed in payment of a vow (*promesa*) after divine healing. If the mortal does not fulfill the vow of undertaking a promised devotional act, the saint may claim his or her due by sending illness or death. Divine healing

Figure 11.6
A traditional *merengue* social-dance ensemble of the northern (Cibao) region, ubiquitous in the Dominican Republic as a folksy musical symbol of national identity. Left to right: *tambora*, button accordion, *güira*, and *marimba*. Cabral, Barahona. Photo by Martha Ellen Davis, 1980.

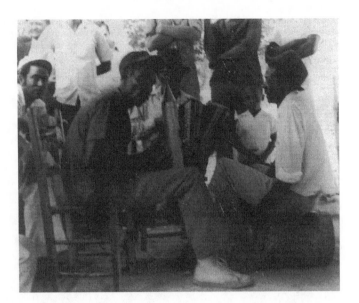

Figure 11.7
The *priprí,* a social dance of the central east and central south. The drum is the *balsié,* known in the colonial Caribbean as the *juba* drum, set on the ground with the player on top, dampening with a heel and beating with the hands on either side of the foot. It is played here for social dancing in the plaza of Villa Mella on Pentecost, the day of the Holy Spirit, patron of the Afro-Dominican brotherhood (*cofradía*) of the Villa Mella region. Photo by Martha Ellen Davis, 1978.

and counseling may be sought through consultation with a medium (*servidor* or *servidora de misterios*), then publicly celebrated; the initiation of new mediums and patron saints' days of the spiritualist center ("altar") and the medium (its "owner") are also celebrated (with longdrums or nonliturgical *Salves*). The *gagá* societies, allied with Haitian Vodou (Vodú in Spanish) and protected by its magic, use the *gagá* drum and aerophone ensemble to express death-and-resurrection and celebration-of-life fertility motifs of the Lenten and Easter season (Figure 11.10).

Afro-Dominican instruments and ensembles

Musical instruments and ensembles of the Dominican Republic include various idiophones, membranophones, chordophones, and aerophones.

Figure 11.8
In Cabral, Barahona, the southwestern ensemble Belí [Belisario Féliz] y sus Muchachos plays a *priprí,* the rhythmic triptych of *carabiné, mangulina,* and *danza* (and today the *merengue*) in their own style. Left to right: a *güira,* a button accordion, a *balsié* (same name, different instrument from that of the east), and a *pandero* (here, large hand-held drum with laced head). Photo by Martha Ellen Davis, 1980.

Figure 11.9
On the patron saint's day of San Pedro de Macorís, carnivalesque mummers of English-island immigrants—the ensembles of Theophilus Chiverton "Primo" (far left) and Donald Henderson (next to drum)—play. Left to right: a side-blown flute, a triangle, and a bass drum. Photo by Martha Ellen Davis, 1976.

Idiophones

A metal scraper (*güira* or *guayo* "grater," Figure 11.4 and Figure 11.6) is a modern version of the gourd (*güiro*) still played in Puerto Rico. The *maraca* is a small shaker with a wooden handle, filled with gourd seeds or pebbles and played in pairs or singly in the *congos* ensemble of Villa Mella, which may represent Taíno-African syncretism. A stick (*catá*) is beaten on the body of a longdrum in the northeast, including Samaná, where it is called a *maraca* (not to be confused with the shaker of the same name). A pair of wooden idiophones (*canoíta* "little canoe") resembles Cuban *claves*, but one is much larger and hollowed out like a little canoe and of softer wood; a *canoíta* is played only with the *congos* ensemble.

A recently introduced, definite-pitched, plucked idiophone is the *marimba* (from the Cuban *marímbula*), a lamellaphone derived from the African *mbira* but much larger and

güira
"Grater" (also *guayo*), Dominican and Cuban metal rasp functioning like the gourd *güiro*, played with a metal scraper

canoíta
"Little canoe," in the Dominican Republic, a pair of wooden idiophones that are struck together, one of which is hollowed out like a little canoe

Figure 11.10
The Haitian-Dominican "*gagá*" (called "*rara*" in Haiti) of the Lenten and Easter season: bamboo tubes of different pitches play in hocket (interlocking fashion), along with *petró* drums, and singing. The dancers twirl staves. Barahona area. Photo by Martha Ellen Davis, 1980.

with fewer metal tongues. The player sits on its plywood box. It was probably imported in the 1930s with the popular *sexteto* of the Cuban *son* and was adopted by the folk-*merengue* ensemble (Figure 11.4 and Figure 11.6).

Membranophones

Except in central Cibao, large membranophones include longdrums (*palos*, *atabales*), hand played throughout the country (Figure 11.5). Except in two enclaves, these are made of hollowed-out logs with cowhide heads. All ensembles include responsorial singing by the drummers plus, if for the saints (rather than the dead), a couple dance (*baile de palos*) symbolizing ritual pursuit, perhaps derived from the colonial *calenda*. In the southwestern *Salve*, the master drum (*palo mayor*), the largest and deepest, is the center drum in an ensemble of three; the other drums are generically called *alcahuetes* ("pimps"). [Listen to "Los Coros de San Miguel"]

Regional variants of longdrum ensembles occur throughout the country except in central Cibao. In the east: two drums with wide, pegged heads and up to three metal scrapers (*güiras*); or one drum plus a pair of *maracas* in the transitional Monte Plata area; or single *maracas* in the enclave of Los Morenos (Figure 11.5) influenced by the *congos* ensemble of greater Villa Mella; or a stick beaten on the drum body in Samaná. The rhythms are *palos de muerto* "drums for the dead" for death rituals and *palo corrido* for dancing. A variant in eastern Cibao (Cotuí, San Francisco de Macorís) uses tiny pegs, and the *alcahuete* is called *adulón*. In the central south, there are three drums (with narrow, tacked heads) and no idiophones. The ensemble is called more specifically *canutos* or *cañutos*. The rhythms are for the dead (*palo abajo* and *palo arriba*), joined in sequence everywhere except in Los Morenos, Villa Mella, though they are also danced somberly (Figure 11.5). In the southwest, there are three drums (with wide, tacked heads) and no idiophones. One *alcahuete* is shorter and called the *chivita*. The rhythm is *palo corrido*, the instruments and the rhythm are called *palos del Espíritu Santo* "palos of the Holy *Spirit*" because of the mysticism of the region and the instrument's association with the Brotherhood of the Holy Spirit.

Two longdrum special enclaves exist. The Afro-Dominican enclave, the Brotherhood of the Holy Spirit (Cofradía del Espíritu Santo) in Villa Mella has two drums (*congos*), one a third the size of the other (with dual goatskin laced heads), one pair of *canoíta* and many single *maracas* as idiophones. The brotherhood's activities entail mainly death rituals: the ninth and final *novena* (*rezo* "prayer") and the anniversary of death (*banco*, probably a Bantu term, meaning unknown). The Afro-Dominican enclave, the Brotherhood of St. John the Baptist from west of Baní (Province of Peravia), now also in town, uses three squat drums of dual goatskin-tacked heads (*tambores*), held between the knees for dance accompaniment or under the arm for procession, and one *güira*. Dance and music are generically called *sarandunga*; dance rhythms are *sarandunga* (pieces include *capitana* for the dead and many others), *jacana*, and *bomba-e*. A procession genre is *morano*, in which drums accompany fixed solo and response quatrains. This brotherhood's rituals entail mainly daytime vows sponsored by devotees.

Smaller membranophones include various squat drums, varying in length from some 25 to 75 centimeters and in diameter from some 23 to 38 centimeters, used as the key instruments in social-dance ensembles; the *tambora* of the northern folk *merengue*; the horizontal, heel-damped tacked-head *balsié* of the *priprí* ensemble of the east and central south (the Caribbean *juba* drum); the vertical *balsié* (same name, different instrument, with a laced head); and the large, laced frame drum (*pandero*) of the *priprí* (same name, different ensemble) of the southwest. The nonliturgical *Salve* ensembles of the central south and east use smaller membranophones: the cylindrical *mongó* or *bongó*, played singly with a polyphonic ensemble of round frame drums (*panderos*). The *pandero* has a tacked head, is 23 to 25 centimeters in diameter and 4 centimeters high, and is similar to the tambourine but with few and irrelevant jingles, representing syncretism between Spanish (Moorish heritage) and African instruments.

Descendants of British immigrants in San Pedro de Macorís imported the ensemble of mummers (*momís*, *guloyas*), consisting of a fife, a bass drum, and a triangle (Figure11.9).

balsié
In the Dominican Republic, the name for two different types of drums: a horizontal drum with tacked head, and a vertical drum with laced head
pandero
A Dominican and Puerto Rican round frame drum like a tambourine but without jingles

Chordophones

A Central African–derived chordophone, the earthbow (*gayumba*, called *tambour maringouin* in Haiti, though it is almost extinct in the island) resembles the American gutbucket, but its resonating chamber is a palm-bark-covered hole in the ground. It plays any kind of music at festive, social occasions.

Aerophones

The conch trumpet (*fotuto*), used for signaling, represents syncretism between a Taíno and an African instrument. Aerophones are also used in the Haitian-Dominican membranophone and aerophone-idiophone ensemble of the *gagá* society, along with *petró* cult drums and an assortment of single-pitched bamboo trumpets (*vaccines* in Haiti, *bambúes* or *fotutos* in the Dominican Republic), whose players beat little sticks on their bamboo tube as they play; plus other metal aerophones (Figure 11.10).

THE EMERGENCE (CREOLIZATION) OF DOMINICAN MUSIC

Today's Dominican culture is best characterized as creole, the product of a process of adaptation and creative evolution that began in the earliest days of the colony. In recent decades, the evolutionary trend within the creole hybrid has been away from the Spanish heritage and toward greater African influence, marked by the gradual loss of acoustic stringed instruments, nontempered scales, antiphonal structures, and traditional vocal genres, including the *romance* and the *mediatuna*.

Dominican rural musical genres and contexts

Some genres, notably dance music and the nonliturgical *Salve*, are the result of creolization. Other contexts, genres, styles, and ensembles, however, are New World continuities of Old World cultures. This musical phenomenon is epitomized in the saint's festival.

The saint's festival

In the religious context of the saint's festival, certain musical genres, as part of the ritual, have been slow to change. These genres include the sung rosary, the liturgical *Salve*, and sacred drumming. This festival is thus a living museum of the most archaic practices of Spanish and African origin. It shows that "traditional" musical culture and its performers may be bimusical—a common Caribbean occurrence (Davis 1987b, 1994a).

Musical activities in the saint's festival have specific spatial and temporal placement, and they often have gender associations. The rosary and the *Salves* are performed at the altar, the sacred European site (erected for the festival against one wall of the folk chapel or of the sponsor's living room), the domain of women's responsibility and authority. Men may participate, but the *Salve* is essentially a women's genre. Drumming (*palos*), a male activity, and the drum dance are situated in the center of the room around a center post (the sacred African site), temporally interrupted with *Salves* (in the southwest), or outside in a covered patio, with the drums being hauled toward the altar for three sacred pieces after each rosary (in the east). If the festival of the east is a nightlong stop along a pilgrimage route, a separate room with a freestanding table is prepared for sung conversation (*tonadas de toros* or "bull songs") among members of a pilgrimage-associated brotherhood, who take donated alms and bull calves to Higüey, Bayaguana, and three other pilgrimage sites. If, as seldom happens, the sponsor is a Vodú medium, spirit possession by deities will occur, and while *palos* or *Salves* are being played in public, spiritual consultations may take place in an adjacent private room.

Depending on the region of the country, social dance music may be interspersed with drumming, played in a separate site on the festival grounds or played in the morning after the fulfillment of the vow. Rural social-dance genres practiced through the mid-twentieth century included variants of the Spanish *zapateado* called *zapateo* (*sarambo* in Cibao, *guarapo* in El Seybo) or derivatives of the English country dance (the *tumba dominicana*, displaced about 1850 by the *merengue*: the *carabiné* of the south; and the Haitian-derived *bambulá* in Samaná). In contemporary rural society, social dance includes the *merengue* from Cibao, the *perico ripiao*; the *merengue redondo* of the east (called *priprí* in the central-south, Figure 11.7); and in the south, the triptych of *carabiné*, *mangulina*, and *danza* or *vals* (Figure 11.8). The same genres may be danced outside the sacred site and on the occasion of the saint's festival. Secular venues of rural social dancing are bars (*cantinas*) and brothels (*cabarets*). The nickname of the northern *merengue*, *perico ripiao* ("ripped parrot"), is said to have been the name of a brothel in the 1930s in the province of Santiago.

Salve

In today's *Salve*, musical elements of different historical origins coexist and have become merged. In the central-south and eastern regions, the *Salve* has evolved into two coexisting subgenres: the Hispanic, sacred, liturgical Virgin's *Salve* (*Salve de la Virgen*) and a less sacred *Salve* with added text (*Salve con versos*). The latter exhibits an appended text and a different, African-influenced musical style: metered and rhythmic, instrumentally accompanied, and responsorial, with a relaxed, mid-register vocal production. Its versos entail a secular response inserted between sacred phrases plus added quatrains at the end. It is accompanied by clapping and/or one small, vertical *mongó* (a drum typically played by a man), several small handheld drums (*panderos*, typically played by women), and a *güira* (played by a man). It reaches its most Africanized extreme in the *Salve de pandero* of the central-south region, especially around Villa Mella and San Cristóbal, with the addition of many small membranophones played polyrhythmically and the elimination of a sacred text. Within the *Salve de pandero*, the variant of the Province of Peravia (Baní) illustrates the coexistence of traditions of two origins within the musical subgenre, with the usual gender associations. Women sing the former positioned in a line in front of the altar, while men, in circular formation at the back of the chapel, accompany them with small membranophones.

Merengue típico (perico ripiao)

Social-dance music, represented today by the folk *merengue* (*merengue típico* or *perico ripiao*) as a musical symbol of national identity, epitomizes the creolism of Dominican culture. The melodic instrument, sometimes a string instrument of the guitar family (Figure 11.4), but more often a Höhner accordion (Figure 11.6), is European; the *tambora* has West African influence; the metal *güira* or *guayo* may represent Taíno-African syncretism; and the *marimba* (since the 1930s) is a large Cuban-evolved version of the African *mbira*. [Listen to "Dice Desidera Arias"] The music is based on the quatrain, rendered partially in African responsorial form to African-influenced rhythms in accompaniment of a European-style couple dance with some African influence in dance style. This is the music and dance that Trujillo promoted as the national dance in ballroom adaptations. Though affirming *hispanidad*, he redefined national culture as creole culture, represented by the *merengue* as his chosen musical symbol of national identity.

DISC ❶ TRACK 35

Dominican urban musical genres and contexts

Since the rise of cities and of literacy, a dialectical relationship of musical exchange bridges rural and urban traditions, as it does literate and nonliterate ones. Cities and towns have literate and nonliterate musical genres, the latter shared among virtually all social classes.

Dominican cities vary in the presence of literate music. The larger cities and regional capitals have a sizeable educated elite and institutions that support fine-arts education and practice. The most musically active and prolific cities in the country are Santiago and Puerto Plata, and secondarily the capital (Santo Domingo) and San Pedro de Macorís. Smaller and newer towns, especially around sugarcane mills, are largely conglomerations of peasants-turned-proletarians. Since 1965, large numbers of peasants have left the countryside, so the rural-urban dichotomy is now also found in the cities.

The elite socialize and dance in a town's exclusive social club (club, casino). A major event is the *fiesta quinceañera*, the coming-out party for fifteen-year-old girls. Soirées (*veladas*) may include art-music compositions, choral poetry (*poesía coreada*), and other musical and theatrical genres. Exclusive dance parties are held on public festive events, such as Carnaval and the patron saint's day.

The neighborhood social-cultural-sports club is a Caribbean urban phenomenon found in cities and towns, and perpetuated in the expatriate community of New York. The club may be the sponsor and organizational site for a Carnival group (*comparsa*) or a sports team; it also serves as a site for dances, parties, and men's domino games. Clubs may have a unit of young people dedicated to research on local popular traditions, or a folk-dance ensemble (*ballet folklórico*), often with the same members.

Taverns (*bares*), often open-air and with no restrictions of gender or age, are popular venues for dance parties. Whole families may enjoy a daylong, daytime Sunday event, called a *pasadía*.

Protestants, who do not participate in Roman Catholic festivities, sing hymns (currently from hymnals from Puerto Rico, translations of United States hymns), and present entertainment programs in their churches, including dramatizations of biblical events and performances of choral poetry. Traditional English-speaking Protestants of Afro-United States and British descent, as in Samaná, end church services with spirituals, called anthems. Seasonal events, such as church anniversaries, include band-accompanied processions; the dead are carried to the cemetery in a cortège with the band. The people of Sanamá have also retained British-derived fife and bass drum ensembles, similar to Mississippi fife and bass drum duos and instrumental groups that accompany English mummers (see *momís* below).

Public music

Public musical events include biweekly concerts of municipal bands and seasonal events—patronal festivals, Carnaval (in some towns), and Christmas. Local patron saints may have little to do with actual devotion. Patronal feasts entail masses and several days of dances played by bands from other towns. They are traditionally prefaced by the *alborada*, a Spanish-derived predawn procession of a local musical ensemble.

Christmas in rural and urban contexts is characterized by *parrandas*, door-to-door singing for money or liquor. *Parrandas*, not so developed in the Dominican Republic as in Puerto Rico, are more African, with drum-based rather than string-based ensembles. A similar door-to-door circuit is undertaken at Christmas by the *momís* or *guloyas* of the "*cocolo*" enclave of San Pedro de Macorís, accompanied by a fife, a bass drum, and a triangle, and in cane settlements (*bateyes*) by the Haitian-Dominican *gagá* groups, with musical ensembles and baton-twirling routines of costumed *mayores*.

Throughout Roman Catholic America, Carnaval is another season for merriment, musical performance, and artistic creativity with masks, costumes, and musical motifs for parade groups. It is celebrated mainly in Santo Domingo, Santiago, La Vega, Cotuí, Monte Cristi, and Cabral, Barahona. Its date is associated not with the start of Lent, but with the political holidays of 27 February (independence from Haiti) and secondarily 16 August (independence from Spain) except in Cabral, where it is celebrated during the three days after Good Friday. The *gagá* societies also celebrate a post–Good Friday Carnaval in cane communities, at least in those near Barahona. Dominican masking on a national scale emphasizes a bovine motif, perhaps representing a syncretism between horned creatures of two different origins: the Christian devil and the Central African totemic ox.

Urban social dance

Social dances, concert bands, and dance bands are major vehicles of musical exchange between localities, social classes, and traditions. Since 1844 at the latest, dance-band musicians have served as conduits for the introduction of rural genres of dancing into the halls of the urban elite and, conversely, for the transmission of urban fashions in social dancing, often of foreign origin, to rural areas. In the late 1700s and early 1800s, the vogue was the *contredanse* and the *quadrilles*, and in the mid-1800s, the Central European waltz, *mazurka*, and polka. The *danzón* of Cuba and the *danza* of Puerto Rico—upper-class urban Latin American creole dance genres that became fashionable in the late 1800s—are still enjoyed on radio in the Dominican Republic and are occasionally danced to. By the 1920s, the rage was U.S. dances: one-steps, two-steps, and fox-trots. In the 1920s, the Dominican *merengue* of the Cibao began to be introduced into dance halls (Alberti 1975); it was promoted after 1930 by Trujillo, who had his own dance bands and bandleader-composers. The *merengue* style of the 1930s to 1950s is still popular as a facet of urban musical patrimony.

At the same time, the orchestrated *merengue* continues to evolve. Since the 1920s, band instruments have been added to the traditional ensemble, starting with the alto saxophone, the most characteristic instrument of the ballroom *merengue* band after the *tambora*. During Trujillo's time, the orchestrated *merengue* was adapted for the ballroom. An initial "stroll" (*paseo*) was added to situate partners on the dance floor. After Trujillo's fall, arrangers added other jazz band instruments to the *merengue* and made stylistic changes in it, including a marked acceleration and middle *montuno* or improvised and responsorial section, as in *salsa*. The contemporary *merengue* bandleader Johnny Ventura (born ca. 1940) is credited with compositions and recordings intended for a broader, international audience. Currently, the modern orchestrated *merengue* is enjoying popularity throughout the Spanish-speaking world as the trendiest Latino dance rhythm (Alberti 1975; Austerlitz 1997), but within Dominican musical culture, the ballroom *merengue* coexists with its unchanging progenitor, the folkloric *perico ripiao*. The vitality of the *merengue* is due to its role as a symbol of national identity. The folk *merengue* represents a rural, traditional identity, and the orchestrated *merengue* represents an urban, modern one.

Urban song

Merengues were composed for dance bands by composers seeking inspiration in rural, nonliterate genres for the creation of songs and dances of the literate tradition with piano or band accompaniment directed toward urban audiences. Leading composer-conductors of this century included Julio Alberto Hernández (b. 1900) (Hernández 1969) and Alberti (1906–1976). Several songs, including "Quisqueya" and danceable *merengues* such as Alberti's "Compadre Pedro Juan," have passed from the literate to the oral urban tradition and are taken as collective musical symbols of national identity.

Another type of urban music is the sentimental song of *trovadores*, crooners of serenades and parties, who strum acoustic guitars and sing amorous courtship songs in settings where alcohol is consumed. Their songs are transmitted largely orally from person to person and more recently through recordings and broadcasts. Their medium and function and certain of their genres (especially the *bolero* and the *vals*) are shared with their counterparts in other Latin American cities and towns. Other genres are Hispanic Caribbean (such as the Cuban-influenced *son*) or specifically Dominican (such as the *criolla*, a lyrical song in 6/8 time, virtually unknown outside the country). The *son* tradition is maintained in Afro-Dominican sectors in the capital by the old Soneros de Borojols and ensembles of younger musicians in Villa Mella.

Urban folk-based music

Two urban musical genres affirm national identity through the performance of folk-based music: the folk-dance troupe (*ballet folklórico*) and the human-rights-based protest song (*nueva canción*, in Cuba called *nueva trova*). Both are genres unto themselves. The first documented fieldwork-based folk-dance troupe was founded in Miches about 1941 by René Carrasco, a self-made folklorist, and the next was established in the capital by Edna Garrido (b. 1913) at the public university about 1945. Later groups, though essentially derivatives of Carrasco's, lack fieldwork-based authenticity and exhibit the accelerated tempi, the uniform costumery, the synchronized movements, and the entertainment and national-identity agenda typical of this genre throughout Latin America. Starting about 1973, Fradique Lizardo founded a presumably research-based troupe, for which he achieved appointment as National Folk-Dance Troupe (Ballet Folklórico Nacional).

Dominican protest songs share the pan–Latin American style of *nueva canción* or *nueva trova*. They are typically guitar-accompanied and, as descendants of the *décima* (the old *trova*), explicitly articulate its ideology. Members of Convite, the group founded about 1975 by Dagoberto Tejeda, were jailed. The lead singer, Luis Días, probably the most authentic and creative of Dominican popular-music composers, was persecuted and now lives in New York. His compositions, based on his rural musical background and later observations, tap Hispanic and Afro-Dominican heritages, fused with the human-rights ideology of *nueva canción*. His compositions have nourished numerous commercial and new-song musicians, including the singer Sonia Silvestre (1994?). Others, mainly of urban origin, have fused Afro-Dominican traditions with new-song verbosity and ideology; they include, in Santo Domingo and New York City, groups led by Toni Vicioso, José Duluc, Edis Sánchez, and William Alemán.

National anthem

The national anthem of the Dominican Republic, titled "Quisqueyanos valientes" ("Valiant Dominicans"), was composed by José Rufino Reyés Siancas (1835–1905) in 1883 to lyrics by Emilio Prud'homme (1856–1932), also written in 1883. It was adopted as the national anthem of the Dominican Republic in 1934.

MUSIC LEARNING, DISSEMINATION, TOURISM, AND PUBLIC POLICY

Education, including musical education, is nationally centralized, administered from the capital. The Ministry of Education, Fine Arts, and Religion is housed in a neoclassical complex built in 1956. The Ten-Year Plan for Education, announced in 1992 by presidential degree and in 1996 awarded a loan of $100 million loan from the World Bank and the Inter-American Development Bank, does not mention music education in its four-volume initial document (Congreso Nacional de Educación 1992) but refers to national culture, art, and folklore. Teacher training in music is still poor: only one music-appreciation class occurs in the teacher-training program at the public university. Public-school teachers, especially of elementary classes, have poor and declining skills and are poorly paid; their classrooms lack audiovisual facilities, materials, instruments, and often electricity.

The National Conservatory of Music was founded in the capital in 1942. Each regional capital has a conservatory that serves elite and middle-class men and women. Young men of the middle and lower classes learn theory and band instruments in public academies of music located in practically every one of the provincial capitals by the 1920s (Anon. 1978:77); these academies are in decline due to underfunding. Their purpose is to train musicians for municipal bands. They were supported by Trujillo, whom they honored with military marches on his visits. There are private academies too. Literacy in music provides income and social mobility for musicians of municipal and military bands, as does military service. During the colonial occupation, the military band represented an arm of military conquest and occupation. Since 1844, the municipal and military bands (most notably of Santiago, Puerto Plata, and the capital) have served as training grounds and laboratories for the great conductors and composers of art music and popular song and dance. Municipal bands also serve public education by providing public access to music. In their regular Thursday and Sunday evening public concerts (*retretas*) in the bandstand (*glorieta*) of the public square (*parque*)—a custom now almost extinct—the band opens the program with the national anthem, then plays musical arrangements, especially of operatic overtures, and then dance music, traditionally ending with a *merengue* and a reprise of the national anthem.

Other performances of many types of music in the capital occur in the theater at the Palace of Fine Arts (built in 1956) and the amphitheater Agua y Luz of the Feria de la Paz government-building complex (1956), the National Theater (1973), neighborhood-club-administered indoor stadiums (including the Mauricio Báez Stadium in the barrio of San Carlos), the national outdoor Quisqueya Stadium (seating about thirty thousand), public basketball courts (including the Sports Palace), the private Casa de Teatro (1974) for counterculture arts, numerous nightclubs, elite social clubs, and public neighborhood cultural-sports clubs. In the southeast near La Romana, the tourist complex Altos de Chavón has a large amphitheater for commercial shows for people mainly from the capital. Venues in Santiago include the Colón Theater, the Centro de la Cultura (about 1982, currently semi-privatized and being expanded into a four-unit Plaza de la Cultura), the Gran Teatro Regional del Cibao (1995, seating eighteen hundred), the Amphitheater of the Pontificia Universidad Católica Madre y Maestra (PUCMM, seating fewer than a thousand), the Cibao Stadium (seating about twenty-five thousand), public basketball courts, and a weekly *peña* (a nocturnal musical gathering in a southern Spanish context, associated with the counterculture in modern Latin America) at the Casa del Arte (in a patio behind the Alianza Francesa, the French language institute), elite social clubs, and popular neighborhood clubs.

Paralleling the role of yesteryear's bandsmen, the recording and broadcast media serve as conduits between urban and rural areas, and between international and national arenas. The first foreign recordings entered the Dominican Republic in 1913, and the first recordings done there were made by Victor in 1928. The first radio station, HIX, was founded in 1928, and its first live broadcast was by the great baritone Eduardo Brito (Incháustegui 1988). HIN, La Voz del Partido Dominicano (The Voice of the Dominican Party), started broadcasting in 1936. Trujillo's absolute dictatorship stunted the recording and broadcast industries, since he promoted or stymied musicians at will.

During the Trujillo era, musical broadcasts favored pieces composed in honor of the dictator. Trujillo's fall (1961) allowed a flourishing of broadcast and publishing media. The event virtually coincided with the Cuban Revolution, when Cubans involved in the music industry fled Cuba; some went to the Dominican Republic. At present, there are more than a hundred radio stations in the country, some with local and others with virtually national range. About three, operated by the Roman Catholic Church, transmit educational programs.

The most popular station among the rural and marginal urban sectors is Radio Guarachita, which has almost national coverage and includes a recording enterprise. Its programming focuses largely on folk *merengues* and the Mexican *bolero* and *ranchera*, as beloved locally as if they were home-grown genres. Since the 1980s, the station has recorded and promoted a newly commercialized genre, *bachata*, a steel-stringed-guitar-accompanied whiny male lament (Pacini Hernández 1995). *Bachata*, derived from the *décima* tradition, has probably been in oral traditions for a century, but has only recently been marketed. In the late 1980s and 1990s, Juan Luis Guerra reinterpreted the *perico ripiao* and the *bachata* for marketing to the urban elite. All social sectors enjoy broadcasts of the romantic *boleros* of *trovadores* and the gentile nineteenth-century dance music, especially the Puerto Rican *danza* and the Cuban *danzón*; more popular sectors enjoy the Cuban *son* and *guaracha*.

In the 1980s and 1990s, television, especially live variety shows, has played an important role in disseminating *merengue*. TV has promoted the showy, nightclub *bolero* (now called *balada*) of pan-Hispanic big business—a far cry from the romantic sincerity and acoustic accompaniment of the *trovador*. Currently, cable television, which brings international broadcasting to the capital, Santiago, and other cities, is a new dimension in broadcast media; it will undoubtedly have some impact on musical taste.

The racial and cultural contrast between the Dominican Republic and Haiti lies at the core of Dominican national cultural policy. In 1804, St. Domingue, through slave revolution, became the second free country in the Americas (the first being the United States), taking on the Taíno name of Haïti and defining itself as a black republic. The Haitian occupation of Santo Domingo (1822–1844) is cited by the twentieth-century Dominican elite as justification for the official affirmation of *hispanidad* (Hispanic racial and cultural purity) and the repulsion of all that is black, African, or Haitian. This policy, promoted by dictator Rafael Leonidas Trujillo Molina (1930–1961), has continued under successive governments.

Despite this policy, most members of the intellectual elite would find Spanish and African-derived extremes of Dominican nonliterate music to sound so foreign as to seem "un-Dominican." This is because of the marked gulf in Latin America between rural and urban and between literate and nonliterate cultures. All modern countries, including the Dominican Republic, are culturally heterogeneous with regard to region, locale (rural or urban), and social class. "Dominican culture" thus represents different realities to different social sectors.

Since the 1970s, nonelite urban youths have opposed *hispanidad* through their ethnographic search for and artistic expression of an Afro-Dominican identity, at home and in New York (Davis 1994b). At the same time, erudite scholarship, filling a niche in the post-Trujillo era, has documented Afro-Dominican history. Eventually, Dominican scholars, musicians, and the public will probably arrive at a realistic view of Dominican culture as essentially a creole composite, born in the New World of the fusion and evolution of multiple cultural components.

FURTHER STUDY

Further basic ethnographic research is needed on nonliterate rural musical traditions, with the publication of texts and particularly audio and visual recordings, with excellent annotation, preferably in English and Spanish, addressed to Dominicans (many of whom are unfamiliar with the panorama of their national musical culture) and non-Dominicans, and intelligible for the public and specialists.

Folkways published several recordings of various genres by Verna Gillis (1976a, 1976b, 1976c, 1978), but she did not have the ethnographic background to prepare in-depth notes; the one on Haitian *rará* and Dominican *gagá* has been republished with the notes revised by Gage Averill (1991). Republishing needs to be done for the other recordings. Morton Marks published a Folkways recording of a longdrum festival in San Cristóbal Province (1983), and John Storm Roberts published recordings with reliable but short notes (recorded in early 1970s). The field collection of Dominican tales by Manuel J. Andrade (1930, 1976) has been crying for classification; this work should be followed with a restudy with audio recording. Ethnographic work should not merely emphasize the trendy Afro-Dominican traditions; it should include the Hispanic heritage, which represents the oldest folk-European continuities in the New World, including Hispanic or creole dance genres that are virtually extinct. The field collections of Garrido Boggs (about 1947 and following) and J. M. Coopersmith (1944) in the American Folklife Center at the Library of Congress should be annotated, guided by Coopersmith's book and Garrido Boggs's publications, and an unpublished manuscript (about 1953).

There is a need to take down oral histories of song-and-dance composers of the written and oral traditions, bandleaders, and *trovadores*, focusing on the history of popular musical culture through life history. Bernarda Jorge's book (1982) does not do this, missing an important source. The study of brass bands is also needed. Such work would require the collection and conservation of scores of compositions by local bandleaders; this could be the job of the National Archive of Music, but it has no operating budget. Scores and recordings of Dominican art-music compositions also need to be published and recorded.

REFERENCES

Alberti, Luis. 1975. *De música y orquestas bailables dominicanas, 1910–1959.* Santo Domingo: Museo del Hombre Dominicano.

Andrade, Manuel J. 1930. *Folk-Lore from the Dominican Republic. Memoirs of the American Folklore Society*, 23. New York: American Folklore Society.

———. 1976 [1930]. *Folklore de la República Dominicana.* Santo Domingo: Sociedad Dominicana de Bibliófilos.

Anon. 1978. "Música." *Enciclopedia Dominicana.* 2nd ed. 5:75–88.

Austerlitz, Paul. 1997. *Merengue: Dominican Music and Dominican Identity*. Philadelphia: Temple University Press.

Congreso Nacional de Educación. 1992. *Un pacto con la patria y el futuro de la educación dominicana*. Plan Decenal de Educación, A, 1. Santo Domingo: Secretaría de Estado de Educación, Bellas Artes y Cultos.

Coopersmith, J. M. 1976 [1949]. *Music and Musicians of the Dominican Republic / Música y músicos de la República Dominicana*. Edited by Charles Seeger. Pan American Union, Music Series, 15. Santo Domingo: Dirección General de Cultura de la República Dominicana.

Davis, Martha Ellen. 1976. "Afro-Dominican Religious Brotherhoods: Structure, Ritual, and Music." Ph.D. dissertation, University of Illinois at Urbana-Champaign.

———. 1980a. "Aspectos de la influencia africana en la música tradicional dominicana." *Boletín del Museo del Hombre Dominicano* 13:255–292.

———.1980b. "La cultura musical religiosa de los 'americanos' de Samaná." *Boletín del Museo del Hombre Dominicano* 15:127–169.

———. 1980c. "'That Old-Time Religion': Tradición y cambio en el enclave 'americano' de Samaná." *Boletín del Museo del Hombre Dominicano* 14:165–196.

———. 1981a. "Himnos y anthems (coros) de los 'americanos' de Samaná: Contextos y estilos." *Boletín del Museo del Hombre Dominicano* 16:85–107.

———. 1981b. *Voces del Purgatorio: Estudio de la Salve dominicana*. Santo Domingo: Museo del Hombre Dominicano.

———. 1983. "Cantos de esclavos y libertos: Cancionero de anthems (coros) de Samaná." *Boletín del Museo del Hombre Dominicano* 18:197–236.

———. 1987a. *La otra ciencia: El vodú dominicano como religión y medicina populares*. Santo Domingo: Universidad Autónoma de Santo Domingo.

———. 1987b. "Native Bi-Musicality: Case Studies from the Caribbean." *Pacific Review of Ethnomusicology* 4:39–55.

———. 1994a. "'Bi-Musicality' in the Cultural Configurations of the Caribbean." *Black Music Research Journal* 14(2):145–160.

———. 1994b. "Music and Black Ethnicity in the Dominican Republic." In *Music and Black Ethnicity in the Caribbean and South America*, ed. Gerard Béhague, 119–155. Miami: North-South Center, University of Miami.

Garrido Boggs, Edna. 1946. *Versiones dominicanas de romances españoles*. Ciudad Trujillo: Pol Hermanos.

———. 1980 [1955]. *Folklore infantil de Santo Domingo*. Santo Domingo: Sociedad Dominicana de Bibliófilos.

———. 1961. "Panorama del Folklore Dominicano." *Folklore Américas*, 11(1–2):1–23.

Gillis, Verna. 1976a. *The Island of Quisqueya*. Folkways FE 4281. LP disk.

———. 1976b. *The Island of Española*. Folkways FE 4282. LP disk.

———. 1976c. *Cradle of the New World*. Folkways FE 4283. LP disk.

———. 1978. *Songs from the North*. Folkways FE 4284. LP disk.

Gillis, Verna, and Daniel Pérez Martínez. 1978. *Rara in Haiti / Gaga in the Dominican Republic*. Folkways FE 4531. 2 LP disks.

Gillis, Verna, and Gage Averill. 1991. *Caribbean Revels: Haitian Rara and Dominican Gaga*. Smithsonian Folkways CD SF 40402. Compact disc and republished notes.

Hernández, Julio Alberto. 1969. *Música tradicional dominicana*. Santo Domingo: Julio D. Postigo.

Incháustegui, Arístides. 1988. *El disco en la República Dominicana*. Santo Domingo: Amigo del Hogar.

Jorge, Bernarda. 1982. *La música dominicana: Siglos XIX–XX*. Santo Domingo: Universidad Autónoma de Santo Domingo.

Las Casas, Bartolomé de. 1958. *Apologética historia sumaria*. Madrid: Biblioteca de Autores Españoles.

Marks, Morton. 1983. *Afro-Dominican Music from San Cristóbal, Dominican Republic*. Folkways FE 4285. LP disk.

Pacini Hernández, Deborah. 1995. *Bachata: A Social History of a Dominican Popular Music*. Philadelphia: Temple University Press.

Roberts, John Storm, compiler. 1972. *Caribbean Island Music: Songs and Dances of Haiti, the Dominican Republic and Jamaica*. Nonesuch H-72047. LP disk.

———. N.d. *Singers of the Cibao*. Tivoli, N.Y.: Original Music OML 403CC. Cassette.

Rosenberg, June. 1979. *El Gagá: Religión y sociedad de un culto dominicano—Un estudio comparativo*. Santo Domingo: Universidad Autónoma de Santo Domingo.

Silvestre, Sonia. 1994? *Quiero andar*. Oi Records, PR 200. LP disk.

Puerto Rico

Héctor Vega Drouet

Puerto Rico is a small Caribbean island just east of the Dominican Republic and west of the Virgin Islands. Like the U.S. Virgin Islands, Puerto Rico is a colony (commonwealth) of the United States, to which it was ceded by Spain in 1898 following the Spanish-American War. It became the Commonwealth of Puerto Rico in 1952, but unlike the people of the Virgin Islands, Puerto Ricans traditionally speak Spanish, though many speak English in urban areas. As a former Spanish colony, Puerto Rico shares much history and culture with Cuba and the Dominican Republic.

THE INDIGENOUS HERITAGE

Archaeological excavations have yielded evidence that thousands of years ago, indigenous people inhabited the island known today as Puerto Rico. Early inhabitants may have used it and other Caribbean Islands as a type of bridge in their travels south from North America or north from South America. Later, Arawak Amerindians from northern South America migrated from Paria Bay into the Caribbean Antilles. By the time Christopher Columbus sailed into the Caribbean, the Arawak-speaking Taíno were firmly established in the island the Amerindians called Borinquen, the present Puerto Rico ("Rich Port"). Excavated pottery, domestic wooden items, and stone sculptures of deities confirm their existence. Archaeological examination of Arawak midden sites has revealed evidence of gourd rasps with scrapers (*güiros*); conch trumpets (*guamos*); wooden trumpets; pieces of a hollowed log with an H-shaped slit (similar to the *teponaztli*, an ancient Mexican hollowed log idiophone); shell, clay, wood, and gourd rattles (*maracas*); clay ocarinas; clay and bone whistles; and a bone flute.

From the descriptions of Arawak musical activities in the writings of the Spanish chroniclers (Cárdenas 1981; Casas 1965; López de Gómara 1965; Pané 1974), we learn that the *areyto* (also *areito*)—a celebration that combined poetry, songs, and dances, with accompanying instruments—was the most important social activity in Taíno everyday life. *Areytos* had a historical, religious, ritual, or ceremonial nature, and the chroniclers describe twenty different types. A principal singer or dancer set the order in which poems, songs, and dances were to be performed. Every child was taught the items appropriate for each occasion and how to improvise *areytos* as new situations arose. The *areyto* was the Taíno's ideal means of communal socialization and reinforcement of shared beliefs and customs. In the performance of an *areyto*, according to chroniclers, Amerindian elders sang the low voices, while the young sang the upper voices; women sang the soprano, alto, and tenor voices; and Taíno singing was not harsh to European ears. There are no other descriptions or analyses of indigenous melodies by the early Spanish in Borinquen.

THE EUROPEAN HERITAGE

Columbus and his fleet of seventeen ships during his second voyage sailed past the southern coast of Borinquen in 1493, perhaps making landfall near the present Puerto Rican town of San Germán (Rouse 1992:147). It was not until 1508, however, that Juan Ponce de León established Spanish settlements in the southwestern and northeastern part of the island, regions where gold was found. The second of these settlements developed into the present capital of San Juan (ibid.:155). Around 1510, the Spanish colonization of Puerto Rico forced the Taíno into hard labor, and many native people succumbed to European diseases for which they had little or no natural immunity. In official records by the early 1600s, the Taíno no longer appeared as a distinct people; however, small bands of them survived by taking refuge in remote and inaccessible hills, areas later called *indieras*.

In Seville, in the *Casa de Contracción* (Contract Clearinghouse), sixteenth-century inventories detailing items sent to Spanish colonies include jingle bells, *vihuela* (early type of guitar) strings, clavichord strings, and fifes. Alfonso de Buenaño, boatswain, brought the first *vihuela* to Puerto Rico aboard the ship *Santiago* on 19 September 1512. A Mr. Quintana also brought a *vihuela* to Puerto Rico on 25 December 1512, when he arrived aboard the *San Francisco*. Subsequently, other *vihuelas* arrived. Juan Martín, a passenger aboard the *San Juan*, brought the first guitar to Puerto Rico on 11 December 1516 (Tanodi 1971).

The 1520s and 1530s were chaotic and disastrous for Puerto Rico, as the discovery of gold in New Spain (Mexico), Peru, and Venezuela lured settlers away. The Spanish population shrank by half. The island became isolated from other colonies; for those who remained, life became austere, and social events were limited. The Roman Catholic Church sponsored the official music activities of the island. Family parties and other informal activities with music were organized by the African slaves and enslaved Indians (*enco-mendados* "charges") officially in Spanish hands. In this population—Spaniards, enslaved Africans and Indians, free Arawaks in the *indieras*—lay the foundation for the creolization (meaning the miscegenation) of Puerto Rico.

By the 1540s, the island was no longer commercially important within the Spanish New World. Most of its merchandise, including musical instruments, was secondhand. For accompaniment to dancing by creole Puerto Ricans, the absence of instruments created a preference for singing, rather than solely instrumental music, and stimulated local craftsmen to build their own instruments.

THE AFRICAN HERITAGE

Compared to the other islands in the Greater Antilles, Puerto Rico's African presence is unique. While African slavery to Puerto Rico was authorized by Spain in 1513, most of the African laborers were freemen (and women) from Spain who were Christians known as *ladinos*. They worked as gold miners, domestic servants, and soldiers. Fewer than two thousand African slaves were forced to work in Puerto Rico in the first half of the sixteenth century, and the island's sugar cane industry did not develop there until the nineteenth century. Spain's interest during the first three hundred years was Mexico and its gold, and Puerto Rico was more important for its ports of call for the Spanish military. As the sugar industry developed in the Greater Antilles, however, African slaves mainly from Guinea and Senegal were imported, and the number of slaves reached nearly twenty-two thousand by the second decade of the nineteenth century and over fifty thousand by mid century, most of the last additions from Ghana, Nigeria, and Congo (Grano de Oro 2004). Slavery was officially abolished in Puerto Rico in 1873.

MUSICAL INSTRUMENTS

Idiophones

Most hard-surface percussive instruments used in Puerto Rico are also found in other Spanish-speaking Caribbean cultures. These instruments include the *claves*, cowbell, and *güiro* scraper used in *salsa* and other dance musics, and the *maracas* used in *jíbaro* music (with the others just listed). Many instruments are machine made, but there are still local makers of the *güiro*, fashioned from a gourd (Figure 12.1).

One distinctly African instrument common in Puerto Rico, as in many parts of the circum-

Figure 12.1
A *güiro* ("gourd scraper") under construction. Photo by Héctor Vega Drouet, 1995.

Figure 12.2
A *marímbula* player.
Photo by Héctor Vega
Drouet, 1995.

Caribbean area, is the *marímbula*, an idiophone similar to the African *mbira* and *kalimba*, with several tuned metal lamellae mounted over a hole in a wooden box. As is still the practice in Cuba, the player would sit atop the box and pluck the lamellae with his fingers, supplying the bass for a small instrumental ensemble. The *marímbula* and its associated musical tradition arrived with slaves between 1800 and 1880 but quickly dissipated at the beginning of the 1900s. The *marímbula* has not been part of the rural tradition of Puerto Rico since the 1950s, and in the previous five decades there had been but a few isolated builders and players of the instrument (Figure 12.2).

Membranophones

The distinctly Puerto Rican *bomba* drum is a single-headed cylindrical instrument resembling an open-ended straight barrel. The drumhead is about 40 centimeters in diameter and about 75 centimeters long. Originally, the tension of the drumhead was fixed by six pegs. However, after Mr. Aquino, the lone drum builder at Loíza Aldea, discontinued making drums in the 1970s, *bomba* drumheads were fixed by screws, just as on commercial drums. Since 1994, Jesús Cepeda has opened a shop in Loíza Aldea, where he builds pegged *bomba* drums, reestablishing the tradition.

The *bomba* drum is placed between a seated musician's knees and played with the hands only. Two *bomba* drums are usually at the center of an ensemble including rattles, responsorial singers, and often other percussion instruments. One *bomba* drum (*sonador*) plays a relatively fixed pattern, and the other (*repicador*) plays a more variable one, improvising in the style of West African drumming.

The *pandereta* is a round frame drum, like a tambourine without jingles. The traditional grouping in Puerto Rico is three *panderetas* of graduated sizes playing three different interlocking parts, with the highest-pitched one having an improvising role. One or more melodic instruments, singers (in a responsorial style with choral refrain), and other percussion instruments are often added.

Many other membranophones are found in Puerto Rico. Most are a part of the Latino tradition, with origins or parallels in Cuba and/or the Dominican Republic. From Cuban background or influence, for example, are the *bongos* and *congas*, and from the Dominican Republic is the *tambora* [see CUBA; DOMINICAN REPUBLIC].

Chordophones

There is no published research on the origins, history, and construction of early European-derived Puerto Rican rural instruments. Notable were four plucked-lute chordophones: *tiple*, *tres*, *cuatro*, and *bordonúa* (Figure 12.3). There are no historical data about, nor are

Figure 12.3
The Puerto Rican luthier Julio Negrón Rivera in his shop in Morovis. Left to right: cuatro, tiple, and bordonúa. Photo by Daniel E. Sheehy.

informants able to ascertain, the exact date or decade in which these instruments were first made. It appears probable, though, that the musical genre called *seis* (discussed below) was always performed on these instruments, and the *seis* was first used in the early 1600s.

Most of these instruments are hourglass shaped, with occasional regional variations. Respondents mention a three-stringed instrument called *requinto*, with the tuning e^1–a^1–c#2. This instrument is a variant of the common *tres*, that is similar in size, but has three triple-stringed courses (for a total of nine strings) tuned to A–d–f#. The *tiple* "treble" appears to derive from the *timple*, a single-coursed vihuela from Andalucía, Spain. It is 56 centimeters long, with a 24-centimeter body, a 16-centimeter neck (*brazo*), and a 14-centimeter pegbox (*pala* or *mano*). The tuning of the five strings is A–e–B_1–G–B.

The *cuatro* is the most popular and common of the melodic instruments. Its earlier, four-double-stringed form gave way to its current, five double-stringed courses. The strings of the *cuatro* are tuned in octaves, except for the first two courses (tuned in unison). The present tuning, B_1–E–A–d–g, is the same as that of sixteenth-century *vihuelas* and lutes. The *cuatro* is about 90 centimeters long, with a 50-centimeter body, a 20-centimeter neck, and a 20-centimeter pegbox.

The name of the *bordonúa* comes from the word *bordón* (similar to the French *bourdon*), roughly meaning "bass." It resembles late-seventeenth-century Spanish instruments on which low-pitched, double-stringed courses include a thick string tuned an octave lower than its companion. The modern tuning of the *bordonúa* is G#–C#–F#–B–e–a, with the first three double-stringed courses tuned in unison and the last three in octaves. It is used primarily to play a bass, rather than a chordal background.

Though craftsmen carve instruments from any native hardwood, they prefer *guaraguao*, *jagüey*, or *maga*. For the soundboard, they use *yagrumo*, a light softwood. To avoid difficulty attaching the neck to the sound box, native makers carve the entire instrument, except the soundboard, from a single block of wood, and then sand the instrument down to the appropriate dimensions and thickness.

Religious forms

The *rosario cantao* ("sung rosary") is an important set of songs, practices, and beliefs that have developed in Puerto Rico around the rosary, a cycle of prayers marked with a circular string of fifty-nine beads. Following Spanish flight from the island around 1530, local versions of Roman Catholic practices began to take shape among the non-Spanish majority population, entirely outside ecclesiastical settings.

There are three types of *rosario cantao*: the *rosario de promesas* ("rosary of promises," to the Virgin Mary or to a saint), the *rosario a la Santa Cruz* ("rosary to the Holy Cross"), and the *rosario para los muertos* ("rosary for the dead"). These sung rosaries are similar to the ecclesiastically sanctioned one, though they are not sung inside a church. Each cycle of fifty-nine prayers (*tercio del rosario* or "third of a rosary"), corresponds to the two-month lunar cycle of fifty-nine days—a reference to the femininity of the Virgin Mary. The Hail Mary dominates the rosary.

The most common poetic forms found in the sung rosary are couplets (*coplas*), *décimas*, and *decimillas*. The typical *jíbaro* ("country people") musical ensemble— *tiple* or *cuatro*, guitar, *güiro*—often accompanies all three types. During the *novenario de difuntos*, it performs only between *tercios*, when the singers take a break.

The *rosario de promesas* is the most common category of these rosaries. The organizer of the ritual offers to the Virgin or to a saint a promise in return for the solution to a problem—an exchange between the metaphysical world and the material world.

The devotee keeps an image of the Virgin or saint on an altar at home. Treated as a member of the family, this image receives prayers, petitions, and supplications—and when necessary, scolding and punishment. The devotee may formally present a petition to the image, with a promise that if the saint intercedes with God and God grants the petition, the devotee will carry out the promise. The promise is specified during the petition, and the quality of the promise will be equal to the importance of the petition. One of the most common promises the *jíbaros* make is to sponsor a complete rosary once a year for so many years.

The rosary of promises begins at vespers the night before the promise is made. It lasts all night. When it ends (usually between six and seven a.m.), the participants say a short daybreak rosary before disassembling the altar. If the organizers have funds left, they will pay the musical group that accompanied the rosary throughout the night or contract a new group to play at a party that will last until noon. Obviously, carrying out a promise can require a lot of effort and money.

The *rosario a la Santa Cruz* follows a similar plan; however, it is performed particularly in May—a remnant of a long-standing Christian tradition of dedicating the month of May to Mary, possibly representing fertility as celebrated in pre-Christian rites of spring (see Davis 1972).

The *rosario para los muertos* is a ritual related to death or dying. It requires thirty-three *tercios*, two novenaries (*novenarios*), and the wake (*velorio*).

This rosary begins with a novenary (nine *tercios*), followed by the wake (thirteen *tercios*). The third section, the novenary for the dead (*novenario de difuntos*), is held for nine consecutive nights after the day of the burial. A *tercio* is said on each of the first eight nights, and three *tercios* are said on the last night. The total of thirty-three *tercios* corresponds to Jesus' supposed age at his death.

Secular forms

Bomba

The first written record of an African musical tradition in Puerto Rico dates from 11 November 1797, when André Pierre Ledrú, a visitor to the island, witnessed an African dance called *bomba* at a party in the farmhouse of a Don Benito in the town of Aibonito (Ledrú 1971:47). Another substantiation is found in a letter dated 9 October 1840 in the Reports of the Spanish Governors of Puerto Rico (entry 23, box 66), whereby Ciriaco Sabat, "King of the Blacks of the Congo Nation," formally requested permission to perform *bomba* dances on the plaza during religious feasts in honor of St. Michael (29 September) and Our Lady of the Rosary (7 October) and reminded the governor that since time immemorial permission to play *bombas* had annually been granted. This suggests that the tradition was then at least a few generations old—which could reasonably date it to the period of 1700–1750. This dating coincides with the belief of the people of Loíza Aldea, who say their tradition of dancing and drumming the *seis de bomba* at the cathedral of San Juan dates to the 1600s as part of the original series of *seises*.

The *bomba* dance was the slaves' and free blacks' most important social event and means of expression. They performed it on special dates, at the end of harvesting, and as part of important festivities and private parties—birthdays, christenings, weddings, and the like. It served as an occasion for meetings and as a signal for rebellions. In the eastern, southern, and western part of the island, the traditions of drumming derives from the *musique de maison* ("house music") of Haiti and Martinique, and resemble the *tumba francesa* of Oriente Province, Cuba. This resulted from migrations of French colonizers with their slaves to the southern coast of Puerto Rico during the Haitian Revolution (1780–1805).

Over time, immigration and cultural change led to musical change. African master drummers associated rhythmic patterns with the words they closely paralleled; the patterns served as mnemonic devices for learning and remembering. The loss of African languages meant the demise of this system. From the 1690s to the 1790s, the promise of freedom for African slaves on their arrival in Puerto Rico attracted slaves from around the Caribbean and resulted in musical acculturation. Consequently, *cunyá*, *leró*, *yubá*, *sicá*, *grasimá*, *holandés*, and *calindá* are among the types of *bombas* brought to Puerto Rico, thus making *bomba* a generic name.

Each type of *bomba* directly relates to the basic ostinato rhythmic pattern on the second drum (*sonador*). The essence of the *bomba* dance was reduced to a challenge between the improvised beats of the first drum (*repicador*) and the dancer's improvised steps. Since about the 1960s, many drummers have felt the economic necessity of performing in *salsa*, *merengue*, or *guaguancó* ensembles and have begun to mix rhythms of these musics with those of *bomba*, drastically adulterating the style.

Today in Loíza Aldea in the north and Guayama in the south (Dufrasne-González 1996), the *bomba* is danced by men and women who move separately, within a circle formed by the audience. On one side of the circle are two *bomba* drums. The elders of the community stand to the right of the drums or sit behind the drums. The second drummer begins to play the basic rhythmic pattern, while the first drummer is idle. The singer begins the song, and the dancer approaches the drums from the opposite side of the circle to get the first drummer's attention and challenge him. The dancer now begins his improvised dance, which consists mostly of steps, jumps, abrupt body movements, stamping of feet or heels, and/or shoulder movements and whirls. Male dancers seem to prefer jumps, with exaggerated foot and leg movements. Female dancers favor whirls and arm movements. The central idea is that drummers should be able to synchronize a beat to each dance movement. Naturally, the improvisation is due to the present lack of a drum language. It is not known if a drum language was ever established. [Listen to "Se Oye Una Voz"]

Décima

The *décima* is one of the oldest, commonest, and most popular creole traditions of the rural people (*jíbaros*) of Puerto Rico. Its performance usually combines poetry and music. A poet, according to rural respondents, is a person who cannot only compose on a theme according to certain rules of rhetoric, but one who can also improvise. Similarly, a *cantaor* is a person who memorizes *décimas* to sing them. Most esteemed is the *trovador*, who can sing improvised texts on a given topic at the spur of the moment.

The *décima* is the metric combination of ten eight-syllable lines, usually rhyming abba: accddc. A pause follows the fourth line (marked by the colon); otherwise, the rhymes of the last five lines mirror those of the first five. This strophe is associated with the Spanish poet Vicente Martínez Espinel (1550–1624), and many people call it the *espinela*.

Another musical-poetic form, the *decimilla* ("little *décima*"), has a similar structure, though with only six syllables per line. In Puerto Rico, *decimillas* are almost as popular as *décimas*. *Decimillas* based on religious topics are called *aguinaldos*, and those based on secular topics are called *seis con décima*. [Listen to "Los Gallos Cantaron"]

There are no restrictions on the number of stanzas a poet may join into one text on a single theme. One-stanza *décimas* and *décimas* of dozens of stanzas occur. Most common, though, are four-stanza *décimas* based on a four-line poem called *cuarteta* ("couplet"). The last line of the stanzas are, respectively, the first, second, third, and fourth lines of the *cuarteta*. The *jíbaros* call this strophe *décima cuarenticuatro* ("forty-four *décima*"), but it is known elsewhere in the Hispanic world as *glosa* ("gloss"). In some *décimas* with an indefinite number of stanzas, the tenth line is always the same; this structure is known as *pie forzado* or "forced foot."

In the verse endings of a *décima*, Puerto Rican classical poets prefer consonant rhymes, whereas *jíbaros* seem to be more tolerant of assonantal rhymes. Rural people also show mastery of the inner rhythms of the verses—the syllabic accents at the beginning and middle of the line. Poetic meter is mostly trochaic, dactylic, or mixed. The inner rhythm synchronizes the poetry to the musical form, the *seis*.

Seis

There is no comprehensive or scholarly publication treating the history of the *seis*, the most important creole musical genre. Most published articles are speculations by historians or literary scholars who lack musical training. The *seis* is by far the largest corpus of creole music. The tradition includes names, rhythms, instruments, and possibly styles of singing that manifest the historical amalgamation, probably begun in the 1520s and 1530s, of African, Indian, and Spanish traditions.

The instruments that accompanied the *seis* in earlier times were the *cuatro*, the *bordonúa*, and the Amerindian gourd rasp now called *güiro*. The *tres* or the *tiple* sometimes replaced the *cuatro*; respondents insist that neither the *tres* nor the *tiple* played simultaneously with it. Eventually, the guitar replaced the *bordonúa*. A second *cuatro* and bongos joined the group, probably in the 1930s (Figure 12.4); for dance-hall settings since about the 1950s, a double bass has given the ensemble a larger sound.

In broad terms, there are two types of *seis*: one, for dancing, is fast and lively; the other, for singing, is slower. Some names of the former type are related to the choreography of the dance: *zapateado* ("with fancy footwork," from *zapato* meanng "shoe"), *amarrao* ("tied"), *valseao* ("waltzed"), *del pañuelo* ("with a handkerchief"), *del sombrero* ("with a hat"), and *juey* ("crab").

The *seis con décima* is the most common slow *seis* for singing. Some *seises* are known by the names of the towns in which they originate: *orocoveño* (from Orocovis), *bayamonés* (from Bayamón), and *cagüeño* (from Caguas). Others are named after the person who composed or popularized a particular example: *seis fajardeño* (after Mateo Fajardo), *seis de Andino, seis de Pepe Orné, seis Portalatín,* and *seis Villarán*. [Listen to "En un Eterno Poema"] *Seises* influenced by Latin American folk music include *seis de milonga, seis gaucho,* and *seis tango* from Argentina; *seis montuno* and *seis habanero* from Cuba; and *seis joropo* and *seis llanero* from Venezuela.

 DISC 2 TRACK 5

Figure 12.4
In a bar in Puerto Rico, a *conjunto jíbaro* performs *música jíbara* ("country music") for their own enjoyment. Left to right: *güiro, bongos, cuatro,* and guitar, with another guitar in back. Photo by Daniel E. Sheehy, 1994.

Seises with African influences probably go back to the mid-1500s. The rhythmic pattern of the melody in the *seis mapeyé* (in the minor mode) and the *seis montebello* (in the major mode) resembles the Ghanaian Akan *mpintín*, which comes from the Dagombas of Burkina Faso. The word *bomba* is not of Spanish origin, yet there are a *seis bombeao*—an instrumental example, in which people yell "bomba!" and exchange pleasantries in couplets—and a *seis de bomba*, the oldest African dance and drumming tradition in Puerto Rico.

The *seis* tradition may have begun in the mid-1500s (López Cruz 1967, Rosa-Nieves 1967). The number of distinct *seises* extant is probably between about ninety and 117. Each *seis* has its own melody, with which its name is most closely identified. The melody is short, usually a phrase or two. The structure of the *seis con décima* is as follows: the instruments play the traditional theme (or melody) twice as an introduction; the singer starts his or her *décima* right after the introduction; the instruments play the theme only once between stanzas and twice to end the performance.

In the modern *seis* ensemble, the first *cuatro* plays the theme and the second *cuatro* plays a duet with it during the introduction and the ending. During other sections of the *seis*, the first *cuatro* improvises, and the second *cuatro* repeats the theme as an ostinato while the *cantaor* sings memorized *décimas* or the *trovador* improvises *décimas* and melodic lines. Proficient *cuatro* players may alternate roles of ostinato and improvisation. The guitar primarily plays a basso continuo, sometimes chordally reinforcing the rhythmic and harmonic framework. The *güiro* player improvises on four basic rhythmic patterns.

Plena

The *plena*, a genre of dance and music, originated in Ponce around 1900. It was first heard in Ponce in the neighborhood Barriada de la Torre, whose population consisted mostly of immigrants from St. Kitts, Tortola, and St. Thomas, who had settled on the island since the late 1800s. At the beginning, sung texts were not associated with the *plena*, which was rendered by guitar, concertina, and tambourine; eventually, in 1907, singing was added.

The first known ongoing *plena* group consisted of Joselito Oppenheimer, tambourine player and leader; Bernabe Aranzamendi, *güiro* player and singer; and Alfredo (last name not known), concertina player. From their base in the neighborhood of Joya del Castillo, the *plena* spread to southern Ponce (San Antón, El Palo de Pan, La Bomba del Agua, and los Pámpanos). It became popular in Guayama and Mayagüez about 1906, and reached its peak popularity between 1918 and 1924, when the most famous *plenas* were "*El temporal*" ("The Storm"), "*Submarino alemán*" ("German Submarine"), "*Mamita, llegó el obispo*" ("Mommy, the Bishop Has Come"), "*Tanta vanidad*" ("Such Vanity"), and "*Juana Peña me llora*" ("Juana Peña Cries for Me"). The *plena* became so popular that people throughout the island sang and danced it—especially at planned or impromptu get-togethers on the street and at nightclubs (*casinos*).

In the late 1990s, its popularity was still in evidence. New *plenas* appear, in many cases with a new sophistication. Often, they are played by an orchestra with a large percussion section—conga, snare, and bass drum added to or replacing the tambourine. Influential groups, such as El Quinto Olivo and Los Pleneros de la Veintitrés Abajo, increased the number of tambourines and their patterns, and other ensembles have followed suit, including three tambourines in a typical instrumentation. [Listen to "El León"] DISC ❷ TRACK 7

Popular commercial musics

Other than folk musics, popular commercial music in the 1800s was mostly Spanish dance and march music. Migration to and from Venezuela, Mexico, and Cuba influenced Puerto Rican music. The Cuban *danzón* and *contradanza* especially influenced the Puerto Rican *danza*. The Cuban *bolero*, *son*, and *son montuno* have influenced the music of professional *jíbaro* ensembles (see Okada 1995: example 19).

The arrival of the U.S. army in 1898 brought American concepts of marching bands, dance bands, and other music, which was locally most obvious in the 1910s. The predominant influences on Puerto Rican music in the twentieth century have been the following, listed chronologically: recruitment of Puerto Ricans by the U.S. army exposed them to dance-band music and big-band music; economic conditions beginning in the 1920s and the Great Depression of the 1930s caused migration to New York, where prominent musicians and composers heard Cuban, Mexican, North American, and other musical traditions; the immigration of Dominicans in the 1950s brought Dominican musical traditions to Puerto Rico; finally, in the 1960s, third- and fourth-generation Puerto Ricans' returning to the island brought North American commercial music traditions.

Today, jazz, *merengue*, *reggaetón* (rap), rock, and *salsa* have strong followings. Stadium or beach concerts featuring any of these traditions are common. Nightclubs present artists from all these traditions every night. Most local radio stations program one particular tradition, though many broadcast four or five hours of country (*jíbaro*) music daily.

National anthem

Although Puerto Rico is a commonwealth of the United States (making "The Star Spangled Banner" its "official" national anthem), the island culture has its own song that functions ostensibly as its very own national anthem. Titled "La Borinqueña," the song's title and lyrics refer to the original native Amerindian's word for the island: "Boriken" or "Borinquen" (the latter the Spanish spelling). The music for the song was composed by Félix Astol Artés in 1867, and was originally dance music with romantic lyrics by Lola Rodríguez de Tió. The present lyrics are by Manuel Fernández Juncos, but they were not officially adopted by the commonwealth government until 1977 (http://david.national-anthems.net/pr.txt), although the music was officially adopted in 1952 when the island became a commonwealth. The original lyrics are still sung by Puerto Ricans, especially those who follow the independent movement (*los independistas*).

MUSIC LEARNING, DISSEMINATION, AND PUBLIC POLICY

The universities of Puerto Rico are teaching institutions. The Fundación de las Humanidades, the local partner of the National Endowment for the Humanities, has a humanistin-the-community program and a video series on rural traditions; copies of these videos are deposited in libraries and cultural centers in towns throughout the island.

The Casa Paoli Folk Research Center in Ponce sometimes sponsors research. The Institute of Puerto Rican Culture sponsors cultural clubs in every town on the island. Hence, towns or regions can generate festivals and other activities according to their needs and goals.

Supplementing the *seis* tradition in rural areas, the Institute of Puerto Rican Culture sponsors annual town, regional, and national competitions of all the major folk-music traditions.

FURTHER STUDY

An important bibliography for the study of Puerto Rican folk music has been compiled by Donald Thompson (1982), who wrote the only study of the *marímbula* in Puerto Rico and the Caribbean—an instrument he calls "the poor man's bass fiddle" (p. 147). Other studies of African-derived music in Puerto Rico are by Héctor Vega Drouet on the *bomba* and *plena* (1969, 1979) and James McCoy (1968) on indigenous and European influences on Puerto Rican music. An important study of a Roman Catholic event, the *rosario* or Fiesta de Cruz in San Juan, was made by the ethnomusicologist Martha E. Davis (1972).

In his annotated bibliography, Thompson (1982) writes: "Recently . . . [ethnomusicological] study has expanded in Puerto Rico to incorporate a growing body of thought concerning urban, as contrasted to rural, folk music" (p. 14). Indeed, since the 1980s, numerous authors have written about Caribbean popular music, including *salsa* and *plena* in Puerto Rico and New York City. The book *Salsiology* (Boggs 1992) has important chapters by Jorge Duany (1992), Juan Flores (1992), and Quintero Rivera (1992) about *salsa*, *plena*, and *danza*, respectively.

REFERENCES

Boggs, Vernon W., ed. 1992. *Salsiology*. New York: Excelsior Music Publishing.

Cárdenas Ruíz, Manuel. 1981. *Crónicas Francesas de los Caribes*. San Juan: Editorial Universidad de Puerto Rico.

Casas, Bartolomé de las. 1965. *Historia de las Indias. Vol. 1.* Edited by Agustín Millanes. México, D.F.: Fondo de Cultura Económica.

Davis, Martha E. 1972. "The Social Organization of a Musical Event: The Fiesta de Cruz in San Juan, Puerto Rico." *Ethnomusicology* 16(1):38–62.

Duany, Jorge. 1992. "Popular Music in Puerto Rico: Toward an Anthropology of Salsa." In *Salsiology*, ed. Vernon W. Boggs, 71–89. New York: Excelsior Music Publishing.

Dufrasne-González, J. Emanuelo. 1996. "Puerto Rico También Tiene . . . ¡Tambó!" *Kalinda*! (Spring): 4–5.

Flores, Juan. 1992. "Bumbum and the Beginnings of La Plena." In *Salsiology*, ed. Vernon W. Boggs, 61–67. New York: Excelsior Music Publishing.

———. 2000. *From Bomba to Hip Hop: Puerto Rican Culture and Latino Identity*. New York: Columbia University Press.

Grano de Oro, Mayda. 2004. "Puerto Rico." http://www.oup.com/us/brochure/africana/puertorico.pdf

Ledrú, André Pierre. 1971. *Viaje a la isla de Puerto Rico*. 5th ed. Edited by Julio L. Vizcarrondo. San Juan: Editorial Coquí.

López Cruz, Francisco. 1967. *La Música Folklórica de Puerto Rico*. Sharon, Conn.: Troutman Press.

López de Gómara, Francisco. 1965. *Historia General de las Indias*. Barcelona: Editorial Iberia.

McCoy, James A. 1968. "The Bomba and Aguinaldo of Puerto Rico as They Have Evolved from Indigenous, African and European Cultures." Ph.D. dissertation, Florida State University.

Okada, Yuki. *The Caribbean. The JVC Smithsonian Folkways Video Anthology of Music and Dance of the Americas,* 4. Montpelier, Vt.: Multicultural Media VTMV-228. Video.

Pané, Fray Ramón. 1974. *Relación acerca de las antigüedades de los indios*. Mexico City: Editores Siglo XXI.

Quintero Rivera, Angel G. 1992. "Ponce, the Danza, and the National Question: Notes toward a Sociology of Puerto Rican Music." In *Salsiology*, ed. Vernon W. Boggs, 45–51. New York: Excelsior Music Publishing.

Rosa-Nieves, Cesarro. 1967. *Voz Folklórica de Puerto Rico*. Sharon, Conn.: Troutman Press.

Rouse, Irving. 1992. *The Tainos: Rise and Decline of the People who Greeted Columbus*. New Haven: Yale University Press.

Tanodi, Aurelio, ed. 1971. *Documentos de la Real Hacienda de Puerto Rico: Volume I (1510–1519)*. Río Piedras: Centro de Investigación Histórica, Universidad de Puerto Rico.

Thompson, Donald. 1975–1976. "A New World Mbira: The Caribbean Marímbula." *African Music Society Journal* 5(4):140–148.

———. 1982. *Music Research in Puerto Rico*. San Juan: Office of Cultural Affairs, Office of the Governor of Puerto Rico.

Vega Drouet, Héctor. 1969. "Some Musical Forms of African Descendants in Puerto Rico: Bomba, Plena and Rosario Francés." M.A. thesis, Hunter College.

———. 1979. "A Historical and Ethnological Survey of the Probable African Origins of the Bomba, including the Festivities of Loíza Aldea." Ph.D. dissertation, Wesleyan University.

Questions for Critical Thinking

Caribbean Latin American Music

1. Compare and contrast the African-derived musical instruments, genres, and contexts from Cuba, Dominican Republic, Haiti, and Puerto Rico, placing them into their proper historical perspective.
2. Place the traditional African-derived music of Cuba, Dominican Republic, Haiti, and Puerto Rico on a continuum from the most to the least African and discuss the characteristics that determine your reasoning.
3. Compare and contrast Spanish-derived musical instruments, genres, and contexts from Cuba, Dominican Republic, and Puerto Rico, placing them into their proper historical perspective.
4. Place the traditional Spanish-derived music of Cuba, Dominican Republic, and Puerto Rico on a continuum from the most to the least Spanish and discuss the characteristics that determine your reasoning.
5. Compare and contrast popular music from Cuba, Dominican Republic, Haiti, and Puerto Rico and discuss the historical and sociological reasons for their differences or similarities.
6. How have Roman Catholicism and traditional non-Catholic expressions worked together to develop unique musical expressions in the Spanish- and French (Creole)-speaking Caribbean?
7. Discuss how Taíno music and dance have been described and explain how Amerindian culture existed after the Encounter with the Spanish and African people during colonial times. How has it continued today?
8. How would you compare and contrast the musical instruments distinctive of music from Cuba, Dominican Republic, and Puerto Rico? Would you say that certain instruments are clearly of African origin? Why or why not?
9. Make an argument for the Caribbean being a musical region different from other major regions of Latin America.
10. Do you think Caribbean music distributed commercially by the popular music industry has a social role different from more local musics? Why or why not?
11. Why do you think that certain Caribbean musics, for example, *salsa*, have been successful in the commercial music world? Which other genres have also been successful? Are the reasons the same?
12. Cuba and Puerto Rico have been called "two wings of the same bird" because of their similarities. Do you think this is particularly true for music? Why or why not? Could the same case be made for the Dominican Republic and Haiti? Why or why not?

Middle Latin America

For this handbook, the term "Middle Latin America" was coined to represent Mexico and the seven countries of Central America—Guatemala, Belize, Honduras, El Salvador, Nicaragua, Costa Rica, and Panama. Arguably, it could be Northern Latin America, since these countries are the northernmost member-states of that cultural domain, the thriving Latino subcultures of the United States and Canada notwithstanding. However, since Middle America is a longstanding archaeological signifier of the indigenous cultures of this area, and since Latin America is our focus, "Middle Latin America" embraces these two concepts.

The region is one of striking cultural contrasts and hundreds of musical threads. In pre-Columbian times, it was dominated by two of the world's most celebrated and musically complex civilizations: the Aztec and the Maya. After the Spanish conquistador Hernán Cortés defeated the Aztec emperor Moctezuma in 1521, the subjugation of all native peoples in the region followed. Over the ensuing five centuries, Spanish colonialism, the emergence of independent nation-states, and economic globalization transformed cultural life, resulting simultaneously in patterns of overall uniformity and of regional diversity. In modern times, two-thirds of Central Americans and three-quarters of Mexicans are mestizos, and two-thirds of Central Americans and three-quarters of Mexicans live in urban areas. Over 85 percent of Central Americans and 90 percent of Mexicans are nominally Roman Catholic, though evangelistic Protestant sects have gained ground. In five of the eight countries, Spanish-speaking mestizos are the majority population. In Guatemala, Amerindians comprise the majority, and most Costa Ricans primarily claim European heritage. In Belize, where the descendants of African slaves who emigrated from English-speaking Caribbean islands account for nearly half the population, English is the official language.

Today, the music of the modern descendants of ancient Amerindian cultures (such as the Tarahumara in Mexico, Maya in Guatemala, and Kuna in Panama, to name just a few), rural-rooted mestizo traditions, African-derived traits, and international urban popular musics exist side by side, giving rise to new musical hybrids. Mexico's population, around

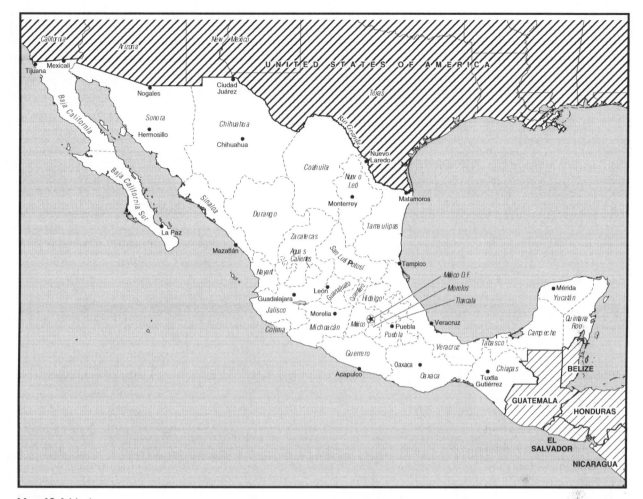

Map 13.1 Mexico

100 million at the turn of the twenty-first century, is nearly three times that of all Central America (about thirty-six million in 1999), and its thriving media industries—radio, recordings, film, and television—have had an enormous impact on the musical life of its southern neighbors. Mexican-rooted popular musics, such as *mariachi* (represented by the musician playing the *guitarrón* on the opposite page), *ranchera*, and others, are played and appreciated in many Latin American countries. At the same time, the evolved popular forms of the Panama-rooted *cumbia* have widespread appeal. The birthrates of Mexico and Central America are among the highest in the world, rapidly increasing the population and giving youth culture a major voice. Musical life in Mexico and Central America is filled with possibilities as an increasingly younger population charts its course into the future.

Francisco Castro of
Guadalajara, a *guitarrón* player
in a strolling *mariachi* orchestra,
poses in a café. Photo by
Daniel E. Sheehy, 1984.

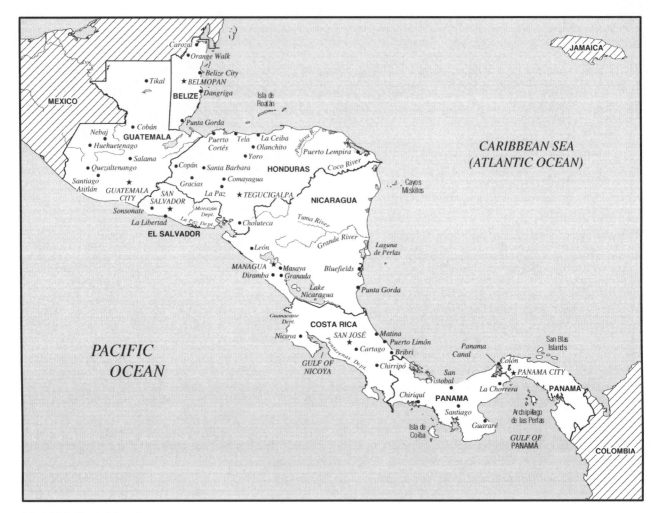

Map 13.2 Central America

Mexico

Daniel E. Sheehy

The Indigenous Heritage
The European Heritage
The African Heritage
The Emergence of Mexican Music
Music Genres and Contexts
Music Learning, Dissemination, Tourism, and Public Policy
Further Study

In 1843, when Frances Calderón de la Barca, the wife of the Spanish ambassador to Mexico, wrote that for Mexicans, "music is a sixth sense," she joined a long line of distinguished observers singing the praise of Mexican musical performance. Evidence of the musical achievements of Mexico's indigenous people is abundant. Archaeological remains bear witness to the complexity of musical instruments and performance in native American cultures more than a millennium before contact with Europeans. Sixteenth-century European chroniclers described the prestige and prominence of musical life among the indigenous peoples they encountered, and twentieth-century documentation has revealed that many distinctive native musical cultures survive nearly five centuries after the Spanish conquistador Hernán Cortés defeated the Aztec Emperor Moctezuma.

Written sources on Mexican music history reflect four major periods: the pre-Encounter era (before 1521); the colonial period (1521–1810); the so-called Independence Period (1810–1910); and the twentieth century after 1910. Most musicological sources were written after 1930. Earlier writings were penned mainly by soldiers and missionaries in colonial times, foreign and urban travelers, journalists, and observers of traditional lifeways in the 1800s, and antiquarians around the turn of the twentieth century.

Since 1325, when Tenochtitlán was founded, Aztec domination had extended over territory extending from north and east of what is now Mexico City south to Central America. A rich store of archaeological and written evidence has allowed scholars to surmise much concerning the importance and centrality of music to Aztec public and ritual life, but fewer archaeological remains of other native American civilizations and their greater chronological distance from European documentarians have greatly limited our knowledge of their music. Most notable among the latter civilizations are the Olmec along the Gulf Coast (circa 1200–400 B.C.), the Maya (flourishing circa A.D. 300–900), and pre-Aztec groups of west-central Mexico.

Extensive historical evidence supports the claims that during many periods before 1521 and in numerous areas of what is now Mexico, music was complex and important. Tubular duct flutes with multiple tubes that were apparently played simultaneously, unearthed on the east and west coasts and perhaps going back more than two thousand years, point to the existence of polyphony. With the possible exception of the musical bow, chordophones are thought to have been absent before their importation by Europeans. Other musical instruments were abundant, and many were found widely throughout Aztec territory. Many tribes used the same instruments, though with names in the local tongue rather than in Náhuatl, the language of the Aztecs.

Important ancient Mexican musical instruments include the following, given in their Náhuatl names. Idiophones included an *ayacachtli*, a gourd or gourd-shaped rattle made from clay or gold; an *ayotl*, a tortoiseshell struck with deer's antlers; a *coyolli* made of clay, copper, dried fruit, gold, or nutshells (Stevenson 1968:40), often strung around a dancer's legs or waist; a rasp (*omichicahuaztli*) made from the bone of a deer or a deerlike animal; and a hollowed log slit drum idiophone (*teponaztli*). Membranophones included a single-headed drum (*huéhuetl*). Aerophones included a conch trumpet (*atecocoli*), a clay whistle (*huilacapiztli*), a wooden or metal trumpet (*tepuzquiquiztli*), and a *tlapitzalli*, an end-blown clay or bone tubular duct flute with four holes. Many similar instruments continue in use among native American peoples.

The Aztec held the *huéhuetl* and the *teponaztli* in particularly high esteem. They considered these instruments sacred and often paired them and situated them at the center of important ritual dances and other events. The *huéhuetl* was typically fashioned from a hollowed log with three supporting legs carved at one end. Its head, of skin, was struck with the hands while the performer sat or stood. The *teponaztli* was most often made of a hollowed log with a slit in the shape of the letter "H" on one side, resulting in two tongues that were struck with sticks. It was placed horizontally on the ground, with a sound hole opening on the side opposite the slit pointing downward. The following account by Spanish chronicler Francisco López de Gómara (1511–1566) is one of many describing the *huéhuetl* and *teponaztli* (1554, quoted in Stevenson 1968:105–106):

> These two drums playing in unison with the voices stood out quite strikingly, and sounded not at all badly. The performers sang merry, joyful, and amusing melodies, or else some ballad in praise of past kings, recounting wars and such things. This was all in rhymed couplets and sounded well and pleasing. … When it was at last time to begin, eight or ten men would blow their whistles lustily. …

Many times a thousand dancers would assemble for this dance and at the least four hundred. They were all leading men, nobles, and even lords. The higher the man's quality the closer was his position with respect to the drums.

Tubular duct flutes were also prominent in Aztec music (see p. 17). An account by Fray Bernardino Sahagún, in his *Historia general de las cosas de Nueva España* (Stevenson 1952:23–24), points to the social and ritual importance of such flutes:

> At the festival of the sixth month they sacrificed a handsome youth whose body was perfectly proportioned. … They selected for this purpose the best looking among their captives … and took great pains to choose the most intelligent … and one without the least physical defect. The youth chosen was carefully trained to play the flute well, and taught … how to walk about as do the nobles and people of the court. … The one chosen for the sacrifice … was greatly venerated by all those who met him. … He who was thus chosen to die at the next great feast went through the streets playing the flute and carrying flowers. … On his legs he wore golden bells which rang at every step he took. … Twenty days before the feast … they married him to four beautiful maidens. …. Five days before the sacrifice they worshiped the young man as one of their gods. … [After four days of preparation, they at last] took him to a small and poorly decorated temple which stood near the highway outside the city. … Upon reaching the foot [of the temple] the young man mounted the steps by himself. As he mounted the first step he broke one of the flutes he had played during the past year of his prosperity; on the second step, another, and so on successively until he had broken them all, and had reached the summit. There he was awaited by the priests who were to kill him, and these now grabbed him and threw him on the stone-block. After seeing him pinned down on his back with feet, hands, and head securely held, the priest who had the stone knife buried it deep in the victim's breast. Then drawing the knife out, the priest thrust one hand into the opening and tore out the heart, which he at once offered to the sun.

In Aztec civilization, music was closely linked to spiritual and material life. Accounts by sixteenth-century Spanish chroniclers, including Toribio de Motolinía (1941 [1858]), Sahagún (1956 [1547]), and Diego Durán (1867–1880), describe many elaborate ceremonies and rituals with music at their center. Robert M. Stevenson has drawn from such accounts to reach numerous conclusions about music in Aztec life. These accounts point to musicians' prestige, the closeness of music's link to ritual and specific ceremonial occasions, the communality of music performance, belief in the divinity and origin of certain instruments, attention to accuracy of pitch and rhythm, and other traits. Music education included formal schools, called *cuicalli* (Martí 1955:112, 115). Unfortunately, there are no known transcriptions of native American melodies from that era (Stevenson 1968:89–91, 125).

THE EUROPEAN HERITAGE

The post-Encounter (also called post-Conquest) era is marked by events that began in 1519, when Spanish conquistador Hernán Cortés and his comrades arrived at what is now San Juan de Uloa, Veracruz. They made their way to Tenochtitlán, slew the Aztec emperor, Moctezuma (1520), and took his nephew Cuauhtémoc captive (1521), bringing an end to Aztec rule over a multitude of Mesoamerican tribes.

During the ensuing colonial period, Franciscan, Dominican, Augustinian, Jesuit, and other Roman Catholic missionaries found European sacred music a valuable means of teaching the indigenous population the tenets and customs of Christianity. Many pre-Conquest indigenous musical practices were easily transferred to Roman Catholic contexts, so church music prospered. Deadly diseases and Spanish oppression, however, diminished the native American population, and African peoples were brought to Mexico as slaves. As Amerindians, Europeans, and Africans intermingled, a new, *mestizo* ("mixed") population gradually rose to prominence. Africans had a profound influence on the shaping of *mestizo* culture and music—an impact not yet fully understood or appreciated.

THE AFRICAN HERITAGE

Before the final quarter of the twentieth century, neglect marked scholarly attention to African contributions to Mexican cultural make-up. The singular exception was Mexican ethnographer and historiographer of the black population in Mexico, Gonzalo Aguirre Beltrán (1976), who summed up African presence:

> There were blacks in Mexico from the moment of the Conquest. … In Mexico blacks were a minority group, representing between 0.1% and 2% of the colonial population; the total number introduced by the slave trade was not much more than 250,000, over a period of three centuries. But there were fewer Spanish than blacks in New Spain. On the other hand, the products of racial mixture, with blacks as well as Spanish, were numerous: at the end of foreign domination in Mexico they represented 40% of the population, of which 10% were considered clearly Afro-mestizo. … The first contacts among blacks, Indians, and Spanish took place by means of the Islamic blacks from the western Sudan area, and the massive invasion of Bantu-speaking blacks from the Congo cultural area, … followed by contact with a few black groups from the gulf of Guinea at the beginning of the last colonial century. From this it seemed certain that the first contacts, because of their primacy, and the second, for their wide extent, were those that left the greatest impression. … The ethnohistorical approach shows the enormous transcendence of colonial blacks in the dynamics of acculturation…

In certain areas, portions of Veracruz and Guerrero in particular, there is abundant racial and ethnohistorical evidence attesting to the presence of blacks. Literate seventeenth-century composers wrote pieces called *guineos* and *negros* portraying blacks as music makers and mimicking their distinctive style of speech and extroverted behavior. Close analysis of regional music today yields strong affinities of certain musical styles, such as the *son jarocho* with its African organizational principles. Many of the more ancient *sones jarochos* are organized around the repetition of a simple, relatively short rhythmic-chordal pattern that drives the music forward in the fashion of the rhythmic cycle that generates much traditional sub-Saharan African music. In contrast, most other *son* styles follow more European-derived song structure marked by more differentiated A and B sung sections separated by an instrumental interlude.

By the late twentieth century, globalization had bombarded Mexico with African sounds from far and near. African artists toured to Mexican cities, and African-derived musics from elsewhere in Latin America brought a passionate following for the Afro-Cuban *son* and *danzón*, Dominican *merengue*, Colombian *cumbia*, Brazilian *samba* and *bossa nova*, and many other genres. African American popular music from Mexico's northern neighbor added yet another African tinge to music in Mexico. Many Mexican musicians themselves consciously explored and promoted African elements of their traditional music, while concerts and film documentaries spread public awareness of the "Third Root" (Tercera Raíz)—the African root of Mexican culture.

Music in the colonial period (1521–1810)

Nueva España (New Spain), as Mexico was called when it was a Spanish colony, enjoyed an active musical life. Most documentation surviving from the 1500s and 1600s tells of the learning, creation, and performance of European fine-art music, particularly that associated with the Roman Catholic Church. Missionaries relied heavily on music as a means of enculturating the indigenous population in the principles and ways of the Spanish Catholic tradition. Native Americans responded by taking up European music in large numbers; many of them attained a high degree of musicianship in choral and instrumental performance. New Spain's church life was a rich vein of European musical production until its decline in the 1700s.

Vernacular European and *mestizo* music outside religious contexts seldom made their way into musical notation. Official documents suggest that musical performance was abundant. It often attracted the reprimand of religious authorities on moral grounds. A violist named Ortiz was among the followers of Hernán Cortés. Locally made Spanish musical instruments were abundant soon after the Encounter. In the 1600s and 1700s, blacks gave profane musical performances (*oratorios, escapularios*) during religious festivities, ridiculing the sacred event. Colonial documents show that blacks played harps and guitars, danced publicly, and played important roles in shaping the people's grass-roots music (Saldívar 1934:220–222).

In the late 1700s, as Spanish influence over the New World waned, the vernacular music of New Spain's *criollos* and *mestizos* took on a more local character, different from its Spanish roots. Spanish *seguidillas, fandangos*, sung verses called *coplas* and *letrillas*, and other folkloric genres were the models for the creation of new pieces called *sones*, first documented as such in 1766 in Spanish Inquisition records. Popular theater performed in the *Coliseo* (Coliseum) in Mexico City around 1800 featured *tonadillas escénicas*—short, simple dramas replete with new *sones* and other local melodies. The *jarabe*, a *son* intended especially for dancing, also emerged around 1800. As *mestizo* culture took shape, the particular cultural blend, the shared life experiences over time, and the isolation of local communities and regions led to considerable cultural diversity among *mestizos*. Musical life was more local and regional than it was national, and this tendency was reflected in the *mestizo* music that had evolved by the 1800s.

Music in the independence period (1810–1910)

Independence from Spain and the decline of ecclesiastical influence brought Mexican secular music to greater prominence. *Sones, jarabes*, and other melodies associated with political insurgence were honored as symbols of national identity. Writers of that time described a Mexican culture alive with musical activity marked by regional traditions and interregional sharing (Calderón de la Barca 1843; Esteva 1844a, 1844b; Prieto 1906:347–351). Traditional Mexican melodies were arranged for piano and exalted in genteel society as national airs (*aires nacionales*) and little *sones* of the country (*sonecitos del país*). *Jarabes* flourished, especially in west and central Mexico, gradually evolving into potpourris of excerpts from *sones* and other popular melodies.

Independence led to the importation of music from Europe, especially Italy and France. Italian opera was imported, imitated, and emulated by Mexican musicians and composers. Outside the confines of the Roman Catholic Church, instrumental fine-art music was virtually unknown in Mexico until the first wave of foreign performers, after 1840 (Mayer-Serra 1941:30). The piano became a standard piece of furniture in the homes of an expanding middle class. European fashions in dancing were adopted unchanged. The waltz (*vals*), introduced by 1815, met frequent condemnation as a "licentious" French import and was quite popular throughout the period. One of the most internationally renowned Mexican compositions of the 1800s was "Sobre las Olas" ("Over the Waves'), a waltz written by the Otomí native American Juventino Rosas in 1891. "La Paloma," the most popular song during the time of the French occupation (1862–1867), had been written in the 1840s by the Spaniard Sebastián de Yradier in the style of a Cuban *habanera*—a form that left a deep mark on Mexican music of later years. A voluminous repertoire of mazurkas (*mazurcas*), polkas (*polcas*), schottisches (*chotíces*), waltzes (*valses*), and other pieces for dancing were written in European styles by Mexicans in the late 1800s (Stevenson 1952:208). In bandstands (*quioscos*) set up in town plazas across the country, brass bands (*bandas del pueblo*) performed *marchas*, European dances, *sonecitos*, and *jarabes*.

The composition of fine-art music in the 1800s largely imitated European models. Some works, such as *Ecos de México* (1880) by Julio Ituarte (1845–1905), drew heavily from Mexican melodies but were entirely European in style. Mexican composers Melesio Morales (1838–1908), Gustavo Campa (1863–1934), and Julián Carrillo (1875–1965) emulated Italian, French, and German musical conventions, respectively (Stevenson 1952:227). Salon music consisted of popular operatic melodies, other diluted versions of elite music (Mayer-Serra 1941:70), and Romantic-style *romanzas*, *contradanzas*, *caprichos*, and so forth. A truly nationalist movement did not occur until the revolution of 1910 put an end to the thirty-five-year presidency of Porfirio Díaz and the hegemony of European cultural models it had encouraged.

Music in the post-revolutionary twentieth century

With the Mexican Revolution, beginning in 1910, came a nationalist movement in cultural thought and policy. Intellectuals elevated and idealized Mexico's Amerindian past, and music scholars combed through archives and archaeological relics, recovering pre-Encounter musical achievements. Native American and *mestizo* songs and dances were collected and published. Mexico's centralized educational system codified and disseminated a select repertoire of music and dance. José Vasconcelos, Secretary of Public Education from 1921 to 1924, directed his agency, through its Aesthetic Culture Department, to encourage traditional dance; on the hundredth anniversary of the founding of the republic (1921), thousands watched as thirty couples danced "El Jarabe Tapatío" in a Mexico City ceremony unveiling the version to be taught throughout the country (Saldívar 1937:9). Rural musicians representing locally distinctive *mestizo* styles migrated to Mexico City in search of professional musical opportunities.

Art-music composer Manuel M. Ponce (1882–1948) successfully blended traditional harmonic and melodic material into a Romantic musical style and was among the first generation of nationalist composers (Mayer-Serra 1941:147). Carlos Chávez led the next generation a step further as he incorporated native American instruments, rhythms, and melodic traits into many of his works to evoke impressions of an ancient Amerindian past. With the indigenous-inspired rhythms of his *Sinfonía India*, he broke all connection to the Mexican Romantic past. Silvestre Revueltas also wrote in a modern musical style, though he took his inspiration from modern Mexico (Mayer-Serra 1941:162–165). In the late 1960s, the avant-garde compositional techniques and aesthetics of Manuel Enríquez, Manuel de Elías, Eduardo Mata, Mario Lavista, Héctor Quintanar, and others signaled a move away from nationalist styles (Béhague 1979:292).

In the 1930s and 1940s, the nationwide expansion of the radio and recording industries created a demand for local musics that possessed the potential for broad appeal. In the same decades, the Mexican film industry, while it created star entertainers singing in pseudo-folk styles, contributed to public awareness of certain styles of traditional music. All these media were powerful vehicles for foreign music to infiltrate local culture. For intellectuals, music from the United States was a major source of concern—a fear that led the music historian Gabriel Saldívar (1937:21) to promote national music as "a barrier of pure nationalism to the avalanche ... of shabby [*quinto patio* 'slum'] songs" that had invaded Mexico.

Post-revolutionary nationalism remains a potent frame of reference among intellectuals, in government cultural policies, and for the population at large, but other social forces have a major bearing on musical life. A high birthrate, bringing Mexico's population to near 100 million at the end of the twentieth century, has made it the most populous Spanish-speaking country in the world, with a high proportion of young people. More than 20 million people reside in metropolitan Mexico City, the most populous city in the world. The country's population is three-fourths urban, though many people have rural roots. The media industry is one of the most influential in Latin America and is in turn greatly influenced by the fashions of the United States. There are more than four hundred radio stations nationwide, most of them commercial. Although the media are the central force in shaping musical tastes, the fabric of Mexico's musical life, like that of most twentieth-century large urban societies, is made up of hundreds of threads, commonly described in several ways: music of "ethnic groups," referring principally to Amerindians; regional musical culture (*música regional*); certain widespread genres of music, such as narrative ballads (*corridos*); folk-derived popular music; international pop-music fashions; and fine-art music.

MUSICAL GENRES AND CONTEXTS

In the century after independence from Spain, many observers published accounts of regionally distinct traditions of music among rural *mestizos*. After the revolution of 1910, many of these traditions were officially promoted as symbols of national identity, or were widely popularized through the power of Mexico's media. Also, from the adoring nineteenth-century accounts of visiting Italian-style opera singers and from the strong following of nationalist composers in the twentieth century, we know that European secular fine-art music did not escape the Mexican attraction to music.

Many musical threads of Mexico's past have continued into the twenty-first century. Rapid urbanization, the intensified commodification of music, an increasingly powerful and centralized media complex, and other twentieth-century trends, however, worked to magnify and co-opt certain musical styles, leaving others to languish in the shadow of neglect, and to introduce and promulgate new musical fashions from abroad, especially from the United States.

Música regional: the *mestizo son*

During the time of self-discovery after national independence, writers such as José María Esteva (1844a:234–235) described many Mexican musical traditions in detail, especially the *mestizo son*:

> The sones danced by the jarochos [of Veracruz] are composed by the jarochos themselves and by other Spaniards [sic], or are from the interior of the republic, and rearranged according to their own tastes; consequently, they dance [the local genres] Canelo, Tusa, Guanábana, etc., along with Manola, Agualulco, and Tapatío [genres from other areas]. Most jarocho women dance the same way, but with much grace, and sometimes in certain sones like the Bamba, one admires the agility with which they tap their heels and make a thousand movements, carrying a glass filled with water on their heads without spilling a single drop, or forming a noose from a sash laid on the ground that they adjust with their feet and which they then untie without using their hands at all.

Jarocho musicians continue to perform most of these *sones*.

In the post-revolutionary era, a national road-building effort, other improvements in transportation, a powerful media industry (which bombarded even the most distant village with the latest musical fads), governmental efforts to educate the population about its national culture, and professional opportunities in urban areas for rural musicians altered these patterns profoundly. But even as local and regional musical distinctions were fading, several regional styles of music were increasingly heard, incorporated into a national canon of region-based national identity. This canon has reinforced regional musical identity at its roots, creating national and international markets for the performance of regional music by professional musicians. Regional musical identity persists, though in part solely as a musical style and as an emblem of an idealized rural, regional heritage. Regional musical distinctions are based on repertoire, typical instrumentation, style of performance, related regional traits such as style of speech and vocabulary, traditional dress, local topics alluded to in song texts, and other factors.

At the core of most regional musical styles that emerged with the formation of *mestizo* culture, particularly those of central Mexico, is the musical genre known as *son*. As the Spanish *seguidillas*, *fandangos*, *zapateados*, and secular forms widely known as *tonadillas* were accepted and reinterpreted by *mestizos*, new genres of music were created, based on their Spanish predecessors. In the early 1800s, the Gran Teatro Coliseo de la Metrópoli in Mexico City and other theaters in the provinces were clearinghouses for a variety of genres of song and dance. Short theatrical interludes featured Spanish and *mestizo* melodies and dances that circulated throughout New Spain. These pieces, often called *sones*, exemplified a variety of forms, including that of *jarabes*, pieces documented as early as the late 1700s. Writing in the 1950s, the folklorist Vicente Mendoza stated that the *son* was "one of the most genuinely Mexican of musical genres," and he estimated that 60 percent of Mexican traditional music, with the *son* as its nucleus, had origins in the *tonadillas* popular nearly 150 years before (1956:59, 66). Indeed, many extant *sones*, including "La Bamba," "El Perico," and "El Palomo," were documented in the early 1800s.

The *mestizo son* continues to be diverse in form, but a few generalizations are possible. It is oriented toward accompanying social dance, with vigorous, marked rhythm and fast tempo. It is performed most often by small ensembles in which string instruments predominate, with notable region-specific exceptions. Its formal structure is based on the alternation of instrumental sections and the singing of short poetic units called *coplas*. The mode is usually major, with harmonic vocabulary mostly limited to progressions drawing from I, IV, II_7, V, and V_7. In contrast to the Amerindian *son*, the *mestizo son* is fundamentally secular as is reflected in its textual amorousness and wit, its overall extraversion, and its performative settings.

When danced, the *son* is usually performed by couples, though some *sones* have special choreography that may call for other groupings. Triple meter (6/8, 3/4, or a combination of both, called *sesquiáltera* in Latin American ethnomusicology) predominates, with many exceptions in duple meter. The performing ensembles include melodic instruments, such as violins and harps, and instruments that provide chordal and rhythmic accompaniment corresponding to specific regional styles, especially guitars. Singing is usually in a high vocal range, often in parallel thirds. Men predominate in the public performance of *sones*, though many women may learn and perform *sones*, particularly in family settings. *Sones* are often among the repertoire of music performed at important life-cycle events (especially baptisms, birthdays, and weddings), in public commemorations of the civic-religious calendar (independence day, patronal saints' days), and in entertainment-oriented venues, including bars, restaurants, and theaters. Many government- and private-sponsored public concerts feature *sones* and other forms of folkloric music and dance.

Coplas performed for *sones* are short poetic stanzas that stand alone as complete thoughts, as opposed to being linked together in a long narrative (as in some other Mexican genres). They usually consist of four to six octosyllabic lines. The even-numbered lines rhyme; the odd-numbered lines may end in consonance or assonance. Two typical *coplas* are the following:

Date gusto, vida mía,	Give yourself pleasure, my love,
que yo me daría otro tanto.	for I'd give myself some.
No vaya a hacer que algún día	Don't let it happen that someday
el gusto se vuelva llanto.	the pleasure changes to tears.
Buenas noches, señoritas;	Good evening, misses;
muy buenas noches señores.	a very good evening, sirs.
A todas las florecitas	To all the little flowers
de rostros cautivadores	with captivating faces
van las trovas más bonitas	go the prettiest verses
des estos pobres cantadores.	from these poor troubadours.

Two major exceptions to this form are textual patterns derived from the *seguidilla* and the *décima*. In the former, seven-syllable lines alternate with five-syllable lines:

Para bailar la bamba,	To dance the *bamba*,
se necesita	one needs
una poca de gracia	a little grace
y otra cosita.	and some other little thing.

Often, filler such as *cielito lindo* ("dear, sweetheart") will be added to the stanza, achieving greater congruence with the accompanying musical phrase:

Ese lunar que tienes,	That mole that you have,
cielito lindo, junto a la boca:	dear, next to your mouth:
no se lo des a nadie,	don't give it to anyone,
cielito lindo, que a mi me toca.	dear, for it belongs to me.

The *décima* is a ten-line stanza rhyming abbaaccddc:

Señora, está usted servida.	Madame, you are served
Sólo le encargo a usted:	I only ask this of you:
que las décimas no se dé,	that the *décimas* not be given away,
aunque el propio rey las pida.	even if the king himself requests them.
Si las tienes aprendida(s)	If you have them learned
y alguno las necesita,	and someone needs them,
no le dé, porque le quita	don't give them to him, because it takes away
la gracia y la decorrupta,	their grace and purity,
que a todo el mundo le gusta(n)	for everyone loves
las décimas bonitas.	pretty *décimas*.

Rhymes may reflect regional pronunciation (*aprendida* for *aprendidas*) or near-rhyme (*gusta* for *gustan*). *Décimas* are present in certain *sones* of southern Veracruz, and in the *valonas*, a musical genre with several declaimed *décimas*, of the hotlands (*tierra caliente*), the western part of the state of Michoacán.

Although these and other unifying traits make a case for a *mestizo son* "supergenre," many regional styles of *son* are easily recognizable by the distinctiveness of their instrumentation, instrumental techniques, treatment of the *copla*, vocal nuances, repertoire, associated dances, and other factors.

Types of regional *sones*

Many regional styles of Mexican music are distinguished by their forms of *sones* and several other styles in which the *son* has been historically influential but not currently central to their identity. Seven principal kinds of *son* that mark regional musical styles are *son huasteco* of the northwestern geocultural region known as the Huasteca; *son jarocho* of the southern coastal plain of the state of Veracruz; *son istmeño* or *son oaxaqueño* of the Isthmus of Tehuantepec, mainly in the southwest portion of Oaxaca, overlapping with Chiapas; *chilena* of the Costa Chica along the Pacific coast of Oaxaca and Guerrero; *son guerrerense* (*son calentano*) of the Balsas River basin hotlands in Guerrero; *son michoacano* (*son calenteño*) from the neighboring hotland region of Michoacán; and the *son jalisciense* of Jalisco. Many regional styles in which the *son* is influential but not central are those found in Yucatán and the northern border area.

Figure 14.1
A *trío huasteco* plays at a member's home in Mexico City. Left to right: Eduardo Bustos Valenzuela, violin; Domitilio Zubiria, *jarana huasteca*; and Mario Zubiria, *huapanguera (guitarra quinta)*. Photo by Daniel Sheehy, 1992.

Son huasteco

The region known as the Huasteca comprises portions of the states of Tamaulipas, Hidalgo, Veracruz, Querétaro, and Puebla. The *son huasteco* is also known as the *huapango*, a term possibly derived from the Náhuatl *cuauh-panco* ("over the wood"), referring to a dance performed on a wooden platform. A *son huasteco* is typically performed by a trio of musicians playing a violin, a *huapanguera* (*guitarra quinta*, a deep-bodied guitar with eight strings in five single and double courses), and a *jarana* (small five-stringed guitar) (Figure 14.1). [Listen to "El Aguanieve"] The violinist plays melodies that are often complex and highly syncopated, requiring a high degree of skill and the ability to improvise. The two guitars play in strummed (*rasgueado*) fashion, with the *huapanguera* player occasionally adding single-string countermelodies. The vocal style includes brief, ornamental breaks into falsetto. *Quintillas* and *sextillas* (five- and six-line *coplas*, respectively) are favored. Singers often improvise texts befitting the particular performance situation. The singing of the *copla* typically involves certain patterns of repeating lines of the *copla* that allow fuller vocal treatment of the text and time for the singer to compose improvised *coplas*. Typical *sones huastecos* are "Cielito Lindo," "La Rosa," "La Azucena," "El Llorar," "El Toro Sacamandú," "El Gusto," and "La Huasanga." The term *huapango* may also include composed songs with fixed texts and two- or three-part vocal harmonies and cast in a rhythmic-chordal accompaniment similar to that of the *son huasteco*.

DISC ❷ TRACK 11

Son jarocho

The *son jarocho* takes its name from a term of uncertain origin (possibly from *jaras*, clubs said to have been wielded by colonial militia) denoting the people of the southern coastal plain of Veracruz. Dancing (*zapateado*) on a *tarima* or raised wooden floor during large social gatherings (*fandangos*) on ranches or in small towns is (was) often a part of the *son jarocho* performance setting.

Figure 14.2
A *conjunto jarocho* in Boca del Río, Veracruz. Left to right: Daniel Valencia on *requinto jarocho*, Rufino Velásquez on *arpa jarocha*, and Inés Rivas on *jarana jarocha*. Photo by Daniel Sheehy, 1978.

DISC❶TRACK30
DISC❷TRACK12

The most widespread typical instrumentation for the *son jarocho* (Figure 14.2) centers on the 32- to 36-stringed diatonic harp (*arpa jarocha*), a *jarana* (shallow-bodied guitar with eight strings in five courses), and a *requinto* ("*guitarra de son*," a four-stringed, narrow-bodied guitar plucked with a 7.5-centimeter plectrum fashioned from cow horn or a plastic comb). [Listen to "Siquisirí," and "La Bamba"] In the southern area, near the border with Tabasco, the harp is rare, and smaller sizes of *jarana* are found. In the central town of Tlacotalpan, a *pandero* (octagonal frame drum with jingles like a tambourine) joins the ensemble. The harpist plays melody and bass. The *jarana* player employs a variety of patterns (*maniqueos*) to strum a rhythmic-chordal accompaniment appropriate to the meter, tempo, and character of the particular *son*. The *requinto* player (*requintero*) supplies an additional, largely improvisatory melodic line, often interacting with the harpist's melody. Six-line *coplas* are most common and are the preferred medium for most textual improvisation, of which a great deal occurs. A revival movement gathered momentum in the 1980s and brought older repertoire and a wider range of local instruments to the fore. The latter include the bass *requinto* (*leona*, "lioness") and *marimbol* (large "thumb piano" in the fashion of the African *mbira* and Cuban *marímbula*).

It is often supposed that the *son jarocho*, more than any other regional *son* tradition, is of African origin. Most *sones jarochos* are based on a short, cyclical rhythmic-chordal pattern (*compás*) that drives the music through continuous repetition in the fashion of the West African timeline and is usually played on a bell or the African-Cuban beat played on *claves*. Certain *sones*—"El Coco" and "La Iguana"—have a responsorial refrain. The style and degree of interaction between musicians, dancers, and audience also suggest a more African style. These factors, with the prominence of African and mulatto people in the region's ethnographic history, further support this notion.

Son istmeño *or* son oaxaqueño

Unlike most regional *son* styles, the *son istmeño* customarily is neither performed by string ensembles nor sung. Wind-and-percussion *bandas* follow the basic pattern of "sung" sections alternating with instrumental interludes, though sections sung in other areas are performed instrumentally in a cantabile style. The *bandas* follow the models of European brass bands of the 1800s. Most *bandas* are composed exclusively of native Americans, the *banda* being a central social institution of many Amerindian communities. The performances at civic and religious celebrations, however, are part of the musical life of *mestizos* and native Americans alike.

In the southernmost state of Chiapas and the southern edge of Oaxaca, the *marimba* (Figure 14.3) is similar to the *banda* in its treatment of the *son*. Though the *marimba* was probably modeled on African xylophone prototypes during colonial times, it has been the domain of primarily *mestizo* musicians since at least the mid-1800s. It has become an important icon of Chiapan identity and is closely associated with the towns of Tehuantepec (Chiapas) and Juchitán (Oaxaca). The *marimba* may be *sencilla* (a single instrument) or *doble* (a combination of a smaller and a larger instrument) and may be played by two, three, or more players. [Listen to "La Llorona"] It is often

Figure 14.3
Near several restaurants in downtown Veracruz, a quartet plays a *marimba* and accompanying instruments. Left to right: two musicians playing the *marimba*, a drummer, and a *güiro* player. Photo by Daniel Sheehy, 1978.

DISC ❷ TRACK 13

accompanied by percussion and other instruments. Although the *marimba* continues to consist of a set of rectangular wooden slats of graduated lengths suspended over resonator tubes (each with a small membrane that buzzes as its slat is struck), the wooden slatboard of the modern *marimba* has been transformed to resemble the piano keyboard, with the black keys located above and set into the white keys. *Marimba* ensembles typically perform a wide-ranging repertoire, from pieces often called *sones* to a special repertoire for Amerindian events to current melodies spread through the popular media. The pieces most closely resembling the *sones* of other regions follow two main models: waltz-rhythm melodies that are instrumental interpretations of songs; and fast-tempo *zapateados* cast in a 6/8 rhythmic mold with frequent shifts to 3/4 (i.e., *sesquiáltera*).

Chilena

Though the cultural antecedents of the *chilena* from the Costa Chica differ from those of *sones* rooted in the colonial era, the overall character and musical traits of the genre argue for its inclusion in the *son* family. It is derived from the *cueca*, a musical genre and dance performed by Chilean and Peruvian adventurers who stopped in Acapulco on their voyage to California during the gold rush of the mid-1800s. Its Chilean origins are found in the structure of the text and in the choreography, with its dancers' use of handkerchiefs. Until its decline in the mid-twentieth century, an ensemble of harp, five-course *jarana*, and some form of percussion typically accompanied the *chilena*. Today, the guitar and six-stringed *requinto*, the latter similar to the guitar, but smaller and tuned a perfect fourth higher, most often fill that role.

Son calentano

From Guerrero, this *son*, also called *son calentano* (from *caliente* "hot," referring to the hotlands of Guerrero and Michoacán), is associated with the ensemble consisting of one or two violins, six-stringed guitar (formerly a smaller *jarana*), a *tamborita* (small, double-headed drum played on the head and rim with two drumsticks), and occasionally a bass (*guitarrón*), borrowed from contemporary *mariachis*. The tradition is found mainly in the area of the Balsas River basin of Guerrero. Most *sones* in this region are called by different names, reflecting differing characters. Those called *son* are usually fast-paced instrumental melodies intended for dancing, those called *gustos* are typically strophic songs in triple meter, and those called *chilenas* resemble those of the Costa Chica.

Son calenteño

DISC **1** TRACK 28
DISC **2** TRACK 10

In the neighboring hotlands of Michoacán, the *son calenteño* (also *son planeco*) is closely identified with a string ensemble consisting of a large diatonic harp (*arpa grande*), two violins, a *vihuela* (five-stringed guitar with a convex back), and a *jarana* (also known as *guitarra de golpe*, a deep-bodied guitar with five strings). [Listen to "Cuaulleros" and "El Perro"] Unlike the *sones* of Veracruz and the Huasteca, the *son michoacano* has fixed musical interludes that separate the sung sections. Occasionally during these instrumental interludes, a violinist or guitarist will kneel down and beat the lower face of the harp with his hands as a percussive accompaniment (Figure 14.4)—a practice that was apparently more widespread in earlier times. Refrains of the *son calenteño* typically are sung in high vocal range in parallel thirds using non-lexical syllables such as "Ay tirararara tirararararararara."

The *son* is central to the ensemble's repertoire, but two other traditional genres, the *jarabe* and the *valona*, are also distinctive of the region. The *jarabe* is similar in form to its counterparts in other regions of west-central Mexico—a string of perhaps five to seven melodies performed instrumentally with each section corresponding to a particular pattern of movement. The *valona* (the word is thought to derive from "Walloon," perhaps introduced during the presence of Flemish troops in the 1700s), more widespread in the 1800s, is a local version of *décima*-based forms found in several parts of Latin America. Generally, a four-line *copla* precedes four *décimas* with the last line of each *décima* duplicating the first, second, third, and fourth lines of the introductory *copla* in that order. A single basic melodic pattern functions as the introduction and as musical interludes between sections of text. The subjects are almost invariably witty or picaresque.

Figure 14.4
A *conjunto de arpa grande* from the hotlands of Michoacán. Left to right: Ricardo Gutiérrez Villa, violin; an onlooker; second violinist (name unknown), momentarily kneeling and beating the harp with his hands; Rubén Cuevas Maldonado, *arpa grande; vihuela* (name unknown); and Osvaldo Ríos Yáñez, *guitarra de golpe* (jarana). Photo by Daniel Sheehy, 1991.

Son jalisciense

The *son jalisciense* (*son* from around the state of Jalisco) is perhaps the most widely known of Mexican *sones* through its performance by *mariachis* throughout the country. [Listen to "El Cihualteco"] The *son jalisciense* is closely related to the *son calenteño* and to a lesser extent to other *sones* throughout territory stretching from southern Sinaloa to Guerrero. A style called *son abajeño* (lowlands *son*) is central to the repertoire of *sones* played by the *mariachi*, lacking the high-pitched vocal refrain of the *son calenteño*. Previous to the introduction and standardization of trumpets in *mariachis* during the 1920s through 1940s, the accompaniment to this *son* was one or two violins, a *vihuela*, perhaps a *guitarra de golpe*, and a harp or a *guitarrón*. Most *sones jaliscienses* are strophic songs in which *coplas* alternate with melodically fixed instrumental interludes. Some *sones* are quite complex rhythmically, with ornate patterns of strumming the guitars and 3/4–6/8 metrical ambiguities (i.e., *sesquiáltera*). With the commodification of *mariachi* music from the 1930s forward came copyrighted standard versions of many *sones* drawn from oral tradition.

Other regional forms

Two other musical regions influenced by the *son*, but not identified by a distinct kind of *son*, are Yucatán and the northern border area. Regional music of Yucatán is distinguished by the *jarana* and the *bambuco*. The *jarana* is a couple dance resembling the Spanish *jota* in its choreography and the meter of its music. The *jarana* is performed instrumentally, most often by a small orchestra of wind and percussion instruments, and has no text, excepting occasional brief breaks, when a dancer declaims a *copla*. The compositions usually consist of a series of short melodies, similar to those of a *jarabe*. Although the *jarana* may have been rooted partially in the *sonecitos* of the 1800s and earlier, its repertoire and overall style show few close similarities with those of regional *sones*. The *bambuco* is a slow, often melancholic genre of song, apparently brought to the region by Colombian musicians around the early 1900s. It is often sung in two or three-part harmony, accompanied by a guitar, a six-stringed *requinto* popularized by Mexican trios in the 1940s, and a percussion instrument or a bass.

El Norte (the north), the vast and arid region stretching from Tamaulipas to Sonora, took shape as a distinctive cultural region in the nineteenth and twentieth centuries. It was sparsely populated through colonial times. In the second half of the 1800s, the growth of ranching and, more important, mining attracted an enormous migration of workers from other regions of Mexico and of professionals and others from European countries such as Germany, Poland, and France. The lack of a strongly unified cultural base made the region fertile ground for the implantation of the European musical and dance vogues that held sway over most of urban nineteenth-century Mexico. Mazurkas, polkas, schottisches, waltzes, and other European dances attained a preeminence that endured throughout the twentieth century. No unique form of *son* emerged in the north. However, songs, *corridos* in particular, were set to the rhythms of the European dances, with the 2/4 polka meter being the most favored. The *son*'s overall form of *coplas* alternating with instrumental melodies and its strong identification with the people (*el pueblo*) may have deeply influenced this

Figure 14.5
A *conjunto norteño* performs for vacationers in Mandinga, Veracruz. Left to right: *bajo sexto*, button accordion, and string bass (*tololoche*). Photo by Daniel Sheehy, 1978.

music, which has long been considered distinctive of the north (Reuter 1985:185). This polkarhythm song, accompanied by accordion as lead melodic instrument, a large twelve-stringed guitar (*bajo sexto*), an acoustic or electric bass, and perhaps a drumset or a *redova* (small, hollow woodblock played with two sticks), much like the *mariachi*, became widely known through its success in the commercial media (Figure 14.5).

Other contexts and genres

Many regional musical customs, genres, and pieces are shared widely, especially by *mestizos*. Religious observances paying homage to the Virgin of Guadalupe or reenacting Mary and Joseph's journey to Bethlehem, songs sung by and for children, *corridos*, serenades (*serenatas*), the song "Las Mañanitas," and a canon of "national" music and dance derived from regional traditions are some of the most pervasive.

Religious music

More than 90 percent of the Mexican population is nominally Roman Catholic. In addition to more universal liturgical music and sacramental events that include secular music (such as baptisms, weddings, and funerals), there are specifically Mexican religious occasions with their own musical repertoires. Key to the conversion of Mexican Amerindians to Roman Catholicism was the belief that in 1531 the Virgin Mary appeared to an Amerindian named Juan Diego on the hill Tepeyac, located in what is now Mexico City. Ecclesiastical authorities confirmed the miraculous appearance, opening the door to the widespread adoration by Amerindians and *mestizos* throughout Mexico and beyond of this figure, closely identified with their own cultural past. Among Mexican communities in Mexico and abroad, 12 December and the preceding weeks have become a time of ceremonial devotion to the Virgin of Guadalupe. Special hymns and other songs of praise to the Virgin of Guadalupe are sung during processions, celebrations of the Mass, and late-evening or early-morning serenades in front of statues of her. Corpus Christi ("Body of Christ") is an important Catholic celebration in Mexico for which music and processional dance is prominent. [Listen to "Danza de Corpus Christi"]

DISC 1 TRACK 29

Early December is one of the most important occasions for devotional performances by musical-choreographic groups often known as *concheros*, named for the guitar many of them play, fashioned from an armadillo shell. *Concheros*, whose performance also may be known as Aztec dance (*danza azteca*), are active in many parts of Mexico and the south-western United States, but especially in the federal district (Mexico City) and in the neighboring states to its north and east. Consisting mainly of blue-collar and lower-middle-class *mestizo* and Amerindian people of both sexes and all ages, these groups take part in many saint's-day celebrations, singing, playing, and dancing while dressed in highly ornate costumes, evoking images of ancient Aztecs. Many carry out long-distance pilgrimages to the Basílica de Guadalupe at the foot of Tepeyac, where they perform tightly coordinated devotional choreographies.

With Christmastide comes *las posadas*, the musical reenactment of Mary and Joseph's journey to Bethlehem. Churches, social groups, and individuals organize these events so children and adults can dress up as characters in local interpretations of the story: Mary, Joseph, shepherds, Bedouins, Romans, devils, and others. The participants divide into pilgrims and innkeepers (*caseros*). The pilgrims ask for lodging (*versos para pedir posada*), and the innkeepers deny them a place to stay. In the following lyrics (after Reuter 1985:101–102), the pilgrims sing the first two stanzas, and the innkeepers sing the second two:

En nombre del cielo,	In the name of heaven,
os pido posada,	I ask of thee shelter,
pues no puede andar	for my beloved wife
mi esposa amada.	cannot go on walking.
No seas inhumano;	Don't be inhumane;
tennos caridad,	have charity with us,
que el Dios de los Cielos	for the God of the heavens
te lo premiará.	will reward you.
Aquí no es mesón;	This is not an inn;
sigan adelante.	continue on your way.
Yo no debo abrir;	I don't have to open;
no sea algún tunante.	don't be a pest.
Ya se pueden ir	Now you can go away,
y no molestar,	and don't bother,
porque si me enfado,	because if I get angry,
los voy a apalear.	I'm going to hit you.

In the end, a door is opened, and the pilgrims are invited in, to the following lyrics (after Reuter 1985:103):

Entren, santos peregrinos;	Enter, holy pilgrims;
reciban esta mansión,	receive this lodging,
que aunque es pobre la morada,	for though the abode is humble,
os la doy de corazón.	it is given to you from the heart.

To the joy of all present, a fiesta begins, at the center of which is a *piñata*. While children are bludgeoning the *piñata*, two melodies are often sung, to the following texts (after Reuter 1985:106–107):

Dale, dale, dale.	Hit it, hit it, hit it.
No pierdas el tino,	Don't lose your aim,
porque si lo pierdes,	for if you lose it,
pierdes el camino.	you lose your way.

No quiero oro;	I don't want gold;
no quiero plata:	I don't want silver:
yo lo que quiero	what I myself want
es romper la piñata.	is to break the *piñata*.

In southern Veracruz and neighboring areas, the Advent tradition known as *la rama* involves groups of adults and/or children going from home to home asking for an *aguinaldo*, a gift of coins, candy, food, or drink. They typically carry with them a decorated branch (*rama*) and sing verses to the melody "La Rama" ("The Branch"). There are local variations of "La Rama," but it is distinguished by verses sung by individuals alternating with the refrain beginning *Naranjas y limas, limas y limones, más linda es la Virgen, que todas las flores* ("Oranges and lemons, lemons and limes, the Virgin is prettier than all the flowers"). An example from Tlacotalpan, Veracruz is the following:

Licencia queremos,	We request permission,
familia decente,	good family,
y sin ofenderlos	and without offending you
dispense a esta gente.	forgive these people.
Naranjas y limas	Oranges and lemons,
limas y limones	lemons and limes,
más linda es la Virgen	the Virgin is prettier
que todas las flores.	than all the flowers.
Dispense a esta gente	Forgive these people
que venga a su casa,	who come to your house,
y si son gustosos,	and if you are pleasant,
verán lo que pasa.	you will see what happens.
Naranjas y limas, etc.	Oranges and lemons, etc.
Ya se va la rama	The *rama* is leaving
muy agradecida,	very thankful,
porque en esta casa	because in this house
fue bien recibida.	it was welcomed.
Naranjas y limas, etc.	Oranges and lemons, etc.

The texts may refer in some way to the birth of Jesus, or they may be entirely secular or picaresque in content.

Corrido

The *corrido* is distributed widely throughout Mexico but has been favored particularly by people in northern and western areas. In simple terms, its historical roots are thought to be in the Spanish *romance*, a long, often epic ballad, structured in a series of *coplas*, and the nineteenth-century printed *décimas* distributed in the fashion of English broadsides as a means of spreading accessible accounts of socially notable events. The revolution beginning in 1910, however, provided the intense popular interest that catapulted the *corrido* to prominence, as it conveyed the events and often heroic exploits of such revolutionary figures as Francisco Madero, Francisco Villa, Emiliano Zapata, and myriad others.

It was in the era of the revolution (1910–1917) that the form and function of the *corrido* became relatively fixed. Structurally, the *corrido* most often consists of a simple melody the length of a *copla* cast in a I–V$_7$ harmonic framework and repeated for a variable number of *coplas* constituting the piece. The meter is usually 3/4, though 2/4 is common, particularly in renditions from later years when *música norteña* with its polka rhythm came into fashion. The emphasis is on the text, sung in a straightforward fashion unfettered by musical complexities. Usually, the first *copla* is a formal introduction, and the final *copla* is a formal farewell. An excerpt from the *corrido* "Valentín de la Sierra" illustrates this structure:

Voy a cantar un corrido	I'm going to sing a *corrido*
de un amigo de mi tierra.	about a friend from my land.
Llamábase Valentín	He was called Valentín,
y fue fusilado y colgado en la sierra.	and he was shot and hung in the sierra.
No me quisiera acordar:	I don't want to recall:
fue una tarde 'el invierno	it was a winter afternoon
cuando, por su mala suerte,	when, from bad luck,
cayó Valentín en manos del gobierno.	Valentín fell into the hands of the government forces.
Vuela, vuela, palomita.	Fly, fly, little dove.
Párate en ese fortín.	Go alight on that fortress.
Estas son las mañanitas	These are the *mañanitas*
de un hombre valiente que fue Valentín.	of a valiant man who was Valentín.

The last stanza (*despedida* "farewell") makes a formal farewell by shifting its stance: after telling of Valentín's capture, interrogation, and execution, it wraps up, under the term *mañanitas* (see below), the information of the previous *coplas*.

The *corrido* continued in its function of memorializing current events, real or imaginary, long after the revolution subsided in 1917. Battles between police and smugglers (*contrabandistas*), assassinations, horse races, and a wide range of tragic and comic stories provide fodder for the composers of *corridos*—on both sides of the Mexico–U.S. border.

Songs by and for children

Children's game-playing songs are "probably one of the most traditional and persistent" musical repertoires in Mexico (Mendoza 1956:55). This conservatism is undoubtedly tied to the group identities that the songs reflect and engender in the children who sing them. Most Mexican game-playing songs are clearly of Hispanic origin, though many variations on those Spanish prototypes have emerged over the centuries of practice in the New World. Circular games (*rondas*), the most prominent, include jump rope and clapping songs, in which the song guides the movements of the game. "La pájara pinta," "Amo ató matarile rilerón," "Doña Blanca," "A la víbora de la mar," "Juan Pirulero," and many others are heard on school playgrounds, parks, streets, and other places where children play. The variety of melodies and texts is great, but most involve constant repetition and the use of nonlexical syllables (Reuter 1985:118).

Mexican children have three other general kinds of children's song: lyric songs not associated with playing games, songs derived from adults' songs, and songs sung by adults to young children. Of the first variety, "La Rana" ("The Frog") exemplifies songs that tell cumulative stories (in the fashion of "Old MacDonald Had a Farm") (after Mendoza 1956: musical example 85):

Cuando la rana se sale a solear,	When the frog goes out to sun itself,
viene la mosca y la quiere picar:	the fly comes along and wants to bite it:
la mosca a la rana,	the fly to the frog,
la rana en el agua:	the frog in the water:
¡cua, cua, cua!	croak, croak, croak!

A new element is added to each successive repetition, resulting in a chain of entities, each trying to do in the one that follows. Death ends the series:

Cuando el herrero se sale a pasear,	When the blacksmith goes out for a walk,
viene la Muerte y lo quiere matar:	Death comes and wants to kill him:
la Muerte al herrero,	Death to the blacksmith,
el herrero al cuchillo,	the blacksmith to the knife,
y el cuchillo al buey,	and the knife to the ox,
y el buey al agua,	and the ox to the water,
y el agua a la lumbre,	and the water to the fire,
y la lumbre al pato,	and the fire to the duck,
y el pato al perro	and the duck to the dog,
y el perro al gato,	and the dog to the cat,
y el gato al ratón,	and the cat to the mouse,
y el ratón a la rana,	and the mouse to the frog,
la rana a la mosca,	the frog to the fly,
la mosca a la rana,	the fly to the frog,
la rana en el agua:	the frog in the water:
¡cua, cua, cua!	croak, croak, croak!

Children's songs derived from adults' songs are of several kinds. Centuries-old Spanish romances, such as "Delgadina," "Mambrú se fue a la guerra," and "El señor don gato," were appropriated and developed by children. Many songs created and recorded especially for children by composer-singers such as Francisco Gabilondo Soler (pseudonym Cri-Cri, El Grillito Cantor "Cri-cri, The Little Cricket Minstrel") have made their way into oral tradition. And of course, the unrelenting presence of commercial advertising jingles and theme songs from soap operas and children's programs in the popular media has left its mark on the songs children sing, particularly in urban areas.

Songs sung by adults to children consist mainly of lullabies (*arrullos*) and coddling songs (*cantos de nana*). *Arrullos* often involve repetition and nonlexical syllables in keeping with the purpose of putting an infant to sleep. *Cantos de nana* often refer to the parts of the body and are combined with movements to develop the infant's physical coordination.

Serenatas

Other musical practices widespread in Mexico include *serenatas*, the related song "Las Mañanitas," and songs and dances (usually associated with a particular cultural region) that have spread through the educational system or the popular media. *Serenatas* (apparently from *sereno* "night watchman," referring to the early hours when their performances traditionally occur) are courting, congratulatory, or devotional serenades. A man may contract or organize a group of musicians and unexpectedly serenade his lover outside her home. The recipient of the serenade may otherwise be a person celebrating a birthday or other happy event—or even a statue of the Virgin of Guadalupe (particularly on 12 December).

The song "Las Mañanitas" is often the first song sung on these occasions. In earlier times, the term *mañanitas* ("early morning") was nearly synonymous with *serenata* and included a range of songs that varied greatly according to local custom. Currently, it often refers to a specific song, an arrangement combining portions of two different *mañanitas*—"Las Mañanitas Mexicanas" and "Las Mañanitas Tapatías."

Folk-derived popular music

Though the recording and broadcasting of regional musics had already been underway during the second and third decades of the twentieth century, the major explosion in Mexico's popular media history did not occur until the fourth decade. The powerful radio station XEW began broadcasting in 1930. It was followed by XEB and others, creating an enormous demand for live musical performances to fill the air time. Seeking opportunities, musicians representing regional musical traditions flocked to Mexico City. In 1935, the Victor Talking Machine Company opened Mexico's first major record-production facility, expanding the availability of recordings of homegrown music. The Mexican film industry prospered in the 1930s and 1940s, and many influential films such as "Allá en el Rancho Grande" (1936), "Cielito Lindo" (1936), and "Ay Jalisco no te rajes!" (1941) portrayed regional musicians, often to evoke an idealized sense of rural life. *Mariachi*, *jarocho*, *marimba*, and other kinds of typical music (*música típica*) were heard and seen throughout Mexico and abroad.

The dramatic growth of the radio, recording, and film industries during this time had major and profound effects on Mexican musical life. Professional composers proliferated, many building on the Mexican tradition of the nineteenth-century romantic song (*canción romántica*). Pseudo-folk and urban derivative styles of music emerged from rural predecessors. The communal character of regional music was displaced by a star system promoted by the commercial media. Foreign folk-derived genres, such as the Cuban *bolero* and the *cumbia*, took hold at the cultural grass roots. American popular-music exports, from the foxtrot to rock and hip-hop, held enormous sway over urban Mexicans' musical tastes.

Canción romántica and canción ranchera

The gamut of Mexican genres, structures, styles of interpretation, and accompanying instrumentation is great. Its range and diversity reflect the musical currents influencing the creation and performance of song in Mexico, particularly since the mid-1800s. It was during this time—of European romanticism, Italian opera, and the rise of the middle class—that a strain of sentimental and nostalgic composition emerged in Mexico. The terms *canción romántica* and *canción sentimental* described this musical vein, which was much in vogue into the early twentieth century and still constitutes a major thread of contemporary Mexican musical life. With Yradier's "La Paloma" (see above), Veracruzan composer Narciso Serradell's "La Golondrina," cast similarly in an *habanera* meter, was an important prototype for songwriters between 1870 and 1900.

In the first decades of the twentieth century, Yucatecan composers, influenced by the Colombian *bambuco* and Cuban parlor music, contributed greatly to the shaping of *canciones románticas*. The prolific Yucatecan songwriter Augusto "Guty" Cárdenas Pinelo (1905–1932) wrote many songs, such as "Rayito de Luna," that became embedded in the growing national musical repertoire. María Grever (1884–1951), based in New York for most of her musical career, created songs such as "Júrame," "Cuando Vuelva a Tu Lado," and "Muñequita Linda" and movie music with wide appeal in the United States, Latin America, and abroad. Agustín Lara (1897?–1970) brought a new urban and more openly sensual sensibility to the *canción romántica* in more than five hundred compositions, such as "Mujer." His early prominence on Mexican radio and in films in the 1930s had a broad impact on musical tastes and contributed to the popularity of his music.

Typically, the *canción romántica* was and continues to be performed by a soloist or a duo or trio of singers, often accompanying themselves on guitars, perhaps with a form of subtle percussion such as maracas or *güiro*. One such group, Trío Los Panchos, which became enormously popular in the late 1940s, contributed greatly to the subsequent prominence of the Cuban-derived, slow-tempo, romantic *bolero*. Its style of interpreting a variety of songs with suave, mellifluous voices singing in two- or three-part harmony forwarded the close association of such groups to *canciones románticas* and the status of the romantic trio as a major Mexican musical stereotype.

The *canción ranchera* came about with the mass migration of rural people to urban areas, Mexico City in particular. Near the end of the twentieth century, urban Mexicans preserved a strong identity with their rural roots. The emergence of the *canción ranchera* is closely linked to the rise of the popular media and to the popularity of folk-derived ensembles such as the modern *mariachi*. Beginning in the 1930s and continuing through the century, popular singer-actor stars of the screen such as Pedro Infante and Jorge Negrete portrayed idealized ranchers, Mexican cowboys (*charros*), and other rural stereotypes, singing country songs (*canciones rancheras*) with straightforward messages of love, romantic betrayal, and adventurous exploits. These songs, finding a niche in the commercial-music market, attracted countless songwriters. The most prolific and influential composer of *canciones rancheras* was José Alfredo Jiménez (1926–1973), who composed and recorded more than four hundred popular compositions beginning in the late 1940s. *Canciones rancheras* are typically in a simple binary form, cast in a slow duple or triple or fast duple meter, and sung by a soloist in a direct, extroverted, passionate style somewhat reminiscent of *bel canto*. The term is often extended to refer to any song sung in a *ranchero* style and particularly such songs accompanied by a *mariachi*. The *bolero ranchero*, for example, is a version of the romantic *bolero* interpreted in a more open-voiced, solo fashion.

Mariachi

Since the 1930s, the *mariachi* (Figure 14.6) has been the most nationally prominent folk-derived Mexican musical ensemble. Post-revolutionary nationalism, which elevated grass-roots cultural expression, and the rising radio and film industries, which disseminated it, contributed to its important role. The term *mariachi* was formerly thought to have derived from the French *mariage* based on the fanciful notion that west Mexican folk string ensembles had played at weddings for the French imperialists who tried to rule the country from 1862 to 1867. Research, however, has unearthed two documents that gainsay this etymology. In one, dated 1852, the priest Cosme Santa Anna in Rosamorada, Jalisco told his archbishop that the diversions called *mariachis* were

Figure 14.6
A *mariachi* in Mexico City poses in front of the historic cabaret Salón Tenampa, located on Plaza Garibaldi, where *mariachis* gather and perform daily. Left to right: men playing two trumpets, two violins, a *guitarrón*, and a *vihuela*. Photo by Daniel Sheehy, 1991.

disrupting holy days. In the other, a diary entry written in Guerrero in 1859, the priest Ignacio Aguilar referred to *Mariache* as a musical ensemble (Jáuregui 1990:15–18). That both these sources predate the French occupation nullifies unsubstantiated accounts of a French imperialist origin.

The old-time *mariachi*—one or two violins, a *guitarra de golpe* and/or a *vihuela*, and a harp or some form of string bass—still exists in some rural communities of Jalisco and Nayarit, where it plays a generations-old repertoire of *sones*, *jarabes*, and religious pieces called *minuetes*. Its presence has been eclipsed almost entirely, though, by the modern *mariachi*, which evolved largely in response to the success of Mexico City's commercial-music industry in radio, film, recordings, and, later, television. The instrumentation was expanded to include sections called *melodía* (two trumpets and three to six or more violins) and *armonía* (a *vihuela*, a guitar, a *guitarrón*, and occasionally a harp). Since the 1930s, the evolution of the *mariachi* was tied closely to that of *música ranchera* and its star system.

The preeminent and archetypal modern *mariachi* since the 1940s has been Mariachi Vargas de Tecalitlán. Under the guidance of the late Silvestre Vargas, Mariachi Vargas came to dominate commercial *mariachi* music. It appeared regularly in the major electronic media, accompanying the most prominent singers of *música ranchera*, and producing countless recordings. Its musical arrangements of traditional pieces and modern compositions set the standard for virtually all modern *mariachis* throughout Mexico and abroad. Since the 1950s, the group's close collaboration with the composer-arranger Rubén Fuentes, who joined Vargas as a musician in 1945, had a profound impact on *mariachi* music. His innovations brought the harmonic language of contemporary popular music and new instrumental techniques and rhythms into the canon of *mariachi* conventions.

Other folk-derived popular musics

The twentieth century saw the creation of many folk-derived musical expressions. In the early decades, the *orquesta típica*, an ensemble of musicians in folkloric garb, played regional melodies on a variety of (primarily stringed) instruments. Miguel Lerdo de Tejada was its leading exponent. The Veracruzan harpist Andrés Huesca, the *requinto* player Lino

Chávez, and others brought standardized arrangements and compositions in a modified *son jarocho* style to audiences in the 1940s and later.

Other regional styles of music penetrated or were co-opted by the mainstream Mexican commercial media. In the 1950s, the accordion-driven *música norteña* entered the commercial market through actor-singers such as the witty Lalo González "Piporro," and, in the 1960s and 1970s, through successful recording artists such as Cornelio Reyna. By the early 1990s, "new" pop groups called *bandas*, emulating the raucous, brass-woodwind-percussion sounds of two closely related ensembles, Sinaloa-style bands (*bandas sinaloenses*) and Zacatecas-style bands (*tamborazos zacatecanos*), dominated Mexican pop. The *marimba* ensemble, though never a major force in the popular media, was an indispensable musical icon, often used to represent the cultural milieu of Chiapas and southern Oaxaca. Although each of these styles reflected the fads of commercial popularity, through widespread recognition as a music representing part of Mexico's national cultural identity, they all filled a long-lasting niche in Mexican musical tastes.

MUSIC LEARNING, DISSEMINATION, TOURISM, AND PUBLIC POLICY

Music learning

Public-school curricula include a small repertoire of traditional songs and dances, and many universities have ongoing ensembles studying and performing folkloric music and dance from a variety of styles. The federal government's social security agency (Seguro Social) sponsors music-and-dance groups and presentations as part of its concern for the well-being of the population. Representations of folkloric traditions are a key element in public and privately funded efforts to promote tourism. Other sectors of government, the armed forces and police departments, for example, may subsidize the performance of such music and dance. The National Conservatory of Music, regional institutions of higher education, and private music schools such as the Escuela de la Música Mexicana in Mexico City offer advanced and specialized music instruction in a range of traditions and styles.

International popular music in Mexico and Mexican music abroad

Although homegrown musical strains, *música ranchera* in particular, account for a major share of the commercially dominant popular music in Mexico, pop-music fashions from abroad hold sway among urban people. Interest in foreign musical models is not new. The Mexican middle class that emerged in the 1800s adored European salon music and opera. A passionate interest in the Cuban *danzón*, kindled in the 1920s and 1930s, waned but continued throughout the century. American dance orchestras of the 1940s and 1950s spawned countless Mexican imitators and internationally popular composer-bandleaders such as Luis Arcaraz. Música tropical—in its most general sense, referring to rhythmically lively urban dance music of Caribbean origin—gained a large following. Beginning in the late 1940s, the *mambo*, the *cha-cha-chá*, the *cumbia*, and, later, *salsa* penetrated Mexican markets and entered the repertoires of many kinds of musical ensembles throughout the country. North American, Brazilian, and other romantic ballad styles were incorporated into the *balada*, an extension of the *canción romántica*. Beginning in the 1950s, large numbers of young Mexicans flocked to American rock. Mexican bands did Spanish-language covers of popular melodies and composed new pieces, though they never managed to forge a long-lasting and distinctly Mexican style of rock.

Much Mexican popular music and, to a much lesser extent, grass-roots traditional music has found a following outside Mexico. With the rise of the commercial music complex in the early twentieth century, Mexican musicians recorded and performed abroad. The first *mariachi* recording is thought to have been made in Mexico City in 1908. Folkloric troupes of dancers and musicians presented theatrical renditions of regional music and dance on every continent, especially in Europe and the Americas. Trío Los Panchos, which formed in New York, toured widely in the United States before settling in Mexico. Commercially aspiring ensembles saw touring abroad, particularly to economically prosperous locations like New York and Los Angeles, as means of gaining greater recognition and profits. Powerful radio stations such as XEW broadcast Mexican music deep into Latin America. Many Mexican musicians resettled in other countries. At the first annual Encuento del Mariachi in Guadalajara in 1994, *mariachis* from the United States, Canada, Costa Rica, Aruba, Venezuela, Italy, Belgium, Japan, and other countries joined their Mexican counterparts. In the final decades of the twentieth century, many Mexican artists, from Mariachi Vargas de Tecalitlán, to singers such as Angeles Ochoa and the veteran Lola Beltrán (d. 1996), to composer-singers such as Armando Manzanero, Luis Miguel, and Juan Gabriel, had major followings abroad. The combination of long-proven Mexican musical productivity and a large and successful Mexican music industry exporting music around the world opened a broad swath in many parts of the world, especially among Spanish-speaking communities.

Music and public policy

In the post revolutionary era, numerous governmental efforts have promoted a common canon of folklore throughout the country. There is no greater archetype of this canon than "El Jarabe Tapatío." *Jarabe* ("syrup" in Mexican Spanish) referred in Mexico to a dance piece as early as 1789, when "El Jarabe Gatuno" was condemned by Inquisition authorities on moral grounds. In the early 1800s, the *jarabe* was still a single, short dance, most likely included in what were called *sones*. Its identity as part of an oppressed *mestizo* culture catapulted it to prominence as the Mexican insurgents won independence from Spain. It thus became one of the earliest musical symbols of national identity. By 1900, it was a series of short *sones* linked together as one composition and was most prevalent in the west-central states of Colima, Durango, Jalisco, Michoacán, and Nayarit. Some of these *jarabes*, such as "El Jarabe Tapatío," were arranged for piano and published, becoming established as standard versions. In performances of "El Jarabe Tapatío" in Mexico City in 1918, the Russian ballerina Anna Pavlova popularized choreographic innovations that further standardized the piece. By 1921, when, in Mexico City, performers premiered the version of "El Jarabe Tapatío" to be taught in the nation's public schools, its primacy and the title of "El Jarabe Nacional" were fixed, though at the expense of losing much of its dynamic quality as a social dance.

At the turn of the twenty-first century, the National Culture and Arts Agency CONACULTA supported a range of musical expression. Many state and local organizations, often known as culture houses (*casas de cultura*), have supported research, documentation, teaching, and presentation of regional music and dance.

National anthem

While exiled in Havana, Cuba in 1851, Mexican general Antonio de López de Santa Anna met the future composer of the Mexican national anthem, Jaime Nunó. Nunó was born in Catalonia, Spain, 8 September 1824 and orphaned by the deaths of his parents at a young age. Placed in the custody of the local bishop, he became a soprano soloist in the Barcelona Cathedral Choir, trained in music in Barcelona and Rome, and became a talented composer and conductor. He was appointed the director of the Queen's regiment in Cuba. After Santa Anna's return to power, he persuaded Nunó in April 1853 to join him in Mexico as director of all of the nation's army bands. On 2 February 1854, a competition convened by Santa Anna's regime to select the best lyrics for a new national anthem awarded Francisco González Bocanegra the honor. In close succession, a second competition picked Jaime Nunó's composition, then titled "Dios y Libertad" ("God and Freedom"), as the official anthem, applauding its combined "simplicity and magnificent effect." Nunó was awarded 300 pesos for his effort, and the anthem was officially debuted that year at the Independence Day celebrations beginning the evening of 15 September. A year after Santa Anna's revolving door leadership once again sent him into exile in 1855, Nunó left for New York state, where he spent most of the rest of his life until his death 18 July 1908. He enjoyed triumphant return visits to Mexico in 1901 and 1904, the latter to celebrate the fiftieth anniversary of the "Himno Nacional." On 6 October 1942, Nunó's remains were transported in a Mexican Air Force plane from Buffalo, New York to Mexico City and placed next to those of Francisco González Bocanegra in the Rotunda of Illustrious Men. On 20 October 1942, President Ávila Camacho decreed the piece the official national anthem and strictly prohibited that its lyrics or music be altered, corrected, or modified.

FURTHER STUDY

English-language sources on pre-Conquest, colonial, and nineteenth-century music in Mexico are few, but Robert M. Stevenson offered a cornucopia of insightful documentation, synthesis, and critical references of previous scholarship in *Music in Aztec and Inca Territory* (1968) and his earlier *Music in Mexico: A Historical Survey* (1952). Peter Crossley-Holland offered new analysis of pre-Aztec musical instruments of West Mexico and an appeal for greater scholarly collaboration among musicologists, archaeologists, anthropologists, physicists, and others in his *Musical Artifacts of Pre-Hispanic West Mexico* (1980). Among the milestone English-language articles on the topic are Charles Boilès' works on flutes and the musical bow (1965, 1966a, 1966b) and E. Thomas Stanford's analysis of music-and-dance terms in three sixteenth-century native-language dictionaries (1966).

Several Mexican scholars have published important works in Spanish on Mexican music history. Gabriel Saldívar broke much new ground through his examination of colonial documents and ancient instruments, resulting in his *Historia de la música en México (épocas precortesiana y colonial)* (1934). Samuel Martí's *Instrumentos musicales precortesianos* (1955; second edition, 1968) offers photographic illustrations of musical artifacts, and his *Canto, danza y música precortesianos* (1961) employs iconography, historical accounts, and ethnographic musical transcriptions in search of knowledge about Aztec song, dance, and music. Articles and book chapters by the folklorist Vicente T. Mendoza (1938, 1956), Daniel Castañeda (1933, 1942), and Carmen Sordo Sodi (1964) are among the many shorter publications treating pre-encounter music. Otto Mayer-Serra's *Panorama de la música mexicana desde la independencia hasta la actualidad* (1941) offered a critical treatment of fine-art music from 1810 to the 1930s.

Though scholarly research on tribal, folk, and popular music in the final decades of the twentieth century has built on and advanced the accomplishments of Saldívar, Mendoza, Stevenson, and others, many musical traditions still lack comprehensive, in-depth, authoritative documentation. Jas Reuter's *La música popular de México* (fourth edition, 1985) offers a brief, introductory overview of tribal and *mestizo* music. The *Serie de discos* edited mainly by Irene Vázquez Valle (1967–1979) is the most comprehensive effort to document a panorama of native American and *mestizo* musical traditions through recordings and descriptive notes. Other important recordings of Mexican music are by Lieberman et al. (1985), Montes de Oca H. (1994), Strachwitz (1992, 1993, 1995), Strachwitz and Sheehy (1994), and many recordings on the Discos Corason label founded by Eduardo Llerenas. In *Historia de la música popular mexicana* (1989), Yolanda Moreno Rivas synthesized much background and biographical detail on the origins, leading personalities, and major trends of popular musical styles. The music of Mexico's Amerindian peoples, particularly that of smaller, more marginal, groups, is acutely in need of further documentation.

REFERENCES

Aguirre Beltrán, Gonzalo. 1976. *La problacíon negra de Mexico, 1519–1810*. Mexico City: Ediciones Fuente Cultral.

Béhague, Gerard. 1979. *Music in Latin America: An Introduction*. Englewood Cliffs, N.J.: Prentice-Hall.

Boilès, Charles Lafayette. 1965. "La Flauta Triple de Tenenexpan." *La Palabra y el Hombre (Revista de la Universidad Veracruzana)* 34 (April-June).

———. 1966a. "El Arco Musical, ¿Una Pervivencia?" *La Palabra y el Hombre (Revista de la Universidad Veracruzana)* 39 (July–Sept.).

———. 1966b. "The Pipe and Tabor in Mesoamerica." In *Yearbook* 2 of the Inter-American Institute for Musical Research, 43–74. New Orleans: Tulane University.

Calderón de la Barca, Frances Erskine. 1843. *Life in Mexico during a Residence of Two Years in That Country*. London: Chapman and Hall.

Castañeda, Daniel. 1942. "Una flauta de la cultura tarasca." *Revista Musical Mexicana* (7 March).

Castañeda, Daniel, and Vicente T. Mendoza. 1933. *Los Teponaztlis, Los Percutores Precortesianos, Los Huehuetls. Anales del Museo Nacional de Arqueología, Historia y Etnografía*, 8. México, D.F.: Museo Nacional de Arqueología, Historia y Etnografía.

Crossley-Holland, Peter. 1980. M*usical Artifacts of Pre-Hispanic West Mexico: Towards an Interdisciplinary Approach*. Monograph Series in Ethnomusicology, 1. Los Angeles: Department of Ethnomusicology, University of California at Los Angeles.

Durán, Diego. 1867–1880. *Historia de las Indias de Nueva-España*. 2 vols. México, D.F.: J. M. Andrade and F. Escalante.

Esteva, José María. 1844a. "Costumbres y trages nacionales: La jarochita." *El museo mexicano*, 3:234–235.

———. 1844b. "Trages y costumbres nacionales: El jarocho." *El museo mexicano* 4:60–62.

Jáuregui, Jesús. 1990. *El mariachi: Símbolo musical de México*. México, D.F.: Banpaís.

Lieberman, Baruj, Eduardo Llerenas, and Enrique Ramírez de Arellano. 1985. *Antología del Son de México*. Discos Corason / Música Tradicional (México) MTCD 01–03. 3 compact discs.

Martí, Samuel. 1955. *Instrumentos musicales precortesianos*. México, D.F.: Instituto Nacional de Antropología.

———. 1961. *Canto, Danza y Música Precorte*sianos. México, D.F.: Fondo de Cultura Económica.

———. 1968. *Instrumentos musicales precortesianos*, 2nd ed. México, D.F.: Instituto Nacional de Antropología e Historia.

Mayer-Serra, Otto. 1941. *Panorama de la música mexicana desde la independencia hasta la actualidad*. México, D.F.: El Colegio de México.

Mendoza, Vicente T. 1938. "Música Precolombina de América." *Boletín Latino-Americana de Música* 4(4):235–257.

———. 1939. *El romance español y el corrido mexicano: Estudio comparativo*. México, D.F.: Ediciones de la Universidad Nacional Autónoma de México.

———. 1956. *Panorama de la música tradicional de México*. México, D.F.: Imprenta Universitaria.

Montes de Oca H., Ignacio. 1994. *Music of Mexico, Vol. 2: Michoacán: Conjunto Alma de Apatzingán, "Arriba Tierra Caliente."* Arhoolie CD426. Compact disc.

Moreno Rivas, Yolanda. 1989. *Historia de la música popular mexicana*, 2nd ed. México, D.F.: Consejo Nacional para la Cultura y las Artes, Alianza Editorial Mexicana.

Motolinía, Toribio de. 1941 [1858]. *Historia de los Indios de Nueva España*, ed. Salvador Chávez Hayhoe. México, D.F.

Pareyón, Gabriel. 1995. *Diccionario de Músic de México*. Guadalajara, México:Secretaría de Cultura de Jalisco.

Prieto, Guillermo. 1906. *Memorias de mis tiempos*. 2 vols. México, D.F.: Viuda de C. Bouret.

Reuter, Jas. 1985. *La música popular de México: Origen e historia de la música que canta y toca el pueblo mexicano*. México, D.F.: Panorama Editoria.

Sahagún, Bernardino. 1956 [1547]. *Historia general de las cosas de Nueva España. New edition, with numeration, annotation, and appendices*, ed. Angel M. Garibay K. México, D.F.: Editorial Porrúa.

Saldívar, Gabriel. 1934. *Historia de la música en México: Épocas precortesiana y colonial*. México, D.F.: Editorial "Cultura."

———. 1937. *El Jarabe, baile popular mexicano*. México, D.F.: Talleres Gráficos de la Nación.

Sheehy, Daniel. 2006. *Mariachi Music in America: Experiencing Music, Expressing Culture*. New York: Oxford University Press.

Sordo Sodi, María del Carmen. 1964. "Los dioses de la música y de la danza en el Códice Borgia." *Revista del Conservatorio* (Mexico City), 7 (June).

Stanford, E. Thomas. 1966. "A Linguistic Analysis of Music and Dance Terms from Three Sixteenth-Century Dictionaries of Mexican Indian Languages." In *Yearbook 2* of the Inter-American Institute for Musical Research, 101–159. New Orleans: Tulane University.

Stevenson, Robert M. 1952. *Music in Mexico: A Historical Survey*. New York: Thomas Y. Crowell.

———. 1968. *Music in Aztec and Inca Territory*. Berkeley and Los Angeles: University of California Press.

Strachwitz, Chris. 1992. *Mexico's Pioneer Mariachis, Vol. 3: Mariachi Vargas de Tecalitlán: Their First Recordings 1937–1947*. Arhoolie- Folklyric CD7015. Compact disc.

———. 1993. *Mexico's Pioneer Mariachis, Vol. 1: Mariachi Coculense de Cirilo Marmolejo, Plus Several Sones by Cuarteto Coculense: The Very First Mariachi Recordings from 1908*. Arhoolie-Folklyric CD7011. Compact disc.

———. 1995. *Music of Mexico, Vol. 3: La Huasteca; Huapangos y Sones Huastecos; Los Caimanes (1995) y Los Caporales de Panuco (1978)*. Arhoolie 431. Compact disc.

Strachwitz, Chris, and Dan Sheehy. 1994. *Music of Mexico, Vol.1: Veracruz: Conjunto Alma Jarocha, "Sones Jarochos."* Arhoolie CD354. Compact disc.

Tapia Colman, Simón.1991. *Música y músicos de México*. México, D.F.: Panorama Editorial.

Vázquez Valle, Irene. 1967–1979. *Serie de discos*. México, D.F.: Instituto Nacional de Antropología. 24 LP disks with notes.

Tarahumara

J. Richard Haefer

Musical Instruments
Musical Contexts and Genres
Further Study

The Tarahumara (Tarahumar, Rarámuri, or "runners") of northwest Mexico occupy the meadows, canyons, valleys, and uplands of central and southern Chihuahua. Numbering some fifty thousand, they have lived in this area for more than two thousand years. They were contacted by Jesuits as early as 1610 (Pérez de Ribas 1944 [1645]). In 1767, at the time of the Jesuit expulsion, they supported nearly thirty missions and more than fifty *visitas* small, nearby suburbs of a mission. The Franciscans replaced the Jesuits in northern Mexico, but mission activity declined among the Tarahumara; many of them retreated into the mountains in the southwest corner of Chihuahua.

Despite the presence of missionaries, miners, and cattlemen, little acculturation occurred before the middle of the twentieth century, when the Mexican government opened facilities for the Indians. In the early 1960s, with the opening of the trans-Sierra Madre railroad (Ferrocarril de Chihuahua al Pacífico), outside influences expanded rapidly. Even so, the Tarahumara have selectively adopted outsiders' cultural traits. Few archaeological investigations have been conducted in their area.

The climate of the Sierra Madre varies from tropical in the valleys to extreme cold in the highlands in winter. Lowland areas are desert, but the mountainous valleys are heavily wooded; in the uplands, heavy rainfalls provide adequate water for junipers, pines, and many other trees. Most Tarahumara live in hamlets (*rancherías*) of several families, each occupying a one- or two-room house. Until early in the 1900s, when outsiders opened local sawmills, houses were made of stone with earthen roofs; many Tarahumara still live in caves in the upper regions of the territory. Local leaders and ceremonial practitioners are elected, or, more often, appointed, as needed.

The only traditional Tarahumara musical instrument in current use is a gourd container rattle. Archaeology has revealed the use of the gourd rattle, a membraphonic drum, and a musical bow during the precontact period (Zingg 1940:63–64). Several instruments were adopted from the Europeans early in the time of contact and are still in use today.

The gourd rattle is normally made from a bottle gourd (*arisiki*), which grows in the valleys. Naturally in pear or globular shape, an *arisiki* gourd is cleaned out and partially filled with seeds or pebbles. The instrument serves for dances, such as the traditional *yúmari* dance and the adopted *matachín* festival. With the coming of sawmills, some Tarahumara began making a distinctive four-sided rattle from thin *uré* wood shavings glued together and supported by two disks where the rattle handle passes through the container. Used by the *matachín* dancers, these rattles are normally topped with a small cross. Additional rattles may also have been made of hide, deer hooves, or cocoons that were tied around the ankles of dancers.

Instruments adopted from Europeans since early times are the guitar and the violin, and possibly the pipe-and-tabor (although there is evidence in pre-Columbian Mexico for the pipe-and-tabor combination). Guitar and violin soundboards are made from local woods, usually pine or ash (*uré, cabari, sawá, watosí*; for scientific names, see Pennington 1963:163), and fingerboards are made from *inóko*, a hardwood. The Tarahumara guitar has less of an hourglass shape than a modern Spanish instrument, and the indentation is well above the center of the sound box. Metal frets are inserted in the fingerboard, and commercial guitar strings are purchased from local stores. Most guitars are undecorated, though occasionally colored tin from a fruit can serves to hold the strings. The guitar is found much less frequently than the violin, and when used, it provides chords strummed beneath the violin melody for the *matachín* dancers.

The violin is somewhat larger than a modern European instrument, nearly the size of a European viola, sometimes with an extremely deep waist. It is made of the same woods as the guitar, with *inóko* used for the fingerboard, pegs, and bow. The bridge may be made of local woods, or sometimes of another material, such as plastic, and the tail piece is made of wood or tin from a can. The head of the scroll box is often carved, usually in the shape of an animal's head (a horse's head is common), and geometric patterns are frequently cut into the lower part of the fingerboard. Commercial violin strings or guitar strings are used, and horsetail hairs are used for the bow, with a peg sometimes used to apply tension. Stringed instruments are normally unvarnished and undecorated, although makers may use colored pencils to outline the eyes of the scroll animal and the large f-holes.

Held in an old-fashioned European way (against the bottom of the collarbone), violins are played in large ensembles for *matachín* dancers, often by as many as eight to twelve violinists; for small fiestas, however, a single violinist will do. The music consists of one to three short phrases, repeated with variations lasting from five to thirty minutes, depending on the dancers' patterns. Velasco Rivero (1983:170–77) outlines some of the typical line-dance patterns as figure-eights, crisscrossing lines, and reverse loops. Melodies may be played in unison or in parts, usually thirds, and infrequently with a drone. Little is known about the songs of

Figure 15.1
A Tarahumara pipe
and tabor player
with members of the
soldiers' society seared
beside him during
Holy Week daytime
ceremonies. Photo by J.
Richard Haefer.

the *matachines*. The system is somewhat complex, with different tunings used throughout a night's performance and possibly different repertoires for different activities, such as playing for private fiestas at home, dancing in front of or inside a church, or in procession (Griffith 1979). After tuning, one performer begins playing, and others will join in as soon as they feel comfortable with the composition.

The pipe-and-tabor consists of a duct flute and double-sided drum. The flute is played by the musician's left hand while he dangles his drum from the little finger of the left hand and strikes it with a stick held in his right hand. Sometimes the musician may rest his drum against his knee or the ground (Figure 15.1). The flute (pipe) is a modified version of the European recorder but with an external duct made by tying a short piece of larger-diameter cane atop the main body of the instrument. It may have as many as four boles for fingering, but three is the norm. The drum is often as large as 60 centimeters or more in diameter and about 10 centimeters deep; smaller ones are made and sold to tourists, especially along the railroad. The drumheads, made of goatskin, may be decorated with red ochre paint, usually in geometric patterns, or left undecorated. Modern drums, made of wooden hoops, usually have several beads strung across one head as a snare. Older drums were fashioned from a hollowed-out section or a log and were deeper in shape. Drums may also be played without the flute—a further indication of their antiquity within Tarahumaran culture.

MUSICAL CONTEXTS AND GENRES

Tarahumara musical performances blend indigenous and European ideas, freely rein-terpreted after the expulsion of the Jesuits from the area (Merrill 1983:296). In local cosmography, the universe consists of seven layers. One god—the father (*ononrúam*), the father god (*tata riósi*), the sun (*rayénari*, called *el padre* 'the father' by González Rodríguez 1982:78)—inhabits the uppermost level, and the god of the lower house—*terégor*, the devil—inhabits the lowest. The Tarahumara live in the middle levels. Other levels are occupied by mother, the moon, the Virgin Mary (*metsaka*, called la *madre* "the mother" by González Rodríguez 1982:79), Mexicans, other non-Tarahumara (*cabóci* "whiskered ones"), and others. The people "conceive of human beings as composed of a body 'sapá' and one or more [autonomous] souls" (Merrill 1988:87).

Tarahumara rituals perpetuate goodness and restore the well-being of particular individuals or the community, but most elements of either kind of celebration are the same. Rituals derived from Christian customs mark the feasts of the Virgin of Guadalupe (12 December), Christmas, the Feast of the Three Kings (Epiphany, 6 January), and Holy Week (especially Palm Sunday and Maundy Thursday through Holy Saturday). During Lenten celebrations, pipes-and-tabors accompany the dancing of the *pariseos* ("Pharisees," in Spanish *fariseos*, associated with Judas).

Less important or localized celebrations may take place for the Immaculate Conception of the Blessed Virgin Mary (8 December), Candlemas (2 February), Corpus Christi (in June), and various local saints. Fiestas normally begin on the eve of the holy day and continue for eight to twenty-four hours, ending with a dinner for all present. The sponsors (*pisteros*, Spanish *fiesteros*), assisted by their relatives, must provide for all aspects of the celebration, including the dancers, musicians, and food.

Traditional ceremonies

González Rodríguez (1982:345) lists eight genres of dances: *tutuguri*, *yúmari*, *matachín* (not precontact), *pascola*, *warishíwami*, *kuwari*, *ayena*, and *yo'é*, indicating that the last four are rare indeed, if found at all. Among Tarahumara ceremonial practices, other sources list *bakánawi* as a curing ceremony, *korima* as a harvest ceremony, and *nawesari* as "ritualized public sermons" that apparently occur within larger ceremonial contexts. Merrill (1988) and Veiasco Rivero (1983) present analyses and examples of sermons, the primary method for presenting reproductions of knowledge through words as a means of restructuring Tarahumaran customs. Merrill discusses curing, including the processes of diagnosis and the prevention and alleviation of sickness, especially in relation to the concept of soul. Such cures are led by a curer (*owirúame*). Other sources describe curing only in relation to *tutuguri*.

Most sources state that *tutuguri* and *yúmari* are names for the same ceremony. It is suspected, however, that further research will show that *tutuguri* is the name for the entire ceremony complex, and *yúmari* may more specifically refer to the dance performed in a circle within the larger ceremony. Some sources indicate that the two names may be specific to particular geographical regions, though that concept seems less justifiable, or that *yúmari* is a generic Spanish term for native dances in this area. *Tutuguri*, a precontact ceremony, is often called a curing ceremony, but is actually practiced to maintain harmony—curing in the most general sense. Led by a chanter (*wikaráame*, *sawéame*) who presents the sermon and with two additional singers leads the singing, the *tutuguri* consists of a synthesis of indigenous and Roman Catholic elements, including a sacrifice of food—a white goat or chickens, plus food to be consumed in the fiesta following—to the sun god, line and circle dancing, and the use of a cross, incense, and a rosary (this resembles the Guarijio *túmari*). *Tutuguri* is also celebrated at eclipses and the winter solstice, with a representation of the sun painted on large drums played during the night.

Tutuguri songs differ from most Middle and North American Indian songs in that they start low and ascend, though the overall structure has successive phrases beginning at lower tones. Songs are usually quite brief, as few as three phrases of only about four seconds each repeated for up to five minutes or more. A rattle pattern is played with downward strokes throughout most of the song, alternating with rolls at the ascent (*Indian Music of Northwest Mexico* 1978). Nearly all sources report the musical texts as being unintelligible, but a seventeenth-century observer (Guadalajara 1683) translated a musical text loosely into a Spanish sentence glossable as "she asks the moon to take care of her sheep so they can have much wool to card, comb, and knit for good blankets" (González Rodríguez 1982:110). *Tutuguri*, therefore, is sung and danced for curing, for propitiation, and for entreating the gods on behalf of all Tarahumara, or as they say, asking forgiveness (*wikálawi tánia*) for a long and healthy life, abundant crops, and many children. *Tutuguri* ends with the offering of food in the early-morning hours, followed by a feast for all in attendance. A *tutuguri* performed during Lent may be accompanied by *fariseos* dancing to the pipe and tabor; the rest of the year, *matachines* may or may not be present.

Several sources, including the seventeenth-century authors Cajas Castro (1992:199–211) and Rodríguez (1982), mention the use of peyote (*jíkuri*) by the Tarahumara. Cajas Castro believes this practice to be older than that of *yúmari*, but few details are known. Peyote celebrations take place only in winter and may involve a *tutuguri a matachín*. González Rodriguez (1982:117) mentions its function for the purification of the dead in a private ceremony led by a *sipáame*. Permission of the local village governor is required, and the ceremony includes the drinking of *tesgüino* plus such Christian elements as a cross.

Acculturated ceremonies

European-derived ceremonies center on the Christian liturgical calendar. In remote locations, they follow an outmoded calendar modified by time and the absence of priests. Being an oral-tradition culture, the Tarahumara are not attuned to changes in the dates for the celebration of various ceremonies as dictated by the ecumenical council known as Vatican II. Therefore, they continue to celebrate the ceremonies as they think they always have, using the dates of the former calendar.

Two main organizations are found: the *matachines* and the societies of Holy Week. *Matachines* dance throughout the year, except during Lent and Easter, especially for Our Lady of Guadalupe day, Christmas, and Epiphany, though they may appear at private fiestas and even dance at *tutuguri*. *Matachines*, introduced from Europe in the 1600s, were first noted in the village of Norogachi in September 1737 by the missionary Lorenzo Gero (González Rodríguez 1982:146), and again in January 1752 by Bartholomé Braun—the latter undoubtedly for an Epiphany celebration, the former probably for the Exaltation of the Holy Cross.

Dancing in front of the church or a private home, the *matachines* (called *awíeme* "dancer") are led by one or two organizers (*monarkos*, rather like booking agents but physically present to lead the group) and a *chapeyó* (another kind of dancer, found principally at smaller, home ceremonies) wearing a deer's head. From four to twenty or more *matachines* move in intricate lines, changing directions at the organizers' shouts and occasionally performing elaborate circle-eight figurations (see Velasco Rivero 1983:170–177, for movement diagrams). On their heads, the *matachín* dancers wear crowns made from a shell of wood covered with bright, meter-long streamers and mirrors or reflective pieces of metal, distinctively different from those of their northern neighbors, the Yaqui and Mayos. Their lower face and shoulders are covered by scarves, as is the front of the waist; brightly colored shirts and jeans are worn beneath. In some regions, colorful bolts of cloth may be draped around the body. In their right hand they carry a gourd rattle and in the left a wand, sometimes shaped like a heart, covered with crepe paper. The dancers, all men, move to the music of violins, in a few places accompanied by one or two guitarists.

Holy Week celebrations are more elaborate and involve two sodalities: *pariseos* and *sontárusi* ("soldiers," in Spanish *soldados*). Leaders appoint appropriate boys and men from the village to dance with each group. Between mass and other ritual devotions, different activities take place daily, including dancing inside and outside the church and processions. A straw-stuffed effigy Judas is hidden by the *pariseos*, and when it is found by the soldiers, it is "killed," burned, or mutilated genitally, depending on local custom. On Holy Saturday, individuals from the two groups wrestle one another, and in some regions one or two *pas-cola*-like dancers appear. Griffith (1983:775) identifies the *pascola* as "a clown and dancer whose appearance enlivens certain fiestas" but who is not part of a separate cult as in other Northern Mexican Indian cultures. *Pariseos* are identified by costuming that includes a bare chest and back with large white scarves or cloth tied over the lower body. Long scarves are tied around the head and hang down the back. The leaders wear turkey-feather headdresses. In some regions, a few dancers have large spots of white clay painted on their chests, backs, and legs, and are accordingly called *pintos*. Elsewhere additional dancers, such as *tenanches'* ("outsider") and *mulatos*, appear. Pharisees dance to the pipe and tabor or the drum alone.

The soldiers dance simultaneously with and against the *pariseos*, are dressed distinctively in long white cloths draped over their bodies, and wear long, red headbands. The leader carries a large red banner of office, and all carry long lances. Holy-Week festivities are sponsored by one or two *pisteros* assisted by their relatives and friends, who may take a year or more to save enough money to pay for the occasion. As with all Tarahumara celebrations, the dancing ends with feasting for all and much drinking of *tesgüino*, often continuing in private homes for several days after Easter.

FURTHER STUDY

Detailed descriptions of the presentations of *matachines* (including more information about organizers and *chapeyos*) are given in Bennett and Zingg (1976 [1935]), Cajas Castro

(1992:154–163), Fontana et al. (1977, 1979), González Rodríguez (1982), Merrill (1983), and Velasco Rivero (1983:152–188). Tarahumara Holy Week celebrations have been studied by González Rodríguez (1982), Velasco Rivero (1983:189–233), Cajas Castro (1992:164–187), and Merrill (1983).

REFERENCES

Bennett, Wendell Clark, and Hubert M. Zingg. 1976 [1935]. *The Tarahumara, an Indian Tribe of Nortern Mexico*. Glorieta, N. M.: Rio Grande Press.

Cajas Castro, Juan. 1992. *La sierra tarahumara o lot desuelos de la modernidad en Mexico*. México, D.F.: Consejo National para la Cultura y las Artes.

Fontana, Bernard, ct al. 1977. *The Other Southwest, Indian Arts mid Crafts of Northwestern Mexico*. Phoenix: Heard Museum.

————. 1979. *The Material World of the Tarahumara*. Tucson: Arizona state Museum

Griffith, James S. 1979. *Tarahumara Matachin Music*. Phoenix: Canyon Records, C-8000. Notes to LP disk.

————. 1983. "Kachinas and Masking." In *Southwest*, ed. Alfonso Ortiz, 764–777. *Handbook of North American Indians*, 10. Washington, D.C.: Smithsonian Institution Press.

González Rodríguez, Luis. 1982. *Tarahumara. La sierra y el hombre*. México, D.F.: Fondo de Cultura Económica.

Guadalajara, Tomás de. 1683. *Compendio del arte de la lengue de los tarahumaras y guazapares*. Puebla: Imprenta Real.

Indian Music of Northwest Mexico. 1978. Canyon Records C-8001. LP disk.

Merrill, William L. 1983. "Tarahumara Social Organization, Political Organization, and Religion." In *Southwest*, ed. Alfonso Ortiz, 290–303. *Handbook of North American Indians* 10. Washington, D.C.: Smithsonian Institution Press

————. 1988. *Rarámuri Souls. Knowledge and Social Process in Northern Mexico*. Washington, D.C.: Smithsonian Institution Press,

Pennington, Campbell W. 1963. *The Tarahumara of Mexico. Their Environment and Material Culture*. Salt Lake City: University of Utah Press.

Velasco Rivero, Pedro de. 1983. *Danzar o morir, religion y resistencia a la dominación en la cultura tarahnmara*. México, D.F.: Centro de Reflexión Teológica.

Zingg, Robert M. 1940. *The Tarahumara. An Indian Tribe of Northern Mexico*. Chicago: University of Chicago Press.

Guatemala

Linda O'Brien-Rothe

The Indigenous Heritage
The European Heritage
The African Heritage
Musical Instruments
Musical Contexts and Genres
The Emergence of Guatemalan Music
Music Learning, Dissemination, and Public Policy
Further Study

Before the Spanish contact in 1524, the territory that is now the Republic of Guatemala was part of the area where Maya civilization developed, flourished, and declined. When the conquistadors arrived, the great Maya temple-cities had long been abandoned, and classic Maya culture lay hidden beneath covers of jungle and time. The Spaniards found the Maya of Guatemala a people divided into more or less mutually hostile, petty kingdoms of the Quiché, Cakchiquel, Ixil, Kekchí, Mam, Pokoman, and Tzutujil clans. The territory won independence from Spain in 1821.

THE INDIGENOUS HERITAGE

From the writings of the ancient Maya (who in the 1500s recorded texts of their myths, clan histories, and dance-dramas using the Western system of writing) we learn about Maya musical life at the time of contact. Principal among the sources are *Los Anales de los Cakchiqueles* (*The Annals of the Cakchiquels*) and the Quiché *Popol Vuh* (*The Book of Counsel*), which contain the history of the people, their myths of creation, and the deeds of their ancestral heroes. Instrumental music, dances, songs, and other arts figure importantly throughout these texts.

These sources show that for the Maya the arts were then, as now, a system of rituals and symbols originated by primordial ancestral heroes. These rituals functioned at the time of Spanish contact, as they do today, to maintain a harmonious relationship between the human world and the world of spirits. In the *Popol Vuh*, the ancestral pair of heroic brothers, Jun Baatz' and Jun Ch'oven (whose names mean "monkey" and "artisan"), are proficient in all the arts, since they became flutists, singers, writers, carvers, jewelers, and silversmiths (Edmonson 1971:59). Also demonstrated in these sources is the Maya belief that their ancestors' music has the power to do what it says. When the younger brothers sang and played the spider-monkey hunter's song for the elder brothers on the flute (*zu*) and drum (*k'ojom*), the elder brothers turned into monkeys. The *Popol Vuh* contains the texts of laments that express the sorrow the people felt when they left their homeland in Tula to migrate into highland Guatemala, such as the following (Edmonson 1971:171):

> Alas, it is not here that we shall see the dawn,
> When the sun is born again
> Brightening the face of the earth.

The Annals of the Cakchiquels and *The Title of the Lords of Totonicapán*, sixteenth-century documents relating the origins and myths of the Cakchiquel and the Quiché, mention a bone flute (*zubac*), a conch trumpet (*t'ot*), a drum (*k'ojom*), and a spiked vessel rattle (*sonaja*). The origin of the latter is related in the following story from the *Popol Vuh* (paraphrase of translation in Edmonson 1971:76):

> The head of the hero, Jun Jun Aj Pu (One One Hunter), was severed by the Lords of the Underworld, and became a living gourd on a calabash tree. The maiden X Kiq (Blood Girl) discovered the head in the branches, and from a drop of spittle the calabash-head let fall on her outstretched hand, conceived the twin heroes Jun Aj Pu (One Hunter) and X Balan Ke (Jaguar Deer).

This story suggests that the magical powers of the spiked vessel rattle stem from its mythical identification with the heroic ancestral twins who conquered the forces of evil, personified as the Lords of the Underworld.

Historical and ethnohistorical records of the music of the Maya in the Audiencia de Guatemala come from journals, letters, and the Spanish colonists' official records, as well as from the accounts of travelers and explorers. References to music and musical instruments in these sources, though scattered and brief, provide a general knowledge of Maya musical instruments and ensembles seen in public performances. An extensive body of manuscripts in Western musical notation of music of European origin or style composed in Spain, Mexico, and Guatemala survives from the 1500s forward. Similarly, after independence, most information collected by ethnographers and anthropologists contains little specifically musical detail but does include valuable information about the contexts of Maya music.

Presently the Maya constitute more than half of the population of Guatemala, speak a Maya dialect as their primary language, and mostly live in rural areas, engaging in subsistence agriculture, small-scale commerce, and home-based crafts. Their customs and traditions are rooted in ancient Maya religion. Their musical culture tends to retain old and traditional musical styles and instruments and to resist outside influences; nevertheless, the loss of traditional styles is more and more evident. Principal among the agents of this loss are the people's conversion to evangelical Christian religions, whose missionaries identify the music of traditional Maya rituals with the powers of darkness, in which they see a hindrance to salvation; the economic pressure that stems from the fact that, unlike popular styles, the performance of traditional music is not lucrative; and the disruptive effect of the long-term oppression and gradual eradication of the indigenous peoples of Guatemala. As a rule, Maya instruments and styles tend to disappear rather than be modified.

THE EUROPEAN HERITAGE

Hernán Cortés, the Spanish conqueror of Mexico, sent his envoy, Pedro de Alvarado, to conquer the territory just to the south, which included territory extending from Chiapas, Mexico, to Costa Rica. The entire area became known as the Audiencia de Guatemala, a portion of the viceroyalty of Nueva España.

The Spanish Roman Catholic missionaries who accompanied the colonists to the Audience de Guatemala introduced Spanish religious musical traditions (predominantly of Seville) to the native peoples (Stevenson 1964). Instruction in singing and the playing of wind instruments for the performance of the sacred polyphony of Western Europe began early in the new territory. In the 1540s, provision was made for an organist and a cantor at the cathedral of Guatemala (in present-day Antigua, Guatemala), and books of plainchant and polyphony from Seville were acquired. The composer Hernando Franco, the first choir director at the cathedral in Guatemala (1570–1575), had a choir that included paid singers and indigenous instrumentalists. Later, the choir director Gaspar Fernandes copied works of Palestrina, Morales, Victoria, and Pedro Bermudes (chapel master from 1598–1603) for use in the cathedral of Guatemala. In 1645, cathedral musicians were performing polychoral music, and Marcos de Quevedo, choir director in 1698, is credited with the composition of polychoral pieces for their use. An exchange of musical resources among Guatemala, Mexico, and Peru began early and was carried on during the colonial period. Choirbooks containing music by Spanish, Flemish, Italian, and Guatemalan composers for voices and wind instruments circulated in remote villages in the 1500s and 1600s, testifying to a musical life similar to that in the city, developed by churchmen among the Maya in the outlands.

In the early 1700s, the cathedral's collection of music included works by Spaniards Francisco Guerrero, Cristóbal de Morales, and Tomás Luís de Victoria, plus Loyset Compère, Jean Mouton, Claudin de Sermisy, and Philippe Verdelot (Stevenson 1980). The Guatemalan-born composers Manuel José de Quiroz (chapel master from 1738 to 1765) and his nephew Rafael Antonio de Castellanos, who succeeded him, composed *villancicos*, *jácaras*, and *negros* that have many ethnic and popular stylistic features. In the mid-1700s, the cathedral orchestra maintained fifteen instrumentalists, including string players, an oboist, soprano and tenor bassoonists, and a harpsichordist.

Music of the Garífuna

The Caribbean coast of Guatemala, especially the towns of Livingston and Puerto Barrios, is inhabited by the Garífuna, descendants of African slaves and Arawak and Carib inhabitants of the Caribbean island of St. Vincent (Arrivillaga Cortés 1990:252). The Garífuna came to coastal Central America in the late 1700s and now inhabit the Caribbean coast from Belize south to Islas de la Bahía in Honduras. Large Garífuna communities live in Laguna de las Perlas, Nicaragua, in New York, and in Los Angeles.

Garifuna musical instruments and ensembles

Garífuna musical ensembles include groups that use at least some traditional instruments and genres. The most traditional combo includes several sizes of *garaón*, *sísira*, and voice. [Listen to "Ámalihaní"] The *garaón* (also *garawung* or *garawoun*) *primera*, the lead instrument, is a membranophone fashioned from the trunk of a tree, perhaps 60 centimeters long, of a slightly conical shape. A deerskin head is laced to a branch that has been bent into a hoop. This is fitted to the larger end, tightened by a cord laced around a second hoop fitted above the first, and from there through holes in the body of the drum near the open end. Threaded between the cords are wooden dowels, rotated to regulate tension. Sometimes snares of nylon guitar string or fishing line are strung across the head. The *garaón segunda* is of the same kind but larger. Two or three of them are used with one *primera*, which plays virtuosically, periodically returning to a basic rhythm between improvisations. The *segunda* often plays an introduction (*llamado*), establishing the rhythm for the other instruments and any dancers; it maintains the basic rhythm throughout. The *garaón primera* is considered male; the *garaón segunda* female (Arrivillaga Cortés 1990: 258). The *sísira*, also called *chíchira*, is a spiked vessel rattle made of a large gourd containing seeds or small stones. Players, often holding two *sísira* in each hand, maintain the basic rhythm. Sometimes a conch trumpet joins the ensemble. These instruments accompany singing led by a soloist and answered by a chorus, gesturing to express the text. The audience participates by singing with the chorus, clapping, commenting, laughing, and sometimes dancing. Afro-Cuban in rhythm and style, the combo's repertoire includes the following genres: *chumba*, *jungujugu*, *jungujugu de Chugu* (*junguledu*), *parranda*, *punta*, *sambay*, and *yankunú* (Arrivillaga Cortés 1990:260–266). Further study is needed to describe these forms and their relation to other Caribbean genres.

Other Garífuna combos include electric guitar, electric bass, electric piano, *batería* (drums and other percussion instruments), congas, sometimes trumpet, trombones or saxophones, and voices. These ensembles play a fusion of traditional rock rhythms in what is called *punta rock*, plus reggae and other popular styles. Neighborhood combos of boys from the same *barrio* may be made up of *garaón*, snare and bass drums, cymbals, tortoiseshell idiophones, spiked vessel rattles, *claves*, and conch trumpets. They play *puntas*, *parrandas*, *calypsos*, and other Caribbean genres. Ensembles of guitar and light percussion, such as *claves*, gourd rasps, and bottle rattles, play at parties, in bars, in the street, at home, and at wakes, provided the deceased enjoyed this kind of music. Their repertoire shows Jamaican influence. In the first half of the twentieth century, municipal brass bands played popular rhythms (fox-trot, blues, and ragtime) in public parks, at private parties, and for square dances (*seti*). Today, brass bands with *garaón* and *sísiras* play religious or funeral marches for religious festivals and processions.

GARÍFUNA SONGS AND DANCES

Garífuna songs include Christian songs (*lemesidi*) for liturgical use at mass or other services of the Roman Catholic Church; ritual songs for the ancestral cult of the gods Chugu and Yankunú (Arumajani), and work-accompanying songs. Most are responsorial between a soloist and a chorus or antiphonal between a small group and a chorus. The *punta* is the most widely known Garífuna dance-song genre. Topical, erotic, or moral, its texts serve as social regulators. Many are old; some are used at the rituals of Chugu and Yankunu; but new ones are regularly composed. The *punta*, for a dance known as the *culeado*, is usually done by women in the center of the circle formed by musicians and audience; they perform for recreation, on San Isidro's day, and at nine-day wakes (*novenarios*).

The *jungujugu de Chugu* (or *junguledu*) is the most sacred Garífuna genre and is used in the ancestor cult of Chugu and Dugu. Drums play a lightly accented rhythm while women and sometimes men dance in a group and may enter a trance in which contact is believed to be made with the ancestors. The *jungujugu de fiesta* is played in procession, and its mood is moderate.

The *yankunú* (probably from "John Canoe," a masked dance known as *junkanoo* in other parts of the Caribbean) is also called *wanaragua* (*enmascarao* in Honduras). This is a majestic warriors' dance usually performed by men, dramatizing victory over Europeans. Musically, it is a dialogue between a drummer and masked dancers, who wear shell rattles (*illacu*) strung around their calves. It is performed on 25 December and 1 and 6 January.

The *parranda* or *zarabanda*, used for celebrating, is usually played while in transit through the streets. Its texts are social regulators of behavior between couples. The *parranda* is done on 12 December for the festival of Our Lady of Guadalupe. The erotic dances *chumba* and *sambay* and the courting song genre *gunyei* have not been studied. There is a growing movement among the Garífuna of Central America, however, to study, rescue, and revitalize traditional Garífuna music and dance. Popular on the commercial media, mainly cassettes, compact discs, television, and radio are the popular Atlantic coastal and Caribbean styles *merengue*, *calypso*, *soca*, and reggae.

Garífuna musical enculturation begins at an early age, usually with children playing the spiked vessel rattle and later with rhythm ensembles of children and youths on the *garaón segunda*. The principal methods of teaching are imitation and example. The development of a clear vocal quality is prized, and singers are usually the composers of their songs. Makers of musical instruments, who often play the instruments, are recognized for their public function during traditional festivals and rituals.

The musical instruments and styles typical of Guatemalan music can be grouped into those commonly used by the indigenous Maya, those more commonly used by the Ladinos (Guatemalans whose primary language is Spanish)—though the lines separating Maya and Ladino music are blurred by an overlapping of cultures—and those used by the Garifuna. Musical instruments and styles are associated mainly with one particular group in Guatemala, rather than all, although the use of the *marimba* and contemporary popular music cross those lines.

Mayan instruments

The Tzutujil classify musical instruments as male or female. Female instruments (*k'ojom*) are those that are struck or plucked; within the Tzutujil cosmos, they represent or are related to the geographic plane or the surface of the earth. The large, double-headed drum is always called *k'ojom* in Tzutujil. Other female instruments may be called simply *k'ojom* or may be called by Tzutujil names derived from Spanish: *ctar* ("guitar"), *arp* ("harp"), or *mrimp* ("marimba"). Male instruments (*xul*) are those that are blown; they are related to or represent the cosmic tree or central axis that penetrates the geographic plane, communicating with the world of spirits under the earth and above it in the sky. Except for the cane flute (always called *xul* in Tzutujil), male instruments may be called *xul* or by Spanish names: *saxofón* ("saxophone"), *chirimía* "shawm"), or *trompeta* ("trumpet"). Traditionally, the playing of musical instruments is limited to men.

Because the Tzutujil have delineated their own taxonomy for musical instruments, which is likely accepted by other Maya subgroups who share the same cosmology, musical instruments are presented that way in this essay.

Female category

Idiophones are abundant in this category. Spiked vessel rattles made of a calabash (Quiché *chin-chin*, Spanish *sonaja*, *maraca*) are pre-Hispanic ritual instruments used in curing and divination. Today, they are made from various materials including calabash, metal, basketry, and terra-cotta and may contain pebbles, seeds, clay pellets, or (in basket rattles) pellet bells. They are used mainly in dance-dramas (dramatic presentations of part of the Maya world myth, many of them undocumented), but also by ensembles of guitars and *guitarrillas* (small guitars used for local music), and by Maya and Ladino ensembles of popular music. Ceramic replicas are sometimes offered for sale in local markets. Terra-cotta vessel rattles surviving from pre-Columbian times, sometimes in figurine form, are often unearthed during cultivation, and such ancient artifacts—including whistles, non-musical figurines, and other shards—are especially valued by shamans for use in divination or curing.

Other idiophones include rattles of coins threaded on string or wire across the face of a metal plate, used in some dance-dramas. Rattlesnake rattles are prized for the buzz they add to stringed instruments, flutes, and whistles, when inserted into their cavities or resonators. A tortoiseshell idiophone (Spanish *tortuga*) struck with a bone, stick, or antler is used by the Ixil of the Department of Quiché in the deer dance (*baile del venado*). It commonly accompanies the singing of *posadas*, mainly a Ladino custom during Advent, the pre-Christmas season.

The *tun* is an idiophone made from a hollowed-out log of lowland hardwood (*hormigo*), into which an H-shaped slit is cut, creating two tuned tongues (Figure 16.1) as with the similar Taino instrument in the Caribbean and the Aztec instrument in Mexico. When struck with a rubber-tipped mallet, deer antler, or stick, the tongues vibrate and produce two pitches about a fourth apart. A third pitch can be produced by beating the side of the instrument. Other names for the *tun* in Guatemala are Tzutujil *c'unc'un* and Quiché *tuntun* or *tum*; in Mexico it is known in Yucatec-Maya as *teponagua*, *teponaguastle*, and *tunkul*. Tzutujil men play it daily at sunrise, noon, and sunset, probably as part of the cult of the sun. In the absence of the appointed male ritual official, his wife may fulfill this duty. The *tun* appears in Maya ritual and dance-dramas, often in differently sized pairs. Probably the most ancient of these is the dance-drama often in colonial documents called *baile del tun* ("dance of the *tun*"), in which a *tun* and long wooden trumpets (also called *tun* or *tum*, which may mean "tube or cylinder") accompany dances and narratives. The log idiophone was used in this presentation with an ensemble of flutes, rattles, skin drums (Spanish *atabales*, *tambores*), conch trumpets (Spanish *caracoles*), and wooden trumpets. Because the dance represented the sacrifice of a captive taken in battle, the church repeatedly proscribed its performance. It persisted, nevertheless, and survives as the dance-drama *Rabinal Achí* (Hero of Rabinal) in Rabinal, *Baja Verapaz*, and as *Ox Tum* in Ilotenango, Sacatepéquez. Today, it is accompanied by valveless metal trumpets about one meter long with one loop, appearing to be nineteenth-century band instruments, and a log idiophone (Mace 1970).

Other idiophones are small metal clapper bells and pellet bells, rasps of gourd, wood, or bone with transverse grooves, and a wooden ratchet (*matraca*) originating in Spain and used principally during Holy Week, when church bells are customarily silent.

The last idiophone included in the female category is the *marimba*, which is discussed below because it is used throughout Guatemala (and beyond: in Mexico, Honduras, Nicaragua, Costa Rica, etc.), not only by Mayas but also by Ladinos and others. The *marimba* could be called Guatemala's national instrument (Figure 16.2).

Membranophones are also within the female category because they are struck.

Those most commonly used by the Maya of Guatemala are cylindrical, double-headed drums with wooden

Figure 16.1
A *c'unc'un* (slit drum) stored under a table with ritual drink, ready to be played during a Mayan ceremony in Santiago Atitlán, Department of Sololá, highland Guatemala. Photo by Linda O'Brien-Rothe, 1971.

bodies, made from a single cedar log or bent plywood. They are of two sizes: small (Spanish *tambor*, Quiché *k'ojom*), and large (Spanish *tamborón*, Quiché *nimaj k'ojom*) about 76 centimeters in diameter. Each head, preferably of deerskin or calfskin, is wrapped around a hoop made from a flexible *membrillo* branch, usually held in place by a looped branch or flat wooden

Figure 16.2
A *marimba de tecomates* from the Cakchiquel area of the shores of Lake Atitlán, Sololá, highland Guatemala. This instrument was converted from a *marimba de arco* by cutting off the arched branch (its stump visible on the left) and adding legs. Photo by Linda O'Brien-Rothe, 1967.

frame, around which tensioning cords are laced, or they are simply laced through the head itself. A small hole, cut into the side of each drum so it can "breathe," is usually ornamented in a style reminiscent of ancient Maya glyphs as a carved six-petaled flower with the hole as its center. The *tambor* and the *tamborón* are each played with one or two sticks, sometimes padded or wrapped with crude rubber. In procession, the flutist usually carries the *tambor* or *tamborón* on his back while another musician plays it.

The snare drum (*caja*, also called *tambor de judía* and *pregonero*) has snares made from knotted cords stretched across the head. Most commonly, the *tambor* or the *tamborón* is found in ensemble with the flute or the shawm (*chirimía*, Figure 16.3); a snare drum customarily joins these in the central departments of Sacatepéquez and Chimaltenango.

The *adufe* is a quadrangular double-skin frame drum, roughly 30 centimeters square, sometimes containing a rattle. It is used in some local dances. The *zambomba* (also *zambudia*) is a small friction drum used in the dance of the twenty-four devils (*baile de los veinticuatro diablos*) in Sacatepéquez.

Because plucking is an action similar to striking, chordophones, therefore, also pertain to the female category among the Maya. However, they stem from stringed instruments introduced from Europe, because there is no evidence of chordophones before the Spanish encounter. Included in this category are the violin, guitar, and harp.

The violin (*violín*, *rabel*) is sometimes crudely constructed, with four holes for tuning pins, but usually only three strings. It is played with a loose horsehair bow, tensioned by the pressure of the thumb. Homemade bows are straight, rather than arched, and are usually gripped partway up the stick. The instrument is held against the chest rather than under the chin. The violin is played as a solo instrument, and it accompanies voices dur-

Figure 16.3
Chirimía and *tambor* players accompany the dance of the conquest for the Tzutujil of Santiago Atitlán, Sololá, highland Guatemala. The musicians, Cakchiquel from another town, are hired for the dance in various towns in the area. Photo by Linda O'Brien-Rothe, 1971.

ing funerals or calendric rituals. It joins a harp for playing *sones* [see MEXICO] and other traditional melodies.

A five-stringed guitar (*guitarra*) is documented among the Tzutujil and Cakchiquel but may be more widespread. It plays alone or accompanies ancestral songs sung by the player. Six- and twelve-stringed guitars tuned in the standard manner are common. In performing *rancheras*, *corridos*, and popular music, two or three guitarists often play together and sing. The *guitarrilla* (*tiple* or treble), a now rare five-stringed guitar with a gourd body as resonator, sometimes plays with the harp. Also disappearing is the twelve-stringed *bandurria* (*bandola*, *bandolín*), an instrument like the mandolin.

The harp in Guatemala resembles that of the Maya of Chiapas, Mexico. It is about 1.2 meters high with a straight, carved pillar and a curved neck that may bear elaborately carved decoration. Its back has five panels; the sound board is of a single piece of wood with three or four sound holes. The tuning pins are of wood, as are the pegs that fasten the strings to the sound board. The harp rests against the player's shoulder and sits on two wooden feet fixed to the base, holding the instrument off the ground. The fingertips of the right hand play the melody on twelve to fifteen diatonically tuned strings of the upper register, and a wooden plectrum held in the left hand is used to play the seven bass strings, tuned to the tonic major triad. There are two or more unstrung pegs between the bass and treble strings. The sound board is sometimes beaten with a padded stick. For playing *sones* and other pieces, the harp often joins a violin, a snare drum, and an accordion (Fgure 16.4).

Male instruments

The Maya of Guatemala use various aerophones, but perhaps the most common is a duct flute made of cane, terra-cotta, or metal. Known in various Maya languages as *xul* (pronounced "shool"), *zu*, *zubac*, *tzijolaj*, and *cham-cham*, and in Spanish as *pito*, this is a 26-to-36-centimeter-long vertical fipple (duct) flute, open at the distal end, usually with six holes (the *tzijolaj*, being smaller, may have three). It combines with a drum (*tambor* or *tamborón*) to make the most widespread and common ensemble in Guatemala (Figure 16.5). The

Figure 16.4
A harp, two violins, and percussion (a man striking the harp body with drumsticks) play for a family celebration at a Tzutujil home in Santiago Atitlán, Sololá, highland Guatemala. The harpist plays the longest strings with a wooden plectrum. Photo by Linda O'Brien-Rothe, 1972.

xul is used with the snare drum in the central departments of Sacatepéquez and Chimaltenango. It may be accompanied by the *marimba*.

A side-blown cane flute (also *xul*) with a rectangular hole for blowing is documented only among the Cakchiquel of San Marcos, Atitlán (Arrivillaga Cortés 1986). It has an inner diameter of about 38 millimeters and is closed at the proximal end by a hollow sphere of black beeswax that has a small perforation over which a thin membrane, usually from a pig's intestine, is stretched as a mirliton. Rattlesnake rattles are inserted into the cavity of the sphere, where they add to the buzzing of the mirliton. The *xul* commonly has six finger holes. The Cakchiquel of Lake Atitlán play it with a gourd *marimba* (Figure 16.6) for the deer dance.

Figure 16.5
In a procession in Sololá, ritual musicians play a cane flute (*xul*) and a drum (*k'ojom*). Photo by Linda O'Brien-Rothe, 1969.

The *chirimía* is a small double-reed instrument of the shawm family, with five or six holes for fingering. Unlike its modern European counterpart, the oboe, it has a cylindrical rather than a conical bore, no keys, and a pirouette (mouth disk) like the shawm of Arab countries. Introduced to the Maya in the early years of Spanish colonization, it is widespread in Guatemala. The reed is fashioned from the dried and smoked leaf of a palm or bromeliad. A shawm is commonly played with a *tambor* or snare drum to accompany dance-dramas, but it is also played in processions and other contexts.

The conch trumpet, now rare, is used in some dance-dramas. Valveless metal trumpets (*tun*) about 90 centimeters long with one loop, probably nineteenth-century European band instruments, have replaced the long wooden trumpets described in colonial sources. They are used with *tun* in the Rabinal Achí and other dance-dramas.

Figure 16.6
Children watch as Cakchiquel musicians in San Marcos La Laguna, Sololá, highland Guatemala play a *marimba sencilla* and the rare side-blown flute with a mirliton in the proximal end (*xul*). This ensemble plays for the deer dance and other rituals. Photo by Linda O'Brien-Rothe, 1972.

Music of the Maya

The music of the Maya of Guatemala is a function of the Maya belief system, in which the ancient Maya religion has accommodated a considerable overlay of Christian beliefs, symbols, and practices. Major public musical events are related to a calendar that mixes Maya and Roman Catholic religious observances with the Maya agricultural cycle. Less-public musical events relate to individual life-cycle events (courting, marriage, funerals) and to human needs, such as curing disease, dispelling evil, and protecting or blessing.

Traditional music is understood by the Maya as having been created and handed down from primordial ancestors who established all the customs, including music, that are pleasing to the spirit-lords (Maya gods), as a means of ensuring the continuing harmony of the cosmos. Tzutujil origin stories relate how the spirit-lord Rilaj Mam (Old Grandfather, Spanish Maximón), to begin his service to the people as their guardian, taught them the songs and dances that must be sung and played to invoke his power. Since their ancestral songs translated "Of the Dead" and "Of the Drowned" call into the singer's presence the spirits of the deceased, special precautions are taken to protect from fright or harm those singing or listening. Other songs bring rain, contain winds, or control human beings' actions. The faithful performance of the ancestors' music is understood as absolutely essential to the people's well-being. The musical genres and instruments that are part of their tradition (and these often include European introductions, including the dance of the conquest and the playing of the guitar) are believed to be the ancestors' legacy.

In the highland Maya towns of Guatemala, social events are marked by the sound of the *marimba*. Many of these events follow the Christian calendar of feasts, which often fall on days of solstice, equinox, or other celestial events important in the Maya calendar or are based on Maya customs relating to the agricultural cycle, such as times to pray for rain or sun, good germination, abundant crops, or successful harvest, each accompanied by its own ritual music.

Mayan Christian feasts

The manner of celebrating saints' days varies from town to town. Most common are colorful processions of townspeople to or from the church and the house of prayer (*cofradía*), preceded by the *xul* and the *tamborón*, whose music heralds what is coming (see Figure 16.5). The officials of the *cofradía* dedicated to the saint being celebrated might hire an ensemble of harp, violin, accordion, and snare drum to accompany the saint's statue while it is being carried in the procession. Festivities (in the town square or the church patio and in *cofradías*) regularly include the playing of one or more diatonic keyboards, sometimes using a special repertoire of pieces (*sones*) particular to the spirit-lord with whom the saint has been identified. The melodies of these *sones* are commonly believed to have been given or taught directly by the spirit-lord being honored on the occasion. Sometimes the *sones* accompany dancing that takes place later in the *cofradía*; at other times, the festivity includes a dance-drama performed in the town plaza. In all these events, a great many people—adults and children—participate by following the processions, listening, watching, and often dancing. The celebration may include a band (*banda*) consisting of an assortment of brass instruments, snare and bass drums, and sometimes violins; the band plays marches or popular songs. Bands achieved great popularity in the late 1800s and continue to be an important tradition in religious festivals. Most of them play a repertoire of marches that the original members of the band learned several generations ago from the founding teacher, who taught them using musical notation. Now the bandsmen, usually descendants of the original performers, continue the repertoire as an oral tradition and add to it their renditions of popular songs.

Holy Week, from Palm Sunday to the Saturday before Easter, is the occasion for the greatest festivities and the widest variety of musical forms. Characteristic of this time is the clacking of the *matraca* (a large wooden ratchet, swung above the head on a long handle); *marimba* combos (*conjuntos*) consisting of three-stringed bass viols, saxophones, and other instruments; and the *xul* and the *tamborón*. On Good Friday, bands customarily play slow marches or dirges (reminiscent of Andalucían *saetas*) during the procession that accompanies Jesus' casket. Among the Tzutujil, the rituals of Holy Week include many ancestral songs, played on a five-stringed guitar and often sung. In some places, survivals of European Renaissance genres of sacred music (including motets and settings of the psalms) are still performed.

Great numbers of dance-dramas are performed in highland towns following the yearly calendar of rituals and customs. Four to twenty costumed dancers recite or sing dialogue and dance to instrumental accompaniment. Dancers themselves may play spiked vessel rattles or rasps. Dance-dramas often last several hours and are customarily performed for eight days in succession, beginning on the saint's day or feast being celebrated. Some clearly predate Spanish contact. These include Rabinal Achí, which is accompanied by the *tun* (and is therefore sometimes called the dance of the *tun*) and two long trumpets, and the deer dance, which may be accompanied by a gourd *marimba* and a *xul* or by other instruments. Other dance-dramas are importations from Spain. These include the dance of Moors and Christians (*baile de moros y cristianos*), accompanied by flute and *tambor*, and the dance of the conquest, accompanied by *chirimía* and *tambor*.

Other Mayan ritual contexts

Life-cycle events, particularly rituals of christenings and weddings, may be celebrated with a *marimba*, by an ensemble that may include strings, *marimba*s, or guitars, or by a band. For wakes, it is common to engage a violinist or a guitarist to play and possibly sing. Following the casket to the grave, women sing laments. At the burial ceremonies, a local specialist in ritual music (*maestro del coro* "choirmaster," *maestro cantor* "song master," or *sacristán* "sacristan, man in charge of ritual") may sing sections of the Roman Catholic burial service, usually in Latin with violin or other accompaniment.

One of the most common means of obtaining what is needed from the spirit-lords is to engage a shaman for a ritual that will include the singing of a prayer. Using formalized but flexible texts praising and petitioning the spirit-lords for what is needed, the shaman sings on a single tone, inflected (at points convenient to the singer and to the significance of the text) by a drop to a lower pitch for a syllable or two before taking a breath to continue.

Vocal quality varies greatly—from a stridently *marcato* style to a relaxed speech-song. This prayer has become a tourist attraction in some places, notably in Chichicastenango, where a shaman lights candles and begins to sing on the steps of the church on cue as the daily tourist bus arrives.

Among the Tzutujil, the yearly rituals for rain and controlling the winds take place in Santiago Atitlán, in a *cofradía* closed and tightly locked to contain the winds the ritual will arouse. A shaman dons a special rainmaking shirt, sings a prayer song, and dances. During these actions, a singer accompanying himself on a five-stringed guitar sings an appropriate ancestral song (*bix rxin nawal*)—apart from the shamanic prayer songs and chants, the only indigenous genre of Maya vocal music documented in Guatemala. Tzutujil ancestral songs are also known as *bix rxin Ruchleu* ("songs of Face-of-the-Earth"), the god whose body forms earth, sky, and underworld. Songs of Face-of-the-Earth are identified by titles that describe their functions, such as "Song of San Martín" (the spirit-lord of wind and rain), "Sad Song" (for women's laments), and "Song of the Road" (where a boy courts a girl). They are improvised by the guitarist-singer on a topic associated with the melody, expressed in a generic title such as "song for courting" and "sad song" (Figure 16.7). Thus the same simple melody with many variations, or more accurately, a melodic contour by which it is identified, serves for all courting songs, whether the singer is narrating a famous courting story from the past or improvising a lyrical song of love; and similarly with melodies for other titles and themes. This may be sung, hummed, or played on a cane flute or a five-stringed guitar. The simple, diatonic melodic formulas with their accompanying chords on I, IV, and V, in 6/8 time with frequent hemiolas (i.e., *sesquiáltera*), and the guitar tuning (which places its origin in sixteenth-century Spain) suggest an origin in Spanish music of the colonial period.

That the Tzutujil have a common origin with the Cakchiquel and the Quiché, whose creation and hero stories and clan histories (*The Annals of the Cakchiquels* and *Popol Vuh*) include musical texts, suggests that the ancestral songs of the Tzutujil are part of an old tradition that probably survives in the broader group but has not yet been documented. Tzutujil texts are in Maya couplets (paired lines in parallel syntax, whose second line usually repeats and varies the first). Some are related to the Quiché origin stories of the Popol Vuh; the history and customs of the people; prayers of ancestors and gods; songs for mourning, courting, traveling, rain, and so on. The following is an example from "Song to the Sun, Lord of the World":

Figure 16.7
A Tzutujil singer of ancestral songs plays his five-stringed guitar at his home in Santiago Atitlán, Sololá, highland Guatemala. Photo by Linda O'Brien-Rothe, 1972.

Green mountain world,
Green mountain Face-of-the-Earth,
You hear us where we stand;
You hear us where we walk,
Face-of-the-Earth, God,
Lamp Samardatina.
You are in the sky;
You are in glory.
Perhaps two hundred,
Perhaps three hundred steps
We will take up and down you,
Oh God, oh World.

The call to be a singer and instruction in singing and playing are received in signs and dreams, and singers belong to the group of ritual specialists who serve the community by maintaining ancestral traditions.

Some traditional Maya music may be heard on commercial recordings, but the most sacred ritual music is rarely issued commercially. In the cities of the United States where Maya refugees from national violence have settled (especially Los Angeles, California, and Indiantown, Florida), traditional Maya music may be heard, usually in a restaurant, at an occasional concert, or at a communitywide social event.

THE EMERGENCE OF GUATEMALAN MUSIC

The *marimba*

The most popular Guatemalan folk-derived instrument is the *marimba*, a xylophone probably introduced from central Africa in the 1500s or 1600s. Evidence for the African origin of the *marimba* is chiefly the similarity of the construction of old gourd-resonator *marimbas* to that of the xylophones of central Africa and the absence of evidence of *marimbas* in pre-Columbian Mesoamerica. Furthermore, the word *marimba* resembles *marimba* and *malimba*, African names for the instrument (O'Brien-Rothe 1982: 99–104).

The *marimba* with gourds (*marimba de tecomates*) is a xylophone of diatonically tuned wooden slats (the "keyboard") made from lowland hardwood (*hormigo* or *granadillo*) suspended above a trapezoidal framework by cord or string which passes through each slat at its nodal point and through threading pins between the slats (Figure 16.2). Tuned gourds for resonation are suspended under the keyboard. Near the bottom of each gourd is a small hole surrounded by a ring of beeswax, over which a piece of the membrane from a pig's intestine is stretched as a mirliton. When the slat is struck, it produces a buzz (*charleo*).

In its oldest form, the *marimba* was carried by a strap that passed around the player's neck or shoulders. Called *marimba de arco* (bow *marimba*, which is more popular today in Nicaragua than in Guatemala), the instrument had no legs. The keyboard was kept away from the player's body by a bowed branch (*arco*), which had its ends fixed to the ends of the keyboard. [Listen to "Los Novios"] Later models, called *marimba de mesa* (table *marimba*), DISC ● TRACK 33 have legs and lack the bow. The diatonic keyboard of the *marimba sencilla* ("simple *marimba*") has from nineteen to twenty-six slats that can be tuned by adding a lump of wax, sometimes mixed with bits of lead, to their undersides; a *marimba* tuned this way may be called a *marimba de ceras* (*marimba* with wax). The slats are struck with mallets (*baquetas*) made of flexible wooden sticks wrapped with strips of raw rubber: larger and softer mallets are used for bass slats; smaller and harder ones for the treble range. The *marimba* with gourds is played by one, two, or three players, each using two to four mallets.

The *marimba* was first mentioned in Guatemala in 1680 by the historian Domingo Juarros (1953), who observed it played by Maya musicians in public festivities. During the 1700s, it became popular and was reported at religious and civil events. Its growth in popularity among Ladinos in the 1800s led to the extension of the keyboard to five, six, and seven octaves and the addition of a fourth player. During the Guatemalan independence celebration of 1821, it became the national instrument. Later, the gourd resonators were replaced by harmonic boxes (*cajones armónicos*), wooden boxes fashioned to emulate the shapes of gourds, and the keyboard was expanded to about five diatonic octaves. This form retained the name *marimba sencilla*, referring to its diatonic scale. The *marimba de cinchos* (also called *marimba de hierro* "marimba with iron" and *marimba de acero* "marimba with steel") with metal slats also became popular, and even varieties with slats of glass or with bamboo resonators were developed. The *marimba* with gourds and the diatonic keyboard, the forms most commonly played by the Maya, may be accompanied by a cane flute (*xul*), a shawm, a saxophone, or other band instruments and a drum (Quiché *k'ojom*, Spanish *tambor*, *tamborón*) or trap set.

The expansion of the *marimba* keyboard to include the chromatic scale is usually attributed to Sebastián Hurtado in 1894. Its names, *marimba doble* ("double *marimba*") and *marimba cuache* ("twin *marimba*"), refer to the double row of slats that accommodates the chromatic scale. Unlike the piano keyboard, in which a raised semitone is found above and to the right of its natural, in many Guatemalan *marimbas* the sharp key is placed directly above its corresponding natural.

The repertoire of the double *marimba* is more popular and contemporary than that of the diatonic keyboard, though the former is often used to play the traditional *son guatemalteco* or *son chapín*, folkloric dance pieces typically in moderate to rapid 6/8 time that may be sung to four-line verses. Many local variations occur. The *son guatemalteco*, the national dance of Guatemala, is danced with stamping (*zapateado*). Music for the double *marimba* ranges from these traditional *sones* to light classics and popular music, often elaborately arranged, in which players display a high degree of virtuosity, precise ensemble playing, and expressive effects.

In villages and towns, the double *marimba* is often combined with saxophones, trumpets, trap set, bass viol with three strings (normally plucked), one or more male singers, and percussion instruments such as maracas, a shaker made of a thermos bottle with pebbles or pellets inside, and percussion sticks to play music popularized in the media.

In larger towns and cities, double-*marimba* musicians are more often Ladinos than Maya. The instrument is commonly played in pairs: the *marimba grande* of six and one-half octaves (usually sixty-eight keys) played by four players and the *marimba cuache* (also *marimba pícolo*, *marimba requinta*, *marimba tenor*), which has a range of five octaves (usually fifty keys), played by three musicians.

The traditional repertoire consists mainly of *sones*. When played in the context of Maya culture, these may belong to a body of melodies reserved for calendric rituals of the saints and spirits, which are often danced but seldom sung. *Sones* played by Ladino musicians are drawn from the traditional folk repertoire of the *son guatemalteco*, *son chapín*, or *seis por ocho*. [Listen to "Los Trece"]

DISC ❷ TRACK 14

Ladino music

Ladinos are people who primarily speak Spanish, tend to live in urban areas where they engage in nonmanual occupations (such as teaching students, keeping shop, driving a bus), and maintain their own customs and traditions, stemming in part from Spanish traditions.

They tend to adopt instruments and styles typical of contemporary Latin American popular music heard on broadcasts, especially those of Mexico and the Caribbean, and more recently, the Andes.

Ladino music flourishes in Guatemala City, in the urban centers of the south coast and eastern lowlands, and among smaller enclaves of Ladinos who live in the predominantly Maya towns of the central cordillera. It does not include Maya ritual music or instruments, but the two cultures share the diatonic keyboard or double *marimba* and much of the *marimba* repertoire of *sones guatemaltecos* and popular music.

In the 1800s, popular music with traditional or local roots—particularly local forms of the *corrido*, the *pasillo*, the *son*, and the *vals*—developed as entertainment in the homes of the elite. Eased by the arrival of printing, songs and dances circulated in elegant salons in Guatemala and other Central American cities and gradually became differentiated from a pan-Spanish-American style into more or less discrete national styles. Popular music in the early twentieth century included the *corrido*, the fox-trot, the *mazurca* (or *ranchera*), the *pasodoble*, the polka, the *schotís*, and the *vals*. By the 1920s, the influence of African rhythms was notable in the *danza* (or *habanera*), the *merengue*, the samba, and other popular styles. The popular music of Guatemala transcends national boundaries, as do the media that transmit it. Nightclubs, restaurants, and hotels support popular styles for urban Ladinos and tourists. Ladinos and urban Maya enjoy *latino* disco music in clubs. Performances of popular music played by Guatemalan *marimba* bands can be heard in U.S. cities where numerous Guatemalan immigrants live.

National anthem

Guatemala's national anthem, with music composed by Rafael Álvarez Ovalle to a text thought to be written by Ramón P. Molina, was selected in a competition in 1887. The first performance of the winning entry occurred ten years later, when the composer was awarded a gold medal, but the lyricist was listed as anonymous. In 1911 it was determined that Cuban poet José Joaquin Palma wrote the lyrics, which were modified slightly by José María Bonilla Ruano in 1934, who removed some of the phrases about war (http://www.david.national-anthems.net/gt.txt).

MUSIC LEARNING, DISSEMINATION, AND PUBLIC POLICY

The publishing (which facilitated learning and dissemination) of music in Guatemala began in 1750 with Fray Antonio Martínez y Coll's *Suma de todas las reglas del canto llano*, which contained music notation. José Domingo Sol was the first published Guatemalan composer with the publication of his composition for guitar in 1829 in England. Guatemala's first musical press was that of Domingo Toyotti, who in 1897 began to publish so-called national music by Guatemalan composers. Benedicto Sáenz de A., appointed organist at the cathedral in Guatemala City in 1802, composed religious and secular music, including Guatemala's first waltzes and polkas for the piano. He directed the first local orchestral performances of operatic works and did much to advance musical appreciation.

Other composers of the late 1800s were Lorenzo Moras (polkas), Rafael Castillo (*valses*, gavottes, mazurkas, *sones*, two-steps), and Fabián Rodríguez (marches).

In the Teatro Oriente in 1853 and 1855, Anselmo Sáenz directed the national premiere of Gioacchino Rossini's *L'Italiana in Algieri*, *La Cenerentola*, and *La gazza ladra*. The Teatro Carrera was opened in 1859, and thereafter the music season in Guatemala usually consisted of the visit of a traveling Italian opera troupe. The National Conservatory of Music, which opened in 1875, was headed first by Juan Aberle, a violinist and conductor from Naples, and later by Guatemalans, many of whom had been trained in Europe. In 1941, Jesús Castillo (1877–1946) of Ostuncalco, Quezaltenango, composed the first Guatemalan opera, Quiché Vinak, which debuted in the Teatro Abril in 1925, and from which selections were played in New York, Washington, and Seville. Other noted composers of the period include Joaquín Orellana (b. 1933 in Guatemala City) whose String Quartet and Trio were premiered at the Inter-American Festivals of 1960 and 1965, and Jorge Álvaro Sarmientos de León, whose *Concerto No. 1 for Piano and Orchestra* was premiered in 1953.

In the 2000s, Guatemala has an active symphonic orchestra and folkloric troupe (*baile folklórico*); the latter presents traditional indigenous and early colonial music and dance, stylized for theatrical performance. Public performances in the central park of Guatemala City by one of the national bands or orchestras are seasonal events. Except when dance music is played, audiences participate passively.

Radio is accessible virtually everywhere, television and other media are available in cities and larger towns, and recordings of popular artists and styles bring to Guatemala the same music being heard in Mexico, Central America, and Los Angeles.

FURTHER STUDY

Ethnomusicological research began with Jesús Castillo's investigations among the Mam and the Quiché, published in *La Música Maya-Quiché* in 1927. In the 1940s, Henrietta Yurchenco, working for the Archive of American Folk Song (Library of Congress), documented and recorded Cakchiquel, Ixil, Kekchí, Quiché, Rabinal, and Tzutujil music. In the 1950s, recordings were made by Lise Paret-Limardo de Vela for the Instituto Indigenista de Guatemala. These collections mainly include music for dance-dramas and other public rituals or festivals. Recordings of Maya vocal and ritual music in homes and *cofradías* were made between 1965 and 1975 among the Tzutujil and Cakchiquel of Lake Atitlán by Linda O'Brien-Rothe, resulting in several studies (O'Brien 1975, 1985; O'Brien-Roth 1976). The body of research is significantly expanded by ongoing contributions of the Centro de Estudios Folklóricos of the Universidad de San Carlos de Guatemala, initiated by Manuel Juárez Toledo.

The Guatemalan *marimba* has been researched by ethnomusicologists Vida Chenoweth (1964), Robert Garfias (1983), and Sergio Navarette Pellicer (2005). These scholars acknowledged a possible African connection for the *marimba*. O'Brien-Rothe (1982) wrote an article about Africanisms in Guatemalan *marimba* music and performance.

The major studies of Garífuna music in Guatemala have been written by Arrivillaga Cortés (1988, 1990), who has focused on drumming ensembles. His anthropological insights and insider status as a Guatemalan scholar make his works particularly useful. Robert M. Stevenson (1964, 1980) has contributed important studies of Guatemalan music in the colonial and preindependence periods. Of particular interest are his analyses of the relationships between the musics of the native people of Guatemala and the Roman Catholic Church.

REFERENCES

Arrivillaga Cortés, Alfonso. 1986. "Pito, tambor y caja en el área Cakchiquel." *Tradiciones de Guatemala* 26:91–102.
———. 1988. "Apuntes sobre la música del tambor entre la Garífuna de Guatemala." *Tradiciones de Guatemala* (Centro de Estudios Folklóricos, Universidad de San Carlos de Guatemala) 29:57–88.
———. 1990. "La música tradicional Garífuna en Guatemala." *Latin American Music Review* 11(2):251–280.
Chenoweth, Vida. 1964. *Marimbas of Guatemala*. Lexington: University of Kentucky Press.
Edmonson, Munro S. 1971. *The Book of Counsel: The Popol Vuh of the Quiché-Maya of Guatemala*. New Orleans: Middle American Research Institute, Tulane University.
Garfias, Robert. 1983. "The Marimba of Mexico and Central America." *Latin American Music Review* 4(2):203–232.
Juarros, Domingo. 1953. *Compendio de la Historia de la Ciudad de Guatemala*. 3rd ed. 2 vols. Guatemala City: Tipografía Nacional.
Mace, Carroll E. 1970. *Two Spanish-Quiché Dance Dramas of Rabinal*. Tulane Studies in Romance Languages and Literature, 3. New Orleans: Tulane University Press.
Navarette Pellicer, Sergio. 2005. *Maya Achi Marimba Music in Guatamala*. Philadelphia: Temple University Press.
O'Brien, Linda. 1975. "Songs of the Face of the Earth." Ph.D. dissertation, University of California at Los Angeles.
———. 1985. "Canciones de la Faz de la Tierra," first part. *Tradiciones de Guatemala* (Centro de Estudios Folklóricos, Universidad de San Carlos de Guatemala) 21–22:55–67.
O'Brien-Rothe, Linda. 1976. "Music in a Maya Cosmos." *The World of Music* 18(3):35–42.
———. 1982. "Marimbas of Guatemala: The African Connection." *The World of Music* 25(2):99–104.
Stevenson, Robert M. 1964. "European Music in 16th-Century Guatemala." *Musical Quarterly* 50(3):341–352.
———. 1980. "Guatemala Cathedral to 1803." *Inter-American Music Review* 2:27–71.

Panama

Ronald R. Smith

The Indigenous Heritage
The European Heritage
The African Heritage
Musical Instruments
Musical Genres and Contexts
Music Learning, Dissemination, Tourism, and Public Policy
Further Study

For over five hundred years, the region today known as the Republic of Panama has shared its entire history with European, Central American, North American, South American, and global development. From the sixteenth century, when Spanish conquistadors first landed on its Caribbean shores, to the nineteenth century and construction of its inter-oceanic canal, and finally political independence in the early twentieth century, the isthmus of Panama has served as the "Bridge of the Americas" and the "Crossroads of the World" (Olsen 2007). As such, it has been the stage upon which millions of people have played out their lives as they traversed the isthmus from the Atlantic Ocean to the Pacific and back, and hundreds of thousands more migrated from Africa, the Caribbean, China, Colombia, and the United States. When we consider the importance of the Panama Canal and the multitude of countries whose ships pass through it continuously, it is easy to see how Panama is the world's crossroads. Millennia and centuries before the Panama Canal, this small and narrow land that separates the northern and southern continents of the Western Hemisphere was also a type of crossroads. First were the Native Americans who traveled south from North America into South America probably as long as twenty or thirty thousand years ago. Many Amerindians stayed in the isthmus, and others came back from South America or from islands in the Caribbean.

This relatively narrow strip of land called Panama has served as a socio-political fulcrum and has provided the means for empire building in the Americas and Europe; yet rarely has it received attention for its beauty, diversity, and vibrant traditional culture. Few people outside of its shores appreciate the rich variety of its peoples, music, material culture, flora, and fauna, although in the twenty-first century tourism is being expanded as a major industry. Nevertheless, there is little recognition for the role that the Isthmus of Panama has played in the development of other areas of the world or even in modern history. For those who have had the occasion to spend time there and to relish its many culinary delights and everyday life, Panama presents an exciting and ever changing social and cultural panorama through which to enjoy the differences and similarities of the world's musical traditions.

Shaped in the form of a large "S" lying on its side, Panama is divided into nine provinces and three *comarcas* or indigenous territories. Each province and *comarca* boasts of its traditions, food, music, festivals, and peoples. Folkloric customs and genres have been associated with particular towns and provinces, though recent internal migration has fostered a dispersion of traditions across Panamanian territory and a concentration of peoples of different regions in the capital, Panamá (Panama City).

Self-identification in Panama does not follow regional lines and alliances to rural beginnings. For music, dance, and verbal traditions, associations and personal preferences are often based on ethnic origins and cultural traditions associated with a particular group. Every ethnic group that forms part of the fabric of Panamanian cultural identity has added something of importance to the mixture. Amerindians, Spaniards, and Africans constituted the principal ethnic groups in colonial Panama; their interaction and exchange in music, dance, and verbal folklore has taken forms that are singular to Panama.

Cultural influences cannot easily be ascribed to the relative numbers within colonial populations. In some regions of Panama, one group or another seems to have predominated in traditional music and dance, though musical instruments illustrate a totally different pattern of dispersion and origin. Officially, Spanish is the national language, spoken by peoples of all groups; nevertheless, Amerindian groups maintain their cultural heritage, and within their own communities speak indigenous languages. Therefore, most verbal forms and vocal music within Panama utilize Spanish as the language of communication. Participants in *congos* (see below) speak a dialect within their communities, though their songs are sung in Spanish (Lipski 1989). People of Antillean descent are essentially bilingual in Caribbean English and Spanish; however, they have had a strong incentive to assimilate, and few examples of Caribbean music and dance survive in their communities.

The provinces of Colón, Darién, and Panamá, plus the central provinces, have been the focus of important studies of Panamanian music and folklore. Though varied musical customs occur in other areas of Panama, there has been little systematic study. It is common for persons who were born and raised in the interior of the country to preserve a lifelong identification and allegiance to their natal province. Frequently, people now living in the capital return to small towns in the interior to celebrate family occasions, local patronal feasts, national holidays, and regional or local festivals.

Archaeologists have dug deep into the soil of Panama to uncover secrets of its pre-Columbian peoples. They have excavated many archaeological sites, though there are no large pyramids or hidden cities to be found as have been in other parts of Middle and South America. Nevertheless, it is clear that for hundreds of years Panama was a major conduit between North and South American Amerindian populations. Researchers have unearthed golden amulets and jewelry; bone, stone, and pottery artifacts; and ceramic tubular and globular flutes. All these objects indicate a flourishing trade and exchange among peoples of different regions over many centuries.

Among twentieth- and twenty-first-century Amerindian peoples in Panama, the only group for whom any significant study and documentation of music and dance exist is the Kuna [see KUNA]. For years, Kuna expressive culture has attracted the interest of European and American researchers. The Kuna people, however, have continued to maintain a degree of independence, and a large portion of their population remains in the Comarca of Kuna Yala in the San Blas Islands. Kuna musical performances and dances are uncommon outside of their own communities. Kuna who reside in urban areas of Panama City or Colón, or in towns within the central provinces, maintain a somewhat separate existence, although communication with and travel to their homelands continues and their social clubs help maintain Kuna identity.

The National Museum and El Pueblito (a folkloric tourist attraction) in Panama City exhibit small collections of Kuna musical instruments and ceremonial artifacts, as does the Götenberg Museum in Sweden (Izikowitz 1970 [1935]). However, some of these instruments are no longer in use in Kuna society. Folkloric performances at national events, cultural fairs, and regional celebrations (especially in Panama City) often include Kuna traditional music and dance to represent Panama's Amerindian populations. The colorful costumes, especially the women's blouses with *molas*, multicolored skirts, and golden earrings and nose rings, attract attention.

THE EUROPEAN HERITAGE

Rodrigo de Bastidas, having received a royal license from Spain to explore in the New World, sailed from Cádiz in October 1501 and late in the year touched the easternmost sector of the Isthmus of Panama, near the Atrato River and the Gulf of Urabá, an area now part of Colombia. Columbus sighted the Caribbean coast of Panama only on his fourth voyage (1502), when he arrived at the western end of the isthmus and the Laguna de Chiriquí. The areas he explored and named—Portobelo and Bastimentos, later called Nombre de Dios (both now in Colón Province)—were to play important roles in the first wave of colonization and the economic boom that drew Europeans to the New World. With economic growth and prosperity, the cultural heritage of Andalucían Spain, especially Seville, was transported to the shores of Panama.

El Camino Real (The Royal Road) was constructed for trans-isthmian travel in the 1500s. Now a collection of cobblestones and streams hidden among luxuriant undergrowth, this road was once the most important highway in Panama, the major route connecting the Caribbean coast (Portobelo) and the Pacific (Panama City). All goods and people who arrived from Spain, the Caribbean islands, and Colombia used the road as a means of communication with Panama City. Traffic, trade goods, and cultural traditions were transported to and from western South America via the Camino Real. Slaves brought from Africa to Portobelo served as muleteers on the roads and oarsmen on the Chagres River, transporting human cargo, gold, silver, wood, manufactured goods, and travelers. Vasco Núñez de Balboa's meeting with native Americans on the isthmus and his sighting the Pacific Ocean encouraged the development of this route, starting the growth of Spanish traditions in this part of the Americas. After the sacking and destruction of Portobelo and Panama City by pirates like Henry Morgan, El Camino de Cruces (Road of the Crosses) became the favored route that incorporated land and river passages (Río Chagres) between Castillo de San Lorenzo on the Caribbean coast with Casco Antiguo on the Pacific (Panama City).

The movement and settlement of Spaniards, captive slaves, fugitive slaves, and indigenous populations during the colonial era set the stage for current Panamanian cultural regions and traditions. The strongest manifestations of Afro-Panamanian traditions appear on the Costa Arriba (Colón Province) and the Costa Abajo (Darién) and on the islands in the Gulf of Panama. The coastal sector of the Caribbean province of Bocas del Toro (Veraguas Province), site of important banana plantations, is also an area of African descendants. Amerindian cultures include the Kuna, who reside in the San Blas Islands (Comarca de Kuna Yara), the Choco in Darién Province, and the Ngöbe-Buglé (formerly known as Guaymí and Teribe) on the Atlantic side in Veraguas Province (Comarca de Ngöbe Buglé). Climatically more temperate, the central provinces—Coclé, Herrera, Los Santos (Azuero Peninsula), and Veraguas—became the center of *mestizo* development and settlement with farmland and cattle ranches. Chiriquí, the westernmost province, has mountains and an extinct volcano with a mean altitude higher than most of the country; suitable for growing vegetables, it is the home of wealthy landowners and *mestizo* farmers.

The construction of the trans-isthmian railroad (in the mid-1800s), mainly to accommodate gold miners traveling to California from the Caribbean and Atlantic regions, and the completion of the inter-oceanic canal (at the end of the nineteenth century) profoundly affected the ethnic mixture and regional identity of Panama. The workforce needed to construct these wonders of engineering was not available in sufficient numbers on the isthmus, so thousands of contract workers from many parts of the world were brought in. Chinese, Greeks, Lebanese, Italians, and others became a new wave of immigrants to cross the "Bridge of the Americas" or "Crossroads of the World" in search of a better life. Communities of their descendants remain in Panama, still practicing ethnic cultural traditions. Among the most numerous contract workers and most visible today are Antilleans, people of African descent from English- and French-speaking Caribbean insular communities, including Antigua, Barbados, Haiti, Jamaica, Martinique, and Trinidad and Tobago.

Spanish influence in traditional Panamanian music is strongly represented by the language of lyrics and such instruments as the *guitarra* and *mejorana* (types of guitar), violin, and castanets. Many dances and especially religious celebrations owe their origins to European festivals. Among the most significant folkloric events are Carnaval, secular holidays that commemorate foundations of towns, and religious commemorations (including Corpus Christi, Holy Week, local patronal feasts, and regional holidays) when music, dance, traditional theater, costume, food, and examples of the plastic arts (traditional masks) all mingle. Although it is often difficult to ascribe a dance or song to one ethnic origin in Panama, the song form known as *décima* and dances such as the *cumbia, pasillo, punto,* and *vals* (waltz), are important representations of Spanish culture and cultural mixing. Known collectively as *música típica* (typical music), distinctions are usually not made between the particular forms, and the most common *música típica* ensemble or *conjunto típico* includes a button accordion, a guitar (or a *mejorana*), a membranophone (usually a *tamborito*), and perhaps a rasp.

When a Panamanian is asked where to find folklore, often the first response is to refer to the folkloric traditions of the central provinces (Coclé, Herrera, Los Santos, Veraguas). There, the singing of *décimas* is most strongly maintained, the *mejorana* (a string instrument and a dance) finds its home, hordes of costumed devils (*los diablicos sucios* "the dirty little devils") dance, musical ensembles (*tunas*) parade through the streets during festivals, military bands play in the central plazas, and festivals of many varieties fill the calendar. Carnaval celebrations in the town of Las Tablas (Los Santos Province) and the roving musical bands that represent its *barrios,* queens, and entourages are famous throughout the country, attracting thousands of people who have never lived in the region. The central provinces are the birthplace of some particularly Panamanian traditions, including *salomas* and *gritos* (discussed below).

THE AFRICAN HERITAGE

The influence of Africans and the traditions that characterized the cultures from which they came is best portrayed in the *congo* tradition and in such other danced genres as *los diablos de los espejos* of Garachiné (Darién Province), the music and dance of the people of the Pearl Islands, and genres such as *bullerengue, bunde, cuenecué, cumbia,* and *el tamborito* (the national dance). Most performing groups within Panama use African-derived drums, though the ensembles are different and the manner of playing varies for each.

Calypso, a Caribbean genre frequently allied with social commentary and criticism, is usually associated with countries such as Trinidad and Tobago and Jamaica, but a Panamanian variety is performed in English or Spanish by Antilleans. Undocumented and virtually unstudied, this Panamanian genre seems to have been popular years ago. It had a resurgence in the 1970s as part of a black awareness and solidarity campaign initiated by bilingual Antillean intellectuals. Though the genre is neither diffused nor performed widely in Panama, it was important in its social context, as it seemed to represent an attempt to build a cultural bridge between English speakers and their Spanish-speaking environment. Calypso is accompanied by guitar, and its text has the same deftness of thought and social commentary that distinguishes calypso in other areas of the Caribbean.

Though virtually nonexistent now, except in self-consciously retrospective cultural presentations by clubs or other organizations, English dances, including the quadrille and the contra dance, once flourished among the Afro-Caribbean residents of Antillean towns within the Canal Zone and in the city of Colón. Today, they are but a memory.

---

cumbia
Panamanian group circle dance
punto
Elegant, steady Panamanian couple genre dance
mejorana
Panamanian term denoting a particular song form, dance, scale, and musical instrument
tamborito
"Little drum," the national couple dance of Panama, featuring drum accompaniment

congo
Afro-Panamanian music, dance, and theater tradition; also, its accompanying African-derived, single-headed drum with wedge-hoop construction
bullerengue
Afro-Panamanian and Colombian responsorial song and dance
bunde
African-derived dance of Panama and Colombia

Unlike the Maya in Guatemala, neither the indigenous people nor the later immigrant cultures of Panama have their own traditional systems for classifying musical instruments. Amerindian groups favor idiophones and aerophones, Panamanians of African heritage often employ membranophones, and Panamanians of European descent and *mestizos* enjoy Spanish-derived chordophones and the button accordion. The following survey examines the instruments of the African- and European-derived musical traditions.

Idiophones

The idiophones of Panama are associated with particular ensembles, genres, or occasions, adding an important percussiveness to the music and dance. Included within ensembles (*conjuntos*) are *maracas* and *güiros*, shaken and scraped idiophones, respectively (Figure 17.1 includes a young musician playing a *güiro*). Dancers such as *los diablicos sucios* use castanets (*castañuelas*) as personal accompaniments (Figure 17.8), and big devils (*gran diablos*) often have jingle bells attached to their ankles or calves (Figure 17.4 and Figure 17.9).

Though widely dispersed within Latin American customs, the most unusual among Panamanian percussive instruments is the *vejiga*, an inflated animal bladder worn by devils as part of their costume; when struck with a stick, it functions as a percussion instrument. Because of its material and construction, it is a sort of combination membranophone and idiophone, being made from nonstretched skin. Devils' slippers or shoes (*cutarras*) also function as percussive instruments: the dancers, as they dance, articulate rhythms, with each foot parallel to the ground, accompanied by their castanets.

vejiga
Air-filled struck idiophone made from the bladder of an animal, played by the dirty little devils

Membranophones

Skin drums are the most widespread instruments in traditional Panamanian musical performances. Though the shapes and sizes vary somewhat from town to town and region to region, most are similar in construction and use. Few musical performances could take place if drummers and singers were not available. The excitement created by drummers and their sonic punctuation of dancers' movements are the main source of the dynamism of performances. A drum ensemble may use drums of various kinds and sizes but usually consists of three or four instruments. The *caja* is played with two sticks, on one head and the side. Most often it is placed on the ground and held with one foot while the performer plays (Figure 17.1).

Other membranophonic drums, played with the hands, may be held between the knees of a seated player or suspended from a cord around his shoulder or neck. Musicians use the latter method to move through streets in parades. All major musical genres and dances are supported by an individual drum with another instrument (such as a guitar or an accordion) or a drum ensemble. The national dance of Panama, *el tamborito*, is the most important drum-accompanied dance within the republic and is danced by couples.

The names of drums vary widely from one town or region to another, but they reveal something important. *Pujador* "pusher," *repicador* "chimer," *caja* "box," *jondo* "deep," and *seco* "dry" are names that indicate relationships and timbral affinities within the ensemble, though they do not seem to make much sense in English translation. Each drum performs a role within the ensemble, and drummers must learn to listen to each other for cues and watch the dancers during a performance. The *caja* often provides a basic rhythmic pattern over which the *pujadar* and the *repicador* improvise complicated patterns. The higher-pitched drums often take turns in the role of soloist. The caller (*llamador*) might accompany *los diablicos sucios* of Chitré.

Figure 17.1
A typical ensemble (*conjunto tipico*) from Panama. Left to right: accordion, *güiro, caja, congo*. Photo by Ronald R. Smith.

Figure 17.2
A *congo* ensemble from Colón Province performs at the Festival de la Mejorana, Guararé, Los Santos Province, Panama. Photo by Ronald R. Smith.

The *congo* ensembles share some of the naming conventions and playing techniques of drummers in other ensembles in Panama (Figure 17.2). Frequently, a *congo* drum will receive a particular name, for example *relámpago* "lightning," though the practice of baptizing drums [see Afro-Brazilian Traditions; HAITI] does not occur. Each group has three or four instrumentalists, a chorus of female singers, and a tradition of mimetic dances that recall colonial slavery.

Though far less common today, *conga* queens, their drum consort, and members of the court travel throughout the Caribbean coastal region in visits (*visitas*) to other so-called kingdoms and palaces (*palacios*). Such visits can be made in cars on the highway, but in earlier days these journeys were quite difficult, as they had to be made in small boats or by walking through the forest. Figure 17.3 shows one of these visits (ca. 1972), when drummers from the court of Lilia Perea (Colón Province) came to the realm of Tomasa Jaen, Queen of María Chiquita, a small village on the Costa Arriba.

Figure 17.3
Congo drummers from María Chiquita, Colón Province, Panama. Photo by Ronald R. Smith.

Chordophones

In most instances, chordophones provide melodies within instrumental ensembles. Traditionally, the violin, and in rustic communities the *rabel*, served in this capacity. The violin is still the instrument of preference for the *punto* because the sweetness and softness of its sound match the elegance and grace of the dance and its participants, but in rural and traditional Panama it has lost much of its importance. More important is the *mejorana*.

The *mejorana* is a small, five-stringed, fretted, guitarlike instrument that in shape and size resembles the Hawaiian ukulele and the Venezuelan *cuatro*. Older instruments used animal material for the strings, but newer ones use synthetics, such as nylon. Its body is made of one piece of fairly soft wood. The front (*tabla* "table"), with its round sound hole, is carved from another flat piece of wood, affixed to the body. Tuning pegs, carved from a harder wood, are placed in a pegbox at the end of a rather short neck. The *mejorana* is made by hand in rural Panama, although factory-made instruments are now on sale. The preferred instruments are those crafted by masters in the interior.

Panama has a set of commonly named *mejorana* tunings, though there does not appear to be any clear relationship between the names given to tunings and the notes that distinguish their configurations. The most common tunings are known as *por veinticinco* "by twenty-five" and *por seis* "by six." Strings are named in a unique pattern: the two outer strings (1 and 5) are designated firsts (*primeras*), the next two strings on each side (2 and 4) are designated seconds (*segundas*), and the fifth string (3, in the middle) is called third (*tercera*).

The *mejorana* is important within the musical traditions of *mestizos* from the central provinces and the capital. Performers (*mejoraneros*) accompany singers of *décimas* and the dance that bears the same name. Players learn from their friends, family, and relatives, and by observation within traditional contexts, and they must master a complex set of *torrentes* "scales" for the accompaniment of *décimas*. The *mejorana* is played with the fingers and can yield single-line melodies, melodic-rhythmic patterns, and chords. Most players do not read staff notation.

Aerophones

Within the *mestizo* tradition, a flute (*pito*) is sometimes heard playing with drummers and accordionists who travel the streets with the dirty little devils (see below). The *pito* is a small, high-pitched, side-blown flute made from cane. Its tone, being somewhat shrill, easily cuts through the din created by the dancers, other musicians, and the crowd.

The accordion has become an important melodic instrument within many ensembles of traditional Panama; in typical ensembles (*conjuntos típicos*), it carries the major share of musical performance (Figure 17.1). Imported from Germany and Austria during the 1800s, it has taken an honored place among musical instruments, often displacing the violin because of its loudness. The accordion used in Panama has buttons for left-hand chords and buttons or a keyboard for right-hand melodies. Although it functions, in most instances, as a melody instrument, it provides harmonic support. Accordions appear in ensembles that play *cumbias*, *puntos*, *tamboritos*, and other popular dances.

Musical genres in Panama, as throughout Latin America, are usually linked to dance. Several Panamanian dances require no lyrics, although melodies may in fact have texts that members of the community know but do not sing while dancing. Each named dance is accompanied by a particular kind of ensemble and is often associated with a specific ethnic group or region.

Among the most popular genres that is also a couple dance is *el tamborito*, a spectacular Afro-Panamanian drum-accompanied style considered the Panamanian national dance. Drums play an essential part in the choreography: they communicate with dancers and with each other, and they enter in rhythmic counterpoint with the dancers and their movements. In each region, specific steps (*pasos*) have names that elicit specific patterns from solo drummers. An important part of the performance, after the entrance of each new couple, is the couple's address to the drummers. The pair steps toward them, moves backward a few steps, and approaches again. They make this gesture three times. The lead drum (*repicador* "chimer" or *llamador* "caller") then "chimes" specific beats (*los tres golpes*), making a high-pitched, bell-like sound on the drum, whereupon each couple makes a fast circular turn and begins the dance. Courtship is the theme, as it is of many dances in the Americas.

Close behind the *tamborito* in popularity is the *cumbia*, a music-dance genre featuring grouped couples, popular also among Panama's Colombian neighbors. It is distinguished by the dancers' counterclockwise movement, describing a circle. The group divides into couples, but men or women may dance as two circles moving in tandem, each partner facing the other. A typical ensemble (Figure 17.1) provides music for the *cumbia* in Panama.

Other important traditional music-dance genres are the *mejorana* and the *punto*. The *mejorana* (which gets its name because it is accompanied by the *mejorana*, a small guitar) features 6/8 or 9/8 rhythms that oscillate between duple and triple pulses (*sesquiáltera*). The *punto*, though also using *sesquiáltera*, is slower. It is an elegant and graceful couple dance, found mostly in the interior of the country. It affords one of the few occasions where the violin finds a significant role within traditional musical ensembles; in the absence of a violin, an accordion is used.

The *bunde* and the *bullerengue*, both of Afro-Panamanian origin, are sung and danced in Garachiné and the towns of the region. The *bunde* is performed at Christmastime in honor of baby Jesus, represented by a doll. Each of these genres is related to the traditions of other Afro-Panamanian groups, especially *congos*, and each is accompanied by drums, a chorus of women, and clapping.

Although most dances in Panama do not have an underlying or background story, there are several important manifestations that do, namely *congos* and various devils (*diablos*); these can be referred to as dance theater.

Congos, originally Afro-Panamanian secret societies during colonial days, today perform a kind of dance theater featuring brilliant costumes, drumming (Figure 17.2 and Figure 17.3), and responsorial singing by people of Afro-Hispanic descent. It is featured

Figure 17.4
Big devils perform in
La Chorrera, Panama.
Photo by Ronald R.
Smith.

during Carnaval, folkloric festivals, and other celebrations. Most people see only the dance and hear the African-derived drums, experiencing the energy of movements and the rhythms. Among the *congos*, however, narratives retell oral histories of slave ships, the devil, the Virgin Mary, runaways (*cimarrones*), and everyday activities. The lyrics that accompany the songs during the dances do not always coincide with the background action, however, and the public must be able to interpret the story and understand what is happening from the dancers' movements and actions.

During the colonial period, liturgical dramas in spoken verse were common in Latin America. They instructed the illiterate population in the wonders and mysteries of biblical narratives. In Panama the mirror devils (*diablos de los espejos*) and big devils (*gran diablos*), respectively from Garachiné and Chorrera, portray variants of the Christian theme of the battle of good and evil. Garachiné, a small town on the gulf of San Miguel, is almost inaccessible except by air or water. The people and traditions of this region are related to descendants of runaways who fled to the jungles and the Pearl Islands of Panama. Chorrera is in Panama Province, closer to the center of the country. Musicians (Figure 17.5 and Figure 17.6) accompany the mirror devils as they enact the defeat of the devil by the Holy Spirit. The big devils (Figure 17.4) speak in verse, although what they are saying is virtually impossible to understand through their wooden masks. As they move through their complicated choreographic

Figure 17.5
An accordionist
performs for mirror
devils in Tucutí, Darièn
Province, Panama.
Photo by Ronald R.
Smith.

Figure 17.6
A drummer performs for mirror devils in Tucutí, Darién Province, Panama. Photo by Ronald R. Smith.

patterns, they act out a drama in which Lucifer, the fallen angel, does battle with the powers of good, personified by the Archangel Michael. Lucifer is vanquished and returned to the grace of God. While the *diablos de los espejos* tradition is related to the *gran diablos* tradition, the style of the mask is distinctive and the theatrical subtext from which they perform their drama is quite different.

Vocal music

Although song and dance are intimately intertwined in the traditional musics of Panama, song is probably the most important part of the equation. Once, when recording music in the Pearl Islands, I had to wait until women had gathered to sing. My friends and I were told that if a chorus could not be formed, there would be no dance that night. A typical vocal group consists of a lead singer (*cantalante* among most groups, *revellín* among *congos*) and a chorus of women (*segundas*), who sing and clap on major subdivisions of the pulse. Songs in this configuration are usually responsorial, as are most of the traditions in Panama. Singing loudly in a high register, the soloist often improvises and varies the text at will. A good voice is a powerful voice, which can rise above the chorus, the drums, all other instruments in the ensemble, and ambient noise.

A solo vocal tradition called *décima* is the province mainly of male singers. It is performed to the accompaniment of the *mejorana*. The singer (*decimero*) must have a powerful voice, but there is an emphasis on the clear and exact enunciation of the text. As one of the singers said, the textual message is the most important part of the *décima*. The *décima* is a poetic form that encompasses elaborate rhymes and melodic improvisation. The following text is an example of a vocal improvisation by the male singer Santo Díaz. It represents just a section of a longer piece, "Me duele tu corazón."

Me duele tu corazón.	Your heart gives me pain.
Tierra, tú me vas matando	Land, you are killing me.
Si acaso me oyes cantando	If by chance you hear me singing,
Yo no grito el mismo son.	I don't shout the same song.
Voy llorando la pasión	I go crying the passion
Que el recuerdo resucita,	That memory revives,
Saber que fuiste mansita	Knowing chat you were gentle
Cuando yo te socolaba,	When I rocked you,
Ay, amor, ¡cómo te amaba!	Oh, my love, how I loved you!
Tierra, tierra, ¡qué bonita!	Land, my land, how beautiful!

Décimas can be sung in a musical duel or competition format between two people. Known as *controversia*, the genre features improvised lyrics in which one singer tries to outwit the other. Like the solo *décima*, the *controversia* is also accompanied by the *mejorana*.

The *saloma*, a vocal melody of undetermined length, appears at the beginning and end of a *décima*. It is a subdued, deeply rhapsodic vocal line, often associated with the *torrente llanto*, used for performances of lyrical themes of sadness and intimacy. It exhibits a striking resemblance to the deep song (*cante jondo*) of Andalucían Spain. Sung in almost a recitative style, it often uses vocables and closely follows the emphasis of spoken verbal rhythms. Most *salomas* are slow, and their major musical cadences coincide with significant textual phrasal endings. Some singers believe that individuals have characteristic *salomas* or manners of performance. They feel that one must sing a *saloma* at the beginning of a *décima* to release the voice and set the mood.

Shouts (*gritos*) ordinarily occur during agricultural activities when it is necessary to communicate in the field. For personal entertainment, men engage in such oral display in homes, on the streets, and in bars. A measure of skill is needed to produce a *grito*, and a degree of stamina is needed to continue it for a concentrated time. It has more musical attributes when men exchange loud, high-pitched yodels. Two or more men sit face to face, or side by side, alternating their *gritos*. Often, after making four or five utterances, they stop for a rest and a drink. When they yodel, each man will often match the alternating pitches and duration of his counterpart in a sort of vocal duel.

Texts within musical compositions are important in Panama's traditional music. Declamations—dramatic recitations of poems, narratives, and *décima* texts—are often part of public celebrations and family occasions. Little has been collected of the texts of dance-theater presentations, and this is a fertile area for potential research.

CONTEMPORARY POPULAR MUSIC

Numerous contemporary popular music forms exist in Panama, most of them borrowed from regions of the Caribbean. Puerto Rican and Cuban *salsa* are very popular, along with Puerto Rican *reggaetón* and *plena*, both forms of rap. Panamanian *plena* should not be confused with traditional Puerto Rican *plena* [see PUERTO RICO], although the element of protest is a similar feature, making it nearly identical to contemporary Nuyorican *plena*, which is also a rap style.

Festivals

For many Panamanians, festivals (*fiestas*) are times of release and abandon—occasions to reestablish ties with the supernatural world, families, and regions, and to make public displays of faith. Some festivals, celebrated on a small scale, involve small numbers of people; others involve neighborhoods, towns, or regions. When a festival is shared by the national community, it permits even more possibilities for creative activity and expression. All festival occasions—secular, religious, national—are commemorated with musical ensembles and singing.

Religious festivals

In the interior of Panama on various occasions during the year, especially the Christian holiday of Corpus Christi, *los diablicos sucios* roam the streets in brilliant red and black striped costumes and musical ensembles (Figure 17.7). This is such a visually attractive tradition that it has been used to represent Panama—within the republic (Figure 17.8) and outside it. Small companies of devils, accompanied by a

Figure 17.7
During the Festival de la Mejorana in Guararé, Los Santos Province, dirty little devils (carrying *vejigas* and sticks and playing castanets) and a guitarist perform. Photo by Ronald R. Smith.

guitarist and maybe a *pito* player and a drummer (Figure 17.9), move throughout towns, performing for visitors. A special trait of their performance is the use of castanets, *vejigas*, and *cutarras*.

National festivals

Independence Day, 3 November, occasions great musical activity, especially in the capital. Thousands of citizens crowd the streets in anticipation of parades that feature marching bands and drum-and-bugle corps from the secondary schools of the city and military units of the government. So many people march that the parades last for about five hours. There are two routes, which the musical organizations exchange on the second day, so each has the opportunity of marching and performing for the maximum number of people and showing its prowess on the main street, Avenida Central. The itineraries, organizational names, and pertinent information on each group are published daily in the local papers. Though the bands are composed of instruments common to military bands in most countries, the percussion sections are greatly enlarged, and the rhythms used for the march are more related to *el tamborito* and other drum-accompanied dances of Panama than to those of John Philip Sousa. A marching band's line resembles a large group of dancers. To discover the more spectacular movements and playing styles, one has only to listen to and watch the bass drum. During each pattern, drummers vigorously lift their drums high in the air, rotating them back and forth so they can alternately strike the heads on opposing sides. Apart from Carnaval (celebrated in Panama and throughout much of Latin America), this parade is the most heavily attended musical event regularly presented in Panama.

Figure 17.8
During the festival of Corpus Christi in Los Santos Province, Panama, a dirty little devil holds castanets in each hand and carries a *vejiga* and a stick. Photo by Ronald R. Smith.

Folkloric festivals

In the early 1970s, Manuel F. Zárate (Panama's most prominent researcher in folklore) and Dora Pérez de Zárate were instrumental in helping to promote an annual event in the former's natal province, Los Santos. Each year during the Festival de la Mejorana, performers within the province and from many other cities

throughout the country come to Guararé to perform and share their traditions for a week.

National anthem

Panama's national anthem, titled "Himno Istmeño" (Isthmus Hymn), was composed by Santos A. Jorge, with lyrics by Jerónimo de la Ossa (http://david.national-anthems.net/pa.txt). "Himno Istmeño" was composed at the turn of the twentieth century and first performed on the day of Panama's independence in 1903. In 1925 it was adopted as the country's national anthem.

MUSIC LEARNING, DISSEMINATION, TOURISM, AND PUBLIC POLICY

Panama supports a national symphony, a children's orchestra, many choruses, a conservatory of music (in the capital city), and Panamanian artists of international reputation present concerts around the world. Historical musicology and ethnomusicology, however, do not have an academic home or a cadre of trained Panamanian specialists, although the study of folklore, including folk music, is found within the faculty of history at the University of Panama. However, there is no university degree program to prepare professionals in this area. Nevertheless, the Panamanian Ministry of Culture has long supported traditional singers, dancers, instrumentalists, and producers of traditional costumes within small schools of performing arts, concentrating their efforts on the teaching of these arts and crafts.

The impact of radio in Panama has been heavy. For some people who live in isolated areas, radio is the only means of contact with urban areas. Panama has a long history of radio broadcasting. Popular programs still commonly feature traditional singers, musical ensembles, reports of folkloric events, and declamatory presentations. The importance of television and the recording industry is more difficult to ascertain, since they have grown in the recent past, and no studies of these media have been made. There is some indication that recordings of traditional musical performances do reach the public, and it is not difficult to find, on tape and disk, commercial recordings of the more popular *conjuntos típicos*.

The lure of Panama—its dances, songs, and festivals—has long been a source of inspiration for Panamanian composers and others in North America. Yet, Panamanian musical composition, often the arena in which fine-art music and traditional musical genres and styles interact, has not been studied with serious attention. The art-music world is probably the most unexplored in the history of the arts in Panama.

There are several venues for traditional music performance aimed at tourists. Most important because of its interest in recreating authentic performances of music and dance is the Las Tinajas restaurant in Panama City. Accompanying traditional cuisine, a nightly floor show includes skillful musicians and dancers in traditional costumes performing most of Panama's folk traditions, including the famous *los diablicos sucios* dance from Los Santos Province.

Some of the best jazz in the Western Hemisphere occurs in Panama City, especially in several jazz clubs in Casco Antiguo, the city's old quarter. An annual jazz festival brings jazz pianist superstar Danilo Pérez back to Panama to often host the event and be featured as a soloist. *Salsa* giant Rubén Blades is the Minister of Tourism in the administration of Martin Torrijos, the son of former president Omar Torrijos. In spite of his high governmental position, Blades has not developed any type of *salsa* festival in Panama, although there are numerous excellent *salsa* ensembles in Panama City.

FURTHER STUDY

There has been no critical research into musical archaeology and the musical practices of ancient Amerindian groups in Panama. Almost no research has been accomplished in the area of music in colonial Panama. Ronald R. Smith has searched in Spanish archives for documents and musical materials that might elucidate this lacuna. It is clear, however, that musical activities were connected to religious brotherhoods (*cofradías*) affiliated with churches: references to musical practices and officers in charge of musical matters appear in their constitutions.

Because the reality of ethnic origins is still strong and provides a basis for a Panamanian worldview, musical terms, musical instruments, and concepts on which people construct interaction, regionalism is an important focus in the study of Panamanian music. Several studies of general interest highlight folkloric traditions in certain regions and among specific ethnic groups, including Amerindian tribes. What is known has been collected by anthropologists, folklorists, and linguists (Carmona Maya 1989; Densmore 1926; Hayans 1963; Lipski 1989; McCosker 1974; Sherzer 1983) from such contemporary groups as the Kuna, the Choco, the Guaymí, and the Teribe. These data focus largely on ritual traditions and musical instruments. There are also studies of communities of African descent (Drolet 1980, 1982; Joly 1981; Smith 1976, 1985, 1994), African-derived and *mestizo* traditions (Cheville 1964, 1977), and *mestizo* traditions (Garay 1930; D. Zárate 1971; Zárate and Zárate 1968).

Recordings of traditional music from Panama have been collected for many years, but most are not publicly available. Recordings that may be consulted are those deposited at the archive of the National Museum of Panamá, the Archives of Traditional Music at Indiana University (Ronald R. Smith collections), and the INIDEF Archive, created by Drs. Isabel Aretz and Felipe Ramón y Rivera in Caracas, Venezuela. Archival field collections contain a wealth of documentation and musical examples that provide the inquisitive listener with an in-depth view of a range of Panamanian genres (Cheville 1964). Since the 1980s, several commercial recordings of Panamanian traditional musical genres have been released (Blaise 1985; Llerenas and Ramírez de Arellano 1987; Stiffler 1983).

REFERENCES

Blaise, Michel. 1985. *Street Music of Panama.* Original Music OML 401. LP disk.

Carmona Maya, Sergio Iván. 1989. *La Música, un fenómeno cosmogónico en la cultura kuna.* Medellín, Colombia: Editorial Universidad de Antioquia. Ediciones Previas.

Cheville, Lila R. 1964. "The Folk Dances of Panama." Ph.D. dissertation, University of Iowa.

Cheville, Lila R. and Richard A. Cheville. 1977. *Festivals and Dances of Panama.* Panama: Lila and Richard Cheville

Densmore, Frances. 1926. *Music of the Tule Indians of Panama.* Smithsonian miscellaneous collections, 77, 11. Washington, D.C.: Smithsonian Institution.

Drolet, Patricia Lund. 1980. "The Congo Ritual of Northeastern Panama: An Afro-American expressive Structure of Cultural Adaptation." Ph.D. dissertation, University of Illinois at Urbana-Champaign.

———.1982. *El Asentamiento cultural en la Costa Arriba: Costeños, Chocoes, Cuevas y grupos pre-históricos.* Panamá: Museo del Hombre Panameño, Instituto Nacional de Cultura. Smithsonian Tropical Research Institute.

Garay, Narciso. 1930. *Tradiciones y cantares de Panamá, ensayo folklórico.* Brussels: Presses de l'Expansion belge.

Hayans, Guillermo. 1963. *Dos cantos shamanísticos de los indios cunas.* Translated by Nils M. Holmer and S. Henry Wassén. Göteborg: Etnografiska Museet.

Izikowitz, karl Gustav. 1970 (1935). *Musical Instruments of the South American Indians.* East Ardsley, Wakefield, Yorks: S. R. Publishers.

Joly, Luz Graciela. 1981. *The Ritual "Play of the Congos" of North-Central Panama: Its Sociolinguistic Implications.* Sociolinguistic working papers, 85. Austin, Texas: Southwest Educational Development Laboratory.

Lipski, John M. 1989. *The Speech of the Negros Congos of Panama.* Amsterdam and Philadelphia: J. Benjamins Publishing.

Llerenas, Eduardo, and Enrique Ramírez de Arellano. 1987. *Panamá: Tamboritos y Mejoranas.* Música Tradicional MT.O. LP disk.

McCosker, Sandra Smith. 1974. *The Lullabies of the San Blas Cuna Indians of Panama.* Etnologiska stüdier, 33. Göteborg: Etnografiska Museet.

Olsen, Dale A. 2007. *Music Cultures of the World: Panama as the Crossroads of the World.* Electronic book posted on Internet for course, MUH 2051, Florida State University.

Sherzer. Joel. 1983. *Kuna Ways of Speaking: A Ethnographic Perspective.* Austin: University of Texas Press.

Smith, Ronald R. 1976. "The Society of *Los Congos* of Panama: An Ethnomusicological Study of the Music and Dance-Theater of an Afro-Panamanian Group." Ph.D. dissertation, Indiana University.

———.1985. "They Sing with the Voice of the Drum: Afro-Panamanian Musical Traditions." In *More Than Drumming: Essay on Africa and Afro Latin American Music,* ed. Irene Jackson-Brown, 163–198. Wesport, Conn.: Greenwood Press.

———.1991. Recording review of *Street Music of Panama: Cumbias, Tamboritos, and Mejorana. Latin American Music Review* 12(2):216–220.

———. 1994. "Panama." In *Music and Black Ethnicity in the Caribbean and South America,* ed. Gerard Béhague, 239–266. Miami: North-South Center, University of Miami.

Stiffler, David Blair. 1983. *Music of the Indians of Panama: The Cuna (Tule) and Chocoe (Embera) Tribes.* Folkways Records FE 4326. LP disk.

Zárate, Dora Pérez de. 1971. *Textos del tamborito panameño: Un estudio folklórico -Literario de los textos del tamborito en Panamá.* Panamá: Dora Pérez de Zárate.

Zárate, *Manuel* F., and Dora Pérez de Zárate 1968. *Tambor y socavón: Un estudio comprensivo de dos temas del folklore panameño, y de sus implicaciones históricas y culturales.* Panamá: Ediciones del Ministerio de Educación, Dirección Nacional de Cultura.

Kuna

Sandra Smith

Kuna Musical Thinking
Musical Instruments
Musical Contexts and Genres
Social Aspects of Music
Further Study

Numbering about thirty thousand, the Kuna (Cuna) live along several rivers in northern Colombia and eastern Panama and along Panama's Caribbean coast and on the San Blas Islands (this coastal and insular region, named Kuna Yala, is a *comarca* or Indian reserve like a state or province within Panama). Kuna expressive culture displays the wealth and imagination afforded by leisure, strong communal organization, and an unbroken heritage of indigenous civilization. The Kuna are among the most extensively documented living Amerindian nations of Latin America. They comprise several slightly different cultural groups sharing a common language and traditions, including music. These groups are distinguished by slight differences in vocabulary, style of speaking, interpretation of oral traditions, and music.

Kuna ancestors once lived in the northern Colombian highlands, where the development of their material and expressive culture reflected a riverine way of life. Some village groups spread along the rivers into the Colombian lowlands toward the Gulf of Uraba. Others spread northward through the mountains into eastern Panama, where they settled along rivers that flow into the Atlantic Ocean. These populations ranged across 300 kilometers and were separated from each other by dense jungle and, in some cases, by other native groups. Offshoots of the mountain and river populations in eastern Panama and northern Colombia formed coastal villages near the mouths of rivers at about the time of earliest European contact there. The people of most of these villages subsequently moved offshore to the San Blas Islands, which stretch from the Colombian border all along Panama's eastern coast. Though these islands have neither fresh water nor soil suitable for farming, they provide a healthier environment than the coastal areas. Island-dwelling Kuna make daily forays to the mainland to farm, hunt, and fetch water. They frequently travel upriver to visit their relatives in the mountains. They associate the variation in their styles of speaking and cultural traditions with each of their populations.

The island-dwelling Kuna, now far outnumbering the mountain- and river-dwelling Kuna, maintain their highland heritage. They travel up and down the coast in canoes, they use the metaphorical structure of rivers and pathways to describe their traditional arts, and they construct many of their musical instruments from materials harvested in the mountains. Each island village maintains social, cultural, and political ties with its mainland relatives, whose linguistic and musical styles are consequently reflected throughout the island population.

Because the Kuna are geographically scattered, interspersed with other native groups and with Latin American populations, they place a high premium on communication between the distant members of each of their cultural groups, and among their different groups as a whole. Much of this communication is carried out musically during periodic gatherings when the cultural leaders of different villages convene to perform tribal oral histories and discuss social and political issues.

Kuna music consists of vocal and instrumental genres. Most of the latter are associated with dance. Individuals of all ages and both genders participate in musical performances, though most musical genres are gender-specific. The following examination of Kuna music uses as a framework Kuna beliefs about the origin and development of their musical traditions and Kuna terminology for musical items and activities.

KUNA MUSICAL THINKING

The Kuna believe that musical traditions, which encompass ways of singing, playing instrumental music, and dancing, exist almost in a Platonic sense in an otherworldly realm. This is the realm of the ancestors and the gods, from where the legendary hero, Ibeorgun, helped bring to the Kuna certain musical instruments, mostly end-blown flutes and panpipes, each with its particular music and dance. The instruments were animate beings that existed in social combinations, such as couples or groups of three or six; they each "sang" their own language and danced their own dance, and they all arrived singing and dancing. The Kuna believe they have undergone legendary and historical periods of cultural decline and renewal, and when they have sought to relearn forgotten traditions, their cultural leaders, like Ibeorgun, have helped them hear the tradition-carrying ancestral voices. The Kuna believe that their musical traditions are continually modified in the slow march of culture, and that new ways of singing, playing instruments, and dancing emerge from ancestral voices to answer current needs.

The Kuna language does not employ terms that correspond directly to English concepts of "music," "chant," "song," and "dance." Most Kuna vocal genres are directly associated with the term *igar* (also *igala*), which can be glossed "way" or "path." *Igar* is more broadly associated with formalized ways of speaking, which can include knowledge about communicating with the world of spirits. Each vocal musical genre with *igar* employs specific linguistic and musical conventions; musicality is part of the *igar* of these specialized ways of speaking. Each piece or text of one of these genres with *igar* has a name and a "way" or manner of expression. It follows a specific "path" that guides expression along a theme or spiritual journey and directs the expression toward an audience of common villagers or trained cultural leaders, Kuna-speakers or Spanish-speakers, nonhuman living things, or spirits or ancestors. Vocal genres with *igar* are learned in formal apprenticeships.

Vocal genres without *igar* use ordinary language. The texts of these genres are neither named nor formalized; they are freely improvised around common themes. Musically, these genres, like those with *igar*, follow certain conventions, but they have greater individual freedom of musical expression than those with *igar*.

Most instrumental genres are associated with musical instruments that have *igar*. Each genre employs a unique musical system, compositional structure, and style of dancing, and all are used in specific social contexts. The pieces within each genre are named, and they are learned in formal apprenticeships. Instruments without *igar* are used for free improvisation or for playing the musical pieces of the instruments having *igar*.

The term *namaked* denotes the performance of vocal genres with or without *igar*; normal speaking is called *soged*. *Namaked* denotes all kinds of human "calling" and individual kinds of flute-produced music. A parallel term, *gormaked*, denotes all nonhuman calling and the sound of flutes in a generic sense ("the calling of the flutes"). Birdcalls are also *gormaked*. To indicate improvisation on flutes without *igar*, the Kuna say the name of the flute followed by the words *binsae* "thinking up" and *namaked* "calling." They use the term *dodoed* to denote flute-produced music associated with dance and the term *dodoged* to refer to the dancing itself. They also use the term *dodoged* to denote the playing of flutes in ensemble, whether or not the performance is choreographed.

I use the term *chanting* to denote vocal *namaked* with *igar* and *singing* to denote vocal *namaked* without *igar*. This usage is consistent with the usage of Sherzer (1983), who has made the most extensive ethnography of Kuna speaking to date. I use *music* to denote human and flute *namaked* and flute *dodoed*. I use "dancing" to denote formally structured human movements.

Considering Kuna beliefs about Kuna musical traditions and the terminology the Kuna use to define musical instruments, compositions, and performances directs attention toward certain features. Broadly speaking, the Kuna do not have an all-encompassing musical system that can be defined tonally or compositionally; rather, musical systems are genre specific. Kuna musical instruments, compositions, and performances are primarily constructed and organized around the interactive roles characteristic of the specific kinds of social groupings represented by the instruments being used or by chanters' or singers' interactions with their audiences. As a vehicle for enhanced communication to certain audiences, music includes formalized patterns of interaction. Cultural leaders are responsible for learning and teaching musical traditions and providing and supporting the contexts that require musical expression.

Each Kuna musical instrument is described below, with emphasis placed on the kinds of groupings in which it is constructed and played. Following this is a discussion of musical contexts and genres, focusing first on vocal genres and second on instrumental genres.

Finally, the social aspects of music, including musical enculturation and acculturation and the role that aesthetic evaluation plays in the homogeneity of Kuna musical traditions are described.

MUSICAL INSTRUMENTS

Kuna instrumental music is represented only by idiophones and aerophones. Musical instruments are neither abundantly nor evenly distributed in Kuna territories, and outside knowledge about their use is limited. There is homogeneity in construction and repertoire among the communities that are in mutual contact. Although variation occurs between community groups that are not in frequent contact, Kuna music on a tribal level shows greater homogeneity than variation.

Idiophones

Of eight reported idiophones, seven are rattles, and one is a humming top. Only one rattle remains in use: the single calabash rattle (*nasis*), shaken by women when singing lullabies and by men when chanting during celebrations of female puberty.

Aerophones

The Kuna have seventeen aerophones, including shell trumpets, voice-modifying instruments made of animal skulls and bamboo, and flutes and panpipes made of wood, bone, and bamboo. Kuna aerophones fall into nine organological classes, distributed among twelve Kuna-defined genres.

Most Kuna aerophones are designed to be played in sets of two, three, or six component instruments. Some paired instruments are made up of a complementary male-female couple; others are composed of a primary and secondary speaker. The three-part aerophone set contains members arranged in a sequential hierarchy, with the members providing different numbers of pitches. The six-part aerophone set contains members that are alike, each producing only one pitch. Each aerophone set is associated with a different genre of dance.

The Kuna do not construct their flutes and panpipes according to a single scale at a standardized pitch. Each kind of aerophone is made to produce a particular array of tones, but its size and range can vary. When matching sets of aerophones are used, as when dancers need three sets of the paired *gammu burui* panpipe, the sets are constructed exactly alike. Different kinds of aerophones are not played together in concert except to produce a cacophony used to drive away harmful spirits.

Flutes

The Kuna distinguish nine kinds of end-blown flutes. The *dolo* or *tolo* is a single end-blown flute with external duct, used for improvisation or for playing the repertoire of the other aerophones. It is referred to in ethnomusicology as a hatchet flute because its mouthpiece assembly consists of an external duct made from a pelican's quill that is embedded in a large

Figure 18.1
Two puberty rite chanters use single end-blown flutes (*gammu suid*) and rattles (*nasis*) in their performances. Around them, Digir Villagers dance in a line at the close of the ceremonies. Photo by Sandra Smith, 1979.

wad of pitch that resembles the head of a hatchet. The *dolo* has four equidistant fingerholes and sometimes one for a thumb.

Supe are paired end-blown flutes that also have external hatchet-shaped ducts. Constructed in male-female pairs that Kuna musicians call primary and secondary speakers, the male flute, with four equidistant fingerholes and one thumb hole, is shorter than the female flute, which has one or two fingerholes. Melodies with many notes, often imitating birds, are played on the male flute, while the female flute intersperses notes between male-flute passages.

The *dede* is a single end-blown vessel flute made of an armadillo skull. It is used to purify the space where musical performances occur. Medicinally, armadillo spirits open pathways or tunnels into Kuna spiritual dimensions.

Four kinds of end-blown internal duct flutes (*sulupgala, gorgigala, mulaqala, uas-gala*) made of wing bones of eagles, pelicans, and vultures were reported to have been used singly and in sets during celebrations of puberty. Several of these flutes are suspended on necklaces and worn by dancers to make a percussive sound while they dance; this use continues in the late 1990s during celebrations of puberty.

Paired end-blown notched flutes called *suara* are constructed like the Andean *kena* [see BOLIVIA and PERU] in male-female couples. The male flute has four equally spaced finger holes and sometimes one for a thumb; the female flute has either no finger holes or one or two holes. The pair is played in interlocking patterns indigenously described as *su-ar-aaa, su-ar-aaa*, with the male flute sounding *su-ar* and the female flute sounding *aaa*. Paired end-blown ductless and unmodified flutes called *gammu suid* (also *kammu suit*) are also constructed as male and female. Both flutes have two finger holes each, and together the set produces four consecutive pitches, spanning a fourth. Two chanters use these flutes to chant through and to play overlapping melodic motifs during celebrations of puberty (Figure 18.1).

The Kuna described one side-blown flute to me that is constructed of bone or wood and has four holes for fingers. Called *galabigbili*, its use has not been reported in print.

Panpipes

The Kuna have two kinds of bamboo panpipes, bound and unbound, which are distinguished in three different groupings: paired panpipes; a panpipe made up of three different tubes; and a panpipe made up of six similar tubes. Each kind of panpipe is played in an ensemble of six players. The paired panpipe is played in three matching sets; the panpipe having three tubes is played in two matching sets; the six-part panpipe is played by six performers.

The paired panpipe, called *gammu burui*, is made up of fourteen lengths of bamboo tubes, giving fourteen consecutive pitches of an equiheptatonic scale, spanning one note short of two octaves. The tubes are distributed alternately between a male and a female instrument that are played in duet. The seven tubes of each instrument are again distributed alternately between two bound raft-like supports. The adjacent tubes within each raft are a fifth apart. Each player holds a three-tube raft and a four-tube raft side by side, with the shortest tubes in the center (Figure 18.3). The interval between the

Figure 18.2
In the dramatic dance performed in Digir Village with the *achunono* and *goenono* voice modifying instruments, the jaguar triumphs over the deer. Photo by Sandra Smith, 1979.

rafts (the two short tubes) is a neutral third. Each tube of the male instrument is one step longer and lower in pitch than the corresponding tube of the female instrument. Melodic statements are produced in an alternating and interlocking pattern between two players. Danced performances use three matching sets, so that six players, all men, dance with six women who each have a rattle (Figure 18.4).

Some *gammu burui* pieces consist of the repetition and modification of two or more melodic statements, each usually closing with the figure presented in the introduction of the piece. The melodic themes are stated and repeated in their shortest forms in the first section; then they are each expanded by a few notes by internal segmental repetition or the insertion of new material. The expanded statements are in turn repeated several times; in the last portion of the piece, the melodic themes contract to their original forms. The total length of a piece is fifteen to twenty minutes.

In a *gammu burui* composition of this sort (Figure 18.5) the last segment of the introduction appears at the end of each theme. Themes A and B are expanded to create A' and B'. The compositional structure is section 1, AABB (four times); section 2, A'A'B'B' (four

Figure 18.3 (left)
A Kuna woman plays a single *gammu burui* panpipe set (two halves). Photo by Ronald R. Smith.

Figure 18.4 (right)
In Digir Village, the head couple of *gammu burui* dancers leads the other dancers through choreographic formations. The men play panpipes and the women shake rattles. Photo by Sandra Smith, 1979.

Figure 18.5
"Buruiguad, Dummad" ("Little Ones, Big Ones"), a *gammu burui* panpipe piece from Nalunega. Interlocking of notes is shown by upward stems for one panpipe and downward stems for the other. Transcription by Sandra Smith.

times); section 3, AABB, A'A'B'B' (once); section 4, AAB'B' (once). In section 3, the entire piece to this point is contracted into a single statement of sections 1 and 2; finally, in section 4, section 3 is further contracted.

Titles given to *gammu burui* compositions name birds and animals, human relationships, techniques of playing the instruments, and activities of the celebrations, with each piece following certain compositional principles. Pieces about birds and animals imitate calls and behaviors in a theme and a series of variations; compositions about techniques of playing instruments feature specific interlocking patterns of movement.

The three-part panpipe called *goke* is constructed from three bound tubes, two bound tubes, and a single tube. The set is duplicated so that six players perform together. The tubes are graduated in size and are arranged to produce six consecutive pitches. The lowest pitch, which I call pitch 1, is produced by the player of the single tube. Pitches 2 and 3 are produced by the player of the two-tube raft. Pitches 4, 5, and 6 are produced by the player of the three-tube raft. The pitches are equally spaced, with the intervals slightly smaller than a whole step; all together, from lowest to highest, the pitches span a sixth. The ensemble plays together, but their musical parts are arranged hierarchically. The music, called *gokedom*, is composed of three short melodic statements of equal length. Each statement can be notated as two eighths followed by a quarter. In each statement, the player of the single tube plays on the quarter, whereas the player of the two-tube raft plays pitches 2, 3, and 2 for each statement. The player of the three-tube raft plays a different sequence in each statement: first he uses only two tubes, playing pitches 4, 5, and 4; then he uses all three tubes, playing pitches 6, 5, and 4; finally, using only one tube, he plays the phrase on pitch 4 as 4, 4, and 4. The three statements are each repeated once, and the entire sequence is played over and over.

The last panpipe, *guli*, has six single unbound tubes producing six closely spaced consecutive pitches spanning a third to a fifth. Six men play single tubes in alternation, interlocking their notes to create a melodic line. *Guli* is an onomatopoeic name of the song of the golden-collared *manakin*, a bird whose sounds and movements are imitated in a dance associated with this panpipe.

Trumpet and voice tubes

An end-blown conch trumpet called *dutu* is used to call performers from their homes. There are two voice-modifying instruments the *achunono* made of a jaguar's skull and the *goenono* made from a deer's skull. Both are constructed with an unmodified open-ended bamboo tube attached to the nape of the skull. Each performer, making jaguar or deer sounds, directs his voice through the bamboo tube into the skull. Together, the performers pantomime a jaguar hunting a deer (Figure 18.2).

MUSICAL CONTEXTS AND GENRES

An outline of Kuna musical genres closely parallels the Kuna division of specialized knowledge into eight named disciplines, all but one of which—the discipline of prophecy and prognosis—involve music. The disciplines of specialized knowledge that utilize music include traditional chanting for history, medicine, exorcism, puberty rites, and funeral rites; traditional *gammu burui* music and dance; and the discipline that includes all other forms of traditional instrumental music.

Chanting

The disciplines involving chanting are practiced by men (called "chanters" in English) who, though not shamans, are trained specialists in traditional medicine, history, exorcism, puberty rites, and funeral rites (Sherzer 1986). Chanters neither transform themselves into spiritual entities nor perform extraordinary acts, but their practices are embedded in a framework that includes beliefs about spiritual matters. Medicinal and exorcistic specialists chant in fixed texts to a collection of wooden doll-like spiritual helpers, informing them how to carry out specific acts. The spiritual helpers then interact with other spiritual entities on behalf of a specialist and his patient.

Addressing the members of their village, historical specialists chant texts woven from fixed stories and accounts to describe mythical and historical events, report on their travels, and recount humorous parables. Christian and other religious groups have established missions, schools, and social projects in some Kuna villages, where the singing of hymns is taught. This music is not combined with indigenous chanting or other Kuna musical traditions, though Christian beliefs and personages are in some places woven into the stories and historical chants.

Funeral specialists perform chants that guide the soul of the deceased to the cemetery and protect the released soul as it begins its journey to the world of spirits. Specialists in puberty rites chant through *gammu suid*, addressing entities in the spiritual world. The word *gormaked* denotes the calling of the chants through, or by, the flutes. The long, fixed texts prescribe all the special preparations and activities of the puberty ceremony, but they are in a linguistic form that the Kuna do not understand. The calling of the *gammu suid* accompanies all the activities, linking the participants and their actions to the spiritual world.

Musically, the performance of all these kinds of chanting, except those used for puberty rites, share stylistic features (Sherzer and Wicks 1982): they are not accompanied by musical instruments; their statements consist of short parallel phrases beginning on a high pitch and ending on a low pitch while diminishing in volume and tempo; and the final phrase of each statement terminates with a long tone. The overall melodic shapes of the phrases suit each chant, but all of them contain strings of syllables on a single pitch: some descend in a steady pattern; others seesaw up and down; others cluster in repeating patterns corresponding to repeated linguistic phrases. As the chanter proceeds, the range of the chanting ascends and increases in volume, strength, and tempo.

Chants for puberty-related rites have a different musical style. The statements are chanted in short notes with a change of pitch on nearly every syllable. One or two musical tones are played on the flutes to introduce each chanted line. Standing side by side, the chanters shake rattles in a continuous, steady rhythm, slowly rotating their bodies as a pair while stepping in place (see Figure 18.1).

Medicinal, exorcistic, and funereal chanters perform alone; historical chanters perform in pairs, the primary one chanting two or more phrases at a time, ending with a long final vowel; the secondary responder overlaps a short phrase of confirmation. The responder uses a single tone, near the midpoint of the range of tones used by the primary chanter. Before the responder finishes, the primary chanter overlaps the beginning of his next statement. In this way, the men create a continuous sound that may last several hours. These men are cultural leaders, and the chants take the form of a dialogue between them in an archaic language, understood only by other trained leaders or their initiates. Afterward, an initiate interprets the chant to the audience.

Chanters of puberty rites perform in pairs and are replaced by their students from time to time during the ceremonies, which last several days. During the celebrations, all villagers participate in four days of ritual and informal music and dance. Though only girls are celebrated in this way, men and women carry out official tasks, participating equally. Before the celebrations begin, many items—food, fermented drink, flutes, rattles, special hammock-supporting ropes, pictographic boards, medicinal materials—are prepared. Male and female specialists are appointed to direct each aspect of preparation; as part of the preparations, some men perform chants. Throughout, the specialists tend to the villagers and the girl or girls being celebrated by serving them food and drink in ritualized, dancelike ways and by performing specific kinds of flute-and-panpipe music and dance at appointed times. This kind of performance is limited because most villages no longer have the proper musical specialists. Outsiders' knowledge of this music is speculative, primarily based on observations in other contexts. Away from the ceremonial activities, men informally perform for each other as entertainment.

At the close of the celebrations, a villagewide dance spirals around the two chanters, first at a running pace in a large circle, and gradually at a slower pace, as the line of dancers closes

Figure 18.6
At an annual dance festival in Digir Village, groups from different villages compete. Here, the host group performs with an unusually large *gammu burui* ensemble of twelve men playing panpipes and twelve women playing rattles. Photo by Sandra Smith, 1979.

in. Alternating along the line, men and women intertwine their arms with their hands on the shoulders of dancers to either side.

Dancing

Only adults perform the chanting traditions and the instrumental music of puberty-related festivals, but people of all ages participate in *gammu burui* music and dance. In several villages, *gammu burui* dancers organize themselves into societies. They hold regular rehearsals and performances; their music is suitable for group learning and participation because once a lead pair of *gammu burui* players has learned a piece, other players can follow in unison. Dancers are led through formations by principal male and female dancers. Sometimes groups of dancers from several villages compete (Figure 18.6).

The defining movement of *gammu burui* dances is a step and a hop in place, which becomes a skip when the dance speeds up. Men and women use the same step, though men perform it more vigorously than women. Choreographies consist of formations such as parallel lines, circles, and squares, with men and women dancing as a group, rather than as couples. In each dance, the tempo and intensity develop from a slow, calm, walking pace to a fast, vigorous, running pace.

Most danced pieces last twenty to thirty minutes; some contexts require shorter versions. Melodic themes and choreographies are sometimes slightly varied by each group; however, the repertoire shows a high degree of homogeneity, and most pieces are known by all the groups. A few troupes perform for tourists who visit the uppermost end of the archipelago. These performances consist of a few dances, each one abbreviated to about five minutes.

Improvised singing

Musical genres that are not named and are not considered to be special disciplines are the vocal genres without *igar*: lullabies sung by women to calm and quiet children, songs women sing to each other during puberty celebrations, and laments sung by women to their dying and deceased relatives. These genres are performed in private, within the household or in a female-only area of a community's festival hall. The texts are improvised in ordinary language, and they are not named.

The singing of lullabies occurs every day and throughout the day. Lullabies are performed within the privacy of the matrilocal household by female relatives of the child: an older sister, cousin, aunt, mother, or grandmother. They are improvised around common themes, but always address the circumstances of the child at hand. Musical phrases are short and rhythmically regular. Their melodic shapes are oscillating, each phrase ending on a low tone and the last ending with a long tone. The singer, sitting in a hammock with a child, shakes a rattle at a fast and steady pace close to the child's head. This sound, combined with the rapid swinging of the hammock, quickly puts the child to sleep.

When women sing beside a dying relative, they use a weeping style. Sometimes several individuals sing simultaneously, though each is singing about her own feelings and memories. This kind of singing has no rhythmic accompaniment, and it is not rhythmically regular. It continues after the relative dies and the body is taken to the burial site, where women may continue singing for a short while after the burial.

A third kind of improvised singing is performed by women in private but outside the home. This is when a village's adult women gather in the festival hall during the first few days of a puberty-related celebration. They are sequestered in a small space and served fermented drink by younger girls. Sitting as close to each other as possible in two facing rows with shoulders, hips, and knees touching, they sing for several hours, one woman at a time. The texts concern the women's mutual friendships. The musical style is like the singing of lullabies, but without rhythmic accompaniment. As the singers become tipsy, the melodies become freer and punctuated by laughter.

SOCIAL ASPECTS OF MUSIC

Kuna chanters, players of aerophones, and makers of instruments are men. For some genres of dancing, rattle-playing women join men. Improvised singing is the purview of women. No classes defined by kinship or economic level occur in Kuna society. Cultural leaders are men who have learned the chants associated with the disciplines of traditional knowledge in history, medicine, exorcism, and puberty and funeral rites. Through one-on-one apprenticeships, they train younger men according to their talents. An apprentice studies sequentially with several teachers, and each teacher may instruct several apprentices. Novices strive to obtain widespread training, often including periods of study at universities in Panama or abroad. Their courses of study might be in history, political science, law, anthropology, social science, or medicine. The Kuna expect that the period of training will last ten to twenty years.

Most Kuna are bilingual in Kuna and Spanish, and some are multilingual, speaking also English, French, or German. They use Panamanian newspapers, radio, and television to follow international, national, and tribal events. With these media, they have become familiar with foreign musics. Nevertheless, they keep their own music compartmentalized

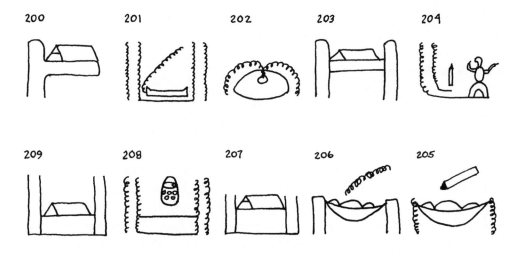

200 201 202 203 204

209 208 207 206 205

Figure 18.7
A pictograph, an indigenous form of Kuna chant notation. Each figure corresponds to a mental map of a chant, depicting spirits and spirit helpers on their travels to different spiritual abodes. Here, the final portion of the first section (called *Gamma* "Flute") of the chant "*Sergan Igala*" ("Way of the Elders"), consisting of 564 pictographs, is shown. Each pictograph corresponds to one or two lines chanted from memory. The pictographs depict midnight (the house), when the cool winds (wiggly lines) from the flutes (shown in 201, 202, 204, and 205) cool the feverish body (hammock), destroying the seeds of sickness (drawing by Sandra Smith, after Holmer and Wassén 1963:32, 49).

and private. They do not incorporate foreign musical instruments with their own in performances, and they do not play foreign music on their own instruments. They keep their music mostly inaccessible to foreigners.

The Kuna have developed a form of notation to help them memorize their long chants (Figure 18.7). Teachers and apprentices use colored pictographs as educational tools. Each pictograph, measuring one to two centimeters square, corresponds to an event, an episode, a character, or an entity. A long tabulation of pictographs, running in boustrophedon, represents the path or way of the chant depicting spirits and spiritual helpers on their travels to spiritual abodes. No forms of traditional notation were developed for instrumental music.

Musical enculturation and acculturation

Beginning with lullabies in infancy, Kuna individuals learn traditional language, song, and customs. Lullabies describe the duties a child has toward other relatives, the village, and the tribe. The singing of lullabies is learned through exposure and imitation, as mothers sing to their children and girls sing to their younger siblings. In nightly or weekly gatherings, villagers listen to their leaders' historical chants. Topics of concern are embedded in the context of mythical and historical tribal lore. In annual puberty celebrations, all kinds of traditional music and dance are displayed. Through music and dance, all villagers participate in the ceremonial rebirth of the girl being celebrated.

Most Kuna musical settings are rural, occurring in indigenous villages. Festivals organized by the *gammu burui* dance societies take place in some villages (see Figure 18.6) and in Panama's cities during folkloric presentations in which national dances are presented. Kuna urban centers for young people organize presentations by and for their members. Dance societies in some villages arrange performances for tourists. Sometimes, for personal use, the Kuna make cassette recordings at festivals.

Electronic media

Electronic media form a small part of the material culture of Kuna music. The Kuna use cassettes to transmit oral letters, and in this way they often send entire speeches and chants from one community to another. Battery-powered radios, phonographs, and televisions expose them to music from outside Kuna society.

Musical evaluation

Most Kuna consider aesthetic judgments inappropriate, and leave evaluations to musical specialists, men who judge the uniformity of dancing and playing, the enthusiasm and vigor of dancers and musicians, and the speed and tightness (or closeness) of interlocking musical parts and choreographic figures.

Kuna women look for similar features in evaluating their textiles, which include appliqué blouses and beaded bands worn on arms and legs. They judge uniformity of colors and designs used by groups of women (such as members of dance groups, the friends of a girl going through the celebrations of her puberty, and even all the women of a single village), brightness and contrast among the colors, intricacy, tightness, closeness, and evenness of interlocking visual patterns. In the images depicted in appliqué blouses, they evaluate humor and the play of multiple levels of meaning. The Kuna similarly value these features in historical chants and their colloquial interpretations and in some *gammu burui* pieces.

Kuna music and dance are meant for human and nonhuman receivers. Most traditional chanting is addressed to nonhuman entities. Human participants are merely witnesses with passive reactions. These relationships characterize the music and dance that occur in the ceremonial contexts of puberty-related festivals. Performances for public entertainment, however, are also addressed to human audiences. Reactions are mostly passive, but exceptionally good performances stimulate bursts of approval.

Some individuals and communities gain reputations for being more innovative than others. Creativity is expected and encouraged from these, while orthodoxy is expected from others. Chanters develop individual styles by combining styles learned from different teachers. In some traditions, they tailor their chanting to specific situations. In this sense, chants are always developing. Women's songs, however, are spontaneously created at each sitting. Each group slightly varies instrumental compositions and choreographies, but new compositions are few, introduced only by leaders of the group.

FURTHER STUDY

Musical texts have been published in translation and in the Kuna language, keyed to transcriptions of indigenous colored pictographs (Holmer and Wassén 1953, 1963; Nordenskiöld 1938); an ethnographic study of curing (Chapin 1983) links the pictographs more closely with Kuna medicinal knowledge than with textual translations. A description of Kuna rites of passage (Prestán 1975) contains detailed accounts of the preparations and ceremonial activities for girls' puberty rites. The Kuna history-chanting tradition is documented in Howe's ethnography on political organization (1985), and general descriptions of the musical aspects of chanting and women's singing were made by Frances Densmore (1925, 1926) and Narciso Garay (1930). (For the Kuna, Densmore uses the name *Tule*, which means "person" in the Kuna language.) Most recently, the singing of lullabies (McCosker 1974) and the performance of instrumental music (Smith 1984) have been studied. A recent detailed and comparative study of the Kuna and Mískito is by Ronny Velásquez (2004).

Museums in Germany, Panama, Sweden, and the United States house collections of Kuna domestic equipment, textiles, and musical instruments. The Kuna construct and use all but a few of their instruments in pairs or sets, but most collections contain only partial or mismatched sets, or instruments in disrepair. Consequently, misinformed photographs, illustrations, and descriptions of construction and usage have persisted.

Few recordings of the musical instruments of the Kuna are commercially available. Moser and Taylor (1987) released excerpts from recordings made in Panama in 1960 for the British Institute of Recorded Sound. The complete recordings are available for study in the Archives of Traditional Music, Indiana University.

REFERENCES

Chapin, Norman A. 1983. "Curing among the San Blas Kuna of Panama." Ph.D. dissertation, University of Arizona.

Densmore, Frances. 1925. "A Study of Tule Indian Music." In *Exploration and Fieldwork*, 115–127. Washington, D.C.: Smithsonian Institution.

———. 1926. "Music of the Tule Indians of Panama." *Smithsonian Miscellaneous Collections* 77(11):1–39. Etnografiska Museum, Etnologiska Studier, 33. Göteborgs: Elanders Boktryckeri Aktiebolag.

Garay, Narciso. 1930. *Tradiciones y Cantares de Panamá*. Panama: Ensayo Folklórica.

Holmer, Nils M., and S. H. Wassén. 1953. *The Complete Mu-Igala in Picture Writing*. Göteborgs Etnografiska Museum, Ethnologiska Studier, 21. Göteborg: Elanders Boktryckeri Aktiebolag.

———. 1963. *Dos Cantos Shamanísticos de los Indios Cunas*. Göteborgs Etnografiska Museum, Etnologiska Studier, 27. Goteborg: Elanders Boktryckeri Aktiebolag.

Howe, James. 1985. *The Kuna Gathering: Contemporary Village Politics in Panama*. Institute of Latin American Studies, Latin American Monograph 67. Austin: University of Texas Press.

———. 1990. "Mission Rivalry and Conflict in San Blas, Panama." In *Class Politics and Popular Religion in Mexico and Central America*, eds. Lynn Stephen and James Dow, 143–166. Washington, D.C.: American Anthropological Association.

McCosker, Sandra Smith. 1974. *The Lullabies of the San Blas Cuna Indians of Panama*. Göteborgs Etnografiska Museum, Etnologiska Studier, 33. Goteborg: Elanders Boktryckeri Aktiebolag.

Moser, Brian, and Donald Taylor, eds. 1987. *Music of the Tukano and Cuna Peoples of Colombia*. Rogue Records FMS / NSA 002. LP disk.

Nordenskiöld, Erland. 1938. *An Historical and Ethnological Survey of the Cuna Indians*. Comparative Ethnographical Studies, 10. Göteborg: Göteborgs Museum.

Prestán, Arnulfo. 1975. *El Uso de la Chicha y la Sociedad Kuna*. Ediciones Especiales, 72. México, D.E: Instituto Indigenista Interamericano.

Sherzer, Joel. 1983. *Kuna Ways of Speaking: An Ethnographic Perspective*. Austin: University of Texas Press.

———. 1986. "The Report of a Kuna Curing Specialist: The Poetics and Rhetoric of an Oral Performance." In *Native South American Discourse*, eds. Joel Sherzer and Greg Urban, 169–212. New York and Berlin: Walter de Gruyter.

Sherzer, Joel, and Sammie Ann Wicks. 1982. "The Intersection of Music and Language in Kuna Discourse." *Latin American Music Review* 3:147–164.

Smith, Sandra. 1984. "Panpipes for Power, Panpipes for Play: The Social Management of Cultural Expression in Kuna Society." Ph.D. dissertation, University of California at Berkeley.

Velásquez, Ronny. 2004. "The Fundamental Role of Music in the Life of Two Central American Ethnic Nations: The Mískito in Honduras and Nicaragua, and the Kuna in Panama." In Malena Kuss, ed., *Music in Latin America and the Caribbean, An Encyclopedic History, Vol. 1, Performing Beliefs: Indigenous Peoples of South America, Central America, and Mexico*, 193–230. Austin: University Press of Texas.

Questions for Critical Thinking

Middle Latin American Music

1. How would you compare and contrast African-derived music from Mexico, Guatemala, and Panama?
2. Place the African-derived music of Mexico, Guatemala, and Panama on a continuum from the most to the least African and discuss the characteristics that determine your reasoning.
3. How would you compare and contrast Spanish-derived music from Mexico, Guatemala, and Panama?
4. Place the Spanish-derived music of Mexico, Guatemala, and Panama on a continuum from the most to the least Spanish and discuss the characteristics that determine your reasoning.
5. Make a list of the popular music genres of Mexico, Guatemala, and Panama, and indicate as many characteristics as you can that make them similar or different.
6. How have Roman Catholicism and traditional non-Catholic expressions worked together to develop unique musical expressions in Middle America?
7. Mexico and Guatemala once were politically unified. Are there historical musical similarities that might reflect this? How have these continued today?
8. Panama is at the southernmost end of Middle America and Mexico at the northernmost. Are there musical contrasts that reflect this separation?
9. In general musical terms, which nation might be considered the most "Indian": Mexico, Guatemala, or Panama? Why? Think about the question with regard to pre-Encounter times, and then compare that period with the present.
10. Is Middle America a unified musical region? Why or why not?
11. How has the past century of urbanization affected music in Mexico, Guatemala, and Panama?
12. Are there certain genres of music from Mexico, Guatemala, and Panama that are popular far beyond their national boundaries? If yes, what are they and what caused them to be popular?

South America

What is the essence of South American music? Many will think of the guitar and its dozens of relatives, or the harp with its dazzling arpeggios. Others may think of skin-covered drums, hand-held rattles, or other rhythm producing instruments. Still others may think of the plaintive sounds of the Andean flutes and panpipes. They are all correct, because South American music includes these and many others. This large land mass in the Southern Hemisphere of the Americas is a region of many heritages and great musical diversity. We think immediately of Spanish, Portuguese, African, and native American backgrounds, but we must also think of *other* Europeans (the British, Germans, and Italians, especially), the *diversity* of Amerindian (over 1,490 indigenous languages spoken at the time of the Encounter) and African cultures (the latter forcibly brought to the New World), and the multitude of other immigrants (Chinese, Japanese, Lebanese, and others) whose musics have become part of the cultural mosaic of South America.

(*Photo on following page*)
Señora Berta Indo, a rural guitarist, is from Curacaví, Santiago Province, central Chile, an area of South America that favors old musical traits, such as the use of metal rather than nylon strings. She holds her instrument in a manner deriving from Renaissance Spain or even relating to performance by Spanish gypsies. Photo by Daniel E. Sheehy, 1973.

The Music of South America

Dale A. Olsen

Linguistic Diversity
History
Musical Threads

South America is a continent of twelve politically independent countries and one department of France (Map 20.1, Map 20.2, Map 20.3, and Map 20.4). Five official or national languages are spoken—Dutch, English, French, Spanish, and Portuguese—as are hundreds of Amerindian tongues, dozens of imported languages [see MUSIC OF IMMIGRANT GROUPS], and several localized ones, such as Creole, Taki-taki, and Papiamento. Most of the continent's three hundred million people, however, speak Spanish or Portuguese.

LINGUISTIC DIVERSITY

Apart from the speakers of indigenous languages, the linguistic diversity of the South American continent originated from its colonial background. In the Treaty of Tordesillas (1494), Pope Alexander VI set a demarcation line that divided the New World between Spain and Portugal. It awarded Spain all lands 370 leagues west of the Cape Verde Islands and Portugal everything east of the line (Goodman 1992). This treaty led to the development of Brazil as an officially Portuguese-speaking country, whereas the other colonies in South America (except the Guianas) officially spoke Spanish. England, France, and the Netherlands, however, eventually established colonial outposts on the northern Atlantic coast of the continent, where their languages prevailed; this area, a sort of coastal buffer between Spain and Portugal, was known as the Guianas—British Guiana (Guyana), Dutch Guiana (Surinam), and French Guiana.

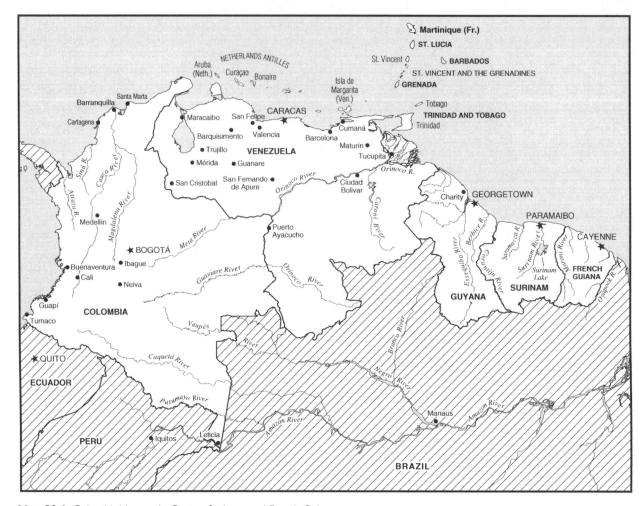

Map 20.1 Colombia, Venezuela, Guyana, Surinam, and French Guiana

HISTORY

For the purpose of governing, Spain divided its lands into four large domains, or viceroyalties (subkingdoms): Nueva España ("New Spain," much of Central America north into the western half of the present United States), Nueva Granada ("New Granada," present Colombia, Ecuador, and Venezuela), Peru (present Chile and Peru), and La Plata (present Argentina, Bolivia, Paraguay, and Uruguay). Portugal's domain became the viceroyalty of Brazil, which grew much larger than the land originally determined by the Treaty of Tordesillas. For almost three centuries, viceroys ruled these areas, representing the crowns of Spain and Portugal.

Unique in South America, Brazil became the home of a reigning European king, the king of Portugal himself, Dom João. He and his royal court escaped the Napoleonic takeover by sailing to Brazil in 1808, and in 1815 he proclaimed himself King of Brazil (Pendle 1963:120–124).

Map 20.2 Ecuador, Peru, and Bolivia

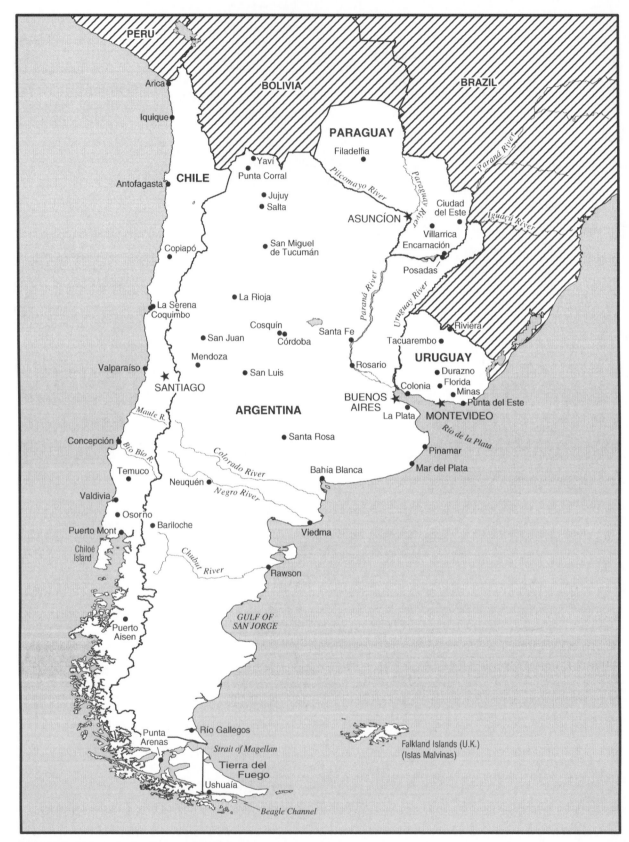

Map 20.3 Chile, Argentina, Paraguay, and Uruguay

Independence movements started in the 1800s. Simón Bolívar and José de San Martín are considered the liberators of Spanish-speaking South America. Brazil, however, was given to Dom Pedro by his father, Dom João who returned to Portugal. Dom Pedro proclaimed Brazil's independence from Portugal in 1822 and had himself crowned emperor of Brazil. The remaining European colonies on the north coast (the Guianas) did not become independent until the 1900s, and French Guiana remains French territory. Since the 1800s, most South American nations have experienced dictatorships, elitist or military rule, and many changes of governments; only since the 1980s have some of them become democratic.

South America is a continent of great geographic contrasts. It contains one of the driest deserts on earth (the Atacama Desert in northern Chile), the highest mountain in the Western Hemisphere (Aconcagua, on the border between Argentina and Chile), one of the world's longest rivers (Río Marañón-Amazon, Amazon), the world's largest tropical forest (the Amazon), the world's highest waterfall (Angel Falls in Venezuela), and many other unique physical features.

In historical times, wars have been fought over some of these regions. From 1879 to 1883, Bolivia, Chile, and Peru fought the War of the Pacific over the discovery of nitrates (Chile won). From melted-down cannons, Argentina and Chile built a large statue of Jesus Christ (Cristo Redemptor, "Christ of the Andes") on their border between Mendoza and Santiago; its inscription translates: "Sooner shall these mountains crumble to dust than Argentines and Chileans break the peace sworn to at the feet of Christ the Redeemer" (Herring 1968:736). Border and internal skirmishes, and even wars, have been waged in the South American rain forests and foothills, mainly because of the desire for slaves, the discovery of minerals and hardwoods, or the possibility of finding deposits of oil. The Brazil-Paraguay War (1864–1870) was one of the bloodiest conflicts in all of South America, and the Chaco War, between Paraguay and Bolivia, was one of the longest (1928–1954) (Herring 1968:815–818). What can be termed genocidal wars against native Americans have continued in South America even into the twenty-first century.

Native South Americans have been affected by the processing of gold, silver, rubber, narcotics, and other products deemed valuable to non Amerindians, and by intrusions into indigenous lands by missionaries and other outsiders. In tropical forests, the Andes, the Caribbean coasts, and elsewhere, indigenous people and species of flora and fauna are in constant danger of extinction—mostly because of greed. Nevertheless, native South Americans have survived, though not without changes to most of their societies. Many musical occasions reveal these changes, as seen in musical instrument usage, ceremonial dress, dance styles, language, and musical genres—or the disappearance of any of the above (Figure 20.1).

But just as the native South American music cultures have evolved, so have the Spanish, Portuguese, and many African music cultures. Most music of South America is a cultural mix, a musical mosaic, as it were (Olsen 1980). South America not only claims some of the world's most populous cities, greatest architectural achievements, and largest slums, it also boasts some of the world's most exciting music and elaborate folkloric events. Much of this is because of the amalgamation of cultures—the fusion of dozens of heritages in a

Map 20.4 Brazil (since this map was originally drawn, the state of Goias has been divided in half to include a new state, Tocantins, in the north, just below the state of Maranhão).

multitude of ways. What are some of the threads that wind their way through this South American musical tapestry?

MUSICAL THREADS

The foremost musical thread, perhaps, is a strong religious belief in Roman Catholicism. Another thread could be the way South America's religions have syncretized and developed into unique Latin American forms, such as Andean folk Catholicism in Bolivia, Ecuador, and Peru; Candomblé and Umbanda in Brazil; and so many others. Another is the performance of music with such Old World instrument derivations as guitar-types (*cavaquinho, guitarra, violão,*

Figure 20.1
During a floor show at the Brizas de Titicaca, a Puno club in Lima's downtown, young migrant musicians from Puno, Peru (or second-generation Puneños), wear ceremonial dress, dance, and play *siku* panpipes and drums while performing for fellow immigrants from Puno, other Peruvians, and tourists. Photo by Dale A. Olsen, 1996.

charango, cuatro, mandolina, etc.), membranophonic drums (*bombo, caja, cuíca, surdo, tambor, tamborim,* etc.), and aerophonic instruments made of brass (*saxofón, trompeta, trombón,* and others). Another is the performance of music with New World manifestations, such as aerophonic instruments made of cane (*kena, pífano, pito, rondador, siku,* etc.). Another is poetry and storytelling through song, realized in such genres as *canción, corrido, cueca, huayno, modinha, paisaje, zamba,* etc. Yet another musical thread is the expression of courtship and joy through dances such as *bambuco, currulao, cueca, joropo, samba, tango,* and others. As these many forms of communal and self-expression are studied, smaller threads can also be seen, as the essays will make clear.

One of the most visible commonalities is the largely urban predilection toward contemporary popular music. Young people in South American cities, as with most youth in cities throughout the world, are influenced by globalization and transculturation in their musical and dance expressions. In particular, Caribbean and West African styles are very influential in nightclubs, on recordings, and through other media. South American rock bands come and go, as they do in Europe and the United States, and the wealthier countries like Argentina, Brazil, and Venezuela have huge music industries. Often, in the name of originality, South American popular music groups fuse many styles, merging the traditions of their countries with the latest sounds from Europe and the United States and from Africa and the Caribbean.

South Americans have great feelings of musical and cultural nationalism; art-music composers have borrowed on traditional themes, and popular-music composers

Figure 20.2
Accompanied by a solo guitarist, an Argentine couple dances the *tango* on a Sunday afternoon in a Buenos Aires street during the weekly San Telmo street fair. To the musician's left is a photo of the famous *tango* singer Carlos Gardel. To his right is a Gardel imitator, dressed like his idol. Photo by Dale A. Olsen, 1993.

have created national expressions. Throughout the centuries, many countries within South America have experienced musical censorship; however, some traditions, such as the *tango* in Argentina, never die (Figure 20.2). Some military leaders prefer German military marches to homegrown *chacareras*, *cuecas*, *huaynos*, or *modinhas*. Most South American countries have ministries of culture that concern themselves with music, and many have institutes of folklore that collect, preserve, and disseminate traditional music and dance. These vignettes suggest that music is highly important to the people of South America: it is one of their most essential elements of life.

REFERENCES

Goodman, Edward J. 1992. *The Explorers of South America*. Norman: University of Oklahoma Press.
Herring, Hubert. 1968. *A History of Latin America from the Beginnings to the Present*. New York: Knopf.
Olsen, Dale A. 1980. "Folk Music of South America—A Musical Mosaic." In *Musics of Many Cultures: An Introduction*, ed. Elizabeth May, 386–425. Berkeley: University of California Press.
Pendle, George. 1963. *A History of Latin America*. Baltimore: Penguin.

The Tropical-Forest Region

Anthony Seeger

Musical Sounds and Processes
Social Hierarchies and Musical Performance
Musical Creativity and Innovation
Immigrant Musical Forms, 1500–1900
Immigration after the 1930s
Cultural Interactions
Conclusion

The tropical-forest region of South America includes much of Brazil and parts of at least eight other countries: Bolivia, Colombia, Ecuador, French Guiana, Guyana, Peru, Surinam, and Venezuela. It encompasses the Amazon and Orinoco river basins [see WARAO] and much of the Guyana shield, extends to the coast of the Guyanas, Surinam, and eastern Venezuela, and reaches into the foothills of the Andes Mountains and toward the savannas of central and southern Brazil. It is huge, with a complex history of indigenous settlement and, later, of colonization and economic transformation.

The music of the region is one of the least known in the world. We do not have enough musical information and analysis to define musical areas on a securely comparative basis and are lucky if we have one or two studies from a given family of languages. A great deal of research remains to be done.

There are several reasons for our lack of information: the physical and cultural disappearances of many Amerindian communities throughout the region, the difficulty of reaching the areas and conducting research, the tendency of ethnomusicologists to focus on some surviving Amerindian traditions to the exclusion of others, and a concentration on other priorities by most other researchers. A few surveys have been prepared, however, including those by Isabel Aretz (1984), Malena Kuss (2004), and Dale Olsen (1980) on South America, Aretz (1991) on Venezuela, and Helza Cameu on Brazil (1977).

Though outsiders think of Amerindians as the primary residents of the tropical forest, other communities live there, and some have done so for centuries. Even before Columbus, Andean peoples probably influenced and were influenced by tropical-forest peoples. Later arrivals who settled in the region and remained there included missionaries, gold miners, rubber tappers, farmers, and ranchers. More recent immigrants include factory workers, oil drillers, prospectors, members of new religious organizations, civil servants, and immigrants from rural areas in other areas or countries.

The Amerindian and nonindigenous communities in the tropical forest have interacted over the past few centuries with profound effects on the music of the former. External influence increased in the last few decades of the twentieth century with the capital-intensive development of the region and the diffusion of shortwave radios, cameras, tape recorders, and television. In the early twenty-first century, musical influences move in several directions as the indigenous Brazilian leader Rauni tours with the British rock singer Sting, Milton Nascimento includes native Brazilian music on his album *Txai!* (1990), and Marlui Miranda (1995) arranges, composes, and performs new Amerindian music.

As with music almost everywhere, two simultaneous musical movements have affected this region. While some musicians looked backward to earlier forms, preserving or reinventing them, other musicians reached out to new forms, incorporating them into their styles to create new traditions. These musical choices are part of specific historical contexts, frequently those of political oppression, economic exploitation, and intentional cultural destruction. In this way, music reflects regional and transnational processes and local communities' reactions to them.

This essay begins with a description of aboriginal South American tropical-forest musical sounds and a discussion of some pertinent musical processes. Later, it addresses the music of the early immigrants to the region. It concludes with a discussion of how these musical forms have interacted and are evolving.

MUSICAL SOUNDS AND PROCESSES

What does tropical-forest Amerindian music sound like? If you could hover over the region and listen to the music emanating from the hundreds of Amerindian communities during a twenty-four-hour period, you might hear a dramatic crescendo with the rise of the morning star (well before dawn) that would reach a peak in the dawn light before sunrise. The sounds would diminish as the day grew hotter then would pick up again in the late afternoon, dying down again around 8:00 p.m., but continuing in some form throughout the night into the predawn crescendo. You would hear flutes of all sizes, played for their overtones; you would hear reed instruments, some played in hocket; you would hear unison men's choruses accompanied by rattles and stamping feet, and unison women's choruses. Shouts, animal cries, whistles, and other sounds would sometimes obscure the text and tune. During the day, you would hear playing children imitating their elder's ceremonies, solo singers, shamans chanting, and lone fishermen and hunters humming to themselves in preparation for the evening's performance.

If your gaze could penetrate the forest and thatched roofs of the villages, you would often see people dancing almost everywhere you heard music. You might see elaborate bodily ornamentation of paint and feathers and ceremonial dress made from palm fronds that would swish with the dancers' movements. Rattles might be hanging from their bodies; wind instruments might appear in various sizes. Men and women would usually be dancing in separate lines, not together, and sometimes the women would be hiding in the houses while the men alone performed. Somewhere you would see a lone shaman, singing over the sick, searching for the cause and cure of the illness. Nowhere would you see a conductor; indeed, the performers would not often be able to see one another while they perform.

In the early morning, when the sounds died down, you would see men heading for rivers and forests to fish and hunt and women hurrying to gardens to gather crops to prepare food and, in some cases, fermented drink. Their labor must produce the sustenance that makes the performances memorable: "When we sing, we eat," say some; "when we perform, we drink," say others.

Somewhere you would see a person listening intently—to sounds coming from an unseen source within, or to a radio or a tape recorder, or to a person from a different community. After a time, the listener introduces to excited colleagues a new song, a new ceremony, a new aesthetic. Then the cacophony will crescendo again.

Ethnohistory

The tropical forest once was a complex mosaic of native communities, interacting with one another in a variety of ways. These groups nearly always lived in small, dispersed settlements. For thousands of years, they traded, intermarried, fought, and learned each others' music. Theirs were mostly traditions of straw and wood, using various kinds of grass, fronds, and vegetal material to construct residences, musical instruments, and symbolically important ritual regalia. As a result, we have little archaeological evidence from the region. Surviving materials include cook pots, charred wood, pollen from gardens, shells, and a few earthworks and other signs of social structure in parts of the region. The archaeology of the region is far richer than it was previously thought, and is revealing impressive populations and population centers in areas where they were thought not to exist. Similarities and possible connections between Amazon and Andean cultures since ancient times are evident through music (Olsen 2001).

Disease, violence, enslavement, missionization, and economic development have dramatically changed tropical-forest Amerindian settlements. Though some communities survived these ravages, the survivors often live in small, isolated settlements, surrounded by immigrant settlers. These communities are discouraged or actually forbidden to perform their traditional music and are often deprived of the lands and resources once essential to their livelihood. Even ethnomusicologists who have gone to the most isolated regions and worked with recently contacted groups are studying a situation greatly altered by the colonization of South America. We do not know exactly what musical life was like before Columbus because no one was asking those questions then; but we can learn something of what it has been like since.

Researchers discussing tropical-forest Amerindians usually talk about language families or cultural areas. The concept of "tribe" is sometimes helpful, but a tribal name is often a historical accident or a bureaucratic convenience. Peoples often have different names for themselves and often distinguish among communities that have been identified as a single people by a tribal name. As names have been used in the scholarly literature, a tribal name (for example, Suyá) identifies a settlement or cluster of settlements with a distinct language or dialect. These linguistic units are themselves then classified as members of language families. Among the largest of these are the Arawak, the Chibcha, the Gê, the Karib, the Pano, and the Tupi (Nimuendajú 1980). Cultural, cosmological, and musical traditions are usually more similar among the members of a language family than between them, but not always. In some regions, communities of several language families share a single social organization, ceremonial life, and musical style: the Upper Xingu (the Xingu National Park, an Indian reserve, was established in 1967) and Northwest Amazon regions are good examples of this.

Regional traits

Despite the variety, some generalizations hold for most of the region: within a given culture, music and dance are often defined by the same word and are inextricably related; music is transmitted entirely in the oral-aural tradition; throughout the region, certain families of instruments are more common than others; societies with strong singing traditions usually have several types of oratory that are distinctly "musical" in the use of rhythm and pitch; much of the music is part of religious and social rituals rather than "entertainment"; music is often associated with transformation (as when a human spiritually becomes an animal) or travel (as when a shaman makes a spiritual journey); and music may be an important means for establishing a communal identity and making distinctions among peoples.

Lexical identity of music and dance

Among the Suyá of Mato Grosso, music and dance are defined in a single word, *ngere*, and this practice seems widespread among land-based cultures. Most peoples seem to comprehend performed sounds and movements as a single, unified event. Often, a set of fairly stable sound structures and fairly consistent movements are identified as a named genre, as among the Xavante (Shavante) of Brazil (Figures 21.1 and Figure 21.2). This practice is distinct from that of societies in which dancers improvise to different musical performances.

In early accounts (1500–1900), observers provided better descriptions of the movements than of the sounds. After the introduction of audio field recorders (twentieth century), better information about the sounds became available. Only in the 1980s, when video recorders became viable field tools in the region, did we begin to get extensive recordings of the two aesthetic systems together.

Participants' costumes and bodily ornamentation and performers' choreography are often important clues to the musical process. When the Waiãpi are dancing the bumblebee ceremony, their instruments are supposed to sound like bumblebees, and they move like

Figure 21.1
Xavante (Shavante, Gê language group) men play side-blown bamboo trumpets (*upawã*) before singing and dancing *daño're*. Amazonas, Brazil. Photo by Laura Graham, 1986.

them (Fuks 1989); a similar association of dance and sounds is evident in Thomas Gregor's film on the Mehinaku (1973).

The oral-aural tradition

All musical traditions are learned and transmitted through the oral-aural tradition. There are no indigenous systems of notation, and if a tradition is not constantly performed, it is forgotten and cannot be revived.

In a purely oral culture, the lack of interest or performance during a single genera- tion can mean the disappearance of the tradition. Musical traditions are as fragile as the tropical-forest ecosystems—once destroyed, they are virtually impossible to reconstruct. Audio and videotape recorders have changed this situation somewhat, and many commu- nities are interested in preserving their traditions and teaching them through these means. Some communities have established archives and cultural centers; others have embarked on extensive documentation projects using sophisticated video technology. They are often doing so with the assistance of national or international grants. In many places indigenous groups are starting to perform ceremonies and practices that had been abandoned in previ- ous decades.

Preferred instruments

Idiophones (mostly rattles) and aerophones (a wide variety of flutes, trumpets [see Figure 21.1], single-reed instruments, panpipes, nose-blown flutes, ocarinas, and so on) are widely distributed. Membranophones, mostly double headed, have played only a small role in the music in this region, though there are some. Chordophones are rare. Musical bows occur among the Shuar in Ecuador and the Yukpa in Colombia. Lute-type stringed instruments are found only in areas where they have been learned from immigrants. The best study on musical instruments of the region remains that of Karl G. Izikowitz (1970 [1935]).

Figure 21.2
After a log relay race, Xavante men sing and dance *daño're*. Photo by Laura Graham, 1986.

Uses of instruments appear to correlate with language families. Members of the Gê family mostly use rattles to accompany singing; their aerophones are usually whistles, played to accompany song, rather than melodic instruments in their own right. In contrast, some Tupi peoples have many wind instruments, classified in considerable detail (Bastos 1978, 1986). Meanwhile, some Chibchan-speakers, such as the Warao, have dozens of musical instruments, but others, such as the Yanomamö, have none (Olsen 1980, 1996).

Everyone a musician

The societies of the region support no full-time native musical specialists or musicologists. Virtually all members of a certain age and gender engage in similar economic tasks and social processes. People make music in addition to all the other things they do in their lives and as part of those other things, rather than distinct from them. This fact distinguishes the tropical forest from some other parts of the world (most court-based societies, for example) and carries with it important implications for studies of tropical-forest music.

Since there are no full-time music specialists, practice is often part of performances. Since there are no full-time scholars of music, discourse about music tends to be phrased in diction borrowed from other domains. This diction appears to be "metaphoric." In fact, many researchers in the region have had difficulty eliciting any "words about music" at all.

The functionality of music

Most tropical-forest music is associated with religious rituals, rites of passage, intercommunal visiting, annual-cycle rituals, or curing. Except for some lullabies and individual songs, most peoples do not set an "entertainment music" apart from these other forms. This tendency means that the contexts for musical performances are quite carefully defined.

In many cases, songs are known by the name of the ceremony to which they belong. Anthropological literature on these peoples frequently includes extensive analysis of rituals but virtually no discussion of music. This is frustrating for ethnomusicologists, but reflects a general tendency in anthropology to avoid discussions of sounds (and scents and feelings).

Song and oratory

Strong singing traditions often coexist with elaborate forms of speaking (Basso 1985; Sherzer and Urban 1986). Virtually all indigenous South American groups distinguish between everyday speech and one or more forms of "oratory" or heightened speech. Elevated forms of speech may serve for formal encounters between humans, to recount myths, or to make political speeches.

Song itself may be considered an extreme of oratory—the extreme employment of fixed tonal relationships and rhythmic forms—and be systematically related to it, as I have suggested for the Suyá and as Olsen (1996) has suggested for the Warao. Instrumental music does not appear to be used to imitate the patterns of speech, even in communities with tonal languages, but to follow compositional rules that differ from those of speech.

Music and reality

Music is associated with cosmological transformations or travel. During ceremonies in many communities, singer-dancers are transformed into a kind of dual being: part-human, part-animal or part-human, part-spirit. Some of the mystery and the efficacy of performances lies in these transformations. Among the Suyá, in the course of the mouse ceremony, the dancers become mice (Seeger 1987); among the Waiãpi, in the course of the bumblebee ceremony, they become bumblebees (Fuks 1989); among the Mehinaku, flutists become spirits.

Shamans are often transformed and travel, and their songs report their travels among the Arawete (Viveiros de Castro 1986), the Tenetehara (Wagley and Galvão 1949), the Kashinaua (Kensinger 1973), and the Shuar (Crawford 1976; Harner 1972, 1973).

What is this all about? Musical performance in the tropical forest appears to be a way to create a bridge between different types of reality. Musical performances bring together humans and animals, humans and spirits, and the past and the present (Seeger 1987; Vidal 1977). These conjunctions are often reflected in sung texts, which may contain referential ambiguities: is the "I" in the text a human? a dead relative? an animal? a spirit?

Music may structure the hallucinogenic experience, acting like a "jungle-gym of consciousness" (Dobkin de Rios 1975). The role of music in these powerful conjunctions of everyday life with spirit-animal-otherworld through music is one of the reasons music plays such a central part in tropical-forest cosmology.

Music and identity

Communities use music to identify themselves in many ways. They may define themselves as against other Amerindian communities by the songs they perform (songs that make them uniquely human), or they may define themselves as "Indians" with respect to the national society around them (singing songs that make them uniquely political).

The use of music in forging and proclaiming an ethnic identity is widespread. In the tropical-forest region, the employment of music to this end varies according to the specific sociopolitical situation of the people. The same song may at one time have an internal meaning with little connection to ethnic identity and only a short time later be performed primarily as a marker of that identity.

SOCIAL HIERARCHIES AND MUSICAL PERFORMANCE

Though in the tropical forest there are no social classes in the Marxist sense (of groups with distinct means of production), notions of hierarchy occur in most indigenous peoples of the region. Hierarchy is established by gender, by age, by knowledge, by occupation, and by other means. The sense of hierarchy seems to become more pronounced toward the Andes.

In virtually all native tropical-forest communities, most public rituals are controlled by adult males. They make most important musical decisions. They select ceremonies, organize performances, and exclude women and children from some of the events. In some societies, men prohibit certain aerophones to women (Gregor 1977, 1985). In others, they let women sing but not play rattles; or women may accompany dancers with rattles but may not sing.

According to a widespread myth about the origin of sacred flutes, women once played flutes, and men were forbidden to touch them. Women at that time are often described as doing other men's tasks, such as hunting and warring. By deceit, men overcame women and took the flutes, which they have kept to this day. When these flutes are played, women are supposed to withdraw into houses and, under pain of severe sanctions, not even to look at them (Hill 1993).

The male dominance in performances is counterbalanced in many cases by ceremonies or musical genres controlled and performed exclusively by women. In the Upper Xingu, women have their own ceremony, Iamuricumã; the Gê have rituals of reversal and rituals in which women play central roles; in the Northwest Amazon, women have their own song genres (Harner 1972, 1973); and in other areas, the lament is an important women's genre, often also performed by men (Graham 1986:87).

Though women frequently know and are capable of teaching or performing certain musical genres, they do not often perform in the absence of a knowledgeable man. It is always important to distinguish between performance and knowledge. Female researchers have often had better access to women's knowledge than male researchers. The dominance of males over public ceremonies does not mean these societies are dominated by adult men; the reality is far more complex.

Age is also an important means of creating hierarchy. Older men tend to direct the activities of younger men and children (and of women), and older women often exercise authority over younger ones. Knowledge often confers status, and older men and women acquire status and authority over younger ones, partly through their knowledge of music, speech, and stories. Their authority lies in their knowledge and their culturally prescribed license to use it.

Other forms of social organization than age and gender may be important in musical performance. In Gê-speaking communities, musical performance of certain rituals may be under the control of name-based social groups. Among the Suyá, each social group has its own songs and sometimes its own way of singing: one moiety is supposed to sing more slowly than the other; young men are supposed to sing certain songs at a higher pitch than older men; and so on. In other areas, a certain community may control the ritual knowledge and musical performance of all the subareas.

MUSICAL CREATIVITY AND INNOVATION

Where does music come from? Contrary to some stereotypes, tropical-forest Amerindians do not sing the same thing all the time, but innovate frequently. New music enters their repertoires in a variety of ways. Among some groups, it comes during dreams, through earplugs, or from necklaces (Aytai 1985; Graham 1986; Olsen 1996). In other groups, songs are brought back from shamanic experiences or illnesses in which individuals have learned songs from spirits.

Many communities are musically multicultural: they perform the music and often entire rituals of neighboring groups. The Suyá are the best documented in this respect: they sing songs from at least ten other societies, including two extinct groups, their former enemies, whose only cultural survivals live on in their music (Seeger 1987). As with all issues of music and identity, under certain circumstances all the music a group sings is "its own" music; under other circumstances, the same group will carefully distinguish the origins of each form.

What makes one performance better than another? Musical aesthetics are often difficult to investigate among tropical-forest communities because music is inextricably bound up with other social events and is rarely discussed dissociated from them. Among the Waiãpi, for example, the success of musical events is judged partly by the quality and quantity of manioc beer served during the performance.

Persistence often yields some forms of evaluation, but it may be worded in a manner that appears to be metaphoric. For example, Suyá descriptions of sound tend to focus on the throat: people with highly appreciated voices are said to have "beautiful throats," people with loud voices "strong throats," and people whose voices are neither strong nor beautiful "bad throats" or "ugly throats."

Children learn music by witnessing or participating in musical performances with their elders. There is rarely any special training, except in the case of shamans, who often undergo long and intensive training and initiations. But shamans' training is more directed toward interaction with spirits than toward musical performance in itself.

Children and young men and women often participate intensively in musical performances, thus gaining musical knowledge and understanding. As there are no full-time music specialists, there are no specialized music schools or other musical-training programs. Children and certain other relatives of particularly knowledgeable musicians often become musicians themselves, having heard a great deal of music during their youth.

Many parts of the tropical forest were not heavily settled by non-Amerindians until the twentieth century. The local economies in the region were based on extractive industries, such as medicinal-plant collecting, lumbering, mining, rubber tapping, subsistence agriculture, hunting, and fishing. These required neither extensive clearing nor large settlements. In parts of the region, the rubber boom of the 1800s and the hunt for minerals profoundly affected the health and well-being of the indigenous populations.

An important and distinct group of long-term immigrants who created communities that remained isolated from their national cultures were slaves who escaped into the tropical forest and founded free black communities. Settlements of this sort were located in parts of French Guiana, Surinam, Guyana, Venezuela, Colombia, and Brazil. Some of these communities, known as Maroons, continued a fairly separate existence even after slavery was abolished in their countries. Some spoke a creole language and developed their own culture from a combination of European, African, and locally indigenous traditions. In regions with large Maroon communities, these people may have had an influence on local Amerindian traditions.

Missionaries and their musical baggage

Important beyond their numbers because of the influence they exercised over other groups, missionaries brought new musical forms to the tropical forest, based on harmony and sacred texts. In the interior of the region, large Roman Catholic missions became important institutions with considerable power and authority. They were often run by international orders and staffed by foreigners. Their effect on the Amerindian communities was often harsh: they forbade traditional music and ceremonies and restricted musical activities.

Later, missionaries of certain Protestant sects intensified the process, some with such success that hymns are the only music performed in certain tropical-forest indigenous communities. Singing hymns may take unusual directions, however, as among the Waiwai, where communities compete in composing hymns.

With a few exceptions, the music of the church and the music of the Amerindians have apparently not mixed: the tunes for Christian services are hymns, and the indigenous melodies continue without harmony where they are sung at all. In unusual cases, Amerindian communities employ some form of harmony that may have its origins in Christian music, as among the Kayabi (strict parallel fifths) and the Javae of Brazil, and the Moxo of Bolivia (Olsen 1976). In Guyana, among the Akawaio, the Makushi, and the Patamona, unusual music developed for the syncretic religion known as Hallelujah (Butt Colson 1971).

Handling the baggage

Why did Amerindian communities let the missionaries make them abandon their traditions? Part of the answer certainly lies with the missionaries' economic power. But part of it may have come from the missionaries' ability to win support among the less enfranchised parts of the Amerindian population—women, children, and young men. The missionaries often started schools for children and for extended periods of time took children away from their parents. They often tried to create new leadership of young men. Since adult men dominated the ritual and public life of the village, part of the missionaries' success may have been the willingness of women and young men to challenge the power of traditional leadership. The tropical forest was not an area of florescence for Christian music, and it did not produce the original Baroque compositions found in other parts of the Americas. Moreover, neither Hallelujah music nor Waiwai hymns have so far had an impact on Protestant hymnals outside the regions where they originated.

Other early immigrants to the tropical forest came from rural areas in the different countries and moved to the region to participate in its extractive economy. They brought with them rural musical traditions and annual celebrations. They played a variety of national styles on guitar, *cuatro*, viola, violin, and other stringed instruments, which they often made themselves. Aside from the music performed in churches, they made music at dance parties, in bars, at birthday parties, and during certain calendrical rituals such as saints' days and Christmas. In some communities, residents formed troupes to perform dance-dramas found in their own country and other Latin American countries, and larger settlements often had brass bands and some instruction in music. In some cases, rural forms survive in the tropical-forest settlements but have disappeared in the places from which they came.

Some itinerant poets and musicians probably made their living from their performances, but many more people now play part-time for their own communities. All music was live, face to face, and, of course, without amplification. The small settlements of Europeans and their descendants often developed distinct regional cultures, incorporating Amerindian material culture and in some cases a basic vocabulary. These communities usually remained economically and culturally tied to the commercial centers of each country, however, if only through an occasional boat that would exchange supplies for natural products. They remained linked to the national culture of which they were a regional part.

IMMIGRATION AFTER THE 1930S

Immigration increased in the twentieth century, and technological changes such as outboard motors, electric generators, recorded sound, radio, and extensive networks of roads in some areas have transformed the economy and the cultures of the entire tropical-forest region. There is now not a single part that lies beyond the reach of a radio transmitter; and, with battery-operated portable radios, phonographs, and tape players, even the residents of the smallest settlements can play the latest music.

Pouring into the region on newly constructed roads or flying into newly enlarged airports, immigrants are rapidly altering the face of the tropical forest, physically and culturally. Quechua- and Aymara-speakers from the highlands have opened new communities in the lowlands; large numbers of gauchos from the southern states of Brazil have moved into Mato Grosso, Rondonia, and Acre; Protestant missionaries are making inroads among Roman Catholic worshipers; regional cities have swelled and created industries, established large governmental bureaucracies, and founded universities that bring wealthier and

cuatro
'Four,' four-stringed small guitar from Venezuela and diffused to regions close to Venezuela

viola
Brazilian plucked and strummed chordophone (from viola de mão, 'of the hand') with five double courses of ten or twelve metal strings

gaucho
In Argentina, Uruguay, and southern Brazil, a rural dweller or cowboy of the pampa

more highly educated people to the region. Each of these groups brings new music to the tropical forest and introduces some new traditions to it.

If you were to hover over the tropical-forest region today, in the haze of the smoke of burning clearings, and listen to the sound of the music, the cacophony would be even greater than before. From tens of thousands of terrible loudspeakers distorting the music from hundreds of sources, you could hear country and rock, industrial products of the world at large; from bars and nightclubs in towns and cities of all sizes, you would hear forms of regional rock, and professional musicians playing styles specific to their region; from Amerindian villages, a thousand tape recorders would be playing national music and even music from other places in the world. The predawn crescendo will have diminished, to be replaced by an evening one as leisure is fitted and fixed into set working hours. The oratorical styles are now often those of sports announcers and politicians, the national anthems of various countries sound out from thousands of rural schools, and religions have made certain days and hours specific to hymns and other religious genres.

If you could see through the smoke, you would see the separation of music and dance, a general secularization of performances, and a continued fascination with bodily ornamentation and swishing adornments, often now in the form of earrings, wristwatches, makeup, and cologne on the one hand, and machine-made clothing on the other.

The centers of the music industry are not to be found in the tropical-forest region, but a great deal of their product sells there. Whether by radio, by prerecorded cassettes, by magazine articles and photographs, or by television, the sounds and images of urban centers bombard the region. Exporting raw materials and importing finished products, the more remote parts of the region have more than a little colonial flavor. Ownership and patronage also come from the urban centers, and many professional musicians in the region eventually leave to pursue their careers elsewhere.

Probably the largest components of the music industry throughout the tropical forest are the country traditions (in Brazil, *música sertaneja*; in Peru, *huayno*; and in Venezuela, *salsa*), which have developed with the spread of recording and playback technology.

Most countries in the tropical-forest region have developed national country or rural-popular genres. Like U.S. country music, most of this music is instrumental dance music or verse-form singing in close parallel harmony by soloists, duets, trios, or quartets accompanying themselves primarily on stringed instruments. It draws heavily from folk music and has had a tremendous influence on it. Widespread and popular but little appreciated by urban sophisticates, this music (and the musical roots from which it draws) is a central part of the repertoire of many immigrants to the tropical forest. Because it does not appeal to middle-class urban sophisticates, we have few good studies of it.

The tropical-forest region continues to preserve some distinctiveness, for it is usually distant from the national capitals and the largest centers of population. The rhythms and songs of Carnaval (Carnival), which dominate the popular music of the coastal cities of Brazil from November to February, are hardly heard in Acre. Hip-hop was not the craze in Roraima that it became in Rio de Janeiro. This pattern probably matches that of other national musical forms elsewhere in the region.

huayno
(also *wayno*) Nataive American–derived (Quechua) Peruvian and other central Andean fast duple-metered song and dance form featuring a long-short-short rhythmical pattern

With increased communication and increased research, the music of the tropical forest has become an object of study in itself. In virtually every national capital, specialists are working to document and preserve tropical-forest musical traditions. They publish the books and recordings that are the best source most of us have for this kind of music. In each country too, bureaucrats are engaged in trying to turn the traditions into possible tourist attractions. In many small cities, the mayor's office works with the local board of tourism and local groups to ensure the continued distinctiveness of their part of the region. Ecotourism, adventure tourism, and the constant search for the exotic have brought new types of visitors to certain areas.

CULTURAL INTERACTIONS

In the intense interaction that typifies the cultures and communities of much of the tropical-forest region, music plays an important part in forging and demonstrating community or ethnic identity and sociopolitical positions. The transnational entertainment industry and the more commercial regional traditions have heavily influenced local populations through recordings, radio, and television. The processes are complex and ongoing. We do not know where they will lead.

For centuries, Amerindians have learned each other's songs, including hymns and other immigrant musical forms. This process continues. Some Upper Xingu Amerindians are great fans of Brazilian rock; elsewhere, country is the rage. Some Amerindian communities have consciously tried to reach accommodations with regional culture. For a while, some Eastern Timbira groups in Brazil were alternating their traditional ceremonies with dances in which regional musicians performed and couples danced together. How enduring such accommodations will be depends on whether new generations of "traditional" singers will emerge.

Amerindian music has become part of the creation and expression of an ethnic identity. Some groups are reviving older forms. To demonstrate authentic Amerindian-ness, by which to assert communal rights to land, health care, and other benefits denied to non-Amerindians, some peoples—whose oral tradition was so interrupted that there is nothing left to revive—are re-indigenizing themselves by learning traditions from other native groups. Music has become part of a complex set of interethnic relations, in which not only Amerindians but also ethnomusicologists and other researchers are often actual participants.

Amerindian music may be important in forging a certain kind of national identity, and indigenous music from the tropical forest is of sufficient interest to the larger national society to support the production of documentary recordings on small independent labels. In an effort to affirm a distinct national identity, nationalist composers in several countries in the Americas have composed operas and other pieces that tried to combine European and Amerindian musical traditions. In Nozanina, for example, the Brazilian composer Heitor Villa-Lobos (1887–1959), with a Brazilian anthropologist, created a piece that combines European compositional styles with a text that is probably in Tupinambá. A similar association of musical forms and ethnic identity is important in certain Afro-Latin American communities, in which fairly isolated cultural forms of the Maroon and other largely black communities of the interior are becoming a source of pride and identity.

Concerns with the future of the tropical forest and the appetite of the transnational popular music industry for novelty have led to manifold results, but not to a great deal of tropical-forest influence on popular music. Some promoters of tropical-forest Amerindian music support the music to defend the tropical-forest ecosystem; others promote the music to broaden their fans' listening habits. Many Amerindian communities are recording their traditions to defend their livelihood and culture. Some tropical-forest Amerindians, active in the defense of their ecosystems, fight against thoughtless industrialization. Through intensive political efforts, they make trips to the United States and to Geneva to talk with international organizations about how to invest in the regions in which they live. The Kayapo leader Rauni toured with Sting in the 1980s, speaking out against the environmental destruction being inflicted on the region.

By the early twenty-first century, however, this activity had not led to a popular musical fusion the way the encounter with South African popular music, Afro-Brazilian music, or Andean music had led to dramatic new styles of popular music in the Americas. Few nonindigenous musicians dealt with the sounds of Brazilian Amerindian music in any serious musical way. When they used native sounds, they tended to opt for direct quotation, rather than for paraphrase or fusion.

Brazilian popular musicians have taken melodies from the tropical forest: in Brazil, Caetano Veloso uses a Juruna flute melody on one recording, and Milton Nascimento includes segments of Brazilian Amerindian songs in his recording *Txai!* (1990). Often laboring under a romantic vision of the noble primitive, many artists have gone to the tropical forest in search of something pure and missing in their own music. Sometimes their encounters have been completely perplexing; sometimes they have been enlightening for both parties; sometimes they have been more useful for one than the other.

CONCLUSION

Why have so few attempts been made to adapt the indigenous music of the tropical forest with other regional musical traditions? I think it is a combination of social and musical features. Most Amerindian music is associated with ritual; it has little harmony or polyphony, and what polyphony it has is unfamiliar to unaccustomed ears. Drums and strings are not common in native tropical forest traditions but are absolutely central to popular music. The long, apparently repetitive performances are foreign to the popular music genre, in which three minutes, rather than all night, is the norm for recorded sound.

In many of these respects, native tropical-forest music differs from most African traditions and the Afro-Latino traditions of the Americas. The indigenous South American form that has had international success is Andean popular music, whose several types are themselves the result of musical fusion in their home countries. Perhaps tropical-forest fusion will someday develop; perhaps it will not. One of the most enlightened and enlightening musical styles of native and pop fusion in the late 1990s, however, is the music of Marlui Miranda (1996), a Brazilian Amerindian.

The reasons for adopting or not adopting a certain musical form are only partly related to the sounds of the music. That is why the development of musical styles can be interesting. It is only slightly predictable. The past is obscured by a lack of archaeological record, the devastation of Amerindian populations before the arrival of the first researchers, and the rapid destruction of communities by the advancing frontier, highly capitalized investment, and large-scale immigration. The present is obscured by its evanescence, and the future has yet to emerge.

The tropical-forest region of South America is huge. Its music is little researched and documented. Yet to the people who live there, music is often an indispensable part of life. Through it, they try to accomplish many different things. As with much music throughout the world, we hear and know about only a small fraction of what is performed there.

REFERENCES

Aretz, Isabel. 1984. *Síntesis de la Etnomúsica en América Latina*. Biblioteca INIDEF, 6. Caracas: Monte Avila Editores.
———. 1991. *Música de Los Aborígenes de Venezuela*. Caracas: Fundación de Etnomusicología y Folklore.
Aytai, Desiderio. 1985. *O Mundo Sonoro Xavante*. Coleção Museu Paulista, Ethnologia, 5. São Paulo: Universidade de São Paulo.
Basso, Ellen B. 1985. A *Musical View of the Universe*. Philadelphia: University of Pennsylvania Press.
Bastos, Rafael Jose de Menezes. 1978. *A Musicológica Kamayurá. Brasilia*: Fundação Nacional do Indio.
———. 1986. "Música, Cultura e Sociedade no Alto-Xingu: A Teoria Musical dos Indios Kamayurá." *Latin American Music Review* 7:51–80.
Becerra Casanovas, Rogers. 1990. *Reliquias de Moxos*. La Paz, Bolivia: Empresa Editora "Proinsa."
Biocca, Ettore. 1966. *Viaggi tra gli indi: Alto Rio Negro-Alto Orinoco: Appunti de un Biologo*. 4 vols. Rome: Consiglio Nazionale delle Ricerche.
Butt Colson, Audrey. 1971. "Hallelujah among the Patamona Indians." *Antropológica* 28:25–58.
Cameu, Helza. 1977. *Introdução ao Estudo da Música Indígena Brasileira*. Rio de Janeiro: Conselho Federal de Cultura.
Claro, Samuel. 1969. "La Música en las Misiones Jesuitas de Moxos." *Revista Musical Chilena* 22(108):7–31.
Coppens, Walter. 1975. Music of the Venezuelan Yekuana Indians. Folkways Records 4104. LP disk.
Crawford, Neelon. 1976. *Soul Vine Shaman*. Notes by Norman Whitten. Sacha Runa Research Foundation Occasional Paper 5. LP disk.
Dobkin de Rios, Marlene, and Fred Katz. 1975. "Some Relationships between Music and Hallucinogenic Ritual: The Jungle-Gym of Consciousness." *Ethos* 3:64–76.
Fuks, Victor. 1989. "Demonstration of Multiple Relationships between Music and Culture of the Waiãpi Indians of Brazil." Ph.D. dissertation, Indiana University.
Graham, Laura. 1986. "Three Modes of Shavante Vocal Expression: Wailing, Collective Singing, and Political Oratory." In *Native South American Discourse*, eds. Greg Urban and Joel Sherzer, 82–118. Berlin: Mouton de Gruyter.
———. 1990. "The Always Living: Discourse and the Male Lifecycle of the Xavante Indians of Central Brazil." Ph.D. dissertation, University of Texas at Austin.
Greenberg, Joseph H. 1987. *Language in the Americas*. Stanford: Stanford University Press.
Gregor, Thomas, ed. 1973. *Mehinaku*. 16-mm film.
———. 1977. *Mehinaku: The Drama of Everyday Life in a Brazilian Indian Village*. Chicago: University of Chicago Press.
———. 1985. *Anxious Pleasures: The Sexual Lives of an Amazonian People*. Chicago: University of Chicago Press.

Guss, David M. 1989. *To Weave and Sing: Art, Symbol, and Narrative in the South American Rain Forest.* Berkeley: University of California Press.

Harner, Michael J. 1972. *Jívaro: People of the Sacred Waterfalls.* New York: Doubleday.

———. 1973. *Music of the Jívaro of Ecuador.* Folkways Records FE 4386. LP disk.

Hill, Jonathan D. 1993. *Keepers of the Sacred Chants—The Poetics of Ritual Power in an Amazonian Society.* Tucson: University of Arizona Press.

Izikowitz, Karl G. 1970 [1935]. *Musical and Other Sound Instruments of the South American Indians.* East Ardsley, Wakefield, Yorkshire: S. R. Publishers.

Keller-Leuzinger, Franz. 1874. *The Amazon and Madeira Rivers: Sketches and Descriptions from the Note-Book of an Explorer.* London: Chapman and Hall.

Kensinger, Kenneth M. 1973. "Banisteriopsis Usage among the Peruvian Cashinahua." In *Hallucinogens and Shamanism,* ed. Michael J. Harner, 9–14. Oxford: Oxford University Press.

Kuss, Malena, ed. 2004. *Music in Latin America and the Caribbean, An Encyclopedic History, Vol. 1, Performing Beliefs: Indigenous Peoples of South America, Central America, and Mexico.* Austin: University Press of Texas.

Menezes Bastos, Rafael José de. 1978. *A Musicológica Kamayura: Para Uma Antropologia da Comunicação No Alto Xingu.* Brasília: FUNAI.

Miranda, Marlui. 1995. *Ihu, Todos os Sons. Manaus,* Brazil: Pau Brasil PB 001. Compact disc.

Nascimento, Milton. 1990. *Txai! Brazil*: Discos C.B.S. 177.228 / 1–464138. LP disk.

Nimuendaju, Curt. 1980. *Mapa Etno-Histórico de Curt Nimuendaju.* Rio de Janeiro: Fundação Instituto Brasileiro de Geografia e Estatística and Fundação Nacional Pró-Memória.

Okada, Yuki. 1995. *Central and South America. The JVC / Smithsonian Folkways Video Anthology of Music and Dance of the Americas,* 6. Multicultural Media VTMV 230. Video.

Olsen, Dale. 1976. "Música vesperal Mojo en San Miguel de Isiboro, Bolivia." *Revista Musical Chilena* 30(133):28–46.

———. 1980. "Symbol and Function in South American Indian Music." In *Musics of Many Cultures: An Introduction,* ed. Elizabeth May, 363–385. Berkeley: University of California Press.

———. 1996. *Music of the Warao of Venezuela: Song People of the Rain Forest.* Gainesville: University Press of Florida.

———. 2001. *Music of El Dorado: The Ethnomusicology of Ancient Andean Cultures.* Gainesville: University Press of Florida (paperback edition, 2004).

Seeger, Anthony. 1981. *Nature and Society in Central Brazil: The Suyá Indians of Mato Grosso.* Cambridge, Mass.: Harvard University Press.

———, ed. 1982. *Musica Indigena: A Arte Vocal dos Suyá.* São João del Rei: Tacape 007 1982. LP disk.

———. 1987. *Why Suyá Sing: A Musical Anthropology of an Amazonian People.* Cambridge: Cambridge University Press.

———. 1991. "When Music Makes History." In *Ethnomusicology and Modern Music History,* eds. Stephen Blum, Philip V. Bohlman, and Daniel M. Neuman, 23–35. Urbana and Chicago: University of Illinois Press.

Sherzer, Joel, and Greg Urban, ed. 1986. *Native South American Discourse.* Berlin: Mouton de Gruyter.

Wagley, Charles, and Eduardo Galvão. 1949. *The Tenetehara Indians of Brazil.* New York: Columbia University Press.

Venezuela

Max H. Brandt

When Spanish explorers encountered the bay of Maracaibo, on South America's north coast, it reminded them of Venice; therefore, they called the land Venezuela "little Venice." Today, the country of Venezuela has a land area of 912,050 square kilometers (more than twice the size of California) and 2,800 kilometers of Caribbean coastline. Its five major cities are Caracas (the capital, founded in 1567), Maracaibo, Valencia, Maracay, and Barquisimeto. From the early colonial period through the first decades of the twentieth century, most of Venezuela's inhabitants lived in rural communities, but today, more than 90 percent of its population resides in urban centers.

Traditional Venezuelan music derives from the cultures that have influenced most Latin American and Caribbean countries: the indigenous, the European, and the African. Venezuela still manifests pockets of unacculturated indigenous music, but most of its traditional music is an assortment of genres and styles stemming from Spain and Africa. Two pioneering twentieth-century ethnomusicologists of Venezuela, Luís Felipe Ramón y Rivera and Isabel Aretz de Ramón y Rivera, have classified traditional Venezuelan music into three categories: indigenous, folk, and popular music—a classification often criticized for being too rigid and simplistic. In it, the indigenous category pertains to essentially unacculturated Amerindian music, and folk music encompasses the music of Spain and

Africa—music that has been transformed in Venezuela and is not attributable to specific authors. According to Aretz and Ramón y Rivera, popular music is music composed by known authors using traditional forms—primarily European. Aretz and Ramón y Rivera recognize art music (academic music) and latter-day popular forms such as *salsa*, but do not view them as "traditional" music.

Though the present overview follows the three categories of traditional music presented above, a more comprehensive study of traditional Venezuelan music might utilize classifications proposed by Rafael Salazar (1992a) or other Venezuelan musicologists. The question of what is indigenous, folk, or popular is widely debated in Latin America today. The term *traditional popular*, for example, is sometimes used in place of *folk*.

THE INDIGENOUS HERITAGE

The Amerindian societies encountered by Europeans during the early 1500s in the area known today as Venezuela were neither as numerous nor as complex in social organization as those found in other territories in South America. Spanish chroniclers documented Venezuelan indigenous music from the 1500s through the 1700s (Quintana 1995). While many of these societies no longer exist, about thirty indigenous languages do survive, spoken by some two hundred thousand people.

Supernatural and symbolic phenomena are associated with most Venezuelan Amerindian instruments. Some groups give human and/or spiritual significance to their musical instruments. Symbolism, as when the handle and the container (usually calabash or gourd) of a rattle represent male and female spheres of influence, respectively, is common, as among the Yekuaná. [Listen to "Yekuaná male shaman's curing song"] Some groups that have few musical instruments rely solely on vocal music, such as the Yanomamö. [Listen to "Yanomamö male shaman's curing song"]

DISC 1 TRACK 2

DISC 1 TRACK 1

The forms of vocal music—solo songs and collective songs, men's songs and women's songs, songs dealing with the supernatural world and songs dealing with mundane activities (such as working and walking in the forest)—vary widely from one indigenous group to another. Musical texts commonly deal with nature and the supernatural world, and songs are sometimes sung by shamans in secret or in bygone languages or even mentally, without sounds [see WARAO].

Musical structure among indigenous Venezuelans is much like that of other aboriginal groups of the Americas. Indigenous groups of Venezuela share no comprehensive system of tonal organization, and the number of tones used in performances varies greatly among individuals and ethnic groups. One song might be sung on a single tone, whereas other songs use five or more (Olsen 1980b:365). Multipart singing may be heterophonic or canonic, as in singing rounds. Rhythmic practices also vary. Free rhythm is common in solo singing, whereas collective singing is often clearly metered, especially when it accompanies dancing.

Among the indigenous peoples of Venezuela, shamans are the key individuals and usually the most important makers of music. Responsible for the mental and physical health of their people and for singing the myths and legends that tell the people's history, they are the vital link between society and the supernatural world. They combine spiritual leadership, divination, healing, and historical narration, and they use their voices (and often rattles) as the paramount implements in conducting their official duties.

Some indigenous groups have several kinds of shaman, each with a unique musical repertoire. The Piaroa (Wothuha) of the Amazon region have two: the *dzuwèwè ruwa*, who fights to protect his people from hostile and evil spirits, and the *mèñeruwa*, the master of the *mèñe*, sacred songs that men perform at nighttime rituals in communal houses (Agerkop 1983:13). *Mèñe* have four functions: combating the fatal illnesses caused by consuming the meat of certain animals; insuring the well-being of agricultural crops and pregnant women; curing acute afflictions, such as snakebites or wounds caused by wild animals; and accompanying the blowing of incense when someone dies or at the beginning of a special ceremony called *warime*.

Musical acculturation among native Venezuelans began in the 1500s with the coming of Europeans and Africans, and especially Christian missionaries. The adoption of Christian music often led to a repudiation of traditional music, which missionaries felt was too closely integrated with indigenous beliefs. Increasing contact with Venezuelan creole culture led indigenous people into new musical realms, affecting their music. Some indigenous groups have been in contact with nonindigenous cultures for decades, but still maintain most of the traditional music they had on first contact. Venezuelan indigenous music was some of the earliest to be recorded by modern technology (around 1900), so to study musical continuity and change, ethnomusicologists can compare early recordings with present-day performances.

THE EUROPEAN HERITAGE

In 1498, when European explorers arrived on Columbus's third voyage to the New World, about fifty thousand native Americans were thought to be living along the central Caribbean coast of Venezuela, an area no longer populated by indigenous peoples. Indigenous music survives primarily in the Amazon region, the Orinoco Delta, and the Guajira Peninsula. European and African influences predominate along the coast of north-central Venezuela, the most densely populated part of the country. Perhaps more than two-thirds of the Spanish who arrived during the first century of colonization came from Andalucía, in southern Spain. With colonization came Moorish influences; thus, when the term *European* is employed here, it is used in its broadest sense, including influences from Arabic, Islamic, and West Asian sources that were part of Andalucía during the colonizing of the Americas.

In the Venezuelan Andes, Spanish influences predominate. Spanish-derived vocal forms and musical instruments, in fact, form a plurality of Venezuela's existing folk music, and Isabel Aretz (personal communication) has identified twelve families of song (*cancioneros*) in Venezuela's folk music, eleven of which she calls Spanish in origin; the remaining one is Afro-Venezuelan. Likewise, though in any survey of musical instruments indigenous-inspired rattles and African-derived drums abound, the stringed instruments of Spanish origin are the most notable. The national instrument of Venezuela, a four-stringed lute (*cuatro*) closely resembling the ukulele, and Venezuela's next most prominent musical instrument, a harp (*arpa*), derive from Spain.

THE AFRICAN HERITAGE

A Caribbean-island character is apparent in much of Venezuela's music, linking this country musically to places such as Cuba, Curaçao, the Dominican Republic, Haiti, Puerto Rico, and Trinidad and Tobago. Much of this influence is African, and the influence of Africa on Venezuela as a whole is much greater than is often perceived. Venezuelans often emphasize their European and indigenous cultural roots, but the African impact on local culture, and music in particular, is undeniable. From the earliest colonial times, Africans were taken to Venezuela directly from the African continent, but the greatest number of Africans and their immediate descendants came indirectly to Venezuela—from Spain, Colombia, and Caribbean islands. These people represented cultures from widely dispersed areas of Africa. In particular, vestiges of West Africa and Central Africa survive in Venezuela today, although Central African influences appear to be more prevalent (García 1990).

No social groups or religious organizations in Venezuela can be traced directly to a specific African ethnic group (Pollak-Eltz 1972, 1994). In Venezuela, the importation of slaves from Africa ended early in the 1800s, while it continued in other countries of the Americas. By 1930, Afro-Venezuelans knew little about the African origin of their principal musical instruments and forms. Not until the research of Juan Pablo Sojo (1976 [1943]), Juan Liscano (1943), Luís Felipe Ramón y Rivera (1950), and others did interest in the African heritage of Venezuela arise.

THE EMERGENCE OF VENEZUELAN MUSIC

Though elite and urbane individuals—from native American shamans and African princes to Spanish priests—have influenced traditional music in Venezuela, the main subjects in this development have been peasants. European and African traits predominate in most folk-musical forms; indigenous phenomena are less apparent. Some Venezuelan folk music blends European and African music, but most of it is European- or African-based. Some songs are obviously European in form. Others feature the leader-response form of African music. Certain ensembles feature Iberian strings, but others feature African-style drums. Occasionally we find a juxtaposition of both, with European-derived lutes and African-derived drums in the same ensemble. Distinctions are sometimes obvious, sometimes subtle. Most of this folk music is associated with the many fiestas that take place in Venezuela throughout the year (Hernández 1993).

The music of Venezuelan peasants of mixed ancestry is often called *música criolla* ("creole music"). Ramón y Rivera (1969) uses the term *folk* in classifying and describing this music, but he and other Venezuelans often use the term *criolla* when discussing the music created in Venezuela since the arrival of the Europeans and Africans. In parts of Latin America and the Caribbean this term is used to identify those of purely European ancestry; in Venezuela, it usually refers to the cultural trinity of indigenous America, Europe, and Africa. Likewise, creole often designates the traditional music of Venezuela. Even music sometimes called Afro-Venezuelan music (Ramón y Rivera 1971) is occasionally designated as creole music by those who perform it.

As in other parts of the Americas, European musical influences are the easiest to trace through written sources. We have not only published accounts of music and musical instruments in Europe during colonial days (elements that may or may not have reached Venezuela), but also explorers', officials', and clerics' inventories of instruments and vocal music brought from Spain. Europeans reported extensively on indigenous music and instruments but hardly mentioned early musical imports from Africa. For those imports, we must rely more on comparisons of existing phenomena with recent ethnomusicological research in Africa.

MUSICAL INSTRUMENTS

The roots of creole music in Venezuela can be traced in part through the study of musical instruments. Two important organological contributions to creole music from indigenous sources are rattles and wind instruments. The major instruments from Spain are stringed instruments, and Afro-Venezuelans are locally known for their knowledge of drums and drumming.

Idiophones

Container rattles (*maracas*), usually in pairs, accompany just about every genre of creole music. Indigenous Venezuelans commonly use a single rattle to accompany singing, but creole ensembles commonly employ a pair. (An exception is the use of a single rattle in some Afro-Venezuelan ensembles of the central coast.) Paired *maracas* are not usually equal in size or sound. One, usually larger, with more seeds, emits a deep, raspy sound; the other, with fewer seeds, emits a clearer and brighter sound. Often, a gender designation is assigned to each: the lower-sounding instrument is male, the higher-pitched is female.

laures
Venezuelan sticks (also palos) beaten on the side of the wooden-bodied mina drum

The most prominent idiophones of African derivation are the sides of wooden-bodied drums, struck with sticks commonly called *palos* and sometimes *laures* (Figure 22.1). They embellish the rhythms of drums, and children often play them while listening to rhythms of drums.

Another African-derived instrument, from the area of

Figure 22.1
During the festival of Saint John the Baptist in Curiepe, Miranda (Barlovento area), Venezuela, two men beat sticks (*laures*) on the side of a *mina* drum. Photo by Dale A. Olsen, 1974.

Barlovento (east of Caracas), is an ensemble of stamped bamboo tubes called *quitiplás* (Figure 22.2), an onomatopoeic word representing the rhythm of the two smallest tubes. The player holds one tube in each hand, striking one to the ground followed by the other, and then striking both against each other, producing the last syllable of the word (*plás*), in a cyclic or continuous rhythm. Two or three other players each hold a larger tube, which they strike on the ground with one hand while using the other hand to cup the top of the tube for special effects. *Quitiplás* sometimes accompany songs and dances of the *redondo* ensemble, using the same basic rhythms performed on these membranophones. Children often play *quitiplás* as a way of learning the rhythms of the drums.

Also of African derivation is the *marímbola* [see DOMINICAN REPUBLIC: Figure 11.4 and Figure 11.6], a wooden box with metal strips or tongues that is plucked by the musician as he sits on the instrument. The *marímbola* is played in various parts of Venezuela and in certain neighboring Caribbean countries. Other African- and European-based idiophones commonly played in Venezuelan folk music are metal triangles, concussion sticks, bells, jaw's harps (*trompa* or *birimbao*), and ridged instruments scraped with a stick (most commonly called *charrascas*). Steel drums are played in some urban centers and in the town of Callao in Bolívar State, where people from Caribbean islands have been relocating for decades.

Membranophones

Though indigenous peoples of Venezuela used numerous kinds of drums, most drums used today are of European and African origin. From Europe came at least two double-headed drums, the bass drum (*bombo*) and the side drum (*redoblante*). The drum found most widely in the country, the *tambora*, may have been inspired by both traditions.

Africa is responsible for the greatest variety of drums. Barlovento ("Windward"), on the central coast in Miranda State, is famous for its Afro-Venezuelan drumming. It has produced three distinct sets of membranophones: *minas*, *redondos*, and *tamboras*. Its stamped bamboo tubes, musically related to *redondos* and sometimes called drums themselves, are part of its heritage. Though multiple sets of drums commonly occur among ethnic groups in Africa (as among the Yoruba of Nigeria, who have different families of drums), they rarely do in communities of the African diaspora in the Americas. Barlovento is an exception. Unlike in Africa, though, where a variety of composite rhythms or instrumental pieces can be played within the context of one family of drums, the drum sets of Barlovento each feature only one composite rhythm. The only exception to this rule is the

mina
Venezuelan set of two single-headed drums; also the longer drum of the mina pair
redondo
Venezuelan double-headed drum with an internal hourglass shape
tambora
A long, tubular Afro-Venezuelan membranophone made from a log with two skin heads and played with one stick while held between the knees

malembe rhythm and song form, performed for processions rather than dancing, primarily by *redondo* ensembles, but also sometimes by *mina* ensembles.

Long, heavy log drums with a skin at one end—*burro, cumaco, mina, tambor grande*—are common in Venezuela. In performance, each is most often placed on the ground. The main drummer straddles the end near the skin, and one or more other musicians beat the side of the drum with *palos* or *laures*.

The Barlovento variant of this drum, the *mina*, is not placed on the ground. When played, it rests on crossed poles (see Figure 22.1). The ensemble consists of two drums, one long (*mina*) and one short (*curbata*), made from the same log, always of strong, heavy wood such as that of the avocado tree. The largest piece, about 2 meters long, becomes the *mina* (*tambor grande*); it is propped up on two long poles tied together in an X, with the upper V of the X being much smaller than the lower. The *curbata*, less than half the length of the *mina*, stands upright on three or four V-shaped legs, cut at its bottom and open end. Each drummer uses two sticks, one in each hand, while one or more (usually two to four) musicians play rhythms on the lower end of the *mina* with sticks (*laures*), one in each hand (Olsen 1980a:403–407). [Listen to "Festival de San Juan"] The ensemble usually includes one *maraca* or a pair of them. DISC ❶ TRACK 27

Two other drum types of the central coast, *redondos* and *tamboras*, have skins at both ends. The most common are *tamboras*, the main instruments that accompany all-night observances for honoring a saint or the Holy Cross. In Barlovento, *tamboras* can be played alone, or in ensembles of up to four or five instruments, by performers who hold the drums between their knees while sitting. The physical traits of the *tamboras* and the rhythms played on them recall those of the *redondo* ensemble. The *tambora*, like the *redondo* drum, is played with one stick, which sometimes (depending upon the particular drum) strikes the side of the drum and the skin.

Redondos, found in a smaller area south and east of Caracas, are longer than *tamboras*, and are held between standing drummers' legs (Figure 22.3). The three drums of the set are made from the same trunk of a balsa tree (called *lano* in Barlovento), whose wood is soft and lightweight. Each drum, varying slightly in size, is hollowed to resemble an hourglass inside and is covered at each end with skins connected to each other with thin rope lac-

ings forming W-shaped patterns. The drummer strikes the drum with a stick held in one hand and the fingers of the other hand. These drums have various individual names and are most commonly called *tamborcitos, tambores redondos*, or *culo 'e puya*. The only other musical instruments accompanying this ensemble are *maracas*.

Figure 22.3
During the festival of Saint John the Baptist in El Tigre, Miranda, Venezuela, three men play drums (*redondos*) with one stick and one hand, as a woman shakes maracas. Photo by Max H. Brandt, 1973.

Neither the *mina* nor the *redondo* tradition seems to have a direct link to a specific community in Africa, although construction techniques suggest that the *mina* has a West African origin and the *redondo* has a Central African origin. The construction of the *mina*, for example, with its skin held in place by ropes tied to pegs that protrude into the body of the drum, recalls construction techniques in West Africa. Likewise, the *redondo* has laced drumheads and recalls drums in central Africa, specifically the Republic of Congo (Brazzaville), according to research made by the Venezuelan scholar Jesús García (1990), a native of Barlovento. Moreover, similarities exist between *redondos* and instruments in the Museum of the Belgian Congo in Tervuren, Belgium (Liscano 1960).

Scholars have not found any drumming traditions in Africa that exactly match those of either ensemble; however, generic links are traceable to parts of Africa. Furthermore, there may be some connection between the term *mina* and the name of Almina, an important port in Ghana from which many slaves embarked for the Americas. In the film *Salto al Atlántico* (Esparragoza 1991), García presents evidence linking Venezuela and Africa.

Scholarly focus has been on Barlovento, but three neighboring areas, also called Barlovento by some people, have similarly Afro-Venezuelan genres and instruments. The Litoral (shore) and the Guarenas-Guatire Valley lie between Caracas and Barlovento proper, separated from each other by a chain of mountains running along the coast. The upper Tuy Valley is the third area, just south of the Guarenas-Guatire Valley and southwest of Barlovento proper, including the towns of Cúa, Ocumare del Tuy, Santa Lucía, and Santa Teresa.

The drumming traditions of the Litoral are closely related to those from Barlovento proper. The *cumaco*, also commonly called *tambor grande*, closely resembles the large *mina* but has a drumhead nailed to one end rather than being fastened by pegs and wedges. Unlike the *mina* (propped up on two poles), the *cumaco* is placed on the ground while the drummer sits on it, playing it with bare hands and sometimes controlling the sound with the heel of one foot. One, two, or three *cumacos* can be played at the same time. Other musicians play sticks on the trunk of the drum. Other names for *cumaco*-like drums in this area are *burro negro*, *campanita*, *mayor*, *piano*, *pujo*, *macizo*, *primero*, and *segundo*. Some communities also have a *curbata*, an instrument much like that of Barlovento with the same name. The town of Naiguata, in addition to having *cumacos*, has drums made of barrels called *pipas*. *Tamboras* or *tamboritas*, much like those of Barlovento, accompany *fulias* at *velorios*. There are no *redondo*-type drums in this area, but *redondo*-type rhythms are played on *cumacos* to accompany songs and dances, much as in the *redondo* tradition of Barlovento.

In the Tuy Valley, southwest of Barlovento, however, *redondos* rule. They are somewhat shorter than the *redondos* of Barlovento, and their rhythms and combinations are somewhat different from those of Barlovento.

In the Guarenas-Guatire Valley, two *tambora*-like drums (*prima*, *cruzao*) and a military-style side drum (*grande*) (Ramón y Rivera 1969:92) accompany *redondo*-like songs and dances during the festivals of the Nativity of Saint John the Baptist (24 June). The best-known fiesta of this area is the Parranda de San Pedro (Saint Peter's Procession), which takes place in the town of Guatire on 29 June. The procession and dancing of this fiesta are accompanied by *cuatros*, *maracas*, foot stamping, and singing. The characters in this reenactment of early colonial days, all of whom are men with faces blackened to represent their African ancestors, are María Ignacia (a man dressed as a woman), one who carries and dances with an image of Saint Peter, a flag bearer, two boys who dance next to María Ignacia, and two dancers with squares of thick, hard leather attached to their sandals, enhancing the sound of their stamping. Other men (often three) play *cuatros* and *maracas*. María Ignacia represents a legendary colonial woman who had promised to dance in honor of Saint Peter every year if the saint would help with a cure for her ill daughter. The daughter survived, but María Ignacia died soon after, so her husband, dressed in María Ignacia's clothes, danced every year in his wife's place. Today, the man portraying María Ignacia carries a black doll, representing the cured daughter.

Around Lake Maracaibo, San Benito (Saint Benedict the Moor, of San Fratello and Palermo) is honored during the Christmas and New Year's season by drumming on *chimbangueles*. The music is primarily Afro-Venezuelan. Documents about *chimbangueles* describe sets of four to seven drums. The communities of Bobures, Gibraltar, and El Batey, at the southern end of Lake Maracaibo, use seven drums, four designated male and three designated female (B. Salazar 1990). The male drums are *el tambor mayor*, *el respuesta*, *el cantante*, and *el segundo*; the female drums are *la primera requinta*, *la segunda requinta*, and *la media requinta*. The drums are conical. At the large end is a skin, held in place by cords attached to a hoop or a loop, also often made of cord, placed near the bottom or narrow end of the drum. This hoop or loop is held in place by wooden wedges placed between the hoop and the body of the drum. Supported by a strap over the drummer's shoulder, *chimbangueles* are played with a stick in one hand. The rhythms played on them have specific names, including *el chocho* ("the doting"), *el ajé* ("the accompaniment"), *el chimbanguelero vaya* ("the chimbanguele drummer goes"), *el misericordia* ("the mercy"), cantica y San Gorongomez ("invocation"), and *saludo a los capitanes* ("salute to the captains").

A single-headed friction drum known as *furruco* (*furro*) is used in *aguinaldo* ensembles (Figure 22.7) during the Christmas season. It is similar to the Spanish *zambomba* and African friction drums, whose sounds are produced by rubbing a stick attached to the skin. It is also related to friction drums from Brazil (*cuica*) and Mexico (Costa Chica region).

Chordophones

The most important Spanish contribution to the instrumental music of Venezuela was the introduction of stringed instruments. Today, the four-stringed *cuatro*, found everywhere in Venezuela, even among indigenous groups, is considered the national instrument (Figure 22.4). The diatonic or creole harp (*arpa*), though found in only two areas of Venezuela, is also recognized as an important symbol of Venezuelan music (Figure 22.4), as attested to by miniature models in the gift shops of Caracas and other tourist-frequented communities.

In large cities, the *cuatro* is played as much as, or more than, in the countryside. It is often called a guitar (*guitarra*), since it is the most commonly used instrument of the guitar family in Venezuela. It is also known by diminutives—*guitarra pequeña*, *guitarrita*, *guitarilla*, *guitarillo*—and by other names, such as *discante*. Primarily an accompanying instrument, it plays chords, mostly the tonic, dominant, and subdominant, but virtuosos such as Fredy Reyna include exquisite melodic techniques in their performances.

chimbangueles
A set of four to seven Afro-Venezuelan conical drums
furruco
A single-headed Venezuelan friction membranophone played by rubbing a long stick attached to and protruding from the top of the drum skin

Figure 22.4
Accompanied by a *cuatro*, the Venezuelan musician Jesús Rodríguez plays a plains harp (*arpa llanera*) in Miami, Florida. Photo by Dale A. Olsen, 1983.

DISC ❶ TRACK 26

Small guitars with nylon strings are used primarily as accompanying instruments. Most, like the *cuatro* ("four"), are named for the number of their strings (A-d-f#-B). Others are the *cuatro y medio* ("four and a half"), *cinco* ("five"), *cinco y medio*, (five and a half"), seis ("six," but smaller than the standard six-stringed guitar), *cuatro con cinco cuerdas* ("cuatro with five strings"), and *cinco de seis cuerdas* ("cinco with six-strings"). In the west of Venezuela, the *tiple* ("treble") is common. Used as a melodic or chordally accompanying instrument, the *tiple* most commonly has four double or triple sets of strings.

Plucked lutes (*bandolas* and *mandolinas*) serve as melodic instruments in Venezuela. The best-known *bandola*, is the *bandola llanera* from the plains, which uses four gut or nylon strings. [Listen to "La Catira"] Barinas is the only plains state where the *bandola* is as popular as the harp—or perhaps even more popular. The *bandola oriental* of the central coast has four courses of double strings, the higher-sounding ones from metal. The *bandola* of the eastern area (more commonly called *bandolín* or *mandolina*), also smaller than the plains *bandola*, has four double courses of nylon strings. The *bandola* of the Guayana area (surrounding Ciudad Guayana, where the Caroní River meets the Orinoco, in Bolívar State) borrows elements from the plains. The *bandola andina* (also known as a *bandurría*), found in the Andes area of western Venezuela, has five or six courses of double or triple strings.

Of the stringed instruments used to play melodies, the violin (*violín*) is the most widely used instrument in Venezuela. It is a European model, like that used throughout the world.

The diatonic harp, once popular in Spain, is an important creole instrument in many countries of Latin America [see Mexico; Paraguay; Peru]. The *arpa criolla* usually has between thirty and thirty-seven strings; thirty-three and thirty-four are the commonest numbers. Its main performance styles in Venezuela are that of the plains (*arpa llanera*) and that of Aragua (*arpa aragüeña*, from the state of Aragua). Because the latter style also occurs in the federal district, the state of Miranda, and states closer to the coast than the plains states, it can conveniently be called the style of the central-coast harp. More commonly, it is specified by adjectives derived from the names of places, including Aragua (*arpa aragüeña*), Miranda (*arpa mirandina*), and the Tuy River area (*arpa tuyera*).

The instruments differ slightly from one area to another. The plains harp has a narrower sound board than does the central-coast harp and now uses only nylon strings. The coastal harp sometimes has gut or nylon strings in its lower register, but metallic upper strings that give it a more brilliant sound. Performance brings out an even more prominent difference between these harps (see below, in relation to the *joropo*).

The diatonic harp was taught to indigenous Venezuelans by Spanish priests during the early colonial period, and its music was fashionable in the salons of the urban upper class. The harp music heard today in Venezuela has roots in seventeenth- and eighteenth-century Spain, when the Renaissance modes had not yet been fully replaced by major and minor tonalities (Garfias 1979:13). Keyboard music was performed on diatonically tuned harps, then popular in Spain. The harp-playing styles of Venezuela closely resemble Spanish Baroque keyboard styles.

Aerophones

Wind instruments are notable in the music of marginalized creoles such as the people of Falcon State, who dance to the music of an ensemble featuring *turas*, end-blown flutes, one male and the other female. Other flutes of this ensemble are *cachos*, made from deers' skulls with antlers attached; these are played in pairs, one large and one small.

Another popular Venezuelan aerophone is the panpipe, locally called by several names, including *carrizo* ("cane") and *maremare* ("happy-happy"), played by creoles in many parts of Venezuela. Especially well known are the panpipes of Cumanacoa, in Sucre State, and those of San José de Guaribe, in Guarico State. There are many other kinds of creole aerophones, including cane and wooden flutes (vertical and transverse types) and conch trumpets (*trompetas de caracol*, *guaruras*). The last instruments play in drum ensembles of the Barlovento area.

MUSICAL CONTEXTS AND GENRES

Folk Catholicism

Venezuelan folk-religious music is based primarily on Christian conventions. There are no clear links to specific African religions, nor do the traces of syncretism between Christianity and African beliefs in Venezuela reveal the same levels of importance found, for example, in musical performances of Cuban Santería or Brazilian Candomblé. The concept of Saint John the Baptist may have syncretic links to African deities and celebrations but no direct links to African prototypes are obvious.

Folk-religious music in Venezuela accompanies rituals that are apparently Christian, though many are not based on formal Roman Catholic teachings. Instead, this music has evolved with a creole version of Roman Catholicism developed from early colonial days to the present. The church was less influential in colonial Venezuela than in such places as Brazil, Colombia, Mexico, and Paraguay, and Spanish priests were not in abundance. Peasants (*campesinos*) observing native American, African, and Spanish beliefs and customs were at liberty to develop and conduct religious ceremonies, embellishing them with music, dance, costumes, and practices not always acceptable to visiting clerics. Even today, representatives of the official church frown on many ritual aspects of Venezuelan fiestas.

Not all this music can be considered entirely religious in design. Much of it is dedicated to Christian saints, but texts and meanings are often interspersed with secular ideas and words. Some aspects of a particular fiesta (such as *salves*, sung at the beginning of a *tamunangue* in Lara) are traditional and acceptable facets of the Roman tradition, yet the music and dance known as *la perrendenga*, performed in front of the image of San Antonio later in the fiesta, has little to do with Christianity. Therefore, although the fiestas described below are Christian in name, creole Roman Catholicism plays a dominant role as they unfold. Furthermore, alcoholic beverages are almost invariably associated with these quasi-religious celebrations; it would be most unusual for the members of a participating music ensemble, usually men, not to share a bottle of rum or some other kind of spirits.

The combination of music and dance as tribute to deities is locally important, as is the concept of *la promesa*, the promise to honor a saint through music and/or dance for certain favors. The interplay and coexistence of beliefs and performances have produced a wealth of religiously inspired creole music and dance.

Velorios

Velorios, nightlong celebrations or night watches to honor a saint or the Holy Cross (not to be confused with wakes for a deceased person, also *velorios*) are common in Venezuela. In the plains, the music of the *velorio* is primarily Spanish in origin, with stringed instruments predominating, whereas in the central coastal region the music is more African in origin, where the *tambora* drums accompany songs called *fulias*. Perhaps the *velorio* most widely celebrated in the Venezuelan plains is the wake of the Holy Cross (*velorio de cruz*) or May Cross (*cruz de mayo*). Table altars are decorated with flowers, and a chapel or a temporary roof is often constructed of fronds, papier mâché, flowers, or other materials to honor a cross, usually made of wood and decorated with the same materials. In the plains and surrounding areas, especially in the states of Apure, Carabobo, Cojedes, Guárico, Lara, Portuguesa, and Yaracuy, the Holy Cross is venerated by performances of three-part polyphonic pieces (*tonos*), usually sung by men, sometimes unaccompanied, but more often accompanied by one or more *cuatros*. The music and texts came from Spain during the early days of the colony. Most harmonic singing in Venezuela is in two parts (usually at intervals of a third), but plains wakes use more complex polyphony, unique in Latin America. The lead singer (*guía* "guide") usually sings a solo phrase and is then joined by two other men improvising a harmonic response—a higher part (*falsa*, also *contrato* and other names), and a lower part (*tenor*, also *tenorete*). In *velorios* of the central coast (especially in the federal district, the state of Miranda, and parts of the state of Aragua), vocal harmony is less important than melody. Here, the *velorios* are centered on the singing of *fulias*, accompanied by at least one *tambora* (but usually three or four), the scraping of a metal plate with a fork, a spoon, or other utensils, and usually one *maraca* or a pair of *maracas*. The *tamboras* are held between seated musicians' knees. The most complex of the drum-accompanied vocal genres of Barlovento, the *fulia* is found in a more widely dispersed area of the central coast than are the songs associated with other drums. It has an alternating solo-chorus form of singing, like the other drum songs. The solo is sung by a man or a woman, and the choruses usually consist of male and female singers. The verses have fairly complex texts, but the choruses almost always include vocables or syllables, such as *o lo lo la lo lai na*.

Though the vigil continues until dawn, *fulias* and the accompanying *tamboras* do not play constantly. The music is broken up every twenty to forty minutes with the recitation of *décimas*, ten-line stanzas of poetry brought from Spain in the early days of the colony. Men and women (usually men) recite this poetry after an order is given to the musicians to stop playing, usually with the words *hasta ahí*, suggesting that the musicians take a pause. Some people, even those who cannot read and write, are recognized as specialists in *décimas*. Dancing is never part of celebrations that employ the singing of *fulias* and the playing of *tamboras*. The *fulia-tambora* tradition is not limited to Barlovento; it occurs in more or less the same form in neighboring areas of the central coast.

Mampulorios

Nightlong *velorios* for the deceased occur in Venezuela, but they are not usually associated with music. An exception to this is angel's wakes (*velorios de angelito*) for infants and young children. In the central coast, these *velorios*, called *mampulorios*, were festive occasions to celebrate the purity of sinless souls, which would ascend directly into heaven. Primarily religious in intent, they lasted all night, with the adorned body of the child present. Attendees ate food, drank alcoholic beverages, and played games. *Mampulorios* rarely occur now, and little is known about their music.

San Juan Bautista (Saint John the Baptist)

From the state of Yaracuy in the west to the state of Miranda, south and east of Caracas, the central Caribbean coast of Venezuela is home to many Venezuelans of African origin. Most of their communities lie along the coast; some are 50 kilometers or more inland. These people claim St. John the Baptist (or simply San Juan) as their patron saint. Juan Liscano (1973), the pioneer twentieth-century Venezuelan folklorist, noted the connection between the celebration of Saint John the Baptist (24 June) and summer-solstice celebrations elsewhere in the world. In central coastal Venezuela, Saint John the Baptist is honored with African-derived music and dancing beginning on 23 June and ending on 25 June, with ritual and musical observations varying from place to place.

Barlovento is known for the music of the festival of Saint John the Baptist. Especially important is one of its major towns, Curiepe, an important slave-trading center in the early 1700s. During the festival of Saint John the Baptist, a standard musical form is associated with drumming on the *mina* and *curbata* drums, and a dance occurs after Mass when many people participate at the same time, usually multiple pairs or three or more people dancing in a line or a circle, each with an arm or a hand on his or her neighbor's shoulder. [Listen to "Festival de San Juan"]

DISC ❶ TRACK 27

Also in Barlovento, *redondo* drums accompany a standard song and dance performed by one male-female couple at a time, the person of each gender being alternately replaced by someone from the audience. A man and a woman dance provocatively in circular movements as spectators form a circular arena around them. The dancers' movements and the

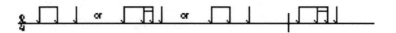

Figure 22.5
Typical rhythms performed on drums (*minas* or *redondos*) to accompany the malembe, sung during street processionals when the statue of St. John the Baptist is carried on the Sunday morning of the saint's feast. Transcription by Max H. Brandt.

formation of the onlookers—not the shape of the drums—are said to give this drum and its music the name *redondo* ("round").

A rhythm and song known as *malembe* accompanies the street processions with the image of Saint John the Baptist. *Minas* or *redondos* accompany the *malembes* and processions with a unison rhythm or its variants notated in Figure 22.5. Though *malembe* means "softly, slowly, take it easy" in various Bantu languages, the people of Barlovento are not aware of its African roots and use it simply as the name of a kind of music.

In some communities, a statue of Saint John the Baptist is kept in the local church or chapel; in others, it may be kept in the home of a devotee or leader of a San Juan society. For his fiesta, the saint is dressed in red vestments and is paraded through the streets. Some larger images of the saint, such as that in Curiepe, are placed on platforms and carried on the shoulders of four or more people, who are more likely to be dancing than walking. At times, because of the carriers' gyrations, it seems that the statue will surely fall off the platform. One or more of the images may be danced about in the hands of a devotee. Saint John the Baptist is said to love dancing, and at certain moments during the festival, libations of rum or cane alcohol are sprinkled over the icon, giving the saint the reputation of a true reveler and the name San Juan Borrachero (Saint John the Drunkard). He is sometimes called San Juan Congo, San Juan Congolé, and San Juan Guaricongo (Liscano 1973:54), revealing a connection to the Congo basin of central Africa.

Tamunangue

One of the most famous expressions of music and dance in Venezuela is the *tamunangue*, from the state of Lara in the northwest of the country. It is a suite of dances and music, usually performed in honor of San Antonio de Padua (Saint Anthony of Padua), the patron saint of Lara. It is regularly performed on 13 June, the saint's feast, but can occur during the weeks before or after.

The music for the *tamunangue* consists of singing accompanied by stringed instruments or *maracas* and a drum of African origin. The *tamunangue* usually begins with the singing of *salves* dedicated to the Virgin Mary in a church or a chapel outside which the dance of the *tamunangue* will be performed. The *salves* are usually accompanied only by stringed instruments—the *cuatro*, the *cinco*, the *quinto*, the *lira*, the *cuatro de cinco cuerdas*, and the *cinco de seis cuerdas*. A *tamunangue* ensemble could have a minimum of two such instruments (one *cuatro* and one *cinco*), but many ensembles, often composed of musicians from diverse communities, have seven to ten.

The principal drum of the *tamunangue* (usually called *tamunango* but also called *tambor grande* and *cumaco*) resembles the *tambor grande* and the *cumaco* from the central coast. With one head nailed in place, the drum normally measures slightly more than one meter long and sits on the ground during performance. In addition to the rhythms played by hand on the drumhead by a drummer who sits on the drum while playing it, sticks (*palos*, also *laures*) are played on its side by one, two, or three men (*paleros* "*palo* players") who bend over one or both sides of the drum behind the seated drummer. On some occasions, and especially when the ensemble graces processions, the large double-headed drum known in most parts of the country as *tambora* is used.

The *tamunangue* begins with the piece "La Batalla" ("The Battle"), also called a game (*juego*). It is followed by distinctive dances and pieces of music that vary slightly from one community to another. Aretz (1970) analyzes the most commonly performed eight pieces of the suite, which she lists in order of performance as "La Batalla," "La Bella," "El Chichivamos" or "Yeyevamos," "La Juruminga," "El Poco a Poco," "La Perrendenga," "El Galerón," and "El Seis Figuriao." "La Batalla" is a graceful stick dance accompanied by music. The stick (*palo*) or staff (*vera*), the size of a walking stick, is usually decorated. The battle, always between two men (regularly replaced), is gracefully executed with stick hitting stick, never touching opponents' bodies. Four lines of verse are sung in 2/4 time.

San Benito el Moro (Saint Benedict the Moor)

Saint Benedict the Moor, also known as Saint Benedict of Palermo and of San Fratello, is the patron saint of people from Venezuela's northwest coast around Lake Maracaibo, especially those of African descent. The festivities for the saint take place after Christmas and into the new year, accompanied by three or four drums mentioned earlier, called *chimbangueles*. The saint is represented by images or statues of a black man. Like Saint John the Baptist in central Venezuela, he takes on the Venezuelan creole mix of traits from Spanish, African, and possibly native American sources, resulting in a zest for both the profound and the sacred. Saint Benedict is associated with the drinking of rum, and he is thought to have an eye for beautiful women.

Los diablos danzantes de Yare (The dancing devils of Yare)

Many central-coastal communities, including Cata, Chuao, Naiguata, Patanemo, and San Francisco de Yare, have organizations of masked devil dancers who perform during the feast of Corpus Christi (Ortiz 1982). The most famous of them is San Francisco de Yare, in the upper Tuy Valley (Figure 22.6). Music is less important in this tradition than in other Venezuelan festivals. The dancing devils of Yare are accompanied by a military-style drum (*redoblante*), single *maracas* carried by many masked dancers, and jingle bells attached to their clothing.

Figure 22.6
During the feast of Corpus Christi in San Francisco de Yare, Miranda, Venezuela, the dancing devils of Yare (*los diablos danzantes de Yare*) perform. Left to right: an unmasked musician-dancer plays a single *maraca*, another plays a *redoblante* (military-style drum), and a masked man dances. Photo by Max H. Brandt, 1973.

Secular genres

The lullabies and children's songs of creole Venezuelans are based on European models. A rich corpus of children's music exists among many African cultures, but this kind of music seems not to have come to the Americas with African slavery. Scholars who have studied children's songs around the world have noted that they are more likely to be passed on from one generation of children to another than from adults to children. (This is not true, of course, of lullabies and other kinds of children's music.) Since few children were brought to the Americas as slaves, this might be one reason that traditional African children's songs are not found among Afro-Venezuelans. European migrations to Venezuela, however, did include children—which may have had some impact on the children's songs sung in Venezuela today and on children's songs fostered by the formal education of the Spanish elite.

Most chores and tasks in the Venezuelan countryside have songs to ease the burden of the labor. The most common are grain-pounding songs and milking songs. A once common sight in the Venezuelan countryside was *el pilón* ("the mortar"), often operated by two women, each with a pestle, to grind or pound grain to the rhythm of a song. These songs, though, are seldom heard today, but we can still hear the milking songs, sung to pass the time and put the cow at ease so the milk will come easily. They are especially popular in the plains states. Other kinds of work-related songs include coffee-picking songs, clothes-washing songs, and songs to encourage beasts of burden that turn the machines that press juice from sugarcane (Ramón y Rivera 1969:30–31).

Year-end music: *aguinaldos* and *gaitas*

Several types of music performed during December (Christmastime) are nonliturgical and bridge the religious and secular categories. *Aguinaldos* are Christmas carols. Their texts can be religious and secular. The word *aguinaldo* in Venezuela also means "Christmas gift." Itinerant musicians perform this music at Christmastime as they go from house to house, a tradition called *parranda*. (In neighboring Trinidad this tradition is called *parang*, a word thought to be an anglicized rendition of the Spanish word *parranda*.) The *aguinaldo* musicians usually expect a gift, which could well be a shot of rum or an *hallaca*, a Venezuelan Christmas delicacy, wrapped in a banana leaf.

The most characteristic musical instrument of the *aguinaldo* ensemble is the friction drum (*furruco*, also *furro*) (Figure 22.7). Other instruments include one or two double-headed *tamboras*, one or more lutes (like the *cuatro* and the guitar), *maracas*, and a *charrasca*. *Aguinaldos* with religious texts usually accompany a Christmas procession called Las Pastoras, but the house-to-house revel (*la parranda*) is more likely to exhibit secular *aguinaldos*.

The music of the plains seems to dominate the traditional music scene during much of the year, and *aguinaldos* can be heard throughout cities, towns, and villages at Christmastime, along with holiday favorites from abroad. It is the *gaita*, though, that reigns at the end of the year, not only in the Lake Maracaibo area (where it originates), but also in Caracas and other communities. The traditional *gaita* of the state of Zulia is accompanied by a friction drum (*furruco*) and drums called *tamboras*, which can be of the standard double-headed type or small barrel-type or *bongo*-like drums. Quite evident is how these

Figure 22.7
Around Christmas, an *aguinaldo* ensemble plays in a Maracaibo home. Left to right: singer, cuatro, two *tambora* drums (played with sticks, rather than hands), and a *furruco* friction drum. Photo by Elena Constatinidou, 1996.

drums are played: the drummer performs with a stick in each hand, one of which beats the side of the drum. *Tamboras* can be played between the legs while the player is sitting or supported by a strap while the player is standing. Standard secondary instruments, such as *maracas* and *charrascas*, also accompany *gaitas*.

Many *gaitas* heard today use electronic keyboards and other modern instruments in addition to the standard percussion instruments. The rapid beats of the *tambora*, though, and the growling of the *furruco*, make this kind of music easy to distinguish from other genres.

Secular dance and music: the **joropo** and its variants

Some creole music is not associated with dance, but most is. Partly because of urbanization, contemporary Venezuelans are less skilled at folk dancing than were their ancestors, though Venezuelan folk dancing is taught in most grade schools; most recorded folk music heard today on public broadcasting systems and on private systems in homes and vehicles is played for listening rather than for dancing. Venezuelan young people are no longer brought up in surroundings where folk dancing is a natural aspect of daily life. Nevertheless, most Venezuelans are aware of the association of dance with most of their folk music. The pieces of the *tamunangue* suite, for example, are more often associated with the dances than with the music accompanying them. Perhaps the greatest joy of participating in the San Juan festival in Barlovento, unless one is a key musician, comes from joining the public dancing to the *mina* ensemble or propelling oneself into the dances of the *redondos*, in which only one couple, through interchanges of partners, is dancing at any one time.

To most Venezuelans, the epitome of folk dance is the *joropo*, a music and dance influenced by both Africa and Europe and known as the national dance of Venezuela. The term *joropo* refers to more than just dance. It also denotes a genre of music and the event in which the music and dance are performed. A person can attend a *joropo* (event), request the performance of a particular *joropo* (musical piece), and then execute a *joropo* (dance). Most often, the term names the dance. This is a couple dance, and each participant normally holds one or both hands of the partner, in the same dance position used by European couples to dance a waltz, for example. (Usually many couples dance at once.) The dance involves both basic and intricate footwork. It is similar in style throughout Venezuela, but the musical ensembles that accompany it vary locally.

The term *joropo* was first used to describe an event in a rural setting with dance, string music, and song, and its meaning as a genre of dancing probably came in common usage around 1850; before then, a dance of this style was probably called a *fandango* (Ramón y Rivera 1969:191). People in the countryside may speak of a particular *joropo* as an event that took place in the past or one planned for the future. It can be on a small scale, organized by a family or a segment of a community, and may take place in a house. An excuse to have a modest *joropo* might be a baptism, a birthday party, or a visit by a special friend. Alternatively, it might be a more public event, perhaps as part of a communitywide fiesta coinciding with a national holiday or a religious celebration, such as that for the local patron saint. Such a *joropo* would probably take place in an outdoor public area or a community hall. Like many fiestas in Venezuela, it would probably start early in the evening and last until sunrise. In the early 1920s, it was much more important than it is today. It included not only musical entertainment and dancing but also special food and drink, children's play, and courtship.

As a musical piece, a *joropo* can be rather complex. There are many names for the musical forms that accompany the dance (Ramón y Rivera 1953). The list includes *joropo*, but four other words are more appropriate for classification: *corrido*, *galerón*, *golpe*, and *pasaje*. Even these are not mutually used in the same context by all musicians. The term *joropo* is often used for pieces that some might call *golpes* and especially for pieces in three, four, or more parts, written by famous composers, such as Pedro Elías Gutiérrez, Francisco de Paula Aguirre, and Carlos Bonet. The *joropos* of urban composers are now often performed in rural areas of Venezuela, and traditional pieces that might once have been called *golpes* or other names forgotten by younger performers are now simply called *joropos* (Ramón y Rivera 1967:54, 1969:191). *Revuelta* is another commonly used term for *joropo* music. It is usually an extended version of a *pasaje*, though both names are often used for the same kind of piece. Yet another commonly used term, *hornada* ("batch" or "ovenful"), denotes a medley of *revueltas* or *pasajes*. Other names usually refer to particular movements, literary texts, or specific pieces, such as the *corrido* called "El Pajarillo" and the *golpe* called "La Refalosa."

Joropo music is rhythmically sophisticated, commonly notated with a double-time signature of 3/4 and 6/8, producing polyrhythms and an always present polymetric sense of simultaneous duple and triple figures (*hemiola* or *sesquiáltera*), which provide creative possibilities for instrumentalists and dancers. The tempo is always brisk (a common pace is 208 quarter notes a minute), keeping dancers and musicians active. Some vocal lines conform strictly to the accompaniment, especially in *golpes*, but much of the singing demonstrates the "melodic independence" that Ramón y Rivera has often written about. This is a free style of singing, in which, except during the beginnings or endings of certain long phrases, much of the vocal line does not coincide rhythmically or metrically with the instrumental accompaniment.

Melodies are clearly Spanish in character, but they have roots in Andalucía. The texts, sung in Spanish, relate to Spanish genres of early colonial days (such as the *romance* and the *décima*). Most melodies have fixed texts, but some texts are improvised. All this music is distinguished by having one musical note for each syllable of text.

The *joropo* and the plains harp ensemble

For accompanying *joropos*, the plains harp ensemble is probably the most famous in Venezuela. This is almost always an all-male ensemble and can be purely instrumental or can have one vocalist, also usually male. It is often presented as the trademark of Venezuelan traditional music, in part because of the attractiveness of the instrumental combination and its repertoire. During the dictatorship of Pérez Jiménez (1950–1958), this music came to the fore as a national symbol, supported by that government.

The *arpa llanera* ("plains harp") is the featured melody instrument of the ensemble, sharing the melody role with the vocalist, who does not usually play an instrument. The other two instrumentalists play a *cuatro* and *maracas*. Since the mid-1900s, a fifth musician, playing an acoustic or electric string bass, has been added to accentuate the bass, traditionally played by the lower strings of the harp. Perhaps the best known harpists and advocates of this style during the second half of the nineteenth century were Ignacio "Indio" Figueredo and Juan Vicente Torrealba.

The *bandola*, a four-stringed, pear-shaped lute that takes the place of the harp in many ensembles (and which may have preceded the *arpa* in some Venezuelan communities), remains the melodic instrument of choice in the states of Barinas and Portuguesa; it is also played in Apure and Cojedes. An eight-stringed version of it appears in Miranda, Sucre, and Anzoategui. The virtuosity possible on the *bandola* has been ably demonstrated by Anselmo López, master of this lute. The instrument is plucked with a pick, so the lower two strings provide an ostinato, much like that of the lower strings of the harp; the higher strings, on alternate beats, play the melody. Performances on the plains harp are usually dashing and impressionistic, but the plains ensemble is equally appealing to most listeners when the *bandola* is the leading instrument.

In the plains ensemble, the *cuatro* provides the basic harmonic framework, plus a rhythmic pulse through its strumming (*rasgueado*). One might expect the *maracas* to provide a basic rhythmic background, but a good player of *maracas* (*maraquero*) can steal the show with rapid rhythmic embellishments, a subtle shifting of accents from triple to duple meter, and a masterful visual display of arm and hand techniques.

Joropo and the central-coastal harp ensemble

The *joropo* of the central coast (especially in the states of Aragua, Miranda, and the federal district, and in parts of Anzoategui, Sucre, and Carabobo) is traditionally accompanied by two male musicians—one who plays the harp and one who sings and plays *maracas*. The best known musician to sing in this style was the late Pancho Prin from the Tuy region of Miranda state.

An eight-stringed *bandola* (four double courses and similar in shape to the plains *bandola*) sometimes takes the place of the harp. The harp also differs somewhat from that of the plains; the sound board is slightly wider at the bottom, and the upper strings are metal, not nylon, though the lower strings are usually nylon or gut.

Central-coastal *joropo* music is less flamboyant than plains *joropo* music, and in form it is quite different. The vocal and instrumental melodies of the plains ensembles are songs with European-based harmonies and fixed texts, but the coastal style features shorter and more repetitive phrases with melodies and texts more likely to be improvised. The harp makes complex melodic patterns.

The African cultural presence is more concentrated on the coast than on the plains. Because Barlovento is at the heart of this area, one would expect to find more African influences in this music than in plains *joropo* music. Indeed, the vocalist's improvisation recalls African musical traditions, as does the repetitiveness of themes and phrases—an important musical trait not always appreciated by those who do not know African music.

The **golpe** of Lara

The *golpe* of Lara State, somewhat northwest of the plains, is a cousin of the plains *joropo* in music and dance (Fernaud 1984). Its standard instrumentation is one or two *cuatros*, a *cinco*, a *tambora*, and a pair of *maracas*. Occasionally, other instruments—a violin, the large drum used for the *tamunangue*, or a standard guitar—substitute the above or join the ensemble. Other instruments (such as *arpa*, *bandola*, and *bandolín*) were formerly used but seldom appear today.

Instrumental and vocal *golpes* are almost always performed by men; women, however, participate in the dancing. Unless a bowed chordophone is involved, the melodies are carried by vocalists, usually a duo singing in thirds. Musicians claim that *golpe* music and dance are distinct from the plains *joropo*, especially in tempo, said to be slower and more sedate.

Other **joropo** ensembles

Though the two harp ensembles mentioned above are conspicuous for performing *joropo* music, other notable *joropo* ensembles exist. Many Venezuelans argue that the vocal part is the most important musical component of the *joropo*, but some *joropos* are purely instrumental, especially in the plains. If only one instrument is used, it probably would be a *cuatro*. If another musician were to accompany the *cuatrista*, it would probably be a *maraquero* ("*maracas* player"). A *joropo* with *maracas* alone or with *maracas* and voice would be possible but rare.

National anthem

Composed by Juan José Landaeta to lyrics written (before the music) by Vicente Salias (http://david.national-anthems.net/ve.txt), Venezuela's national anthem is titled "Gloria al bravo pueblo" (Glory to the Brave Nation). It was adopted in 1881, although its inspiration came much earlier in the 1810s, during the country's struggle for independence. The anthem was written and composed, with the lyrics written first and the music added later, under the inspiration of the first attempt of the Venezuelans to win their independence in the 1810s. Venezuela's national anthem has been called the "Venezuelan Marseillaise" because of its birth in the independence movement and the martyrdom of several of its early freedom fighters.

SOCIAL STRUCTURE AND PERFORMANCE

Presentations of Venezuelan folk music in urban settings, at home and abroad, have since the 1960s often been organized and performed by university students and middle-class devotees of these traditions—citizens of ethnic and social backgrounds somewhat different from those who claim this music as their own. With the decline of the petroleum market in the final two decades of the twentieth century, a change that has brought economic strife to Venezuela, the number of urban performances by young people with roots in rural areas has surged. The core of this music remains in the countryside, performed by agricultural workers who, though not always having the educational and financial resources of their urban cousins, do have access to the carriers and surroundings of traditional culture. It has been passed on to them orally by older relatives and neighbors, who in turn lend their musical skills from earlier generations of local contacts. Since the 1980s, a revival of interest in creole traditions has produced hundreds of community-based performance groups scattered throughout the *ranchos* (poorer neighborhoods of Caracas), where few existed in the 1960s and 1970s.

Most instrumentalists continue to be men. Women contribute in an equally important way to the vocal music and dancing. Drummers in Barlovento, harpists in Apure, and players of cane flutes in the states of Zulia and Falcón to Sucre are almost always men, reflecting similar practices in native American, Iberian, and African cultures. Often a woman will play a *maraca* or another supporting instrument, but seldom do women serve as lead instrumentalists. In addition to enhancing vocal music, they usually play a prominent part in organizing fiestas, without which performances would not occur.

Middle-age and older men and women usually take the most prominent musical roles, but young people—from babies to teenagers—are always present at fiestas, encouraged to participate in making music. Children are expected to clap and sing, and certain instruments, such as sticks struck on the wooden bodies of the large drums, provide access for young people to play minor parts, even at the height of important celebrations. During less festive occasions, as when instruments are being made or prepared for performances, children are encouraged to touch and play them. Formal courses of instruction in folk music are more likely to be found in the schools of cities and major towns than in rural settings.

Most music described here was once maintained solely by rural people, including people of European descent, whereas the upper classes in towns and cities, especially the elite descendants of Europeans, regarded this music as inferior. This situation has changed, and Venezuelans of all social classes and walks of life tend to be proud of their folk music. In the last decade of the twentieth century and the first decade of the twenty-first, sometime during their schooling most Caraqueños (people from Caracas) are encouraged to learn to play the *cuatro*, dance the *joropo*, and absorb other aspects of Venezuelan folklore.

MUSICAL CHANGE

Venezuelan folk music began to undergo substantial change during the mid-1900s, when large migrations from rural areas to urban centers began. The Afro-Venezuelan area of Barlovento is a good example of musical change.

Though Barlovento is close to Caracas, it was until the 1940s isolated by mountains, the lack of modern roads, and a reputation for malaria and other tropical illnesses. Isolation had an impact on the cultivation of African music, leading to its present fame. Since the early 1950s, these traditions have undergone major transformations, primarily because Venezuela's major eastern highway now penetrates Barlovento, allowing wealthy Venezuelans from the capital to purchase and develop its land. Likewise, in a reverse migration, many Afro-Venezuelans who have called Barlovento home for generations have moved to Caracas for better jobs, education, and health care. These changes at first had a detrimental impact on traditional drumming, since these people usually did not bring the instruments and their music, but folk music from the countryside became much more acceptable during the last decade of the twentieth century.

MUSIC LEARNING, DISSEMINATION, AND PUBLIC POLICY

The cities of Venezuela, especially Caracas, have genres of popular music, influenced in varying degrees by the music of the Venezuelan countryside and of other countries in the Americas and Europe. Ensembles and individual performers who became popular in the 1960s for drawing on Venezuelan folk music in their compositions and performances include such famous recording artists as the *cuatro* player Fredy Reyna, the internationally known folk singer Soledad Bravo, and popular groups such as El Cuarteto, Gurrufío, Quinteto Contrapunto, and Serenata Guayanesa.

Perhaps the best-known group to perform and promote both folk and popular music in Venezuela during the last decade of the twentieth century is Un Solo Pueblo, which has produced many CDs. Other important groups that feature African-Venezuelan music of the central coast and especially the region of Barlovento includes Grupo Madera, Tambor Urbano, and Huracán de Fuego. In 1998 the group known as ODILA (Orquesta de Instrumentos LatinAmericanos), the performance component of the Fundación de Etnomusicología y Folklore (FUNDEF), celebrated its fifteenth anniversary promoting not only Venezuelan folk music, but also music from various other countries of Latin America and the Caribbean. The performances of ODILA are based primarily on recordings and research conducted since the 1950s under the auspices of the former Instituto Nacional de Folklore (INAF), the former Instituto Interamericano de Etnomusicología y Folklore (INIDEF), and their succeeding organizations, such as FUNDEF. Venezuela has also made its mark on pop, rock, and especially *salsa* music. Oscar D'León is probably the best known of Venezuela's superstars of *salsa*.

The music of Venezuela portrays an exquisite model of the Amerindian, European, and African layers of culture that make up the identity of this important region of Latin America. Intertwined with rituals, fiestas, and dances, the music unique to this vibrant South American country continues to endure and embodies a fundamental ingredient of the national psyche. To experience Venezuelan music is to capture the essence of a positive national pride and beauty that is truly remarkable.

FURTHER STUDY

The most comprehensive study of indigenous Venezuelan music is by Aretz (1991), who presents a survey of twenty-three Venezuelan societies that exist in various states of acculturation. A brief synopsis of her work on this subject appears as an article in *The World of Music* (1982). Before making a detailed musical inventory of each ethnic group, Aretz discusses the consequences of musical contact with Europeans, gives an overview of studies, and presents the general traits of Venezuelan indigenous vocal and instrumental music. She cites publications that deal with the missionaries and explorers of early colonial days, the scientific expeditions of the eighteenth and early twentieth centuries that mention musical culture, and the more concentrated efforts of ethnomusicologists and other scholars interested in this subject. Photos, illustrations, and charts make this publication important, even for those who do not read Spanish. Other important studies (including recordings) of Venezuelan Amerindians include Agerkop (1983), Coppens (1975), Olsen (1996), and Ramón y Rivera (1992).

A publication on the music of Caracas (R. Salazar 1994) surveys the music of the Caracas valley from the time of the first known encounters between Amerindians and Europeans to the most famous popular groups of the late twentieth century. It covers scores of urban genres and performers—those with minimal ties to rural Venezuela and individuals and ensembles using Venezuelan rural sources in their works. A perspective on the music of the *joropo*, the first major work on this subject since Ramón y Rivera's classic work of 1953, is a book and compact disc by Rafael Salazar titled *El Joropo y Sus Andanzas* (1992a). The *décima* has been studied in detail by Ramón y Rivera (1992). Other relevant works by Rafael Salazar are *Latinoamérica es Música* (1992b) and *Memorial del Canto* (n.d.).

Since music is an important part of most festivals and fiestas in Venezuela, at least two books are important. One is *Fiestas Tradicionales de Venezuela* by Daria Hernández and Cecilia Fuentes (1993), with photographs by Nelson Garrido. The other is *Diablos Danzantes de Venezuela*, edited by Manuel Antonio Ortiz (1982).

A study of Afro-Venezuelan music by Max H. Brandt (1994) focuses on the aspect of music as identity among the people and musicians of Barlovento. It includes photos of Afro-Venezuelan drummers. In addition to written sources that address musical instruments (especially Aretz 1967), excellent recordings outline the distribution of creole instruments in Venezuela, such as *Folklore de Venezuela* (1971), *The Music of Venezuela* (1990), *Música Popular Tradicional de Venezuela* (1983), and those by Lares (1969, 1978a, 1978b).

REFERENCES

Agerkop, Terry. 1983. *Piaroa*. Caracas: Cajas Audiovisuales INIDEF.

Anuario FUNDEF, Año IV. 1993. Caracas: Fundación de Etnomusicología y Folklore.

Aretz, Isabel. 1967. *Instrumentos Musicales de Venezuela*. Cumaná: Universidad de Oriente.

———. 1970. *El Tamunangue*. Barquisimeto: Universidad Centro Occidental.

———. 1982. "Indigenous Music of Venezuela." *The World of Music* 25(2): 22–35.

———.1991. *Música de Los Aborígenes de Venezuela*. Caracas: Fundación de Etnomusicología y Folklore.

Brandt, Max H. 1994. "African Drumming from Rural Communities around Caracas and Its Impact on Venezuelan Music and Ethnic Identity." In *Music and Black Ethnicity: The Caribbean and South America*, ed. Gerard H. Béhague, 267–284. Miami: North-South Center, University of Miami.

Coppens, Walter. 1975. *Music of the Venezuelan Yekuana Indians*. Folkways Records FE 4101. LP disk.

Danzas y Canciones Para Los Niños. 1981. Caracas: Ediciones Fredy Reyna. LP disk.

Esparragoza, Maria Eugenia. 1991. *Salto en el Atlántico*. Research by Jesús García. 16mm film.

Fernaud, Alvaro. 1984. *El Golpe Larense*. Caracas: Fundación de Etnomusicología y Folklore.

Folklore de Venezuela. 1971. Caracas: Sonido Laffer. 8 LP disks.

García, Jesús. 1990. *Africa en Venezuela: Pieza de Indias*. Caracas: Cuadernos Lagoven.

Garfias, Robert. 1979. "The Venezuelan Harp." *Folk Harp Journal* 24:13–16.

Hernández, Daria, and Cecilia Fuentes. 1993. *Fiestas Tradicionales de Venezuela*. Caracas: Fundación Bigott.

Lares, Oswaldo. 1969. *Música de Venezuela: Indio Figueredo (Homenaje al Indio Figueredo)*. Caracas: Oswaldo Lares. LP disk.

———. 1978a. *Danzas y Cantos Afrovenezolanos*. 1978. Caracas: Oswaldo Lares. LP disk.

———. 1978b. *Música de Venezuela: Cantos y Danzas e La Costa Central*. Caracas: Oswaldo Lares. LP disk.

Liscano, Juan. 1943. "Baile de tambor." *Boletín de la Sociedad Venezolana de Ciencias Naturales* 8(5):245–252.

———. 1960. "Lugar de origen de los tambores redondos barloventeños." *Revista Shell* 8(35): June.

———. 1973. *La Fiesta de San Juan El Bautista*. Caracas: Monte Avila Editores.

The Music of Venezuela. 1990. Memphis: Memphis State University. High Water Recording Company, LP1013. LP disk.

Música Popular Tradicional de Venezuela. 1983. Caracas: Instituto Nacional del Folklore. LP disk.

Olsen, Dale A. 1980a. "Folk Music of South America—A Musical Mosaic." In *Musics of Many Cultures: An Introduction*, ed. Elizabeth May, 386–425. Berkeley: University of California Press.

———. 1980b. "Symbol and Function in South American Indian Music." In *Musics of Many Cultures: An Introduction*, ed. Elizabeth May, 363–385. Berkeley: University of California Press.

———. 1996. *Music of the Warao of Venezuela: Song People of the Rain Forest*. Gainesville: University Press of Florida. Book and compact disc.

Ortiz, Manuel Antonio. 1982. *Diablos Danzantes de Venezuela*. Caracas: Fundación La Salle de Ciencias Naturales.

Pollak-Eltz, Angelina. 1972. *Cultos Afroamericanos*. Caracas: Universidad Católica Andres Bello.

———. 1994. *Black Culture and Society in Venezuela*. Caracas: Lagoven.

Quintana M., Hugo J. 1995. "Música aborigen en los cronistas de Indias." *Revista Montalbán* 8:157–175.

Ramón y Rivera, Luís Felipe. 1950. "La percusión de los negros en la música americana." *Boletín de la Sociedad Venezolana de Ciencias Naturales* 8(5):245–252.

———. 1953. *El joropo, baile nacional de Venezuela*. Caracas: Ediciones del Ministerio de Educación.

———. 1967. *Música Indígena, Folklórica y Popular de Venezuela*. Buenos Aires: Ricordi Americana.

———. 1969. *La Música Folklórica de Venezuela*. Caracas: Monte Ávila Editores.

———. 1971. *La Música Afrovenezolana*. Caracas: Universidad Central de Venezuela.

———. 1992. *La Música de la Décima*. Caracas: Fundación de Etnomusicología y Folklore.

Salazar, Briseida. 1990. *San Benito: Canta y Baila Con Sus Chimbangueleros*. Caracas: Fundación Bigott.

Salazar, Rafael. N.d. *Memorial del Canto*. Caracas: Banco Industrial de Venezuela.

———. 1992a. *Del Joropo y Sus Andanzas*. Caracas: Disco Club Venezolano. Book and compact disc.

———. 1992b. *Latinoamérica es Música*. Caracas: Ediciones Disco Club Venezolano.

———. 1994. *Caracas: Espiga Musical del Ávila*. Caracas: Disco Club Venezolano. Book and compact disc.

Sojo, Juan Pablo. 1976 [1943]. *Nochebuena negra*. Los Teques: Biblioteca Popular Mirandina, Gobernación del Estado Miranda.

Warao

Dale A. Olsen

Musical Instruments
Musical Contexts and Genres
Performers and Performances
Further Study

"Tropical-forest spirits singing with beautiful voices, fruit scattering on the forest floor, a scissors-tailed kite circling high above the forest canopy—it's time to sing a magical protection *hoa* song, or you will die!" So believe the Warao of eastern Venezuela, deep within the tropical forest of the Orinoco River Delta. "And so many Warao die because they do not know the songs," says Jaime, a Warao elder and religious leader.

The Warao (also spelled Warrau, Guarao, Guarauno), which is their name for themselves, are the "canoe people" (*wa* "canoe," *arao* "owners of"), whom I call the "song people" (*wara* "ritual song communication," *arao* "owners of"), because magical singing is as essential to them as canoeing (Olsen 1996). The Warao speak and sing in a language believed to belong to the Chibchan-Paezan phylum, making them related to the Yanomamö, Kogi, Kuna, and other Amerindians in northwestern South America (Greenberg 1987:382).

The traditional world of the Warao is the swamp of the Orinoco River Delta, known politically as the Delta Amacuro Federal Territory, and most of them live in houses built on pilings over the water. Each extended family shares a cluster of houses. Because the delta is a web of rivers and streams, constituting about 26,500 square kilometers, the Warao are a riverine fishing people, though they were not always so. In ancient times, they lived in the jungle, building their villages next to groves of moriche palms. This palm, then as today, has provided the Warao with essentials of life, including mortal food for themselves and spiritual food for their patron being, Kanobo ("Our Grandfather"). Also during ancient times, the Warao were primarily gatherers and occasionally hunters; today, they have added horticulture to their food-quest activities. They have always needed to travel through swampy jungles, by land as well as by water, in search of food or cosmological sustenance.

Until about the 1950s, isolation kept the Warao relatively free from contact with European- and African-derived cultures. For this reason, they are large in number and rich in traditional culture. The Warao population is over twenty-five thousand individuals, settled in about 250 villages (Girard 1997:332). Extensive missionization of the Warao began in 1925, when Spanish Capuchín missionaries founded mission schools in the delta. Even into the twenty-first century, these missionaries control the area, and Protestant missionization, common in other parts of the South American tropical forest, has not been possible.

Other locally acculturative forces of the late twentieth century are creole-owned sawmills, with their attraction of outside traders, adventurers, and frontiersmen; exploration for oil; the building of roads and dikes; and research by anthropologists and other scientists. An additional but much smaller number of Warao, the "Spanish Warao," inhabit the swampy coasts of Guyana between the Orinoco Delta and the Pomeroon River; they have mixed with the Spanish and are an acculturated group.

The Warao live closer to the Caribbean Islands than the people of any other native South American culture. Trinidad is a short distance by sea, north of the delta. Some musical traits of extant Warao culture resemble those noted in historical accounts of indigenous Caribbeans, especially the Taíno or Island Arawak; the most important of these traits involve musical instruments, festivals, and shamanic tools common to the Warao and the Taíno. These peoples share some religious and musical similarities with the Yanomamö, a thousand kilometers to the southwest.

MUSICAL INSTRUMENTS

The Warao use ten traditional musical and noisemaking instruments in shamanistic rituals, other ceremonies and musical occasions, and signaling. They play two borrowed instruments for entertainment and retain knowledge of three other instruments, the latter belonging to an extinct part of their culture and no longer used.

The ten surviving traditional instruments are four idiophones including the *sewei* (strung rattle), *habi sanuka* (small container rattle), *hebu mataro* (large container rattle), and a small woven wicker container rattle; one membranophone, the *ehuru* (double-headed hourglass-shaped drum); and five aerophones including the *muhusemoi* (deer-bone notched vertical flute), *hekunukabe* (cane vertical flute), *isimoi* (clarinet), *heresemoi* (conch trumpet), and *bakohi* (bamboo or cow-horn trumpet). The recently borrowed instruments are two chordophones: *sekeseke* (violin) and *wandora* (Venezuelan *cuatro*).

The following classification, based on the production of sounds, serves for an objective study. The Warao themselves suit their instruments to certain cultural contexts, such as religious rituals and dance, shamanism, traveling in the jungle or on water in search of food, entertainment, and tourism. Some of these contexts cause the overlapping use of certain instruments.

Idiophones

The religious dances known as *habi sanuka* (for fertility) and *nahanamu* (for harvest) are occasions for attaching *sewei* strung rattles to male dancers' right ankles. Consisting of numerous small hoofs, seeds, nuts, fruits, or beetle wings threaded on a string, these rattles are sacred, although their sounds simply enhance the rhythms of the dancing. Women never use strung rattles. As gifts from Kanobo, they have great value, and only village chiefs or shamans own them.

The *habi sanuka*, a small container rattle, is used by Warao men (and occasionally women) during the fertility festival also called *habi sanuka* (see below). It is made from the fruit of the calabash tree (*Crescentia cujete*) known as *mataro* or *totuma* in the delta. Filled with small stones, pieces of shells, or black seeds, the fruit (the container) is pierced by a wooden handle. The total length of this rattle is 23 centimeters.

The *hebu mataro* is a huge calabash container rattle about 70 centimeters long. It serves for the festival of *nahanamu* and in *wisiratu* shamanism (see below). No instrument among the Warao is more important than this rattle, whose size, sound, symbolism, and supernatural power are unsurpassable. When not used, it is stored in a *torotoro* basket (Figure 23.1). The Warao believe the *hebu mataro* is capable of providing profound spiritual help as a "head-spirit" (Wilbert 1993:133). The handle (the "leg"), which pierces the calabash (the "head"), is made from a stick of wood, and the stones (the "voice") are small quartz pebbles, which are not found in the central delta but must be brought from Tucupita, the territorial capital. When the *hebu mataro* belongs to a powerful *wisiratu* priest-shaman elder (as opposed to a less powerful younger *wisiratu* shaman who has not yet inherited the position of priest), the instrument is adorned with feathers (the "hair") where the handle protrudes from the top of the calabash. Selected red and yellow tail feathers from a live *cotorra* parrot are sewn into a long sash wound around the tip of the shaft. Two vertical and two horizontal slits (the "mouth") always appear in the sides of the container, and geometric designs (the "teeth") often adorn the slits. The shaft symbolizes fertility, an obvious power symbol for the festival of *nahanamu* and curing rituals, in which male and female power unite to restore a patient's health.

The *hebu mataro* is usually gripped and shaken with both hands while the player dances during the festival of *nahanamu* and while he cures illnesses. In

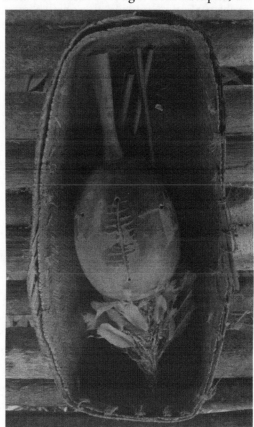

Figure 23.1
A Warao wisiratu shaman's *hebu mataro* rattle in a *torotoro* basket. Photo by Dale A. Olsen, 1972.

Figure 23.2
Bernardo Jiménez Tovar, a *wisiratu* shaman, uses his *hebu mataro* rattle in an attempt to cure a girl. Photo by Dale A. Olsen, 1972.

the latter context, a *wisiratu* shaman will usually begin his work of curing by sitting on a bench, singing, and shaking his *hebu mataro* (Figure 23.2). He will later stand to lean over his patient and shake it with all his strength. At this time, the *hebu mataro* often produces a fiery glow seen only by the shaman and the patient during a nighttime curing séance. When the *wisiratu* shaman vigorously shakes his rattle during the transitional part of the séance, the quartz pebbles repeatedly strike against the wooden handle, producing a fine dust. This dust, which has a low flashpoint, is in turn ignited by the heat produced by the concussion of pieces of quartz. Seeing a glow through the slits of the rattle has a psychological effect on the patient, reinforcing his or her belief in the shaman's curative powers.

Tourism accounts for the existence of one Warao musical instrument—a small, finely woven, wicker rattle, about the same size as the *habi sanuka*. It is simply a toy and most often made for sale to tourists in the Venezuelan towns of Tucupita and Barrancas.

Membranophone

A double-headed skin drum known as *ehuru* (or *eruru*) is used by the Warao while traveling through the jungle in quest of food and to the *morichal* (grove of *moriche* palms) to prepare for the *nahanamu*. In those contexts, it often accompanies singing; it has the secondary function of letting those behind the drummer and those ahead at the destination know where they are. Additionally, the Warao use the *ehuru* to frighten off jaguars and evil spirits that lurk in the jungle when the Warao go off to gather the starch for *nahanamu* (Turrado Moreno 1945:227).

A hollowed log cut into the shape of an hourglass, the *ehuru* has heads usually made from the skins of howler monkeys. The player strikes one end with a single stick; the other end has a snare made of twisted *moriche*-fiber string and toothpick-sized thorns.

Chordophones

Solely for entertainment, the Warao use two stringed instruments: *sekeseke* (a violin) and *wandora* (a small, four-stringed guitar like the Venezuelan *cuatro*). The *sekeseke* is an often crude copy of a European violin, especially of the Renaissance prototype of the modern violin. A bow, slightly arched at each end, is made from a branch with several dozen loose strands of cotton fibers attached. Warao bowing especially resembles European Renaissance bowed-lute technique. According to Warao lore, the *sekeseke* was first fabricated and transported to the Warao in a ship captained by Nakurao, a man-monkey from a far-off land. This creature, who had the upper torso of a man and the lower torso of a monkey, learned how to make the violin in a dream.

Aerophones

The *muhusemoi* (*muhu* "bone," *semoi* "wind instrument") is a bone flute made from the tibia of a deer (Figure 23.3). Its mouthpiece consists of a wide, obliquely cut notch, against which the flutist focuses his stream of air; the flute's body has three holes for fingering. The Warao flutist has a unique way of fingering his *muhusemoi*: he opens only one hole at a time, producing a musical scale quite unlike any Western example. No two *muhusemoi* are alike, because no two deer's tibias are ex-

Figure 23.3
Juan Bustillo Calderón plays a *muhusemoi* deerbone flute. Photo by Dale A. Olsen, 1972.

actly the same size—and, more importantly, each maker uses his own fingers as rulers for placing the holes.

During the *nahanamu* festival, several *muhusemoi* are played in ensemble with two *isimoi* clarinets, several strung rattles, and *hebu mataro*. Men may play several bone flutes with the *ehuru* drum while traveling by foot in the jungle. If a man does not own a *muhusemoi*, he may fabricate a *hekunakabe*, a disposable plant-stalk flute with the same proportions as the bone flute. After the travelers have reached their destination, the men play their instruments again while women collect and prepare *moriche* palm starch (*yuruma*) for Kanobo—a process undertaken in preparation for the *nahanamu*.

The most sacred wind instrument played during the festival is the *isimoi*, a heteroglot clarinet without fingerholes, made and played by the musical leader of the festival, the *isimoi arotu* "owner of the *isimoi*." The Warao believe that, according to the ancients, the *isimoi* has a spirit that is the same as Kanobo.

The owner of the *isimoi* plays his instrument in duet with another *isimoi* played by an apprentice (the former instrument has a lower pitch). Though the *isimoi* does not have fingerholes, by increasing and decreasing the air pressure a skillful player can produce two distinct notes at the interval of a minor third plus limited microtonal glissandi. Like the first interval produced by most *muhusemoi* flutes, and like the basic interval of Warao shamanistic music for curing, an approximate minor third is the interval that fundamentally identifies most Warao music.

An end-blown conch trumpet, *heresemoi*, is an important instrument among the

Warao, although it is associated primarily with canoeing during the crabbing season. Basically a signaling instrument used for giving directions to canoes at night and to signal the departure and arrival of the crabbing canoes, it can also be blown to announce the death of a tribal member, to signal the annual trek to the *morichal* in preparation for *nahanamu*, to announce the completion of a newly made canoe (Furst 1965:27), and "to herald each new phase in the process of building a canoe" from a living *cachicamo* tree (Wilbert 1993:55).

Electronic sound devices

Generally, modern Venezuelan material culture has had little effect on Warao music. A transistor radio may occasionally appear in a village, but the lack of receivable broadcasts and the expense of batteries work against its use and survival. In Warao villages adjacent to Roman Catholic missions, small phonographs were once found, and children could occasionally be seen dancing to Venezuelan creole music from scratchy 45-rpm records.

MUSICAL CONTEXTS AND GENRES

By far the most important Warao context for making music is theurgy (supernatural communication), and the most common kind is healing. Sickness and accidents abound, and though their causes are always attributed to the supernatural, some require the help of a shaman. Song, however, is always the most powerful medium for curing.

Music and the work of shamans

The Warao view of the world specifies three types of cosmological practitioners loosely classifiable as shamans: *wisiratu*, who oversee the apex of the Warao celestial dome and communicate with ancestral spirits; *bahanarotu*, who communicate with the eastern part of the cosmos where the sun rises, a good place; and *hoarotu*, who appease the spirits of the dead in the west where the sun sets, a bad place.

One of the most important duties of these specialists is curing illnesses caused by the intrusions of foreign essences. Through an ecstatic technique culturally induced with the aid of music and tobacco smoke, shamans transform themselves into powerful entities able to sustain contact with the spiritual world to determine the illness-causing essences and how they got into their patients. Each type of shaman has a melodically and textually distinct set of songs for curing.

In all cases, the curer must name the illness-causing spiritual essence. When properly named within a descending melody, the malevolent essence is removed, and the patient recovers. While curing, *hoarotu* shamans sing alone or in twos or threes (as do, to a lesser degree, *wisiratu* shamans). Singing together, prescribed when the patient is an important person, results in a complex, multipart texture like a free round.

The **wisiratu** shaman

Only the *wisiratu* regularly rattles a large *hebu mataro* while curing illnesses. [Listen to "Warao male *wisiratu* shaman's curing song"] With this tool and its powerful properties,

DISC ❶ TRACK 3

he is the most commonly consulted Warao doctor, primarily in charge of curing everyday respiratory and febrile diseases. Furthermore, as the mediator between man and ancestors, he can communicate with the major Warao supreme beings, known as *Kanobotuma* (Our Grandfathers). In addition to his curing role, therefore, he often functions as a priest in charge of Kanoboism, a Warao temple-idol religion in which the patron, Kanobo, is represented by a stone; and as a person in direct communication with the ancestors, he is greatly admired by all Warao.

The *wisiratu* shaman has three melodically and textually differentiated sections to his curing-song cycle. These respectively function to release and communicate with the helping spirits that reside within his chest, to name the illness-causing essence, and to communicate with the spirit essence after it has been removed and before it is blown off into the cosmos.

The first of these musical sections, characterized by masking of the voice, has the narrowest melodic range, consisting of two or three notes based on the terminating interval (cadence) of a minor third (such as fourth, minor third, tonic). This section of his curing song is accompanied throughout by the *hebu mataro*, which is at times vigorously shaken as a means to punish the illness-causing *hebu*. The second is the naming section, in which the shaman seeks out the illness-causing spirit within the patient. It does not include masking of the voice, and in it the rattle is only minimally played. Guided by the patient's symptoms, the *wisiratu* names animate and inanimate objects from the Warao physical, vegetable, or cosmic world—objects that he suspects are causing the illness. The naming section is characterized by the widest melodic range, again based on the terminating interval of a minor third (such as fifth, fourth, minor third, tonic). In the naming excerpt transcribed in Figure 23.4, the shaman begins by establishing rapport with his patient as he sings, "My friend, my friend, my friend, my friend, you are sad; my friend, you are sad." The third section of the *wisiratu* curing-song cycle, when the shaman communicates with the illness-causing spirit, is an unmasked, high-pitched, one-note recitation.

Figure 23.4
A naming section of a *wisiratu* shamanistic curing-song cycle. Transcription by Dale A. Olsen.

The **bahanarotu** shaman

The *bahanarotu* shaman cures gastrointestinal and gynecological illnesses caused by the intrusion of essences of material objects (believed to be the material objects themselves) that living or ancestral malevolent *bahanarotu* shamans have placed into a victim via magical arrows. He is the ritual specialist pertaining to *hokonemu*, the misty, easternmost part of the Warao cosmos and the tobacco-smoke home of Mawari, the supreme *bahana* bird.

Like the *wisiratu*, the *bahanarotu* sings musical sections that differ melodically and functionally. The first, in which the shaman communicates and releases his helping spirits from his chest, is characterized by masking of the voice, and has a narrow range that emphasizes major-second and minor-third terminating intervals in about equal proportion. This is followed by a second section, similar to the first except that the voice is not masked, and the function includes dialogues with helping and malevolent spirits. When the *bahanarotu* finishes the second part of his ritual, he begins to suck on the patient's body where the illness is believed to be located, removing the illness-causing material object. Accompanied by noisy slurps and gagging sounds, the shaman produces a saliva-covered object from his mouth, such as a thorn, a nail, or a piece of rope. This, he says, was causing the illness. If the *bahanarotu* shaman does not detect and remove an object, or if the removal causes no relief, he will continue singing a third section, in which he names what he believes to be the illness-causing object itself and its supernatural cause. This third part, the naming section, which has the widest melodic range of his curing ritual and melodically resembles the naming section of *wisiratu* curing, is used only when an object has been placed within the patient via the magical arrows of the supernatural *bahana* wizards living in *hokonemu*. The curing wizard names as many objects as he can, until the patient's body begins to vibrate, when he once again applies suction to extract the pathogen.

The **hoarotu** shaman

The third type of Warao shaman, the *hoarotu*, sings in his attempt to cure deadly diarrheal or hemorrhagic illnesses, believed to be caused by the supreme deity of the western part of the Warao cosmos. [Listen to "Warao male *hoarotu* shaman's curing song"] This cosmic place where the sun dies is the abode of Hoebo (symbolically represented by a scarlet macaw) and his accomplices, the living-dead *hoarotu* shamans of eternity. Hoebo and his court, who feast on human flesh and drink human blood from human bones, must be fed by living *hoarotu* shamans. Through dreams, a living *hoarotu* receives a message to provide food for his supernatural leaders, which he accomplishes through inflicting songs ("sung" mentally) for killing other Warao (Olsen 1996), especially children. (Warao cite this practice in explanation of high infant mortality among them.) This inflicting genre employs an ascending two-note melody based on a major second (sung aloud only when being taught to an apprentice) in which the shaman names the essences that he will place into his victim.

Living *hoarao* (plural form) are called upon by the families of the patients to cure what are believed to be *hoa* illnesses. Through performing a curing ritual characterized by singing a descending naming melody similar to those employed by the *wisiratu* and *bahanarotu* shamans, but with different words and spiritual intent, a *hoarotu* tries to effect a cure; masking the voice does not occur. Inspired by the symptoms of the patient, a curing *hoarotu* names anything he can think of, from any aspect of the Warao tangible or intangible, mortal or immortal world. Many Warao die, it is said, because of the nearly impossible task of naming the correct intruding spiritual essence that is causing the *hoa* illness.

The power of music can be used malevolently. Only the *hoarotu* shaman, however, inflicts illness—and even death—through song. This genre employs an ascending two-note melody, in which the shaman names the essences he will place into his victim.

Other uses of music in healing, inflicting, and protecting

A fourth kind of affliction among the Warao requires musical healing, though the healer need not be a shaman. This is a physical and often external ailment of the body, such as a wound from a knife or a hatchet, the sting of a bee or a scorpion, the bite of a snake, a bruise, an internal problem during childbirth, an abscessed tooth, and others. These ailments are believed to be caused by supernatural powers possessing the objects or animals and causing them to harm the Warao. A cure is effected by knowing the proper prayerful song (*hoa*), sung directly to the body or the object or animal that inflicted the condition, and by blowing tobacco smoke over the patient.

Another kind of *hoa* serves for magical protection against supernaturally altered animals and ogres (Olsen 1996). These songs rely on the power of naming the danger, and on the melodic aspect of the song itself. The following musical text is for protection from a transformed *mera* ("lizard") about which the singer said: "The *mera* comes transformed to eat us. This isn't from here, but is in the jungle. It comes to hunt us and to kill us. This *hoa* is good for saving yourself, when you leave for the jungle":

> You are arriving.
> You were born in the earth.
> This is your movement; this is your name.
> You were born in the earth.
> You are a small lizard of the earth, a little lizard of the jungle.
> This is your movement, and this is your name.
> Go away from me.
> Make your path, because the world is large.
> This is your movement, small lizard of the jungle, little lizard of the earth.

Like other Warao songs for controlling the supernatural, these have their own individual melodic patterns.

A supernatural charm, the *mare-hoa*, is employed for enticing a woman to love a man: the man names all the parts of a woman's body, causing her to find him irresistible. Another kind of *hoa* is sung during the ritual for felling a large tree from which men make a canoe: a shaman's song in which the man has supernatural intercourse with the tree, the mythical mother of the forest.

Songs of utility

Another common Warao context for music is utility, including lullabies and songs for working and traveling in the jungle, often with drum accompaniment.

Figure 23.5
A *dakoho* song about a stingray (*húe*). Transcription by Lawrence J. App.

Lullabies are sung by men and women, and often have texts that teach older children about Warao life and beliefs, including the dangers of ogres and animals. "Go to sleep, little child, or the jaguar-ogre which has no bones will think you are a deer and eat you" is a common theme. The educative aspect of the lullabies is an important form of Warao enculturation.

Work-related songs once had an entertainment context. Known as *dakoho*, they are dance songs whose dance context is obsolete. They are more commonly sung to ease the work of men and women, to accompany the paddling of canoes, to augment drinking, or just for relaxing around the house. The excerpt transcribed as Figure 23.5 is of an old *dakoho* about the stingray (*húe*), which can be seen in rivers during high tide. Most of its text contains vocables, such as the words *yanera, lanera, kwanera,* and *da-na-na-na-na*. It is a happy song, originally meant for dancing.

Unlike theurgical songs and the other songs of utility, most work-related songs have Western melodic traits. Many of them can effectively be accompanied with standard tonic, dominant, and subdominant harmonies, though the most common practice is to sing them unaccompanied. They are occasionally played on the *seke-seke*, or less often accompanied on the *wandora*. When and how this aspect of acculturation occurred is unknown. *Dakoho* from the 1930s and 1940s notated by the Spanish missionary Basilio María de Barral (1964:253–574) display more traditional traits than those I collected in the 1970s.

When the Warao walk through the forest to get to the *morichal* to find large *cachicamo* trees, to visit neighboring villages not easily accessible by canoe, or to gather food, they sing songs. Led by a male player of the *ehuru* drum, the songs keep the group together and help maintain the walking pace.

PERFORMERS AND PERFORMANCES

Most Warao musicians are adults, though children, because of the constancy and closeness of family and village contact, learn all kinds of songs informally from adults. Occasionally children will sing *hoa* prayers to themselves to ease their pain from cuts, stings, or bruises. Likewise, dance songs and popular Venezuelan songs are a part of some children's musical repertoire, especially those who attend Roman Catholic mission schools in the delta.

Though women have been shamans, most singers of theurgical songs are men. The older the male adult, the more likely he knows the important theurgical songs, whether he is a shaman or some other leader of his village. Because Warao male elders are highly respected as leaders of families, knowledge of the songs increases the opportunity to sing them.

All Warao men must have a role within their society. Without a social position—as shaman, maker of baskets or canoes, keeper of the *isimoi*, and so forth—men would have no place to go with their wives after death except to the western part of the cosmos, the place of eternal death. And nearly all Warao roles, from shaman to artisan, include songs of power.

The underlying structure of Warao theurgical music is not an aesthetic one. It is based on the proper knowledge of the melodic formulas determined by context, and on the ability to choose words that will effectively communicate with the proper supernatural entities for accomplishing the appropriate tasks. This lack of aesthetic concern is typical of lullabies and other secular songs. The Warao sometimes, however, comment that someone is a good singer of *dakoho*—a reference to knowledge and ability. Other than the knowledge of *dakoho* or Venezuelan popular songs, there is no musical creolization or miscegenation between the Warao and African- or Spanish-derived Venezuelans—a factor caused by the Warao's physical isolation.

FURTHER STUDY

Recent books about the Warao are by Dale A. Olsen (1996), which explores the role of Warao music as power and pleasure, and by Johannes Wilbert (1993, 1996), which studies Warao cosmology, including some uses of music. Additionally, Charles L. Briggs (1993, 1996) has studied several areas of Warao music, including ritual wailing and healing.

REFERENCES

Barral, P. Basilio María de. 1964. *Los Indios Guaraúnos y su Cancionero*. Madrid: Consejo Superior de Investigaciones Científicas, Departamento de Misionología Española.

Briggs, Charles L. 1993. "Personal Sentiments and Polyphonic Voices in Warao Women's Ritual Wailing: Music and Poetics in a Critical and Collective Discourse." *American Anthropologist* 95(4):929–957.

———. 1996. "The Meaning of Nonsense, the Poetics of Embodiment, and the Production of Power in Warao Healing." In *The Performance of Healing*, eds. Carol Laderman and Marina Roseman, 185–232. New York: Routledge.

Furst, Peter T. 1965. "West Mexico, the Caribbean and Northern South America." *Antropológica* 14:1–37.

Girard, Sharon. 1997. Review of Music of the Warao of Venezuela: Song People of the Rain Forest, by Dale A. Olsen. *Latin American Music Review* 18(2):331–337.

Greenberg, Joseph H. 1987. *Language in the Americas*. Stanford: Stanford University Press.

Olsen, Dale A. 1996. *Music of the Warao of Venezuela. The Song People of the Rain Forest*. Gainesville: University Press of Florida. Book and compact disc.

Turrado Moreno, A. 1945. *Etnografía de los Indios Guaraúnos*. Interamerican Conference on Agriculture III. Cuadernos Verdes 15. Caracas: Lithografía y Tipografía Vargas.

Wilbert, Johannes. 1993. *Mystic Endowment: Religious Ethnography of the Warao Indians*. Cambridge, Mass.: Harvard University Press.

———. 1996. *Mindful of Famine: Religious Climatology of the Warao Indians*. Cambridge, Mass.: Harvard University Press.

Brazil: Central and Southern Areas

Suzel Ana Reily

The European Heritage
The Emergence of Central and Southern Brazilian Music
Musical Instruments
Music Genres and Contexts of Central and Southern Brazil
Music in Migrant Communities
Learning, Dissemination, and Public Policy
Further Study

The music of central and southern Brazil is as diverse as the one hundred million people that populate the area. Gross topological contrasts occur throughout the rural areas of central and southern Brazil, which cover about 2,224,000 square kilometers, and an equally wide range of musical activities occur in such urban centers as Rio de Janeiro and São Paulo. These and other cities provide opportunities for hearing many kinds of Brazilian musics, including Brazilian popular music genres that have become known all over the world; traditional southeastern rural genres of medieval origin and their later developments; a wide variety of Afro-Brazilian traditions; northeastern traditional genres, brought by migrants searching for a better life in the south; and the musical traditions of the immigrant groups (Chinese, Germans, Italians, Japanese, Middle Easterners, Poles, Spaniards, and so on) that came to Brazil from the early 1800s on and particularly after 1888, when slavery was abolished in the country [see MUSIC OF IMMIGRANT GROUPS]. Concerts of Western art music are given regularly, and outlets of mass communication bombard the Brazilian public with the latest popular hits from abroad.

There are further distinctions between the musical preferences of different Brazilian social classes, ages, religious communities, professional categories, and even political parties. In effect, musical activities and preferences have become markers of identity for the social groups that make up Brazilian society.

The settling of Brazil began in 1500 when Pedro Alvares Cabral (who was appointed commander by Dom Manuel I, king of Portugal) and his fleet of thirteen ships, carrying a combined crew of 1,200 men, arrived accidentally to the east coast of South America from Lisbon, Portugal. They thought they were following Vasco de Gama's route around Africa's Cape of Good Hope on their way to India. However, they saw land in the west and went to explore what later came to be called Brazil. The late 1400s and early 1500s were a time of exploration for the Portuguese as well as for the Spanish and other Europeans.

Little is known of the music of central and southern Brazil before the area's first encounter with Portuguese explorers on 22 April 1500, and information is also scant regarding the first three hundred years after that. During the colonial period, documents detail the musical activities of the major Roman Catholic cathedrals and the parlors of the upper classes, but data about musical life outside these domains are sparse. Some information is available in writings left by such travelers as Jean de Léry, who lived in Brazil from 1557 to 1558 and produced the first known transcriptions of native American music: two chants of the Tupinambá near Rio de Janeiro (Léry 1980:150, 162). From his description of a "savage ritual" it is clear that, like other Europeans, he was shocked by the rattles and flutes made from human skulls and bones. Other early documents on colonial musical life appear in the journals and graphic representations of such travelers as Theodor de Bry, Pero Vaz de Caminha, Gabriel Soares de Sousa, Hans Staden, and others.

The European settlement of Brazil was undertaken as a joint venture between Portugal and the Roman Catholic Church; with the sword came the cross. The Portuguese were allotted the landmass east of the demarcation set in the Treaty of Tordesillas in 1494, which included a large section of present-day Brazil. The colonization of the area combined economic, political, and religious objectives. Despite the Christianizing model of colonization, the Roman Catholic Church in Brazil was weak, and its weakness had important implications for colonial musical life: without ecclesiastical subsidies, musical performance—even for religious rituals—became almost exclusively the prerogative of lay people.

Since 1179, when the Portuguese crusade against the Moors began, the Portuguese crown had been on good terms with Rome, and a series of papal bulls had granted the king concessions over Portuguese religious institutions, rendering the church in Brazil subservient to the state. Though in the first years of colonization the goals of Portugal were seemingly congruent with those of the church, the crown's greater interest in gold than in souls had important consequences. About 250 years after the first encounter, Portugal had scarcely fulfilled its part of the bargain; there were but eight dioceses in the colony and only a few thousand priests to serve a population of 1.4 million freemen and others. Most of the priests were employed on northeastern plantations to administer the sacraments to owners and their families.

Central and southern Brazil were especially affected by the crown's neglect. Unlike the northeast, where sugarcane had started generating profits almost immediately after the arrival of the Portuguese, the southern areas had little economic importance to the metropolis. The land was settled by Portuguese subsistence farmers, who moved farther and farther into the hinterland, displacing the indigenous population. They formed small, scattered communities (*bairros*) of around ten to fifteen households, which helped one another with tasks that a single family could not complete. These circumstances led to the emergence of a peasant ethos, marked by nomadism, community solidarity, and an emphasis on personalized social interaction.

In these communities, Christian festivities were the primary sociable contexts. In the absence of priests, colonists developed devotional forms based on rituals brought from Portugal, many rooted in late medieval musical traditions. Households alternated in promoting popular religious festivities. It was up to the host of the festival (*festeiro*) to invite musicians to lead the ritual proceedings at his house. The only leadership roles in these communities were those of popular Christian traditions. In rural areas, in such traditions as the baptism of Saint John the Baptist, the Saint Gonçalo dance, and the *folia de reis* (see below), the legacy of the household forms of popular Christianity can still be observed.

The communal work party (*mutirão*) was another important venue for making music and socializing in rural communities. At the end of the day, the host offered the workers a meal, followed by the *cateretê* (also *catira*), a widely practiced double line dance. In some areas, musical traditions developed to amuse the workers while they worked. In the Paraíba Valley, which lies between the cities of Rio de Janeiro and São Paulo, the *mutirão* is still accompanied by sung riddles (*brão*) sustained throughout the day (Figure 24.1).

In southern Brazil, the church was far more active with the indigenous population than with the Portuguese. Jesuit missionaries, who arrived around 1550, were particularly fervent in their desire to convert the native Americans. By the late 1500s, more than five hundred Jesuits were in Brazil, baptizing and domesticating the Tupinambá, the Guaraní, the Botocudos, and other indigenous groups, and the Jesuit order played an important role in the history of Brazilian music.

Music was often included in morality plays (*autos*) that priests enacted for the natives,

Figure 24.1
Brão singers rest for a moment to introduce new clues to help other singers solve the riddle. Photo by Suzel Ana Reily, 1985.

and it is thought that even before the foundation of the Indian Theater of São Lourenço in Rio de Janeiro, there had been a native American theater in São Vicente. The first morality play believed to have been written in Brazil was the *Auto da Pregação Universal*, attributed to the missionaries José de Anchieta and Manoel da Nóbrega. It was first performed in Piratininga (now São Paulo) in 1567 before being taken to other coastal settlements.

The Jesuits were successful in acculturating Amerindians through music and musical instruction, particularly within the missions (called *reducciones* "reductions") they organized in the extreme southern parts of the country. By the mid-1600s, the Guaraní were not only playing European organs, harpsichords, woodwinds, and stringed instruments but masterfully manufacturing instruments (Preiss 1988). Native orchestras accompanied religious songs sung in Latin, Portuguese, and native languages. Their ability to perform European music became a major argument in a scholastic debate as to whether or not native Americans had souls.

Although cultural interchange within the missions was essentially unilateral, some musicologists have claimed that the *caٍ٢eterê* had a native origin (Andrade 1933:173). Anchieta (and later other Jesuits) supposedly used it during religious festivals held among the Tupinambá, though evidence of this is weak. The acculturation of the native Brazilian population seems to have been so effective that, at the level of the greater society, native American influence in almost all areas of life in Brazil is small. In the domain of musical expression, it may be limited to the preservation of a few indigenous terms, certain choreographic practices, and the occasional use of *maraca*-type rattles. In 1759, the Jesuits were expelled from Brazil, and the Amerindians they had domesticated were enslaved. An important era of musical life in Brazil came to an end, and Rome lost its only strong ally in the colony.

Near the end of the 1600s, lay brotherhoods (*irmandades*) began to appear in urban centers throughout the colony. These voluntary associations became the main colonial institutions linking church and society. They built churches and maintained charitable institutions. Their main public activities involved the celebration of patronal festivals. Thus, they became particularly important in promoting the musical life of the colony.

THE EMERGENCE OF CENTRAL AND SOUTHERN BRAZILIAN MUSIC

Among countries in Latin America, if not the world, Brazil is unique because it was an empire ruled by a European king. Portuguese influence was strong, and the royal blood line of Brazil's leadership lasted into the period after the country's independence. Several important eras can be distinguished during Brazil's long colonial period.

The gold era

The significance of the lay brotherhoods becomes particularly evident with the rise of what has been called the *barroco mineiro* ("baroque of Minas Gerais"). This phase of artistic development occurred as a consequence of *bandeiras*, expeditions led by Portuguese colonizers from the São Vicente Captaincy into the interior of the country searching for gold. The rugged frontiersmen who left São Vicente and São Paulo on expeditions usually returned only with natives, whom they kept for themselves or sold as slaves to prosperous local aristocrats. Though these expeditions did not bring immediate prosperity to the colonizers of the São Vicente Captaincy, they paid off in the long term.

In 1698, prospectors found gold in the Serra do Espinhaço, and, during the 1700s, the mines of Minas Gerais, Goiás, and Mato Grosso were producing 44 percent of the world's supply of gold. Gold attracted prospectors from all over the country and even from Europe. New communities grew up overnight, particularly around the major mining sites of Minas Gerais but also along the routes used for transporting the gold to the ports.

Figure 24.2
Typical rhythmic
sequence of a *cateretê*.

From about 1750 to about 1800, the concentration of wealth in gold-rush areas led to the development of an urban life-style in several of the important towns of Minas Gerais; unlike at any other moment in the colonial period, artistic activity in sculpture, painting, and music flourished. Though the music of the period, studied extensively by Francisco Curt Lange (1965, 1966), has been termed *barroco mineiro*, it is more closely associated with a preclassical homophonic style (like that of C. P. E. Bach and Franz Joseph Haydn), yet no single European musician stands out as the main influence on local composers. Many *mineiro* compositions involved a four-part mixed chorus with an orchestral accompaniment provided by two violins, a viola (or cellos), a bass, and two French horns, and occasionally oboes, flutes, and a harpsichord.

Between 1760 and 1800, nearly a thousand active musicians were associated with lay brotherhoods in Minas Gerais, primarily concentrated in Vila Rica (now Ouro Preto), Sabará, Mariana, Arraial de Tejuco (now Diamantina), São João del Rei, and São José del Rei (now Tiradentes). Many were free mulattoes, trained in family-based musical establishments, who studied Latin, voice, and instruments, and learned to read and copy music and to set liturgical texts to melodic lines.

The most outstanding local composer of the period was José Joaquim Emérico Lobo de Mesquita (ca. 1740–1805), who composed more than three hundred pieces, of which about forty have survived. Other important composers were Marcos Coelho Netto (d. 1823), Francisco Gomes da Rocha (d. 1808), and Ignacio Parreiras Neves (ca. 1730–1793). By 1820, the gold in the mines was becoming exhausted, and the golden era of Brazilian music was declining.

The coffee era

The gold-rush developments were followed by a boom in coffee, and the establishment of coffee plantations (*fazendas*) affected musical practices. In the early 1800s, coffee had become popular in Europe and the Americas. Coffee plants could be cultivated profitably in the soil of the Paraíba Valley, an area soon taken over by large landholdings, modeled on the northeastern plantation system. Around 1860, coffee moved westward to the areas around Campinas and into Ribeirão Preto. By 1900, the state of São Paulo was producing nearly 75 percent of the world's supply. In the mid-1940s, northern Paraná became the locus of the new boom. Today, as coffee takes over the scrub lands of central Minas Gerais, fortunes are still being made.

Figure 24.3
Toada paulista, a rural
traditional genre,
showing a typical
cadential pattern
using parallel thirds.
Transcription by Suzel
Ana Reily.

As coffee made its westward march, rural communities were absorbed as sharecroppers into the plantation life-style. The coffee economy brought vast numbers of African slaves and their descendants, mostly of Bantu origin [see AFRO-BRAZILIAN TRADITIONS], plus European and other immigrant groups. The musical traditions of these social groups existed side by side, but in time they began to borrow from one another.

As in other rural communities, sociability on plantations centered on Christian festivities. On special saints' days, landowners provided a hefty meal and entertainment for their workers. At these festivals, the landholding elites congregated in the parlor of the plantation house for European-style dancing in couples; sharecroppers participated in the *cateretê* in the front patio of the house; and slaves amused themselves in *batuques* near the slave quarters (*senzalas*). In the *batuque*, individual dancers entered a circle to perform acrobatic steps to other participants' singing, clapping, and percussive accompaniment. The soloist ended his or her performance with a belly bump (*umbigada*) against someone in the circle, transferring the role of soloist to that person.

batuque
Afro-Brazilian round dance of Angolese or Congolese origin

As the population increased, patronal festivals became common in towns throughout the coffee-producing areas. The hosts (*festeiros*) of these festivals were mostly large landholders. To confront labor shortages, they competed with one another to produce ever grander festivals, demonstrating their benevolence toward their workers. As the festivals became more and more elaborate new musical styles emerged to enhance them. Many communities founded brass bands, derived from the European military-band tradition, to lead their processions, and various Afro-Brazilian dramatic traditions of dance and music emerged, amalgamating Portuguese and African musical and ritual practices.

These ensembles still perform for patronal festivals throughout central and southern Brazil. In many rural communities, the patronal festival is the most important event of the calendar, bringing crowds of people to the streets, where they are bombarded with sounds, music, dancing, smells, and visual stimuli.

Musical life in Rio

Outside the mining areas, the only other colonial town of significant size in southern Brazil was Rio de Janeiro, where musical life centered on the monastery of São Bento and the cathedral of Saint Sebastian. In 1763, Rio became the capital of the colony, and throughout the 1800s it was Brazil's cultural center. The new musical trends and fashions that emerged in Rio radiated to other parts of the country. Thus, Rio set the tone for the country's art music and urban popular music.

Rio was the birthplace of Domingos Caldas Barbosa (1739–1800), the first known composer of *lundus* and *modinhas* whose texts are extant. His songs scandalized the Portuguese court because their manner of addressing women in the audience struck the court as being indecently direct (Tinhorão 1990:92–93). Gregório de Matos Guerra of Bahia (1623–1695) may already have written and sung *lundus* and *modinhas*, but none of his works has survived.

lundu
Early Brazilian song type derived from Afro-Brazilian folk dance
modinha
Brazilian sentimental song genre, originating in late colonial period

The *lundu* and the *modinha* developed in the early 1700s, competing for the distinction of being the first "truly Brazilian" musical form. The *lundu* made its way into upper-class parlors from the *batuque* circles, but the *modinha* evinces influences from Italian opera. The *lundu* is faster, and deals with comical and satirical themes. The *modinha* is more melodic, and incarnates the Brazilian romantic spirit, appropriate for serenades. Even essentially art music composers such as the famous mulatto chapel master José Maurício Nunes Garcia (1767–1830), Francisco Manoel da Silva (b. 1812), and Carlos Gomes made their contributions to the repertoire, exemplifying how fluid the dividing line between Brazilian popular music and art music has been.

In 1808, to escape the Napoleonic threat, the Portuguese court moved to Rio. Though the king, Dom João VI, remained in the colony only thirteen years, his presence gave new vitality to musical life in the capital. A patron of the arts, he stimulated musical activity, and Garcia, one of Brazil's most renowned priest-composers, soon found himself in the monarch's favor, much to the annoyance of the former court-based composer Marcos Portugal (1762–1830), who had also followed the king to the colony.

When Dom João returned to Portugal, he left the kingdom in the hands of his son, Dom Pedro I, who declared its independence in 1822. Though Dom Pedro was himself a composer (having received instruction from José Maurício, Marcos Portugal, and Sigmund Neukomm), he lacked his father's commitment to the arts, and cut state patronage to local musicians. In 1831 when he abdicated, the musical activities of the Brazilian imperial chapel had practically come to a standstill, with only twenty-seven musicians still under imperial patronage.

In 1840, his successor, Dom Pedro II, assumed the throne, and musical life in Rio was revitalized. This was due to the efforts of Francisco Manoel da Silva (1795–1865), the master composer of the imperial chapel, whose most famous work is the current Brazilian national anthem. In Rio in 1847, Da Silva founded the Music Conservatory, which he directed until his death. In 1860, the National Lyric Opera was founded; its first production was *A Noite de São João* by Elias Alvares Lôbo (1834–1901), who based his libretto on poems by the Indianist writer José de Alencar. It was also through the National Lyric Opera that Brazilian audiences were introduced to Carlos Gomes (1836–1896), Brazil's most successful composer of operas. In his most celebrated pieces, *Il Guarany* and *Lo Schiavo*, he drew on the romantic image of the native Brazilian—which made him especially popular in Europe. Reminiscences of native Brazilian motifs and popular Brazilian urban genres were present in his music.

The arrival of the Portuguese court had other important implications for colonial musical activities. With the entourage came the first pianos, which families with sufficient means soon acquired. By 1834, pianos were being constructed in Brazil, and the piano remains an important status symbol for the upper classes. By 1834, Brazilian publishers were editing the music of the latest European dances (country dances, polkas, quadrilles, schottisches, waltzes, and others), which amateurs throughout the country played with enthusiasm. Popular composers, such as Chiquinha Gonzaga (1847–1935) and Ernesto Nazaré (1863–1933) Brazilianized these dances, providing the country's amateur pianists with a locally flavored repertoire. The influence of the *modinha* could be observed in the waltz, while the fusion of the polka with the *lundu* provided the matrix for the Brazilian *tango* and the *maxixe*, an early form of the *samba*.

While the upper classes gathered around their parlor pianos, Rio's bohemians were playing the same repertoire in the streets on *violões* (guitars) and *cavaquinhos* (small, four-stringed, guitarlike instruments similar to ukuleles, with metal strings). During the 1870s, a standardized ensemble evolved, consisting of an ebony flute (which played the melody), a *cavaquinho* (for the harmony), and a *violão* (guitar, which provided a bass). The musicians who played in this manner became known as *chorões*. Many early *chorões* were employed in military bands, which became important venues of musical instruction for those who could not afford private piano tuition. Near the end of the century, other band-derived wind instruments (such as the flute, the ophicleide, the clarinet, and the saxophone) would often play the melody. The repertoire became progressively faster and required greater virtuosity. It eventually evolved into a distinct musical genre, the *choro* (also *chorinho*).

Even in the late 1990s, the masterpieces of such popular composers as Pixinguinha, Zequinha de Abreu, Anacleto de Medeiros, and others were still being played and recorded, though *choros* were performed by larger ensembles, including tambourines and other percussion instruments. Small stringed instruments came to be used as melodic instruments.

violão
(Portuguese, "guitar") The common Iberian six-stringed guitar
choro
Afro-Brazilian musical genre based on polka-maxixe rhythm

MUSICAL INSTRUMENTS

Numerous musical instruments are used during central and southern Brazilian social events; rhythmic percussion instruments are used in ensembles, while melodic instruments are played solo or in ensembles. The former include a great variety of idiophones and membranophones; the latter include aerophones, many influenced by use in military bands, and chordophones derived from colonial times. Only the most common musical instruments are included here.

Idiophones

The idiophones of central and southern Brazil are mostly small percussion instruments used to give timbral diversity to various ensembles. The *ganzá* (also *guaiá*, cylindrical shaker), *melê* (also *afoxé* and *cabaça*, friction rattle), *rêco-rêco* (spring or bamboo scraper), and triangle are used in many different settings in urban and rural contexts. The double bell (*agogô*) is used exclusively in Afro-Brazilian urban traditions such as Candomblé (an Afro-Brazilian possession cult) and the Carnaval (Carnival) associations known as *samba* schools (*escolas de samba*). Knee-tied bells (*paiás*) are unique to certain rural Afro-Brazilian dances, especially the *moçambique* of the Paraíba Valley. Large cymbals are an integral part of the percussion section of town bands.

Membranophones

Membranophones of various shapes and sizes are common throughout central and southern Brazil. Like idiophones, some are used in numerous traditions; others are only found in specific contexts. The tambourine (*pandeiro*, often known as *adufo* in some rural areas), and the *caixa* (a medium-sized double-headed drum, with or without snare) (Figure 24.4)

Figure 24.4
A man plays a *caixa* ("box," a snare drum) for a *folia de reis* in Batatais, São Paulo. Photo by Suzel Ana Reily, 1988.

are the most versatile membranophones in the area, found in such diverse traditions as *samba* ensembles, *choros*, and popular Roman Catholic rural traditions of Portuguese or African influence.

Afro-Brazilian traditions, which use several drums of different sizes, often have distinct names for the different membranophones. In the popular traditions of Roman Catholic dramatic music and dance, the three most commonly found are a small drum (*repico*), a medium-size drum (*caixa*), and a large drum (*bumbo*). Two drums are used in the *jongo*: the larger *tambu* and the smaller *condonqueiro*. A friction drum (*puíta*) is also used. *Baterias*, the percussion ensembles of *samba* schools, may have any number of *tamborim* (small, single-headed frame drum; Figure 24.5), *caixa*, *repique* (also *repinique*) (medium-size single-headed drum), *atabaque* (large narrow single-headed conical drum), *cuíca* (single-headed friction drum), and *surdo* (large double-headed bass drum). In these traditions, each drum type is characterized by its own basic rhythmic pattern, often in a polymetric relation to the other parts.

Aerophones

DISC ❶ TRACK 15

One of the most popular aerophones in Brazil is the accordion. Throughout the country, it is known as *sanfona*, but in the extreme south, it is called *gaita*. [Listen to "Forró de sanfona"] The *sanfona* was introduced into the country by German immigrants in the early 1800s, but became popular with the population at large only after 1870. In southern Brazil, it is commonly associated with the *fandango*, a social dance; in southeastern and central Brazil, it often accompanies the *quadrilha*, danced during festivities in honor of Saint John the Baptist.

Figure 24.5
The *tamborim* ("frame-drum") section in a *samba* school in São Paulo. Photo by Suzel Ana Reily, 1982.

Military bands have left their legacy throughout central and southern Brazil, and many small towns maintain bands that perform for patronal and civic festivities. The wind instruments used in these ensembles often include flutes, clarinets, alto and tenor saxophones, cornets, trombones, saxhorns, tubas (*bombardinos*), and sousaphones (*baixos*). Their repertoire consists primarily of *dobrados* (marches in 2/4 time), appropriate for processions. Flutes, clarinets, and saxophones also serve as melodic instruments in *chorinhos*.

In many percussive ensembles of African influence, the leader uses a whistle to cue stops and transitions.

Chordophones

The most common stringed instruments in the area include the *viola* (a guitar with five single or double courses of strings), the *violão* (the ordinary Portuguese term for guitar), the *cavaquinho* (a small, four-stringed guitarlike instrument similar to the ukulele, with metal or nylon strings), the *bandolim* (a small mandolinlike instrument with four double courses of strings), and the *rabeca* (folk-derived violin, the term reflecting the European word *rebec*).

The *viola*, the Brazilian descendant of the Spanish *vihuela*, is the most important instrument of central and southern Brazil, and it exists in a variety of types. A form of the instrument found in Mato Grosso do Sul is known as a *viola de cocho* ("trough guitar"). The body of the instrument is dug out of a single trunk of soft wood and is covered with a thin layer of wood. Some instruments have a few small sound holes, but others have none. The *viola de cocho* has five single courses of strings, made of animal gut or fishing line. It produces a deep, hollow sound, more percussive than harmonic.

In southeastern Brazil, the most common *viola* is the *viola caipira* ("country guitar"). It is smaller than a guitar, and has five double courses of metal strings. In contrast with the *viola de cocho*, it has a full, metallic timbre. It can be tuned in many ways, the most common being the *cebolão* ("big onion") and the *rio abaixo* ("downriver"; Figure 24.6). These tunings make the viola especially adequate for doubling the singers' parallel thirds. Quite often, other four-stringed instruments are tuned like the *viola* by eliminating the lowest string. Currently, the *viola dinâmica* (Figure 24.7) is gaining popularity. Though larger than a *viola caipira*, it can be tuned in the same way, and it produces a louder sound.

A *violeiro* (*viola* player) must be competent to play in a tonality other than the one in which the instrument has been tuned. *Música sertaneja* (the Brazilian equivalent of North American country music) is accompanied by a *viola* and a *violão*, an instrumental configuration that has come to be known as *o casal* ("the couple"). Since the 1960s, however, the *violão* has been taking the place of the *viola*, since it is considered more modern and versatile.

Though the *viola* is the quintessential instrument of the Brazilian lower classes, the *violão* epitomizes the popular musical traditions of the upper and middle classes. It was celebrated in many pieces by Heitor Villa-Lobos, and it was the primary instrument of the *bossa nova* movement. Nonetheless, it is used in popular Roman Catholic traditions in rural areas, just as it is included in *samba* styles of the urban underprivileged. The *choro* musician (*chorão*) Horondino Silva created a seven-stringed guitar (*violão-sete-cordas*) to give him a wider range for his bass notes. The instrument continues to be used for *choros*.

The *cavaquinho* is primarily an urban instrument, used to accompany *choros* and *samba*. The *bandolim* is also used in the *choro* tradition, often as a melody instrument.

Figure 24. 6
Viola tunings: a, *cebolão*;
b, *rio abaixo*.

Figure 24.7
A man plays a *viola dinâmica* in Monsenhor Paulo, Minas Gerais. Photo by Suzel Ana Reily, 1988.

The *rabeca*, however, is fundamentally a rural instrument, played primarily during popular Christian festivities.

MUSICAL CONTEXTS AND GENRES

Contemporary musical traditions in central and southern Brazil resonate with the processes of interaction of the social groups in the area. Although Portuguese material has been substantially reinvented over the centuries, the strong sense of solidarity that had united peasant communities prior to the invasion of coffee culture has guaranteed the persistence of a marked Lusitanian-Hispanic legacy in the area. Iberian stylistic traits include arched melodies, conjunct melodic movement, parallel thirds and sixths, tonality, stanza-refrain alternation or strophic form, and the extensive use of stringed instruments.

Secular music in rural contexts

Many contemporary musical traditions associated with blacks and mulattos evince the influence of the *batuque*. These traditions often involve responsorial singing, syncopated rhythms (irregular accentuation and anticipation), and the extensive use of percussive accompaniment organized around an eight-pulse timeline.

In the process of acculturation or mestization, unique musical styles developed, reflecting the amalgamation of European and African musical practices. Many African traditions incorporated parallel thirds, functional harmony, and stringed instruments of European origin; likewise, the eight-pulse timeline became ubiquitous in the traditions of the Portuguese peasantry, as in the typical rhythmic sequence of the *cateretê* (Figure 24.2).

Some forms (*embolada*, *moda-de-viola*, *xácara*, and others) have fixed texts, but many genres—particularly those involving musical duels, including the *cururu paulista* and the *porfia* of the extreme south, known as *cantoria* in the northeast—involve textual improvisation within the form of the Iberian quatrain. [Listen to "É bonito cantar"] In these genres, two singers take turns improvising versified insults about each other until one is declared the winner. The texts of the *jongo*, the *brão*, and other riddle-based genres are also improvised, and the exposition of the enigmas and the quest for their answers involve song, as seen in the following example of a *jongo* improvisation. After a quatrain for the enigma, it has a quatrain for the answer.

DISC ❶ TRACK 13

Debaixo de papai velho,	Under old father,
Menino tá sepurtado.	Boy is buried.
Quero contar no meu ponto:	I want to tell you in my verse:
Menino foi interrado.	Boy was interred.

Meu irmão, sendo mais velho,	My brother, being older,
Licença peço pr'ocê.	I ask you to excuse me.
Vou desinterrar o menino	I'll now exhume the boy
Pra nós tudo aqui beber.	So all of us here can drink.

The "old father" is the *tambu*, the largest drum used in the *jongo*; the "boy" is a bottle of cane spirits. To protect the singer's knowledge from others' envy, he has hidden the drink under his instrument (Borges Ribeiro 1984:38).

In many popular Roman Catholic traditions of Brazil, competence in improvising verses is fundamental to ritual leadership. More than in other domains of performance competence, this ability is viewed as evidence of the leader's gift. Though age is a determining factor, criteria based on musical competence are important in constructing the internal hierarchies common to most popular Roman Catholic musical ensembles.

Some genres are sung solo (the *cururu paulista* and improvisations in the *carangueijo*) and others are sung collectively (processional prayers and refrains between improvisations in the *carangueijo*), but a common configuration throughout central and southern Brazil is that of the *dupla*, singing in parallel thirds or sixths. Its *modas* and *toadas* ("melodic sequences" and tunes) often encapsulate narrations related to rural social and religious life and traditional values.

One of the most typical features of rural traditional music is the consistent use of parallel thirds. The main voice is in the higher register, considered the more salient. Yet for the last chord of each verse, the first voice takes the mediant (the third note of a scale), while the second takes the tonic (the first note of a scale), rendering the first voice tonally subordinate to the second (Figure 24.3). The two voices are perceived as a unity; when one is not present, people feel something is missing. This kind of vocal construction can be viewed as a way of reconciling notions about the equality of the participants with the hierarchical aspects of vocal organization. Rendering the role of the first voice ambiguous causes its dominance to become structurally muted, and the two voices conjoin to form a complementary unit. Far from being merely an aesthetic preference, parallel thirds have probably been stable because they provide a sonic means of reconciling the asymmetry of social relations with notions of human equality—a fundamental issue of the Roman Catholic and socially oriented ethos of rural Brazil.

Only in the extreme south did the stereotype of the cowboy (*gaúcho*), androcentric and individualist, so influence the formation of the Lusitanian-Brazilian personality that parallel thirds and other polyphonic traits are less prevalent. There, male solos are far more common, and groups are more likely to sing in unison (Mendoza de Arce 1981). Distinctively, the southern Brazilian states have received the musical legacy of waves of European immigrants, particularly Germans, who, in isolated communities, maintain their language and musical traditions.

Music within popular Roman Catholicism

Musical activities in rural areas are associated with religious events, and many popular rituals still take place with little or no ecclesiastical intervention. Many saints who have become the objects of popular devotion in Brazil—the Virgin Mary, Saint John the Baptist,

Figure 24.8
Women of Atibaia, a suburb of São Paulo, dance with Saint Gonçalo. Photo by Suzel Ana Reily, 1983.

Saint Sebastian, and many others—are depicted with all-too-human traits, and quite frequently they are fun-loving musicians and dancers. Devotion to these saints typically involves making merry, eating heavily, performing music, and dancing.

The Saint Gonçalo dance

Saint Gonçalo of Amarante (flourished about 1250), patron of *violeiros*, is invariably depicted with a *viola*. It is said that every Saturday night he would take his instrument to the brothels of Amarante, Portugal, rounding up prostitutes, with whom he played and danced, tiring them so much that on Sunday they would not sin.

For this reason, the saint is honored through the Saint Gonçalo dance, a double line dance similar to the *cateretê*, involving rhythmic clapping and stamping. It is usually performed on a Saturday night in someone's yard to fulfill a promise made to the saint in return for a miracle, often a miraculous cure involving a person's legs. People with promises often dance holding the saint's image (Figure 24.8). An entire social network assumes the responsibility of an individual's obligations toward the saint by attending the dance and participating in the activity. In this way, the institution of the promise and the actual event are as means of promoting social solidarity (Brandão 1981).

Folias de reis

The biblical Magi became musicians, according to stories told by people who participate in mummerlike ensembles known as *folias de reis* ("the kings' *folias*"). In Brazilian folklore, the wise men received their instruments—a *viola*, an *adufo*, a *caixa*—from the Virgin Mary; they returned to the east, singing from house to house to announce the birth of Jesus. [Listen to "Folia de Reis"] Acting out this story, the *folia de reis* members go from house to house during the twelve days of Christmas, collecting donations to promote a festival on Epiphany (6 January), celebrated in Latin America as the day of the three kings (Figure 24.9).

DISC❶TRACK 11

The tunes (*toadas*) used by *folias de reis* often involve an accumulation of voices (usually six), leading to a loud and prolonged major chord. The voices make successive entrances, each entrance tonally higher than the previous one; with each entrance, the texture becomes denser. Thus, the structure of the music reflects the ritual role of these ensembles: it is a sonic representation of the accumulation of donations, which, once collected, allows the community to stage its festival (Reily 1994b:13).

Ternos

In central and southern Brazil, ensembles of dramatic music and dance known as *caboclinhos*, *caiapós*, *congadas*, *moçambiques*, and others are collectively called *ternos*. They often perform in the streets during patronal festivals. They are usually dedicated to the Virgin Mary in her capacity as Our Lady of the Rosary and to Saint Benedict the Moor (d. 1589), but they may come out for festivals in honor of other saints. [Listen to "Moçambique"]

DISC ❶ TRACK 12

Their typical choreography consists of a symbolic battle—between Christians and Moors, or Africans and slavers, or Indians and Portuguese—enacted through dialogues (*embaixadas*) and various uses of batons (Figure 24.10). Symbolically, good (or the oppressed group) prevails over evil (or the oppressing group), thanks to the honored saint's intervention.

Figure 24.9
A *folia de reis* collects donations for the Festival of the Three Kings in Monsenhor Paulo, Minas Gerais. Photo by Suzel Ana Reily, 1988.

At large festivals, several *ternos*—some local, and others from neighboring municipalities—roam the streets. Each ensemble has unique uniforms and a unique combination of colors, and all the ensembles compete with one another, beating their instruments as loudly as possible.

In some areas, people distinguish between the music and the choreography of each type of *terno*. In the Paraíba Valley, *congadas* do not use batons and knee-tied bells, because these are associated with the poorer *moçambiques*. In other areas, *moçambiques* do not perform *embaixadas*, though both ensembles battle with batons.

Ternos are voluntary associations, but membership tends to be almost exclusively male; women may participate as bearers of banners (*porta-bandeiras*), leading the procession of musicians and dancers. The ensembles perform in two parallel lines, in which the leaders stay behind the instruments, in front of the dancers (*soldados* "soldiers"). The dancers are organized in pairs according to their ages, with elders in front.

The musical performances of these ensembles begin with a slow *toada* sung in parallel thirds by the captain (*capitão*) and his helper (*ajudante*), immediately answered by the responder (*resposta*) and his helper (also *ajudante*). After this introduction, the first singers break into a faster *toada*, which, once presented, is repeated by the responder and his helper before the dancers behind them take it up (Figure 24.11). Once the singing is under way, the captain blows his whistle, and the dancers begin to strike their batons in choreographed routines.

Figure 24.10
Moçambiques dance at the Festival of the Divine Holy Spirit (Pentecost) in São Luís do Paraitinga, São Paulo. Photo by Suzel Ana Reily, 1982.

Figure 24.11
A *toada de moçambique* performed at the Festival of the Divine Holy Spirit (Pentecost) in São Luís do Paraitinga, São Paulo. Transcription by Suzel Ana Reily.

The parallel thirds and the harmonic accompaniment of the *toada* in Figure 24.11 are signs of European input, but several of its features show African influence. Note the eight-pulse timeline underlying several parts, particularly the melody and those of the bass drum, the knee-tied bell, and the sticks. The other parts are in polyrhythmic relations to the timeline. Musical associations such as *congadas* and *moçambiques* may be Brazilian analogs to the tradition of secret societies brought to the New World by the slaves from the Kingdom of the Congo (Kazadi wa Mukuna 1979).

Secular music in urban contexts

At the turn of the twentieth century, musical activities in the urban centers of central and southern Brazil were clearly defined along class lines: the elites congregated in enclosed spaces (parlors, concert halls, ballrooms) to participate in events involving European and national art music and dancing in couples; the middle classes were associated with *chorões,* which performed in the street, though in respectable places; and the lower classes, who were restricted to the hills overlooking Rio and poor peripheral neighborhoods, were recreating musical forms that had developed in *batuque* circles during the slave era. By the 1930s, however, *samba* had become a national phenomenon, cutting across these class-drawn barriers.

Samba

Samba is the best known of Brazil's musical expressive forms. Almost an international synonym for Brazilian music, it has become something of an umbrella term to designate a range of popular styles, including *samba carnavalesca* (Carnaval *samba*), *samba-enredo* (theme *samba*), *samba baiana* (Bahian *samba*), *samba-lenço* (handkerchief *samba*), *samba rural* (rural *samba*), *samba de morro* (hill *samba*), *samba da cidade* (city *samba*), *samba de terreiro* (yard *samba*), *samba de breque* (break *samba*), *samba de partido-alto* (specialist *samba*), *samba corrido* (verse *samba*), *samba-canção* (song *samba*), *samba-choro* (choro *samba*), and many others. All these genres have elements that at some level can be traced to African origins, particularly to Bantu traditions organized in eight- and sixteen-pulse timelines.

These timelines generate some rhythmic patterns (*batucadas*) played by several instruments in the percussion ensembles (*baterias*) of the urban Carnaval associations known as *samba* schools (*escolas de samba*) (Figure 24.12). Note the eight-pulse cycle in the accents of the *caixa* and the *rêco-rêco*, and how the rhythmic patterns of the *agogô* and the *tamborim* are structured around a sixteen-pulse timeline. Other instruments such as the *surdo,* the *ganzá,* and the *cuíca,* are accented on offbeats creating a rich, polyrhythmic texture.

Brazilian musicologists argue about how and where the *samba* originated. Most concur that the word developed out of the Quimbundo (a Bantu language) term *semba*, which denotes the belly bump, one of the distinctive choreographic features of the *batuque*. According to Sílvio Romero (1954), the term was associated with a specific Bahian dance in the second half of the 1800s; Bahian ex-slaves then brought it to Rio de Janeiro, where it fused with such urban styles as the polka, the *habanera*, the *modinha*, and the *lundu*. Kazadi wa Mukuna (1979), however, argues that it may have developed on the coffee plantations of the Paraíba Valley before reaching the capital. Many rural forms of the *samba* are still danced throughout the coffee-producing areas, where they are known by various terms, such as *samba* rural and *samba-lenço*. In the contemporary forms of rural *samba*, the belly bump has been suppressed to make the dances more respectable. José Ramos Tinhorão (1986) argues that the *samba* was the product of a middle-class elaboration of Afro-Brazilian musical practices by professional musicians in Rio. It was then reappropriated in its more complex form by blacks and mulattos for their Carnaval parades.

Whatever the antecedents, *samba* first became associated with Carnaval in Rio de Janeiro. At Carnaval around 1900, mobile associations (*ranchos*, also *blocos*), made up of

Figure 24.12
A rhythmic pattern played by a *samba* school's percussion ensemble. Transcription by Suzel Ana Reily.

blacks, mulattoes, and unskilled white laborers danced down the streets to the rhythm of percussive instruments, singing responsorially to the short improvised verses of a leader. In Rio, this *samba* style became known as *samba baiana* or *samba carnavalesca*.

The new 2/4 rhythm proved particularly suitable for keeping unity in the movements of the mobile associations while allowing each dancer to move freely. By appearing to be more organized, these ensembles were less likely to attract official repression. Soon the *samba* became extremely popular among the lower-class inhabitants of Rio de Janeiro (*cariocas*), displacing practically all other musical genres. *Samba* and Carnaval would remain linked from then on, each lending its prestige to the other.

One afternoon in 1928, a group of *samba* musicians (*sambistas*) belonging to an association known as Deixa Falar (Let Them Speak) was rehearsing in a field in front of a teacher-training college. Inspired by this situation, they decided to call their own association a *samba* school (*escola de samba*). Thereafter, other Carnaval associations adopted the term, and *samba* schools began turning up in Rio neighborhoods.

Samba-enredo

During the 1930s, *samba* schools began presenting themes (*enredos*) in their parades, and these presentations soon led to the development of the *samba-enredo*, *samba* with a narrative text. Various uniformed dancers (*alas*) became clearly demarcated, each representing part of the story of the *samba-enredo*. Floats carrying *destaques* (people in special outfits placed on the floats) were added, also relating to the theme.

It did not take long for local politicians to perceive the political utility of the *samba* schools, for these were among the few associations capable of organizing the urban popular masses. In 1930, Getúlio Vargas came to power, and by 1937 he had instituted a nationalist regime, the new state (*estado novo*), modeled on Mussolini's Italy. The Vargas government was quick to coopt Rio's *samba* schools, incorporating them into its nationalist project.

In 1934, Carnaval in Rio was made official, and only legally registered schools could receive public funds to help cover the costs of their exhibitions. By 1937, these groups had to develop themes that would stimulate nationalist feelings among the participants by glorifying patriotic symbols and national heroes. National glorification remained a dominant thematic trait of *samba*-school performances long after the Vargas era, which ended in 1954. In the mid-1960s, literary figures and Brazilian folklore became dominant themes.

With the onset of the 1980s, as the country faced redemocratization, many *samba* schools began to use the parades as a venue for addressing national issues, such as direct presidential elections, inflation, poverty, ecological devastation, discrimination against minorities, and other social and economic problems that afflict Brazil's people. One of the best examples of this change was "O Luxo e o Lixo" ("Luxury and Trash"), the 1989 theme developed by the producer (*carnavalesco*) Joãozinho 30 (whose surname is a number) for his *samba* school, Beija-Flor; it starkly depicted the inequalities of Brazilian society.

Hill *samba* and city *samba*

The distinction between hill *samba* and city *samba* emerged in the 1930s, when members of the ascending middle classes within urban contexts took to the new rhythm. Styles classed as *sambas* from the hills were those used by the lower classes that lived in shantytowns (*favelas*) overlooking the respectable neighborhoods. These included the various forms of Carnaval *samba* (*samba carnavalesca*, *samba baiana*, and *samba-enredo*), *samba de terreiro* (*sambas* played by *samba* school musicians outside the Carnaval period), *samba de partido-alto* (*sambas* in which prominent musicians improvised long verses between refrains), and *samba corrido* (a style of *samba* without refrains). City *sambas* catered to middle-class tastes; they emphasized melody and text, and their composers had better access to recording studios. Their dominant form was song *samba* (*samba-canção*), but *break samba* and *choro samba* were also included in this category.

The first recording of a *samba*, made in 1917, was of the composition "Pelo Telefone" ("By Telephone"). Only in the 1930s, when the radio was more widely diffused, did *samba* become a quasi-national phenomenon. With the popularization of the genre, the demand for it was no longer restricted to Carnaval, and composers of *sambas* responded by creating a new modality: *samba-canção*, *samba* for any time of the year. Performers and composers such as Ary Barroso, Noel Rosa, Araci Cortes, Carmen Miranda, Ataúlfo Alves, and many others could be heard year-round, all over the country.

As were the *samba* schools, the most popular musicians were quickly co-opted by the Vargas government, which contracted with them to perform on National Radio, a state agency. During this period, Ary Barroso composed the internationally famous *samba*

"Aquarela do Brasil" ("Watercolor of Brazil"). Grandiloquence became the trademark of the genre, as it exalted the country's greatness.

In the 1980s, a new form of *samba*, *samba de gafieira*, became popular in large urban centers. *Gafieiras* are large dance halls patronized by the urban working class, and *samba de gafieira* is the style of *samba* used in these establishments. In the early 1990s, the *samba* was fused with reggae to produce *samba-reggae*.

Bossa nova

After more than two decades of *samba-canção*, Brazilian audiences in the late 1950s welcomed the change brought by *bossa nova*. During the Vargas era, the country had undergone dramatic changes; as industry spearheaded the country's economic growth, rural bases of power had lost ground. Juscelino Kubitschek was elected president in 1955, espousing a platform encapsulated in the slogan Fifty Years in Five. He promised to lead the country in a developmental drive that in a single term of office would reduce its fifty-year lag in relation to the developed world. National pride was at a high, and the urban population was resolutely behind him.

In this era of national euphoria, the urban middle classes centered their preoccupations on making the most of the modern conveniences industrialization had brought them. By now, the lower and upper social classes of Rio had become spatially isolated from one another, and for the first time in Brazilian history, a new generation had grown up with only a superficial experience of interclass contact.

Youths who grew up within this context lived a carefree existence of sun, beaches, and romance, secure in their belief that Brazil was finally taking its place on the international scene. They were searching for a musical style that suited their self-image: it had to be simultaneously Brazilian and nonexotic, and it had to be able to speak of traditional guitars and Rolliflex cameras.

Furthermore, nightlife for Rio's upper classes had moved out of the large big-band halls to the intimate dark setting of nightclubs, and such establishments were proliferating in the city's affluent neighborhoods. The nightclub context called for a mellow musical style, which could promote the romantic intimacy young, dreamy-eyed couples were seeking.

Bossa nova answered all these requirements. While drawing on various traditions, the mellow sound of the guitar and the soft percussion highlighted their complex principles of rhythmic organization rather than their visceral qualities; the timid and quiet vocal style of *bossa nova* negated the stereotype of Brazilians as an overemotive, exuberant race to portray them as contemplative, intimate, and sophisticated.

The first recording of *bossa nova* was made in 1958. The song was "Chega de Saudade" ("No More Longing"), which united the heavyweights of the movement, epitomizing their individual contributions. Antônio Carlos Jobim (1927–1994) wrote the music, which had a modal feeling set against altered and compact chords; the lyrics, by Vinícius de Morães (1913–1980), had a colloquial ethos and were crafted to make full use of the timbre of each word in a manner reminiscent of the symbolist poets of the late 1800s. João Gilberto's (b. 1931) nasal, speechlike vocal style was ideally suited to *bossa-nova* aesthetics.

Gilberto's guitar technique attracted special attention: he slotted the chords between the syncopations of the melody, avoiding coincidences, a style that became known as the "stuttering guitar" (*violão gaga*). Gilberto derived the upper snaps of his beat from the rhythms of the *tamborim*, while the thumb reproduced the thump of the *surdo*. He produced chords with up to five tones by using the little finger of his right hand to pluck the highest string (Cabral n.d.:12).

Classics of the *bossa nova* repertoire, such as "Desafinado" ("Off Key," Antônio Carlos Jobim and Newton Mendonça), "Samba de Uma Nota Só" ("One-Note Samba," Jobim and Mendonça), "Garota de Ipanema" ("Girl from Ipanema," Jobim and Vinícius de Morães), "Insensatez" ("How Insensitive," Jobim and de Morães), "Corcovado" ("Quiet Night of Quiet Stars," Jobim), "Wave" (Jobim), and many others, became known internationally (Reily 1996).

Popular music after *bossa nova*

After *bossa nova*, Brazilian popular music (*música popular brasileira, MPB*) took many directions. The 1960s saw the rise of a protest movement in which musicians such as Carlos Lyra, Geraldo Vandré, Chico Buarque, and others somewhat naively proposed to use their music for raising the consciousness of the underprivileged masses.

Various local styles were reformulated within the *bossa-nova* framework, and musical texts moved away from love, sun, and beaches to depict the harshness of life, especially for poor people. Though too distant from the reality of the lower classes to have any effect on them, these songs did help incite intellectualized sectors of the upper classes, who began to organize in opposition to the military dictatorship. But the 1960s was the decade of the young guard (*jovem guarda*), a romantic and alienated movement, which helped set the foundations for Brazilian rock (*roque brasileiro*). Trying to place Brazilian popular music back onto its "evolutionary track" (an expression used by Caetano Veloso in an interview with Augusto de Campos [1986a:63] in 1966), the *tropicália* movement of the late 1960s depicted Brazilian society as an amalgam of diverse and contradictory elements. In text and music, *tropicália* exposed the contradictions of this diversity. But the movement was cut short with a new law, Institutional Act No. 5 (1968), which led to the imprisonment of Veloso and Gilberto Gil and their subsequent exile in London.

The 1970s saw a series of revivalist and locally oriented movements. With the recognition that the national repertoire was made up of more than *samba*, Brazilian popular music in the 1980s became particularly heterogeneous; it was the decade of the independents. Alongside Brazilian rock, the *mineiros*, led by Milton Nascimento, were reinventing their local styles; the nativist (*nativista*) festivals of Rio Grande do Sul were reviving the cowboy-derived traditions; and various reformalized northeastern tendencies found niches in the southern commercial recording market.

In the early 1990s, traditional southeastern genres were being stylized, reviving for urban audiences the *viola caipira* and its repertoire. *Pantanal*, a prime-time television soap opera (*novela*) set in an ecological reserve on the border between Brazil and Bolivia, provided a strong impulse in this direction by featuring Sérgio Reis, a leading figure of *música sertaneja*. Prime-time soaps are major setters of style in Brazil, influencing many domains of urban life-styles, including musical taste.

National anthem

Brazil declared its independence from Portuguese rule in 1822, and during the period between 1822 and 1890, the Empire of Brazil's national anthem was titled "Hino a Independência" (Hymn of Independence) and was composed by Dom Pedro I, the Emperor of Brazil and son of the King of Portugal. The lyrics (http://www.david.national-anthems. net/br-90.txt) were written by Evaristo Ferreira da Veiga, but the anthem was usually performed without words. When the bloodless *coup de etat* occurred in 1889 that brought about the Republic of Brazil, the national anthem was redone and attributed to composer Francisco Manoel da Silva. Its melody was adopted in 1890 and new words were added in 1909, selected from a song text competition. The anthem with its new words were officially adopted in 1922 during the Brazilian centennial of its independence.

MUSIC IN MIGRANT COMMUNITIES

During the 1930s, Brazil began developing its industrial focus, and with that development the country moved from an essentially rural society to an urban one. From the 1950s, more and more migrants from the rural areas flooded into the large urban complexes, particularly those of the southeast, bringing with them their rural values and musical heritages. In the late 1990s, 75 percent of Brazil's population lived in cities or towns. Greater São Paulo and greater Rio de Janeiro together are home to nearly 20 percent of all Brazilians.

Unskilled on arrival, most migrants have been forced into marginal markets. They eke out a hand-to-mouth existence in the shantytowns surrounding the major industrial centers. Even so, they claim they are better off in the city than they were in the country, for in the urban centers they have access to cultural and technological benefits that are not rurally available. In effect, the experience of migration is marked by the development of strategies that can reconcile traditional values based on personalized social relations with projects of social ascent within a greater context based on impersonalized relations, and these contradictory aspirations can only be partially fulfilled.

In such contexts, participation in musical activities based on traditional rural genres has played an important role in providing the migrants with a means of processing their experience and of constructing mutual support groups in new contexts. Urban *folias*, *ternos*, and other devotional ensembles attract fellow townsmen (*conterrâneos*), providing the structure around which they can reconstitute their towns of origin in the big city. Northeasterners unite around their *repentistas* (performers of northeastern musical duels), and they congregate in establishments where they can dance the *forró* (a northeastern couple dance). [Listen to "Forró do pife"] But it is in *música sertaneja* ("music from the *sertao*") that the best example of a migrant musical creation appears. It is the most popular genre among the migrant populations of greater São Paulo, and the industry catering to this audience is booming.

DISC ❶ TRACK 14

Country in the city

Traditional southeastern genres of *dupla*, particularly the *moda-de-viola*, became *música sertaneja* when they started to be recorded commercially in the late 1920s. The musicians for these recordings were recruited from itinerant professional performers active in the circuses that have roamed the countryside throughout the year since 1900. Though the performances took place under circus tents, the attractions they offered were mostly melodramatic plays and comedies. *Duplas* were performed before the play, between acts, and after the play. Since the 1980s, many circus owners have dispensed with the play altogether, offering only performances of *dupla* in their tents. The term *música sertaneja* became current only in the late 1950s, replacing the more pejorative term *música caipira* (*caipira* might best be glossed "hillbilly," though it officially refers to the inhabitants of the interior of the state of São Paulo). The change in nomenclature coincides with the formation of the migration chains moving from the interior of the country toward the southeastern industrial centers.

No doubt "modern" *música sertaneja* is far removed from its rural origins, as it has taken the direction of technological sophistication and full-scale production. Música sertaneja proper, however, is typified by duos such as Tião Carreiro and Pardinho and Pena Branca and Xavantinho, who have been able to derusticize traditional genres by using "correct" Portuguese and a more sophisticated vocabulary, while their sung narrations refer to themes related to the experience of migration.

Yet they have maintained some fundamental musical elements of the *caipira* aesthetic, such as continuous parallel thirds and the *viola* and *violão* accompaniment. Their performances pay attention to tuning, instrumental technique, and vocal simultaneity. The vocal timbre has lost some of its nasality without acquiring excessive vibrato. The music sounds like that of the *duplas caipiras*, but it has been cleaned up, so to speak. Furthermore, these duos are the ones most likely to be found performing in the circuses of the periphery, allowing the audience more personalized contact with them.

Through these elements, urban migrants have created a means of using music as a symbolic representation of those traits they feel they have acquired through migration and access to urban life. Just as the music has become more organized and "cleaner," so have those who participate in the performances; and inasmuch as the language in the verses has become more grammatical and sophisticated, it expresses the migrants' image of themselves as more cultured and better educated. The incorporation of these elements can thus be viewed as an attempt to create sound-based structures that represent the process of social ascent they view themselves undergoing or, at least, aspire to. By maintaining traditional elements associated with values that focus on the family and on personalized social relations, they are making a parallel statement that they have not been contaminated by the negative side of the metropolitan experience, the excessive individualism that breeds greed, selfishness, arrogance, and other antisocial traits.

Migrant musical creations stand as symbols of the possibility of reconciling urban economic mobility with a rural ethos of noncompetitive sociability. Through music, migrants have constructed a symbolic universe in which they have reconciled contradictory experiences of urban and rural life, creating a positive image of themselves. In the long term, this process may give them dignity and confidence enough to confront the society that marginalizes them.

Music learning and dissemination of its music began in Rio de Janeiro during the nineteenth century, and its greatest impetus was the movement in Brazil known as musical nationalism, whereby Brazilian composers worked to create a style representative of their large country.

Musical nationalism

By the late 1800s, musical nationalism had become a feature of Brazilian art music, particularly in the work of Joaquim Antônio da Silva Callado (1848–1880), Alexandre Levy (1864–1892), and Alberto Nepomuceno (1864–1920). These nationalists drew primarily on Rio's urban musical traditions: the *lundu*, the *modinha*, and the *choro*.

Without doubt, Heitor Villa-Lobos (1887–1959), a native of Rio, was Brazil's most talented and prolific nationalist composer. He composed numerous orchestral pieces including twelve symphonies, thirteen tone poems, twelve suites, and more than twenty concertos. He also composed seven operas, numerous chamber and choral pieces, and a vast repertoire for solo instruments, especially piano and guitar. As a youth, he played with *chorões*, and later he traveled around the country, acquainting himself with the national soundscape, drawing on this material in his compositions. Among his most celebrated works are a series of *Choros*, composed between 1920 and 1929; the *Bachianas Brasileiras*, composed between 1930 and 1945; and his piano music, particularly the *Lenda do Caboclo*, composed in 1920; and suites based on children's songs, *A Prole do Bebê*, No. 1 and No. 2, composed between 1918 and 1921.

The intellectual leader of Brazil's nationalist music movement was Mário de Andrade (1893–1945), born in São Paulo. In a book about Brazilian music (1964 [1928]), he called on Brazilian composers to participate in the construction of a national serious music tradition through the use of Brazilian expressive elements. Though he was himself not a composer, he used his literary work to introduce his project to Brazilian music circles. Much of his work (especially 1975, 1982, 1983) was dedicated to the collection and analysis of the national repertoire, which provided composers with raw material for their compositions. His research inspired other artists and intellectuals to collect the musical folklore of the country. Among these are Oneyda Alvarenga (1946, 1982), Alceu Maynard de Araújo (1964), Augusto Meyer (1958), Baptista Siqueira (1979), and others.

Musical nationalism remained a hallmark of Brazilian art music well into the twentieth century, spearheaded by Camargo Guarnieri (1907–1993). The only composers who openly rejected it were those associated with Música Viva, a movement that congregated around Hans-Joachim Koellreutter (b. 1915), a German Jew who fled to Brazil to escape Nazi persecution, bringing with him the techniques of dodecaphonic composition. Some exponents of Música Viva did try to produce nationalist twelve-tone music, most notably Cláudio Santoro (1919–1989) and César Guerra-Peixe (1914–1993).

Other compositional styles

It was not until the 1960s that Brazilian composers began to break away from the nationalist mold. Through organizations such as the New Music Group in Santos and São

Paulo, the Brazilian Society of Contemporary Music in Rio de Janeiro, and festivals of avant-garde music, Brazilian composers began to experiment with new compositional techniques—serialism, electronic music, aleatory procedures, atonality, and composition in mixed media. Major contemporary Brazilian composers active in central and southern Brazil include Gilberto Mendes (b. 1922), Willy Corrêa de Oliveira (b. 1938), Marlos Nobre (b. 1939), and Jorge Antunes (b. 1942).

FURTHER STUDY

Brazilian art music has received the attention of numerous scholars. General histories of it include Renato Almeida (1942), David Appleby (1983), Gerard Béhague (1979), Bruno Kiefer (1976), Vasco Mariz (1983a), and others. Other historical musicologists have focused on specific periods or important figures in Brazilian art music; these include José Maria Neves (1981), Vasco Mariz (1983b), and Bruno Kiefer (1986). Studies of the social history of Brazilian art music are contained in Léa Vinocur Freitag (1986), José Miguel Wisnik (1978, 1983), Enio Squeff (1983), and others.

Documentation of the rural musical traditions of central and southeastern Brazil abounds, but much of this research is purely descriptive. Since the early 1980s, anthropologically oriented studies have emerged, though scholars have tended to emphasize Amazonian and northeastern musical traditions. Studies of interest for central and southern Brazil include Carlos Rodrigues Brandão (1981, 1985), Suzel Ana Reily (1994a), Kilza Setti (1985) for central and southeastern Brazil and Daniel Mendoza de Arce (1981) and Richard Pinnell (1984) for the south of the country.

Special interest has been shown toward urban popular musics. Researchers in this sphere include Edgar de Alencar (1965), Augusto de Campos (1986b), Chris McGowan and Ricardo Pessanha (1991), Charles A. Perrone (1989), Claus Schreiner (1993), José Ramos Tinhorão (1981, 1986), Ary Vasconcelos (1977), Hermano Vianna (1995), and many others. More recently, scholars have been turning their attention to the musical traditions of rural migrants in the urban context. Northeastern musical traditions in São Paulo have been studied by Maria Ignez Novais Ayala (1988); southeastern genres have been studied by Waldenyr Caldas (1979), José de Souza Martins (1975), and Suzel Ana Reily (1992). Overviews of musical research and annotated bibliographies can be found in Gerard Béhague (1985, 1991), Charles A. Perrone (1986), and Suzel Ana Reily (1994a).

REFERENCES

Alencar, Edgar de. 1965. *O Carnaval Carioca através da Música*, 2nd ed. 2 vols. Rio de Janeiro: Freitas Bastos.
Almeida, Renato. 1942. *História da Música Brasileira*, 2nd ed. Rio de Janeiro: F. Briguiet.
Alvarenga, Oneyda. 1946. *Melodias Registradas por Meios Não-Mecânicos*. São Paulo: Departamento de Cultura.
———. 1982. *Música Popular Brasileira*, 2nd ed. São Paulo: Duas Cidades.
Andrade, Mário de. 1933. *Compêndio de História da Música*, 2nd ed. São Paulo: Miranda.
———. 1963. *Música, Doce Música*. São Paulo: Martins.
———. 1964 [1928]. *Ensaio sobre a Música Brasileira*, 2nd ed. São Paulo: Martins.

———. 1975. *Aspectos da Música Brasileira*, 2nd ed. São Paulo: Martins.

———. 1982. *Danças Dramáticas do Brasil*, 2nd ed. São Paulo: Martins.

———. 1983. *Música de Feitiçaria no Brasil*, 2nd ed. São Paulo: Martins.

Appleby, David P. 1983. *The Music of Brazil*. Austin: University of Texas Press.

Araújo, Alceu Maynard. 1964. *Folclore Nacional*. 3 vols. São Paulo: Melhoramentos.

Ayala, Maria Ignez Novais. 1988. *No Arranco do Grito: Aspectos da Cantoria Nordestina*. São Paulo: Atica.

Béhague, Gerard. 1979. *Music in Latin America: An Introduction*. Englewood Cliffs, N.J.: Prentice-Hall.

———. 1985. "Popular Music." In *Handbook of Latin American Popular Culture*, eds. Herald Hinds, Jr. and Charles Tatum, 3–38. Westport, Conn.: Greenwood Press.

———. 1991. "Reflections on the Ideological History of Latin American Ethnomusicology." In *Comparative Musicology and Anthropology of Music*, eds. Bruno Nettl and Philip Bohlman, 56–68. Chicago: University of Chicago Press.

Borges Ribeiro, Maria de Lourdes. 1984. *O Jongo*. Rio de Janeiro: FUNARTE.

Brandão, Carlos Rodrigues. 1981. *Sacerdotes da Viola*. Petrópolis, Brazil: Vozes.

———. 1985. *A Festa do Santo Preto*. Rio de Janeiro: FUNARTE.

Caldas, Waldenyr. 1979. *Acorde na Aurora: Música Sertaneja e Indústria Cultural*, 2nd ed. São Paulo: Nacional.

Campos, Augusto de. 1986a. "Boa Palavra sobre a Músic Popular." In *Balanço da Bossa e Outras Bossas*, 4th edition, ed. Augusto de Campos, 59–65. São Paulo: Perspectiva.

———, ed. 1986b. *Balanço da Bossa e Outras Bossas*, 4th ed. São Paulo: Perspectiva.

Cabral, Sérgio. N.d. "Em Busca da Perfeição." In *Songbook: Bossa Nova*, ed. Almir Chediak, 10–17. Rio de Janeiro: Luminar.

Freitag, Léa Vinocur. 1986. *Momentos de Música Brasileira*. São Paulo: Nobel.

Kazadi wa Mukuna. 1979. *Contribuição Bantu na Música Popular Brasileira*. São Paulo: Globo.

Kiefer, Bruno. 1976. *História da Música Brasileira*. Porto Alegre, Brazil: Movimento.

———. 1986. *Villa-Lobos e o Modernismo na Música Brasileira*. Porto Alegre, Brazil: Movimento.

Lange, Francisco Curt. 1965. "Os Compositores na Capitania Geral das Minas Gerais." *Revista de Estudos Históricos* 3–4:33–111.

———. 1966. *A Organização Musical durante o Período Colonial*. Coimbra, Brazil: Separata do Volume IV das Actas do V Coloquio Internacional de Estudos Luso-Brasileiros.

Léry, Jean de. 1980. *Viagem à Terra do Brasil*, trans. Sérgio Milliet. São Paulo: Universidade de São Paulo.

Mariz, Vasco. 1983a. *História da Música no Brasil*, 2nd ed. Rio de Janeiro: Civilização Brasileira.

———. 1983b. *Três Musicólogos Brasileiros: Mário de Andrade, Renato Almeida, Luiz Heitor Correa de Azavedo*. Rio de Janeiro: Civilização Brasileira.

Martins, José de Souza. 1975. "Música Sertaneja: A Dissimulação na Linguagem dos Humilhados." In *Capitalismo e Tradicionalismo*, ed. J. S. Martins, 103–161. São Paulo: Pioneira.

McGowan, Chris, and Ricardo Pessanha. 1991. *The Billboard Book of Brazilian Music*. New York: Billboard Books.

Mendoza de Arce, Daniel. 1981. "A Structural Approach to the Rural Society and Music of the Río de la Plata and Southern Brazil." *Latin American Music Review* 2(1):66–90.

Meyer, Augusto. 1958. *Cancioneiro Gaúcho*. Porto Alegre, Brazil: Globo.

Neves, José Maria. 1981. *Música Contemporânea Brasileira*. São Paulo: Ricordi.

Perrone, Charles A. 1986. "An Annotated Interdisciplinary Bibliography and Discography of Brazilian Popular Music." *Latin American Music Review* 7(2):302–340.

———. 1989. *Masters of Contemporary Brazilian Song: MPB 1965–1985*. Austin: University of Texas Press.

Pinnell, Richard. 1984. "The Guitarist-Singer of Pre-1900 Gaucho Literature." *Latin American Music Review* 5(2):243–262.

Preiss, Jorge Hirt. 1988. *A Música nas Missões Jesuíticas nos Séculos XVII e XVIII*. Porto Alegre, Brazil: Martins Livreiro-Editor.

Reily, Suzel Ana. 1992. "Música Sertaneja and Migrant identity: The Stylistic Development of a Brazilian Genre." *Popular Music* 11(3):337–358.

———. 1994a. "Macunaíma's Music: National Identity and Ethnomusicological Research in Brazil." In *Ethnicity and Identity: the Musical Construction of Place*, ed. Martin Stokes, 71–96. Oxford: Oxford University Press.

———. 1994b. "Musical Performance at a Brazilian Festival." *British Journal of Ethnomusicology* 3:1–34.

———. 1996. "Tom Jobim and the Bossa Nova Era." *Popular Music* 15(1):1–16.

Romero, Sílvio. 1954. *Cantos Populares do Brasil.* Rio de Janeiro: José Olympio.

Schreiner, Claus. 1993. *Música Brasileira: A History of Popular Music and the People of Brazil.* New York: Marion Boyars.

Setti, Kilza. 1985. *Ubatuba nos Cantos das Praias: Estudo do Caiçara Paulista e de sua Produção Musical.* São Paulo: Atica.

Siqueira, Baptista. 1979. *Modinhas do Passado*, 2nd ed. Rio de Janeiro: Folha Carioca.

Squeff, Enio. 1983. "Refexões sobre um mesmo Tema." In *O Nacional e o Popular na Cultura Brasileira: Música*, ed. Enio Squeff and José Miguel Wisnik, 13–127. São Paulo: Brasiliense.

Tinhorão, José Ramos. 1981. *Música Popular—Do Gramofone ao Rádio e TV.* São Paulo: Atica.

———. 1986. *Pequena História da Música Popular: Da Modinha a Canção de Protesto*, 5th ed. Petrópolis, Brazil: Vozes.

———. 1990. *História Social da Música Popular Brasileira.* Lisbon: Caminho da Música.

Vasconcelos, Ary. 1977. *Raízes da Música Popular Brasileira.* São Paulo: Martins.

Vianna, Hermano. 1995. *O Mistério do Samba.* Rio de Janeiro: Jorge Zahar.

Wisnik, José Miguel. 1978. *O Coro dos Contrários: A Música em Torno da Semana de 22.* São Paulo: Duas Cidades.

———. 1983. "Getúlio da Paixão Cearense (Villa-Lobos e o Estado Novo)." In *O Nacional e o Popular na Cultura Brasileira: Música*, eds. Enio Squeff and José Miguel Wisnik, 129–191. São Paulo: Brasiliense.

Afro-Brazilian Traditions

Gerard Béhague

Religious Musical Traditions
Secular Musical Traditions
Urban Popular Musical Traditions

Both nationally and around the world, Afro-Brazilian traditions most clearly identify the musics of Brazil. Afro-Brazilian traditions shape the unique character of the musics of Brazil as recognized at the national and international levels. These traditions must be viewed, however, in their specific historical and regional contexts in order for their true meanings to be understood. A multiplicity of black identities emerges from the ambiguity of ethnic self-identities and the complexities of Brazilian social stratification.

Although historically Afro-Brazilians have remained at the lowest of the social strata and discrimination continues at certain levels, Brazil has seen deep racial integration throughout the twentieth century. Official segregation never became a reality in the post-slavery period. All of this facilitated the true nationalization of certain originally Afro-Brazilian popular musical expressions.

The history of African cultural transfers to Brazil is imprecise and often confused. The aftermath of the abolition of slavery brought such an overwhelming sense of national shame on the part of some governmental officials that in 1891 the minister of finances, Rui Barbosa, ordered the destruction of a large amount of archival documents relating to slavery in the naïve hope that such negative aspects of national history would be forgotten. Our sources of knowledge of early Afro-Brazilian musical traditions, therefore, are primarily oral, written, and iconographic sources dating mainly from the 1800s and throughout the twentieth century (Almeida 1942).

Traditional Afro-Brazilian musical manifestations are centered essentially in three parts of the country: the northeastern and northern states of Alagoas, Bahia, Maranhão, Pará, Paraíba, Pernambuco, and Sergipe; the southeastern regions of Espírito Santo, Minas

Gerais, and Rio de Janeiro; and parts of São Paulo. As far south as Rio Grande do Sul, however, religious worship of African gods, as in the Batuque of Porto Alegre, survives. Moreover, significant aspects of Afro-Brazilian traditions are an integral part of some of the most significant genres of Brazilian popular music of the twentieth century.

Despite various racist policies at the beginning of the twentieth century (including advocacy of the cultural whitening of the black population), Brazil at the beginning of the twenty-first century retains the position of being the second-largest black country in the world, after Nigeria. This, however, does not make it an African or neo-African culture, despite the establishment of trade and cultural contacts with West Africa following the abolition of slavery (1888) and an official opening to Africa since the 1970s.

After a period of sociopolitical vindication since the late 1970s, and especially after the centenary of the Brazilian abolition of slavery, the position of black musicians in the national market of the late 1990s remained ambivalent. In Bahia, these musicians have come of age in terms of their own involvement, freedom in, and control over their activities. In other areas, their future is uncertain. In general, however, at the beginning of the twenty-first century, Afro-Brazilian musics command nationwide an unprecedented recognition and respect.

Brazilian racial democracy has remained a myth, yet the multicultural expressions of contemporary Afro-Brazilians are a reality. Indeed, Afro-Brazilian musical traditions cover a wide continuum—from traditional, Afro-related music integrated in religious systems inherited from Africa but developed independently, to obviously Iberian songs and dances also prevailing in nonblack Brazilian communities. This spectrum of musical expressions is not contradictory because it reflects the actual cultural experience and heritage of contemporary Afro-Brazilians (Tinhorão 1988). More than any other expressive means in numerous contexts, music in Brazil transcends social and ethnic boundaries. As some Afro-Brazilian musical traditions affect nonblack Brazilians, some Luso-Brazilian traditions are faithful expressions of Afro-Brazilians.

RELIGIOUS MUSICAL TRADITIONS

The stylistic continuity that can be observed in Afro-Brazilian religious music is most probably a case of cultural resistance during centuries of cultural confrontations—centuries that also involved cultural sharing. Afro-Brazilian religions present a complex configuration of dogmas and practices resulting from the local adaptation and transformation of systems of beliefs inherited from Africa and Europe, encapsulating the historical national experience.

The most nationally acknowledged popular religion, Umbanda, is found almost everywhere. Other religions, such as various types of Candomblé (Candomblé Gêge-Nagô, Congo-Angola, de Caboclo in Bahia and Sergipe, and Macumba in Rio de Janeiro), Xangô (Pernambuco) (Carvalho 1993), Tambor de Mina (Maranhão), Batuque (Pará), Pajelança (Amazonas), and others, are specific to certain regions. In varying degrees, they all recognize some aspects of the African Yoruba and Fon pantheon and the basic beliefs and practices of traditional African religions.

Animism, divination, initiation, ancestor worship, various kinds of offerings to the deities, ritual use of sacred plants, ritual music and dance, and specific social hierarchical organization prevail in all Afro-Brazilian religious communities. In Brazil, African religions underwent a great deal of transformation. On the one hand, Yoruba-Fon religions (of the *orixá/vodun* complex) exerted considerable influence on Bantu (Congo-Angola) religions; on the other hand, Roman Catholicism, imposed on slaves in Brazil, became integrated in varying degrees with African beliefs—which explains the so-called syncretism of Afro-Brazilian religions.

In the most traditional Candomblé religions of Brazil (Gêge-Nagô and Congo-Angola, in Bahia and Rio de Janeiro), syncretism is not so evident as it is in Candomblé de Caboclo, Macumba, Umbanda, and other religions, though African deities (*orixás* and *voduns*), usually have counterparts in Roman Catholic saints. Thus, the cult of *orixás* and *voduns* eventually became fused with that of *santos*, if only as a result of a historical accommodation, in which during the period of slavery, saints served to camouflage African deities.

Candomblé

In Candomblé, the center-leader, known as *babalorixá* or *pai de santo* (if a man) or *ialorixá* or *mãe de santo* (if a woman), assumes full responsibility in general liturgical matters and in the musical and choreographic training of the initiates and their subsequent position in the center. The ultimate authority in the knowledge of music and dance, he or she usually leads the performance of the proper sequence of songs. The religious leader also exercises power through the authority recognized and acknowledged by all. This power emanates primarily from ritual knowledge, including music and dance, in addition to the whole complex of esoteric knowledge of the precepts operating in the ceremonies. Among these, the most dramatic and richest is undoubtedly the cycle of initiation rites, representing the highest degree of participation in religious life. Initiates go through a severe education in ritual behavior, ritual language, music, and dance, all for serving their particular deity. In effect, this liturgical behavior results from a deep sociocultural conditioning, of which the performance of sacred songs and of specific dances represents an integral part. The relationship of music and spirit possession also results from this conditioning; that is, initiates are taught the meaning of certain songs within the mythology of their specific *orixá* and the corresponding expected behavorial response. It is therefore the association of such sacred ritual songs and corresponding accompanimental rhythms with their respective god that triggers the trance behavior, not necessarily fast and loud drumming as is usually believed. Initiation, the ultimate degree of participation in religion, consists in "placing the orixá in the candidate's head" (in local terminology, the *obrigação da cabeça*) so as to predict that deity's behavior when he or she takes possession of devotees. In actuality, spirit possession indicates the presence of the supernatural among humans (see Okada 1995: example 4). The possessed initiate is identified as the *orixá* himself or herself. Whether or not anyone should go through initiation is determined by the *ifá*, a divination game interpreted by the diviner (*babalaô*), frequently the same *pai* or *mãe de santo*.

The music of the Gêge-Nagô groups retains a strongly Yoruba style, both in the pentatonic and hexatonic melodic structures and in the rhythmic organization of the accompaniment. Overlapping responsorial singing prevails, the solo vocal lines performed in general by the cult leader, the master drummer, or less frequently by any of the official civil protectors of the group, known as *ogans*. The monophonic choral responses are provided by the initiates and any members of the congregation, male and female, who may wish to participate. The lyrics and most ritual speech of Gêge-Nagô groups are still in the Yoruba and Fon languages, though these languages are not spoken in Brazil as a rule, and few participants can give a word-for-word translation of the texts. This does not prevent them, however, from knowing the overall meaning and function of the songs. Portuguese dominates in Candomblé de Caboclo and Umbanda.

The extensive repertoires of song originate from the association of specific songs with each deity, with all private and public ceremonies, and within each ceremony with a rigorous sequence of ritual events. Each event or gesture has its corresponding songs. Thus, repertoires are classified according to their ritual functions: botanical songs, sacrificial songs, songs of offering, songs for calling the gods, songs for sending them away, and so on. The ritual power of musical sounds, combined with the liturgical significance of lyrics as components of myths, explains the length and complexity of Candomblé ritual songs.

The rhythmic structure of Candomblé music reveals a typically African sense of rhythm whereby regular motoric, unchangeable parts are contrasted with improvised parts. Ritual drumming occurs as an accompaniment to sung performances and in solos. Specific rhythmic patterns are associated with specific gods, such as *alujá* for Xangô (god of thunder and fire), *bravum* for Ogum (warrior deity and god of metal tools), *aguerê* for Oxossi (god of hunting), and *igbim* for Oxalá (god of creation). To each rhythm corresponds a given choreography associated with the specific god. The interlocking rhythmic organization common in traditional West African and Afro-Cuban religious music does not prevail in Brazil; however, the African type of hemiola is quite frequent. Cone-shaped, single-headed drums, known in Bahia as *atabaques*, are played in a battery of three sizes (Figure 25.1). The largest drum, *rum*, is played with a stick and a bare hand by the master drummer, who, by improvising, controls the ritual dance. The middle-sized drum (the *rumpi*) and the smallest drum (the *lê*), played with sticks in Gêge-Nagô music, perform standard, unchanging patterns. The double bell (*agogô*), played with a metal stick, completes the accompanying ensemble. As drums constitute a significant symbol of communication with the *orixás*, they go through a sort of baptism before they can be used in ritual contexts (Béhague 1975, 1977, 1984, 1988, 1992b). The sacred role of drummers (*alabês*) is recognized by means of a ceremony of confirmation. The drummers' primary function is to call gods (Figure 25.2), hence to bring about initiates' spirit possession (Figure 25.3), but drummers themselves never fall into trance while drumming.

Figure 25.1
Atabaque drums for Candomblé: from left, *lê, rumpi,* and *rum.* They are painted to match the colors of the main god of the Candomblé house. Salvador, Bahia, Brazil. Photo by Gerard Béhague, 1978.

Umbanda

Since the 1950s, Brazilian religious music has gained a greater following as a result of the countrywide popularity of Umbanda, the religion that combines Candomblé beliefs, popular Roman Catholicism, spiritualism, and Kardecism (a Brazilian spiritualist movement based on the writings of Allan Kardec). Umbanda music displays stylistic changes that illustrate how completely national values permeate strong regional and urban cultural settings. Indeed, Umbanda music caters to all segments of urban society, especially the lower middle class, by relying on a nationally omnipresent and familiar style, the folk-urban type of dance music most readily associated with the *samba*.

In contrast to traditional Candomblé religions, the repertoire of Umbanda music is in constant elaboration, albeit stylistically restricted. But this stylistic limitation appears the most effective in attracting worshippers from all social strata. In effect, Caboclo, Umbanda, and their expressive means (mostly music and dance) may be the most important factors contributing to the cultural and regional integration of Brazil in the last three decades of the twentieth century.

SECULAR MUSICAL TRADITIONS

The ancestry of secular traditions is not always easily established whenever the elements of a given musical genre and of specific sociocultural contexts of performance cannot be unequivocally related to an African derivation. Regardless of origin, one should consider traditions that are fully integrated in contemporary music making among self-defined Afro-Brazilian communities. Criteria of use, function, origin, and structure define the identification of traditions.

"Sacred" and "secular" are relative concepts, especially in Afro-Brazilian culture, in which songs and dances functioning outside a religious context frequently refer to sacred topics. As in Africa, religion sustains expressive culture in all its dimensions.

Capoeira

The game-dance known as *capoeira* is considered by some to have come from Angola, and by others to have been the creation of Brazilian blacks during slavery. Most probably, it is a local elaboration of some African model (Rego 1968). From a game fight believed to have been practiced by slaves during resting periods in the fields, it developed into a sort of martial art with subtle choreographic movements and rules—a well-defined musical repertoire of songs and accompanimental rhythms. It originated in Bahia but has extended to other major coastal cities, especially since the 1940s, and it became a main martial art taught in military schools. The traditional dance is known as *capoeira Angola*—a term that gives a linguistic justification to believers in the Angolese origin. [Listen to "Brincando na Roda"] The choreographic development involves a series of figures known as *golpes*, in which a swaying motion (*ginga*) is fundamental. Pairs of male dancer-fighters (*capoeiristas*) perform figures that include simulations of various motions of attack and defense (using the feet only), plus head-over-heels turns. The synchronization of movements between the attack of one dancer and the defense of the other (and vice versa) is remarkable (see Okada 1995: example 5; Fujii 1990: example 28-8).

Capoeira is accompanied by an ensemble (Figure 25.4) of musical bow (*berimbau de barriga*), tambourine (*pandeiro*), double bell, and at least one drum (*atabaque*), and the singing is responsorial. The main instrument, the *berimbau* has a calabash resonator and is played by a wooden stick with a basket rattle (*caxixi*) (Figure 25.5). By using a coin as a stopper on the string (like a movable bridge), the player of the *berimbau* can produce two distinct pitches (usually a second apart), but the simultaneous performance of several bows of different sizes allows multipart and harmonic textures. Specific rhythmic pat-terns (*toques*) include the *São Bento grande*, the *São Bento pequeno*, the *Iúna*, the *Santa María*, the *Angola*, and the *cavalaria*, with specific functions and references to the dance. They differ mostly in tempo, rather than in rhythmic structure.

Capoeira songs—some 139 have been collected—constitute a rich source of Afro-Bahian expressive culture relating to slavery, the local lingo, and poetics. Except for the "hymn of the *capoeira*" and litanies (*ladainhas*), the repertoire of *capoeira* songs borrows a great deal from other repertoires, such as children's game songs of the *ciranda*

Figure 25.4
A *capoeira* group. Salvador, Bahia, Brazil. Photo by Max Brandt, 1996.

Figure 25.5
A *berimbau* player with *caxixí*. Salvador, Bahia, Brazil. Photo by Gerard Béhague, 1985.

genre. Other songs, such as "Santa Maria, mãe de Deus" ("St. Mary, mother of God"), invoke religious themes and figures.

Traditionally, *capoeira* has been taught and practiced in academies (*academias*) led by masters (*mestres*). Among historically known masters, none has enjoyed as much fame as Mestre Bimba, who developed a new form, *capoeira regional*, adding a number of dance figures resembling some of the strokes of other martial arts (Pinto 1991).

Since the 1960s, the influence of tourism has resulted in the impoverishment of the *capoeira* tradition, in the performance of *golpes* and *toques* and the knowledge of songs. In addition, the popularity of *capoeira* abroad, primarily in Western Europe and the United States, has brought about fundamental changes in traditional performances.

Dramatic dances

Originating in missionaries' activities during the early colonization of the country, dramatic dances (*bailados*) have survived in contemporary Afro-Brazilian communities. These dances include processions and actual dramatic representation, with numerous characters, spoken dialogues, songs, and dances accompanied by small instrumental ensembles. The major themes of such dramatic dances relate to the Iberian medieval catechistic theater, including conversion, resurrection, and battle scenes between Christians and infidels (Moors). Among significant dramatic dances enacted by Afro-Brazilians are the *bumba-meu-boi*, *congada*, *congo*, *marujada*, and *taieira*, all known by many different local names.

Bumba-meu-boi

The *bumba-meu-boi*, perhaps the most popular of all folk dramas, is known and practiced in various styles in several regions of the country, north and south. It has its origins in the triethnic heritage, but its Afro-Brazilian elements are especially evident in the northeastern and northern states. The main character is the bull (*boi*), representing for some an African totemic survival. The dramatic action enacts regional variants of a legend concerning characters of the colonial period—the Portuguese master, the black slave (variously named Mateus or Francisco), his wife Catarina, the captain (*cavalo marinho*), and others. Fantastic figures and animals participate in the representation, but only human characters actually sing. According to Mário de Andrade (1982), the dance includes fixed and variable elements, the former consisting of the main characters' entrances and dances, the latter also involving the secondary characters. Most of the songs exhibit characteristic elements of *mestizo* folk music, including the style of cattle-herding songs known as *aboios*.

Documentation of the dance in Maranhão (Kazadi wa Mukuna 1994) reveals the presence of three distinct styles, the *boi de zabumba* (*zabumba* is a double-headed bass drum), the *boi de matraca* (*matraca* is a type of wooden rattle), and the *boi de orquestra* (mostly brass-band instruments). Of these, the first is considered to represent a truly Afro-Brazilian tradition, not only through its instrumentation (including, besides the *zabumba*, the friction drum [*tambor onça*] and other percussion instruments), but also its musical and choreographic structures. The criticism of the dominating characters, hence of the ruling class, evidenced in the comic scenes of the bull's death and resurrection, is seen as an important clue that the drama originated in slaves' culture.

Marujada

The *marujada* (from *marujo* "sailor") of the coastal area of the state of Bahia is performed entirely by black associations on specific feast days. It combines and celebrates Portuguese maritime feats and the confrontation of Christians and Moors. Performers representing Christians, dressed in Brazilian white navy uniforms, reenact episodes of exploration, including the hardship of life at sea, the battle with the Moors (dressed in red capes) and their imprisonment, the wounding and symbolic death of the leader of the Moors, and his eventual resurrection as a Christian, welcomed into his new community in a final scene. The performance includes choral numbers in a processional type of march by the sailors and several solo and duet numbers in scenes by naval officers and Moors. Some scenes are spoken, and others are sung. Each community has developed a traditional oral script for the dramatic scenes. Responsorial singing between officers and sailors is common, with the sailors accompanying themselves on small hand-held drums. The melodic structures of the tunes belong almost entirely to the tradition of Luso-Brazilian folk songs. To a great extent, the *marujada* illustrates pertinently the biethnicity of Afro-Bahians' cultural heritage, for its participants are Candomblé worshipers, who obviously see no contradiction in their biculturalism.

Social dances

Dance music of a predominantly Afro-Brazilian tradition includes a variety of genres and instrumental ensembles. Quite frequently, collective singing forms an integral part of such genres, so singing combines with dancing. The performance of this music occurs on numerous social occasions, from spontaneous, informal performances in party gatherings to formal contexts associated with cyclical celebrations of life.

The substantial Afro-Brazilian contribution to and influence on Brazilian folk dances in general is reflected not only in the larger number of specific Afro-Brazilian dances, but also in the Brazilianization—that is, Afro-Brazilianization—of European dances, an important aspect of Brazilian urban popular music. The most common traits of folkloric choreographic structure are circular formation, frequently with solo dancers, and the presence of *umbigada* (from Portuguese *umbigo* "navel"), the symbolic bumping of the couples' navels, signifying an invitation to the dance or challenge—and an indication that the dances originated in Africa.

Music and dance are inseparable—which explains why the name of a dance is applied to the music it accompanies. Among the dances of predominantly Brazilian blacks are the *batuque* and the *samba*, the *caxambu*, the *jongo*, the *côco*, the *baiano* (*baião*), and the former *lundu* and *sarambeque*, all with numerous regional names. Only a few can be considered here.

Batuque

A round dance given an Angolese or Congolese origin, the *batuque* is no longer performed as such, and the term has acquired the generic sense of black dance accompanied by singing and heavy percussion. However, in Rio Grande do Sul and Belém, Pará, *batuque* now designates Afro-Brazilian cults associated with different religious groups, and in São Paulo state, it is a specific dance of local Afro-Brazilian cults. The accompanying instruments of the latter include drums (*tambu*, *quinjengue*) and rattles (*matraca*, *guaiá*).

Samba

Many regional varieties of *samba* exist. As a folk dance, it was formerly important, but its importance has diminished in most regions of the country because of the popularity of some types of the urban *samba*. In the southern-central areas, the folk *samba* is known as *samba-lenço*, *samba de roda*, and *samba campineiro*. The choreographic arrangement of the *samba-lenço*—dancers with a kerchief (*lenço*) in their hand—resembles the old *batuque*, again in circular formation. With texts in the form of quatrains, the songs are performed in parallel thirds with snare drum and tambourine accompaniment. The songs are usually eight bars long, in duple meter with an anacrusis, and have a range of up to an octave, a descending motion with repeated notes, and isometric rhythm. The accompaniment exhibits typical Afro-Brazilian syncopation.

Mário de Andrade studied the *samba campineiro* of São Paulo (calling it Paulista rural *samba*) in 1937 and observed that *samba* was defined by its choreography rather than by its musical structure. The latter shows an arched melody in duple meter, syncopated rhythmic figuration, strophic and variable textual forms, and the relative importance of textual improvisation. The dance itself stresses collectivity—which explains the absence of the *umbigada*. Besides the instrumentalists (who also dance), the main participants are women. The *samba de roda* has lost its former importance in São Paulo, but in the northeast (especially in Bahia) it is still the most popular social dance. As a round dance involving soloists, it is usually performed responsorially with frequent overlapping between the vocal soloist and the choral response.

The Bahian *samba de viola* is a type of *samba de roda* from a choreographic standpoint, but *violas* (various sizes of guitars with five double-stringed courses as a rule) are the central instruments of the ensemble, completed by a *prato-e-faca* ("plate and knife"), a *pandeiro*, a triangle, an occasional *atabaque*, and hand clapping. The lyrics (*chulas*) set this *samba* apart from others in their extreme eclecticism in form and subject. In the 1980s and 1990s, the tradition of *samba de viola* lost its former importance and was known and performed by only a handful of older musicians (Waddey 1981).

Côco

The *côco* (coconut) is a dance of poorer people in northern and northeastern Brazil. Its name derives from the fact that the dance is commonly accompanied by clapping with hands cupped to create a low-pitched sound, like that of a coconut shell being broken. Sometimes a drum or a rattle may be used, in which case the dance is named after the instrument: *côco-de-ganzá* (shaker), *côco-de-mugonguê* (drum), and so on. In the northern states, different names refer to the type of song associated with the coconut, such as *côco-de-décima, côco-de-embolada,* and *côco-desafio* (Alvarenga 1982). The choreographic structure dictates the alternation of stanza and refrain in the song: a solo dancer in the middle of the circle improvises a stanza and is answered by the other dancers. A frequent feature of coconut-song melodies (also present in *côco-de-embolada*) is the peculiar rhythm of short durations (usually sixteenth notes in 2/4 time) repeated continually, resulting in exciting ostinatos.

Maculelê

The Afro-Bahian *maculelê*, another martial dance, is believed to have originated in the city of Santo Amaro in the 1890s in celebration of the abolition of slavery. Strongly reminiscent of black African stick-fighting dances, the *maculelê* is performed with sticks used as mock weapons and percussive instruments. Responsorial singing with drum accompaniment praises two figures as having been responsible for the abolition of slavery: Our Lady of Conception is the main religious one, and Princess Isabel de Bragança (1846–1921) is the historical one. The songs are in Portuguese with numerous African words in the choral refrains. Some of the dance figures resemble those of *capoeira*, but in no way can it be said that *maculelê* functions as a preparation for *capoeira* practice, since it has its own autonomous repertoire and performance contexts.

URBAN POPULAR MUSICAL TRADITIONS

Brazilian popular music owes much of its character and creativity to Afro-Brazilians (Béhague 1985). In the 1700s, the Afro-Brazilian dance known as *lundu* had already been assimilated by upper-class composers as an expression of the tropical colony, and it had influenced the *modinha*, a sentimental genre (opposed to the Portuguese *moda*) in its characteristic syncopated rhythmic accompaniment (Araújo 1953; Béhague 1968). In the 1800s, the black flutist-composer Joaquim Antônio da Silva Callado, professor of flute at the Imperial Conservatory, Rio de Janeiro, began to nationalize European dances (including the polka, the schottische, and the waltz) by incorporating into his compositions in these genres melodic and rhythmic patterns associated with the popular scene of Rio de Janeiro. Reinforced by the introduction in Brazil in the mid-1800s of the *habanera*, with its typical dotted rhythm (dotted eighth, sixteenth, and two eighth notes), the Brazilian *tango* emerged. In effect, the systematic application of subtle variants of the *habanera* pattern, and the frequency of occurrence of syncopation such as the sixteenth-eighth-sixteenth pattern in a duple meter, created the *maxixe*, at first the name only of a fast, syncopated style.

The semipopular composer Ernesto Nazareth wrote for the piano many polkas and tangos that are true *maxixes* from a rhythmic point of view.

Rio de Janeiro

Urban popular music in Brazil found its most important early cultivators in Rio de Janeiro, which became the capital of Brazil in 1763, replacing Salvador de Bahia, the first colonial capital of the country. The first Afro-Brazilian composer of note was José Maurício Nunes Garcia (or Padre José Maurício, as he is known in Brazil), a *mulatto* who became the chapel master of the Rio de Janeiro Cathedral in 1798 at the age of forty. When the word came that the Portuguese royal family was arriving, he began immediate preparations for a mass to celebrate their arrival. The royal family tradition of musical patronage was continued in Brazil with the establishment of the Royal Chapel in Rio de Janeiro in 1808. Padre José Maurício became the royal chapel master, until the arrival of several Portuguese composers a few years later, especially Marcos Portugal, who was named the royal chapel master in 1811. Padre José Maurício, however, had won favor from King João, and wrote many important works during that time. His output during this period has been estimated at about seventy compositions, including a number of urban popular songs in the *modinha* genre, a type of love song with nostalgic sentiment (*saudade*), unique to Brazil but influenced by the Portuguese *moda* and other European song lyrical song styles. Padre José Maurício's *modinhas* were among the first composed, and the genre had a great impact on later popular Brazilian music styles, such as the *choro* and *bossa nova*.

Chorões and the *choro*

In Rio between 1875 and 1900, popular instrumental ensembles of strolling street musician-serenaders known as weepers (*chorões*) appeared, performing dance music (*maxixes* and polkas) and arrangements of sentimental songs of the *modinha* type. This kind of ensemble, which came to be known as *choro*, typically included guitars (*violões*, sing. *violão*), a *cavaquinho* (small four-stringed guitar of Portuguese origin), a flute, a *pandeiro* (tambourine), and later a saxophone. While the ensemble's performance stressed improvisation and virtuosity, the musical genre *choro*, which developed after 1900, continued to use the same rhythmic foundation as *maxixes* and polkas. Many black popular musicians active during the period 1900–1930 became composers and performers of *choros*.

The urban *samba*

The urban *samba*, which came to epitomize Brazilian popular music in general, has been strongly identified with Afro-Brazilian expressive urban culture. The first commercially recorded *samba*, "Pelo Telefone" (1917), was the work of the black composer Donga (Ernesto dos Santos). Sinhô, called the King of Samba in the 1920s (Alencar 1968), and Caninha, both black musicians, contributed greatly to the popularity of the genre; but it was Pixinguinha (Alfredo da Rocha Viana), another black composer, who had the greatest influence. With his bands Os Oito Batutas (1922), Orquestra Típica Pixinguinha-

Donga (1928), and Grupo da Velha Guarda (1932), he popularized the urban *samba* among different social classes in the 1920s and 1930s (Alves 1968; Efegê 1978–1979).

In emphasizing a percussive ensemble and traditional responsorial singing, the so-called *samba* of the slums in the hills (*samba de morro*) maintained a closer identity with the folk *samba*. Out of this ensemble developed the *batucada* (percussion ensemble and percussive dance music) associated with the *samba* school (*escola de samba*), first organized as a Carnaval (Carnival) association in 1928. The music history of the *samba* school since then has been primarily associated with Afro-Brazilians as composers, arrangers, and performers (Alencar 1965). In addition to the *samba de morro*, other subgenres appeared from the 1920s to the 1940s, especially the *partido-alto* (a folklike dance of the primarily black connoisseurs) and the *samba de enredo* (*samba* with a story or plot), used by each group of *samba* schools.

In the 1970s and 1980s, the *samba* from Rio (*samba carioca*) regained vitality with the works of Martinho da Vila and others, especially the emergence of the *pagode*, as part of the complex world of Rio's slums (*favelas*). Some *pagode* pieces in the performance of Bezerra da Silva, such as "O Preto e o Branco" ("The Black and the White"), picture vividly the issues of racial relations and the deterioration of city life in the slums (Carvalho 1994).

Salvador de Bahia

The state of Bahia followed Rio in importance for the cultivation of urban popular music. As early as the mid-1930s, the Afro-Bahian Dorival Caymmi, through his fisherman or beach songs (*canções praieiras*) and his *sambas* (even before the advent of *bossa nova*), created an innovative style based on authentic, empathetic references to Afro-Bahian folklore and music. For several decades, his popularity throughout the country remained strong, perhaps because he was able to convey even to listeners alien to Bahia the essence of his cultural experience as a black Bahian worshiper of Candomblé and a cultivator of the most modern popular genres and styles. In addition, his lyrics, deeply rooted in the African linguistic and emotional tradition of his native state, represent a chief asset of his creativity (Risério 1993).

The innovations brought about in the *samba* tradition by *bossa nova* musicians beginning in the 1950s were the work of sophisticated musicians, primarily middle- and upper-class whites (Béhague 1973; Castro 1990). Some black performers, however, participated in the new trend, indicating their integration in the modern era of Brazilian popular music. In addition to Johnny Alf, Jair Rodrigues, Wilson Simonal, and especially the great guitarist of the 1960s, Baden Powell, *bossa nova*'s second generation of black musicians included the internationally successful composers Gilberto Gil and Milton Nascimento, who each used a variety of styles and subjects to express and transcend their ethnic identity (Béhague 1980; Perrone 1989).

The city of Salvador, Bahia, the traditional bastion of Afro-Brazilian artistic expressions, has become a significant locus of popular-music developments since the 1960s. Besides the avant-garde movement of *tropicália*, whose members were mostly Bahians, a new Carnaval music appeared in the 1970s and 1980s. The Afro-Bahian phenomena of *afoxé*, *carnaval ijexá*, and *bloco afro* had significant sociopolitical and economic repercussions at that time. The traditional music and culture of Candomblé played an important role as a creative source and force in the concept of black ethnicity in the 1970s and 1980s. The emergence of an African consciousness among young people of African descent represents a social and human history of great significance, in which traditional music has had a fundamental function in the movement of ethnic and political vindication. Local black and *mestizo* young people have contributed to the re-Africanization of Carnaval (Risério 1981; repeated by Crook 1993). The process of a new black-consciousness movement, though it has much to do with the ideology of negritude, was never based on the cultural incorporation of contemporary African elements; rather, it originated in a new interpretation and rendition of the most traditional elements of Afro-Bahian culture. It would appear more accurate, therefore, to refer to a re-Afro-Brazilianization within a new concern of validation of the contemporary black culture and the necessity of expressing a new ethnicity.

The revitalization in the 1970s of the Afro-Bahian Carnaval associations called *afoxés* gave the new black movement a starting point. *Afoxés* whose members were devotees of Candomblé represented the first attempts in Bahia to transfer to the street, during Carnaval, the aura of the mythical world. The name of the oldest *afoxé*, Filhos de Gandhi (Sons of Gandhi), paid homage to the great statesman a few months after his assassination (1948) and revealed the ideological affinity of the group with Gandhi's anticolonialism, philosophy of nonviolence, and activism against European domination. Traditionally, the music performed in the Carnaval parades of *afoxés* was actually Candomblé music, specifically *ijexá* songs and rhythms. Filhos de Gandhi developed its own music but retained the main stylistic features of *ijexá* music.

By extension, the new Carnaval of the 1970s and 1980s became known as *carnaval ijexá*, primarily to establish a direct relationship with some of the most essential aspects of black culture. In a general sense, however, the word *ijexá* implied at that time Afro-Bahian culture associated with Candomblé, in which the term designates a specific drum rhythm resembling that of a slow *samba*. Actually, several lyrics composed for *afoxés* call *ijexá* a rhythm, a style, and a dance.

Beginning in the mid-1970s, new Carnaval organizations called *blocos afro* began to appear. The first one, founded in 1974, bore the linguistically and politically significant name Ilê Aiyê (from Yoruba *ilê* "house, temple," and *aiyê* "real world" in Yoruba cosmovision and mythology as opposed to Yoruba *orum* "supernatural world"). At first, Ilê Aiyê barred white people's participation, and its compositions constantly mentioned the *aiyê* as the living, exciting, beautiful world of black people. The themes "black is beautiful" and "the living world is the black world" became part of the ideological manifesto of *blocos afro*. Reinforced by the appearance of the militant political group known as Movimento Negro Unificado (MNU), *blocos afro* took on the form of true activism in the 1980s. Their support of the MNU, however, was more a symbol of black identity and power than a direct political militancy. Their songs not only evoked the Afrocentricity of their origins, but also addressed the issues of racism and socioeconomic injustice. The creation of a new aesthetic involved the imitation and transformation of African and Afro-Caribbean models of music, dance, and dressing, known or imagined. The choice of instruments was limited at first

Figure 25.6
The *bloco afro* group Axé. Salvador, Bahia, Brazil. Photo by Max Brandt, 1996.

to drums—several *surdos* (low pitched), *repiques* (high pitched), and snare drums—and other percussion, supporting a responsorial vocal structure (Figure 25.6). In the beginning the basic rhythmic organization, known as the toque *afro-primitivo*, consisted of a slow-to-moderate-tempo *samba* in a rich and forceful percussive texture. *Bloco afro* songs referred to a variety of Afro-Brazilian and other Afro-diaspora subjects, always expressing the black world, its history, and its problems.

Bloco afro is to Bahia what *escola de samba* is to Rio de Janeiro, and Carnaval in Salvador da Bahia features only the former. In the mid 1980s Ilê Aiyê and other *bloco afro* groups began to incorporate electric guitars and keyboards into their musical peformances, a process of electronic modernization that was influencing many formerly acoustic ensembles in other parts of Latin America and the Caribbean. Another development, also common in Brazil's northeast (Recife and elsewhere), included the use of flatbed trucks upon which electric/acoustic groups perform as they are slowly pulled through the streets. In the northeast the *trio eléctrico* was developed, including electric bass and two guitars on the back of a pickup truck playing *frevos* and *maracatús rurais* (Amerindian-African-inspired music and dance that includes mock battles and partially improvised narrative songs with choral responses (Crook 1998:337). [Listen to "Boa noite todo povo"] In Salvador da Bahia, two-story high trucks carrying *bloco afros* were used during the 2005 Carnaval. These musical groups played to people down below or up in trees (Julie Hill, personal communication with Dale Olsen, 2007).

With the new *afoxés* and *blocos afro*, the direct relationship to Candomblé diminished considerably, since the young leaders were no longer Candomblé priests, the musicians not necessarily Candomblé drummers, and the songs no longer derived from liturgical repertoires. The members of the new groups, however, did not fail to recognize and adhere to some aspects of Candomblé traditions, as some members are Candomblé worshippers. Before celebrating an important festivity (such as Carnaval), people sometimes perform rituals of offering to the *orixás* in the name of the groups. Some Candomblé rhythms have occasionally been incorporated into *bloco afro*'s rhythmic section. In general, however,

DISC ❶ TRACK 16

whether or not they are close to the Afro-Bahian religions, leaders of *blocos afro* are aware of and in tune with Candomblé's traditional function as a center of cultural resistance and of social and ethnic identity.

Among the Afro groups that emerged in the 1980s (including Araketu, Badauê, Ebony, Malê Debalê, and Muzenza) the most successful *bloco afro* undoubtedly has been Olodum, founded in 1979 by former members of Ilê Aiyê. Musically innovative, Olodum had by the mid-1980s introduced different patterns into their fundamental *samba* beat. These patterns were reminiscent of Afro-Caribbean rhythms (*merengue, salsa*), but the influence of Jamaican reggae was so strong that the new patterns of drumming, having acquired the interlocking structure of Afro-Caribbean rhythms, became known as *samba-reggae* (Béhague 1992a). Cuban *timbales* joined the percussive group of Olodum. Ideologically, the reference to Jamaica created a sense of affinity and solidarity with the Bahian-black movement. Through reggae and Rastafarianism, Jamaican black culture had been recognized the world over, and Bob Marley and Jimmy Cliff were idols of Afro-Bahian youths. Eventually Olodum created its own Banda Reggae, which toured extensively. The success of Olodum's sociopolitical program—schools, shelters, and jobs for street children, a variety of community services—was due to the vision and determination of various leaders of the group, and to the inevitable selling out to the music industry. Though its first commercial success was local, its international popularity, translated into multimillion-dollar activity in a few years, has tarnished the ideological grounding of its beginnings, since Olodum is now viewed as another style of worldbeat.

In Bahia, *samba-reggae* was so successful that in the late 1980s several popular commercial bands, especially Banda Mel and Reflexu's, jumped at the opportunity to flood the pop market with synthesized renditions of the style. Among Afro-Bahian composers who specialized in the new genre has been Edson Gomes, one of the best representatives of resistance reggae (*reggae resistência*). Bahian mass-mediated popular music ended up establishing a trend called *axé* music (from Yoruba *axé*, denoting the vital spiritual force of Candomblé and everything and everyone associated with it)—an obvious misnomer, as this music has little or none of the Afro-Bahian religion's spirituality. The justification actually comes from the fact that this is music of Salvador, Bahia, often labeled the African city of Brazil, or the African Rome of the Americas, and, as such, its music needs to be qualified as African. *Axé* music, as in the works and interpretations of such figures as Margareth Menezes and Daniela Mercury, combines a variety of Afro-Bahian styles, *ijexá afoxé, bloco afro samba, samba-reggae*, and even occasionally *lambada* and *fricote*, all with heavily electrified accompaniment. As opposed to *bloco afro*, however, *axé* music has penetrated into the national pop market and, with the support of the multinational music industry, has resulted in a worldwide craze.

Another development that capitalized on *bloco afro*'s success was the early 1990s *timbalada*, so called because it involved an instrumentation in which the timbre of the *timbal* is the focus, provided with a plastic head and special tunings, in trying to approximate the percussive sound of *bloco afro*. Carlinhos Brown and others had a central role in popularizing *timbalada*, nationalizing a primarily regional style of popular music.

In 1993 the former director of Olodum and reputed founder of *samba reggae*, Neguinho do Samba (born Antonio Luiz Alvez de Souza), founded the first *bloco afro* for women in Salvador da Bahia, named Escola Didá (Hill 2006:55–56). Dedicated to helping poor women and homeless children through music, young girls in particular learn self-esteem through *bloco afro* drumming and dancing, as Hill explains:

> As part of the forces of developing their own inner strength and confidence, the girls are required to assist other women and children that are not a part of the project by helping to organize donations of food, medicine, and cleaning supplies for the homes of the poor in Salvador. Other project goals include instilling in the young girls a feeling of responsibility that women have to their families in terms of education and work ethic. Their role is not taken lightly and they must encourage all family members to become educated and learn about their own history and black heritage. Escola Didá has become a symbol for the potential in all women, the strength and independence they may show while at the same time being the strong center of their family units and instilling in their children the same ideals.

In the first decade of the twenty-first century there are approximately ten such all-women *bloco afro* groups in Salvador da Bahia.

The Bahian pop star Luís Caldas, a light *mulatto* sometimes called the Brazilian Michael Jackson, won wide popularity in the 1980s with his *lambadas*, *reggaes*, and another genre of Carnaval dance music, *fricote*. His hit "Fricote" combines elements of *ijexá* and *bloco afro* rhythms, a *lambada* type of tune, and lyrics that have double meanings and overt sexual connotations. The *lambada* popularized in Bahia is actually an adaptation of the established popular dance from Pará known as *carimbó*. The market for international recordings fostered another short-lived craze for the *lambada*, of easy musical access and suggestive, acrobatic, sensual dancing. In Brazil, *lambada* continued in the 1990s only as a tourist attraction in the Bahian coastal resort of Porto Seguro.

Many Brazilian black pop musicians have been busy in adapting North American pop-music trends, such as funk and rap. Rock in Brazil has been associated predominantly with the white middle class. Funk and rap, introduced in Brazil in the 1980s, are heavily supported in big cities by people—especially teenagers—of the lower socioeconomic class, primarily blacks. Some musicians and singers of these styles "have associated themselves openly with the various black movements" (Carvalho 1994:30). In addition, funk musicians have frequently commented in their songs on the racial situation in Brazil and expressed black pride openly. In the late 1990s in Rio de Janeiro, newspaper articles reported that funk and rap were being used by the drug lords of the city for recruitment.

Around 1990, in homage to the gangs, the "kings" of Rio rap, William Santos de Souza and Duda (Carlos Eduardo Cardoso Silva), who earned about $80,000 a month in 1995, recorded a famous rap, "Rap do Borel" ("Rap of Borel"), about a slum in the Tijuca neighborhood, where drug dealers operate. Raps exist for almost all the main *favelas* of Rio, and even as a challenge to drug enforcement, for the Division of the Repression against Drugs, as in the "Rap da DRE" ("Rap of the Divisão de Repressão a Entorpecentes"). Comando Vermelho ("Red Command"), the famous organized crime group, is known to have subsidized funk parties to recruit kids for dealing drugs. The more radical types of funk and rap, however, have served mostly for sociopolitical messages on local, regional, or national issues, as demonstrated by the rap groups Câmbio Negro ("Black Exchange") and Chico Science. In opposition to hip-hop, Câmbio Negro adheres to consciousness rap (*rap consciência*). The noncompromising ideology of this group reflects militancy against racism and social injustice in deliberately shocking and foul language.

Charm, another form of urban popular music of the 1990s, attracts predominantly lower-to-middle-class blacks in Rio and São Paulo. A form of well-behaved, apolitical funk, it stresses bourgeois values.

REFERENCES

Alencar, Edigar de. 1965. *O carnaval carioca através da música*. 2 vols. Rio de Janeiro: Livraria Freitas Bastos.
———. 1968. *Nosso Sinhô do samba*. Rio de Janeiro: Civilização Brasileira Editora.
Almeida, Renato. 1942. *História da música brasileira*. 2nd ed. Rio de Janeiro: F. Briguiet.
Alvarenga, Oneyda. 1982. *Música popular brasileira*. São Paulo: Livraria Duas Cidades.
Alves, Henrique L. 1968. *Sua excelência o samba*. Palermo, Brazil: A. Palma.
Andrade, Mário de. 1982. *Danças dramáticas do Brasil*. 3 vols. Belo Horizonte, Brazil: Itatiaia.
Araújo, Mozart de. 1953. *A modinha e o lundu no século XVIII*. São Paulo: Ricordi Brasileira.
Béhague, Gerard. 1968. "Biblioteca da Ajuda (Lisbon) MSS 1595 / 1596: Two Eighteenth-Century Anonymous Collections of Modinhas." *Yearbook / Anuario* (Inter-American Institute for Musical Research, Tulane University) 4:44–81.
———. 1973. "Bossa & Bossas: Recent Changes in Brazilian Urban Popular Music." *Ethnomusicology* 17(2):209–233.
———. 1975. "Notes on Regional and National Trends in Afro-Brazilian Cult Music." In *Tradition and Renewal*, ed. Merlin H. Forster, 68–80. Urbana and London: University of Illinois Press.
———. 1977. "Some Liturgical Functions of Afro-Brazilian Religious Music in Salvador, Bahia." *The World of Music* 19(3–4):4–23.
———. 1980. "Brazilian Musical Values of the 1960s and 1970s: Popular Urban Music from Bossa Nova to Tropicalia." *Journal of Popular Culture* 14(3):437–452.
———. 1984. "Patterns of Candomblé Music Performance: An Afro-Brazilian Religious Setting." In *Performance Practice: Ethnomusicological Perspectives*, ed. Gerard Béhague, 222–254. Westport, Conn.: Greenwood Press.
———. 1985. "Popular Music." In *Handbook of Latin American Popular Culture*, eds. Charles Tatum and Harold Hinds, 3–38. Westport, Conn.: Greenwood Press.
———. 1988. "Fonctions Socio-Liturgiques de la Musique Religieuse Afro-Brésilienne, à Salvador, Bahia." In *Les Musiques Guadeloupéennes dans le Champs Culturel Afro-Américain, au Sein des Musiques du Monde*, ed. Michel Bangou, 195–208. Paris: Éditions Caribéennes.
———. 1992a. "La afinidad caribeña de la música popular de Bahia en la década de 1980." *Anales del Caribe* (Havana: Centro de Estudios del Caribe, Casa de las Américas) 12:183–191.
———. 1992b. "Regional and National Trends in Afro-Brazilian Religious Musics: A Case of Cultural Pluralism." In *Competing Gods: Religious Pluralism in Latin America*, Occasional Paper 11:10–25. Providence, R.I.: Thomas J. Watson Institute for International Studies, Brown University.
———, ed. 1994. *Music and Black Ethnicity: The Caribbean and South America*. Miami: North-South Center, University of Miami.
Carvalho, José Jorge de. 1993. "Aesthetics of Opacity and Transparence. Myth, Music, and Ritual in the Xangô Cult and in the Western Art Tradition." *Latin American Music Review* 14(2):202–231.
———. 1994. *The Multiplicity of Black Identities in Brazilian Popular Music*. Brasilia: Universidade de Brasilia.
Castro, Ruy. 1990. *Chega de saudades. A história e as histórias da bossa nova*. São Paulo: Companhia das Letras.
Crook, Larry. 1993. "Black Consciousness, Samba Reggae, and the Re-Africanization of Bahian Carnival Music in Brazil." *The World of Music* 35(2):90–108.
———. 1998. "Brazil: Northeast Area," in *South America, Mexico, Central America, and the Caribbean*, Vol. 2, *The Garland Encyclopedia of World Music*, eds. Dale A. Olsen and Daniel E. Sheehy, 323–339. New York: Garland Publishing.

Efegê, Jota. 1978–1979. *Figuras e coisas da música popular brasileira*. 2 vols. Rio de Janeiro: FUNARTE.

Fujii, Tomoaki, ed. 1990. *The Americas* II. Produced by Katsumori Ichikawa. *JVC Video Anthology of World Music and Dance*, 28. Video.

Hill, Julie. 2006. "The Percussion Music of Brazil: An Emphasis on Social Reform for Women and Children through Escola Didá." Ph.D. dissertation, University of Kentucky.

Kazadi wa Mukuna. 1994. "Sotaques: Style and Ethnicity in a Brazilian Folk Drama." In *Music and Black Ethnicity: The Caribbean and South America*, ed. Gerard Béhague, 207–224. Miami: North-South Center, University of Miami.

Okada, Yuki. 1995. *Central and South America. The JVC Smithsonian Folkways Video Anthology of Music and Dance of the Americas*, 5. Montpelier, Vt.: Multicultural Media VTMV-229. Video.

Perrone, Charles. 1989. *Masters of Contemporary Brazilian Song: MPB 1965–1985*. Austin: University of Texas Press.

Pinto, Tiago de Oliveira. 1991. *Capoeira, Samba, Candomblé: Afro-brasilianische Musik im Recôncavo*, Bahia. Berlin: Staatliche Museen Preussischer Kulturbesitz.

Rego, Waldeloir. 1968. *Capoeira Angola: Ensaio sócio-etnográfico*. Salvador, Brazil: Itapuã.

Risério, Antonio. 1981. *Carnaval ijexá*. Salvador, Brazil: Editora Corrupio.

———. 1993. *Caymmi: uma utopia de lugar*. São Paulo: Editora Perspectiva.

Tinhorão, José Ramos. 1988. *Os sons dos negros no Brasil*. São Paulo: Art Editora.

———. 1991. *História social da música popular brasileira*. São Paulo:

Waddey, Ralph C. 1981. "Viola de Samba and Samba de Viola." *Latin American Music Review* 2(1):196–212.

Paraguay

Timothy D. Watkins

The Indigenous Heritage
The European Heritage
The African Heritage
Musical Instruments
Musical Contexts and Genres
Social Structure and Musicians
Popular Music and Electronic Media
Further Study

Paraguay is often called by its citizens the heart of South America because of its landlocked position in the center of South America and national pride in its cultural riches. About 95 percent of the population is of mixed Spanish and Guaraní Indian descent. Though little else of Guaraní culture has survived, the Guaraní language has left a strong mark, and its use is a focus of national pride. Most of the population is bilingual; 90 percent of the population speak Guaraní, and 75 percent speak Spanish. Widespread bilingualism has led to frequent mixing of the languages, creating a linguistic hybrid, Jopará. Racial and linguistic mixtures contribute to the ethnic, cultural, and social homogeneity of the population. This homogeneity, in turn, contributes to a strong sense of cultural identity, often expressed in music.

Though the landmass of Paraguay (406,750 square kilometers) is almost the size of California, most of the 6.5 million population has traditionally occupied an area within 160 kilometers of the capital, Asunción. Large-scale migrations to the east and south since the early 1970s have reduced this concentration, but most of the population still lives in the eastern half of the country. Though the western area accounts for 60 percent of the landmass, only about 4 percent of the people live west of the Paraguay River, in the area known as the Chaco.

THE INDIGENOUS HERITAGE

The Paraguay River serves as a cultural divider between the country's Amerindians. The four native groups in eastern Paraguay all speak varieties of Guaraní or Guayakí, a related language. Those in the Chaco represent five language families: the Ayoreo and Chamakoko belong to the Zamuko family; the Angaité, Guana, Lengua, and Sanapana belong to the Maskoy family; the Chorotí, Chulupí (Churupí), and Maká belong to the Matako family; and the Guaykurú family is represented by the Toba language. The only Guaraní group in the Chaco is the Chiriguano. The Guaraní language often serves as a *lingua franca* among the native populations.

The archaeological musical record of pre-Columbian Paraguay is scant; it includes only a few bone vertical end-blown ductless flutes (*mimby'*) of Guaraní origin. Besides the climate and the soil, among the reasons for the paucity of archaeological musical artifacts is that the indigenous inhabitants led a seminomadic way of life, occasioned at least in part among Guaraní tribes by the belief that the souls of the dead continued to inhabit the structures that were their homes during life.

THE EUROPEAN HERITAGE

The historical musical record begins with the arrival of the Portuguese explorer Aleixo García in 1524. Among the chroniclers, Martín del Barco Centenera (1982 [1602]), who in 1572 accompanied the expedition of Juan Ortiz de Zárate, mentioned the *mbaraká* (large rattle), horns, and drums. Ruy Díaz de Guzmán (1945:187) wrote of trumpets (*cornetas*) and horns (*bocinas*), sounded by the Indians before an attack. Ulrich Schmiedel, a Bavarian soldier who accompanied Pedro de Mendoza in the exploration up the Paraná and Paraguay rivers, recounted that music was played while the chief of the Jerús—scholars have not identified this culture; it may have been the name of a village—ate his meals, and that at noon, if the chief so wished, the most attractive men and women danced before him (1942:60).

Some of the most informative accounts of natives' musical performance come from Jesuit records. The *Cartas anuas*, annual reports made by each Jesuit province to the Jesuit general in Rome (Leonhardt 1927–1929), tell us that some Guaraní surrounded the house of a certain Spaniard and for several nights played their horns and drums "in a warlike manner." The Jesuit historians praised Guaraní musical abilities, which they used for missionizing other Indians. Gonzal Carrasco recounted how the missionaries would travel into new areas by canoe, taking Indian converts. As they headed upriver, the missionaries, echoed by their recent converts, sang songs to attract the attention of other Guaraní, who came out of the forest to the riverbanks, and sometimes even swam after the canoes, at least in part because of their fascination with the music they heard (Charlevoix 1769 [1756]:60).

The Jesuit accounts focus on life in the thirty mission towns (*reducciones* "reductions") established by the Jesuits among the Guaraní. These accounts have little to say regarding native musical practices among the Guaraní, but they do attest to the extent to which the missionaries instructed the Indians in European musical styles. As early as 1609, the year the first mission towns were founded, the Jesuit provincial (the highest-ranking Jesuit in the province), Diego de Torres, ordered that the Indian inhabitants should be taught "not only doctrine and singing, but to read and write music with ease." By 1620, Pedro de Oñate reported that in the mission town of San Ignacio the missionaries had taught the Indians to sing well in three voices, and there was a good trio of *chirimías* ("shawms"). By about 1700, all the mission towns had choirs and instrumentalists trained in European styles, whom observers frequently compared favorably with European performers. The Guaraní musicians performed music imported from Europe and written by Jesuit missionaries, including the Italian composer Domenico Zipoli (1688–1726).

In addition to the musical instruction available in each mission town, Guaraní youths who showed musical talent were sometimes sent to the music school established at Yapeyú, near the Uruguay River. The most important figure in the musical life of Yapeyú was Anton Sepp von Reinegg (1691–1733) from Tirol, whose accounts (1696, 1973 [1710]) of his life as a missionary shed important light on the development of music not only at Yapeyú but in all the mission towns. He is credited with the introduction of the harp, an instrument that has obtained musical primacy in Paraguayan folk music, and he built the first organ to have been constructed in the mission towns. This organ seems to have been moved from Itapúa, where it was built, to Yapeyú.

Guaraní from the mission towns sometimes visited Argentine cities, including Córdoba and Buenos Aires. In 1628, Francisco de Céspedes, governor of Río de la Plata, wrote about having seen in Buenos Aires a group of more than twenty Indians from San Ignacio. He described them as "great musicians" who played "the organ, violin, and other instruments" and performed the "dances of the Sacrament." He insisted they were as skilled as if they had been educated in Spain (Peña 1916:173).

THE AFRICAN HERITAGE

Though Paraguay never had as many African slaves as did regions along the Atlantic and Pacific coasts, there was in the 1800s a small number of Paraguayans of African ancestry. They have mostly been absorbed into the population at large, leaving little trace of their African heritage except the musical bow (*gualambau, guyrambau, lambau,* and other names) and possibly the *mbarimbau.* The one exception is the community of Laurelty, where the celebration of the feast of Saint Balthazar is observed by the descendants of the blacks who had followed the Uruguayan General Artigas into exile. This celebration retains certain Africanisms, especially the primacy of drums, which are played exclusively by men.

In the 1980s and 1990s, African-Brazilian cults including Umbanda and Candomblé made inroads into Paraguay, principally because of large numbers of Brazilian immigrants in the western part of the country. There has been little study of these cults in Paraguay and even less of their music. Given the relative homogeneity among African-Brazilian cults from Belem and Bahia in the Brazilian northeast to Asunción, Montevideo, and Buenos Aires, it is to be assumed that the music of these cults in Paraguay is similar to that practiced by their adherents in Brazil. The most important *terreiros* (centers of African-Brazilian worship) in Paraguay are in Asunción, Caaguazú, Campo Nueve, Coronel Oviedo, Itá, and Itaguá (Gallardo 1986:43).

MUSICAL INSTRUMENTS

Inventories made of the mission towns on the expulsion of the Jesuits from Spanish lands show the use of a remarkable number and variety of musical instruments. Among them were harps, guitars, *vihuelas*, *bandurrias*, violins, violas, harpsichords, spinets, horns, trumpets, trombones, *chirimías*, *bajones*, flutes, and organs. Some of these instruments had been imported from Europe, but many had been made by the Guaraní. The only instrument with precontact roots recorded in the inventories was a conch trumpet.

In addition to the written inventories, an iconographic record of some instruments found in the mission towns still exists. High on the walls of the church in the partially restored ruins of the town of Trinidad is a frieze depicting angels playing many of the instruments mentioned in the written accounts of musical life in the Jesuit mission towns (Figure 26.1).

Numerous musical instruments are in use today among the indigenous, *mestizo*, and European-descended inhabitants of Paraguay, though there is no record that indigenous instruments were used in Jesuit mission towns.

Idiophones

One of the most important idiophones in use among the Guaraní is the *mbaraká*, a spiked calabash rattle with small stones or seeds inside and a wooden handle usually adorned with feathers. It is regarded as a shamanistic instrument.

The *takuapú*, a Guaraní word for an indigenous bamboo stamped tube, is played only by women among themselves and other groups. Among the Maká and other Chaco indigenous groups, the length may vary between 1.5 and 2 meters. The *takuapú* tubes in the Chaco may have strings of rattles attached and are used in women's dances to mark the beat. Strings of rattles, such as those attached to the *takuapú*, may be worn around dancers' ankle, waists, or wrists. They are traditionally made from deer hooves, tortoiseshells, or other materials or may even consist of bottle caps strung together (Boettner n.d.:20).

Membranophones

Indigenous groups use various types of drums. Water drums are used by the Toba, the Maká, the Guaykurú, and other groups living in the Chaco. The bodies of these drums may be made of wood, ceramic, or

Figure 26.1
Section of a frieze in the ruins of the church of Trinidad, Itapúa, Paraguay. Left to right: violin, harp, and guitar. Photo by Timothy D. Watkins, 1992.

Figure 26.2
Two Aché-Guayakí women play *krywá* resonating tubes. Photo by Timothy D. Watkins, 1992.

tin and are covered at their tops with deerskin or lizardskin. The heads are beaten with a single stick, a gourd, or the hand.

Aerophones

Flutes are the most frequent type of aerophone among all indigenous groups in Paraguay. The generic term for flutes among the Guaraní is *mimby´*, but a wide variety exists. One of the most notable flutes among the non-Guaraní Paraguayan groups is a wooden globular flute found among the Chulupí.

The *krywá*, a resonating tube played exclusively by Aché-Guayakí women, consists of a simple cane tube open on both ends but with no holes for fingering (Figure 26.2). It is held so the player hums into one of her hands, which acts as a duct to the proximal end of the tube. The player's other hand alternately covers and uncovers the distal end of the tube, producing a rhythmic change of timbre. Individual players may use single or double tubes. In the latter case, the alternate covering and uncovering of the distal end occurs on only one of the two tubes. Though the *krywá* is used exclusively by women, there does not appear to be any taboo against its handling by men, and it is frequently played in mixed gatherings.

Chordophones

Traditional chordophones played by members of indigenous groups in Paraguay include several types of musical bows. The *cajuavé* is a small, mouth-resonated bow found in the Chaco. It is held between the front teeth and struck with a small stick; the musician's mouth serves as a resonator and a means of changing the amplitude of the overtones. The sound of the *cajuavé* is soft, and it is a personal instrument, played by men on occasions such as the death of or separation from their wives (Boettner n.d.:30).

The Aché-Guayakí hunting bow (*rapã*) serves as a musical instrument. Players place it over a resonating container and strum it to produce a monotone ostinato. Traditionally, clay pots were the resonators of choice, but metal buckets are sometimes used. A possibly related chordophone used by the Aché-Guayakí is the terokará, a board zither with five to seven strings. One end of it is placed inside (rather than over) a resonating container, which, like that used for the *rapá*, may be of pottery or metal.

A one-stringed violin is used by the Maká and the Lengua of the Chaco, probably as a result of contact with missionaries. The hairs of the bow are moistened by the player's mouth to produce sound when drawn across the string. The body of the violin is made from wood or a tin can.

The most ubiquitous instruments in the folk music of the population of Paraguay are the guitar (*guitarra*) and the harp (*arpa*). These are considered indispensable for folkloric ensembles (*conjuntos*). The guitar, called *mbaraká* in Guaraní, is of standard European design, with six nylon strings.

Harps and harpists

The diatonic *arpa paraguaya* ("Paraguayan harp," sometimes called *arpa india* "Indian harp," though it is of European descent) is usually the featured instrument of a *conjunto*, and the harpist is often the director of the group. The Paraguayan harp produces a bright, powerful sound. The neck is made of two halves of laminated wood through which the tuning pegs pass, and the strings (usually 36 to 40) come out of holes in the bottom side of the neck. This construction causes a centralization of pressure in the neck, which allows a high string tension that creates a bright sound. This construction allows for a lightweight instrument, usually between 3 and 5 kilograms. Tuning pegs were traditionally made of wood, though most harps now feature guitar-type mechanical pegs. The body of the Paraguayan harp is about 1.4 meters long and about 40 centimeters wide at its widest point. The sound resonates from the body through a single, large, round hole in the base of the sound box. Traditionally, harpists made their own instruments—a practice that can still be observed in the interior of the country. However, a thriving harp-making industry now exists in and around Asunción, providing harps for professional harpists in Paraguay and throughout the world. The popularity of the Paraguayan harp has spread widely since 1970, even as far as Japan (Figure 26.3).

An important aspect of harp-performance technique in Paraguay is the lack of standardization. Harpists learn by experimentation and observation. This results in widely varying techniques and special effects, which become part of the tradition. Techniques of muffling and glissando are especially important in harp pieces such as "Pájaro Campana" ("The Bellbird"), "Cascada" ("Waterfall"), and "El Tren Lechero" ("The Milk Train") and are based largely on natural or human-made sounds.

guaránia
National song genre tradition of Paraguay created in 1925 by José Asunción Flores
conjunto
"Ensemble," throughout the Spanish-speaking Americas, a musical ensemble that performs folk music

Figure 26.3
A young Japanese woman, "T-san," who immigrated to Asunción, Paraguay specifically to study the Paraguayan harp, poses with her instrument. Photo by Dale A. Olsen, 1993.

The most influential Paraguayan harpist-composer was Felix Pérez Cardozo (1908–1952), composer of the onomatopoeic "Llegada" and "El Tren Lechero" and arranger of the famous traditional melody "Pájaro Campana." He was one of the first harpists to popularize the Paraguayan harp outside the country. Other famous harpists include Luís Bordón, who lived for many years in Brazil; Digno García, the original harpist with the internationally acclaimed Trío Los Paraguayos and the composer of "Cascada"; and Santiago Cortesi, who in addition to his fame as a performer has gained wide renown as a harp teacher.

When the harp is played at home or in concert as a solo instrument, the harpist is usually seated; in a *conjunto* performance, usually with two or three guitars, the harpist usually stands, sometimes placing the legs of the instrument on a small stool to obtain the correct height. In addition to the harp and standard guitars, a *requinto* (a smaller guitar) is sometimes used in folkloric ensembles.

MUSICAL CONTEXTS AND GENRES

Religious

Religious contexts form an important part of musical life in Paraguay. Music is an important part of shamanism among the Indian groups, where sickness is often believed to be caused by intrusion of substances into the patient. Healing results from naming and extracting the intrusion, which follows several hours of chanting by the shaman.

About 95 percent of Paraguay's population is Roman Catholic, and most of the other 5 percent are Mennonites, Baptists, Pentecostals, or belong to smaller Protestant denominations. Beginning with the Jesuit mission towns, Roman Catholicism has been a significant cultural force through Paraguay's history. Given the greater freedom that began after the second Vatican Council (1962–1965), liturgical music has been somewhat influenced by the *coritos* (short choruses) prominent in many of the Protestant churches. Much music associated with the Roman Catholic Church, especially in religious festivals, is greatly influenced by folkloric traditions. Traditional religious songs include *gozos* "joys," *alabanzas* "praises,", and *villancicos* "rustic songs.".

Roman Catholic fesivals

An important musical event that occurs during Holy Week is the activity of the *pasioneros* (relating to the Passion of Christ), also called *estacioneros* (relating to the Stations of the Cross). These are associations of men who process to the church or to a replica of Calvary, the hill on which Jesus was crucified. Dressed in uniforms, they carry the banner of the association and a cross. The uniforms usually consist of black or navy pants, plain or with yellow stripes down the legs, or white pants with colored stripes; black belts; and white shirts with the association's own emblem or a cross enclosed in a triangle on the pocket. Sometimes a black or purple sash, crossing from the right shoulder to the left side of the waist, is worn. A short cape, which may be black, purple, blue, dark yellow, or gray, decorated with a cross, is also part of the uniform. Sometimes a white cap is worn. As these uniformed *pasioneros* process, they sing somber songs, known as cried song (*purahéi jahe'ó*) or mournful song (*purahéi asy'*), on the subject of the Passion, stopping every few steps to kneel, as if observing the Stations of the Cross. The songs, which may be in Spanish, Guaraní, or a mixture of the two, are sung in unison or in thirds and have mostly conjunct melodies, simple harmonies (usually only tonic and dominant), and rather free rhythm. Musical instruments are not used.

Patronal festivals are especially important musical occasions in which a complex of religious and secular ceremonies forms a unified whole, providing an occasion for celebration and strengthening of communal bonds that is often marked by the return of family members who have moved away from the community. The festivals are usually organized by a festivity commission (*comisión de festejos*) composed of prominent men and women in the community. The religious observance begins nine days before the feast of the patron saint. Masses are said for community members who have died in the past year and for the sick. Weddings are an important part of the celebration.

Traditionally, the image of the patron saint is kept in the home of a caretaker, but this custom is no longer widely observed. From the caretaker's home, the image is taken in a large procession to the church for the beginning of the *novena*. In communities where the image is kept in a chapel, the procession from the chapel to the church takes place on the eve of the feast, accompanied by a joyful celebratory procession marked by fireworks, band music, flying flags, and people on foot and (in rural areas) on horseback. After the image of the saint arrives in the church, masses are celebrated.

The feast proper begins before dawn with a trumpet signal (*diana mbajá*) the pealing of bells, brass-band music, and fireworks. The national flag and the standard of the patron saint are raised in the central plazas. If the patron saint is female, young men may serenade her, accompanying themselves with guitars and harps.

The central ceremony of the patronal feast is a high mass (always sung) in which a *conjunto* often supplies the musical accompaniment. Frequently, especially in rural areas, the mass is in the Guaraní language. The church is highly decorated for the occasion. The entire town attends the mass, as do residents of neighboring localities and towns. Many pilgrims or *promeseros*, children and adults, come dressed as the patron saint or at least wear elements of clothing such as habits, cloak, belt, or tiara associated with the saint. They may carry the standard or insignia of the saint and as a sign of penance may carry stones on their heads. These *promeseros* may walk great distances; in the days immediately before 8 December, the feast of the Virgin of Caacupé, attended by pilgrims from all over the country, it is common to see *promeseros* walking for many miles up rugged hills on their knees in supplication or in recognition of answered prayers.

After mass, the image of the saint is carried in a solemn procession through the streets of the town, which have been adorned with bamboo arches, small flags, flowers, ticker tape, and aeolian noisemakers, which sound in the wind. The procession is led by a brass band, followed by the various religious confraternities, brotherhoods, and associations each carrying its standards and flags and led by its own color guard. The patronal festivals of some isolated towns still feature bands composed entirely of men and boys who play *mimby'* and drums resembling those used by the Guaraní. These include the Banda Para'í in the town of Tobatí and Peteke (also known as Angu'a Pararä) in the town of Guayaiv-ity. Peteke and Pararä (Parará) are onomatopoeic words recalling the sound of the drums (Gómez-Perasso and Szarán 1978).

More secular events also take place. In the plaza in front of the church or on a vacant lot, a temporary amusement park (*kermese*) is usually set up. Tents and booths provide cover for various activities, including raffles, darts, target shooting, cards, and other games. Typical foods and drinks, alcoholic and nonalcoholic, are sold, as are local arts and crafts. A merry-go-round is an indispensable part of the festivities. Bullfights are frequent occur-rences, as is the *toro candil* ("lighted bull"), in which one or two men inside a mock-bull play the part of a fighting bull. The bull's body is made of cowhide or canvas over a wooden frame; its head is fashioned of a cow skull to the horns of which are tied flaming torches.

An important part of the celebration surrounding patronal festivals is the concerts provided by military bands (from the local army post) or by similar civilian bands (*banda koyguâ*) and by *conjuntos* performing folk music, which may accompany folk dances like the *polca paraguaya*, the *galopa*, and the *golondriana*. Groups of musicians may go from house to house serenading ecclesiastical, civil, and military authorities and prominent families.

Social and athletic clubs hold their own festivities. These events frequently feature rock bands, and are characterized as *bailes*. Those who attend come to dance. Dances (*danzas*) are not so frequent in the celebrations at these clubs.

Alongside the feasts of local patron saints and of the Virgin of Caacupé, the other most important patronal festivals are those of San Blas (the patron saint of Paraguay, 3 February) and Saint John the Baptist (24 June). The festivities of the night of 23 June are anticipated the entire year. Besides the typical revelry, musical performance, and dancing, a particular feature of this celebration is fire. Around dusk, a large bonfire (*fogata de San Juan* or, in Guaraní, *San Juan ratá*) is lighted. Around midnight, when the fire dies down, the white-hot coals are raked out into a uniform bed on the ground about 1 meter wide by 4 or 5 meters long over which the faithful walk barefoot after exclaiming "Viva San Juan!" This practice, which apparently does no harm to the practitioners' feet, is known as *tatá ari jehasá* ("to walk on fire"). Other important activities of this feast involving fire are the crowd's kicking around a fireball (*pelota tatâ*), a ball of rags soaked in tar and kerosene and set afire, and the burning of Judas in effigy (*Juda kái*). The figure of Judas is often filled with fireworks, causing a great commotion. The *Juda kái* and *tatá ari jehasá* mark the high-light of the festivities and for that reason bring the music to a temporary halt.

Protestant music

The music of the Protestant churches formerly tended to resemble that of the denomina-tions in the United States and Europe to which they were related. Many of the Protestant hymns were Spanish translations of European and North American hymns and gospel songs. Since the 1970s, however, short repetitive choruses (*coritos*), written originally in Spanish, have been gaining popularity. These may or may not be settings of Scripture. Their texts are much more subjective and emotionally charged than those of traditional hymns. Musically, they tend toward diatonic, conjunct melodies with uncomplicated har-

polca paraguaya
"Paraguayan polka," the preeminent national genre of Paraguay, vastly different from the European polka
galopa
"Gallop," Paraguayan outdoor fast dance consisting of two contrasting musical sections

monies easily accompanied by guitars, frequently even in churches that have a piano or an electronic keyboard.

Secular music and dance

Folkloric music, a primary vehicle for expressing Paraguayan ideology, is particularly linked with a sense of national identity. Much of this musical nationalism is related to the importance of the Guaraní language and mythology in *mestizo* culture. Many musical texts are in Guaraní or Jopará. Several songs of wide renown are based on Guaraní mythology. Much folkloric music is composed by individuals but is generally conceded folkloric status based on preconceived notions of genre. The executive branch of the government demonstrated the nationalistic importance of music in a 1959 decree, which ordered that 50 percent of the music played on the radio be by Paraguayan composers.

The musical genre known as *guaránia*, created in 1925 by José Asunción Flores (1904–1972) and later adopted by other composers, is widely acknowledged as an important national tradition. Often in minor mode, the *guaránia* is slower than a *polca*, though it makes use of the same dual-meter (*sesquiáltera*) rhythmic device. It is defined primarily by the characteristic *rasgueado*, or guitar strum. The texts of many *guaránias* assume a nostalgic viewpoint, expressing a yearning to return to a particular locality, as does the song "Asunción," or remembering a lost love, as does "Recuerdos de Ypacaraí," which became famous throughout the world. The following partial text of "Recuerdos de Ypacaraí" reveals the typical nationalistic and romantic flavor of the *guaránia*, including the Guaraní term for "girl" (*cuñataí*):

> **sesquiáltera**
> A Spanish-derived dual meter consisting of superimposed 3/4 and 6/8 and often with alternation or hemiola

Chorus:

Donde estás ahora cuñataí,	Where are you now, cuñataí,
Que tu suave canto no llega a mí?	That your gentle song does not reach me?
Donde estás ahora?	Where are you now?
Mi ser te adora	My being adores you
Con frenesí.	With frenzy.
Todo te recuerda, mi dulce amor	Everything is reminiscent of you, my sweet love.
Junto al lago azul de Ypacaraí,	Near the blue lake Ypacaraí,
Todo te recuerda.	Everything is reminiscent of you.
Mi amor te llama, cuñataí.	My love calls you, cuñataí.

The *polca* ("polka," though vastly different from the European and American dance by that name), in various forms, is a preeminent national genre. The texts of the sung *polca* and the related genre of song (*canción*, Guaraní *purahéi*), commonly known together as *polca canción*, are frequently about explicitly nationalistic, military, or political subjects. Accounts of important battles in the Triple Alliance War (1864–1870) against Argentina, Brazil, and Uruguay and the Chaco War (1932–1935) against Bolivia, are common topics. The use of music to declare ideological and organizational allegiances can be seen in the fact that all major political parties and even soccer teams have official *polcas*.

Dancing frequently accompanies folkloric music. Especially prominent are several varieties of *polca*. The dance music of the *polca paraguaya* is unlike that of the European and North American polka. Whereas its most prominent feature is the melody's duple rhythm, it uses a dual meter—a syncopated compound binary in the melody against simple triple meter in the bass. [Listen to "Pájaro Chogüí"]

Polcas are often qualified by terms that describe how they are danced: *polca syryrý* "smooth (or slippery) polka," *polca popó* or *jeroky popó* "jumping polka," or "jumping dance," *polca jekutú* "stationary polka" (in which the dancer does not cover much space), *polca valseado* "waltzed polka" (characterized by a smooth balance of the dancer's body as in the waltz).

The gallop (*galopa*) consists of two musical sections: the first resembles a *polca*, but the second has notable syncopation emphasized by percussion instruments. It is performed by an instrumental ensemble usually consisting of brass and woodwind instruments, bass drum, snare drum, and cymbals. The dancers (*galoperas*) are women who dance to fulfill religious vows. The *galopa* usually takes place outdoors in a space prepared for the occasion, lit with torches and adorned with flowers and paper pennants. The *galoperas*, in traditional dress, improvise steps as they dance with pitchers of water or bottles of alcoholic *caña* balanced on their heads, from which they offer drinks to observers. Formerly, some *galoperas* would carry baskets of fruit on their heads rather than pitchers or bottles. The symbolism of water and fruit and sensuous motions of the dancers, most of whom are young, seem to identify this dance as a type of disguised fertility ritual.

Other important folkloric dances include the *chopí* (also known as the Santa Fe), the *palomita*, the *golondriana*, the *london karapé*, the *pericón*, the *solito*, and the *cazador*. All of these are couple dances and are performed in traditional clothes.

Steakhouses and touristic performance

An important context for Paraguayan folkloric music and dance can be found in the steakhouses (*parrilladas*) of Asunción, especially those catering to tourists from Argentina, Brazil, the United States, Japan, and other parts of the world. These restaurants, featuring typical Paraguayan cuisine, frequently offer performances of *conjuntos* of singers accompanying themselves with harp and guitars, as well as performances of folk dances.

One of the most impressive dances, and a popular tourist attraction, is the bottle dance (*danza de las botellas*), usually accompanied by *polca* music (Figure 26.4). Probably derived from the *galopera*, it can be danced by couples, a group of women, or by solo women. The steps are often improvised, and the distinguishing mark of the dance is the balancing of bottles on the heads of the female dancer(s). As the dance progresses, more and more bottles are added, one on top of the other (the top of one may fit into a groove in the bottom of another).

Figure 26.4
In a Paraguayan steakhouse, a woman performs the *danza de las botellas* ("bottle dance"). Photo by Timothy D. Watkins, 1992.

Sometimes feats such as picking up a handkerchief from the dance floor with the teeth emphasize the dancer's agility and balance. In particularly lavish productions, as many as fourteen or fifteen bottles may be placed one on top of the other on the dancer's head by a helper, who may need to ascend a ladder to stack them. The final bottle is usually decorated by the insertion of flowers or by the attachment of a tricolor ribbon.

National anthem

Paraguay's national anthem is titled "Paraguayos, República o muerte!" ("Paraguayans, The Republic or Death!"). Written in the early nineteenth century during the independence movement by Francisco José Debali, with lyrics by Francisco Esteban Acuña de Figueroa (http://david.national-anthems.net/py.htm), it was adopted as the country's national song in 1846 and officially recognized as the national anthem in 1934.

MUSIC AND LIFE-CYCLE EVENTS

Life-cycle rituals are frequently settings for musical performance in Paraguay. Especially notable is the *quinceañera*, a girl's fifteenth-birthday celebration. This event marks her coming of age and is celebrated as lavishly as her family can afford. Dances featuring rock bands are often held; if the family's resources do not permit a live band, recordings are played.

Serenades

The serenade (*serenata*) is a frequent occurrence at a *quinceañera*, often performed by a young woman's suitor, who may be accompanied by his male friends. The serenade may be a surprise to the recipient, or she may have had prior knowledge of the event, usually as the result of gossip. The music usually begins with a love song, frequently a *guárania*, sung to the accompaniment of guitars, and is followed by two or three faster songs such as *polcas*. At the end of the serenade, the recipient and her family are expected to thank the musicians graciously, and if they had prior knowledge of the event, to invite them into the house for an *ambigú*, food and drink. Longer *serenata*s are sometimes called *musiqueadas*. Both are performed as a sign of respect for family members, important members of the community, and girlfriends.

Wakes

A wake (*velorio*), especially that of a young child, is an important musical event. According to popular belief, the spirit of a young dead child (less than about eight years of age) bypasses purgatory and goes directly to heaven, where he or she becomes an angel or even a star. For this reason, the wake of a young child is called a little angel's wake (*velorio de angelito*) and is the scene of festivities (González Torres 1991:312–313). The child wears a white crown; the clothes are white or pink for a girl or light blue for a boy. A small crucifix or palm leaves are placed in the child's hands, folded on the chest. The body is placed in a white casket whose edges are decorated with white flowers and is displayed on a table covered with a white sheet. Candles are lighted at the head of the casket. Family members and friends who attend the wake place flowers and sometimes money on the body or on the table.

During the wake, a *conjunto* (an ensemble of harp, guitar, and flute, or at least two guitars) plays and sings. Alcoholic beverages, including *caña* (sugarcane alcohol) and beer, flow freely. Those attending the wake frequently dance all night, and fireworks are not uncommon. The mourning parents of the deceased child usually remain in a separate room, where friends and family console them.

A burial procession is headed by musicians. The casket may be carried by four children—friends, relatives, or schoolmates—or may be carried by the mother or godmother on her head. The lid of the casket is carried by other children. Once at the cemetery, the crucifix or palm leaves are taken out of the child's hands, and the casket is closed for burial. In some parts of the country (such as Alto Paraná and Itapúa), store owners commonly pay for the expenses of wakes and provide money to deceased children's parents. This service entitles store owners to sell food and drinks to the guests.

LEARNING, DISSEMINATION, AND PUBLIC POLICY

Most musical education in Paraguay takes place informally, based on oral tradition. Basic study of music is part of the public school curriculum, but not many people learn to read music. The Ateneo Paraguayo, founded in 1883, is one of the oldest and most highly regarded musical institutions of the country. It offers lessons in applied music and music theory. The Escuela de Bellas Artes, part of the National University of Asunción, was established in 1957; it is made up of departments of music, voice, classical dance, and plastic arts. More or less advanced musical training is available at the Baptist and Mennonite seminaries, which also sponsor choirs. The offerings of these educational institutions are supplemented by the Orquesta Sinfónica de la Ciudad de Asunción, which, in addition to concert seasons of art music from the Western tradition, carries on educational activities for young people.

Individual teachers, primarily in Asunción, provide private music lessons. The most frequently studied instruments are harp, guitar, and piano. The study of classical guitar is particularly prestigious, and Paraguayans take pride in the two guitarists of world fame Paraguay has produced: Agustín Barrios Mangoré (1885–1944) and Cayo Sila Godoy (b. 1920).

Musical performance in Paraguayan culture is widespread among all ages and social classes. Singing among groups of friends is perceived to have great entertainment value and is a frequent pastime. Guitars are widely played, though mostly by ear; few players have any formal training in music. Men and women play guitars, but few women play harps. Some professional and semiprofessional *conjuntos* include women, who tend to be singers rather than harpists or guitarists.

The intentional role of music in the promotion of cultural identity can also be seen among various ethnic groups of foreign extraction, such as the communities of Japanese, Koreans, Germans, Russians, Ukrainians, and Arabs, some of whom maintain cultural centers that occasionally sponsor concerts to promote the traditional music of the group. Particularly notable are the Japanese, who operate cultural centers in Asunción, Ciudad del Este, Encarnación, and smaller towns [see MUSIC OF IMMIGRANT GROUPS].

Paraguayan folk music such as *polcas* and *guaránias* continues to exercise great appeal, but other styles are popular. Local rock bands are in constant demand for public dances (*bailes*). These bands perform music of their own composition, plus covers of songs that have obtained success through recordings or on the radio, including those by musicians from the United States, Europe, and the rest of Latin America. Rock bands are somewhat influenced by popular Caribbean styles. The influence of Argentine rock is especially apparent.

Electronic musical culture in Paraguay includes a widespread network of forty-two AM and forty-eight FM radio stations, covering the entire country. Eight television stations and a cable television system cover the main population centers, in the eastern half of the country. Television and radio signals from Brazil and Argentina can be received in the areas bordering those countries. Several small recording studios are located in Asunción; these produce mainly cassette recordings by Paraguayan folkloric and popular musicians.

FURTHER STUDY

The Jesuit accounts provide most of the historical records regarding music in Paraguay during the 1600s and 1700s. Most important are those by Pierre François Charlevoix (1769 [1756]), Anton Sepp von Reinegg (1973 [1710]), Martin Dobrizhoffer (1784), and Florian Paucke (1696).

One of the best sources on Paraguayan folklore is Mauricio Cardozo Ocampo's *Mundo folklórico paraguayo* (1989). The first volume, *Paraguay folklórico*, is devoted almost entirely to Paraguayan folkloric music and is notable for the number of musical texts included. Most of the music in the volume has been arranged for piano by the author.

The definitive work on Paraguayan dance is Celia Ruiz Rivas de Domínguez's *Danzas paraguayas, método de enseñanza: Reseña histórica de la danza en el Paraguay y nociones sobre el folklore* (1974b), an excellent overview of the history and choreography of Paraguayan folk dances. It is supplemented by the same author's *Album musical: Suplemento del libro de Celia Ruiz Rivas de Domínguez "Danzas tradicionales paraguayas"* (1974a).

Brief biographies of Paraguayan musicians can be found in Miguel Angel Rodríguez's *Semblanzas biográficas de creadores e intérpretes populares paraguayos* (1992). More extensive works about individual musicians include Armando Almada Roche's *José Asunción Flores: Pájaro musical y lírico* (1984), and Richard Stover's *Six Silver Moonbeams: The Life and Times of Agustín Barrios Mangoré* (1992).

For further information on the Paraguayan harp, see Alfredo Rolando Ortíz's *Latin American Harp Music and Techniques for Pedal and Non-Pedal Harpists* (1984) and John M. Schechter's *The Indispensable Harp* (1992), the latter work about Ecuador's harp tradition, but containing a valuable history of the harp in Latin America.

The section on Paraguay in Paulo de Carvalho-Neto's *Estudios afros: Brasil, Paraguay, Uruguay, Ecuador* (1971) is an invaluable overview of the sources on African descendants in Paraguay. Josefina Plá's *Hermano Negro: La esclavitud en el Paraguay* (1972), in addition to discussing the history and social context of slavery in Paraguay, dedicated a chapter to the cultural legacy of Paraguayans of African descent.

REFERENCES

Almada Roche, Armando. 1984. *José Asunción Flores: Pájaro musical y lírico*. Buenos Aires: Ediciones el pez del pez.

Barco Centenera, Martín del. 1982 [1602]. *Argentina y conquita del Río de la Plata*. Madrid: Institución Cultural "El Brocene" de la Excelentísima Diputación Provincial de Cáceres.

Boettner, Juan Max. n.d. *Música y músicos del Paraguay*. Asunción: Autores Paraguayos Asociados.

Cardozo Ocampo, Mauricio. 1989. *Mundo folklórico paraguayo*. 3 vols. Asunción: Editorial Cuadernos Republicanos.

Carvalho-Neto, Paulo de. 1971. *Estudios afros: Brasil, Paraguay, Uruguay, Ecuador*. Serie de Folklore—Instituto de Antropología e Historia, Universidad Central de Venezuela. Caracas: Instituto de Antropología e Historia, Facultad de Humanidades y Educación, Universidad Central de Venezuela.

Centurión, Carlos R. 1961. *Historia de la cultura paraguaya*. Asunción: Biblioteca Ortiz Guerrero.

Charlevoix, Pierre François. 1769 [1756]. *Histoire du Paraguay*. Translated as The History of Paraguay. London: L. Davis.

Díaz de Guzmán, Ruy. 1945. *La Argentina*. Buenos Aires: Espasa-Calpe.

Dobrizhoffer, Martin. 1784. *Historia de Abipones*. Translated by Sarah Coleridge as *An Account of the Abipones: An Equestrian People of Paraguay*. 3 vols. London, 1822. Reprint, New York: Johnson Reprint Corporation, 1970.

Gallardo, Jorge Emilio. 1986. *Presencia africana en la cultura de américa latina: vigencia de los cultos afroamericanos*. Buenos Aires: Fernando García Cambeiro.

Gómez-Perasso, José Antonio. n.d. *Ava guyrá kambí: notas sobre la etnografía de los ava-kué-chiripá del Paraguay oriental*. Asunción: Centro Paraguayo de Estudios Sociológicos.

Gómez-Perasso, José Antonio, and Luís Szarán. 1978. *Angu'á parará. Estudios Folklóricos Paraguayos* 1(1). Asunción: Editorial Arte Nuevo.

González Torres, Dionisio M. 1991. *Folklore del Paraguay*. Asunción: Editora Litocolor.

Leonhardt, Carlos, ed. 1927–1929. *Cartas anuas de la provincia del Paraguay, Chile y Tucumán, de la Compañía de Jesús*. 2 vols. Buenos Aires: Instituto de Investigaciones Históricas.

Ortiz, Alfredo Rolando. 1984. *Latin American Harp Music and Techniques for Pedal and Non-Pedal Harpists*. 2nd ed. Revised and enlarged. Corona, Calif.: author.

Paucke, Florian. 1696. *Florian Pauckes Reise in die Missionen nach Paraguay und Geschichte der Missionen S. Xavier und S. Peter Brixen*. Translated by Edmundo Wenicke as *Hacia allá y para acá*. Tucumán: Universidad Nacional de Tucumán (1942).

Peña, Enrique. 1916. *Don Francisco de Céspedes, noticias sobre su gobierno en el Río de la Plata (1624–1632)*. Buenos Aires: Coni Hermanos.

Plá, Josefina. 1972. *Hermano Negro: La esclavitud en el Paraguay*. Madrid: Paraninfo.

Rodríguez, Miguel Angel. 1992. *Semblanzas biográficas de creadores e intérpretes populares paraguayos*. Asunción: Ediciones Compugraph.

Ruiz Rivas de Domínguez, Celia. 1974a. *Album musical: Suplemento del libro de Celia Ruiz Rivas de Domínguez "Danzas tradicionales paraguayas."* Asunción: Impresa Makrografic.

———. 1974b. *Danzas paraguayas, método de enseñanza: Reseña histórica de la danza en el Paraguay y nociones sobre el folklore*. Asunción: Impresa Makrografic.

Schechter, John M. 1992. *The Indispensable Harp: Historical Development, Modern Roles, Configurations, and Performance Practices in Ecuador and Latin America*. Kent, Ohio: Kent State University Press.

Schmiedel, Ulrich. 1942. *Viaje al Río de la Plata*. Buenos Aires.

Sepp von Reinegg, Anton. 1971 [1696]. *Reissbeschreibung*. Translated by Werner Hoffman and Monica Wrang as *Relación de viaje a las misiones Jesuíticas*. Buenos Aires: Eudeba.

———. 1973 [1710]. *Continuation oder Fortsetzung der Beschreibung deren denkwuerdigeren paraguarischen Sachen*. Translated by Werner Hoffman as *Continuación de las labores apostólicas*. Buenos Aires: Editorial Universitaria de Buenos Aires.

Stover, Richard D. 1992. *Silver Moonbeams: The Life and Times of Agustín Barrios Mangoré*. Clovis, Calif.: Querico.

Argentina

Ercilia Moreno Chá

The Indigenous Heritage
The European Heritage
The African Heritage
Secular Musical Contexts and Genres
Learning, Dissemination, and Public Policy

Located in the southern "cone" of South America, the Republic of Argentina constitutes the southeastern extreme of South America with an area about 2.77 million square kilometers. Its territory has a varied topography in which several cultural areas (with their provinces) can be distinguished: Patagonia (Chubut, Neuquén, Río Negro, Santa Cruz, and Tierra del Fuego), the pampa (Buenos Aires, La Pampa, Santa Fe, the south of Córdoba), Cuyo (Mendoza, San Juan, San Luis), the northwest (Catamarca, Jujuy, La Rioja, Salta, Tucumán), the central area (Santiago del Estero, the center and north of Córdoba), the Chaco (Chaco, Formosa, the east of Salta), and the littoral region (Corrientes, Entre Ríos, Misiones).

About 85 percent of the country's population is of European descent. Amerindians and *mestizos* have been pushed aside or absorbed. A famous character, immortalized in literature, is a kind of *mestizo* called *gaucho*, a human stereotype synonymous with the country, especially the pampa (hence, a type of cowboy). The most representative music of Argentina, known all over the world, is *tango*, a popular dance for couples, with sensual and complex choreography.

THE INDIGENOUS HERITAGE

Archaeological evidence for pre-Encounter Argentine music comes almost totally from the northwest (Jujuy Province), while the historical record covers more of the country. Ancient aerophones include different types of end-blown flutes, globular flutes (ocarinas), raft pan-pipes of three or four closed tubes, and trumpets made from stone, ceramic, bone, and wood. Oval and pear-shaped ductless ocarinas were occasionally zoomorphic and mostly abstract in design; one was made from an armadillo cranium, with an avian humerus for a duct (Vignati 1982:93).

Historical sources for the study of Argentine music began as early as 1520, and include the chronicles of explorers, travelers, colonizers, and missionaries, most describing indigenous music from Patagonia, Tierra del Fuego, Río de la Plata, and the Chaco (see Furlong 1909, Gallardo 1910; Lothrop 1928; Segers 1891, Vignati 1982). Music of the Yámana and the Ona (now extinct) in Tierra del Fuego included collective songs and solo shamanistic songs related to birth, childhood, curing, and death. There is no agreement about Yámana and Ona musical instruments, because the chroniclers could not competently determine whether or not an object was a musical instrument; only an aerophone and a women's rhythm stick have been mentioned with certainty. Fifty-one Tehuelche (related to the Mapuche) melodies were recorded by Robert Lehmann-Nitsche in 1905; more than forty recordings of the Fueguian Yámana and the Selk'nam were made between 1907 and 1908 by Colonel Charles Wellington Furlong; and work in Tierra del Fuego was continued by Father Gusinde in 1923–1924 (all these audio recordings went to the Phonogramm-Archiv Berlin). Much later, Anne Chapman completed the last recordings of the Selk'nam (1972, 1978).

Indigenous musical instruments

Beginning in 1931, documentary recordings of the music of indigenous and creole cultures were made by Carlos Vega, Isabel Aretz, and others. These are preserved in the archives of the Instituto Nacional de Musicología "Carlos Vega" in Buenos Aires.

Idiophones, the most common types of musical instruments among the current indigenous populations, include jingle rattles (Mapuche and Mataco people), rhythm tubes (Mbyá people), and gourd rattles (Mataco-Mataguayo and Mbyá-Guaycurú). Gourd rattles are symbolic and used for different types of shamanistic rituals, including female initiation, fermentation of drinks, weather phenomena, birth-related rites, and curing.

Membranophones include the *kultrún*, a single-headed kettledrum played with one stick, used only by the Mapuche [see MAPUCHE], who believe it has existed since the beginning of the world and that the gods of music (*tayiltufe*) teach the shaman (*machi*, always female today) how to paint the symbolic designs on its drumhead and how to play it. The *kultrún* is very symbolic: as a shamanic tool it represents the *machi* in her transcendent roles; and it represents the Mapuche universe, conceived as a "complex network of relationships among diverse elements related through a good-evil polarity: colors, cosmic supernatural and natural areas, the cardinal directions, the stars, and earthly regions" (Grebe 1979–1980:12). The supernatural world is represented on the drumhead, always painted with abstract motifs. The natural world is represented by the body of the drum, constructed from the wood of a sacred tree, to which is attributed the power to help the shaman during her trance. In the drum's cavity various symbolic elements are placed—rocks, feathers, medicinal herbs, and the hair of animals—which will confer efficacy to the shamanic endeavor (Pérez Bugallo 1993:42). The *kultrún* is always the leader of the instrumental ensemble in which it is played, carrying out the function of ritual communication in relation to sickness, death, initiation, and fertility. At death, a *machi* is transformed into a mythic being that goes to the place in the supernatural world where the spirits of the other deceased shamans, other ancestors, and gods live. Her *kultrún* is buried with her or destroyed by her before death, because no other person is allowed to play it.

Two aerophones—*pifülka* and *trutruka*—are used by the Mapuche. The *pifülka*, a wooden pan-pipe, whose sound recalls the whistle of a mythic vampire that musically announces his disgrace, is constructed so its shape suggests the mythic creature's wings (Pérez Bugallo 1993:92). Originally used in shamanic curing, fertility rites, human sacrifices, battle, petitions, exorcisms, and funeral rites, the *pifülka* is currently played with the *trutruka* trumpet in the *nillipún* (*ngillatún*) festival, the most important supplicatory ceremony of the Mapuche. The *trutruka* is a long (up to 3 meters), end-blown natural trumpet made from a hollowed bamboo pole covered with horse gut and adorned with a cow's horn at its distal end (Figure 27.1). It resembles the *erke* (*erque*), used in the northwest by *criollos*, a side-blown trumpet whose length can be up to 7 meters.

Other indigenous aerophones in the Andes of northern Argentina are *siku* panpipes (see BOLIVIA and PERU), played as double-unit instruments consisting of two halves that play in an interlocking fashion, accompanied by military drums. The *kena* (*quena*), the ubiquitous notched vertical flute of the central Andes, is also found. A double reed shawm with a cowhorn bell called *erkencho* is also used in Jujuy province.

Figure 27.2
A Mapuche artisan tries a recently finished *trutruka*. Junín de los Andes, Río Negro. Photo by Cristina Argota, 1983.

Several mouth-resonated musical bows (chordophones) were reported during the last decades of 1800s, but the first mention was made by d'Orbigny, who saw a mouth bow among the Auca in 1829. In the past, the Mapuche may have used a musical bow called *cunculcahue*. Amerindian use of violin in the Chaco and Misiones is borrowed from European colonists and Jesuit missionaries, and the small *charango* guitar is borrowed from Bolivian folklore.

Indigenous musical contexts and genres

Every January, the Mbyá (Mbïá) of Misiones province celebrate the *ñemongaraí*, a ceremony related to the ripening of fruits (Ruiz 1984). Its three principal objectives

Figure 27.3
Four Mapuche boys dance the *lonkomeo* during a *nillipún* celebrated in Anecón Grande, Neuquén. Photo by Cristina Argota, 1990.

are making offerings to the gods in thanksgiving for blessings received, making supplication for the people's health and prosperity, and naming of children beginning to walk. The importance of naming consists in the belief that a child's soul is sent by one of the four deities, and the group's religious leader (*pa'i*) must ascertain which of the deities is responsible; only then can it be known what name the child will have. On the morning of the ceremonial day, women prepare an offering of bread, men search the forest for the sacred *gwembé* (fruit of a local philodendron), and the *pa'i* waits within the ceremonial enclosure. After noon, adults enter the ceremonial enclosure—first the men, led by the ceremonial assistant and musicians playing a *rabel* (early violin) and a guitar, followed by the women, led by the wife of the *pa'i*. After placing the offerings, they leave, only to return soon after sundown. The second stage also takes place in the ritual enclosure, which adults enter after dancing to the music of *rabel* and guitar. Once inside, the communication of the children's names takes place, followed by sacred songs to the accompaniment of guitar and rhythm sticks.

Daily at sundown, Mbyá men, women, and children dance to honor their deities. Also accompanied by *rabel* and guitar, they perform in an open space in front of the ritual enclosure. After an hour or more they enter the enclosure where the *pa'i* leads the religious ceremony with more dancing and singing, accompanied by guitar and rhythm sticks.

In the northern and northeastern provinces of Argentina, celebrations (often known as *minga*) include the spontaneous and free collaboration of rural people for the labor of the harvest and related tasks. The workers include employees, friends, and neighbors, who by day gather in a given field for the necessary amount of time and at night participate in traditional dances and other diversions.

In the northern region of Argentina, people collectively gather the fruit of the *algarrobo* from which *chicha*, one of the most popular local drinks, is made. At the end of spring (October–November) when the *algarrobo* pods are ripe, entire families go into the woods for several days of gathering, followed by nightly parties with music and dancing.

The ritual marking of animals is another context for music making. Usually celebrated at the beginning of winter (June) in the northern provinces, it is called *señalada* because the marking takes the form of a shaped cut (*señal* "signal") on the ear of each goat or sheep born the previous year. The *señalada* is followed by a fertility ritual in which two persons take two animals, position them as if they are mating, and then feed Pachamama (Mother Earth) in supplication of the production of manure [compare with Q'EROS]. The entire celebration is accompanied by the music of an *erkencho* (a single-reed concussion aerophone), a snare drum, and the singing of *bagualas* (nostalgic tritonic songs accompanied by a *caja* membranophone).

THE EUROPEAN HERITAGE

Spanish explorer Juan Díaz de Solís and his crew discovered the land that became Argentina ("Land of Silver") when they made landfall on the banks of what became known as the Rio de la Plata (River of Silver) in 1516. Santa María de los Buenos Aires was founded in 1536, then abandoned and refounded in 1580. During the sixteenth century the provinces of Tucumán and Córdoba flourished in the north, and the influence of Jesuit missionaries was great, extending into the Misiones region.

Roman Catholicism

Roman Catholicism was introduced by the Spanish, who used it as a tool for cultural penetration and domination. Jesuit missionaries established numerous mission villages called *reducciones* ("reductions") in the Indian lands along the Iguazú and Paraguay Rivers, where they taught the Guaraní and other Amerindians how to play European music and build musical instruments (see PARAGUAY). The cathedrals of Buenos Aires and Córdoba became important locales for the performance of European baroque music. Famous Italian composer and missionary Dominico Zippoli composed hundreds of sacred works while working in Córdoba, and his influence was important in many regions beyond Argentina, from Paraguay to Bolivia.

Many of the religious celebrations in the rural areas of Argentina are syncretic religious expressions that show characteristics of indigenous beliefs and practices that have joined with either Roman Catholic or Protestant characteristics. Even into the twentieth and twenty-first centuries, festive folk Catholic celebrations that utilize traditional music are found in Argentina's northern provinces and, to a lesser degree, in the rest of the country. There are several types of folk Catholic musical occasions, some using an ecclesiastical repertoire that has fallen out of official use but appears in processions and masses. Others have local traits and texts obviously conceived for occasions such as patronal (i.e., pertaining to a patron saint) festivals, whereas still others include only instrumental performances that accompany the moving of saints' images.

Another folk Catholic repertoire, though not overtly religious, accompanies feast-day celebrations of the saints at night in places equipped for dancing, eating, and drinking. These celebrations include some or all of the following events: pilgrimage to the shrine,

Figure 27.4
Men play a button accordion and a guitar, a common duet for dancing *chamamé, ranchera, polca,* and *vals.* Victorica, La Pampa. Photo by Ercilia Moreno Chá, 1975.

mass, vigil, *novena*, procession, and a fair where local artifacts, food, and drink are sold. This procession can be carried out with publicly venerated saints or family ones and is usually accompanied by instrumental music performed on the violin and *bombo.*

A procession that attracts the largest number of faithful is that of the Virgin of Punta Corral in Jujuy province, where the religious statue is carried every year from Punta Corral to the church in the village of Tilcara (Cortázar 1959). Including a ten-hour march over steep mountains, the procession is the occasion for the most splendid gathering of panpipe ensembles in Argentina, playing *waynos* (*huaynos*) and *marchas* ("marches") and making themselves heard during four stops made for the purpose of prayer and rest. These ensembles are made up of *siku* panpipes of three or four different sizes, military drums of three kinds, and a rattle.

According to Silvia P. García (1978), the summer solstice, celebrated in pre-Christian antiquity, was changed by the Roman Catholic Church to the feast of the Nativity of Saint John the Baptist, celebrated throughout Latin America on 24 June. As with all festivals at the end of spring and the beginning of winter, rites of fertility and purification had great importance. Saint John the Baptist became associated with rites of water and fire. In the four northern Argentine provinces, where Brazilian and Paraguayan influence is felt, this celebration is more vigorous and features bonfires, games with fire, and barefoot walks on burning coals. The nighttime celebration features music often played on button accordion and guitar (Figure 27.4) and traditional dances, especially the *chamamé* (derived from the Paraguayan *polca*), the *polca*, and the *rasgueado doble*. It is interrupted periodically by four men dressed as women pretending to fight a bull of wood and rags carried by two youths. The bull's head is actually a bull's skull, but in place of horns are lighted torches.

Patronal festivals in Argentina have acquired various features ranging from the official form, emanating from its use in Rome and predominating in urban centers, to forms typified by localized traits. In patronal celebrations, situations when the church is more influential, only the ecclesiastically approved form can be observed. In rural areas of the northwest, however, a different kind of festival is found. Examples are the fiestas of Saint James (Santiago) and Saint John the Baptist (San Juan); the latter, as the patron saint of sheep, inspires devotion among shepherds.

Both celebrations occur in front of family shrines with neighbors and friends in attendance or at the churches, to which some of the saints' statues are carried. In some towns of Jujuy, both celebrations use a dance known as *cuarteada*, so named because the dancing couples carry the hindquarter of a sacrificed sheep or goat, advancing or retreating with it in front of the saint's statue, placed on a table in an open space. This dance shares some of the traits of the country dance, and is usually accompanied by the sounds of long cane trumpet (*erke*). Displaying traits of a fertility ritual, it culminates with an attempt to rip the meat; whoever pulls at it with the most force keeps it, unless it tears in two.

In the town of Yavi, bordering Bolivia in Jujuy province, an example of what the celebration of Holy Week was formerly like can be seen in small groups called *doctrinas*, originally formed to teach Christian doctrine to those preparing to take first Communion. These classes, commonly seen in Andean villages until about 1900, can still be found in Yavi (Moreno Chá 1971). The entire ceremony on Good Friday night includes unaccompanied songs learned by the groups from their teachers through oral tradition. Many of the texts refer to Christ's passion and Mary's pain and are sung to pentatonic scales. They include *gozos* ("praises"), *alabanzas*, *glorias*, *salves*, and other named genres. The study of Roman Catholic doctrine is no longer the purpose for the gatherings, now composed mainly of women and adolescents; instead, the occasion simply affords a chance for people to sing together.

Another type of religious occasion with a peculiar repertoire is the celebration of the Child-Mayor (Niño-Alcalde) in the province of La Rioja. A local veneration of the baby Jesus, this celebration goes back more than three hundred years. It relates to events in which, some people believe, the mediation of the baby Jesus made local Amerindians submit to Spanish rule. In the ceremony, celebrated for three days starting on 31 December, the principal images are those of the Child-Mayor and Saint Nicholas, each having its own devotees who form its court in a hierarchical organization similar to those of European religious brotherhoods across Latin America (Aretz 1954). Music is performed during the processions and the *novena*, which is said before both images. During the *novena*, *alabanzas* and *gozos* are sung. During the procession to the church and the *novena*, a special song for the occasion ("Año Nuevo Pacari" 'Pacari New Year', using the Quechua word *pacari* "origin, beginning") is sung in Quechua to the accompaniment of a snare drum played by the Inca, a character who, representing indigenous vassals, belongs to the court of the Child-Mayor. The entire musical repertoire, however, is European derived, syllabic, and in a major key.

Other European dances occur on 26 December in the province of San Juan during the celebration of the Virgin of Rosario de Andacollo; the major source of inspiration for this celebration is probably the fiesta of the same name occurring in the north-central Chilean town of Andacollo. The celebration usually consists of a *novena* prayed to the Virgin, followed by a procession and the climax of the fiesta, the presentation of the *chinos* (Quechua "humble servants"), persons who honor the Virgin by dancing in fulfillment of vows (Olsen 1980:410). Many prayers and songs derived from the Chilean *chinos* interrupt this dance. Accordion, guitar, and triangle accompany the dances and marches of the procession.

While numerous indigenous life-cycle rituals have disappeared in Argentina, a few remain among the *criollo* populations of certain northwestern provinces. The *rutichico* is a barely surviving Inca ceremony in Catamarca, Jujuy, Salta, and Santiago del Estero, in which a boy's first haircut serves as a transition between his first and second childhoods.

The haircut is initiated by the boy's godfather and is continued by the guests, who give the child gifts. The ritual is often syncretic because the freshly cut hair is frequently offered to the Virgin Mary—an example of an old European practice superimposed on an indigenous one. The ceremony always ends with dancing.

At funeral rituals in the province of Santiago del Estero, women are hired to pray and sing Roman Catholic songs such as *salves* and *alabanzas* in the presence of the deceased. Once common, wakes for children now occur only in remote areas. Argentine Roman Catholics, who believe that children's souls go directly to heaven, do not see a child's death as a sorrowful loss. For this reason, manifestations of happiness, such as songs with couplets (*coplas*), are sung to the child and its parents, accompanied by a snare drum or a guitar. The Passion of Christ, similar to a wake, is dramatized in remote locales of this area. Calvary is simulated, and an effigy of Jesus is taken down from its cross, placed in a crystal coffin, veiled, and nocturnally paraded around villages.

The most vigorous dramatizations occur during Carnaval ("Carnival"), when the women's ceremony known as *topamiento de comadres* occurs (a similar ceremony for men is now extinct). Women parody the baptism of an infant, thus sealing their relationship as godmothers (*comadres*). The *topamiento de comadres* includes the exchange of fruits, seeds, or homemade cheese. In some places, cheese in the shape of a baby is placed on the table, and a man in the role of a priest mimics the sprinkling of baptismal water on it.

After the ceremony, which includes singing accompanied by drumming, the godmothers and their invited guests dance. After the Carnaval, a symbolic burial is enacted. Carnaval can be represented by a human being, a rag or wooden doll, or the statue of the devil. Its death is symbolized by its burial or destruction by fire. This process is observed by all the revelers, and a mother of the personification (Quechua *pujllay*, in many places Carnaval) accompanies this death with tears of farewell. In towns and cities, Carnaval has no dramatizations among the masqueraders (*murgas*).

murga
Urban Carnaval song genre in Argentina

Protestantism

Protestant Christianity was introduced to Argentina in 1838, when Anglican missionaries began working in the south of the country among the indigenous people of Tierra del Fuego. In 1914, Protestants began proselytizing to the Mataco (Chaco province). Anglican Protestantism spread quickly in the north and has competed since the 1940s with Pentecostalism, which has gained more adherents.

The first organized indigenous Pentecostal religious congregation, recognized officially in 1958, was the Iglesia Evangélica Unida (United Evangelical Church), which prospered most among the Toba living in their native Chaco and in the outskirts of larger cities. In addition to its religious function, it provides a feeling of identity and protection from global society. Dance and music are extremely important in Toba Pentecostal worship. In only one of the five parts of the service are these genres absent. Different types of songs can be distinguished. Some have texts and music composed by the Toba; others have texts (in Toba or Spanish) taken from North American hymnals, though the original music (when it is available) is ignored. Most of the service is sung in unison by the congregation; sections are sung by small ensembles in two or three parts and by soloists. Until the 1970s,

Toba Pentecostal singing was unaccompanied, but since then the guitar, the *bombo*, and the tambourine, and in the 1990s the *charango*, the *kena*, and the accordion have been introduced. Influence of folk-derived music and lore can be seen in the incorporation and treatment of *criollo* instruments and in the use of *chamamé* and *zamba* musical forms.

Pentecostalism has been understood in indigenous terms (Roig 1990). The healing effected by the shaman as mediator is not replaced but is superimposed on the healing effected in worship by the pastor and the faithful. Originally the communication between the shaman and the supernatural was verified by song and rattle; now, power is realized through the song and dance of the pastor and the faithful, accompanied by *criollo* instruments. The gift of song to the shaman now comes from the Holy Spirit and often the learning of an instrument requires isolation, as it did for the shaman. In certain conventions or important meetings of the Toba Pentecostal church, dedications of musical ensembles of young people are reminiscent of forgotten initiation ceremonies, in which youths, in addition to marking their passage to adult life, entered the world of music.

THE AFRICAN HERITAGE

Though Argentina does not have a traditional black population, it once had a considerable one, which disappeared rapidly under mestization after the national abolition of slavery in 1853.

The presence of African-derived beliefs in Argentina today includes two variants of African-Brazilian religions: Umbanda and Batuque. The official opening of the first African-Brazilian temple was in 1966, and by the mid-1990s there were some three hundred churches, most in the Buenos Aires metropolitan area. Most of the adherents of Umbanda and Batuque are of the lower middle class (Frigerio 1991:23). In most of the temples, both religions are practiced, but Batuque is sometimes replaced by other cults of the same origin, such as Candomblé. According to Alejandro Frigerio (personal interview, 1990), music and dance are of minimal importance in the Argentine versions, probably because the musical transplantation is abrupt and the repertoire has little in common with traditional or popular Argentine culture. The repertoire of songs is learned through repeated listening to Brazilian recordings; the texts are in Portuguese and Yoruba, languages incomprehensible to most followers. The instrumental music is played on drums (and sometimes bells), often different from those used in Brazil. For Umbanda, however, the drums are Brazilian; for Batuque, they are locally available commercial instruments. A drummer's training is brief.

There is a relative homogeneity among these African-Brazilian cults from Belem do Pará (Brazil) to Asunción (Paraguay), and from Montevideo (Uruguay) to the Brazilian Northeast (Gallardo 1986:46). In the northeastern province of Corrientes, a syncretic celebration honors the black Saint Balthasar, not canonized by the Roman Catholic Church but popularly accepted as a saint to whom masses are offered. According to Roman Catholic traditions, Balthasar was one of the Magi, the three kings who journeyed to pay tribute to the baby Jesus. In the present celebration of Saint Balthasar, African traits of social organization and music are superimposed on the structural base of the Roman Catholic saint's celebration (Kereilhac de Kussrow 1980). An African-influenced ritual called *candombe*

bombo
European-derived cylindrical double-headed bass drum membranophone, played with sticks
charango
In the Andes of northern Argentina, Bolivia, and southern Peru, a small guitar made with wood or an armadillo shell

was found in Buenos Aires until about 1800 and is still found in Montevideo, Uruguay. In certain localities in Corrientes province, *candombe* (known locally as *charanda* or *ramba*) is also danced. In *candombe*, the coronation of African kings is represented and homage is given to them. Today, this dance appears with no racial connotations but with social ones because it is danced by members of marginal social classes with remote Amerindian or African ancestors. Some traditional characters in *candombe*, such as the king and the *escobillero*, an acrobatic dancer (who dances with a small broom), have been replaced by others of local significance and with Guaraní names such as *cambá-caraí* and *camba-ra-angá*. The music consists of simple melodies sung in Spanish and Guaraní in a major key and in binary rhythm, accompanied by *bombo* and triangle. Unlike the *bombo* of Andean music, for *candombe* the *bombo* is a double-headed conical membranophone with two heads attached to rings fastened by cords; it is played with the hands or with small sticks by two players seated astride it. The type of drum, its position on the ground, and its being played with the hands are unique features in traditional Argentine music. They suggest an African origin.

Formerly a dance of black brotherhoods during the Carnaval of Montevideo and Buenos Aires, the *candombe* has become a votive dance found in the context of a Roman Catholic festival, which has assimilated it as the fulfillment of a vow to a saint. The dancers gather in pairs (of the same or opposite sex), forming parallel lines.

SECULAR MUSICAL CONTEXTS AND GENRES

Music as entertainment is particularly important among Argentine *criollos*, who with music and dance often celebrate family events such as weddings or birthdays. They celebrate patriotic celebrations in much the same way but on a local level. Since the 1960s, music has gained importance at sporting events and political rallies, where, as an expression of support, ridicule, or happiness, it occurs as multivoiced songs, usually improvised as quatrains or pairs of lines, or transmitted orally by ensembles. A large, double-headed bass drum occupies a privileged place in this type of musical performance and is used with a European trumpet and a wooden noisemaker. The melodies emphasize duple meter, are conjunct, and are always in a major key, similar to the melodies used in *murgas* (urban Carnaval song genre).

Apart from these musical traditions for public events, several large traditions stand out for having local, national, and international importance. These are *tango*, folkloric music, tropical music, and rock. *Tango*, especially, reflects social and cultural events that occurred in Argentina during the end of the nineteenth century and during the early twentieth century, when heavy immigration from Europe (mainly France, Germany, Italy, Poland, Russia, and Spain) and Asia (China and Japan [Okinawa]) took place. Beginning in the 1880s or 1890s, continuing after World War II until the end of the 1940s, immigration expanded again in the 1950s, with new waves arriving from the bordering countries and more coming from Japan (Olsen 2004). This situation mainly oriented Argentine society toward European cultural life, greatly influencing the origin of *tango* because *tango* permitted the immigrants to blend with other sectors of society.

Another migration took place within the country when large numbers of people from rural areas moved to the urban centers, attracted by industrial growth. This is credited for the appearance of folkloric music in the cities.

Tango

Tango is music and dance of nostalgia and melancholy, centered on one city—Buenos Aires. Beginning ca. 1880, *tango* went through various stages. The first, called *la guardia vieja* ("the old guard") lasted until 1917; the second, *la guardia nueva* ("the new guard") lasted until 1930; the third, called the Peronist *tango* (from Juan Perón, Argentina's president) or the "golden age" of *tango* went from 1935 until ca. 1950; and the fourth, vanguard *tango*, began in 1955, led mostly by Astor Piazzolla. Traditional *tango*, golden age style, has experienced a revival of sorts and continues to be danced in halls and clubs and heard in *tanguerías*, a recent name for *tango* clubs given by its fans.

In its first stage of development, *tango* did not reach the central locales of Buenos Aires but remained marginalized among lower-middle-class people and seedy characters. Beginning in 1912, political and social changes brought together various social classes in Buenos Aires. With the opening of cabarets downtown, *tango* encountered more demanding venues, where it won not only new audiences but also new musicians who, being better trained, could make a living by playing it.

One musical instrument stands out as the essence of *tango* music—the *bandoneón*, a square-shaped concertina or small button accordion named after Heinrich Band, a German music store owner who was the first to advertise and sell the instrument in ca. 1850. The *bandoneón* arrived in Argentina ca. 1890 and is characterized by having seevnty-one buttons (thirty-three for the left hand fingers and thirty-eight for the right), each producing a different note when the bellows is pushed or pulled. The early instrumentation of *tango* ensembles included one *bandoneón* and two guitars; or a *bandoneón*, a violin, a flute, and a guitar; or a clarinet, a violin, and a piano; or a violin, a piano, and a *bandoneón*; or a similar trio or quartet. The 1920s saw the appearance of solo performers and the formation of the typical orchestra (*orquesta típica*): two violins, two *bandoneones*, a piano, and a string bass.

During the heyday of *tango*, different genres and expressions developed within the idiom. These included sung *tangos* (*tango canción* and *tango característico*), instrumental *tangos* (*tango romanza*, *milonga*, and others, performed by virtuosic ensembles), important lyrics, the appearance of prolific writers (such as Pascual Contursi and Celedonio Flores), and male and female singers who acquired tremendous popularity, of whom the most important was Carlos Gardel (ca. 1890–1935), the greatest idol in the history of *tango*.

The most prominent musicians of this time were Julio De Caro, an icon in the development of the composition, arrangement, and performance of instrumental *tangos*, and Osvaldo Fresedo, who singlehandedly did away with the *tango*'s chamber-music character (in which solo instruments were important) by consolidating the orchestra so groups of instruments were treated as single voices.

The beginning of the 1930s was a difficult time for the *tango* and its musicians. Since most *tango* performances accompanied silent films, the arrival of movies with sound

Figure 27.5
Two of the most outstanding tango dancers—Milena Plebs and Miguel Ángel Zotto—in their show Perfume de Tango as performed at Sadler's Wells Theatre, London, 1993.

took away much of the market. From 1935 to 1950, however, the *tango* recovered its popularity and gained a new audience, particularly through the media of film and radio. Cabarets attracted a new audience, the middle class, which adopted the *tango* as its favorite dance because it acquired a stronger rhythm and became easier to dance. Instrumental parts continued to be treated homophonically (like voices in a chorus), and solos decreased.

The great orchestras of the 1930s and 1940s were those of Miguel Caló, Carlos Di Sarli, Enrique Mario Francini, Osmar Maderna, and Osvaldo Pugliese; major figures were Aníbal Troilo, Alfredo Gobbi, and Horacio Salgán. Singers acquired a new importance as soloists because they began to sing all the lyrics rather than just the refrains. The vocalists Edmundo Rivero and Roberto Goyenche became highly popular.

The 1950s marked the end of *tango*'s greatest creativity and popularity. It became associated with closed intellectual circles, which did not dance to it but listened to and studied it as a relic of earlier times. Beginning in 1955, however, a new stage of *tango avant-garde* began, headed by Astor Piazzolla and his octet of two *bandoneone*s, two violins, piano, and electric guitar. New venues opened where the *tango* could be heard, including Gotán 676, La Noche, and other clubs, frequented mainly by upper-middle-class *porteños* (people of the port, Buenos Aires) and international tourists.

The 1960s marked the appearance of Editorial Freeland, dedicated to the publication of the lyrics from the "golden age" of *tango*. Studies of dictionaries on the subject appeared, and the Academia Porteña del Lunfardo opened. It was a center for the study of the dialect (*lunfardo*) used by the social classes among which the *tango* originated and which is still used in some lyrics.

During the 1970s and especially in the 1980s, the *tango* had a resurgence, not so much in terms of new compositions but in the appearance of new singers and small instrumental ensembles (trios, quartets, sextets). The principal reason for this resurgence was *tango*'s recovery as a dance. Since Piazzolla, beginning in 1955, the *tango* became just a music to listen to because of its rhythm. The success of *tango* shows abroad, especially *Tango Argentino* (Paris, 1983; Paris and Venice, 1984; New York's Broadway, 1985), brought a renaissance of the dance in middle and high classes, especially in big Argentine cities;

however, much of the *tango*'s popularity in Europe resulted from the international activity of Astor Piazzolla, Osvaldo Pugliese, Horacio Salgán, the Sexteto Mayor, and the singer Susana Rinaldi.

In 1990, the Academia Nacional del Tango (National Academy of Tango) was founded, and since then several scholars have developed research on, preserve, and diffuse the *tango* through conferences, publications, courses, and concerts. Other factors are important for *tango*'s renewed popularity: the establishment in 1990 of FM Tango, a radio station dedicated exclusively to the genre, and the creation in 1991 of the University of the Tango of Buenos Aires, dedicated exclusively to the study of the *tango* from literary, historical, sociological, choreographic, and musical perspectives. Sólo Tango (Just Tango), the first TV channel devoted only to *tango*, was created in 1995.

Since the 1970s, *tango* as a dance has attracted the attention of important choreographers, including Maurice Béjart (Belgium), Dimitri Vassiliev (Russia), and Pina Bausch (Germany), and outstanding dancers, including Mikhail Baryshnikov (United States), Julio Bocca (Argentina), Milena Plebs, and Miguel Angel Zotto (Figure 27.5).

Since the 1980s, *tango* has been going through another phase of splendor and has occupied prominent places in such countries as Japan, Germany, and Finland. In Argentina, it has been preserved by some sectors of Buenos Aires that never abandoned it and transmitted it by tradition. *Tango* began to obtain more visibility through films, literature, and research and by embracing new audiences. These came from abroad and from the Argentine middle and upper class, especially young people, anxious to learn from professional dancers called *maestros* (Moreno Chá 1995). In addition, folkloric singers like Suni Paz have recorded *tangos* as part of their interest in representing Argentina's musical patrimony, even though their style differs from that of the traditional *tango* masters. [Listen to "Sueño de Barrilete"]

DISC **2** TRACK 16

Folkloric music

Since the 1960s, spectacles known as *jineteada* or *jineteada y doma* have appeared in rural and semi urban areas mostly in the central part of the country, organized by traditionalist societies, local municipal authorities, or special brokers. These spectacles include daylong displays of outdoor skills with ropes, horses, and colts. They are always accompanied by traditional *pampa* musical forms such as *cifras*, *estilos*, *milongas*, and *rancheras*, invariably used to set the mood while people display their skills. Some famous musicians often provide entertainment with their guitars for these events. At night, dancing marks the end of the celebration. Recordings are usually used, but instrumental ensembles occasionally accompany dances such as *chacarera*, *chamamé*, *gato*, *ranchera*, and *vals*.

Folkloric festivals (*festivales de folklore*) have occurred in Argentina since the late 1950s. The most important one, begun in 1960, takes place every year in Cosquín in the province of Córdoba. Similar festivals have appeared in neighboring countries. These festivals are competitions of singing, dancing, or both, usually celebrated annually in a consistent location under the auspices of local authorities. In addition to singing and dancing, the Cosquín competition features parallel events such as conferences, seminars, and craft-oriented fairs. The music heard throughout a week by an enthusiastic crowd of about

estilo
"Style," Argentine traditional musical form from the pampa region
milonga
Argentine song genre
chamamé
Argentine polka-derived social dance form
gato
"Cat," Argentine social dance genre

twenty-five thousand is not traditional, however, but revivalistic, composed in traditional styles by famous musicians who sometimes perform it themselves. A good performance in a competition like the Festival de Folklore de Cosquín can launch a performer's career at the national or international level, especially when followed by recordings and live appearances. The singer Mercedes Sosa started her career in this manner.

Many of the most popular folkloric music and dance genres of Argentina in the twenty-first century are revivalist in intent, although some of them reflect ideologies such as the search for cultural and national identity, often represented by the nativist or traditional *gaucho*. These ideologies formed in the late 1800s in defense of a nationality seen as endangered by the great European and Asian immigrations, which are still active preservers of the *gaucho* tradition (seen as the archetype of everything Argentine). As in many regions of Latin America that display Iberian musical characteristics, improvised sung verse is a prominent *gaucho* musical tradition. In Argentina the process of singing spontaneous verses is known as *payada*, and the singer is a *payador*. Often, as a musical duel, two *payadores* alternate their verses in *décimas*. One of the most common genres for the dueling *payadores* is the *cifra*, a syllabic and somewhat recited song form in *décimas* characterized by a descending melody in a major key. A *cifra* begins with a guitar introduction and includes guitar interludes between every other verse. Another popular genre used by *payadores* is the vocal *milonga*, which is often performed without a pause between the verses of the duelers.

Milonga

There are two types of *milongas*: rural and urban. The rural *milonga* came first and is generally instrumental, played by a solo guitar. The urban *milonga*, by contrast, is vocal. *Payadores*, although mostly from rural areas in Argentina, have preferred to perform their improvised verses in the style of the urban *milonga* since the beginning of the twentieth century. While perhaps a paradox, the process is part of the revivalist tradition, which has contributed to the survival of the *milonga* as the mostly rural singers seek out urban audiences for their performances, which has often included circuses. Perhaps the greatest exponent of both the rural and urban *milongas* was singer, songwriter, poet, and guitarist Atahualpa Yupanqui, his stage name (he was born Héctor Roberto Chavaero). His song "Los Ejes de mi Carreta" ("The Axels of my Cart") is one of the best known urban *milongas* that expresses the Argentine *gaucho* sentiment of loneliness and abandonment.

In another context, the urban *milonga* was a popular dance form in the poor and often decadent suburbs of Buenos Aires during the end of the nineteenth century. At the beginning of the twentieth century, it became one of the prototypes of the Argentine *tango* with its syncopated rhythm and often satirical lyrics.

Chacarera

More of a rural dance than an urban one, the *chacarera* is believed to have derived its name from *chacra* "farm," especially in the provinces of Jujuy, Salta, Santiago del Estero, and Tucumán, far away from the city of Buenos Aires. As a revivalist genre, however, it is well known in the capital and other cities. The *chacarera* is a fast song and dance genre that often features *sesquiáltera* rhythm, emphasized by a complex and intricate *bombo* accompaniment to guitar strumming (*rasqueo, rasqueado*). Song texts are usually comical or satirical, and dancing includes *zapateo* (*zapateado*) "foot stamping" by individual dancers as they show off their skills.

Gato

Another rural song and dance genre featuring *sesquiáltera* rhythm, the *gato* is a fast couple dance in which the male and female do not hold each other but exhibit a type of dancing duel. One of the male exhibitions is a rapid *zapateo* and foot-swinging movement known as *escobilleo*. The female dancer exhibits her foot work by lifting her skirt to show her agile movements. In the northern provinces of Argentina it is said that some dancers can perform more than fifty types of *zapateo* and *escobilleo* combinations.

Zamba

Siimilar to the *gato* but slower in tempo, the *zamba* is a scarf or handkerchief dance (*danza de pañuelos*) that is related to the colonial Peruvian *zambacueca* (also *zamacueca*, later *marinera*) and later Chilean *cueca* (which is also found in western Argentina near the border with Chile). Although similar in name to the Brazilian *samba* (and pronounced alike), the Argentine *zamba* is not related to the *samba*. The Argentine *zamba* is a conquest dance between a man and a woman in which the man advances, the woman retreats but flirts, the man continues his advance, the woman continues to evade him, and both show off their skilled foot work in the process. The entire performance is repeated, as this is a dancing duel between male and female that, like its prototypes in Peru and Chile, are said to have once been imitative of the mating ritual of a rooster and a hen.

Tonada

Numerous song forms that are not danced are found in Argentina, and many derive their names from their musical characteristics: *canción* "song," *copla* "couplet," *estilo* "style," *tonada* "tune," and others. The *tonada* is a medium-paced love song in a major key often sung by two women in parallel thirds. Characteristically, the *tonada* usually includes cadences on the third by a solo singer or top singer in a duo. When accompanied by guitar (the most common accompaniment), the typical *tonada* rhythm includes vertical *sesquiáltera* during strumming; the vocalized melodies feature horizontal *sesquiáltera* or *hemiola*, a shifting of duple and triple meters.

Other ideologies besides humor, satire, and love include those of a protest nature, which can be seen in protest songs (*canciones de protesta*) that are partly as a consequence of the Cuban revolution of 1959, and these expanded throughout Latin America, culminating in the *nueva canción chilena* in the 1960s. Rock also became a vehicle for protest.

Folkloric performance venues and processes

Public performances of traditional and popular musics can involve various scenarios. In rural areas, venues are set up for particular occasions, with buildings constructed from straw, canvas, or wood. As temporary structures, they provide spaces for nights of music and dancing after days of fairs. The structures where music and dance occur on a permanent basis acquire different names in different areas: *almacén*, *carpa*, *chichería*, and *ramada*. The music for these events may be recorded or live.

In urban areas, folk-derived music is performed in *peñas*—places where people of the same area meet, typical dances are performed, and local foods are consumed; they may be in the headquarters of traditionalist societies or in social or sports clubs. Some concerts by musicians of established fame take place in concert halls in large cities. Folk music reached its peak of popularity in the 1960s and has gradually lost its audience to national and international rock, which the middle and upper-middle classes enjoy.

The so-called *música de proyección folklórica*, or simply "folklore," is nothing more than the result of the process of urbanization of traditional rural repertoires that has occurred since the late 1800s. This was provoked by several internal and some external reasons. Internal reasons were the collection and documentation of traditional elements, the important activity of theater, circus, and *payadores* (singers of challenges and poets who sing with guitar), the emergence of musical nationalism, and the development of *peñas*. External reasons were the different streams of migration from Europe and Asia—streams that generated a local tendency to defend ethnic identity through music (Moreno Chá 1987). Since the 1920s, this process has been assisted by various official measures for the study, appreciation, and transmission of musical folklore and by internal migrations in which many rural inhabitants moved to the Buenos Aires metropolitan area in search of work. Aided by nationalistic fervor and governmental support, traditional music and culture have reached new geographical areas and social groups previously unfamiliar with them. Numerous ensembles (*conjuntos*) and instrumental groups of different kinds appeared with repertoires not strictly traditional but based on traditional music. Different geographic areas were somewhat unequally represented by these groups, and there was a marked influence of the central and northwestern parts of the country.

Concurrently, between 1960 and 1965 a professionalization of composers and poets occurred, with an explosion of a movement known as the folklore boom. Famous singers, instrumentalists, and poets appeared widely on radio, television, and records. Theatrical events featuring music and dance were produced, the Festival de Folklore de Cosquín was founded, and several magazines covering the movement began to be published. The most famous magazine, *Folklore*, achieved a circulation of a hundred thousand in 1961. The most lasting and most internationally renowned works of the folklore revival were produced during this period. Perhaps the most representative work is the *Misa Criolla*, a musical setting of the mass composed by Ariel Ramírez and recorded with orchestra, chorus, and soloists on different occasions; one of the most outstanding performances was by the Spanish tenor José Carreras in 1990.

In the 1990s, the folklore revival experienced a soft revitalization, due in part to support by the national government through two radio stations—Radio Nacional and Radio Municipal. Folkloric music received a good amount of airplay on other radio stations (though little was on television) and was still performed in some of the more traditional festivals. It no longer had the widespread popularity that it did during the 1960s but is alive in the *peñas* and at family reunions of people with provincial roots. To a great extent, the repertoire is that of prior decades and is performed by old and new musicians.

The most widely known folkloristic performers on the international stage who rose from this process—Eduardo Falú, Ariel Ramírez, Mercedes Sosa, Jaime Torres, and Atahualpa Yupanqui—remain influential through their recordings. Many of them have attracted audiences of a size that characterized this type of concert in its most glorious years.

Tropical music

Caribbean music has been represented in Argentina since the 1960s by the *cumbia*, a Colombian dance that became enormously popular. Ensembles such as Wawancó, Cuarteto Imperial, and Charanga del Caribe experienced such great success that their music, consisting mostly of *cumbias*, was widely recorded. Moreover, Caribbean music has been represented since the 1980s by genres like *salsa*, *son*, *guajira*, and *reggae*.

Caribbean-style music in Argentina is known generally as tropical music (*música tropical*). It gained popularity during the 1980s and is heard in dance halls (*bailantas* or *bailables*, from *bailar* "to dance") and in sport clubs and stadiums. In addition, the success of tropical music has revived an earlier genre, *música de cuarteto* or *música cuartetera*, which originated in the province of Córdoba and has become widely known because of the activities of the Cuarteto Leo. In the interior of the country, some ensembles do not hesitate to play a traditional melody to the rhythm of the *cumbia*.

Caribbean percussion is important as a defining element of tropical music. The genre may incorporate different mixtures of keyboards, accordion, electric bass, trumpets, trombones, saxophones, and other European-derived instruments. The lyrics are short, simple, and repetitive and straightforwardly deal with dancing and love.

In Buenos Aires and its suburbs, a hundred thousand people visit no less than eighty tropical music venues every weekend, contributing to the proliferation of tropical music. The people who frequent these locales are of the middle and lower-middle classes, and the success of tropical music in the resorts of Mar del Plata and Pinamar and in the Uruguayan Punta del Este since the summer of 1990–1991 showed that the higher classes also enjoy this music.

The success of recordings has accompanied the popularity of this music. Each LP disk by popular singers such as Ricky Maravilla and Alcides surpasses two hundred thousand in sales. Two recording companies, Magenta and Leader Music, are dedicated to tropical music, and they produce vinyl discs at a cost one-third that of multinational record companies. Although the composers are unknown to the general public, they often share the credit with the performer who records the music for the first time.

The tropical music of the dance halls has enjoyed a boom that goes beyond the music to reach its typical locales, its own record labels, its specialized magazines, and its FM radio stations (Radio Fantástica and Radio Tropical) dedicated exclusively to the genre. It is a massive phenomenon based primarily on the desire for amusement through dancing, in couples or large groups, to sounds and lyrics that denote simple and contagious joy, often shared by entire families. It has variants defined by the origin of its principal performers and its fusion with traditional local genres. Some refrains of popular songs are sung with adapted lyrics at soccer matches.

Rock

Other popular musics, national and international, are danced to nightly in locales known as discos, *disquerías*, or *boîtes*, in social and sports clubs, and are heard in open-air or enclosed stadiums. These styles, known in Spanish by the English word "rock," have become most widespread in the mass media.

Argentine rock began about 1965 under the name *música progresiva nacional* "progressive national music," in an attempt to differentiate it from the commercial music of the time and from British and American rock. Like those forms, it began as a young people's musical expression, challenging adult culture. The first stage in its development saw tension between an international rock-blues style and protest music based on urban concerns directed at a working-class audience (Vila 1989). It included a fusion of *tango*, jazz, and Argentine folklore dealing with lyric, personal themes. This stage reached its peak with the development of an ideology that sought to identify with the working class and resist the military dictatorship then in power. This ideology made rock a movement in which young people sought to construct their identity during the fifteen years when military dictatorships blocked or diverted their channels of expression.

Argentine rock also attracted another audience, the middle class, and between 1975 and 1977 it typically incorporated Brazilian music, *tango*, Argentine–Latin American musical folklore, jazz, English rock, traditional rock, and ballads. This peculiar combination, which also included a search for identity, different musical genres, and protest ideology, gave the movement great originality; however, it lost its meaning when the political stage again changed.

In 1981, university student organizations began to function once more, and young people were again able to participate in political parties. At that point, some national bands began to deal with the traditional themes of international rock for the first time, with lyrics centered on the body and leisure. This created a crisis in the movement, aggravated by the intervention of the recording industry and its broadcasting capabilities.

Then in 1982, the war over the Islas Malvinas (Falkland Islands), claimed by both Argentina and the United Kingdom, provoked the prohibition of any music sung in English. From then on, *rock nacional* began to gain the airplay that for years had eluded it: television and recording studios at last opened their doors to it without reservation. Finally, the arrival of democracy in 1983 saw a flowering of new musical styles, and the movement lost the need to keep its branches united.

Since the 1970s, *rock nacional* has received the support of the written press through magazines such as *Pelo*, *Expreso Imaginario*, *Mordisco*, and *Estornudo*; but whereas radio programs have been dedicated to the genre since 1972, the support of radio stations was generally lacking. This changed in 1985, with the magazine *Rock & Pop*, followed by the appearance of additional magazines and inserts in the most widely distributed newspapers in Buenos Aires.

Other factors that played an important role in the development and popularity of *rock nacional* are related to technological advances: the amplification and electrification of musical instruments from the United States, Japan, and England; the development of recording studios with new resources; and festivals that incorporated high-tech sound-

and-lighting effects, which attracted more enthusiastic followers. *Rock nacional* has always incorporated different styles, such as pop, heavy metal, blues, folk, symphonic rock, *tango* rock, jazz rock, new wave, folklore rock, techno, reggae, and rap, many of which were influenced by styles current in England and America and by the concerts of its famous performers in the large cities. Others had more local roots.

Rock nacional is no longer a locally Argentine phenomenon. Since about 1990, it has been the third most exported national variety of rock—after those of the United States and the United Kingdom (Vila 1989:1). It has had success in other Latin American countries. The existence of about six hundred bands and soloists and the production of more than five hundred recordings attest to the development of this genre. In Argentina, *rock nacional* competes with British and American rock, which attracts a high-economic-level audience that can understand English. This music benefits from a great amount of airplay and record distribution, and the important support of music videos, broadcast nationally on Argentine television and internationally on cable television—including MTV, Music 21, and Much Music.

The displacement of *rock nacional* by imported music has been notable since 1988. In 1989, 9.23 percent of the music broadcast on the ten privately owned radio stations in Buenos Aires was sung in Spanish, Portuguese, or other languages, whereas 90.77 percent was sung in English. In the 1990s, this situation continued, improving the presence of U.S. rock groups and U.S. alternative music like that of Pearl Jam.

National and international rock (represented by famous performers from the United States and England) are featured in numerous festivals and concerts, and Argentine and foreign musicians often share the same stage. The festivals that take place every year in Buenos Aires, Córdoba, and elsewhere are special occasions that occur in theaters and stadiums. Argentina's audience for rock tries to identify itself with artists through appearance, dress, haircuts, and other details. Fans are young and strongly enthusiastic, often participating in concerts by singing along, clapping, swaying to the rhythm, and showing approval by whistling and lighting cigarette lighters. Some of these manifestations have become common in folk-music concerts when musicians incite enthusiasm with their rhythms and lyrics.

The music-video industry began in Argentina in 1985 with local stars such as Soda Stereo, Virus, and Charly García. Though its product has seen success in Europe and the United States, the industry has not yet reached maturity. In the opinion of producers of videos, the reason for such underdevelopment in this part of the music business is the lack of economic support, despite the existence of numerous television programs dedicated to the genre. There are ten recording studios in Buenos Aires, but many of them cannot carry out the entire process of production.

National anthem

Argentina's national anthem, titled "Marcha de la Patria" (March of the Fatherland), was composed by José Blas Parera to lyrics (nine verses) by Vicente López y Planes. It was adopted in 1813 and officially decreed in 1900 as the country's national anthem.

The 1990s saw the rise of institutions that provided training in popular music. The Taller Latinoamericano de Música Popular (Latin American Popular Music Workshop), with headquarters in Rosario, has as its purpose the development of popular musicians and the awakening of critical and creative attitudes in composers, performers, teachers, journalists, and listeners. To train musicians of jazz, *tango*, and folk in a four-year program, the Escuela para Instrumentistas de Música Popular de América Latina (School for Instrumentalists in Popular Music of Latin America) was created in 1985 in Avellaneda, a suburb of Buenos Aires. In reality, however, pop musicians get their musical training almost exclusively from private teachers, sometimes the most famous musicians in the field, who own and operate workshops or labs for that purpose.

Another kind of institution eases the study of folk music: the secondary school with an artistic focus. In addition to studies leading to the *bachillerato* (high-school diploma), these schools offer specialization in different artistic fields, including folk-derived dance. Something similar takes place at the National Schools of Dance, where the same specialty is offered. All the schools of music have some course about traditional music of Argentina, and one of the most important ones, the Conservatorio Municipal, offers a career in ethnomusicology. In addition to a systemized pedagogical approach, some social and sports clubs and traditionalist societies offer training in the same areas.

Courses in musicology are offered at the university level. The Universidad Católica Argentina offers a major in musicology, in which students study music of oral traditions and others. Similar subjects are taught in the fields of arts or humanities at other universities. In general, however, the faculties of Argentine universities treat these subjects from highly theoretical and Western viewpoints.

Musical change and dissemination

Because of newly introduced musical genres, mass communication has been the most

Figure 27.6
Ivoti, one of the best-known bands dedicated to *chamamé*. Corrientes, 1995.

profound agent of change in rural Argentina. Typical rural instrumental ensembles began to disappear, replaced by records and cassettes of folk and fashionable international musics.

These factors of change had consequences that differed from one place to another. In the northwest Andean area, the native tritonic scale disappeared, native pentatonic and *crio-llo* heptatonic major-minor scales yielded to European major and minor scales, and singing in parallel thirds gradually disappeared. In the central and northeastern area, European salon dances (such as the polka, the mazurka, and the waltz) were introduced in the early 1800s and become extremely popular. These changes initiated a process of creolization, resulting in genres with truly local traits. One of them, the polka, gave birth to other genres, such as the *chamamé* and the *rasgueado doble*. Since the 1970s, the *chamamé* has been the only traditional Argentine music and dance form that is expanding and spreading more and more (Figure 27.6 and Figure 27.7). It has even reached southern Chile.

Figure 27.7
Wearing clothes typical of rural areas of Corrientes, a couple dances the *chamamé*. Photo by Jorge Prelorán, 1964.

Public policy

Some Argentine governments have ignored the political aspect of music, but others have paid attention to it. Among the latter have been those of strong nationalistic and populist character, such as the Perón regime, which mandated the broadcasting of a certain percentage of music of national origin over all radio stations and in all places of entertainment. In 1949, a minimum of 50 percent of Argentine music was required to be aired; in 1969, that mandate was reiterated. In 1971, the proportion was increased to 70 percent, with the specification that this amount was to be divided equally between urban, folk, and "modern" musics. After 1983, with the return of democracy, all these requirements were abrogated.

Because rock was associated with subversive ideas, additional governmental actions included the suppression of rock concerts. Through censorship, the military governments impeded the activities of some folk musicians because of the musicians' sympathies with leftist ideologies. In contrast, the creation of a *tango* orchestra in the Subsecretariat for Culture dates from 1938, and in 1980 the first musicological study of *tango* (Antología del Tango Rioplatense) was published—by a state agency, the Instituto Nacional de Musicología "Carlos Vega."

Since the early 1990s, music of all types has been broadcast on about 2,100 radio stations and 330 television channels in Argentina. Especially important is the Servicio Oficial de Radiodifusión (SOR), made up of LRA Radio Nacional and its forty affiliates, and the Argentina Televisora Color (ATC) television channel. About another 470 closed-circuit channels and several cable broadcasts come from Europe and the rest of America.

—Translated by Timothy D. Watkins

REFERENCES

Aretz, Isabel. 1954. *Costumbres tradicionales argentinas*. Buenos Aires: Huemul.

Barco Centenera, Martín del. 1836. "La Argentina o la conquista del Río de la Plata." In *Colección de Obras y Documentos Relativos a la Historia Antigua y Moderna de la Provincias del Rio de la Plata*, ed. Pedro de Angelis, 2:183–332. Buenos Aires: Plus Ultra.

Chapman, Anne, ed. 1972. *Selk'nam Chants of Tierra del Fuego, Argentina*. Ethnic Folkways FE 4176. 2 LP disks.

———. 1978. *Selk'nam Chants of Tierra del Fuego, Argentina*. Ethnic Folkways Records FE 4179. 2 LP disks.

Cortázar, Augusto Raúl. 1959. "Usos y costumbres." Folklore Argentino, ed. José Imbelloni et al., 158–196. Buenos Aires: Nova.

Despard, George Pakenham, ed. 1854. *Hope Deferred, Not Lost: A Narrative of Missionary Effort in South America, in Connection with the Patagonian Missionary Society*, 2nd ed. London: J. Nisbet.

Díaz de Guzmán, Ruy. 1969–1972 [1612]. "Historia argentina del descubrimiento, población y conquista de las Provincias del Río de la Plata." In *Colección de Obras y Documentos Relativos a la Historia Antigua y Moderna de la Provincias del Rio de la Plata*, ed. Pedro de Angelis, 1:11–111. Buenos Aires: Plus Ultra.

Dobrizhoffer, Martin. 1784. *Historia de Aiponibus Equestri: Bellicosaque Paraguariae Natione*. 3 vols. Vienna: Kurzbek.

Ferrer, Horacio. 1977. *El libro del tango*. 2 vols. Buenos Aires: Galerna.

Frigerio, Alejandro. 1991. "Umbanda o Africanismo en Buenos Aires: Duas etapas de um mesmo caminho religioso." *Comunicações do ISER* 35:52–63.

Furlong, Charles Wellington. 1909. "The Southernmost People of the World." *Harper's Monthly Magazine* 119(June).

Gallardo, Carlos R. 1910. *Tierra del Fuego: Los Onas*. Buenos Aires: Cabaut y Cía.

Gallardo, Jorge Emilio. 1986. *Presencia africana en la Cultura de América Latina: Vigencia de los cultos afroamericanos*. Buenos Aires: Fernando García Cambeiro.

García, Silvia. 1978. "La fiesta de San Juan en la Provincia de Formosa." *Cuadernos del Instituto Nacional de Antropología* 8:125–148.

Grebe, María Ester. 1979–1980. "Relaciones entre música y cultura: El kultrún y su simbolismo." *Revista INIDEF* 4:7–25.

Hernández, Juán Antonio. 1910 [1836]. "Diario que el capitán … ha hecho de la expedición contra los indios teguelches." In *Colección de Obras y Documentos Relativos a la Historia Antigua y Moderna de la Provincias del Río de la Plata, ed. Pedro de Angelis*, 4:547–563. Buenos Aires: Librería Nacional.

Kereilhac de Kussrow, Alicia. 1980. *La fiesta de San Baltasar*. Buenos Aires: Ediciones Culturales Argentinas.

Lothrop, Samuel Kirkland. 1928. *The Indians of Tierra del Fuego*. New York: Museum of the American Indian, Heye Foundation.

Lozano, Pedro. 1874–1875. *Historia de la conquista del Paraguay, Río de la Plata y Tucumán*. 5 vols. Buenos Aires: Imprenta Popular.

Moreno, S. J. 1890–1891. "Exploración arqueológica de la provincia de Catamarca." *Revista del Museo de La Plata*, vol. 1.

Moreno Chá, Ercilia. 1971. "Semana Santa en Yavi." *Cuadernos del Instituto Nacional de Antropología* 7:1971.

———. 1987. "Alternativas del Proceso de Cambio de un Repertorio Tradicional Argentino." *Latin American Music Review* 8(1):94–111.

———, ed. 1995. *Tango tuyo, mío y nuestro*. Buenos Aires: Instituto Nacional de Antropología y Pensamiento Latinoamericano.

Morris, Isaac. 1750. *A Narrative of the Dangers and Distresses Which Befell Isaac Morris, and Seven More of the Crew. …* London: S. Birt.

Olsen, Dale A. 1980. "Folk Music of South America: A Musical Mosaic." In *Musics of Many Cultures: An Introduction*, ed. Elizabeth May, 386–425. Berkeley: University of California Press.

———. 2004. *The Chrysanthemum and the Song: Music, Memory, and Identity in the Japanese Diaspora to South America*. Gainesville, FL: University Press of Florida.

d'Orbigny, Alcide Dessalines. 1835–1847. *Voyage dans l'Amérique méridionale*. 7 vols. Paris: Pitois-Levrault.

Pérez Bugallo, Rubén. 1982. "Estudio etnomusicológico de los chiriguano-chané de la Argentina: Primera parte: Organología." *Cuadernos del Instituto Nacional de Antropología* 9:221–268.

———. 1993. *Pillantún: Estudios de etno-organología patagónica y pampeana.* Buenos Aires: Búsqueda de Ayllu.

Pigafetta, Antonio. 1800 [1534]. *Primo viaggio intorno al globo terracqueo.* Milan and Paris: Amoretti.

Robertson, Carol E. 1979. "Pulling the Ancestors: Performance Practice and Praxis in Mapuche Ordering." *Ethnomusicology* 23(3):395–416.

Roig, Elizabeth. 1990. "La música toba en el contexto de la Iglesia Evangélica Unida." Paper presented at the "Séptimas Jornadas Argentinas de Musicología" of the Instituto Nacional de Musicología "Carlos Vega," Buenos Aires.

Ruiz, Irma. 1984. "La ceremonia ñemongaraí de los Mbïá de la Provincia de Misiones." *Temas de Etnomusicología* 1:45–102.

Sánchez Labrador, Joseph. 1936 [1772]. *Paraguay cathólico: Los Indios Pampas—Puelches—Patagones.* Buenos Aires: Viau y Zona.

Segers, Polidoro A. 1891. "Tierra del Fuego: Hábitos y costumbres de los indios onas." *Boletín del Museo de Historia Natural* 19(5–6).

Transilvano, Maximiliano. 1837 [1829]. "Relación escrita por … de cómo y por quién y en qué tiempo fueron descubiertas y halladas las islas Molucas." In *Colección de los viajes y descubrimientos que hicieron por mar los españoles desde fines del siglo XV.* Madrid: Imprenta Nacional.

Vaulx, Comte Henri de la. 1898. "À travers la Patagonie du Río Negro au détroit de Magellan." *Journal de la Société des Américanistes* 6:71–99.

Vignati, María Emilia. 1982. "La música aborigen." *Historia General del Arte en la Argentina,* 1:58–102. Buenos Aires: Academic Nacional de Bellas Artes.

Vila, Pablo. 1989. "Argentina's Rock Nacional: The Struggle for Meaning." *Latin American Music Review* 10(1):1–28.

Zeballos, Estanislao S. 1881. *Descripción amena de la República Argentina: Viaje al país de los araucanos.* 3 vols. Buenos Aires: Peuser.

Mapuche

Carol E. Robertson

Musical Instruments
Musical Contexts and Genres
Acculturation
Further Study

The Mapuche (People of the Land) inhabit the lands between the Bío-Bío River and Chiloé Island in Chile and adjacent areas in western Argentina. Anthropologists and government officials often use the name *Araucano* to designate these native Americans who share a common language (Araucanian), though many continue to identify themselves as Pehuenche, Puelche, Tehuelche, Ranquel, Huarpe, and Pampa-Boroga. The politics of naming and specifying cultural identities in this area of Chile and Argentina is a puzzle that can be solved only through a discussion of archaeological records, musical forms, and ritual practices. The history of the southern Andes unites traditions of warriors, prophets, shamans, and nomadic pastoralists under a linguistic umbrella, *mapudungun* ("words of the land").

Archaeological records and oral histories trace several migrations across the Andes Mountains. For millennia, peoples of the eastern pampas traded with their western neighbors and utilized the natural resources of the Atlantic and Pacific oceans. Ancient Moluche warriors and hunters from the pampas conquered the agriculturalists between the Bío-Bío and Toltén rivers more than a thousand years ago (Berdichewsky 1971). Between the 1400s and 1700s, the Chilean Mapuche reversed the direction of this influence by extending their military and trade empire all the way to what is now Buenos Aires (San Martín ca. 1919; Schoo Lastra 1928).

Clay vessels and stone panpipes suggest that trade routes extended from Patagonia to the southern borders of the Nasca, the Wari, and (much later) the Inca empires of Peru. In the late 1400s, the Inca incorporated the Kolla Suyu (Southern Kingdom) into their extensive domain and established military outposts south of the Maule River to protect their claims (Aldunate del Solar 1992). Thus, by the time of the Spanish invasions in the 1500s, the people we know as Mapuche had become a heterogeneous mixture of autonomous communities, formed into military confederations to resist incursions from Inca and Spanish forces.

Several centuries of contact between peoples on both sides of the Andes produced an intricate cosmology and a body of ceremonial lore loosely shared by peoples with differing systems of social organization (Faron 1956, 1961, 1964; Robertson 1979; Robertson-DeCarbo 1975). Until about 1900, Mapuche military success was reinforced by a system of elaborate rituals in which animal sacrifice and agricultural offerings to ancestors played a central part. For horses, women wove intricate wool blankets and belts covered with protective signs and invocations of each warrior's personal power. To deepen the spiritual and physical fortitude of absent husbands and sons, wives and mothers performed lineage songs daily. To ensure the prosperity of those in battle and those at home, shamanic practitioners were consulted throughout the year.

Present-day Mapuche oral historians assert that formerly there were no permanent chiefs among Mapuche peoples; rather, in wartime, prominent citizens (often male diviners or heads of lineages) would be installed as military chiefs, expected to step back into the ranks once peace had been secured. Prominent women were consulted on matters of military strategy. Authority was negotiated through a system of lineage exchanges. The social and ritual power of each lineage was embodied in characteristic songs and dances.

The persistence of warfare over five centuries radically changed Mapuche social organization. Once the Argentine and Chilean armies usurped control of Mapuche lands, they established land-distribution patterns (Chile) and a system of reservations (Argentina) that altered access to the people's water, trade routes, animal herding, and authority structures. With men at war for long periods, social authority, ritual life, food gathering, and animal herding had fallen increasingly into the hands of women.

The Argentine and Chilean national governments were slow to recognize the rights of Mapuche women and restricted their claims to land and herds. The power arrangements that had prevailed in peacetime were replaced with permanent, hereditary chieftainships. Despite the conqueror's misogyny, several Mapuche women inherited the title of community chief (*lonko*) in Chile and Argentina. Each chief now answered to the white (*hninca*) military or provincial authorities of each territory (Martínez Sarasola 1992).

The ritual power of the shaman (*machi*) was undermined by missionization, public education, and governments, which feared shamans' power to energize the will of a subjugated people. Decreased access to fertile land and to the new economic system diminished a community's ability to provide feasts, horses, silver ornaments, and personnel requisite for important rituals, including seasonal rites of increase and female rites of passage (*katán kawil*).

MUSICAL INSTRUMENTS

The Mapuche have always challenged scholarly reduction, for while engaging in many musical practices common to other South American peoples, they have fashioned their dialogue with the sacred through unique uses of vocal and instrumental techniques.

The archaeological record offers extensive examples of *pitucahue,* stone panpipes of up to eight tubes, linking the Mapuche to panpipe traditions reaching as far north as Panama (Pérez de Arce 1986, 1987). Some Chilean *pitucahue* were carved as early as the tenth century. Stone, an unyielding medium, was eventually replaced by wood and cane. Though stone panpipes were used to make melodies, their cane and wood counterparts (*pifülka*) were used as markers of rhythm. Most *pifülka* are double-tubed pan-pipes, yielding a fundamental and an overblown fourth, fifth, or octave. Wooden varieties became scarce in the 1900s and have been replaced by ensembles of single canes of varying lengths. Rather than playing them in melodic groups (as in the northern Andean traditions), Mapuche musicians play each tube separately: to create rhythmic patterns, each player coordinates the pitch of his tube with his fellows' pitches. When large numbers of *pifülka* players gather to dance around the altar (*rewe*) during the annual rites of increase (*ŋillipún,* also *nguillattún* and *kamarrikún*), the exact pitch of each cane is not important; instead of focusing on melody, the ensemble creates rhythmic patterns for movement.

Many other kinds of flutes have been found in archaeological sites, as have straight trumpets with oblique or transverse mouthpieces. Among the latter, the *trutruka* (with oblique mouthpiece) continues to be an important sonic element in the annual rites of increase [see ARGENTINA: Figure 27.2]. This kind of trumpet, found in the Andes all the way to the Bolivian border, usually consists of a thick cane 2 to 5 meters long wrapped in horse intestine (earlier, guanaco intestine) and capped with a cow horn. Many *trutruka* players, having learned to play the trumpet in the army, often insert European military signals into the patterns traditionally associated with the annual rites of increase (Robertson-DeCarbo 1975). Because the *trutruka* can be heard at a distance, it is still used for signaling in remote areas of the Andes.

Another instrument that has pre-Columbian antecedents is the *kultrún,* a single-headed kettle drum central to Mapuche healing and ceremony. It consists of a wooden bowl (*mamül ralí*) covered with hide of *guanaco,* dog, or (in recent times) cow or horse and fastened with human hair or sinew. Drums are painted with symbols that denote the four directions, the four lines of ancestors, the sun, the moon, spirals, planets, and other forces of nature (Aldunate del Solar 1992; Grebe 1979–1980). They often appear in ancient rock drawings in scenes depicting important social changes, hunts, or spiritual revelations.

Many other instruments within the archaeological record have fallen out of use: shell rattles (*chunan*), calabash rattles (*huada*), shell rasps (*cadacada*), musical bows (*quinquerche* or *quinquercahue*), diverse flutes made of bone and cane, and a sucked trumpet (*lolkiñ* or *nolkín*). Of all the instruments mentioned, the *kultrún* is by far the most important, for it offers a point of entry into Mapuche cosmology.

MUSICAL CONTEXTS AND GENRES

In Mapuche ideology, each individual has two souls. The first, *alwé* or *almén,* is distinctly personal: it is born with each individual and yet survives the physical limitations of that individual. It is the source of each individual's creative energy. When a person dies, this soul wanders across the earth until it reaches the end of the western horizon, through which it enters the realm of gods and ancestors.

The second soul, *kimpén,* is an inherited soul embodying the life force of a lineage. It originates in the sacred ancestral past, but it is transmitted across the boundaries of time to the contemporary descendants of a lineage. This soul is individualized only in that it enters a person at birth. Its nature is cumulative, compounded through time, and contributed to by all deceased and living members of each lineage. Lines of kinship are traced through an individual's four grandparents. Though this soul can be traced to an individual's father's father, each person may invoke up to four sets of ancestors according to circumstance and need.

The power of each *kimpeñ* is coded in its song, known as *tayil.* Each *tayil* is a signature—a shorthand statement of the natural powers and physical properties associated with a particular lineage, its guiding spirits, its animal totems, its spiritual history. As Andrés Epullán, a Mapuche elder of Andean Argentina, put it in 1978, "*Tayil* is a way of feeling. When the women pull out *tayil,* they do it with great emotion. In that moment, they are feeling everything that has ever flowed through the veins of those who hold that chant. They feel it through their wombs." This genre can be performed only by women, for it is a form of giving birth to spirit. The verb used for vocalizing a *tayil* is the same verb used for the process of going through labor and giving birth. Many variations of *tayil* melodies exist, but women say they know they are "tracking" the song correctly when they feel a certain tension in their wombs.

Specific melodic contours and coded syllables are combined to signal the character of a lineage (Figure 28.1). For example, the word for sheep is *ufisha,* but the specific sung syllable identifying the sheep lineage is *we.* Likewise, the water lineage (*kó*) is coded into song as *yo-le-le.* When combined with the right song path or melodic contour, these syllables become the signature that identifies a specific family in the presence of ancestors and supernaturals.

The goal of performing *tayil* is to bridge the present and the past. Each performance consists of four phrases, and each phrase articulates the lineage soul in a different sphere of time and space. When a woman performs her husbands *tayil* (Figure 28.2), phrase one departs the body of the singer and enters the body of the person whose lineage soul is being sung. Phrase two pulls this soul out of the husband's body and into the ritual space of the performance. Phrase three sends the performance into the realm of supernaturals. Phrase four brings it back into the body of the individual whose *à tayifàf* is being performed (Robertson 1979).

Figure 28.1
Ufisha tayil ("sheep lineage-soul chant"), melodic contour or "path." Transcription by Carol Robertson.

"We" - -

Figure 28.2
Ufisha tayil as performed by Tomasa Epulef, Zaina Yegua, Nenguén. Transcription by Carol Robertson.

We   we   we—   a   we—   we   we—   a

we   we   we   we—   a—   we   we   we—   we we—   a

Tayil are critical to the Mapuche process of ritual and healing. In Mapuche belief, most disease is caused by the wandering of the personal soul (*alwé*). This detachable aspect of self can become entangled in the spirit world or can be captured by another human being. An individual whose soul has been tampered with may suffer illnesses, exhibiting physical and spiritual symptoms. Treatment may be approached through several methods. In Chile, the most common is the *machitún,* wherein the *machi* uses her voice and her *kultrún* to journey for her patient and take the diseased soul through a cathartic process that will bring a release into wellness (Grebe 1979–1980; Grebe, Pacheco, and Segura 1972).

Persecution, intimidation, and missionization have made Argentine Mapuche wary of acknowledging the presence of shamanic practitioners in their midst (Robertson 1991). As in Chile, healers on the eastern slopes of the Andes are usually women. Men in this profession have always dressed and behaved socially as women, developing an artificial womb through which to channel healing.

In Argentina, ceremonial leaders are known as *witakultruntufe* ("women carrying the drum"). Like the Chilean *machi,* the *witakultruntufe* combines chant and drumming with herbal medicine and ritual action to create a healing gestalt in which the spiritual and social patterns and behavior of the patient may be modified. If illness is the result of a personal soul's wandering, the patient may be strengthened when the healer "pulls" the *tayil,* fusing past and present, creating a union of the mundane and sacred worlds. The healer may resonate sounds in parts of her body that correspond to affected parts of the patient's body. To treat respiratory diseases, she may sound tones in her chest and project the sound from her body into the patient's lungs. These techniques, developed over centuries of empirical experimentation, are based on a world view that perceives sound as central to the movement and balance of the universe, the community, and the individual.

Vocal genres

Several traditional vocal genres persist among the Mapuche. A precomposed style of ceremonial song (*öl*) accompanies dances at the annual rites of increase. Improvised songs (*kantún*) are often denoted by a Spanish term, *romanceo* (or *romancero*). Spontaneous creations, these usually describe recent events and may cleverly juxtapose Spanish and Mapuche texts to cultivate the metaphors and puns of Mapuche humor. The melodies and rhythms of many *kantún* have been influenced by the Chilean *cueca,* and by *chamamé, chotis, milonga,* polka, and *vals,* styles introduced by frontier soldiers and *gauchos.* Early twenty-first-century examples may show traces of melodies by Mexican *mariachis* and even the Beatles. *Kantún* may be composed and sung by men and women, unaccompanied or with guitar and accordion. The *öl* are often sung by women simultaneously with the hocketed melodies of *pifülka* ensembles; but *tayil* are the exclusive domain of women's voices.

Because Mapuche homes are often at great distances from one another, whole communities do not gather frequently. Men who work on road construction sites or on cattle farms owned by non-Mapuche settlers may gather at makeshift *pulperías,* where alcohol lubricates the throat and loosens *cuecas* and *romanceos.* Since the 1960s, women have begun to join their men at *ramadas,* song-and-dance feasts held in *criollo* towns, in which participants may dance until they collapse from exhaustion.

The Mapuche are famous for their endurance in song and dance. Some boast that they have been well honed for *ramadas* by years of participation in the annual rites of increase, held at the end of each harvest season, and involving three or four days and nights of perpetual dancing and ceremony. The goal of the ceremony is to draw the ancestors' and deities' attention to the needs of their earthbound children. Sheep and horses are sacrificed and offered on an altar (*rewe*); women sing *tayil* and *öl* to fortify ritual actions that link the community to sacred time.

The dances of these rites vary from one community to another, depending on the mix of Andean and pampa groups that has resulted over centuries of migration and intermarriage. Among the most widely known dances are *puel purrún* and *lonkomeo,* performed in areas of Chile and Argentina. Their rhythms are signaled by the *kultrún* and are sometimes accompanied by young male dancers playing *pifilka* and *trutruka.*

Puel purrún means "dance to the east," whence come light and life. The *puel purrún* involves the whole community. Women dance in one direction around the altar, and men dance in a circle in the opposite direction, or men and women face each other in parallel lines, dancing first to the right, and then to the left.

The *lankomeo'* means "moving the head" and differs from *puel purrún* in that it is a virtuosic display of individual skill. The choreography of this dance depicts five stages in the life of the *choike,* a rhea (like an ostrich), whose size and power impede its flight but which at death soars heavenward to meet the ancestors. Drummed rhythms accompany the emergence of the rhea from the egg, its wobbly attempts to walk, its strut as a mature bird, and its death and ascent. Old and young men alike are selected to form groups of four or five dancers representing the major lineages in a community. Kinswomen pull forth the lineage soul of each dancer so the dance, a ritual metaphor for life on earth, will evoke compassion in the beings of the spirit world.

Mapuche performance spaces often accommodate more than one event at a time, so instrumental and vocal genres often occur simultaneously without the need for synchrony. Thus, though dances, chants, and instrumental passages may accompany the same ritual action, they may do so as separate artistic statements. This is especially evident in group performances of *tayil,* in which each woman may begin her rendition on any pitch and perform at her own speed, for each woman is pulling her lineage soul forth as a separate, personal effort (Figure 28.3).

This approach to performance often carries over into some of the musical genres learned from Argentine *gauchos* and performed at annual *señaladas,* when animals are branded, separated, and prepared for journeys to higher pastures where they will spend the summer. These events are capped in the late afternoon by house parties at which hosts provide meat, wine, and song. Guitars, accordions, and Western band instruments seldom seen in colder months may be brought down from the rafters for renditions of a late-nineteenth-century *vals* or *chotis,* and an occasional polka. Many of these styles were learned by grandfathers of the present generation while in captivity in frontier

Figure 28.3
Ufisha tayil as it might be performed by two kinswomen in the same ritual space. A composite transcription by Carol Robertson.

forts. Sometimes, an accordion, a guitar, and a trumpet may play in different keys and at different tempi, for, although they are part of the same event, each performer asserts a degree of independence.

ACCULTURATION

Though many Mapuche children have been estranged from traditional world views by schools, missionization, and a world that hawks "modern" values and rejects old ways, they continue to participate in the agricultural and ritual cycles of their communities. Since the 1970s or earlier, Salesian missionaries have stressed traditional weaving and leatherworking as part of the curriculum, and Mapuche artisans have been receiving recognition for their textiles, pottery, silversmithing, and dance regalia. In turn, Mapuche communities continue to absorb influences from the outside, especially those transmitted by radio and village dance festivals. New generations are mediating the impact of military defeat through agricultural and animal-husbandry programs, and the Mapuche language is still spoken in many areas of the southern Andes.

In 1981, Gregorio Cayulef, a Mapuche elder from the Argentine-Chilean border, said: "Chile and Argentina may declare war on each other forever. But we know that though our grandfathers came from many places, we are now one Mapuche people. We find seashells in the mountains and know these Andes were not always there. Change will come; but as for us, we must keep two things: our language and our chants."

FURTHER STUDY

The Chilean composer and scholar Carlos Isamitt was one of the first to study and write about the music and dance of the Mapuche, whom he called *los araucanos* (1937, 1938, 1941). Another Chilean composer interested in musical nationalism, Carlos Lavín, also published about the music of the Mapuche (1967). The Chilean composer, musicologist, and

Indiana University professor Juan Orrego-Salas drew on the findings and publications of these Chilean scholars, those of Pedro Humberto Allende, and also his own research, resulting in an article in *Ethnomusicology* (1966) entitled "Araucanian Indian Instruments." This was one of the first studies in English on Mapuche music. With the expansion of the foremost Chilean scholarly journal, *Revista Musical Chilena,* into more ethnomusicological topics and themes, numerous articles on Mapuche music appeared in the 1970s and 1980s. Most important are those by María Ester Grebe (1973, 1974), Ernesto Gonzàlez (1986), Luis Merino (1974), and Carlos Munizaga (1974).

An early but important anthropological study of Chilean Mapuche music is by Titiev (1949), entitled *Social Singing among the Mapuche.* His studies (also 1951) and those by Louis Faron (1964, 1968) are important ethnographic works for contextualizing Mapuche music.

Two commercial recordings that include Mapuche music are by Dannemann and Wenzel (1975) and Clair-Vasiliadis, et al. (1975). Dannemann and Wenzel include several excerpts of *trutruka* music and a lengthy example of a *machi* shaman accompanied by a *kultrún,* Clair-Vasiliadis's recording includes numerous social songs, love songs, marriage songs, and other vocal examples, plus a short excerpt of a *trutruka* solo. *The JVC/Smithsonian Folkways Video Anthology of Music and Dance of the Americas* (Okada 1995), Vol. 5, has excellent footage of Mapuche ceremonial music (examples 12 and 13).

REFERENCES

Aldunaie del Solar, Carlos. 1992. *Mapuche: Seeds of the Chilean Soil.* Philadelphia: Port of History Museum and Museo Chileno de Arte Precolombino

Berdichewsky, Bernardo. 1971. "Fases culturales en la prehistoria de los araucanos de Chile." *Revista Chilena de Historia y Geografía* 139:105–112.

Clair-Vasiliadis, Chrisios, et al. 1975. *Amerindian Music of Chile: Aymara, Qaqashqar, Mapuche.* Ethnic Folkways Records FF. 4054. LP disk.

Dannemann, Manuel, and Jochen Wenzel. 1975. *Amerindian Ceremonial Music from Chile.* Unesco Collection. Musical Sources, Pre-Columbian America XI-1. Philips 6586 026. LP disk.

Faron, Louis C. 1956. "Araucanian Patri-Organization and the Omaha System." *American Anthropologist* 63:435–456.

———. 1961. *Mapuche Social Structure.* Urbana: University of Illinois Press.

———. 1964. *Hawks if the Sun: Mapuche Morality and Its Ritual Attributes.* Pittsburgh: University of Pittsburgh Press.

———. 1968. *The Mapuche Indians of Chile.* New York: Holt, Rinehart and Winston.

González, Ernesto. 1986. "Vigencias de Instrumentos Musicales Mapuches." *Revista Musical Chilena* 40(166):4–52.

Grebe, María Ester. 1973. "El kultrún mapuche: Un microcosmo simbólico. *Revista Musical Chilena* 27(123-l24):3–42.

———. 1974. "Presencia del dualismo en la cultura y música y mapuche." *Revista Musical Chilena* 28(126-127):47–79.

———. 1979-1980. "Relaciones entre música y cultura: El kultrún *y* su simbolismo." *Revista INIDEF* 4:7–25.

Grebe, María Ester, Sergio Pacheco, and José Segura. 1972. "Cosmovisión Mapuche." *Cuadernos de la Realidad National* 14. Santiago: Universidad Católica de Chile.

Isamitt, Carlos. 1937. "Cuatro instrumentos musicales araucanos." *Boletín Latino Americano de Música* 3(3):55–66.

————.1938. "Los instrumentos araucanos." *Boletín Latino Americano de Música* 4(4):307–312.

————. 1941. "La danza cntre los araucanos."*Boletín Latino Americano de Música* 4(5):601–605.

Lavín, Carlos. 1967. "La música de los araucanos." *Revista Musical Chilena* 21 (99):57–60.

Martínez Sarasola, Carlos. 1992. *Nuestros paisanos los indios: Vida, historia y destino de las comunidades indígenas en la argentina*. Buenos Aires: Emecé.

Merino, Luis. 1974. "Instrumentos musicales, cultura mapuche y el Cautiverio feliz del Mestre de Campo Francisco Núñez de Pineda y Bascuñán." *Revista Musical Chilena* 28(128):56–95.

Munizaga, Carlos. 1974. "Atacameños, araucanos, alacalufes: Breve reseña de tres grupos étnicos chilenos." *Revista Musical Chilena* 28(126–127):7–20.

Okada, Yuki. 1995. *Central and South America. The JVC/Smithsonian Folkways Video Anthology of Music and Dance of the Americas*, 5. Montpelier, Vt.: Multicultural Media, ML3410.C362 1999 VD5 (1 videocassette).

Orrego-Salas, Juan A. 1966. "Araucanian Indian Instruments." *Ethnomusicology* 10(1):48–57.

Pérez dc Arce, José. 1986. "Cronología de los instrumentos sonoros del area extremo sur andina." *Revista Musical Chilena* 166:68–123.

_____, 1987. "Flautas arqueológicas del extremo sur andino." *Boletín del Museo Chileno de Arte Precolombino* 2:55–87.

Robertson, Carol E 1979. "'Pulling the Ancestors': Performance Practice and Praxis in Mapuche Ordering." *Ethnomusicology* 23(3):395–4l6.

_____. 1991. "The Ethnomusicologist as Midwife." In *Music in the Dialogue of Cultures: Traditional Music and Cultural Policy*, ed. Max Peter Baumann, 347–364. Wilhelmshaven: Florian Noetzcl Verlag.

Robertson-DeCarbo, Carol E. 1975. "Tayil: Musical Communication and Social Organization among the Mapuche of Argentina." Ph. D. dissertation, Indiana University.

_____. 1976. "Tayil as Category and Communication among the Argentine Mapuche: A Methodological Suggestion." *Yearbook of the International Council for Traditional Music* 8:35–52.

San Martín, Félix, ca. 1919. *Neuquén*. Buenos Aires: Rodríguez Giles.

Schoo Lastra, Dionisio. 1928. *El indio del desierto*. Buenos Aires: Jacobo Peuser.

Titiev, Mischa. 1949. *Social Singing among the Mapuche*. Anthropological Papers of the Museum of Anthropology, 2. Ann Arbor: University of Michigan Press.

_____. 1951. *Araucanian Culture in Transition*. Ann Arbor; University of Michigan Press.

Bolivia

Henry Stobart

The Indigenous Heritage
The European Heritage
Musical Instruments
Musical Contexts and Genres
Musical Performers and Performances
Musical Ideologies and Aesthetics
Musical Change
Learning, Dissemination, Tourism, and Public Policy
Further Study

Over 75 percent of Bolivia's people live in the Andean highlands, an area dominated by the cold, high central plain known as *altiplano* ("high plain" in Spanish and *puna* in Quechua). At an altitude of 4 kilometers, the *altiplano* is bordered by two steep mountain ranges. The western cordillera follows the border with Chile, and the eastern cordillera drops through intermontane valleys toward the Amazon basin. The hot, eastern lowlands, which make up more than 60 percent of the country's area, are much less densely populated and comprise plains and tropical forest.

The official national languages of Bolivia are Spanish (spoken by 87 percent of the population), Quechua (34 percent), and Aymara (23 percent) (van Lindert and Verkoren 1994:72–73). In the lowlands of eastern Bolilvia some forty Amerindian languages (including Guaraní, Moré, Moxo, and Yurakaré) are spoken, but mainly by small, dispersed groups. With Peru, Bolivia is notable among South American countries for the strongly native American aspects of its culture and population (comprising nearly 60 percent, followed by 35 percent *mestizo*).

Archaeological evidence of musical activity in the Andean highlands of Bolivia is poorly preserved in comparison with the wealth from early Peruvian coastal cultures. The earliest finds, said to date from 900 B.C. to A.D. 300, include clay panpipes, vessel flutes, and three-holed bone notch flutes. These are on deposit in the university museum at Cochabamba. Tiwanaku (Tiahuanacu, Tiawanaku), at its height around A.D.1000, was one of the most important early highland cultures, centered a few kilometers south of Lake Titicaca. The *zampoñero*, a large stone statue found there (kept in the Gold Museum, La Paz), is believed to represent a man holding a panpipe to his lips. Other finds include three bronze figurines depicting musicians holding end-blown flutes, a drum, and a four-tubed panpipe (Díaz Gainza 1988), and what appears to be a workshop for constructing panpipes.

The mythological record for Bolivian music, by contrast, is rich. As early as 1653, for example, a creation myth was documented by the seventeenth-century Spanish priest and chronicler Bernabé Cobo (1990 [1653]) that tells how humans were fashioned from mud at Tiwanaku, each endowed with language to sing their multiplicity of songs. Song and dance are often featured in accounts describing early mythological ages when humans freely transformed themselves into animals. Even today, rural Andean music is especially linked with metamorphosing beings that may be said to take the form of humans or mermaids or to transform themselves into animals, and musical instruments are commonly said to have arrived with Inkarrí, the Inka (Inca) king.

Music and musical practices in Bolivia are often associated with enchantment and myth. These range from the consequences of breaking musical taboos to pacts with the devil to gain special musical powers and enchant members of the opposite sex. A Bolivian version of the almost universal story of the singing bones tells of a priest from Potosí who dug up his lover's body and fashioned a flute from her tibia. A more rural version of the same story (told as far north as Ecuador) tells of a young man who fashioned a flute from the bone of his lover (a partridge), which his parents had killed and eaten.

In many highland peasant communities of Bolivia, the image of three maidens connected with music is common. The Callawaya call these maidens Tusuy, the goddess of dance, who is compared to a spinning distaff; Wancay, the singer, who has the mouth of a toad; and Munakuy, love, the beautiful, who wears her heart outside her chest (Oblitas Poblete 1978 [1960]). In other areas, three maidens with enchanting voices are said to have been invited to a wedding, but partway through the ceremony they turned into toads (Torrico 1988).

History records that the expansion of the Inka empire from Cuzco, Peru around 1450 included all of today's highland Bolivia. Before this, the region was divided into kingdoms and ethnic groups, principally speaking Aymara, Pukina, and Uruqilla. The constant wars and shifting alliances among these kingdoms were exploited by the Quechua-speaking Inka, who introduced elements of their own culture, including music.

The Inka achieved uniformity and stability through implanting groups of loyal Quechua-speakers into troublesome parts of the empire, such as the valleys of Cochabamba, southern Potosí, Chuquisaca, and Tarija—areas now predominantly Quechua-speaking. The continued use of Aymara was accepted by the Inka, and Aymara remains the dominant indigenous language of the high plains of La Paz and Oruro departments.

In a late-sixteenth-century account of the musics of the Inka Empire, the Spanish chronicler Guamán Poma de Ayala (1980 [1600?]) depicts *altiplano* women playing a large drum suspended from a frame, accompanying men who each blow across a two-tone pipe. The *jantarka*, a similar percussion instrument, is still played by women during Carnaval in the village of Calcha, Potosí Department (Stobart 1987).

THE EUROPEAN HERITAGE

The Spanish invasion of the southern Andes in the 1530s followed less than a century of Inka rule. It brought from Europe new instruments that profoundly influenced indigenous music. In contrast, the invaders often viewed Amerindian instruments with suspicion. They associated panpipes with those played back home in Spain by lowly castrators of pigs and grinders of knives. Spanish efforts to evangelize often repressed indigenous musical instruments, but the native Americans were immediately attracted to European instruments, and musical instruction was among the methods of Roman Catholic indoctrination. Lessons were given in plainsong and polyphony, and instruments such as shawms (*chirimías*) and recorders (*flautas*) were taught to provide processional or liturgical music.

Jesuit missions not only encouraged the use of instruments such as violins and transverse flutes, but also, unlike other Roman Catholic sects, sometimes adapted indigenous instruments to play European-style music. In the lowlands, these include the huge *bajones*, a multiple-tubed, double-unit, raft trumpet (resembling *sikuri* panpipes, but played as trumpets rather than flutes), and the *pífano*, a bird-bone flute. In secular music, the introduction of the *vihuela* and guitars resulted in imitations and hybrid instruments, such as the *charango*. Many European forms, styles, and rhythms were adopted; and even musical concepts, such as that of the siren (Spanish *sirena*) were blended into what appear to be pre-Hispanic musical practices.

In the 1570s, with the adoption of compulsory labor (*mit'a*, Spanish *mita*) to work the silver mines of Potosí, native Americans were drafted from communities all over the highlands, walking sometimes up to 1,600 kilometers from southern Peru. This glittering city was a melting pot of indigenous and foreign cultures. Descriptions of its legendary feasts by the chroniclers Arzans de Orsúa and Vela (1965) mention native American instruments such as cane flutes, trumpets (of conch, cane, or gourd), and a kind of marimba. These were played alongside instruments from every level of Spanish society, including bugles, guitars, harps, hornpipes, pipe and tabors, trumpets, *vihuelas*, and rebecs (Baptista Gumucio 1988).

Potosí and nearby La Plata (today Sucre) boasted theaters dating from the early 1600s, for which much music was composed. Several accounts mention the importance of persons of African descent as entertainers, and in 1568 a black and a mulatto were contracted in La Plata to open a school of music and dance (Stevenson 1968). Few manuscripts from that period survive, but a large collection of sacred pieces, dating mainly from the 1700s and 1800s, is held in the national archives in Sucre, mostly scored for voices, sometimes with violins and basso continuo, specifically harp and organ.

Bolivia is remarkable for the diversity of its musical instruments, which vary according to cultural group, area, time of year, and ritual function. In many highland zones, cane is the most common material, because of the proximity of the tropical valleys of the Yungas and Cochabamba; to the south and west, wood and bamboo are frequently used.

The names of many instruments are interchangeable, and a single generic term may refer to a variety of instruments of different construction. Confusions often arise in orthographic conventions between Spanish and indigenous languages; for example, the Spanish *quena* or *kena* is written as *qina* in standardized Quechua (originally it was *qina-qina* in Aymara). Alterations and inconsistencies in spelling and pronunciation often make a word almost unrecognizable, as with the Spanish word for "flute," spelled variously *flauta*, *flawta*, *flawata*, *lawuta*, and *lawatu*. This essay uses standardized spellings for indigenous languages and common Spanish spellings.

Idiophones

Highland percussive instruments include triangles, bronze llama bells (*sinsiru*, *cencerro*), cog rattles (*matraca*), and heavy metal spurs attached to wooden sandals (*suila jut'as*). Among the lowland percussive instruments are seed-pod rattles (*paichochi*), worn on many dancers' ankles, drums and various idiophones, such as the gourd and beeswax *toá* of the Moré, a friction idiophone (Leigue Castedo 1957), and pestles and mortars played by paired women among the Chacobo (Prost 1970).

Membranophones

Double-headed drums are used throughout the highlands to accompany wind ensembles. Among the larger types are long cylinder drums (*phutu wankara*), commonly played

with panpipes, as are shallower, military-style bass drums (*pumpu*, *bombo*). Military-style side drums (*tambora*) are particularly common in the *altiplano*, while vertically held drums (*wankara*, *caja*), often with a single beater and a snare of string, and sometimes porcupine quills, are universal there. Women sometimes play these types (*quchana*, *chinki*) in special rituals.

Aerophones

Panpipes are common throughout the highlands and are found in several parts of the lowlands. Among the lowland Chacobo, four tubes are simply grasped in the player's right hand; but in other regions, the tubes, ranging from two to seventeen, are usually tied together.

Figure 29.1
Julajula players kneel to perform a *kulwa* outside a church. Charka Province, northern Potosí, Bolivia. Photo by Henry Stobart, 1986.

DISC ❶ TRACK 6

DISC ❶ TRACK 5

Figure 29.2
Suna, a processional dance played on paired *julajula*, often precedes ritual battles. About fifty musicians play their instruments in parallel octaves. Upper stems represent the four-tubed *qia* (the leader of the pair); lower stems the three-tubed *arka* (the follower). Charka Province, Northern Potosí, Bolivia. Transcription by Henry Stobart.

Highland panpipes are usually played in consort on instruments of graduated sizes (tube lengths of 2.5 to 109 centimeters for the *julajula* of northern Potosí), typically tuned to play in parallel octaves or fifths (Figure 29.1). For many types (double-unit panpipes), the tones of the scale are apportioned between two half instruments—a distribution of resources that requires two players to perform a melody in hocket or interlocking parts. With the pentatonic *julajula*, one person plays a four-tubed half (tuned to D–G–B–e), while the other plays a three-tubed half (tuned E–A–d). Thus, with a single half it is impossible to perform a complete melody (Figure 29.2)—a performance aspect that has considerable social and symbolic significance. [Listen to "Kulwa"]

Other double-unit panpipes played without drums range from the simple three-tubed (male) and two-tubed (female) bamboo pipes of the Chipayas (Baumann 1981) to three- and four-tubed varieties, such as the *julajula* (northern Potosí), the *chiriwanu* (La Paz and Cochabamba departments), and the *julujulu* (La Paz Department). These are respectively associated with ritual fighting, dances imitating combats, and hunting dances (Baumann 1982a).

Double-unit panpipes played with drums usually have more tubes (for example, pairs of eight and seven tubes) and are often constructed in double rows of pipes per unit of which only the row held nearer the player's lips is sounded (Figure 29.3). Through sympathetic vibration, the outer, unstopped row (whose tubes are of similar lengths) enriches the harmonics of the stopped tubes. Such types of panpipe are commonly known as *siku*, *lakita*, or (Spanish) *zampoña*. They are played throughout the highlands and are often tuned approximately to a seven-note diatonic scale. In contrast, the seventeen-tube *siku* panpipes are played in parallel fifths and tuned so the tubes are arranged as a series of four five-note scalar units, each with a flatted third. [Listen to "Sikuriada"]

Figure 29.3
During a Bolivian religious festival, a man plays a *siku* and a drum. Photo by Peter Smith, 1960s.

DISC❶TRACK7

Figure 29.4
During a Bolivian religious festival, men play notched flutes (*lichiwayu*). Photo by Peter Smith, 1960s.

The end-blown notched flute (*quena*, *qina*, *qina-qina*, *lichiwayu*, *chuqila*, *mullu*, and others), commonly made of cane, is widespread in the highlands (Figure 29.4). [Listen to "Lichiwa-yu"] These are primarily played in consorts with drums and are tuned in unison or parallel fifths. Most have five or six holes, but the *mukululu* (La Paz Department) has only four, of which the lowest is never stopped—a practice common among many Bolivian flutes. In urban and *mestizo* contexts, the notched flute (*quena*, *kena*) is popular and has become a highly expressive and virtuoso solo instrument.

The six-holed cane side-blown flute (*flauta*, *pífano*) is common among lowland groups, especially those influenced by the Jesuits. In the highlands, it is played in consort to accompany certain dances, such as the *ch'unchu*, which caricatures lowland native Americans.

Several types of duct or fipple flutes (*pinkillus*, *flawtas*) are played in consort with drums in most highland regions and some lowland ones. Most types have six holes for fingering, but techniques of construction vary widely. Some types, such as the *pinkillu* (*flawta*) of northern Potosí, are made from branches with a pithy core, burned away with red-hot irons to form a hollow tube. Exceptional among flutes, groups of *pinkillu* of northern Potosí are played in hocket and are not accompanied by drums. In southern Potosí, among the Chipayas and in parts of La Paz Department, another form of *pinkillu* is made from curved branches that are split lengthways, hollowed out, and tied back together with

DISC❶TRACK8

Figure 29.5
At Carnaval, men play duct flutes (*saripalka*) and drums (*caja*). Calcha Province, Potosí Department, Bolivia. Photo by Henry Stobart, 1987.

tendons from an ox or a llama. Such instruments as the *saripalka* (Figure 29.5) the *lawatu*, the *rollano*, and the *ch'utu*, like the northern Potosí *pinkillu*, are often wetted to swell the wood and fill any cracks before use.

Most notable among the cane duct instruments of La Paz and Oruro departments are the *musiñu* (*mohoceño*) (Figure 29.6). [Listen to "Walata Grande"] Within a consort, the flutes range from the end-blown *sobre requinto* of 54 centimeters and the slightly longer *requinto* to the huge *liku* of 169 centimeters (5 centimeters in diameter), with the end-blown *irasu* in the middle. The *liku* is played transversely with the aid of a narrow parallel extension-tube duct, enabling the player to reach the fingerholes. The intermediate instruments of the consort are organized in parallel fifths, octaves, and sometimes dissonant intervals.

Tarka (or *anata*) are duct flutes played throughout the highlands in parallel fifths and octaves (Mamani 1987). They are usually bored and cut from a solid block of wood (Figure 29.7). [Listen to "*Tarkeada*"]

The three-holed pipe-and-tabor (*waka pinkillu* "bull flute"), a flute and drum played by the same person, is performed in many highland areas. It is sometimes made from a condor's wing bone when it is known as the *quri pinkillu* "golden flute" (Figure 29.8). Likewise, the wing bone of a local wading bird (*batu*) is used for the six-hole *pífano*, a duct flute that accompanies *macheteros*, dances of Trinidad, in lowland Beni Department (Olsen 1976).

Figure 29.6
A duct flute (*musiñu*) and drum ensemble of Villa Aroma, Aroma Province, Oruro Department, Bolivia. Photo by Henry Stobart, 1987.

DISC❶TRACK9

Highland natural trumpets include those made from conch shells (now rare), animals' horns (*pututu, corneta, pulilitu*), and cane and gourd (*pululu*). Trumpets are often played nonmelodically in combination with wind ensembles or for signaling. However, certain types may be played melodically. These include the *caña*, a spectacular 3-meter-long cane of Tarija, with a bell formed from the dried skin of a cow's tail (Calvo and Guzmán 1984) and the equally long *pututu* (or *tira-tira*) of northern Potosí, made of wood and the horns of oxen. Though resembling panpipes in shape, the huge *bajón* of the lowland Jesuit mission of San Ignacio de Moxos (Beni Department) is a multiple-tube trumpet (Becerra Casanovas 1977) that plays the bass in a European-style ensemble that usually includes violin and flute.

A simple single reed instrument or clarinet type (*irki* or *erke*), consisting of a single idioglot reed inserted into the narrow end of an animal's horn, is played in many regions of the southern highlands, especially by the Jalq'as (near Sucre), where men and women play at distinctive pitches at Carnaval (Martínez n.d.). Such performance is especially notable in Tarija, where the *erke* is played as a solo instrument with a drum (*caja chapaca*).

Chordophones

Musical bows are played by many lowland groups, such as the Moré in Beni Department and others in Pando Department; they appear to be the only indigenous chordophones. In the highlands, chordophones are for the most part found among the Quechua-speakers of the central highlands and valleys. However, the

Figure 29.7
At Carnaval, men play duct flutes (*tarka*). Eucalyptus, Cercado Province, Oruro Department, Bolivia. Photo by Henry Stobart, 1987.

Figure 29.8
One man plays a "golden" flute (*quri pinkillus*) and a drum; the flute is made from a condor's wing bone. Chayanta Province, Northern Potosí Department, Bolivia Photo by Henry Stobart, 1991.

charango, a small four- or five-course double-stringed (some have three strings) mandolin-like instrument, and the *guitarilla*, a deep-bodied five-course guitar, are particularly common among the Aymara-speakers of northern Potosí and the Chipayas of Oruro Department.

The peasant *charango*, often traditionally made using the carapace of an armadillo or half of a gourd, is especially associated with courtship (Figure 29.9). Gut strings were originally used, but metal strings are used today with a variety of tunings that in some regions alternate according to the time of year. Peasant *charangos* are strummed and act primarily as a percussive and melodic, rather than harmonic, accompaniment to singing. In contrast, city and village styles tend to use full chords, fast strumming (*rasgueado*), and picking (*punteado*). Urban-style instruments are usually more finely constructed, are often carved from wood, use machine heads and nylon strings, and are commonly played in combination with the Spanish guitar, which is also popular as a solo instrument or as an accompaniment to songs (Cavour 1988).

The peasant guitar (*kitarra, guitarilla, qunquta, talachi, guitarrón*) is strummed to accompany singing. It uses sheep-gut (archaic), nylon, or metal strings, or a combination of nylon and metal. The depth of the sound box varies from 6 centimeters to more than 20. Many types are painted bright colors, depicting the growing crops of the rainy season, when these instruments are usually played.

Figure 29.9
On Easter, a young man in ritual-battle dress plays a *charango* with metal strings. Ayllu Macha, northern Potosí Department, Bolivia. Photo by Henry Stobart, 1991.

Though widely used in churches and played in rural towns in the early 1900s, harps became rare by the end of the century. Violins, played in the valleys of Tarija, Chuquisaca, and Potosí to accompany dancing, are usually held below the shoulder, as was the practice in Europe before 1800. Locally constructed instruments may be made of a variety of materials, including cane of wide diameter.

Other Western instruments

Common in many larger towns, brass musical instruments from the West are becoming increasingly popular in the countryside. Most notable are the brass bands of Oruro and other mining centers, considered some of the finest in Latin America. These incorporate mostly imported trumpets, baritones (*bajos*), sousaphones, and, less commonly, trombones (often valve trombones).

The accordion sometimes replaces the *charango* and is commonly played in combination with saxophone or trumpet and percussion to supply music for dancing. Because Western instruments are costlier than local ones, they remain beyond the resources of most peasants.

The introduction of the brass band, most especially in mining towns such as Oruro, had a huge impact on Bolivian popular music in the twentieth century. Similarly, accordions, saxophones, electric guitars, and keyboards (synthesizers) are widespread and exert increasing influence over popular styles of urban music.

The technology of music

Traditionally, many instruments, especially panpipes and flutes, were made in the communities where they were played. In valley regions with abundant wood, instrument-making traditions have tended to be stronger, and instruments are still commonly exchanged or bought by highland herders of llamas on their visits to the valleys in the dry winter months (June–August). However, certain highland communities specialize in manufacturing instruments, and some supply a variety of regions. These artisans have been influential in maintaining, revitalizing, and dispersing musical traditions.

Every large town has at least one radio station, and many stations broadcast in native American languages such as Quechua, Aymara, or Guaraní. Popular Latin American musical styles predominate, and outside the main cities most music broadcast on radio is local or national. Though peasant families living in remote regions often do not own a radio or are unable to afford batteries, radio–cassette recorders are common in most other regions, where they are used to listen to radio networks and record local music. On the high plains of La Paz and Oruro departments, traditional music (such as a *musiñu* ensemble) may be recorded by as many as thirty to forty villagers using portable radio-cassette recorders.

Televisions are common in towns with electricity but rare in the countryside; the national average is one set per sixteen people (Myers 1992:470). The city of La Paz boasts more than seven channels with a surprisingly large amount of time dedicated to music, mainly of the urban variety.

Neither musical notation nor other practical mnemonic devices are commonly used in peasant music; however, players in brass bands can often read Western notation and may use it when learning new melodies. In the 1990s, the famous *charango* player Ernesto Cavour developed forms of nonrhythmic notation for the *charango* and certain other instruments.

MUSICAL CONTEXTS AND GENRES

Maintaining a stable and creative relationship with the spiritual world is the central concern of most Andean and lowland ritual shamanic practices and curing. Traditional indigenous beliefs are highly complex, localized, and related to the surrounding environment, though most cosmogonies feature spirits of ancestors, the sun, the moon, lightning, and the earth, such as the Andean Pachamama (Mother Earth) and mountain deities. These beliefs are deeply syncretized with those of the Roman Catholic church, the official and dominant religion. In certain areas, the sun and moon are called *tata santísimu* "holiest father" and *mama santísima* "holiest mother," respectively, and thunder and lightning are called *gloria*, Santa Barbara, or Santiago "St. James."

Musical sound, often said to be the manifestation of spirit (*animu*), plays a central role in many rituals, especially at climactic moments. Most processions and many ceremonies are considered incomplete without the presence of appropriate music. In highland animal-fertility rituals such as *k'illpa*, special songs may refer directly to the animals or *pinkillu* may be played. The sound of the flutes is said to engender the animals (causing them to multiply) and console the peaks (where the animals graze).

Seasonality and music

One of the most remarkable features of highland peasant music is the strong association of certain instruments, genres, and even tunings with specific times of year, the agricultural cycle, and other cyclical activities or celebrations. Over the course of a year, individual players from a single community may play as many as twelve instrumental types, each linked to a prescribed feast or season.

Musical instruments are often believed to influence agricultural production directly, and their sound is considered to affect the weather. Among the lowland Moré, for example, the *toá*, a friction idiophone, is considered to control rainfall. In highland northern Potosí, the high-pitched sound of the *charango* is said to attract the frost, necessary in the winter months for the preparation of *chuñu* (freeze-dried potatoes). In contrast, flute music is commonly said to bring rain and prevent frosts.

During periods of drought, people sometimes play *pinkillu* to call the rain, but the hoarse sound of the *tarka* is said to attract dry spells and is especially associated with Carnaval, when continued rain would spoil the ripening crops. In some regions during the growing season, *pinkillu* and *tarka* are alternated as required: the *pinkillu* bring rain, and the *tarka* attract dry spells (Buechler 1980). Some instruments (such as *kitarra* and *pinkillu*) are played continuously throughout a prescribed season, while others (such as *lichiwayu* and *julajula*) are confined to specific fiestas within a specific period.

The rainy season (November to March) is especially associated with the souls of the dead, said to participate in agricultural production. According to Aymara legend, they "push the potatoes up from inside the earth" (Bastien 1978:81). At the feast of Todos Santos (1 and 2 November), the dead are invited back to the world of the living and are ritually fed in family houses and the cemetery. In northern Potosí, *pinkillu* and *kitarra* begin to be played a few weeks before All Saints (1 November), when planting is begun or completed; their music continues until Carnaval, the ritual end of the growing season. On the final night of Carnaval, dancers imitating the spirits of the dead and devils dance out onto the mountainsides. At a climactic moment, the instruments of the rains are dramatically hushed and hidden away, and the people start singing the songs of the dry season to the strumming of the *charango* (Harris 1982a).

In contrast, the ritual start of the dry season is sometimes linked with the resurrection of Christ, following Lent and Holy Week, when music is often banned. During the vigil of Easter in Ingavi Province, La Paz Department, the musicians stand silent until the church bells ring *kalan kalan* (mnemonic, onomatopoeic vocables) to announce the resurrection. At this signal, musicians begin to play the *qina-qina*, which are not put away again until October. In many areas, the most intensive festal activity occurs between July and September, when a series of patronal festivals (saints' days) occurs. But in some areas (as Yura, Potosí Department), such activity is almost entirely confined to the growing and harvesting season between the solstices of December and June (Rasnake 1989).

Strummed chordophones such as *charango* and *kitarra* commonly change tunings and performance techniques according to the time of year. As with the construction of instruments, many localized variations occur.

Fiestas and music

Most traditional musical performances occur at fiestas, events that serve a broad range of functions and mark a wide variety of celebrations and anniversaries. Carnival and All Saints are celebrated in most of the country, but the dates of other fiestas are subject to local variations. Besides acting as foci for ritual activity, celebration, recreation, and opportunities for courtship and social interaction, fiestas sometimes serve to provide contexts for public expressions of injustice or dispute.

In northern Potosí, full-scale battles may occur during fiestas, often within the context of ritual fighting (*tinku*). Some of the most intense moments of confrontation occur in the music itself, with aggressive stamping dances (*zapateo*) to the music of the *charango* and provocative performance on the *julajula*. This fighting expresses individual courage and communal solidarity, especially in territorial disputes.

Huge crowds of people simultaneously playing different musics, widespread inebriation from alcohol, raised passions, fighting, and the spilling of blood—all are said to be essential to the success of a fiesta. From this chaos and creativity emerges a new order. The fiesta marks a turning point, reflecting the Andean concept of *pachakuti* "world turning", the end of an old period and the beginning of a new one. Time is specified in terms of the local cycle of fiestas rather than in months. The activities of these cycles are sometimes mirrored in the fiestas themselves, commonly accompanied by music. Participants may humorously mimic the mating of their domestic animals, making phallic allusions to their *pinkillu*; or, to the sound of *zampoña* and llama bells (*sinsiru*), they may carry sacks on their backs, imitating llamas journeying to the valleys to collect maize.

Some fiestas are centered on the sites of miracles or on villages with important patron saints and may involve pilgrimages of several days' walk carrying the community cross or standard, accompanied by almost continuous music *para alegrar el señor* "to make the saint joyful." On the participants' arrival, music is commonly performed in each corner of the village square and then inside or facing the main door of the church in adoration or consolation of its patron. Social investment is another important aspect of fiestas through sponsorship of fiesta-related activity and in the common experience of collective participation.

Many lowland peoples perform special dances at initiations and marriages. At the lip- and ear-piercing ceremony of ten- to twelve-year-old children, the Moré dance the *chiquít* to the sound of a gourd rattle of the same name. In the highlands, informal musical performance may follow baptisms and the ceremony of a child's first haircut, but it is almost always an important aspect of nuptial feasts, when special songs (*ipala*) are often sung by the bridegroom's sisters or songs of insult (*takipayanaku*) are improvised between in-laws. Music may be provided for dancing by local wind instruments, brass bands, or *charangos*, for which a special tuning (*kasamintu*) is used in some areas.

For certain fiestas, married couples are expected to take part in hierarchical series of *cargo*s, ritual-sponsorship obligations. In northern Potosí, for fiestas where *julajula* are played, the main sponsor (*alférez*) provides food and drink over the course of the festivities, while the minor sponsor (*mayura*) obtains the instruments, teaches the new melody, and carries a whip to discipline the dancing and control the ritual fighting (*tinku*). In other traditions, the sponsors (*pasantes* or *cabezas*) may contract local musicians who perform out of goodwill, or musicians from outside the community who for their services are paid with money or local produce. The sponsorship of fiestas in some regions alternates between sponsors (*alfereces*) and communal authorities (*kuraqkuna*) or *cabildos*. These positions of authority are rotated each year, and each married couple is obliged to take a turn.

Music is not usually played at funerals, but in La Paz Department, bamboo *alma pinkillus* are sometimes played for the Misa de Ocho Dias, a mass held on the eighth day after a death. Traditions vary widely for the feast of the dead at All Saints; in many areas, music is banned in favor of weeping in cemeteries, while in others the strains of *pinkillu* may replace prayers at the sites of graves. There is a special relationship between music and the ancestors or the recently dead.

Dance

In most Bolivian genres, music and dance are inseparable, and the physical action of dancing is often of great ritual significance. Dances in a circle are universal. Among the Tobas of the Gran Chaco, they were used in curing and life-cycle rituals. Encircling the patient would supposedly make the malignant spirits possessing the body depart with the dancer's perspiration (Karsten 1923). The courtship dance songs of the highlands often alternate sung verses with energetic stamping dances; the ring of dancers breaks periodically to rush energetically from one household or bar to another. Similarly, with much ritual wind music (played by flutes and panpipes), circles are formed at crossroads or the corners of village squares. At Carnaval, a band of musicians and dancers commonly accompanies the local authorities on a tour of territory and boundaries and dances in a circle in the patio of each homestead.

In processional *julajula* dances of northern Potosí (linked with ritual battle), single files of sometimes up to a hundred players snake into village squares for major fiestas. For this dance, participants wear ox-hide fighting helmets identical in shape to those of the Spanish conquistadors.

In the highlands of La Paz Department, many dances include a burlesque or pantomimic aspect (d'Harcourt and d'Harcourt 1959; Paredes Candia 1980), such as the *waka tokori*, which caricatures a bullfight; other dances represent mock combat or hunting, such as the *chuqila* (*chokela*), a ritual hunt for *vicuñas* (Baumann 1982b). Lowland dances are often connected with hunting or sometimes with the conversion of warlike tribes to Christianity. On Palm Sunday, *macheteros*—dancers with feather headdresses and large knives (machetes)—process through the streets of Trinidad (Beni Department) in a bowing dance of supplication before an image of Christ on a donkey (Rivero Parada 1989).

The most famous processional dances of Bolivia are the costumed and masked dances of Oruro Carnaval, which developed among urban miners and occur in other towns (Guerra Gutiérrez 1987). Two of its most spectacular dances are the choreographed *diablada* "devil dance" and *morenada* "black-slave dance," which feature huge, colorful, costly masks and are accompanied by brass bands. Among the many other urban dances of this type are those that caricature ethnic populations from other regions of Bolivia (such as Toba and Kallawaya) and even native North Americans. Partner dances or dance songs between men and women, such as the duple-time *huayño*, the compound-triple-meter (i.e., *sesquiáltera*) *cueca* (a dance with handkerchiefs), and the *takirari* of the lowlands are popular in middle-class contexts but less common among traditional peasants.

The mimed dances, the extravagant costumes, and the dramatic aspect of many rituals are evidence of the popularity of theatrical presentation. A play based on the murder of the Inka Atahualpa by the Spanish is one of the few traditional dramas still performed. It appears as part of Oruro Carnaval, but early in the twentieth century it was staged in rural towns (Lara 1989). Music is an important aspect of the performance, especially in the laments of the Inka princesses.

National anthem

Bolivia's national anthem is titled "Canción Patriótica" (Patriotic Song). It was adopted in 1852 with music by Italian composer Leopoldo Benedetto Vincenti and words (http://david.national-anthems.net/bo.txt) by Bolivian patriot José Ignacio de Sanjinés. The music resembles an Italian operatic aria.

MUSICAL PERFORMERS AND PERFORMANCES

The variety of musics and types of instruments is one of the salient markers of Bolivian cultural identity and differentiation, especially with the steady decline of traditional dress. People use music to express solidarity and competition at various levels. Some instruments and musical forms are closely associated with the immediate community and local agricultural production. Others are linked with the larger sociopolitical groups and may relate to the maintenance of territorial boundaries.

Competition often occurs between wind ensembles from different highland hamlets, communities, *ayllus*, or wards. Each attempts to dominate the other during a fiesta in volume and assurance of melody, ideally causing their opponents to falter. But within the ensemble itself, there is a strong sense of solidarity, social leveling, and reciprocity, which reflect traditional forms of social organization and exchange.

Gender-based roles

With few exceptions, instrumental performance is the role of men. In the highlands, women are the main singers, and a song is said to be incomplete with only men's voices and without women's. Historically, women have often played drums to accompany singing and men's instruments, but the playing of drums by women is restricted to a few specific ritual contexts. Symbolically, men are commonly associated with the dynamic and engendering force of breath, while women are linked with the creative substance of water (Arnold Bush, Domingo Jiménez, and de Diós Yapita 1991).

In the highlands and the lowlands, music is a central aspect of courtship. Many instruments—such as the *moráo*, a ten-tube panpipe of the lowland Moré, and the *pinkillu* and guitar-type instruments of the central highlands—are specifically associated with the young and unmarried. Songs of courtship are often laced with erotic metaphors, continually refer to marriage, and, like the instruments themselves, are often linked with agricultural fertility.

North of Potosí, many couples meet only in the context of song and dance at fiestas and do not regularly spend time together until, after obtaining the permission of the woman's parents, the woman steals away to live with the man's family in concubinage. Following marriage (or concubinage), musical activity by women is sometimes frowned on because of its associations with courtship. In some regions, women are prohibited from singing and dancing. However, males of all ages, including boys, are expected to play in the massed panpipe bands that perform at certain highland festivals; in some places, older men are said to be better musicians because they have greater experience and know more tunes.

Class and ethnicity

Class structures are transitory and highly complex; they vary considerably according to region. Ethnicity, residence, wealth, education, occupation, and physical type may all contribute to the construction of class position. Distinctions of class as cultural identity are often clearly defined by the use of specific musical styles, techniques, rhythms, genres, and instruments. In many places, the choice of nylon or metal strings on a *charango* is not so much an issue of musical taste as one of class and ethnic identity. A peasant who uses nylon rather than metal strings may be understood to be rebelling against his ethnic origins and aspiring to a higher class.

The peasants (*campesinos, indios*) of the highlands are subsistence farmers or herders who principally speak Quechua or Aymara. In some regions, people retain traditional dress and strong ethnic identity. Their music is often closely linked to social considerations, cosmology, and agricultural production. Some dispersed indigenous groups remain in the lowlands, speaking a mosaic of languages, but few traditional musical practices survive among them.

The broad spectrum of middle classes ranges from those who speak indigenous languages and Spanish and retain localized music traditions to educated monolingual Spanish-speakers with a strong sense of national cultural identity. The brass band developed among urban miners, but strong localized *charango*, guitar, and accordion styles developed among the more rural middle classes. A repertoire of nationally popular songs and dances called *música folklórica*, including many highland and lowland dances, is constantly played on the larger radio networks. Other Latin American styles and performers, such as the Colombian *cumbia* and the Peruvian *huayno* (*huayño* in Bolivia), are often heard, while younger generations sometimes favor rock and the fusion of these elements into the so-called commercial tropical style, known in Peru as *chicha* music.

The culture of the small, white, and wealthy *mestizo* population is more aligned with that of Europe and the United States, as is the growing migrant population of the lowlands, which includes many Okinawan Japanese [see Music of Immigrant Groups]. African Bolivians still perform *sayas* "praise songs" in the streets of Cochabamba, and the *saya* is a popular musical form among Bolivian *música folklórica* or pan-Andean groups.

Composition

In rural communities of the highlands, the performance of new melodies each year and sometimes for individual fiestas (especially Carnaval) is commonly considered a ritual necessity. Old tunes are said to have no power and in Quechua are called *q'ayma* "insipid." In the high plains of La Paz and Oruro departments, new melodies are sometimes obtained through a process of collective composition. They may consist of no more than a few short motifs treated according to consistent formulae with, for example, rhythmic repetition at intervals of the fourth or fifth, or repetition of pitches with rhythmic variation.

It is often said that new melodies cannot be made up inside a house. Players describe how they are inspired when alone on a mountainside, beside a river, or sometimes when playing in an ensemble of *pinkillu*; often, a new tune appears under their fingers as if by magic, "played by the *sirínus*." Musical abilities and new melodies are commonly attributed to the *sirínus* "sirens" or the *yawlus* "devils" (Martínez 1990; Sánchez 1988) said to live beside streams and waterfalls or in caves or large rocks; these places are described as (Spanish) *lugares feos* "ugly-evil places." The *sirínus* supposedly take various forms, including that of humans, and can transform themselves into animals such as toads, doves, cats, dogs, and foxes.

Men sometimes visit *sirínus* late at night after buying a new instrument or shortly before fiestas, to endow their instruments with special magical powers. After making ritual offerings that may include the sacrifice of a red cockerel (made to crow before being killed), they leave the instruments beside a rock or a spring and retreat to a safe distance; they may leave the instruments for several nights. Traditions vary widely: in some places, people say if you hear the music of the *sirínus*, you will become mad; other people claim to listen to the music and copy it; in some parts, to frighten off the *sirínus* and collect the tuned instruments, people make a noise by throwing a tin can as soon as they hear the first tuning note. The tuned instruments are then said to have magical powers that attract girls with their enchanted music, as suggested in a text from Bustillos Province, Potosí Department:

Kay charanguytuyki	This *charango* of yours
Kasaru kustillu	Wants to get married
Sapa waqasqampi	Each time it weeps
Sirínu kustillu	With the desire of the *sirínu*

MUSICAL IDEOLOGIES AND AESTHETICS

In the tropical lowlands, music is often performed in a gentle, meditative manner; the Sirionó, for example, frequently sing while lying in hammocks (Key 1963; Riester 1978).

Such meditative and day-to-day performance is rare in highland peasant communities, where most music is confined to fiestas, when women usually sing in a vigorous and often high-pitched style (called *ñañu*, "fine"), sometimes reaching two octaves above middle C. This style is sometimes matched by shrill strumming from the *charango*, whose metal strings are often tensioned almost to the breaking point. Similarly, wind instruments are blown strongly in high registers, and gentle, mellow sounds are untypical and considered aesthetically unsatisfactory. [Listen to "Lunesta, Martesta"]

DISC ❶ TRACK 10

The dynamic aspect of musical performance emphasizes its ritual and socializing role in the reciprocal exchange of energies between paired performers (using interlocking technique) and between the worlds of humans and spirits. Such an exchange is analogous to the tradition of reciprocal labor in which work performed as aid to others is later returned with produce or a similar form of labor (Harris 1982b). In fiestas, dynamism and aesthetic saturation (food, drink, music, color) are considered ritually essential, contrasting vividly with the austerity of everyday life. Complaints about the quality of performance are rarely made, but if the music falters and stops, people are swift to criticize, even when the musicians are almost too drunk and exhausted to stand.

Many traditional wind instruments, especially of highland Oruro and La Paz departments, are played in consorts (*tropas*) of a single type of instrument made in graduated sizes and tuned in unison, parallel fifths, or octaves. Blending is essential, and people say the tonal color of the ensemble should be consistent, with each voice heard equally and no single voice standing out from the solidarity of the ensemble. In weaving, color is also often blended through chromatic graduations, *k'isas* "sweetness" (Cereceda 1987); and what from a distance appears as a monochrome may be blended from, perhaps, fourteen shades and colors.

In contrast with the pure harmonics of the European flute, a broad tone, rich in harmonics (*tara*), is usually preferred in the highlands. *Tarka* or *taraka* probably derive their name from the Aymara word *tara*, which denotes a hoarse voice. When blown strongly, the sound of these flutes divides so the fundamental tone and the octave above are of near-equal intensity.

Rich, dense, and often dissonant tonal color is sometimes consciously added by an instrument that plays in parallel to the rest of the ensemble, but at a dissonant interval. For example, in the *tropa recto* (an ensemble of *musiñu*), all the instruments are tuned to play in parallel octaves or fifths; however, the single *sobre requinto*, tuned a fifth above the *irasu*-sized instruments, is pitched a tone above the four *requintos*. The resulting consistent parallel dissonance enlivens and enriches the timbre of the ensemble, *como órgano* ("like an organ").

Fascination with sound is emphasized rather than developed instrumental technique, and little individual practice is necessary. Musical performance is essentially a socializing activity in which general participation and interaction are encouraged, reflecting traditional egalitarian social structures while discouraging excessive power or subordination. The notion of a soloist is contrary to many traditional highland musical practices. This presents a marked contrast to urban ensembles (*conjuntos*), which, following Western practices and tastes, combine a variety of instruments with contrasting timbres, use harmony and polyphony, and feature one person playing both panpipe halves to form a single instrument with the player periodically acting as a soloist.

Many types of double-unit panpipes and the *pinkillu* ensembles of northern Potosí divide the notes of the scale between paired instruments. The combination of paired instruments (that is, two halves), such as the three-tubed male panpipe and the two-tube female panpipe of the Chipayas, is usually stated to be "like older and younger brothers" but is sometimes compared with heterosexual intercourse. These concepts may be understood in terms of the organizing principle of duality or complementarity (Quechua *yanantin*) by which paired elements are said to belong together and to be incomplete or uncreative alone (Platt 1986).

Similarly, the hoarseness of *tara*, which refers to the timbre of some highland wind instruments, can be glossed "double." This vibrancy, rich in harmonics, is said to be in tune and creative like the balancing of male and female and the sexual union of a man and a woman. But when instruments produce a thin tone with few harmonics, do not sound well, or are out of tune with the rest of an ensemble, they may be called *q'iwa*, a concept said to imply singleness or aloneness and used to denote castrated animals, infertile plants, homosexuals, and misers with money or food. Associated with the inability to produce and with imbalance, *q'iwa* is understood in terms of agency and is of central importance to concepts of regeneration. In traditional communities, musical timbre is directly related to regeneration, productivity, and creation (Stobart 1992).

Poetry and music

The universality of dualistic principles in Bolivia may be attributed to certain musical forms and aesthetics, particularly in the poetry of Quechua songs. Each line is a union of two halves, and adjacent lines are commonly paired through common or opposing ideas or through vocabulary of similar sound, often as wordplay, as seen in a text from Ayllu Macha, Chayanta Province, Potosí Department:

Walli q'iririnqa,	Valley *q'iririnqa*,
Puna q'iririnqa:	Highland *q'iririnqa*:
Warmi wachakuqtin,	When the woman's giving birth,
Cholay q'ipirinqa.	My girl will be carrying.

This verse, sung by women, likens the *q'iririnqa* (a bird) to highland men who travel to the valleys with llama caravans each year to exchange salt for maize—a journey associated with amorous intrigue. The first and second lines suggestively contrast low and high (valleys or birth versus highlands or child on its mother's back). By semantic coupling, the single idea of "woman" is expressed in two contrasting words, *warmi* and *chola*; the words *q'iririnqa* and *q'ipirinqa* are almost identical in sound, though different in meaning.

MUSICAL CHANGE

Throughout history, highland Bolivian music has been subject to change with the reinterpretation of new musical ideas, often brought from other cultures, within a cosmology centered on traditional economics, social structures, and agricultural production. But the latter half of the twentieth century, even more than the Spanish invasion hundreds of years before, saw an upheaval in the basis of Andean life. Music serves to reflect and motivate traditional values and structures, but, as these concepts are abandoned or replaced by Western ideologies, music is no longer the necessity it was.

The introduction of radios and tape recorders and widespread migration to the cities has meant increased contact with urban *mestizo* and Western music in the countryside. The high prestige of such music, accompanied by increasing orientation toward Western values and aesthetics, means that traditional practices tend to be devalued and their significance forgotten. With increased ownership of tape recorders, tunes are becoming fixed, and taped music is beginning to replace live musicians, even in ritual contexts. Musical scales and melodic structures appear to be increasingly influenced by Western-based diatonic music; for example, a series of *lawatu* (flute) melodies recorded in southern Potosí in 1977 included a six-note scale, but *lawatu* tunes played in the same village ten years later commonly used a seven-note scale.

Among the middle classes, recorded music is heard in most buses, bars, and cafés. There are numerous radio networks, and sales of vinyl records and cassettes are high. Styles are diverse, but some of the most popular are the rhythmic lowland dance songs of such groups as Trío Oriental, who combine vocal harmonies with accordion, bass, and percussion. Besides incorporating forms such as the *taquirari* and the *saya* from Bolivia's own indigenous and black populations, this so-called tropical style is often influenced by African-Caribbean rhythms (such as the Columbian *cumbia* and the Peruvian *chicha*). Some highland bands have adopted similar forms and rhythms; for example, Maroyu's commercial style combines voice, electric guitars, organ, and percussion. Countless electric bands of this type, with considerable awareness of rock, are found in urban centers; typically, they supply music for dancing at weddings.

Traditional music is being rediscovered and valued again by many urban migrants. Far more than a hundred indigenous ensembles (*grupos autóctonos*) regularly perform in La Paz. Numerous urban ensembles (*conjuntos*) tour internationally on a regular basis. Andean music is often identified internationally with folkloric ensembles (*grupos folklóricos*), whose instruments typically include *charango*, guitar, *quena*, panpipes, and percussion, sometimes using highly developed instrumental techniques. Such ensembles are commonly seen on tour in international concert halls or as migrants busking on sidewalks in Europe and the United States. Kjarkas, Rumillajta, and Savia Andina are among the most famous Bolivian ensembles of this type; their original songs and stylized versions of traditional dances are famous throughout the middle classes and are recognized as the popular national culture. Other groups, including Awatiñas, Los Masis, Norte de Potosí, and Los Yuras, often include examples of more traditional peasant styles in their programs. Many more localized *mestizo huayños* or other forms of dance and song are recorded and sold in large numbers, typically sung in a high, plaintive, full-voiced style accompanied by *charango* and guitar or accordion.

nueva canción
"New song," generic name for pan-Latin American neofolk-protest music that began in Chile in the 1960s and spread throughout the Americas

The group Wara has combined more traditional folkloric instruments with electric guitars and a drum set, but the progressive exponents of a new style, *nueva canción* "new song," often use traditional instruments alongside, for example, piano and flute. This intellectual movement represents an expression of broader Latin American identity and solidarity; such songs are popular in more educated circles. Famous artists include Emma Junaro, Jenny Cardenas, and Savia Nueva.

Formal concerts of classical music on Western instruments, and even new music especially composed for native instruments, take place in La Paz and other large towns. But public performances of more urban folk-derived music usually take place in the more informal setting of music clubs (*peñas*), where an array of professional and semiprofessional ensembles play styles likely to appeal to urbanites' and tourists' tastes; the most famous is Peña Naira in La Paz. One of the most famous groups to come out of the music clubs in La Paz is Los Jairas, featuring the virtuosic *charango* playing of Ernesto Cavour and the florid *quena* playing of the Swiss-born Gilberto "El Gringo" Favre.

peña
In Andean cities where tourism is common, a private gathering place or touristic nightclub where folk musicians perform

LEARNING, DISSIMENATION, TOURISM, AND PUBLIC POLICY

Traditionally, music is learned informally and socially through collective imitation and repetition. In the rural highlands, children and young men carry instruments while herding or on journeys; they learn to play their instruments alongside friends or while they are passing the time alone. New tunes on wind instruments are usually taught in collective contexts, through continual repetition of the complete melody.

Ensembles usually consist of members of existing social groups—a hamlet, a community, an *ayllu* (ethnic group), a ward, or even an urban migrant neighborhood or cultural center. But the brass bands and troupes of Oruro and several other towns are much institutionalized and autonomous, in themselves serving as a social focus.

A school of military music was founded in La Paz in 1904, as were the National Conservatory in 1908 and the National Symphony Orchestra in 1944. Twentieth-century Bolivian composers adopted a nationalistic style, often through incorporating traditional elements or forms into their music. This was most successful, for example, in the stylized traditional dances (*cuecas*) for piano by Simeón Roncal (1870–1953). In the late twentieth century, composers tried to incorporate traditional instruments in a classical format, as in the Orquesta Experimental de Instrumentos Nativos (Experimental Orchestra of Native Instruments) of La Paz.

The teaching of music in schools is mostly confined to singing local or national songs (especially the national anthem) and depends largely on the enthusiasm of individual teachers. Players in urban *conjuntos* sometimes take individual or collective lessons, and they may study Western classical music at the National Conservatory.

Since the agrarian reforms of 1953 and a policy of cultural unification, the state has encouraged folkloric festivals in certain regions. Many developmental agencies, radio stations, and political parties continue to organize competitions of peasant music, often with Westerners or *mestizos* as judges. These practices have served to transform essentially participatory music into a medium that differentiates musicians and audience. The radical reversal in ideology has often been accompanied by the abandonment of seasonal considerations, the encouragement of virtuoso instrumental techniques, and the development of new forms.

Major competitions are held annually for folk-derived music in *mestizo* style, often resulting in prestigious coverage, recording contracts, and opportunities for the winners of prizes to travel abroad. Regional competitions are held for music from peasant communities and smaller towns, usually organized by radio stations or foreign-aid groups.

FURTHER STUDY

One of the earliest books about Bolivian music in the twentieth century is Marguerite and Raoul d'Harcourt's seminal study titled *La musique des Aymaras sur les hauts plateaux Boliviens d'après les enregistrements sonores de Louis Girault* (1959). A type of "armchair" analysis of Aymara music from recordings by Louis Girault, it is an early hallmark study in Latin American ethnomusicology. Another European ethnomusicologist who has done exceptional research in the Bolivian highlands is Max Peter Baumann. His articles and recordings from the 1980s among the Chipayas and other Andean cultures are published in several American and European journals and compact discs. The most recent study of Bolivian music from the Andes is by Henry Stobart (2006), a book titled *Music and the Poetics of Production in the Bolivian Andes*. Dale Olsen has researched the music of Japanese immigrant societies in the Bolivian lowlands in and around Santa Cruz, which constitutes a chapter in his book *The Chrysanthemum and the Song: Music, Memory, and Identity in the South American Japanese Diaspora* (2004).

REFERENCES

Arnold Bush, Denise, Domingo Jiménez, and Juan de Diós Yapita. 1991. "Scattering the Seeds: Shared Thoughts on Some Songs to the Food Crops from an Andean Ayllu." *Amerindia* 16:106–178.
Baptista Gumucio, Mariano. 1988. *Potosí: Patrimonio cultural de la humanidad.* Santiago: Compañía Minerva del Sur.
Bastien, Joseph W. 1978. *Mountain of the Condor: Metaphor and Ritual in an Andean Ayllu.* St. Paul: West Publishing.
Baumann, Max Peter. 1981. "Music, Dance, and Song of the Chipayas (Bolivia)." *Latin American Music Review* 2(2):171–222.
———. 1982a. "Music of the Indios in Bolivia's Andean Highlands." *The World of Music* "Latin America" 25(2):80–98.
———. 1982b. *Musik im Andenhochland: Bolivien.* Berlin: Museum für Völkerkunde MC 14. 2 LP disks.
Becerra Casanovas, Rogers. 1977. *Reliquias de Moxos.* La Paz.
Buechler, Hans. 1980. *The Masked Media.* The Hague: Mouton.
Calvo, Luz María, and Roberto Guzmán. 1984. *Música tradicional de Bolivia. VI festival folklórico nacional "Luz Mila Patiño."* Cochabamba: Centro Portales y Lauro. LP disk.
Calvo, Luz María, and Walter Sánchez C. 1991. *Música autóctona del Norte de Potosí: VII Festival Folklorico "Luz Mila Patiño."* Cochabamba: Centro Portales y Lauro. LP disk and commentary.
Cavour, Ernesto. 1988. *El Charango.* La Paz: CIMA.
Cereceda, Verónica. 1987. "Aproximaciones a una estética andina: de la belleza al tinku." In *Tres Reflexiones sobre el pensamiento andino*, ed. T. Bouysse-Cassagne, Olivia Harris, T. Platt, and Verónica Cereceda, 133–231. La Paz: Hisbol.

Cobo, Bernabé. 1990 [1653]. *Inca Religion and Customs*, trans. and ed. Roland Hamilton. Austin: University of Texas Press.

Díaz Gainza, José. 1988. *Historia Musical de Bolivia*. La Paz: Puerta del Sol.

Guamán Poma de Ayala, Felipe. 1980 [c1600]. *Nueva crónica y buen gobierno*, ed. John V. Murra and Petena Adorno. México, D.F.: Siglo Veintiuno.

Guerra Gutiérrez, Alberto. 1987. *El carnaval de Oruro a su alcance*. Oruro, Bolivia: Editora Lilial.

d'Harcourt, Marguerite, and Raoul d'Harcourt. 1959. *La musique des Aymaras sur les hauts plateaux Boliviens d'après les enregistrements sonores de Louis Girault*. Paris: Société des Américanistes, Musée de l'Homme.

Harris, Olivia. 1982a. "The Dead and Devils amongst the Bolivian Laymis." In *Death and Regeneration of Life*, ed. Maurice Bloch and Jonathan Parry, 45–73. Cambridge: Cambridge University Press.

———. 1982b. "Labour and Produce in an Ethnic Economy, Northern Potosí, Bolivia." In *Ecology and Exchange in the Andes, ed. David Lehmann*, 70–96. Cambridge: Cambridge University Press.

Karsten, Rafael. 1923. "The Toba Indians of the Bolivian Gran Chaco." *Acta Humaniora* 4, iv. Helsinki: Academiae Aboensis.

Key, Mary. 1963. "Music of the Sirionó (Guaranian)." *Ethnomusicology* 7(1):17–21.

Lara, Jesús. 1989. Tragedía del fin de Atawallpa. Cochabamba, Bolivia: Los Amigos del Libro.

Leigue Castedo, Luis D. 1957. *"El Itenez Salvaje": Influencia selvicola e indigenal sobre el Río Itenez*. La Paz: Ministerio de Educación y Bellas Artes.

Mamani P., Mauricio. 1987. *Los instumentos musicales en los Andes Bolivianos*. La Paz: Museo Nacional de Etnografía y Folklore.

Martínez, Rosalia. 1990. "Musique et démons: Carnival chez las Tarabuco (Bolivie)." *Journal de la Société des Américanistes* 76:155–76.

———. n.d. "Instrumentos de la zona Jalq'a." In *Guía de los instrumentos Bolivianos*. Cochabamba, Bolivia: Centro Portales.

Myers, Helen, ed. 1992. *Ethnomusicology: An Introduction*. London: Macmillan.

Oblitas Poblete, Enrique. 1978 [1960]. *Cultura Callawaya*. La Paz: Ediciones Populares Camarlinghi.

Olsen, Dale A. 1976. "Música Vesperal Mojo en San Miguel de Isiboro, Bolivia." *Revista Musical Chilena* 133:28–46.

———. 2004. *The Chrysanthemum and the Song: Music, Memory, and Identity in the South American Japanese Diaspora*. Gainesville: University Press of Florida.

Orsúa, Arzans de, and Bartolomé Vela. 1965. *Historia de la Villa Imperial de Potosí*. Providence: Brown University Press.

Paredes Candia, Antonio. 1980. *Folklore de Potosí*. La Paz: Ediciones ISLA.

———. 1984. *La danza folklórica en Bolivia*. La Paz: Ediciones ISLA.

Platt, Tristan. 1986. "Mirrors and Maize: The Concept of Yanantin among the Macha of Bolivia." In *Anthropological History of Andean Polities*, eds. John Murra, Nathan Wachtel, and Jacques Revel, 228–259. Cambridge: Cambridge University Press.

Prost, Marian D. 1970. *Costumbres, habilidades y cuadro de la vida humana entre los Chacobo*. Riberalta, Bolivia: Instituto Lingüístico de Verano, y el Ministerio de Educación y Cultura.

Rasnake, Roger. 1989. *Autoridad y poder en los Andes: Los Kuraqkuna de Yura*. La Paz: Hisbol.

Riester, Juergen 1978. *Canción y producción en la vida de un pueblo indígena*. La Paz and Cochabamba: Los Amigos del Libro.

Rivero Parada, Luis. 1989. *Principales Danzas y Danzarines de los nativos de San Ignacio de Mojos, Departmento del Beni—Bolivia*. Santa Cruz, Bolivia: Casa de la Cultura "Raúl Otero Reiche."

Sánchez, C. Walter. 1988. *El proceso de creación musical (Música autóctona del norte de Potosí)*. Cochabamba, Bolivia: Centro Pedagógico y Cultural de Portales, Centro de Documentación de música Boliviana. Bulletin 7.

Stevenson, Robert M. 1968. *Music in Aztec and Inca Territory*. Berkeley: University of California Press.

Stobart, Henry. 1987. *Primeros datos sobre la música campesina del norte de Potosí*. La Paz: Museo Nacional de Etnografía y Folklore.

———. 1992. "Tara and Q'iwa—Worlds of Sound and Meaning." In *Cosmología y música en los Andes*. Berlin: International Institute of Traditional Music.

———. 2006. *Music and the Poetics of Production in the Bolivian Andes*. Aldershot: Ashgate.

Torrico, Cassandra. 1988. "Toads and Doves: The Symbolism of Storage Sacks' Design amongst Macha Herders."

van Lindert, Paul, and Otto Verkoren. 1994. *Bolivia in Focus*. London: Latin American Bureau.

Peru

Raúl R. Romero

The Indigenous Heritage
The European Heritage (and Indigenous Encounters)
Musical Instruments
Musical Genres and Contexts
Tradition and Musical Change
Learning, Dissemination, Tourism, and Public Policy
Further Study

Peru is a country of diverse geographical regions: the Andean highlands running through the center from north to south; one of the driest deserts in the world along the Pacific coast; and the Amazonian rainforest to the east and on the slopes of the Andes. Spanish and Quechua (Kechua) are the principal languages in coastal and Andean Peru, with Aymara around Lake Titicaca, and numerous indigenous languages in the vast Amazonian watershed area.

In pre-Hispanic times, indigenous cultures had occupied the coast and the mountains of what is today Peru, but during the colonial domination, the Spaniards settled mostly along the coast while the mostly Quechua and Aymara peasants inhabited primarily the Andean regions. Thus, coastal Peru became a bastion for Spanish and creole culture, with pockets of African-derived cultures because of the presence of black slaves who were eventually liberated in 1854 (see AFRO-PERUVIAN TRADITIONS). By contrast, the Andes became a stronghold for Amerindian and *mestizo* communities. The geographical and cultural partition of the country began to blur with massive migrations to the capital, Lima, beginning in the 1950s and later the revolutionary régime of 1968–1980, which implemented radical agrarian reforms and structural changes crucial to the Peruvian economy. The Peruvian Amazonian region continued to be occupied by more than fifty scattered and seminomadic ethnolinguistic groups, which for centuries remained isolated from the national scene.

The pre-Hispanic cultural heritage of Peru can be traced back to about 1400 B.C. when the Chavín culture flourished in the central Andes of Peru. One of the oldest samples of music iconography is from the Chavín horizon, showing musicians playing conch trumpets (Bolaños 1985:11, 14). Among the earliest musical instruments are a sixth-century B.C. panpipe and an endblown notched flute found in the Chilca region. Throughout the centuries after Chavín's decline, successive prosperous regional cultures developed. The Moche (Mochica) culture from Peru's northern coast (ca. 100 B.C.–A.D. 700) was one of the richest in Peru, and Moche pottery depicts musical instruments, costumes, and dances in detail. Among the most significant representations is that of two panpipe players facing each other, their instruments attached with a string—evidence that these instruments were played in pairs in pre-Hispanic times.

The Nasca culture on Peru's southern coast (ca. 200 B.C.–A.D. 600) produced clay panpipes that have been the most studied and debated pre-Hispanic musical instruments. The excellence of their condition (most are housed in the National Museum of Anthropology and Archaeology in Lima) has enabled several investigators to measure their pitches and hypothesize about pre-Hispanic musical scales. Carlos Vega (1932) and Andrés Sas concluded that blowing the panpipe produces a series of semitones and quarter tones. Sas also maintained that Nasca musicians used diatonic and chromatic scales (1936:232). Later, Stevenson (1968), Haeberli (1979), Bolaños (1988), and Olsen (2002) studied Nasca panpipes with more systematic methodologies, providing new data and arriving at similar conclusions about ancient musical scales. These studies rejected the conclusion by Raoul and Marguerite d'Harcourt (1990 [1925]) that pentatonicism was the dominant scale in ancient times [see STUDYING LATIN AMERICAN MUSIC]. All of these cultures were either gone or subdued by the Inca culture in the 1400s.

Spanish chroniclers of the 1500s and 1600s first documented the musical practices of the Inca period. Guamán Poma de Ayala (1956) contributed many pages to describing musical expressions and activities of the Incas, making drawings of Amerindian life in which he depicted musical instruments and performance settings. Other chroniclers, such as Pedro Cieza de León (1967), Bernabé Cobo (1956), and Garcilaso de la Vega (1959), also profusely described various pre-Hispanic musical occasions. Colonial dictionaries of Quechua and Aymara by Diego Gonzales Holguín (1608) and Ludovico Bertonio (1612), respectively, contain important definitions of musical genres, musical instruments, and dances at the time of the Spanish Encounter.

Among the issues addressed by these chroniclers were regional and ethnic diversity in music and dance. Guamán Poma de Ayala (1956:242) and Cobo (1956:270) agreed that each province or part of Tawantinsuyu (the Inca empire) had unique songs and dances and that certain kinds of music were performed only by elites during particular rituals and thus were not intended for popular use. On one occasion, Cobo described forty different dances that occurred in the Corpus Christi procession in the province of Collao (Cobo 1956:270–271). The reason for the high number, perhaps, is because the chroniclers characterized songs and dances on the basis of texts rather than on musical traits. Therefore, most of their references to musical genres are in the domain of literary pictures, and their information does not provide a clear understanding of the musical structure of actual pieces. Guamán Poma (1956:233–235), for instance, mentioned various musical genres, indicating their character and transcribing their lyrics, among them the *harawi* (a nostalgic love song), *kashwa* (a cheerful song), *wanka* (a love song), and *haylli* (a harvest song) as the most important ones. Cobo described the *kashwa* as a dance of men and women joining hands in a circle, Holguin portrayed the *haylli* as a joyful, victorious songs, sung during the sowing of the fields, and *harawi* included songs about unrequited love (Stevenson 1960:169).

Musical instruments are probably the most fully documented musical phenomena of pre-Hispanic times. Chroniclers described numerous Incan idiophones, membranophones (*huancar*), flute- (*pincullu, pingollo, kina-kina* [*quenaquena*], *antara*) and trumpet-type aerophones (*k'epa*), and the absence of chordophones. Although allusions to musical performances are scanty, they constitute the only extant references for the pre-Hispanic period. Garcilaso de la Vega, for example, described panpipe ensembles as using an interlocking technique of performance between individual instruments and suggested that fifths were the foremost intervals in those ensembles. He also noted the presence of larger intervals at the expense of smaller ones in musical scales, which Carlos Vega (1932:350) interpreted as a description of a pentatonic scale. Guamán Poma de Ayala referred to the musical accompaniment of the *pingollo* and the *kina-kina* in several dances and songs and highlighted two cases of antiphonal dances of men and women (1956:233). The first of these, *uaricza araui*, he explained was sung by the main Inca and his women, the *cuyas* and the *ñustas*, and that the Inca's chant, which imitated the gentle moan of an animal, was repeated over and over again until it resembled the high sound of a dying animal. This chant was answered by the women. The second description of an antiphonal chant was the *saynata*, in which a man responded to a women's chorus.

THE EUROPEAN HERITAGE (AND INDIGENOUS ENCOUNTERS)

The Spanish incursion of the 1500s caused an abrupt end to the autonomous development of indigenous cultures in coastal and Andean Peru and introduced an era of economic exploitation of the Peruvian Amerindians through such institutions as *encomienda* (a system by which land and peasants were governed by Spanish landlords called *encomenderos*), *mita* (coercive labor for the colonial administration), and the collection of forced tribute (Indian contributions in kind to the Spanish crown). With these tactics, ideological struggles against indigenous religious practices, such as the extirpation-of-idolatries campaign conducted by the Spanish clergy in the 1600s, were enforced. These actions and the diseases brought by Europeans caused a dramatic depopulation of indigenous peoples in the region the Spanish called the Viceroyalty of Peru. The importation of African slaves added another ethnic dimension to the colonial social framework.

Distinctive social and ethnic groups began to emerge in Peru soon after the arrival of Europeans, such as the Spanish born on the Iberian Peninsula and those born in the colonies; the former Peruvians (*peninsulares*) considered themselves superior to the latter, who were called *criollos* (creoles). Early miscegenation between Spanish men and Amerindian women created a *mestizo* racial group, which during most of the colonial period occupied an ambivalent social position between Spanish and native American.

In the second half of the 1700s, Bishop Baltazar Martínez Compañón included notations of seventeen traditional Amerindian songs and three instrumental dances in the ninth volume of his encyclopedia of life and nature in Trujillo, the province to which he was assigned. Likewise, in a five-hundred-page encyclopedia, the Franciscan brother Gregorio de Zoula, who served in Cusco in the late 1600s, left seventeen musical transcriptions of anonymous songs. In contrast to the more regional flavor of Martínez Compañón's collection, Zoula's transcriptions revealed a marked Renaissance style. A *zapateo* (a creole form of music and dance) and a hymn to the Virgin Mary were transcribed by Amédée François Frézier. Amerindians were converted to Roman Catholicism by Spanish missionaries, and music was one of the tools of conversion. A colonial composition based on an autochthonous theme, extant today, is the well-known four-part polyphonic piece titled "Hanacpachap Cussicuinin" published in Quechua by the Franciscan Juan Pérez Bocanegra (1631) (facsimiles in Quezada Machiavello 1985:76 and Stevenson 1960:48–49). It is possible, scholars argue, that the piece was composed by an Amerindian trained in the Lima cathedral choir.

The modern nation of Peru resulted from the political and economic independence of the creoles from Spanish jurisdiction in 1821 (the beginning of the republican period), after which a new sector of rich and influential plantation owners (*hacendados*) replaced the *encomenderos*. Thus, the political and economic structures of the new nation remained in the same hands, and the subordination of Peruvian Amerindians and *mestizos* persisted.

THE AFRICAN HERITAGE (SEE ALSO AFRO-PERUVIAN TRADITIONS)

The practice and performance of African-derived music, dances, and rituals by black slaves in Peru since the early years of the conquest is well established in colonial and republican sources. The 1700s marked the beginning of creolization of the music of Peruvian blacks, and with their integration into the dominant society, people of African heritage began to accept and adopt creole cultural and musical expressions. During the 1800s, after the abolition of slavery, this process intensified. By the 1950s, only a small number of specialists remembered a few genres of song associated with their ancestors, the repertoire had dwindled to a minimum, and choreographies of most were lost.

This repertoire was the subject of a revival and reconstruction that labeled it Afro-Peruvian, as put forward by the brother and sister Nicomedes and Victoria Santa Cruz, who performed, produced, and promoted Afro-Peruvian music and dances (Romero 1994). The movement singled out black-associated genres that had previously been intermingled with the white creole repertoire. Genres such as the *festejo*, *ingá*, *socabón*, and the *panalivio* were commercially disseminated by the Santa Cruz family in the late 1950s. In the next decade, the *landó* (or *zamba-landó*), the *son de los diablos*, *habanera*, *zaña*, *samba-malato*, *agua de nieve*, *alcatraz*, and other genres were favored.

Because of the uniqueness of Peru's three main topographical zones, the following sections are subdivided accordingly.

The Andean area

Many pre-Hispanic musical instruments are still used in the Peruvian Andes, and other instruments developed during the colonial domination period. Various European musical instruments, including the guitar, the accordion, the harp, and the violin, were introduced by the Spaniards, and since the 1890s additional Western instruments have been adopted by the Andean peasantry, such as the trumpet, the saxophone, the clarinet, and other band instruments.

Membranophones

Skin drums receive different names according to their sizes and localities, including the Quechua terms *tinya* and *wankara*, and the Spanish terms *bombo*, *caja*, and *tambor*. Most are double-headed cylindrical drums of different sizes, ranging from a *tinya* of about 20 centimeters in diameter to a *caja* of 70 centimeters in diameter. Small drums like the *tinya* are mostly played by women on such occasions as the marking (*marcación*) of animals (also called *herranza*), while bigger drums are played by men, mostly to accompany ensembles.

Aerophones

Aerophones are played only by men. Traditional panpipes, *ayarachi*, *chiriguano*, and *sikuri* in Puno, are tuned to a diatonic scale. They are double-unit panpipes, designed to be played with two halves (double units) of a *siku* (each unit or half of the *siku* has comple-

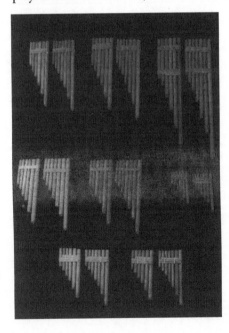

Figure 30.1
A set of *sika* panpipes of the Aymaram Quechua, and/or mestizo people of Puno, Southern Peru, represents the *ira* "leader" (male) and *arka* "follower" (female) pairs in their assorted four sizes. Photo by Raúl R. Romero, 1985.

mentary pitches to the other half) and always in a collective manner. Among the *sikuri*, one half of the double-unit set is designated *ira* "leader" and the other half *arca* "follower." *Sikuri* ensembles consist of different sizes of panpipe (Figure 30.1): some are tuned in octaves, whereas others are tuned to the fifth (called *contras*). An ideal orchestration would include eight different groups of instruments, but not all ensembles always present all the possible combinations (Valencia Chacón 1989:46–53). Other panpipe traditions, such as those of the *ayarachi* and *chiriguano*, are subdivided in three groups, each of which is tuned to the octave (Valencia Chacón 1989:65, 71). *Sikuri* and other panpipe ensembles perform intensively throughout the annual calendar of fiestas, in weddings, and other life-cycle events, such as a child's first haircut (*corte de pelo*, Turino 1993:46). In several traditions in the Puno area and in Lima among migrants from Puno, individual players of each panpipe half play a drum at the same time (Figure 30.2). Elsewhere, a single-unit panpipe is played as a solo instrument, like the *antara* (*andara*) in Cajamarca (Instituto Nacional de Cultura 1978:209–210).

Different kinds of vertical end-notched flutes (*quena*, pronounced and often spelled *kena*), vertical duct flutes (*pincullo*, *tarka*), and side-blown flutes (*pito*) are widely disseminated in the Andes. The *quena*, also known by local names (*lawata*, *chaqallo*, and *quenacho*), is usually made from cane but also from wood and plastic (since the 1970s). *Quenas* can have diverse lengths (between 25 and 120 centimeters) and from three to eight fingerholes. One of the most ubiquitous types, measuring 30 to 40 centimeters long, has six fingerholes in the front and one thumbhole. The *quena* can be played as a solo instrument in private and contemplative situations (while herding, for example), but in public performances it is usually played with contrasting instruments in ensembles, such as in *música folclórica* groups or *conjuntos* in Cusco, or with large ensembles of other *quenas* for *choquela* dances in Puno (Cuentas Ormachea 1982:59) and Carnaval dances in the Colca valley in Arequipa (Ráez 1993:286).

Figure 30.2
In a street in La Victoria, a *barrio* in Lima, a panpipe group consisting of migrants from the department of Puno and their descendants performs for an event. The ethnomusicologist Thomas Turino is in the left background. Photo by Cathy Collinge Herrera, 1984.

Since no archaeological evidence has been discovered proving the origins of duct tubular flutes in Peru (although globular flutes with duct mouthpieces are found archaeologically; see STUDYING LATIN AMERICAN MUSIC), it is generally thought they originated during the colonial period. The term *pingollo*, however, was usually employed by the early chroniclers to denote pre-Hispanic flutes, and today's duct flute has nearly the same name (*pincullu*, also spelled *pincullo*, *pinkillo*, *pinkuyllo*); other names are the Spanish term *flauta* in many areas and *chiska* or *rayán* in Ancash. Most frequently made of wood or cane, the duct flute is of different sizes (from 30 to 120 centimeters long), and often has a variable number of fingerholes. One of the most disseminated types is the three-holed one-handed duct flute, played in a pipe-and-tabor mode. In northern Peru, pipe-and-tabor duct flutes are of two types: *roncador* "snorer" [Listen to "*Huayno*"], characterized by a harsh sound (in Ancash and Huánuco), and *silbadora* "whistler" (also *flauta*), with a more mellow timbre (in Cajamarca and La Libertad). Pipe-and-tabor players perform widely in public festivals, fulfilling a central role in ceremonies associated with communal labor in the fields (Figure 30.3) and in the construction of buildings in Junín (Romero 1990:14) and Ancash (den Otter 1985:112). In the Colca Valley, a six-holed *pinkuyllo* measuring 120 centimeters long, is played by one performer accompanied by a drum played by a woman; it is used exclusively in fertility rituals (Ráez 1993:291). Duct flutes can be played in ensembles of instruments of the same type, including the five- and six-holed *pinkillo* in Conima, Puno;

DISC ❶ TRACK 21

Figure 30.3
During a communal work effort in the fields of Paccha, Jauja, Peru, a *pincullo* and *tinya* pipe-and-tabor musician performs. Photo by Raúl R. Romero, 1985.

from eight to fifteen performers play them in "dense unison" (caused by the folk intonation of the instruments), accompanied by drums (Turino 1993:48).

The *tarka*, another harsh sounding duct flute, is played only in the southern department of Puno. The feature that distinguishes it from other duct flutes is its hexagonal cross-sectional shape [see BOLIVIA]. Usually with six fingerholes, it is played in large ensembles (*tarkeadas*) during public festivals and as a solo instrument by shepherds in the mountains (Bellenger 1981:24).

In the Andes, a side-blown flute is known by several local names, such as *flauta*, *pito*, *phalahuita*, and even *quena* (Instituto Nacional de Cultura 1978:221). In Puno, where it is called *pitu*, it is made of cane, has six fingerholes, and is played in large ensembles of similar instruments during community festivals (Turino 1993:57). In Cusco, two six-holed *pitus* are accompanied by drums in war bands (*bandas de guerra*), ensembles recurrent in public festivals throughout the region.

Different kinds of locally constructed trumpets are widely used, including the *wak'rapuku* in the central Andes, the *clarín* in the northern Andes, and the *pampa corneta* in Huancavelica. The *wak'rapuku* (Figure 30.4), made of cattle-horn pieces spirally joined together, is usually played in pairs (*primera* and *segunda*) tuned a third apart. It is played but once a year, during animal-marking fertility rituals. Its origins are no doubt colonial, because cattle were introduced by Europeans. The *clarín*, popular in Cajamarca, is a cane side-blown trumpet 3 meters long, used in festivals (Figure 30.5 [Listen to "Festival de la Virgen del Carmen"]) and in agricultural music (Canepa-Koch 1993:150). The *pampa corneta* is a straight wooden trumpet, 3 to 4 meters long. Restricted to Ayacucho and Huancavelica, it is usually played only in the ritual marking of the animals. The *pututu* (conch trumpet) is still used in the southern Andes for signaling, opening special com-

DISC ❶ TRACK 22

Figure 30.4
Two *wak'rapuku* coiled cow-horn trumpets: *cacho primero* "first horn" on left, *cacho segundo* "second horn" on right. Pitched a third apart, they are traditionally played in Junín, Peru, for the *herranza* "marking of the animals" fertility ritual, often with a violin and *tinya* drum. Photo by Raúl R. Romero, 1985.

munal ceremonies, and communal labor (*faenas*) in Pisac and Paucartambo, Cusco province.

The Spanish introduced double-reed instruments such as the *chirimía* (a shawm made of wood), which during colonial times was frequently played for official ceremonies related to municipal affairs in urban centers. The *chirimía* is still played in the northern coastal and Andean areas in public festivals (Casas Roque 1993: 324–326) and in highland Lima, Huancavelica, and Ayacucho, where it is known as *chirisuya* (Jiménez Borja 1951:79).

Chordophones

Since ancient Peruvians used no chordophones, it is reasonable to conclude that the many string instruments currently in use (*guitarra, mandolina, bandurria, arpa,* and *violín*) were introduced by the Spaniards during the colonial period. The *charango* (in certain localities also called *quirquincho* "armadillo" and *chillador* "screamer") is a small guitar made of armadillo shell, wood to resemble the roundness of the armadillo (Figure 30.6), or wood to resemble a small flat-backed guitar. Common to southern Peru (and believed to be invented in Potosí, Bolivia), it is from 23 to 45 centimeters long (Bellenger 1981:42). It has diverse tunings and regionally variable numbers of strings; the most common tuning for the ten-stringed *charango* is G–G–c–c–e–E–A–A–e–e. The six-stringed variant usually duplicates only the third string, one of which is tuned to the octave of the other. In Cusco, the *charango* is played by Andean peasants with a predominant strumming style while a single string carries the melody; *mestizo* performers play it in a plucked melodic mode, interspersed with strumming sections (Turino 1984:259) [Listen to "Quien a visto aquél volcán"].

DISC ❶ TRACK 24

The Spanish guitar (*guitarra*) has not changed much since its adaptation to Andean musical practices, though its tuning varies by region. Besides the standard tuning, others depend on the locality, each with a specific name. In Ayacucho the most common tuning, *comuncha* (G_1–B_1–D–G–B–e), predomi-

Figure 30.6
Nicanor Abarca Puma, a *charango* maker and player from Arequipa, Peru, plays a *charango de caja*. Resembling a small guitar, it has five triple courses of metal strings. Photo by Dale A. Olsen, 1979.

Figure 30.7
The late Fausto Dolorier Abregu, professional harpist and former professor of harp at the National School of Folkloric Arts, Lima. Photo by Dale A. Olsen, 1979.

nates in rural areas and serves primarily for playing peasant *huaynos* (pronounced and often spelled *waynos*) in E minor. Other tunings, such as harp tuning (*temple arpa*, $F\#_1–A_1–D–F\#–B–e$), used to play *huaynos* and *carnavales* in B minor, and devil tuning (*temple diablo*, $G_1–B_1–D–G–c–e$), used to play *yaravies* in G minor, are also widely used (Pinto 1987:84–86). In the village of Jesús in Huánuco, Villareal Vara (1958:35) found six different tunings in Carnaval guitar music, one of which, called plain (*llano*), corresponds to the standard European tuning $E_1–A_1–D–G–B–e$.

Spanish missionaries propagated the European harp and the violin throughout all the Andean area, and today both instruments are widely dispersed in the communities of the Peruvian Andes, played individually or together as part of larger ensembles. The harp, contrasting with the guitar and the violin, has experienced considerable morphological adaptation, ranging from the triangle-shaped *arpa indigena* (Figure 30.7) to the smaller *domingacha* type with a pear-shaped sound box (Olsen 1980a and 1986–87). The Peruvian harp is diatonic, usually tuned to the C major scale. It uses from twenty-six to thirty-six metal or nylon strings and has no pedals. It is so lightweight that it can be easily played upside down in a sling around the musician's neck during processions and festivals (see Figure 30.9 and Figure 30.10).

Harp performance styles vary by region. Dale Olsen (1986–1987) has distinguished six principal regional styles in Peru: Callejón de Huaylas–Huánuco in the northern Andes, Mantaro in the central Andes, Ayacucho in the south-central Andes, Urubamba–Abancay in the southern Andes, Chancay in the central coastal region, and urbanized in Lima. The harp can be played solo and in ensemble, where it provides bass and harmonic functions. In some regions of the country, it is played as an accompanying percussion instrument by a *tamborero*, a person who beats his fingers on its body while someone else plucks the strings.

Ensembles

Andean music has adopted the accordion, widely used throughout the region but especially in *conjuntos* in Cusco, in string ensembles in the Callejón de Huaylas (den Otter 1985:91), and in the *estudiantina* group of stringed instruments in Puno. Wind instruments—clarinet, saxophone, trumpet, trombone, tuba—make up brass bands (Figure 30.8). Saxophones (alto, tenor, baritone), clarinets, harps, and violins form the basis of the typical orchestra (*orquesta típica*), the most popular ensemble in the central Andean department of Junín and neighboring areas (Figure 30.9). [Listen to "No lo cuentes a nadie"]

tamborero
In Peru, a person who beats on the box of the harp as on a percussion instrument while the harpist plucks the strings
estudiantina
"Student ensemble," an ensemble in Puno that includes guitars, *charangos*, mandolins, and an accordion
orquesta típica
"Typical orchestra," an ensemble in the central Peruvian highlands consisting of saxophones, clarinets, violins, and a harp

DISC ❶ TRACK 23

Regional instrumental ensembles play in various contexts. Throughout the Andes, a combination of harp and violins are pervasive, as is the ensemble of flute and drum played by a single performer or by several, as in the *banda de guerra* of Cusco, which combines *quena* flutes, accordion, mandolin, harp, and a violin. The *banda típica* in northern Cajamarca mixes *quenas* and percussion instruments (snare drum and cymbals). Large ensembles of one instrumental type—for example, aerophones such as *pitu*, *pinkillu*, and *tarka*—are also common in the south. The *estudiantina* ensemble of Puno includes guitars, *charangos*, mandolins, violins, and an accordion. The *herranza*, an ensemble that accompanies herding rituals in the central Andes, merges a violin, several *wak'rapuku*, and a *tinya*. The string ensemble (*conjunto de cuerdas*) of Ancash combines a violin, a mandolin, and sometimes a harp or a *quena* and an accordion.

Figure 30.8
A military band performs in procession during a patronal festival in Los Baños del Inca, Cajamarca, Peru. The musicians are reading music affixed with clothespins to each other's backs. Photo by Dale A. Olsen, 1979.

The coast

The Spanish introduced the lute (*laúd*) and the *bandurria* along Peru's coast, but after they were discontinued the guitar became the most important instrument in creole music in urban areas (Santa Cruz 1977:49), serving as a solo instrument or for voice-accompanying duos and trios, especially in the *vals criollo*. After the 1950s, when creole music began to be disseminated primarily via commercial records and the mass media, the creole repertoire began to be performed by various musical instruments and ensembles. Although the guitar remained the most vital instrument in live performances, percussion instruments such

Figure 30.9
The *orquesta típica* "typical orchestra" Los Piratos del Centro (the Pirates from the Center [central Mantaro Valley]), from Huancayo, perform in Junín, Peru. Left to right: baritone saxophone, three tenor saxophones, four alto saxophones, a harp carried upside down, a clarinet, a violin, and another clarinet. Photo by Raúl R. Romero, 1985.

as the *cajón* "big box" and Iberian castanets (usually replaced by a pair of spoons in live performances) were introduced. The *cajón* is a variably sized wooden box with a hole in its back (compare with Cuba). Commonly used by Afro-Peruvians, a performer sits atop the instrument and strikes it with both hands.

In the rural areas of the Peruvian coast, other instruments can be found. Many of them—such as the *pinkullo* and the *caja* (played by a single performer, as in the highlands), the harp, the *chirimía*, and the instruments that form the brass band in Lambayeque—are also played in the Andes. For *marineras* (dance music in *sesquiáltera* meter), a *tamborero* beats on a harp's sound box while the harpist plucks the strings and sings. The banjo, introduced in some areas of the north Peruvian coast around 1900, is now used to play *valses* and *marineras* (Casas Roque 1993).

The guitar is the most important instrument in the Afro-Peruvian tradition. Peruvian blacks incorporated it and the harp in street fiestas as early as the 1700s, but this tradition has been forgotten (Estenssoro 1988:163). Still in use is the *quijada* (or *carachacha*), which is the jawbone of an ass, mule, or horse, whose teeth rattle when the jawbone is struck with a hand. After the 1950s, when a process of revitalization of Afro-Peruvian music took place, Caribbean instruments (including *congas*, cowbell, and *bongos*) were incorporated.

The Amazonian region

An extensive assortment of musical instruments can be found among the nearly sixty ethnolinguistic groups that inhabit the Amazonian region (see Okada 1995: examples 9–11). Among numerous types of wooden slit drums and membranophonic drums are those used to send messages and signal the group or other parties. Many classes of musical bows are employed, as are diverse types of European-derived wooden zithers and violins. Cane and bamboo trumpets, the conch trumpet (*churu* in Amazonas and *quipa* in San Martín), and vertical and side-blown flutes of different sizes and number of holes are also common. The panpipe is played as a solo instrument or in ensembles.

MUSIC GENRES AND CONTEXTS

The Andean area

Current Andean musical expressions are often re-creations of pre-Hispanic indigenous genres, local developments based on colonial European models, or recent configurations derived from the encounter with national and transnational urban musical forms. Among the pre-Hispanic genres of song cited by early chroniclers and still persisting among Andean peasantry is the *harawi*, a monophonic genre of song that consists of one musical phrase repeated several times with extensive melismatic passages and long glissandos. It is associated with specific ceremonies and rituals (including farewells and marriages) and agricultural labor (including sowing and harvesting) in the southern Andes. It is usually sung in a high-pitched, nasal voice by a group of elder women called *harawiq* (Cavero 1985:237). In Cusco, this genre, known as *wanka*, is associated with the same ritual contexts (Arguedas, cited in Pinilla 1980:390). The *kashwa*, a pre-Hispanic genre usually associated with nocturnal harvest rituals, is performed in a circle by young, unmarried men and women (Roel Pineda 1959). *Haylli* is a responsorial genre, performed during communal agricultural work in the fields.

Among other Andean musical genres associated with specific contexts is the *carnaval*, a song and dance for the festivity known as Carnaval. This genre has several regional variants and designations, such as *wifala* and *puqllay* (in Ayacucho, Puno, and Cusco), *araskaska* and the recently introduced *pumpín* (Ayacucho), and the more disseminated *pasacalle* (in Ancash and the southern Andes). The *walina*, a genre linked with the ritual cleaning of the irrigation channels in the highlands of the department of Lima, is customarily sung by men, with a *chirimía* playing a countermelody.

Some genres have become dissociated from their original contexts. These include the *santiago* (originally a kind of song from the Central Andes, performed by women during the ritual marking of animals), the *huaylas* (once a ritual harvest song, also from the Central Andes), and the *carnaval* of the southern Andes. These genres became accepted beyond their villages, achieving regional significance in traditional fiestas. Later, they began to be distributed by the record industry, achieving national coverage and eventually emancipating themselves from their original ritual contexts.

The most widely disseminated and popular song-dance genre in the Andes is the *huayno* (*wayno*). In view of meager early colonial references to it as a musical form, Roel Pineda (1959) has postulated that its popularity grew during the colonial period, and that this acceptance was achieved to the detriment of the *kashwa*. He has further explained that the *kashwa* as a collective and rural manifestation could not survive within a colonial system that implied spatial and ideological limitations. In this sense, the *huayno* as a freely choreographed couple dance was better suited to urban, narrow spaces.

The *huayno* has many regional variants and adopts different names, including *chuscada* (Ancash), *pampeña* (Arequipa), *cachua* (Cajamarca), *chymaycha* (Amazonas and Huanuco), *huaylacha* (Colca Valley), and *sikuriada* (Puno). Usually in duple meter, it consists of a pair of musical phrases in periodic form (AABB). Like other Andean genres, it may have a closing section, called *fuga* or *qawachan*, which consists of a contrasting theme in a faster tempo. Today, it reflects the styles of the different social and ethnic groups that perform it. As an autonomous expression of contextual and ritual constraints, it can be performed at any time and in various settings (see Cohen 1984).

The *yaraví* is a slow, lyrical, *mestizo* genre in triple meter and binary form. [Listen to "Quien a visto aquél volcán"] Mostly sung in the southern Andes (especially in Arequipa), it is usually associated with afflicted love affairs and nostalgic moods. Arguedas has suggested that in Cusco the *mestizo yaraví* evolved from the indigenous *harawi*, from which it took its main sentimental theme (Pinilla 1980:390). Its melody is built on a minor tonality, is usually sung in parallel thirds, and has a flexible tempo (Carpio Muñoz 1976; Pagaza Galdo 1961) (see Okada 1995: example 13). Having analogous musical characteristics is the *triste*, pervasive in northern Peru. In the central Andes, the *muliza*, though distinctive in style and form, is similar to the *yaraví* and serves the same evocative function. These genres are usually followed by a *fuga de huayno*, a fast closing section.

DISC ❶ TRACK 24

Contrasting with fixed genres are nonfixed genres organically linked to specific ritual contexts, including fertility rituals, agricultural communal work, the cleaning of irrigation channels, the building of edifices, and life-cycle ceremonial phases (baptism, courting, marriage, funerals). In many cases, the accompanying music bears the name of the ritual involved, though in some cases a fixed musical form may be associated with the ritual.

In the Mantaro Valley in the department of Junín, the nocturnal harrowing of grain was until the 1950s accomplished by young unmarried men and women who sang unaccompanied or with guitar accompaniment and danced on top of a mound of grain, separating the seeds from the husks. In the same region, the music of a *pincullo* and a *tinya*, played by one performer in a pipe-and-tabor fashion, is reserved for times when the peasant community gathers to work in the fields in specific moments of the agricultural calendar, especially the first tilling of the soil and the harvest. Each musical repertoire pertains solely to its corresponding performance context, and although each tune is given a descriptive name, the whole repertoire lacks any concrete name other than the occasion for which it is intended. In Cajamarca in the northern Andes, the *clarín* is played during the *minka* (communal work in the fields), especially during the harvest of grain (Cánepa-Koch 1993:150; Jiménez Borja 1951:75).

The marking of animals is one of the most ubiquitous fertility rituals in the central and southern Andes of Peru. Associated with the Andean mountain deities (the *wamani*, the *apu*, or the *achachila*, depending on the region), it is usually performed during specific seasons of the year [see Q'EROS]. In the highland areas of the Colca Valley, the music of a large *pincuyllo* and a *tinya* is played in the *tinka*, a ceremony during Carnaval when a llama is sacrificed and ritual offerings are buried for the deities. Music accompanies the steps of the ritual and is played during rest periods when, after the ritual, the participants dance and relax. An ensemble of eighteen *quenas* or *chaqallos* accompanied by two *bombos* and a snare drum fulfills the same function during a similar ritual called *wylancha* in Puno (Canepa-Koch 1991). In the Mantaro River Valley, the musical ensemble of the marking of animals consists of one or two *wak'rapuku*, a violin, a singer, and a *tinya* (see Okada 1995: example 16) The repertoire of this ensemble is strictly linked with each step of the ritual and like the previously mentioned cases is exclusively reserved for this occasion.

The cleaning of irrigation channels (*michicoq, fiesta del agua* "festival of the water") is a ceremonial task performed by all the members of the peasant community. It is an especially strong tradition in Puquio, Ayacucho, and San Pedro de Casta, Lima (see Okada 1995: example 15). Here, the *walina* is a fixed genre associated exclusively with this ritual. A large repertoire of *walina* is sung only by the men, who perform the ceremonial cleaning; it is accompanied by the *chirimía*, which plays a relatively independent countermelody to the lead singer's melody.

The communal construction of buildings (*pirkansa*) is an event in which communal labor fulfills an indispensable function and in which music is ceremonially vital. In the Mantaro Valley, the *pirkansa* occurs when the walls of an edifice are being built: during the ritual, a performer of *pincullo* and *tinya* music (as in agricultural music) participates. A similar instrumental combination is employed in Ancash (*flauta* and *caja*) in the same setting (den Otter 1985:113).

Ceremonial life-cycle phases (baptism, courting, marriage, and funeral) are also contexts for major musical repertoires. The role of music in courting rituals is particularly solid in Cusco. In Canas, young unmarried men summon their chosen women by playing the *tuta kashwa* ("night dance," a particular melody) on their *charangos* during the fiestas of Saint Andrew (San Andrés) and the Holy Cross (Santa Cruz) (Turino 1983:85). Funeral music is usually sung by specialists at the wake or actual burial as in the festivity of the Día de los Muertos (Day of the Dead). In the Mantaro Valley, items in the repertoire of the funeral-song singers (*responseros*) have Quechua texts with strong musical-liturgical influence. In other areas, the relatives of the deceased themselves may weep and grieve, combining spoken passages with musical cadences. When an infant dies in Puno, a lively *huayno* is sung with *charango* accompaniment because it is believed that the dead baby goes to heaven in a state of grace; thus, the death is an occasion to celebrate rather than grieve.

The annual festival calendar is the natural context for the numerous dance-dramas that exist in the Peruvian Andes. The fiesta calendar, prolific throughout the Andean region, is the result of the blending of the pre-Hispanic agricultural calendar with the Christian annual calendar. Different types of festivals are celebrated with greater or lesser intensity according to each region and locality. Some fiestas have achieved pan-Andean relevance. These include the Purification of Our Lady (Virgen de la Calendaria, 2 February), Fiesta de la Cruz (3 May), the Nativity of St. John the Baptist (San Juan, 24 June), Saints Peter and Paul (San Pedro y San Pablo, 29 June), Our Lady of Mount Carmel (16 July), St. James the Apostle (Santiago Apóstol, 25 July), St. Rose of Lima (Santa Rosa de Lima, 30 August), the Nativity of the Blessed Virgin Mary (8 September), and Christian seasonal observances such as Christmas, the Epiphany, Holy Week (especially Palm Sunday), and Corpus Christi. Carnival is celebrated throughout the Andes, often closely linked with the Purification of Our Lady.

Frequently, the actual fiesta lasts from three to five days, depending on the type of festivity and the region. The main events usually occur during vespers the evening before the central day, on the central day itself, and on the closing day or the farewell. In the Colca Valley, fiestas usually consist of five parts, coinciding with the five days of the fiesta. First is the *antealba*, when the communal preparations are concluded and the musicians begin to rehearse. Second, the *alba* constitutes the evening of the principal day, when fireworks are set off. Third is the *principal*, the main day, when all the dance-dramas are performed and the customary bullfights or horse races are presented. Fourth is the *bendición*, when the fiesta continues and the organizers for the next year are chosen; during that night, a general farewell takes effect with music and dance and continues until the following day, the fifth and closing day, known as *kacharpari* (Ráez 1993:278–279). In Ishua, Ayacucho, the fiestas have a similar temporal division, but different names: *anticipo, víspera, día, cabildo*, and *despacho* (Bradby 1987:200).

Music and dance are integral parts of the Andean fiesta (Figure 30.10). The music for dance-dramas follows the structure of the dance-dramas themselves—a multisectional form of two to six parts, each with different tempos and styles. The dance-drama choreography is usually fixed and repeats itself year after year. In Cusco, most dances include formations

Figure 30.10
On Sunday, the main day of the patronal festival of San Juan Bautista (Saint John the Baptist) in Acolla, Junín, Peru, dancers known as *tunantadas* and *chunginos*, representing Spanish nobility, perform to the accompaniment of an *orquesta típica* (only the upside-down harp is in view). Photo by Dale A. Olsen, 1979.

in columns, zigzag movements, and circular patterns—figures that ultimately express local concepts of social space and hierarchy (Poole 1991:325). Similar choreographic patterns have been observed in the province of Cajamarca in the dances of the *chunchu* and the *palla* (Canepa-Koch 1993:170). Dance-drama music is unique exclusively linked with the choreography of the dance from which it takes it name. Besides the dances in the fiestas, other festive music includes music for fireworks, bullfights, horse races, processions, special offerings, and orchestral salutes (welcomes and farewells).

Music for dance-dramas can be performed by a single musician, several performers (Figure 30.11), or a large ensemble. The performers may be members of the community or hired musicians who play professionally in regional markets. In many regions, *mestizo* sponsors of fiestas hire Indian performers to be closer to the tradition. In this sense, performers of music for dance-dramas may have a less conspicuous profile than the dancers themselves. In some contexts, the latter usually dance because of a religious promise to the Virgin, whereas musicians are usually hired to play (Canepa-Koch 1994:270). Brass bands (winds, drums, and cymbals) became widely popular in the Andes in the beginning of the twentieth century, largely because military service had become mandatory and few young men could avoid it (Romero 1985:250). Brass bands remain one of the most popular vehicles for dance-dramas in the southern Peruvian Andes.

There are numerous dance groups (*comparsas*) and choreographic representations in the Andes, and their classification has seldom been agreed on. Using thematic criteria, Luis Valcarcel (1951:11–13) distinguished the following thematic types in Andean dances: religious, totemic, martial, associational (guilds), satirical, regional, pantomimes, entertainment, agricultural, and strolling dances. Mildred Merino de Zela (1977:70), preferring to use a chronological model, classified them as pre-Hispanic, conquest, colonial, independence, and republican dances. Poole (1990:101), however, has highlighted the fact that ethnic or historic representation, if in fact the most important external trait that these classification systems emphasize, is not necessarily the most important factor involved in Andean dance. The significance of local concepts of time, space, and hierarchy in representing "the other" go beyond the plain illustration of a personage.

Musical competition is pervasive in the Andes, where competitiveness is an essential trait intended to encourage social productivity and solidarity (Montoya 1987). In the Mantaro Valley, after a ceremonial labor day, the laborer who worked fastest and best was elected to inspire the other workers. During traditional festivals throughout the Andean region, contests in which a jury of selected personalities chooses the best music-and-dance group are pervasive. In other instances, a jury is not involved, but the participants themselves decide which group is best. Competition is indispensable in the scissors dance (*danza de tijeras, dansaq*), performed in the context of public fiestas in Ayacucho and adjacent areas. In this dance, two groups compete, each including a harp, a violin, and one or two dancers who play the scissors as an idiophone (see Cohen 1984). Competing dancers alternatively perform up to twenty-one choreographic segments of increasing difficulty (Núñez Rebaza 1990:18–21). Competition also involves singing, as in the Carnaval songs called *coplas* in Cajamarca. In a succession of challenges and responses among musicians, each singer sings a *copla* in open competition with the others (Canepa-Koch and Romero 1988). In these instances, the principal competition is immersed in Andean established values, but in new contexts (such as the *concurso* "contest"), the focus shifts to external and formal elements. Dances and musical groups are taken out of context to compete in the urban theater or stadium, and competition is based on formal and ornamental criteria.

Figure 30.11
During a festival in central Peru, a bass drum, snare drum, and two violins are played. Photo by Raúl R. Romero, 1985.

The coast

Coastal Peruvian music is generally called creole music (*música criolla*), and the creole waltz (*vals criollo*) is the most representative genre of the repertoire and many Peruvians consider it the foremost national music. A development of its European counterpart, it had achieved regional consolidation by the end of the 1800s. It developed from the Spanish *jota* and *mazurca* and from the Viennese waltz, popularized in Lima by the mid-1800s (Santa Cruz 1977). The Peruvian *vals* originated in the lower classes and neighborhoods of Lima. It was the genre the working classes in the *barrios* (suburbs) preferred, while the upper classes rejected it (Stein 1982).

The polka, now seldom performed, is also part of the creole repertoire. The *marinera*—until about 1900 known as *zamacueca, chilena, mozamala,* and *resbalosa* (it was renamed *marinera* after the sailors who lost their lives in the 1880s War of the Pacific with Chile)—is one of the most widely disseminated song-and-dance genres in the country. Originally from coastal Peru, it is widely performed in Andean regions. In *sesquiáltera* rhythm (compound duple and triple meter, 6/8 and 3/4), it has three distinctive parts: the song (three stanzas), the *resbalosa* (one stanza), and a closing *fuga* ("flight," not a fugue in the European sense). The *tondero*, a related genre, followed a parallel evolution in the northern coastal departments of La Libertad, Lambayeque, and Píura. In music and choreography, the *tondero* resembles the *marinera*, but it exhibits a distinctive harmonic structure: the first section (*glosa*) begins in the major mode, the second is in the relative minor mode (*dulce*), and the piece returns to the major mode in the third (*fuga*). Both genres are usually accompanied by guitars and a *cajón*. In northern Peru, the latter is replaced by a harp and often a banjo.

Creole musical contexts in Peru are mostly limited to the city of Lima and adjacent coastal areas. In coastal Lambayeque, dance-dramas (including *pastoras, margaros,* and *diablicos*) are accompanied by a *pincullo* and a *caja* (played in pipe-and-tabor style), brass instruments, and a *chirimía* (Casas Roque 1993:304–318).

The Amazonian region

Among the groups that inhabit the Amazonian region (i.e., the rainforest or tropical forest, including the eastern slopes of the Andes), the musical cultures of the Aguaruna (border with Ecuador), the Huitoto (frontier with Colombia), the Culina (frontier with Brazil) and the Campa, Cashibo, Shipibo, and Yagua (central Amazon) are better known than others. In the Peruvian tropical forest, music is customarily linked with ritual and festival cycles, which (as in the Yagua group) are strongly influenced by the Roman Catholic calendar. Ritual songs are most prominent in healing ceremonies such as the *ayahuasca* ritual (in which a hallucinogenic drink made from a vine is imbibed) and other shamanistic activities. Vocal music is more pervasive than instrumental music. The vocal imitation of animal and jungle sounds is especially emphasized by the Cashibo. Widely various scales have been reported, ranging from two to seven pitches. Among these, pentatonic scales are quite common in groups such as the Culina. Although heterophony is most commonly observed in musical renditions, two-voice polyphony in intervals of fourths and canonic singing has also been observed (Pinilla 1980:380–384).

National anthem

Peru's national anthem is titled "Marcha Nacional" (National March), which was composed by José Bernardo Alzedo with lyrics by José de la Torre Ugarte (http://david.national-anthems.net/pe.txt). It was selected in 1822 after a national anthem composition contest took place following Peru's independence, and after its first performance in the Teatro Principal in Lima on September 24, 1821. It was officially adopted in 1913 after a few revisions of the song text. The current version of "Marcha Nacional" has six verses.

Most Andean communities are concerned about safeguarding their traditions, which, for them, represent the past, though their origins are not necessarily thought archaic. Several musical expressions in the Andes are locally considered traditional, though their origins can be traced back only to the beginning of this century. In the cities of Puno, young people regard the panpipe group Qantati Ururi of Conima as the true keepers of the pan-pipe tradition, although this band uses intervals of thirds—a practice introduced as a result of urban influence in Conima during the first decades of the twentieth century (Turino 1993:130). In the Mantaro Valley, a variant of the typical orchestra—clarinets, violins, harp—is considered to represent authentic performance, though clarinets were introduced into the valley only in the 1920s. In Cusco, the dance *los majeños* "the men of Majes" (a town in Arequipa), normally accompanied by a brass band, is considered traditional re-gional folklore, though it became popular only in the 1960s (Mendoza-Walker 1994:55).

Trends in musical change include the spread of brass bands throughout the Andean region at the cost of smaller traditional ensembles with less dazzling instrumentation. This change happened especially in the case of dance-dramas. In the Mantaro Valley (Romero 1985:21), in the Colca Valley (Ráez 1993:280), and in most of the Andean region, brass bands have displaced Indian and rural ensembles and have achieved intense popularity. One of the factors in their expansion is that they are more elastic in repertoire than are the regional ensembles. They can play any musical genre—*cumbia, marinera, pasodoble,* tropical music, and even the latest popular music hit—and this versatility adds to their popularity among younger people.

Cumbia and chicha

Cumbia, originally a genre from Colombia, is immensely popular in the Peruvian Andes. It is commonly performed by the ubiquitous brass band and is danced at special times in traditional fiestas. In regional ensembles, called jazz bands by the people of Cusco, its basic rhythmic pattern has influenced the rhythmic accompaniment of *mestizo* genres like the *huayno* and those of festival music. The similarity of this rhythmic pattern with that of the *huayno* is striking.

During the 1960s, the popularity of the *cumbia* among Andean residents and migrants was boosted by the appearance of a new urban musical genre, called *chicha* or *cumbia an-dina*, which blended musical elements from the *huayno* with the *cumbia*. *Chicha* achieved great approval among the younger generations of Andean origins, and became especially important in its center of operations, Lima, though many of its principal performers came from the central Andes. *Chicha* style and the instrumental makeup of its musical groups reflect the influence that since the early 1960s international Latin American popular styles and American and British rock have had on young Andean migrants (Turino 1990:19). A typical group (Figure 30.12) consists of two electric guitars, an electric organ (replaced in the 1990s by a synthesizer), an electric bass, Latin percussion (*timbales, congas, bongos,* cowbell), and a vocalist, who performs in a style recalling that of Andean *mestizo* songs.

Chicha music became a nucleus around which young unmarried men and women

Figure 30.12
On stage in Lima, Peru, the *chicha* (also known as *cumbia andina*) ensemble Alegría performs. Left to right: musicians play *bongos*, electric bass, *timbales*, keyboard, and electric guitar. Photo by Raúl R. Romero, 1985.

from first- and second-generation cohorts in Lima congregated every Sunday and holidays. Several *chichódromos* (locales for *chicha* events) opened in downtown Lima and in the outskirts, and such groups as the Shapis, Alegría, and Chacalón y la Nueva Crema gained fame. Although most *chicha* lyrics deal with romantic love, other themes directly linked to the problems of the migrant in Lima also prevail. As a product of migrant Andean people, *chicha* was regarded by the upper classes and by the mass media as a low cultural product in bad taste, and its performances were considered dangerous and promiscuous. With time, however, *chicha* has opened new channels for migrant music on FM radio stations and during prime-time television. This reversal does not mean that upper and middle classes in Peru have changed their attitudes toward *chicha* music but rather that Andean migrants have achieved an influential position in Peruvian society. The role of *chicha* as the urban expression of a new Andean cultural identity transcending regional characters to achieve national significance has been emphasized by Peruvian social scientists since the 1980s (Hurtado Suárez 1995).

In rural areas, as in Paccha in Junín, *chicha* is usually played in public buildings at night in social dances (*bailes*) organized during the traditional fiestas. Without disturbing the normal development of the fiesta during daytime, the *bailes* in Paccha gather young unmarried men and women together. In this setting, they may interact freely and independently in ways that they cannot during traditional festivities. In the context of a social dance, *chicha* functions as a courting ritual, does not require heavy expenses, and may be enjoyed at any period of the year (Romero 1989:131).

MUSIC LEARNING, DISSEMINATION, TOURISM, AND PUBLIC POLICY

Andean migrant music in the cities

Andean music had been present in Lima since the 1930s in the festival of Amancaes every *día del indio* (24 June) and well before that through the works and performances of

Peruvian academic composers who have borrowed Andean musical materials and themes (Núñez and Llorens 1981:54–55). Since the late 1940s, processes of massive migration and the presence of Andean peoples in the urban centers of the country, especially in Lima, have continued and expanded highland traditions (see Figure 30.2) and generated new musical styles, which combined Andean musical traditions with the popular musical trends available in the cities. The appearance of the first commercial records of Andean music marked the birth of a new style of urban *mestizo* popular song. These records were distributed in Lima in 1949 because of an initiative by José María Arguedas (1975:125), who promoted the pilot edition of a series of 78-rpm records on the (now locally extinct) Odeon label. The success was overwhelming, so Odeon began to mass-produce them independently of Arguedas.

In the 1950s, the sale of Andean records grew considerably in urban sectors of Peru, mainly because of the increasing migration of Andean rural peoples into the capital. The appearance of the first folkloric programs (*programas folklóricos*) on commercial radio stations in Lima dedicated to the diffusion of Andean music and the promotion of folkloric festivals contributed to this success (Llorens 1991:180). In the 1960s, as a result of this outburst of production and consumption, Andean *mestizo* celebrities—songwriters, instrumentalists, performers—achieved popularity and recognition. Singers including the Pastorcita Huaracina, el Jilguero del Huascarán, and Picaflor de los Andes sold thousand of records and became celebrities. The effort was not limited to records but also included live performances in marginal spaces where migrant musicians could play and migrant consumers could attend, such as live radio shows, open theaters (*coliseos*), and regional associations.

Coliseos were the most influential musical settings for these musical styles. Beginning in the late 1940s, masses of Andean migrants congregated in them, usually on Sundays and holidays, to watch their favorite professional and amateur performers. Today, these venues have disappeared, replaced by public performances and musical festivals in provincial clubs and athletic stadiums. Many provincial associations celebrate their regional fiestas in Lima, recreating their own music and dances (Núñez and Llorens 1981:66–70).

The mass media and popular musics

The mass media have been responsible for disseminating transnational musical genres and styles since the first decades of this century. Peruvians with access to the radio and movie theaters became familiar as early as the 1920s with the Argentine *tango*, the Mexican *ranchera*, and the North American fox-trot, one-step, and charleston (Basadre 1964). Local orchestras disseminated these genres in social and private dances and events. Jazz has been played in Lima since the first decades of the twentieth century, especially by orchestras influenced by the styles of New Orleans. In the late 1960s, Jaime Delgado Aparicio, a pianist, arranger, and musical director trained at Berklee College in Boston, returned to Peru and became a jazz advocate. He was the main disseminator of modern jazz until his death in the early 1980s. He recorded three jazz LPs and performed and conducted widely in public concerts in Lima. Despite his advocacy, however, jazz audiences in Lima remained limited to a narrow circle, drawn mainly from the middle and upper classes. In the early 2000s, live jazz performances in Lima are scarce, though recorded performances are broadcast on radio regularly alongside Brazilian popular music, which has been present in the Peruvian media since the 1960s.

In the 1960s, rock and roll became popular among the younger generations in urban centers thanks to the massive influence of radio, the LP-recording industry, and national television. In that decade, local singers and groups sang rock in Spanish (*rock en español*), gaining for the genre a sudden, though short-lived, fame. In 1985, rock and roll in Spanish reemerged as Micky Gonzales, a performer and composer, sold thousands of copies of his first rock album and suggested the same path to subsequent rockers. In the 1990s, rock in Spanish, with lyrics based on nationally significant themes, regained popularity among young people of different social sectors. Other bands have been equally open to influences of pop, reggae, rap, and worldbeat, but the most consequential musical influence is Argentine *rock en español*, whose popularity in Peru preceded the development of Peruvian rock in the 1980s. Unlike Argentine rock bands, however, Peruvian bands have had only a limited international distribution. The most commercially successful band in writing lyrics portraying national reality with a satiric touch is "No Sé Quien y No Sé Cuantos" (I Don't Know Who and I Don't Know How Many), the best-selling Peruvian rock band of all time. Most Peruvian bands have begun producing CDs, cassettes, and videos, all of which the national media broadcast intensively.

Until the 1970s, commercial records were produced by major Peruvian record companies, including FTA, IEMPSA, Mag, Sono Radio, and Virrey. Only the first two survive and are now the biggest record producers in Peru. Both maintain an Andean music division, one of their most important production departments. It was not until the 1970s that small and independent record companies in open competition with IEMPSA and Virrey began to record nonprofessional peasant performers. Consequently, *huayno* songs were less emphasized by these companies, and widely various songs and dance genres (including ritual music) began to be recorded on commercial discs. These recordings are not distributed on a national scale but prevail in local and regional markets (Romero 1992:198).

In the early 1970s, the movement known as *nueva canción latinoamericana* "new Latin American song" began to influence politically conscious university students. As a result, many performing groups emerged. The main influences that had achieved immense popularity among university students were groups performing *nueva canción chilena* "new Chilean song" and *nueva trova* "new song," a Cuban genre. In the early 1980s, the movement lost its vitality in Peru, and political-oriented Peruvian musical groups dissolved. Among them were ensembles formed within the Taller de la Canción Popular (Popular-Song Workshop), which the composer Celso Garrido Lecca had established at the National Conservatory of Music in the 1970s.

The *nueva canción* movement in Peru precipitated the rise of numerous neofolkloric groups that later achieved worldwide popularity. Mainly directed to the foreign-tourist market, these groups, which usually combine the *siku*, the *quena*, the *charango*, the guitar, and the Argentine *bombo*, play Andean musical genres, usually in faster tempos and altered in their rhythmic, harmonic, and instrumental aspects, furthering their commercial aims. In the 1990s, it is common to find these groups playing in *peñas folklóricas* (coffeehouses and/or restaurants featuring neofolkloric music) or as street musicians in Europe and the United States. Record production and sales of these groups in Peru is minimal, despite their national ubiquity.

In the 1950s, Cuban and Caribbean popular genres such as the *son*, the *rumba*, and the *bolero* began to gain wide acceptance in Peru, as did (later) the most commercial versions such as the *cha-cha-chá* and the *mambo*. The regular visits of renowned Cuban and Caribbean performers and bandleaders consolidated the popularity of these genres throughout the years. Today, *salsa* music is one of the most popular genres throughout Peru. Live performances of *salsa* are frequent in *salsódromos* (nightclubs for dancing to salsa) around the country, and numerous AM and FM radio stations exclusively broadcast *salsa* music at all hours. Most local *salsa* activity consists of the performance of covers of hits from New York and Puerto Rico. Peruvian composers and performers of *salsa* have not yet achieved international distribution, with the exception of the singer-composer Antonio Cartagena.

Latin pop dominates Peruvian markets and record sales. In the mass media, it is the most disseminated genre, closely followed by Top 40 international hits. Both are highly popularized by the media, and both styles fill the stacks at local record stores. A survey of the musical preferences of *limeños* (people of Lima) in the early 1990s revealed that more than 57 percent of *limeños* who listen to radio prefer Latin pop and *salsa*, 19 percent prefer Andean and creole music, and 17 percent prefer rock and roll. Jazz and classical music were the least-represented categories with 3 percent total (Bolaños 1995:111). The remaining 4 percent is accounted for by other categories.

Today, the Peruvian recording industry is in a transitional stage. Recordings in the LP format ceased to be produced in the late 1980s, and since then the cassette industry has controlled the market. Though the bigger companies are slowly switching to the CD format, they are unable to compete with small and informal companies that market inexpensive cassettes. Illegal copying and cassette piracy are common throughout the country, as are ambulatory retailers who frequent the busiest streets and local markets.

Radio is a powerful medium in contemporary Peru. It reaches even distant rural communities. In 1992, there were 331 AM and 180 FM radio stations in the country. Of these, only forty-seven AM and thirty-nine FM stations were located in Lima. In the 1980s, television networks experienced a notable growth. Today, Peru has six private television stations and one state-supported channel, most with national coverage. Cable television, available only in the capital, airs TV programming from Europe, the United States, and other Latin American countries. Parabolic antennas, which pick up satellite waves, are widely dispersed in the rest of the country, providing television to rural communities that cannot receive signals from national television stations.

FURTHER STUDY

An excellent survey of traditional musical instruments in Peru is Jiménez Borja's seminal book on the subject (1951). A more recent and exhaustive organological inventory for all three geographical regions of Peru can be found in the *Mapa de los Intrumentos Musicales de Uso Popular en el Perú* (Instituto Nacional de Cultura 1978).

The first known wax-cylinder recordings made in Peru were made by the French husband and wife team, Raoul and Marguerite d'Harcourt, in the 1920s. The d'Harcourts recorded extensively throughout the Andean areas of Ecuador, Peru, and Bolivia, and used these recordings as the basis for a book (1990 [1925]). The current location of these recordings is unknown, and it is widely assumed that they are lost. Around 1900, Heinrich Brünning recorded wax cylinders in the north coast of Peru, documenting musical renditions and oral expressions in the Mochica language, now largely extinct. The location of Brünning's materials is unknown.

The first recordings of Andean Peruvian music known to be extant are those made in the 1940s by the South American ethnomusicologists Isabel Aretz and Luís Felipe Ramón y Rivera, who recorded extensively on reel-to-reel tape in the southern Andes of Peru. Their collection is deposited in the National Institute of Musicology in Buenos Aires, Argentina, and in the Fundación Interamericana de Etnomusicología y Folklore in Caracas, Venezuela. More recent recordings of Peruvian traditional music are deposited in the Library of Congress and the Archives of Traditional Music of Indiana University, Bloomington. The largest collection of unpublished audiovisual materials is housed in Lima, in the Archives of Andean Traditional Music of the Catholic University of Peru.

REFERENCES

Archivo de Música Tradicional Andina. 1995. *Catálogo del Archivo de Música Tradicional Andina.* Lima: Pontífica Universidad Católica del Peru, Instituto Riva Agüero.

Arguedas, José María. 1975. *Formación de una Cultura Nacional Indoamericana.* México: Siglo XXI.

———. 1985. *Indios, Mestizos y Señores.* Lima: Horizonte.

———. 1989 [1938]. *Canto Kechua.* Lima: Horizonte.

Bellenger, Xavier. 1981. "Les Instruments de Musique dans les Pays Andins: Deuxième Partie." *Bulletin de L'Institut d'Études Andines* 10(1–2):23–50.

Basadre, Jorge. 1964. "Notas sobre la Música en el Perú." In *Historia de la República del Perú*, ed. Jorge Basadre, 10:4603–4619. Lima: Editorial Universitaria.

Bolaños, César. 1985. "La Música en el Antiguo Perú." In *La Música en el Perú*, 1–64. Lima: Patronato Popular y Porvenir Pro Música Clásica.

———. 1988. *Las Antaras Nasca.* Lima: Instituto Andino de Estudios Arqueológicos.

———. 1995. *La Música Nacional en los Medios de Comunicación Electrónicos de Lima Metropolitana.* Cuadernos CICOSUL. Lima: Universidad de Lima, Facultad de Ciencias de la Comunicación.

Bradby, Barbara. 1987. "Symmetry around a Centre: Music of an Andean Community." *Popular Music* 6(2):197–218.

Canepa-Koch, Gisela. 1991. *Wylancha.* 28 mins. Lima: Pontificia Universidad Católica del Peru, Archivo de Música Tradicional Andina. Video, VHS-NTSC.

———. 1993. "Los chu'nchu y las palla de Cajamarca en el ciclo de la representación de la muerte del Inca." In *Música, Danzas y Máscaras en los Andes*, ed. Raúl R. Romero, 139–178. Lima: Pontífica Universidad Católica del Perú.

———. 1994. "Danzas, Identidad y Modernidad en los Andes: Las Danzas en la Fiesta de la Virgen del Carmen en Paucartambo." Anthropológica 11:255–282.

Canepa-Koch, Gisela, and Raúl R. Romero. 1988. "Música Tradicional de Cajamarca." Lima: Pontífica Universidad Católica del Perú, Instituto Riva-Agüero. Notes to LP disk.

Carpio Muñoz, Juan. 1976. *El Yaraví Arequipeño.* Arequipa: La Colmena.

Casas Roque, Leonidas. 1993. "Fiestas, Danzas y Música de la Costa de Lambayeque." In *Música, Danzas y Máscaras en los Andes*, ed. Raúl R. Romero, 299–337. Lima: Pontífica Universidad Católica del Perú.

Cavero, Jesús A. 1985."El Qarawi y su Función Social." *Allpanchis* 25:233–270.

Cieza de León, Pedro. 1967 [1553]. *El Señorío de los Incas*. Lima: Instituto de Estudios Peruanos.

Cobo, Bernabé. 1956 [1653]. *Historia del Nuevo Mundo*. Vol. 2. Madrid: Ediciones Atlas.

Cohen, John. 1984. "Mountain Music of Peru." New York: Cinema Guild. Film, video.

Cuentas Ormachea, Enrique. 1982. "La Danza Choquela y su Contenido Mágico Religioso." *Boletín de Lima* 4(19):54–70.

de la Cadena, Marisol. 1995. "Women Are More Indian: Ethnicity and Gender in a Community near Cuzco." In *Ethnicity, Markets, and Migration in the Andes: At the Crossroads of History and Anthropology*, eds. Brooke Larson and Olivia Harris, 329–348. Durham, N.C.: Duke University Press.

den Otter, Elisabeth. 1985. *Music and Dance of Indians and Mestizos in an Andean Valley of Peru*. Delft: Eburon.

Estenssoro, Juán Carlos. 1988. "Música y Comportamiento Festivo de la Población Negra en Lima Colonial." *Cuadernos Hispanoamericanos* 451–452:161–166.

Garcilaso de la Vega, El Inca. 1959 [1603]. *Comentarios Reales de los Incas*. Vol. 1. Lima: Universidad Nacional de San Marcos.

Guamán Poma de Ayala, Felipe. 1956 [?1567–1615?]. *La Nueva Crónica y Buén Gobierno*. Lima: Ministerio de Educación.

Haeberli, Joerg. 1979. "Twelve Nasca Panpipes." *Ethnomusicology* 23(1):57–74.

d'Harcourt, Raoul, and Marguerite d'Harcourt. 1990 [1925]. *La Musique des Incas et ses Survivances.* Paris: Paul Geuthner. Reprinted in Spanish, 1990, as *La música de los Incas y sus supervivencias*. Translated by Roberto Miro Quesada. Lima: Occidental Petroleum Corporation of Peru, Luis Alberto Sánchez, and Ismael Pinto.

Hurtado Suárez, Wilfredo. 1995. *Chicha Peruana: Música de los Nuevos Migrantes*. Lima: Eco-Grupo de Investigaciones Económicas.

Instituto Nacional de Cultura. 1978. *Mapa de los Instrumentos Musicales de Uso Popular en el Perú*. Lima: Instituto Nacional de Cultura.

Jiménez Borja, Arturo. 1951. "Instrumentos musicales Peruanos." *Revista del Museo Nacional* 19–20:37–190.

Llorens, José Antonio. 1991. "Andean Voices on Lima Airwaves: Highland Migrants and Radio Broadcasting in Peru." *Studies in Latin American Popular Culture* 10:177–189.

Matos Mar, José, and Jorge A. Carbajal. 1974. *Erasmo: Yanacón del Valle de Chancay*. Lima: Instituto de Estudios Peruanos.

Mendoza-Walker, Zoila. 1994. "Contesting Identities through Dance: Mestizo Performance in the Southern Andes of Peru." *Repercussions* 3(2):50–80.

Merino de Zela, Mildred. 1977. "Folklore Coreográfico e Historia." *Folklore Americano* 24:67–94.

Montoya, Rodrigo. 1987. *La Cultura Quechua Hoy*. Lima: Mosca Azul.

Núñez Rebaza, Lucy. 1990. *Los Dansaq*. Lima: Instituto Nacional de Cultura, Museo Nacional de la Cultura Peruana.

Núñez Rebaza, Lucy, and José A. Llorens. 1981. "La música tradicional andina en Lima metropolitana." *América Indígena* 41(1):53–74.

Okada, Yuki. 1995. *Central and South America. The JVC Smithsonian Folkways Video Anthology of Music and Dance of the Americas*, 6. Montpelier, Vt.: Multicultural Media VTMV-230. Video.

Olsen, Dale A. 1980a. "Folk Music of South America–A Musical Mosaic." In *Musics of Many Cultures: An Introduction*, ed. Elizabeth May, 386–425. Berkeley: University of California Press.

———. 1980b. "Symbol and Function in South American Indian Music." In *Musics of Many Cultures: An Introduction*, ed. Elizabeth May, 363–385. Berkeley: University of California Press.

———. 1986–87. "The Peruvian Folk Harp Tradition: Determinants of Style." *Folk Harp Journal* 53:48–54, 54:41–48, 55:55–59, 56:57–60, 57:38–42, 58:47–48, 59:60–62.

———. 2002. *Music of El Dorado: The Ethnomusicology of Ancient South American Cultures*. Gainesville: The University Press of Florida.

Pagaza Galdo, Consuelo. 1961. "El Yaraví." *Folklore Americano* 8–9:75–141.

Pinilla, Enrique. 1980. "Informe sobre la Música en el Perú." In *Historia del Perú*, vol. 9, ed. Juan Mejia Baca, 363–677. Lima: Juan Mejia Baca.

Pinto, Arturo. 1987. "Afinaciones de la Guitarra en Ayacucho." *Boletín de Lima* 9(49):83–87.

Poole, Deborah A. 1990. "Accommodation and Resistance in Andean Ritual Dance." *The Drama Review* 34(2):98–126.

———. 1991. "Rituals of Movements, Rites of Transformation: Pilgrimage and Dance in the Highlands of Cuzco, Peru." In *Pilgrimage in Latin America*, eds. Ross Crumrine and Alan Morinis, 307–338. New York: Greenwood Press.

Quezada Macchiavello, José. 1985. "La Música en el Virreinato." In *La Música en el Perú*, 65–102. Lima: Patronato Popular y Porvenir Pro Música Clásica.

Ráez Retamozo, Manuel. 1993. "Los ciclos ceremoniales y la percepción del tiempo festivo en al valle del Colca." In *Música, Danzas y Máscaras en los Andes*, ed. Raúl R. Romero, 253–298. Lima: Pontífica Universidad Católica del Perú.

Roel Pineda, Josafát. 1959. "El Wayno del Cusco." *Folklore Americano* 6–7:129–245.

Romero, Raúl R. 1985. "La Música Tradicional y Popular." In *La Música en el Perú*, 215–283. Lima: Patronato Popular y Porvenir Pro Música Clásica.

———. 1989. "Música Urbana en un Contexto Rural: Tradición y Modernidad en Paccha, Junín." *Anthropológica* 7(7):121–133.

———. 1990. "Musical Change and Cultural Resistance in the Central Andes of Peru." *Latin American Music Review* 11(1):1–35.

———. 1992. "Preservation, the Mass Media and Dissemination of Traditional Music." In *World Music, Musics of the World: Aspects of Documentation, Mass Media and Acculturation*, ed. Max Peter Baumann, 191–210. Wilhelmshaven: Florian Noetzel.

———, ed. 1993. *Música, Danzas y Máscaras en el Perú*. Lima: Pontífica Universidad Católica del Perú.

———. 1994. "Black Music and Identity in Peru: Reconstruction and Revival of Afro-Peruvian Musical Traditions." In *Music and Black Ethnicity: The Caribbean and South America*, ed. Gerard H. Béhague, 307–330. Miami: North-South Center, University of Miami.

Santa Cruz, César. 1977. *El Waltz y el Vals Criollo*. Lima: Instituto Nacional de Cultura.

Sas, Andres. 1936. "Ensayo Sobre la Música Nazca." *Boletín Latinoamericano de Música* 4:221–233.

Stevenson, Robert M. 1960. *The Music of Peru*. Washington, D.C.: Organization of American States.

———. 1968. *Music in Aztec and Inca Territory*. Berkeley: University of California Press.

Stein, Stephen. 1982. "El vals criollo y los valores de la clase trabajadora en la Lima de comienzos del siglo XX." *Socialismo y Participación* 17:43–50.

Turino, Thomas. 1983. "The Charango and the Sirena: Music, Magic, and the Power of Love." *Latin American Music Review* 4(1):81–119.

———. 1984. "The Urban-Mestizo Charango Tradition in Southern Peru: A Statement of Shifting Identity." *Ethnomusicology* 28(2):253–270.

———. 1990. "Somos el Perú: 'Cumbia Andina' and the Children of Andean Migrants in Lima." *Studies in Latin American Popular Culture* 9:15–37.

———. 1993. *Moving Away from Silence: Music of the Peruvian Altiplano and the Experience of Urban Migration*. Chicago: University of Chicago Press.

Valcarcel, Luís E. 1951. "Introducción." In *Fiestas y Danzas en el Cuzco y en los Andes*, ed. Pierre Verger. Buenos Aires: Editorial Sudamericana.

Valencia Chacón, Américo. 1983. *El Siku Bipolar Altiplánico*. Lima: Artex Editores.

———. 1989. *The Altiplano Bipolar Siku: Study and Projection of the Peruvian Panpipe Orchestra*. Lima: Artex Editores.

Vega, Carlos. 1932. "Escalas con Semitonos en la Música de los Antiguos Peruanos." *Actas y Trabajos Científicos del XXV Congreso Internacional de Americanistas* (La Plata) 1:349–381.

Villareal Vara, Felix. 1958. "Las Afinaciones de la Guitarra en Huánuco, Peru." *Revista Musical Chilena* 12(62):33–36.

Q'eros

John Cohen and Holly Wissler

Musical Instruments and their Contexts
Other Musical Contexts and Genres
Social Structure, Ideology, and Aesthetics
Recent Musical Changes
Further Study

The Q'eros are a Quechua-speaking people living high in the Andes Mountains, east of Cusco, Peru. Although it is tempting to see the Q'eros as an Inca survival, their unique musical practices probably reflect an even earlier Andean diversity with an Inca overlay.

All past orthographies refer to this group as "Q'ero," but today it is common for the people to call themselves Q'eros. Q'eros also refers to the entire cultural region that comprises eight Q'eros communities, located approximately 100 miles southeast of the ancient Incan capital of Cusco, in the province of Paucartambo. This region includes the communities of Kiku, Hapu, Totorani, Marcachea, Pucara, K'allacancha, Kachupata, and (Hatun) Q'eros. These communities all have their own corresponding annexes, or hamlets, consisting of small isolated clusters of houses. In response to current political developments in Peru, five of these communities recently banded together as a statement of solidarity to form la Nación Q'eros, "the Q'eros Nation."

In terms of population, Hatun Q'eros is the largest of these communities, consisting of approximately 24 percent of all Q'eros. It is also the most remote of all Q'eros cultural communities, and therefore, the most traditional and least acculturated. For these reasons, this article focuses on Hatun Q'eros. It presents the names and language in use by the Q'eros people today, though these may differ from previous orthographies and descriptions.

Q'eros ceremonial music is heard throughout seasonal cycles, and the Q'eros exploit every local ecological zone from the mountaintops to the jungle. Centered on flocks of llamas and alpacas, music is an integral part of Q'eros rituals. The Q'eros share many social, economic, and cultural ties with their Andean neighbors, but they have been sufficiently isolated to have preserved their own cultural and musical traits in coexistence with contemporary elements.

Living at an elevation of approximately 14,200 feet (4,300 meters), the Q'eros are essentially herders near their homes. They raise potatoes in the middle ecological zone (11,000–14,000 feet; 3350–4200 meters), and corn, melons, and peppers in the high jungle farther down (6000–7500 feet; 1800–2300 meters). Each family has temporary wood shelters in the jungle, large stone houses in the ceremonial center at an elevation of 11,200 feet (3,400 meters), and small stone houses located in isolated clusters in the high valleys. The total population is about one hundred and twenty families (roughly seven hundred people) distributed in six hamlets. This is a major increase when compared to a forty-family count in 1922 and eighty-two families in 1970.

The Q'eros share certain musical traditions with the entire region of Cusco, but they have distinctly emblematic songs and music, heard only in their highland home. Their major festivals coincide with Spanish calendrical festivals, but with little or no European or colonial elements. Each of their festivals has songs and instruments specifically associated with it, but the emblematic and uniquely recognizable Q'eros style consists of descending three-note melodies sung and played on the indigenous flute (*pinkuyllu*). Their songs serve many functions, including Carnaval celebration, animal veneration, and Catholic-influenced festivals. The music associated with each ritual varies from endogenous to exogenous musical styles. For this reason, their music cannot be characterized by a single style, musical scale, or musical function. This diversity within the music of a single community is inherent in Andean cultural life.

MUSICAL INSTRUMENTS AND THEIR CONTEXTS

Q'eros autochthonous music is not influenced by European elements: it uses neither instruments introduced by the Spanish, nor any of the stringed instruments (like the *charango* and the *bandurria*) or the brass instruments that evolved in the Andes in the colonial era. Although the Q'eros have had transistor radios since 1980 and can hear Andean radio programs of *huayno* (also *wayno*, a popular Andean dance genre) music broadcast from Cusco, they still use only musical instruments extant at the time of the Inkas: end-blown and side-blown flutes, panpipes, conch trumpets, and drums. Two Q'eros musical styles consist of distinct musical instruments found only in Q'eros territory, the Q'eros-style panpipes and *pinkuyllu*, an end-blown flute.

Panpipes

The Q'eros have single-unit raft panpipes that are two bound rows of seven reed tubes each. One row is never played, yet holding two sets is representative of *yanantin*, or the Andean system of duality. The pipes have three names for the same instrument: *qanchis sipas* "seven young unmarried women," *qori phukuna* "golden blow-pipe," and *choqewanka* "golden song of echo." The women sing pentatonic songs to sheep, cows and alpacas, as well as about the *Apu* (mountain deities) who protect these animals, while the men play the pipes. The sheep and cows are venerated in a ritual known as Sinalay (from the Spanish *señalar*, or marking of the animals). This festival is also called Santos since the ritual is performed in October before the Catholic festivity of Todos Los Santos on November 1. [Listen to "China Uha Taki" or "Female Sheep Song"] The alpacas are venerated soon after, before the end of the year. These rituals are performed much less today than a few decades ago. In one song the women sing the following (English translation by Holly Wissler): DISC ❷ TRACK 18

> Because you eat, we eat.
> Because you drink, we drink.
> Because you are, we are.

Another says the following when they sing to the cows:

> Your *choqewanka* is guiding you.

This statement has layers of meaning, from the most evident being "Your panpipes (the cow's) are guiding you." However the Q'eros believe that all panpipes originally came from the cow protector mountain deity who also has his own set of panpipes and is herding all cows by way of humans. Therefore the panpipes are the connector between the protector spirits, the humans who are herding, and the cows.

In the department of Cusco, panpipes are rare, but they are common in the *altiplano* (high plateau) around Lake Titicaca. The presence of these panpipes (and the Q'eros' use of four-stake looms) therefore suggests an earlier cultural connection to the Titicaca basin.

Flutes

The *pinkuyllu*, an end-blown notched flute, produces the music most uniquely associated with Q'eros. It is played in conjunction with women's singing in two fertility rituals: Aqhata Ukyachichis (for the male llamas) and Phallchay (for alpacas and female llamas). It is also played to accompany the body of Carnaval songs (*Pukllay taki*) that are composed of subject matter in the Q'eros world, such as "Phallcha," after a gentian that grows at an elevation of 14,000 feet (4,500 meters) and blooms in February and March; "Wallata," after the name for wild Andean geese that fly in pairs over the mountains in Q'eros territory; "Sirena," after a mythical mermaid who lives in waterfalls; and "Thurpa," the name for a high-altitude flower used for healing coughs and washing the women's hair. A translation of some Q'eros words in "Thurpa" includes "*Panti thurpa*, why have you come to these desolate ravines?" The text of "Wallata" includes these words in translation:

> *Wallata*, black and white, with eyes of pearls;
> *Wallata*, black and white, with scalloped wings:
> The running waters which you drink in the highlands.

The Q'eros sing their ever-changing present world and landscape, and as this changes so do the contents of their songs. Because of this there are also older *Pukllay taki* that are no longer sung and are slowly dying with the older generation of Q'eros who remember them. Examples of these songs are "Pariwa," about an Andean flamingo that used to be in the Q'eros region and is no longer, and "Sortija" (Carnival rings), sung during the time when *hacendados* owned the Q'eros land (fifty years ago and before) and Q'eros were forced to take their llama trains to Bolivia to exchange agricultural goods for metal from the mines (they made their Carnaval rings or *sortija* from this Bolivian metal).

Pinkuyllu are notched flutes made from cane or bamboo obtained in the lower elevations of the cloud forest where the Q'eros grow corn. They randomly range from 15 to 71 centimeters long, depending completely on the flute maker's choice, and always have four rectangular finger holes and no thumb hole. From the bottom or distal end of the tube, the flutist measures with two or three widths of his fingers, and there he makes his first finger hole, followed by three others that he evenly spaces toward the proximal end of the instrument. This creates a standard scale for each flute that can produce the desired three notes comprising the Q'eros' *pinkuyllu* melody. Like their three-note songs and weaving patterns, their specific *pinkuyllu* and its melody are unique to them.

The outline of the *pinkuyllu* rhythm and melody follows that of the sung melody. Although each plays a three-note melody, they are not the same three notes. The flute part differs from the vocal part in that it shares the central two notes of the melody, but then the woman's voice goes lower while the *pinkuyllu* goes higher. In this sense, the two parts together make a melody consisting of four notes. This unprecedented combination of flute and voice, male and female, is consistent with the Andean sense of "*yanantin*" (duality), and introduces a dimension of gender into the musical structure.

Always in connection with animals, shepherds play the *pinkuyllu* in pastures while herding. Usually, several such flutes can be heard playing independently of each other across the high pastures (*puna*). The music directs and comforts the animals by locating their shepherd in space. This custom of playing *pinkuyllu* while herding is now giving way to portable radios.

A person plays the *pinkuyllu* by uncovering the four holes in sets of one, two, and sometimes three fingers rather than one finger for each tone. The timbre is breathy, composed of many overtones. Sometimes only the outline of the melody is heard with segments conceived under the breath without being audibly played (the musician plays mentally, silently). In addition, coloration is sometimes given to the music when the flutist overblows on the notch, producing short and high overtones or octaves. A technique frequently used in transitions from one note to another is to rapidly touch down two fingers, covering and uncovering two holes, producing a sound akin to a trill. Yet it is important to note that *pinkuyllus* are neither tuned to each other nor played together in unison. People, however, sometimes sing in unison, but more often they do not, depending on the context. Three men playing in the same room will play the same tune together, and three women will sing the same song, though not at the same pitches, and not with shared starting or stopping points. In this way the music is both communal and individual at the same time.

Other musical instruments

The Q'eros also use musical instruments found in other Andean communities. Of these instruments, the *pututu* is a conch trumpet, played by communal authorities as a sign of their position. The conch produces a blast of sound to announce the beginning of an event or a ceremony. The *pututu* is an old instrument, dating back to Inca and pre-Inca times. Conch shells come from the sea, hundreds of kilometers away, and originally were traded for and carried to the mountaintops.

A side-blown six-note flute, *pitu*, is used principally for melodies of the *ch'unchu*, a dance with pre-Hispanic roots that represents Amazonian jungle culture. This music is played during the festival of Qoyllur Rit'i, southeast Peru's largest pilgrimage festival, a one-day's walk from Q'eros where hundreds of troupes worship a combination of Catholic and Andean elements through colorful costumed-dance and song. The theme of the Qoyllur Rit'i pilgrimage is the *ch'unchu* melody, a pentatonic tune which sometimes ends with a sequence of notes unrelated to the tonal center of the melody. Dancers representing the *ch'unchu* dress in brightly colored feather headdresses, carrying long pieces of jungle wood (from a bow), festooned with short feathers. The *ch'unchu* as a visual motif is also seen in Q'eros' weaving. The Q'eros will continue the *ch'unchu* music and dance just after Qoyllur Rit'i during the Corpus Christi festival in Hatun Q'eros. In addition, the *pitus* and drums are used to play *huaynos* at Easter, also held in Hatun Q'eros.

OTHER MUSICAL CONTEXTS AND GENRES

The Q'eros celebrate their annual festivals in their hamlets or at a lower elevation at the ceremonial center, Hatun Q'eros, where the entire community gathers several times a year for major feasts. In addition, they make a pilgrimage to Qoyllur Rit'i during Corpus Christi. In sequence, the major festivals are Chayampuy, Phallchay, Carnaval (with Tinkuy), Pascuas (Easter), Corpus Christi, Aqhata Ukyachichis (Santiago), and Sinalay (Santos).

The most unusual and emblematic Q'eros festivals are the ones for animal veneration: Phallchay, Aqhata Ukyachichis, and Sinalay. Phallchay focuses on alpacas and llamas, Aqhata Uyachichis is for the male llamas that successfully carried the corn harvest from the high jungle to the homes above, and Sinalay is for the cows and sheep. Each animal type has its own song and there are no specialized musicians; rather all women sing the songs and all men play the *pinkuyllu* and sing.

At Phallchay (occurring on the Monday before Ash Wednesday, based on the Christian calendar), individual Q'eros families hold rituals in their houses. Starting on Monday morning, the woman of the house sings, and the man plays *pinkuyllu*. They pour corn beer (*chicha*) onto grass from the pasture, and onto little statues of the animals. Then several families join together outside and throw flowers (*phallcha*) over their gathered herd of llamas and alpacas while singing and playing *pinkuyllu*. Five or more women may sing the song for the animals at the same time, sometimes interspersing ritual phrases (usually song refrains) with improvised complaints about their daily lives. Each tells her own story in song, often expressing deep grief. At times, the musical texture consists of different people singing personalized songs simultaneously. Only occasionally do they meet on ritual phrases or on final notes.

The following translation from one woman's singing of a floral song is adapted from Cohen and is the text the woman sang in 1984, translated at that time; the performance can be seen in Cohen's 1984 film *Mountain Music of Peru*:

Scatter the flower, Huaman [a mountain spirit].
What suffering you leave me, my brother [refers to alpaca],
Huaman, my brother sun [a mountain spirit].

Don't leave me, mother [refers to the lineage of alpacas].
The red flower that I gather,
The earth hill that I climb [site of the ritual],
You will make blossom.
Come here, my mother [lineage of alpacas],
Where I sleep with my lover.
Leave those ancient things [old, male, infertile alpacas]:
Black alpaca with red feet,
You eat by the side of another,
Or with the alpacas of Santo Domingo [a nearby mountain spirit].
You drank to the earth.
You gave me flowers, Huaman.
Suffering takes away the happiness of my valley.
Alpaca who leads the way,
Flower that I have to give,
Wouldn't you nurture me?
Together you are sleeping.
Don't look at me, mother [for you are sacred].
Scatter the panti [flower], Huaman.

Recently (2006) it has been revealed that this song was expressing the woman's feelings about her father's death. In the new translation of a portion of this 1984 recording, which can be heard on Smithsonian Folkways 1991 CD, *Mountain Music of Peru*, track 38, the references to *phallcha* flowers, female alpacas and llamas, dead people drinking, red hail, colored vicuñas, and "please eat me quickly," as well as the places her father lived in his lifetime, reflect the complexity of Q'eros symbolism. [Listen to "Pantilla T'ika" or "My sacred *phallcha* flower"]

DISC ❷ TRACK 19

My sacred *phallcha* flower
Come here my mother, let's celebrate in the corral
[refers to the female llamas/alpacas]

Until my death arrives
My sacred *phallcha* flower
He left me with all the animals [referring to her father]

I am without nothing
My sacred *phallcha* flower
How am I not going to drink?

Do, perhaps, the dead people still drink?
My sacred *phallcha* flower
He who dies, who goes, no longer drinks

Like this why don't we get drunk
My sacred *phallcha* flower
For the years to come

The people who die, they go
My sacred *phallcha* flower
I am the young woman from *Qowasani* [her father's birthplace]

My *yana orqo*, of red hail [another place her father lived]
My sacred *phallcha* flower
Please eat me quickly

Poncho with the color of Santo Domingo vicuña
My sacred *phallcha* flower
White waterfalls of the *Kusi Way'qo* ["Joyful Canyon"]

I would like to be only in my home
My sacred *phallcha* flower
I would be with my family

Why did you raise me?
My sacred *phallcha* flower
You should not have raised me

Are you "sleeping" happily? [she is asking if her father is "resting in peace."]
My sacred *phallcha* flower
My beloved Apasa [her father's name]

The ritual is repeated late in the day, with the animals in their corrals.

The following day, Tuesday, many elements come together. For Carnaval, the entire community descends from the isolated mountain hamlets, gathering at the central village, Hatun Q'eros, which serves as the ceremonial center overlooking the jungle. Each Q'eros family has a large house here, used only for community rituals. The male authorities are greeted with exchanges of conch trumpets in the central plaza in front of the church, while other men play *pinkuyllu* and do a stomping dance. Groups (according to hamlets or families/friends) make their rounds to many houses, singing and playing the year's chosen Carnaval song all night long. Twenty people may be packed together inside, drinking, dancing, and singing heterophonically (overlapping the same melodic line) with conch trumpets blasting. Sometimes, late in the night, the individual qualities become less apparent as people find accord between them, reaching a degree of musical consensus. At this point, the sustained final note of a phrase provides a drone beneath the individual voices. Yet the "wide" heterophonic overlapping of voices and *pinkuyllu* creates a dense texture and the whole event takes on a choral sound.

On the principal day of Carnaval, Ash Wednesday, everyone gathers at the plaza. While the men dance, sing, and play *pinkuyllu*, the women sing separately or in unison in groups. In this way, many groups of women will sing the same song in overlapping "disregard" for each other. The women are arranged in a single line that arcs around the men, who dance, sing, and heterophonically play *pinkuyllu*. There is a rich, pulsating, and dense texture to the event. This kind of heterophony does not occur elsewhere in the Andes, but it resembles celebrations in the Amazon basin. The structure of this Q'eros music may therefore suggest a cultural connection between the Andes and the Amazon.

The prevalent song at Carnaval is chosen by the *carguyoq* (*cargo* holder, or main organizer of Carnaval for a particular year). The song is selected two weeks prior to Carnaval by the *carguyoq* and his *regidores* (officials and assistants elected from all six hamlets) during the ritual known as Chayampuy held in Hatun Q'eros. After officially receiving their authority, these chosen men stay up all night long in a type of song competition, where they sing Carnaval songs (*Pukllay taki*) for one another until one song "emerges" as that year's song. This song is only announced to the community on the Monday morning of Phallchay. In past times, before the Q'eros had their own town council and needed to ride on horseback one whole day to Paucartambo (district capital) to receive their authority, the *carguyoq* would compose a new song by "reading the landscape"; that song became the song of the year. Today there is an existing body of Pukllay *taki* from which one song is chosen, and no new songs are composed (the chosen songs for 2005 and 2006 were "Thurpa" and "Phallcha," respectively).

Similar celebrations with music are held at the hamlets in the high valleys. From late August into September, individual families thank the gods for the strength and fertility of their male llamas. In the *mullucancha* (sacred, chosen corral for this ceremony), they mark the male animals by putting tassels in their ears and forcing them to drink corn beer (*aqha*). This festival is known as Aqhata Ukyachichis ("Let's Water [the animals] with Corn Beer," referring to the act of sharing their nutritive corn beer with the llamas). Each family's ritual differs slightly from that of its neighbors. Though families celebrate on separate days, they all employ similar ritual items. A special cloth, *unkhuña*, is set on the ground as an altar on which ritual objects are placed. These are special ritual versions of items used in daily life: ropes, bells, and offerings of corn beer and coca leaves. The women sing and men play *pinkuyllu* in the *mullucancha* in amongst all male llamas, creating a dense and rich texture of overlapping sound and activity (like at Carnaval): singing, playing *pinkuyllu*, dancing with the lead llama's bells, "inviting" the llamas to drink corn beer then putting tassels on their ears, drinking, talking, laughing, crying, all simultaneously.

The ritual moves from the corral into the house. As it progresses through the night, the men increasingly mimic the animals, shaking llama bells and ropes, hitting each other with whips as if they themselves were llamas, and whistling as they do when they drive the animals along. Some men sing in a low, forced growl, in imitation of the llamas' humming. Often the women sing intensely, and some men play *pinkuyllu*.

The music goes on continuously, but individuals start and stop as they please, sometimes not completing a phrase. After the ritual items are put away, the celebration becomes an expression of human fertility as couples go off to bed. This musical style allows for expression of the individual while retaining a distinctive communal identity.

SOCIAL STRUCTURE, IDEOLOGY, AND AESTHETICS

Because Q'eros music functions as an integral part of ritual, considering music as a separate entity may be a mistaken notion. The Q'eros explain music this way: "It's always like this, we sing this song of the Inkas. We compose the song from all things. Every song comes on its appropriate date. If there is no song, there is no fiesta; and without the fiesta, there is no song."

Q'eros songs reflect a complex cosmology that moves freely between mountain spirits (*Awki* and *Apu*) and personal events from daily life. The texts speak of parallels between the lineage of animals and humans; they include metaphorical references to flowers as symbols of love and representatives of the gods. Wild birds and animals are seen as representatives of mountain spirits, whereas domesticated animals (llamas and alpacas) are associated with human counterparts. Songs that celebrate the fertility of the animals are mixtures of courtship, floral symbols, and giving thanks to the gods. The songs may contain calendrical and landscape references.

Though men and women know and sing the songs, women are the primary singers; only men play the accompanying *pinkuyllu* or panpipes. (Consistent with indigenous Andean tradition, Q'eros women do not play instruments.) At rituals for the fertility of the animals, gender differences in styles of singing are defined in terms of the animals: men imitate the sound of male alpacas, while women imitate the sound of female alpacas.

Often the flute serves as a prod to initiate women's participation, and the flutist will delineate a melody in anticipation of the singing. The women's singing is more intense than the flute. At communal gatherings, the maximal female vocal qualities find fullest expression. The women's singing becomes more emotional and intense rather than formal or dutiful, and often loss and grief are expressed spontaneously through song. Men's singing can become an expression of a constrained explosion, a forceful assertion of local conceptions of maleness, complete with growls and explosive yelps.

The general Q'eros musical aesthetic allows different pitches, texts, and rhythms to sound at the same time. Though the Q'eros sometimes sing in unison, their songs are structured to be sung individually. There is no sense of choral singing or harmony. A family, or extended group, may be singing and playing the same song at the same time, but each singer sets her or his own pace, pattern of breathing, and point of starting and stopping. Yet the melodies sung at communal occasions have a sustained note at the end of a phrase, permitting the other singers to catch up and share this prolonged duration, which serves as a drone. When the new verse starts, the heterophony begins anew.

RECENT MUSICAL CHANGES

In the midst of maintaining ancient musical traditions, the Q'eros are experimenting with new musics as well. They have danced *ch'unchu* at Qoyllur Rit'i for decades, but recently the younger generation decided to learn and implement the *qhapaq qolla* folkloric dance (representative of merchant traders/llama herders of the high plateau) in their pilgrimage to the sacred site. The songs of the *qhapaq qolla* are mostly *huaynos*, the most popular dance genre throughout the Peruvian Andes. The typical instrumentation accompanying this dance includes *quenas* (notched flutes), violin, harp, accordion, and manufactured drumset complete with pedal bass and cowbell. The Q'eros acquired an accordion (2003) and a drumset (2004) to accompany their *quenas* and simple hand-made drums, which brought a sense of pride when performing alongside the many other *qhapaq qolla* dance groups at Qoyllur Rit'i. Many of the younger generation have purchased their own string instruments, namely the 16-string *bandurria* and 10-string *requinto*. They teach themselves to play popular *huaynos* and *carnavales* by listening to the radio and cassette recordings on battery-operated tape players, and watching music videos on television in nearby

Ocongate or Cusco. After a typical ritual during the day, late at night the youth will play, dance, and sing to these instruments. One young Q'eros man said they wanted to learn songs of other Andean communities because they are all "*runa*" ("country people") and "*kuska sonqoyoq kayku*" ("we are of the same heart"). The Q'eros are aware of which music is uniquely their own and which is of the larger Andean community, to which they also belong and identify with. They have the ability to keep all of their various musics separate in function and performance, and the Q'eros' strong identity allows them to maintain musical tradition and experiment with musical modernization simultaneously.

FURTHER STUDY

The material presented here is based on John Cohen's visits to the Q'eros over a thirty-five-year period, when he attended most of their major festivals, and Holly Wissler's regular visits to Q'eros for doctoral dissertation research from 2003–2007. Cohen's recordings of Q'eros music (1991 [1964]) have provided ethnomusicologists with ways to construct a model for Inka-Andean tradition and to augment or refute d'Harcourt and d'Harcourt's pentatonic theories. Alan Lomax (1968) used a Q'eros example from this recording to characterize the Andes in his global musical map for cantometrics; Rodolfo Holzmann (1980, 1986) used this music to establish a tritonic basis for Inka music; Dale Olsen (1980) transcribed an excerpt to explain the use of tetratonic scales and to demonstrate the use of microtones; and Bruce Mannheim (1984) used a Q'eros example from the same source in his studies of subliminal verbal patterning in southern Quechua folk song. In Peru, Oscar Núñez del Prado has made recordings of Q'eros music (unissued). A published Peruvian mention of Q'eros music (Ochoa and Fries n.d.) derives from his writing or the sources above. Holly Wissler made numerous recordings of Q'eros music from 2005–2007. Peru's National Institute of Culture recently published the book *Q'ero: El Ultimo Ayllu Inca* (2005) with articles about Q'eros spanning from 1955 to the present, covering a wide range of subjects such as geography, social organization, ideology, mythology, weavings, and music. Holly Wissler's dissertation (2008) provides new insights into Q'eros traditional music, its functions, and changes.

REFERENCES

Cohen, John. 1957. "An Investigation of Contemporary Weaving of the Peruvian Indians." M.F.A. thesis, Yale University.
———. 1979. *Q'eros, the Shape of Survival.* New York: Cinema Guild. Film, video.
———. 1980. *Peruvian Weaving, A Continuous Warp.* New York: Cinema Guild. Film, video.
———. 1984. *Mountain Music of Peru.* New York: Cinema Guild. Film, video.
———. 1988. *Your Struggle Is Your Glory.* Music from films by John Cohen. Arhoolie Records.
———. 1990. *Carnival in Qeros.* Berkeley: University of California Extension Media Center. Film, video.
———. 1991 [1964]. *Mountain Music of Peru.* Smithsonian/Folkways CD SF 40020. 2 compact discs, re-issued with additional material.
d'Harcourt, Raoul, and Marguerite d'Harcourt. 1990 [1925]. *La musique des Incas et ses survivances.* Paris: Librairie Orientaliste Paul Geuthner.

Holzmann, Rodolfo. 1980. "Cuatro Ejemplos de Música Q'eros (Cuzco, Perú)." *Latin American Music Review* 1(1):74–91.

———. 1986. *Q'eros, pueblo y música*. Lima: Patronata Popular y Porvenir, Pro Música Clásica.

Lomax, Alan. 1968. *Folk Song Style and Culture*. Washington, D.C.: American Association for the Advancement of Science. Publication 88.

Mannheim, Bruce. 1984. "Subliminal Verbal Patterning in a Southern Quechua Folksong." In *Symposium of Latin American Indian Literatures.*

Okada, Yuki. 1995. *Central and South America. The JVC/Smithsonian Folkways Video Anthology of Music and Dance of the Americas,* 6. Montpelier, Vt.: Multicultural Media. VTMV-230. Video.

Olsen, Dale A. 1980. "Symbol and Function in South American Indian Music." In *Musics of Many Cultures: An Introduction*, ed. Elizabeth May, 363–385. Berkeley, Los Angeles: University of California Press.

Ochoa, Jorge Flores, and Ana María Fries. n.d. *Puna, Qeshwa, Yunga—El Hombre y su Medio en Q'eros*. Lima: Banco Central de Reserva.

Wissler, Holly. 2005. "Tradición y Modernización en la Música de las dos Principales Festividades Anuales de Q'eros: Qoyllurit'i (con Corpus Christi) y Carnaval." In *Q'ero: El Ultimo Ayllu Inca*, Second Edition, eds. Jorge Flores Ochoa and Juan Nuñez del Prado, 375-413. Lima, Peru: Nacional Institute of Culture,

———. 2008. "Musical Tradition and Change in the Quechua Community of Q'eros, Perú." Ph.D. dissertation, Florida State University.

Yábar Palacios, Luis. 1922. "El Ayllu de Q'eros." *Revista Universitario*, No. 38: 3–26. Universidad Nacional del Cusco.

Afro-Peruvian Traditions

William David Tompkins

Musical Instruments
Africa/Spanish Musical Encounters
Traditional Afro-Peruvian Traditions
Creole Musical Traditions
Twentieth-Century Urban Popular Musical Traditions
Further Study

The African presence in coastal Peru began with the Spanish Encounter in the early 1500s and increased over the next three centuries. Afro-Peruvian musical development was a function of black exposure to the musical traditions of African, Spanish, and indigenous people. Though the link with Africa was reinforced with each new arrival of slaves, blacks in colonial Peru worked closely with the Spaniards, for receptivity to Spanish culture, language, and religion was the key to their social advancement. Interracial mixing and the eventual decline of the black population relative to others on the coast also promoted acculturation.

The strength of the African heritage varied in intensity, following social and cultural changes in Peru that affected black behavioral attitudes—particularly the growth of political and folkloric nationalism, and ultimately, in the early twenty-first century, the world-wide movement of negritude. Despite Afro-Peruvian eclecticism, however, blacks in Peru not only retained much of the integrity of their musical style, but also profoundly influenced the development of national music in coastal Peru.

One of the principal sources of cultural unity and community for Peruvian blacks from about the 1550s to the 1850s was the *cofradías,* religious brotherhoods or sodalities for black slaves, established by the Roman Catholic Church in the 1540s. Each *cofradía* was devoted to a particular saint and served the members' spiritual and physical well-being. Though much activity of the *cofradías* was supervised by the church, it apparently included African ritual elements.

The *cofradías* were a major factor in the preservation of African musical traditions, as evidenced by descriptions of them in colonial literature. Though most accounts of the music and dance of non-Hispanicized slaves (*bozales*) in the *cofradías* were biased and critical (Lee 1935:144), the municipal leaders of Lima still required the *cofradías* to take part in the city's state and religious processions. An ordinance called the *cofradías* to assemble according to their respective nations of origin with their typical dress and musical instruments, and to dance and sing their traditional music.

MUSICAL INSTRUMENTS

From the descriptions of musical instruments in the colonial literature, blacks showed a marked preference for percussion instruments. Their only aerophone was a nose-blown flute ("Rasgo ... de los Negros Bozales" 1791), and their only chordophone was a musical bow, strung with catgut and struck with a small cane (W. B. Stevenson 1825:304). They had several membranophones, particularly those formed from hollow logs or large conical, ceramic vessels (*botijas de barro*). Both types are described in eighteenth- and nineteenth-century sources and are remembered by elderly consultants as being used in rural areas until the early 1900s.

Among now obsolete idiophones, the *marimba* was once one of the most popular. It consisted of wooden slabs placed on an arch of wood over the mouths of gourd resonators. The slabs were struck with sticks by a player who squatted in front of them. The existence of the *marimba* in northern Peru in the 1780s is documented by Martínez Compañón (1978: plate 142), who ordered a watercolor made of it. The last known reference to it is in a travel account from the first decades of the nineteenth century (Rushenberge 1834:39).

Black slaves also employed other idiophones, including a notched stick, a bamboo rasp, and a long stamped pole hung with pieces of tin, ribbons, and tinsel, the base of which was struck on the ground.

Perhaps the most unusual musical instrument used by Afro-Peruvians until the first decades of the twentieth century was a *mesa de ruidos* "table of noises," called *tamborete* in Lima and *tormento* in Chile. It consisted of a sheet of wood placed on four legs, with a possible box resonator underneath. On top of the sheet were (perhaps partially nailed) bottle tops with chips of wood on top of them. Agile fingers played rhythms on top of the sheet, causing the bottle tops and wood chips to vibrate.

Among the idiophones still extant are the *cajita* and the *quijada*. The *cajita* "small box" consists of a small wooden box with a hinged

Figure 32.1
In Lima, Peru, Rodolfo Arteaga Barrionuevo, a member of Perú Negro plays a *cajita*. Photo by William David Tompkins, 1974.

Figure 32.2
In Lima, Peru, Lalo
Izquierdo, a member
of Perú Negro plays
a *quijada*. Photo
by William David
Tompkins, 1974.

wooden lid. It is suspended in front of the player by a cord that passes around his neck or waist. He plays rhythms by striking the side of the box with a stick and opening and closing the lid (Figure 32.1).

The *quijada*, also called *carraca* or *caracha-cha*, is the lower jawbone of an ass, mule, or horse, stripped of its flesh and with the teeth loosened so they can rattle in their sockets (Figure 32.2). While the left hand holds the jawbone at the chin, the right scrapes a piece of sheep rib across the face of the jaw or the surface of the molars, or the clenched fist strikes the side of the jaw, buzzing the molars in their sockets.

A watercolor by Pancho Fierro from the mid-1800s illustrates the use of the *cajita* and the *quijada* to accompany the *son de los diablos*, a dance performed during Carnaval (Figure 32.3). The *cajita* is still used primarily in stage renditions of the *son de los diablos*, and the *quijada* accompanies various Afro-Peruvian genres, most notably the *festejo* (described below).

In northern Peru, the idiophones *angara* and *checo* are also used. Each is fabricated from an empty calabash with one of its sides opened. The player puts it between his thighs, the aperture facing down, and strikes its top with his hands. Ignacio Merino (1817–1876) painted the *angara* as it was played during the 1800s.

The Afro-Peruvian idiophone used most widely in the twentieth century is the *cajón* "box," a simple wooden box about 50 centimeters high, 30 wide, and 25 deep, with a sound hole about 10 centimeters in diameter in the back. The player normally sits on top of the *cajón*, rhythmically striking the front and sides of it with his hands (Figure 32.4). During the late 1800s, the nails in the planks of the *cajón* were purposely loosened to add a kind of vibration when the *cajón* was struck (Fuentes 1925:112). The instrument probably developed during the 1800s and became popular shortly after 1850; before then, membranophones had more commonly been used. Today, the *cajón* provides rhythmic accompaniment to various forms of Afro-Peruvian and other coastal music.

Many of these instruments seem to be of African origin or inspiration. The African affinity for percussive instruments is evident, and the buzzing produced by numerous African instruments reappears in the Peruvian *marimba*, rasps, *quijada*, *cajón*, and *tamborete*. After the 1950s, as folkloric groups strove to reconstruct their African musical heritage, they rediscovered some of these instruments.

AFRICAN/SPANISH MUSICAL ENCOUNTERS

Colonial literature shows that blacks in Peru used two forms of musical expression. Music rooted in African traditions continued to be performed in the *cofradías* into the 1800s;

son de los diablos
Choreographed musical spectacle performed in the streets of Lima during Carnaval
festejo
Afro-Peruvian form often interrupted at phrase endings by a sudden pause or a long-held pitch
cajón
"Big box," Afro-Peruvian and *criollo* idiophone made from a wooden box with a soundhole in the back

Figure 32.3
Watercolor by Pancho
Fierro (1803–1879)
showing players of a
cajita, a harp, and a
quijada, accompanying
a *son de los diablos*
performed during
Carnaval. Municipality
of Lima. Used with
permission.

however, blacks skilled in playing Spanish musical instruments had long performed military music, and soon Afro-Peruvian musicians became commonplace in all facets of social, religious, and musical life in Spanish Peru.

As early as the 1500s, but especially during the 1800s, many blacks developed proficiency in the graces of European salon music and dance. Some black dance masters attained considerable fame (Fuentes 1925:110–111; R. M. Stevenson 1968:304). Even the church exploited blacks' musical talents: in the 1600s, the College of San Pablo had a fine band of black musicians who played trumpets (*clarines*), shawms (*chirimías*), drums, flutes, and various kinds of plucked lutes (Bowser 1974:246).

As black musicians encountered more European music, they adapted and reinterpreted elements into their own music. New Afro-Peruvian genres emerged. Some of them were indigenous to Peruvian blacks; others were black stylizations of Spanish musical forms. The pantomimic *morros y cristianos* ("Moors and Chistians"), one such musical tradition, was eventually absorbed into black culture from Spanish folklore. Several chroniclers wrote about it during the 1800s, and Pancho Fierro portrayed it in a watercolor in 1830. This mime-drama has probably disappeared from coastal Peru, and already by the 1970s, only the oldest people in rural areas remembered having seen it.

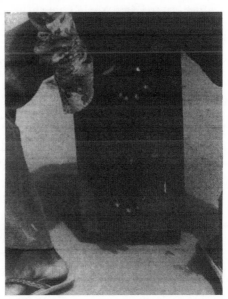

Figure 32.4
Fernando Cartagena
Peña of Guayabo
plays a *cajón*. Photo
by William David
Tompkins, 1974.

Another Afro-Peruvian genre that originated in Spanish traditions is the *son de los diablos,* danced by several blacks dressed in devil costumes and masks (Figure 32.3). This dance seems to have its more remote origins in the short religious plays of Corpus Christi and the processions of Low Sunday (Quasimodo Sunday). After 1817, it passed to the secular context of Carnaval (Fuentes 1925:80). Various written accounts of it, and paintings by Pancho Fierro, show that the performing group normally consisted of a major devil (*diablo mayor*) and several minor devils, masked and dressed in pantaloons, accompanied by musicians playing the harp or a guitarlike plucked lute (possibly the *vihuela*), the *cajita,* and the *quijada.* The group formed a circle on street corners, and each devil would dance in turn. During the first few decades of the twentieth century, the *son de los diablos* gradually disappeared from Lima's Carnavales. It was revived in the mid-1950s in the context of a staged Afro-Peruvian folk dance.

Celebrations of Christmas

Christmas in Peruvian homes takes place around often elaborate creches (*nacimientos, belenes*). In some rural areas and small towns, late December also brings out the *hatajos de negritos* (see Okada 1995: example 22), boys dressed as Magi, who sing and dance in adoration of the Infant Jesus to the accompaniment of a solo violin in front of creches. *Mestizos* and even indigenous peoples have *danzas de negros* that imitate blacks. The songs and dances of the *hatajos* from the more densely black-populated areas of Chincha, however, are rooted in their own history and heritage. In their performances, boys represent not only kings and shepherds, but also enslaved blacks.

The costumes of the *negritos* vary from group to group but generally consist of an ornate cap representing a crown, and a band of bright red or blue cloth, crossing diagonally over the upper body like a royal sash. The crown and the band bear a profusion of tinkle bells, bits of bright paper, bolts of cloth, and tiny mirrors—and paper currency, donated to the dancer. Each *negrito* holds a handbell (*campanilla*) and a decorated rope whip (*chicotillo*). At one time, small jingle bells (*cascabeles*) attached to the dancers' ankles would sound with each movement of their feet. The *negritos* dance repetitive choreographic figures in two lines, employing rhythmic stamping reminiscent of the *wayno* (*huayno*) but with more frequent use of *zapateado* (rhythmic striking of the heels and toes of the shoes against the floor or against each other) and *escobillada* (a brushing movement of the shoe or bare foot along the floor or ground).

DISC ❶ TRACK25

The songs and dances of the *hatajo de negritos* from the town of El Carmen, province of Chincha, represent a notable example of acculturation and assimilation of Spanish, African, and highland native musical elements. [Listen to "Zancudito"] Like the nineteenth-century Spanish *villancico,* the songs of the *negritos* employ pastoral, amorous, or sacred Christmas themes set syllabically to a simple melody in a short strophic form. The dramatic element in the performances of the *negritos* probably owes much to the *villancico's* occasional association with the theater and the old Christmas plays (*autos*) introduced by the Spanish missionaries.

Some songs reveal Amerindian influences in the texts and melodies, and occasionally even in the vocal style—particularly the broken, wailing voice at points where the melody suddenly descends. The *hatajo* of El Carmen, composed mainly of blacks, employs a more kinetic style than does that of *mestizo* groups. Residents of the area consider black dancers particularly skillful in *zapateado.* Many of the texts employ black dialect and make frequent references to life under slavery.

Spanish prosody

Afro-Peruvian traditions have absorbed several recited or competitively sung Spanish poetic forms, some of which may be recited or sung competitively. Among the most important of these is the *décima,* a poetic form consisting of ten octosyllabic lines, developed in Spain during the 1500s and popularized throughout Latin America. The *décima* deals with biblical subjects (*a lo divino*) or themes of philosophy, politics, satire, or love (*a lo humano*). It is usually recited, but may be sung in a declamatory, syllabic style with guitar providing an unobtrusive chordal accompaniment (*socabón* or *socavón*).

Décimas can be presented *sueltas* "individually" or *de pié forzado* "with forced foot." The structure of the *décima de pié forzado* varies in different regions of Latin America. In Peru, it consists of four *décimas* preceded by an octosyllabic quatrain (*glosa*) that becomes the skeleton on which four ten-line strophes hang, thematically and structurally. Each line of the quatrain in turn becomes the final line of one of the corresponding *décimas.*

The *cumanana* and *amor fino,* less complicated coastal poetic forms, are sung in declamatory style. They are accompanied by the guitar and, like the *décima,* are often performed competitively by two or more poet-musicians. The *cumanana,* found in the northern Peruvian departments of Piura and Lambayeque, consists of four octosyllabic verses of text set to a melody, the style of which closely resembles that of the *triste* and the native *yaraví.* When it is performed in competition, the singers alternate *cumananas* but must retain the same melody throughout. Their texts present a dialogue in which each singer draws from his own repertoire or demonstrates his improvisatory skill in responding to the thoughts or questions presented by his opponent. An almost obsolete sister form of the *cumanana* is the *amor fino* (in the department of Lima), also based on a quatrain of essentially octosyllabic lines but with an optional two-line refrain (*estribillo*), making it somewhat similar to the Argentine *payada.*

The *décima,* the *cumanana,* and the *amor fino* have roots in the Spanish poetic tradition. They are represented in all cultural groups in coastal Peru, they do not belong exclusively to any one group. Nevertheless, many African-derived cultures demonstrate an affinity for verbal dueling, and my oldest consultants in Peru remember many of the masters of these poetic forms as being of African descent.

TRADITIONAL AFRO-PERUVIAN TRADITIONS

As blacks became integrated into the social and economic order of colonial Peru, they developed musical genres that reflected the realities of the New World. The *penalivo* or *panalivio* "ease-pain," a satirical dance and song of lament dating from the 1700s, commented on the conditions of slavery. Afro-Peruvian work songs, street vendors' songs (*pregones*), and songs accompanying the watermelon-harvest festival (*maca-maca*) in lca also reflect something of the nineteenth-century black life-style (Vizarreta 1941).

Festejo

Probably the most important Afro-Peruvian musical form is the *festejo* (see Okada 1995: examples 19 and 20), whose rhythms occur in several genres. A typical *festejo* melody consists of short phrases with a surging rhythm, frequently interrupted at phrase-endings by a sudden pause, or by a tone of longer duration. The question-answer character of the melodic line in consecutive phrases is exaggerated in the final section (*fuga*), composed of melodic fragments sung responsorially by soloist and chorus. Considerable metric variety and even simultaneous use of two different meters can be found, but the underlying meter is essentially 6/8 with a stilted iambic rhythm.

A typical example (Figure 32.5) has balanced four-bar phrases (repeated), rhythmic contrasts, the use of *fugas,* accent displacement, and a responsorial nature:

A don Antonio Mina	Sir Anthony Mina
lo pican y lo mataron.	They stabbed and killed.
Arriba en la huaca grande	Up at the old ancient tomb
al don lo vido yo.	I saw the gentleman myself.
Atiralalá, atiralalá, atiralalá	Throw it, throw it, throw it
desde Lima a Lunahuana.	from Lima to Lunahuana.
Cachaplaca, chaplaca, chaplac.	Mark of the blade.
Un jarro de agua y un dulce.	A jar of water and a candy.
El turronero de yema.	The candy maker.

The texts often follow a set strophic form. They usually treat a festive theme, often in a historical setting reflecting the era of slavery. Texts and melodies are sometimes interchanged between *festejos,* and texts may even be borrowed from another musical genre and set to a *festejo* melody and rhythm. This swapping of melodies and texts is common in the Afro-Peruvian musical tradition as elsewhere in the world (Levine 1977:196–198). The guitar, the *cajón,* and clapping provide the basic instrumental accompaniment. The use of the *cajón* in the *festejo* is an innovation of the 1950s, replacing the ceramic vessel or hollow log membranophones that were used previously, and most modern performances include the *quijada.*

The *festejo* was probably danced in free style. In addition, several other genres of dance are based melodically and rhythmically on the *festejo.* These include the *son de los diablos* (described above), the *alcatraz,* the *ingá,* the *zapateo* (*zapateado*) *criollo,* and the *agua 'e nieve.*

There are several novelty dances based on the *festejo,* including the *alcatraz* and the *ingá.* My oldest consultants remember them only as sources of entertainment. The *alcatraz* is performed in a circle. One male-female couple at a time dances in the center. Either or both dancers carry a flaming stick or candle, with which he or she tries to light a paper streamer attached like a tail behind the partner, while the other makes such pelvic movements that the streamer flicks about, dodging the flame. To perform the *ingá* (also called *ungá*) and *baile del muñeco* "doll's dance," the dancers also form a circle. In its center, embracing a large doll, pillow, or anything that could be used to represent an

fuga
"Flight," Afro-Peruvian musical appendage used as a lively closing section

alcatraz
Afro-Peruvian novelty couple dance

ingá
Afro-Peruvian novelty circle dance

Figure 32.5
Excerpt from "*Don Antonio Mina*," a typical *festejo*. Transcribed by William David Tompkins, from *El Festejo* (n.d.:B4).

infant, one performer dances alone. After several minutes of dancing, the soloist passes the doll to someone of the opposite sex within the circle. This person takes a turn, and the sequence proceeds in that manner until all have danced.

Two dances utilizing *festejo* rhythms in a competitive demonstration of skill are the *zapateo* (*zapateado*) *criollo* (or the *pasada*) and the *agua 'e nieve* (or *agüenieve*). The *zapateo criollo* is danced by a solo male who demonstrates his skill by improvising intricate rhythmic patterns with his feet, supplemented by rhythmic slapping (see Okada 1995: example 21). An element of virtuosity and even acrobatics is often present. The dance is usually performed competitively by two or more individuals who take turns trying to impress onlookers or to score points with the person chosen to judge their contest. The *agua 'e nieve* is essentially the same, but based on *escobillada* technique.

The only rhythmic accompaniment used in these dances comes from the guitar, which provides a simple, unobtrusive musical framework on which the dancer improvises. When these dances are performed by the *hatajo de negritos,* however, rather than using the *festejo* rhythm, the violin plays an accompaniment resembling that used for *villancicos,* and boys combine *zapateado* and *escobillada* techniques.

Landó

Another Afro-Peruvian musical genre, rhythmically distinct and more complex than the *festejo,* is the *landó.* Colonial-period literature provides no information that reliably confirms the origin of this dance. Because the original choreography for the dance has essentially been lost, modern Afro-Peruvian troupes have created their own steps, utilizing accentuated movements of the hips. The original rhythm of the *landó,* which has also been lost, was replaced by a rhythm created by the guitarist Vicente Vásquez Díaz (Vásquez Rodríguez 1982:44).

zapateo
From *zapateado* "foot stamping," a dance technique involving rhythmic hitting of heels and toes against the floor or each other
landó
Afro-Peruvian song and dance form, said to have come from the Brazilian *lundú*

Figure 32.6

Excerpts from a traditional *landó* from Guayabo, Chincha Province, Peru, arranged and performed by Perú Negro: (a) instrumental introduction, showing polyrhythms on guitar and *quijada*; (b) call-and-response pattern between a male soloist and a chorus of men and women. Transcribed by William David Tompkins, from *Perú Negro* (Byrne and Evelev 1995: track 13).

Fragments of a few traditional *landós* have survived, and new ones are being composed. The *landó* exhibits richly syncopated rhythmic variety using six units per bar, conceivable as (4+2)/4 time. The primary accentuation is on the first and fifth quarter notes; a secondary accent occurs on the third. Contrasting meters, especially 6/4 time, often occur in instrumental and vocal parts, producing polyrhythms and cross-accents (Figure 32.6a). Frequently in minor mode, the music of the *landó* is in a responsorial format: a soloist sings a one- or two-bar phrase answered by a chorus singing a short refrain (Figure 32.6b). As they alternate, the soloist repeats the same melodic fragment using different verses in a kind of miniature strophic form, and the chorus repeats a refrain, such as "*Samba landó, landó/Samba malató landó.*" Some *landós* also employ a contrasting lyrical section (see Byrne and Evelev 1995: example 13).

CREOLE MUSICAL TRADITIONS

The nineteenth century was a critical period in the development of Peruvian culture. Political and cultural alienation from Spain led to national independence (1821), the abolition of slavery (1865), and the War of the Pacific with Chile (1879–1883). In all these movements and events, blacks played important roles.

Concurrently, nationalism in folk music was evidenced by the emergence of new national genres of music. Thus, even as the mixture of races along the Peruvian coast produced a distinctive *mestizaje,* the blending of Hispano-European, native American, and African music traditions gradually synthesized a creole music (*música criolla*), truly representative of coastal Peruvian culture.

Zamacueca and its variants

Probably the most important new national musical genre of the nineteenth century was the *zamacueca* (or *zambacueca*), which appeared in coastal Peru not long after 1800. Its choreographic theme, shared with dances derived from it, was a courtship pantomime, performed by a man and a woman amid a crowd that accompanied them with rhythmic clapping and supportive shouting. As the dancers advanced and retreated from each other, they rhythmically and provocatively flipped a handkerchief about. The instrumentation varied, but frequently consisted of plucked stringed instruments and a percussive instrument such as the *cajón.*

Other coastal dances choreographically related to the *zamacueca* appeared during the 1800s. The most notable were the *tondero* and the *resbalosa.* These dances are distinctive in their musical form and style. The *tondero,* still found in northern coastal Peru, has a ternary structure: *glosa* (always in minor mode), *dulce* or *canto* (always in the relative major), *and jitga* (in the original minor mode). The *resbalosa,* found in the areas closer to Lima, is musically more syncopated, and its steps are based on *escobillada.*

The *zamacueca* became popular in many Latin American countries during the mid-1800s, and numerous regional and national variations developed. In the 1860s and 1870s, the *zamacueca chilena,* a Chilean version of it, was the most popular form in Peru. After the War of the Pacific, however, Peruvians, not wanting their national dance to carry their enemy's name, renamed it the *marinera,* honoring their seamen who had died in the war. Modern, commercial Afro-Peruvian renditions of the *zamacueca,* which began with Victoria Santa Cruz's popular "*Ven a mi encuentro,*" bear little resemblance to the historical version.

The *marinera* has choreography similar to that of the *zamacueca,* with regional variations throughout Peru (see Okada 1995: example 24). Most important to a study of Afro-Peruvian music is the *marinera* of Lima (*marinera limeña*), which functions in one of two contexts: first, as a competition (*contrapunto*) between or among singers (this is referred to as *canto de jarana* or just *jarana*) and second, as a noncompetitive performance of a simple *marinera* with singing and/or dancing. Unlike the *marineras* of other regions, the *marinera limeña* follows strict rules of performance in dancing and singing. The essential accompaniment consists of two guitars, a *cajón,* and clapping. The poetic structure of a *marinera limeña* is ternary, consisting of three strophes, each of which must adhere to set poetic and musical structures.

The *jarana* song competition is performed by two or more singers who sing alternate strophes in a series of *marineras.* A singer may choose strophes from traditional Spanish poetry or from verses composed before the competition, or he may even improvise strophes. According to strict rules, the texts of the strophes of a given *marinera* must be adapted spontaneously to fit the melody, chosen or improvised by the performer who sings the first strophe (Hayre 1973).

A complete performance of a *jarana* consists of three to five *marineras,* each having three strophes followed by a *resbalosa* and *fugas.* The *resbalosa,* the complementary movement to the *marinera,* consists of two or more strophes sung in a somewhat livelier and more syncopated rhythm than that of the *marinera,* with fewer metrical and musical restrictions than its counterpart. The *fugas* are the climax of the piece and the competition. In them, the competitors test each other's knowledge by singing couplets or quatrains of verses back and forth to each other in rapid succession. If a singer makes an error during the *jarana,* or is unable to answer at all, his opponent wins. Many of the greatest interpreters of the *marinera* and performers of *jaranas* have been Afro-Peruvian, including Bartola Sancho Dávila, Manuel Quintana, Elías and Augusto Ascuez, Augusto Gonzales, and Abelardo Vásquez. Only a few individuals who know how to sing *jaranas* are still alive. The only commercially available recorded traditional performances are the LP disk *La Marinera Limeña es Así* (n.d.), and *Jarana's Four Aces*, a CD published in 2005 by José Durand that is a testament to four of the best *jarana* singers of modern times, all of whom are now deceased (2005, British Library Sound Archive TSCD926).

Vals criollo

The creole waltz (*vals criollo*) is the most popular national form of music among most races and social classes in coastal Peru. Though it has its roots in the Viennese waltz, it bears little resemblance to its aristocratic progenitor. Many of its national traits reflect black influences.

By the 1850s, the *vals* already differed considerably from the European waltz. It had, and still has, a free choreography consisting of short, slow steps with considerable rhythmic movement of the hips, arms, and shoulders. Its melody usually abounds in displaced accents, anticipated and retarded beats, and occasional use of rubato. In the early 1900s, the traditional instrumental accompaniment of two guitars was enriched by the addition of the *cajón.* Most composers of *valses* have been whites or *mestizos,* but Afro-Peruvians are among the carriers of the tradition, and their influence has helped make its character unique.

TWENTIETH-CENTURY URBAN POPULAR MUSICAL TRADITIONS

Folkloric nationalism or *criollismo* continued to develop throughout the twentieth and into the twenty-first century in Peru, with the black population always playing an important role. Many musical genres identified principally with Afro-Peruvian culture, however, began to fall into disuse in the late 1800s and the early 1900s.

Only a few families of black musicians in Lima and rural areas remained familiar with the forms. Black composers, singers, and dancers showed little interest in traditional Afro-Peruvian music. Instead, they dedicated themselves to creole music in vogue, especially the *marinera,* the *resbalosa,* and the *vals,* plus imported popular music such as the *tango* (from Argentina), the *boston* and *shimmy* (from North America), and even the *zarzuela.*

Beginning in the 1920s, semiprofessional musical ensembles of Afro-Peruvian musicians and singers attained renown in the performance of creole music, often entertaining on stage or at late-night parties (also called *jaranas*). These groups, usually living in and identified with particular neighborhoods of Lima, developed repertoires of *valses,* polkas, *marineras, resbalosas,* and *tonderos.* One musician of Afro-Peruvian heritage, Samuel Márquez, formed the ensemble Ricardo Palma, which in addition to popular creole genres performed some old Afro-Peruvian songs. In 1936, he presented this repertoire in the theatrical performance *Del 96 al 36* ("From [18]96 to [19]36"). Much Afro-Peruvian music had already been lost by then, and often only portions of choruses survived; therefore, Márquez made arrangements based on surviving fragments. His presentation was a success, and, for the next couple of decades, Ricardo Palma performed Afro-Peruvian folkloric music at many kinds of celebrations.

The first attempt to bring an entire program of Afro-Peruvian music to the stage was achieved through the efforts of José Durand, a white creole. Frequenting festivities where the foremost black singers and musicians performed, he collected information and songs from knowledgeable elderly blacks. The result was La Cuadrilla Morena de Pancho Fierro (The Moreno Company of Pancho Fierro), which made its début in the Teatro Municipal of Lima in the summer of 1956. This engagement marked the beginning of organized commercial companies of Afro-Peruvian musicians and dancers.

Though Durand's ensemble eventually disintegrated, it inspired other commercial Afro-Peruvian groups. During the 1960s, Victoria and Nicomedes Santa Cruz formed Danzas Negros del Perú and Cumanana. Other groups initiated in the 1970s included Perú Negro (founded by Ronaldo Campos), Gente, Morena, Los Frijoles Negros, and the Afro-Peruvian ensembles of the Conjunto Nacional de Folklore (led by Victoria Santa Cruz). The following decades saw the formation of many more commercial Afro-Peruvian groups in Lima and some smaller coastal towns. Several scholars' research has confirmed that most of the repertoire of these commercial groups since the 1950s has been stylized, newly invented, or Africanized "folklore" with few roots in Afro-Peruvian tradition (Vásquez Rodríguez 1982:44–53).

Festejos, landós, and other Afro-Peruvian music can now be heard in nightclubs, *peñas criollas, centros musicales*, and on compact discs by such well-known singers as Eva Ayllón and Susana Baca. Though *peñas* were originally where amateur performers of creole (and occasionally Andean) music met for jam sessions, the term is now loosely used by entrepreneurs to describe cover-charge dinner concerts of popular Peruvian music with professional performers or even dinner dances with Latin American music provided by a disk jockey. Numerous vinyl records, cassettes, and compact discs of commercialized Afro-Peruvian music have been issued.

In Cañete every August, the Festival Negroide promotes Afro-Peruvian musics. It gives awards for the best black dancers, vocalists, and composers. Governmental agencies promote creole and Afro-Peruvian music by requiring a certain portion of the programming of radio and television stations to include national music.

Academic folklorists and authenticity

The twentieth century saw the beginning of scholarly research on Afro-Peruvian music. In the 1930s and 1940s, Fernando Romero began studying African influence on Peruvian coastal music. Other scholars—including Abraham and Felipe Arias Larreta, Fernando Assuncao (1969), José Mejía Baca (1938), José Durand (1961, 1971, 1973), Carlos Havre (1973), Arturo Jiménez Borja, Robert M. Stevenson, Rosa Elena Vásquez Rodríguez (1982), and Carlos Vega (1936, 1953)—have researched diverse aspects of coastal creole and black culture.

Possibly the most popular Afro-Peruvian folklorist and prolific writer of the 1960s and 1970s was Nicomedes Santa Cruz. Most scholars have taken issue with his theories, especially those concerning the nature and origins of colonial Afro-Peruvian and creole musical instruments and genres, but no other folklorist during this period did more to make Peruvians aware of the richness of their Afro-Peruvian heritage.

Most Afro-Peruvian consultants who remembered traditional black music as it was performed around 1900 have now died. They asserted that contemporary Afro-Peruvian "folklore" is an invention of modern black ensembles that wish to Africanize performances to make them more exotic. Afro-Peruvian music has entered into the commercial music industry. To succeed, it must be marketable and competitive with other youth-favored music, particularly Caribbean dance music. Only the *hatajo de negritos* has remained relatively noncommercialized and within the realm of tradition. However, the growing public interest in African-Peruvian music has led to an increase in tourism to the Chincha area, which has benefited the province commercially. Tourists now visit Chincha and the smaller provincial towns of El Carmen, San José, and Guayabo, especially during major feasts, to see the *hatajos de negritos* and other groups dance.

Despite the arguments about "true" Afro-Peruvian traditions, however, one must avoid the misconception that the only authentic Afro-Peruvian music is that which has remained unchanged from former centuries. Culture is not static, and African-derived culture has been characterized by resilience throughout history as it interacted between the past and present, absorbing and reinterpreting elements from the musical traditions around it.

Similarly, modern Afro-Peruvian music reflects the ethos and group consciousness of the present-day black population. The social struggles of the 1800s (calling for greater cultural integration) had taken a turn by the late twentieth century, when blacks were beginning to take new pride in their African heritage, inspired by the worldwide development of negritude. Many Afro-Peruvians have embraced these new musical expressions as their own and consider them to be rooted in their history and traditions as they perceive them, expressive of their values and views.

FURTHER STUDY

Recent studies of the Afro-Peruvian music and dance revival are by Heidi Feldman with her 2006 book titled *Black Rhythms of Peru: Reviving African Musical Heritage in the Black Pacific* and her article in *Ethnomusicology* (2005), "The Black Pacific: Cuban and Brazilian Echoes in the Afro-Peruvian Revival." An excellent twenty-page booklet by Guillermo Durand and David Mortar accompanies a compact disc of *jarana* music, compiled by Peruvian folklorist José Durand (2005). A review of the publication by Dale A. Olsen (2006) provides some information about the tradition. David Mortara, an Associate Research Fellow in the Centre for Latin American Cultural Studies at King's College, University of London, is responsible for the archiving of Afro-Peruvian sound recordings from the Durand and Tompkins collections. William David Tompkin's dissertation

(UCLA, 1981) has been published in Peru as *La Música Tradicional de Los Negros de la Costa del Perú* (2007).

REFERENCES

Assunçao, Fernando. 1969. "Aportaciones Para un Estudio Sobre Los Orígines de la Zamacueca." *Folklore Americano* 17(16).

Bowser, Frederick Park. 1974. *The African Slave in Colonial Peru 1524–1650.* Stanford, Calif.: Stanford University Press.

Byrne, David, and Yale Evelev. 1995. *Afro-Peruvian Classics: The Soul of Black Peru.* Warner Brothers Records CD-9-45878-2. Compact disc.

Durand, José. 1961. "Del Fandango a la Marinera." *Fanal* 16(59): 10–15.

———. 1971. "De la Zamacueca a la Marinera." *Mensajes* 15:23–27.

———. 1973. "La Resbalosa Limeña." *Mensajes* 19:8–14.

———. 2005. *Jarana's Four Aces: Vocal Duels from the Streets of Lima.* Compact disc with commentary by Guillermo Durand Allison and David Mortara. Topic Records TSCD926.

El Festejo. N.d. Lima: Sono Radio LPL9239. LP disk.

Feldman, Heidi. 2005. "The Black Pacific: Cuban and Brazilian Echoes in the Afro-Peruvian Revival." *Ethnomusicology* 49(2):206–31.

———. 2006. *Black Rhythms of Peru: Reviving African Musical Heritage in the Black Pacific.* Middletown, Conn.: Wesleyen University Press.

Fuentes, Manuel. 1925. *Lima: Apuntes Históricos, Descriptivos, Estadísticos y de Costumbres.* Lima: E. Moreno.

Hayre, Carlos. 1973. "Apuntes para el análisis de la marinera limeña." Mimeogram, 23 pp. Lima: author.

Lee, Bertram T, ed. 1935. *Libros de Cabildos de Lima.* Vol. 6, part 2, 16 de agosto, 1563. Lima: Consejo Provincial.

Levine, Lawrence W. 1977. *Black Culture and Black Consciousness.* New York: Oxford University Press.

La Marinera es Así. N.d. Lima: Odeon ELD-2215. LP disk.

Martínez Compañón, Baltasar Jaime. 1978. *La Obra del Obispo Martinez Compañón Sobre Trujillo del Peru en el Siglo XVII.* Madrid: Ediciones Cultural Hispánica del Centro Iberoamericano de Cooperación.

Mejía Baca, José. 1938. *Algunas Noticias Sobre la Conga.* Lima.

Okada, Yuki, director. 1995. *Central and South America. The JVC Smithsonian Folkways Video Anthology of Music and Dance of the Americas,* 6. Montpelier, Vt.: Multicultural Media VTMV-230. Video.

Olsen, Dale A. 2006. Review of *Jarana's Four Aces: Vocal Duels from the Streets of Lima.* Compact disc with commentary by Guillermo Durand Allison and David Mortara. Topic Records TSCD926 (2005). *Ethnomusicology* 50(1):168–171.

Perú Negro, Lima. 1974. Virrey Recording VIR 920. LP disk.

"Rasgo. de los Negros Bozales." 1791. *Mercurio Peruana.* 16 June.

Rushenberge, William. 1834. *Three Years in the Pacific.* 2 vols. Philadelphia: Carey, Lea & Blanchard.

Stevenson, Robert M. 1968. *Music in Aztec and Inca Territory.* Berkeley: University of California Press.

Stevenson, William Bennett. 1825. *A Historical and Descriptive Narrative of Twenty Years Residence in South America.* 3 vols. London: Hurst Robinson.

Tompkins, William David. 1981. "The musical traditions of the blacks of coastal Peru." Ph.D. dissertation, University of California, Los Angeles.

———. 2007. *La Música Tradicional de Los Negros de la Costa del Perú.* Spanish translation by Juan Luis Dammert. Lima: CEMDUC (Centro de Música y Danza de la Pontificia Universidad Católica del Perú).

Vásquez Rodríguez, Rosa Elena. 1982. *La Práctica Musical de la Población Negra en el Perú.* Havana: Casa de las Américas.

Vega, Carlos. 1936. "Eliminación del Factor Africano en la Formación del Cancionero Criollo." *Cursos y Conferencias* 10(7):765–779.

———. 1953. *La Zamacueca (Cueca, Zamba, Chilena, Marinera).* Buenos Aires: Editorial Julio Korn.

Vizarreta, Juan Donaire. 1941. *Campiña Iaueña.* Lima: Imprenta La Moderna.

Questions for Critical Thinking

South American Music

1. Compare and contrast the musical instruments and musical styles of the Mapuche, Aymara, and Q'eros. Why are they similar or different?
2. Compare and contrast traditional African-derived music and dance from Venezuela, Brazil, and Peru, and give reasons for their similarities and differences.
3. Place the traditional African-derived musics and dances of Venezuela, Brazil, and Peru on a continuum from the most to the least African, and discuss the characteristics that determine your reasoning.
4. Compare and contrast the traditional Spanish- and Portuguese-derived musical instruments in South America.
5. Make a list that compares and contrasts the popular music genres in South America, and describe your examples.
6. How has Roman Catholicism functioned to create musical unity in South America?
7. How have African religious expressions functioned to create musical unity in South America?
8. Of the South American countries covered, which is most closely musically related to the Caribbean? Why is this so? Describe the musical and dance characteristics that support your argument.
9. List as many factors as possible that have led to musical diversity among the South American countries covered. Give examples to support your argument.
10. Name three genres of music from South America that have become popular far beyond their national boundaries of origin, and explain why you think this occurred.
11. Trace the origins, development, and diffusion of the *zamacueca* and all its variants in South America, describing the music and dance for each.
12. Compare and contrast Amerindian music, musical instruments, and dance from the tropical forest region with those from the Andes.

Conclusion

Dale A. Olsen[1]

Musical Threads Revisited
New Wine in Old Bottles
Cultural Identity vs. Cultural Blurring
Looking at the Past; Seeing the Future

Music in Latin America is a reflection of its history, and each musical genre follows the path taken by particular people to produce its unique style (Gelabert 2006). Indeed, the music genres studied in this book have followed particular paths by the people who create and perform those genres to produce their melodies, lyrics, rhythms, and dances. The many authors in this book have presented a series of musical descriptions, narratives, and analyses of many genres, musical instruments, dances, contexts, performance venues, and much more, most of which are not always restricted by political boundaries. Rather, they exist like threads that wind themselves throughout many countries, cultures, and subcultures. Although the diffusion of a certain musical trait may reach particular regions of Latin America, in other sectors that trait may be nonexistent (Gelabert 2006).

Most simply stated, *The Garland Handbook of Latin American Music* is a history of Latin American music or, rather, a history of many musics in Latin America (Mardirosian 2006). As a history (or perhaps an ethnohistory), however, the book is really a series of snapshots in time, because writing about history is never definitive and can never be concluded. It is constantly evolving and expanding with every passing moment. This book has shown, however, that many of those numerous threads which weave through the historical musical tapestry of Latin America are just as strong today as they were decades and even centuries ago. In the various introductions to the large geographic areas that make up this book, I often asked some form of the following question: What are some of the threads that wind their way through this [CARIBBEAN LATIN AMERICAN, MIDDLE LATIN

AMERICAN, or SOUTH AMERICAN] musical tapestry? The same question is once again asked but now with reference to the entirety of the region called "Latin America."

MUSICAL THREADS REVISTED

From the earliest times, the first thread is the indigenous heritage, which has created a multiplicity of musical colors, contexts, meaning, and symbolism that has emanated from a wealth of diverse Amerindian cultures from below the Rio Grande River to Cape Horn. Another complex series of threads were created by the Spanish and Portuguese immigrants from the time of their Encounter (they called it "discovery") with the New World to the present. Another series of threads were created by the diversity of African slaves and their descendants over the centuries. Since independence in Latin America and the subsequent end of the colonial periods, these three major populations have broadened into complex variants that were unimaginable at the time of their inception, aided by centuries of cultural and racial mixing, additional migrations, technological mediation, transculturation, and globalization. All of this has already been said, but the essays have made the points very obvious.

NEW WINE IN OLD BOTTLES

Parting from the initial Amerindian-derived, European-derived, and African-derived musics, we can now say that these three major groups have been influenced in turn by contemporary genres as much as technological advances. For example, we can now hear *huaynos* from Peru, *sayas* from Bolivia, *chacareras* from Argentina, *cuecas* from Chile, *joropos* from Venezuela, and *sambas* from Brazil with synthesizers and in the style of pop tunes but without loosing their traditional musical characteristics, sentiment, and energy. Likewise, *cumbia* can now be heard as *techno-cumbia*, samba as *samba-reggae*, bossa nova as *rap-bossa*, *tamborito* as *tamborito-remix*, *música norteña* as *nor-tech*, and so forth.

CULTURAL IDENTITY VS. CULTURAL BLURRING

More than twenty countries make up the vast region referred to as Latin America. Each country experienced its own fight for independence, projects for nation building, and struggles to develop. Many of these concepts of formation are often continuous for developing countries, where issues of identity have been put into question many times. Indeed, the foundation and success of a nation often lies in the formation of its national identity. Along with the conquest of the late fifteenth and early sixteenth centuries, however, cultural imperialism and globalization in the present have transformed Latin America into a smaller place where differences are blurred to the point that many societies think of themselves as one community living within a kind of global Latin American village (Gelabert 2006). Music has served to emphasize cultural identity as well as to blur it.

Many Latin American politicians have taken advantage of music and used it for and against their people: from the creation of national anthems that are supposed to embody the essence of nationalism in a country; from the claim of a certain genre as part of the country's identity (as *samba* is to Brazil, *plena* is to Puerto Rico, *merengue* is to Dominican Republic, and *tango* is to Argentina, for example); to the censoring of certain musical genres and musical instruments in order to establish a determined agenda with a country (as in Chile in the mid-1970s, for example). When Latin American countries suffered from dictatorships and struggled with injustices, it was often music, along with dance, art, film, and literature (and soccer) that played important unifying roles, providing not only voices for the voiceless but sometimes creating calls for social change and national unity by giving a voice to its people (Gelabert 2006).

LOOKING AT THE PAST, SEEING THE FUTURE

If history repeats itself, as the adage goes, then the knowledge gained from investigating the past should be contemplated and applied in order to better understand, anticipate, and prepare for the future (Mardirosian 2006). Therefore, a thorough understanding of the history of the musics of Latin America should lead to the anticipation of the shape of the future of Latin America's music. What are some of these facets of the past (and present) that may shape the future?

The investigation into the history of Latin America's musics, as presented in this book, reveals example after example of syncretism. The last thirty years of the twentieth century and into the twenty-first have seen a noticeable growth in the musical styles of Latin America, and instances of syncretism throughout Latin America and beyond have increased at an exponential rate. The "Latino" (or "latino") world started becoming a smaller place because of transculturation, migration, and technological innovation (Mardirosian 2006). As Latin America enters the third millennium, given the understanding that history does repeat itself and that the music of Latin America has a history full of syncretism, it is feasible to assume that the future of Latin American music will include a continued syncretistic pattern. It is impossible to minimize and simplify the musics of Latin America of the past into one name or under one umbrella. They are all quite different from each other due to their multi-cultured heritages. However, if syncretism and cultural hybridity continue, which is likely since it is seen repeatedly in the history of the Latin American musical world, and as the global world becomes a smaller place leading to more sharing and blending of cultural lines, some Latin American musics may indeed have the potential of eventually being combined and referred to as one style. Already *salsa* and *reggaetón* have that capability on their surface levels. Syncretism, cultural hybridity, and globalization are inescapable, and accounting for that and the unavoidable and constant desire of the "outside" world to define (i.e., minimize, label, and market) cultural products, it is important to consciously protect and, more importantly, to celebrate the musical diversity that existed historically and still exists in Latin America (Mardirosian 2006). This book represents an effort to make Latin American music (as part of the musics of the world) available to those who wish to understand it and learn about the historic, cultural, and social background that makes Latin America what it is (Gallardo 2006).

NOTE

1. In the process of using this book as a textbook in my Music of Latin America 1 course at Florida State University, I received many comments and student input since 2000, when the book was first published. Several students wrote short conclusions for the book as a final exam in 2006, synthesizing its materials and addressing particular issues. Therefore, portions of this conclusion are written with collaboration from Gonzalo Gallardo, Carla Gelabert, and Gregory Mardirosian. Their works are referenced above.

REFERENCES

Gallardo, Gonzalo. N.d. "Final 'Take-Home' Exam." Final Exam for Music of Latin America 1. Florida State University (December 10, 2006).

Gelabert, Carla. N.d. Final Exam for Music of Latin America 1. Florida State University (December 10, 2006).

Mardirosian, Gregory. N.d. "Latin American Music: Entering a New Millennium." Final Exam for Music of Latin America 1. Florida State University (December 10, 2006).

Questions for Critical Thinking

Latin American Music

1. What impact have women had on traditional music in Latin America? Give specific musical examples.

2. What impact have women had on popular music in Latin America? Give specific musical examples and provide names when known.

3. Explain the reasons for the similarities and/or differences in your answers to questions one and two.

4. Compare and/or contrast the five major harp traditions found in Latin America (Mexico, Guatemala, Venezuela, Paraguay, and Peru) as regards physical characteristics, playing techniques, musical contexts, musical genres, and performance details.

5. What impacts have dictatorships, political ideologies (e.g., Marxism, right-wing politics, etc.), and war had on music in Latin America? Describe these and use specific country examples and time periods.

6. Make a list of and describe the many variants of guitar types found in Latin America. Why are there differences in so many regions?

7. Describe the historical/social/political elements that have contributed to the development of *mariachi*, *samba*, and *tango*. Conclude your essay by explaining why there are differences and similarities among them, and discuss what makes them national symbols and enduring traditions.

8. Choose one musical genre from each of the countries included in this book and discuss each one as a representative nationalistic and emblematic genre for its country. Conclude by using your examples to argue for either unity or diversity in Latin American music (or both).

9. Compare and/or contrast how the countries studied in this book make and employ public policies to disseminate, foment, and preserve their traditional musics.

10. Discuss how music and tourism are integrated in Latin America, giving examples from particular countries.

11. What types of acculturative influences have been felt throughout Latin America? Discuss them within four Latin American countries of your choice that represent the greatest amounts of change, choosing one country from Caribbean Latin America, one from Middle Latin America, and two from South America.

12. Define *sesquiáltera* and discuss its use through Latin America, providing examples of particular musical genres. Why is it so prominent? Where is it not very common, and why?

13. Delineate five common characteristics found in African-derived music and discuss where and how they are found throughout Latin America, from the Caribbean and Mexico in the north to Argentina and all points between.

14. Based on the particular Amerindian essays and similar portions within the country essays, discuss the most important commonalities found within indigenous music and dance.

15. Write an essay on the uses and functions of music and shamanism within the Amerindian cultures discussed in this book. What are the similarities and differences and why do they exist?

16. List one culture other than Amerindian, African, Portuguese, and Spanish that has contributed significantly to the shaping of Latin American music and explain what music(s) it impacted and how.

17. How has geography determined or influenced musical diversity throughout Latin America?

18. Discuss how the national anthems of Latin American countries do or do not represent the musical reality of particular nations and their people.

19. Give some examples of "music as power" throughout Latin America. How is this "power" manifested? Does music function as physical power, political power, sexual power, social power, spiritual power, or what? Think of some examples.

20. The Conclusion to this book states that "writing about history is never definitive and can never be concluded. It is constantly evolving and expanding with every passing moment." With that in mind, think about current events in Latin America (i.e., things that are happening right now as you read this study question). How is music being used in Latin America for events that you read about or see on television? Listen carefully. Do you hear protest songs? Do you hear loud rock or *samba* during an event? Listen to your local Spanish-speaking television channel; what types of music do you hear? Whatever type it is, first you have to listen! Write about it daily or weekly, making entries in a journal.

Glossary

aboio
Brazilian *cantoria* cowboy cattle-herding song genre featuring the imitation of cattle

acculturation
Changes that occur when members of different cultures come into continuous contact, involving complex relationships of cultural, economic, and political dominance

acordeón
"Accordion," in many regions of Spanish-speaking America, a multiple single-reed-concussion aerophone with bellows, either with buttons or keyboard for melody, and buttons for bass notes; see index under aerophones

adufe
Guatemalan quadrangular double-skinned frame drum, with or without rattle inside the body

aerophone
"Air sounder," a musical instrument whose sound is produced by vibrating air, often a column of air

afoxé
(1) Contemporary Afro-Brazilian Carnaval music; (2) a Brazilian friction idiophone, also *cabaça* and *melê*

agogô
Brazilian double or triple cone-shaped bell played with metal stick

agua 'e nieve (also *agüenieve*)
Afro-Peruvian male competition dance

aguinaldo
Song genre throughout Hispanic America that is usually sung around Christmas and that involves gifts of coins, candy, food, or drink in exchange for music

aires nacionales
"National songs," traditional Mexican and other Latin American melodies arranged for piano

alabado (also *albao, alavado*)
"Praised," an announcement played by the *clarinero* in Peru

alabanza
"Praise," unaccompanied religious praise song in Argentina and elsewhere in Spanish-speaking America in two, three, or four voices

alabês
Afro-Brazilian drummers in Candomblé

alborada
Municipal band music for patronal festivals

alcahuete (or *adulón*)
Drums other than *palo mayor* used in the *palos*

Alcatraz
Afro-Peruvian novelty couple dance

alferez (also *alferez, alferece*)
Administrative director, conductor, or main sponsor of a *baile* or *cofradía* dancing group in Chile

altiplano
"High plain," the cold, high central plain of southern Peru and Bolivia (also used for the region around Bogotá, Colombia)

amarrao
"Tied," Puerto Rican dance choreography

anata
Bolivian wooden duct flute, another term for *tarka*

angelitos
"Little angels," songs and instrumental music for deceased infants and children

antara (also *andara*)
Quechua term for single-unit panpipe in Peru, played by one person

arca (also *arka*)
"Follower" in Aymara, one of the halves (female) of the *siku* (and several other) double-unit panpipe in the central Andes (counterpart of *ira* half, "leader")

areito (also *areyto*)
Pre-Columbian music and dance celebratory event of the Taino Indians of the Caribbean

arpa
"Harp," a diatonic harp without pedals, found in many regions of Hispanic America, especially Chile, Ecuador, Mexico, Paraguay, Peru, and Venezuela; see index under chordophones

Arrullo
Children's game song and lullaby

atabales
(1) Large Nicaraguan and Guatemalan drums the size and shape of standard snare drums but made of wood;
(2) longdrum music and instruments associated with saints' festivals

atabaque
Brazilian and Uruguayan conical single-headed drum

auto
Early religious musical drama and allegorical or religious play throughout the colonial Americas, used by priests for teaching about Christianity

axé
(1) Brazilian popular music genre; (2) Yoruba word for vital spiritual force of *Candomblé*

ayacachtli
Náhuatl name for a gourd or gourd-shaped rattle, made from clay or gold

ayarachi
Peruvian panpipe tradition subdivided in three different groups of instruments tuned to the octave

ayotl
Náhuatl name for a tortoiseshell idiophone struck with antlers

babalaô
Brazilian "diviner" of initiation rite

babalorixá
Female temple leader in Brazilian Candomblé

baguala
Argentine song with or without allusive texts

baião
Brazilian social dance music from Northeast Brazil typically played by trios of accordion, triangle, and *zabumba* drum

bailados
Afro-Brazilian country dramatic dances

bailanta (also *bailable*)
Argentine large dance hall

baile
"Dance" in Spanish, referring to dozens of costumed folkloric events in the Hispanic Americas; see index under dance and movement

bajo
"Bass," (1) Bolivian baritone horn; (2) *bajo sexto*, large twelve-stringed Mexican guitar

bajón
"Big bass," Bolivian multiple-tubed trumpet

bakohi
Warao bamboo and/or cow-horn trumpet used as substitute for conch-shell trumpet

balada
Commercially called Latin pop, can be considered the continuation of a long-standing pan-Hispanic tradition of guitar-based romantic song

ballet folklórico
"Folkloric ballet," often a Latin American country's professional troupe that performs nationalistic or ideological reinterpretions of rural music and dance practices

bambuco
(1) Mexican romantic, slow, often melancholic vocal genre; (2) fast music/dance from Colombia

bambúes
Set of bamboo tubes played in interlocking fashion

banda
"Band," usually either a brass band, a large ensemble of mixed European-derived wind instruments, or any ensemble of aerophones and percussion instruments; see index under instrumental ensembles

bandola
(1) A relative of the mandolin and direct descendant of the Spanish *bandurria*; (2) four-stringed pear-shaped lute chordophone

Bandolim
From Italian *mandolino*, small double-course Brazilian chordophone

bandoneón
Argentine button accordion used in tango music, invented in Germany by Heinrich Band in 1854 and brought to Buenos Aires about 1890

bandurria
A multi-stringed plucked lute introduced by the Spanish during the colonial period and still in use in Cuba, Guatamala, Paraguay, and Peru

banjo
Fretted, plucked-lute chordophone with circular membranophone resonator

baquetas
Guatemalan *marimba* mallets

baquiné (also *baquiní*)
Ecuadorian, Dominican, and Puerto Rican festive wake, celebrated at the death of an infant or young child

batucada
(1) Brazilian percussion ensemble and percussive dance music; (2) drumming session or performance of a samba percussion ensemble

Batuque
From Portuguese bater "to hit," (1) Afro-Brazilian religion and dance in Pará, São Paulo, and Rio Grande do Sul states; (2) *batuque,* Afro-Brazilian round dance of Angolese or Congolese origin; (3) Argentine variant of Afro-Brazilian religion

bayamonés
Style of *seis* from Bayamón, Puerto Rico

berimbau
(1) Struck musical bow with a calabash resonator common to Bahia, Brazil, and derived from Angola; (2) *berimbau de Angola,* another more complete name for the *berimbau*; (3) *berimbau de barriga,* "berimbau of the belly" another name for the Afro-Brazilian musical bow, so called because the calabash resonator is stopped by pressing it against the player's stomach

bhajan
Hymns of devotion and praise sung at Hindu religious services in Trinidad

birimbao (also *birimbau*)
(1) Argentine criollo jaw's harp; (2) Venezuelan jaw's harp

bix rxin nawal
Songs of the ancestors in Guatemala

bloco afro
Contemporary Afro-Brazilian Carnaval music

bocinas
Colonial Spanish term for "horns" sounded by the natives in Paraguay prior to an attack

boi
"Bull" in Portuguese (1) Afro-Brazilian bull character; (2) *boi de orquestra,* Afro-Brazilian aboio brass-band style; (3) *boi de zabumba,* Afro-Brazilian aboio style

bolero
Cuban-derived song genre for listening and dancing, attributed to José "Pepe" Sánchez

bolero-son
Cuban genre that combines elements of the *bolero* and the *son*

bomba
Afro-Puerto Rican drum and music/dance genre

bombo
(1) European-derived cylindrical double-headed bass drum membranophone, played with sticks; (2) for *candombe,* African-derived double-headed conical membranophone

bongos
Cuban and Puerto Rican membranophone consisting of two small drums joined by a piece of wood

bordonúa
Puerto Rican low-pitched, plucked lute chordophone with six double courses of strings

botija
Cuban aerophone made from earthen jugs with small hole in the side, through which the performer blows

brão
Brazilian enigmatic musical genre performed during *mutirões*

brazo
"Arm," referring to neck of lute chordophones from Puerto Rico

bumba-meu-boi
Dramatic Afro-Brazilian dance that is the last dramatic dance of the *reisado* cycle

burro
Venezuelan single-headed log drum

cabildo
(1) Secret society in Cuba and other Hispanic-Caribbean areas; (2) Bolivian community authority who may sponsor fiestas

caboclinho (also *terno de caboclos*)
Brazilian children's dramatic dance, same as *caiapó*

cacho
(1) Peruvian circular valveless trumpet made of connected bull-horn sections; (2) *cachos,* Venezuelan ductless deer-skull flutes played in pairs

cagüeño
Puerto Rican *seis* from Caguas

caiapó (also *terno de caiapós*)
Brazilian dramatic dance group that combines Native American, African, and Portuguese elements

caja
"Box," small membranophone in many Spanish-speaking countries, either single headed or double headed, often with a snare

cajón
"Big box," (1) Cuban and Afro-Peruvian *criollo* idiophone made from a wooden box with a soundhole in the back; (2) *cajones harmónicos,* Guatemalan wooden-box *marimba* resonators

cajuavé
Small mouth-resonated bow among the Chaco of Paraguay

calypso
Caribbean song form attributed to Trinidad, characterized by humorous language, rhyme, and the improvisational treatment of text and music which are often satirica

caña
(1) Bolivian long cane trumpet; (2) Paraguayan "cane" alcohol in bottles securely balanced on heads of *galoperas*

caña de millo
Colombian idioglottal transverse clarinet made from cane see also *pito*

canchis sipas
Q'ero panpipes with a double set of seven reed tubes

canción de protesta
"Protest song," any Latin American protest song, often influenced by Cuban revolution

canción ranchera
Mexican song type linked to the rise of the popular media and to the popularity of folk-derived ensembles such as the modern *mariachi*

canción romántica
Mexican tradition of the nineteenth-century romantic song

canción trovadoresca
Cuban genre created by singer-composers of Santiago de Cuba

canções praieiras
Afro-Brazilian fisherman's or beach songs

candombe (also *charanda, ramba*)
(1) Argentine entertainment dance; (2) Uruguay, a Brazilian-derived relgious cult

Candomblé
(1) Afro-Brazilian religion in Bahia; (2) Argentine variant of Afro-Brazilian religion observed in place of Batuque; (3) Candomblé de Caboclo, Afro-Brazilian religion in Sergipe

cantaor (also *cantador*)
Person who memorizes Puerto Rican *décimas* in order to sing them

cantos de nana
Mexican coddling songs

cantoria
Brazilian folk singing usually involving improvised duel, also known as *desafio*

capoeira
(1) Afro-Brazilian game-fight dance; (2) capoeira Angola, Afro-Brazilian traditional dance of possibly Angolan origin; (3) Capoeira regional, Afro-Brazilian innovative form developed by Mestre Bimba

capoeiristas
Afro-Brazilian couples of (usually) male dancer-fighters in *capoeira*

carabiné
Dominican Republic imitation dance of nineteenth-century occupying Haitian soldiers

carachacha (also *carraca, quijada*)
Idiophone, scraped or struck, that is made from the lower jawbone of an ass, mule, or a horse

caracol
Conch-shell trumpet

carangueijo
Brazilian circular social dance of many variants, especially popular along border areas of Uruguay

cargo
During patronal festivals, the musician's role of service to the community to placate the gods and ensure the well-being of the people

carimbó
Afro-Brazilian popular dance from Pará

Carnaval
"Carnival," secular celebration prior to Lent in Brazil and throughout most of Hispanic America

cartas anuas
Annual reports made by each Jesuit province to the Jesuit general in Rome

cascabeles
Argentine metal bell jingles

cashua taki
Inca line dance

catá
(1) Stick used to hit the body of the longdrum in the Dominican Republic; (2) Cuban idiophone made from hollowed-out log and struck with two sticks

cateretê (also *catiretê*)
Brazilian social dance genre found in rural areas

cavalaria
Afro-Brazilian rhythmic pattern

cavaquinho
Four-stringed treble guitar used in Brazil, mostly for *choro* and *samba* music

caxixí
Afro-Brazilian basket rattle, played by the same musician who plays the *berimbau*

cencerro
(1) Cuban metallic idiophone, similar to a bell with no clapper; (2) Bolivian bronze llama bells

chacarera
Argentine social dance performed during *jineteada*

chac-chac
In Grenada and Trinidad and Tobago, gourd-constructed rattle

cha-cha-chá
Cuban genre created by Enrique Jorrin during the 1950s

chamamé
Argentine polka-derived social dance performed during a *jineteada*)

changüí
Cuban genre belonging to the *son* family

charanga (also *charanga típica,* or *charanga francesa*)
Cuban ensemble combining piano, violin, and flute with percussion

charango
In the Andes of Argentina, Bolivia, and southern Peru, a small guitar made of wood or an armadillo shell with eight to fifteen metal or nylon strings tuned in five courses

charm
1990s Brazilian popular music form

charrasca
Venezuelan ridged idiophone scraped with a stick

chéquere (also *shekere*)
Cuban rattle of African origin, with external beaded net rattles

chicha
(1) Argentine popular alcoholic drink made from *algarrobo* tree; (2) distinctly Peruvian variant of *cumbia* that creolized the Colombian *cumbia* rhythms with highland *huayno* melodies (also *cumbia andina*)

chilena
(1) Chilean couple dance, with Afro-Hispanic rhythms and Spanish stanzas, related to the *zamacueca* and the *cueca* of the coast of Peru and Chile; (2) Mexican regional style of the Costa Chica, along the Pacific coast of Oaxaca and Guerrero states

chillador
"Screamer" in Spanish, in the Andes (especially northern Chile) a small guitar (like a *charango* but smaller) of five or six courses made of wood or armadillo shell)

chimbangueles
A set of four to seven Afro-Venezuelan conical drums whose single skins are tightened by hoops and wooden wedges

chino
"Humble servant" in Quechua, Chilean dancers who honor the Virgin and who are the oldest type of dancing group comprised of miners in Chilean patronal festivals

chiquit
Bolivian special dance for initiation and marriage ceremonies, and the name for a gourd rattle that accompanies it

chiriguano
(1) Bolivian tradition of panpipes subdivided into three different groups tuned to the octave (also *chiriwanu*); (2) in the Andes and Paraguay, the name for an Indian culture (also *Chiriwano*)

chirimía
(1) In Bolivia, Guatemala, Mexico (among Purépecha, Maya, and Nahua especially), and parts of Peru, an oboe-type instrument of early Spanish colonial importation played by native Americans or *mestizos*

chirisuya
Type of oboe played in highlands of the Peruvian departments of Lima, Huancavelica, and Ayacucho

chopí
Paraguayan folk couple dance

chordophone
"String sounder," a musical instrument whose sound comes from the vibrations of a stretched string

choro
(1) Brazilian dance music ensemble; (2) Afro-Brazilian musical genre based on polka-*maxixe* rhythm

chorões
"Weepers," Brazilian strolling street musician-serenaders)

chulas
Brazilian song texts of *samba de viola*

chumba
Guatemalan erotic dance

ch'unchu
Bolivian caricature dance

chuqila
(1) Bolivian ritual vicuña-hunt dance; (2) Bolivian vertical end-blown notched flute

churu
Conch-shell trumpet in Amazonas

cifra
Argentine traditional *pampa* musical form performed during *jineteada*

cinco
"Five," (1) Venezuelan small guitar with five strings; (2) *cinco de seis cuerdas,* Venezuelan small guitar with six strings; (3) *cinco y medio,* Venezuelan small guitar with "five and a half" strings

ciranda
Brazilian children's game-song genre

clarín
(1) In Cajamarca, Peru, a long cane side-blown tranverse trumpet in Peru); (2) a long valveless, transverse wooden or cane trumpet in Peru

clave
"Key," (1) Cuban rhythm consisting of 3 + 2 or (reverse clave) 2 + 3; (2) *claves,* in Cuba and other Latin American regions, two hardwood dowels struck together to mark the clave or basic meter

coco
(1) Afro-Brazilian coconut dance; (2) *côco-de-décima,* Afro-Brazilian dance based ten-line stanza song structure; (3) *côco-de-embolada,* Afro-Brazilian dance based on tongue-twisting song form; (4) *côco-de-ganzá,* Afro-Brazilian shaker dance

cofradía
"Confraternity," (1) Roman Catholic religious brotherhood founded for African slaves and their descendants; (2) Guatemalan Indian prayer house

coliseos
Open theaters that were venues of Peruvian music in 1970s in Lima

columbia

Cuban music and dance genre belonging to the *rumba* family

combo

Cuban name given musical ensembles toward the end of the 1950s

comparsa

Cuban characteristic dance in Carnaval

comuncha

Ayacucho guitar tuning pattern (E–B–G–D–B–G) used primarily to play peasant *huaynos* in E minor

conchero

Nahua dance accompanied by armadillo-shell guitar, also called by the same name

congo

(1) Also *congada*, Brazilian dramatic dance group that combines African and Iberian influences; (2) *congos*, ensemble music of the Brotherhood of the Holy Spirit of Villa Mella

conjunto

"Ensemble," (1) throughout Spanish-speaking Americas, a musical ensemble that performs folk music

contradanza

Cuban genre with French origins, belonging to the *danzón* family

contrato

High voice part of Venezuelan *tonos* ensemble

copla

"Couplet," Spanish-derived narrative musical genre from Chile, Colombia, and other Hispanic-American countries

copla de carnaval

Chilean "Carnaval couplet," main musical genre of the Atacameño Carnaval

corneta

"Cornet," Andean animal-horn lip-concussion aerophone

corpophone

"Body sounder," the body used as a musical instrument by striking or popping a body part (or parts), such as a hand clap, thigh slap, and so on

Corpus Christi

Annual Catholic festival and liturgical holiday in honor of the Eucharist, June 15

corrido

Narrative song genre of Chile and Mexico

coyolli

Náhuatl name for idiophone rattle made of clay, copper, dried fruit, gold, and nutshells

criolismo

"Creolism," (1) a mixing of African and European cultural traits; (2) referring to European descendants born in the New World

criolla

"Creole," Cuban urban genre with rural themes belonging to the *canción* family

criollo

"Creole," (1) originally, a black born in the New World, as opposed to an African brought from Africa (2) later applied to anyone born in the colonies; (3) more recently applied to a person, a behavior, a music, a style, or some other element that displays or promotes the distinctive traditions, sentiments and customs of the culture of coastal Peru

criollos

Whites, Spanish-Americans

cronistas

"Chroniclers," early Spanish or Portuguese writers

cuarteada

Argentine couple dance named after carried hindquarter of sacrificed animal

cuarteta

"Couplet," four-line Puerto Rican poem

cuarteto

Pop music from Córdoba, Argentina

cuatro

"Four," (1) four-stringed small guitar originally from Venezuela and diffused to Colombia, Grenada, Trinidad, and other regions close to Venezuela); (2) Puerto Rican ten-stringed guitar with double courses; (3) *cuatro y medio*, Venezuelan small guitar with "four and a half" strings

cuíca

Single-headed Brazilian friction membranophone used in *samba*, sounded by rubbing a short stick attached to and protruding from the bottom of the drum skin into the wooden or metal body

cuicalli

Aztec formal schools that included music education

culeado

Guatemalan women's *punta* dance**cumaco**

Large African-derived drum of Venezuela

cumbia

Colombian and Panamanian genre of Caribbean music, existing in both rural and urban forms, the latter popular throughout Latin America's Pacific rim regions from Chile to Central America and Mexico

cunculcahue

Argentine musical bow

curbata

In the Venezuelan longdrum ensemble, the short drum that is paired with the *mina*

cururu

Musical or dance style in Brazil

dakoho

Warao dance or entertainment song

dansaq

Scissors dance in Ayacucho, Peru

danza

"Dance," Cuban genre belonging to the *danzón* family, part of the evolution of the *contradanza*

danzón

Cuban instrumental dance genre created by Miguel Failde in 1879; the national dance of Cuba

danzonete

Cuban genre belonging to the *danzón* family)

décima

(1) Spanish and Hispanic-American song containing ten-line stanzas, eight syllables per stanza, and a particular rhythm scheme; (2) sung genre for courtship or expression of religious and social commentary

decimilla

"Little décima," same as *décima* but with six syllables per line

deculturation

Loss of culture without the implication of the replacement of it by another

desafío

Iberian song duel; see *cantoria*

dholak

Guyanese drum for popular music

diablada (also *diabladas*)

"Deviled," Bolivian Carnaval and patronal festival devil dance and dancers

diana mbajá

Dawn trumpet signal to begin patronal feast days in Paraguay

discante

Alternative Venezuelan name for *cuatro*, a four-stringed small guitar

distal

In organology, the portion of the musical instrument farthest from the mouthpiece

doble

"Double," (1) Argentine dance; (2) combination of a smaller and a larger Chiapan *marimba*

domingacha

Small Peruvian diatonic harp with pear-shaped sound box

ehuru

Warao double-headed hourglass-shaped drum with skins of howler monkeys and a snare on one end, played with one stick

el pilón

Venezuelan large mortar and pestle used during grain pounding songs

electrophone

"Electronic sounder," a musical instrument whose sound is produced by a vibration or action made by electronic means

embolada

Brazilian "tongue-twister" song genre performed by dueling singers accompanying themselves on *pandeiro* or *ganzá* (257)

encomienda

System by which land and peasants were governed by Spanish landlords

erke

(1) Bolivian animal-horn single-reed-concussion aerophone; (2) small trumpet made from a single cow or bull horn; (3) *erque*, Argentine very long lip-concussion aerophone made from cane

erkencho (also *erquencho*)

Argentine single-reed-concussion aerophone without finger holes

escapularios

Profane musical performance given by blacks during religious festivities in colonial Mexico

escobillero

Acrobatic dancer in Argentine *candombe*

escola de samba

Brazilian "*samba* school," urban *samba* group for Carnaval

espinela

Ten-line structure of *décima*

estilo

"Style," Argentine traditional *pampa* musical form used during a *jineteada*

estudiantina

"Student ensemble," (1) group of musicians playing instrumental music with Spanish-derived instruments, especially common in Colombia and Peru, and in late-nineteenth-century Cuba (see also *lira*, *rondalla*, *tuna*); (2) ensemble in Puno that includes guitars, *charangos*, mandolins, and accordion

falsa

High voice part of Venezuelan *tonos* ensemble

fandango

(1) Venezuelan predecessor of the *joropo*; (2) Brazilian generic term for a dance event

favela

Brazilian hillside slums

festejo

Afro-Peruvian form often interrupted at phrase endings by a sudden pause or long, held pitch

festivales de folklore

Argentine "folkloric festivals," annual revivalistic competitions and exhibitions of song and dance

fiesta

"Party," (1) celebration of the feast of a patron saint of the town, according to the Catholic calendar; (2) occasion for communal sharing of foods, drinking, dancing, music making, and merriment; see index under festivals

flauta

"Flute," common Spanish term for cane or bamboo transverse flute, usually with six finger holes

flawta

Bolivian duct flute

Florentine Codex

Nahua early colonial codex by Fray Bernardino Sahagún

FM Tango

A 1990s Argentine radio station dedicated exclusively to *tango*

folia

Brazilian ensemble that goes from house to house, singing, playing instruments, and collecting donations for popular Catholic festivals, such as the *folia de reis*, "festival of kings" (Magi) around Christmas

forró

Brazilian social dance music

fotuto

Archaic Colombian gourd, shell, or wooden trumpet

fricote

Brazilian Carnaval dance music

fuga

"Flight," (1) a type of faster coda in Andean music; (2) Afro-Peruvian musical appendage used as a lively closing section; (3) in Andean music, a contrasting theme in a faster tempo, usually a *huayno* following a *yaraví*

fulia

Drum-accompanied Venezuelan responsorial song genre

furruco

Single-headed Venezuelan friction membranophone sounded by rubbing a long stick attached to and protruding from the top of the drum skin

gafieiras

Brazilian large dance halls patronized by the urban popular classes

gagá

Haitian-derived ensemble in the Dominican Republic, and the Dominican term for Haitian *rara*

galerón

Venezuelan dance music genre

galopa

"Gallop," Paraguayan outdoor fast dance consisting of two contrasting musical sections: a polka and a syncopated section

galoperas

Paraguayan women "dancers" who dance to fulfill religious vows

ganzá

Brazilian shaken metal tube filled with beans, seeds, shells or other material

garaón (also *garawung*)

(1) *Garífuna* single-headed, conical drum in Guatemala; (2) *garaón primera*, the smaller drum of the set; (3) *garaón segunda*, the larger drum of the set

gato

"Cat," (1) Argentine social dance performed during a *jineteada*; (2) *gato polqeado*, fusion of German polka and Argentine *gato*

gaucho

A rural-dwelling nativist, traditionalist, or cowboy of the *pampa* region of Argentina; also found in Uruguay and in the southern state of Rio Grande do Sul, Brazil

gayumba

Central African–derived earth bow in the Dominican Republic

ginga

Brazilian swaying motion, common to *capoeira*

glorias

Argentine unaccompanied religious songs

glosa

"Gloss," Spanish term for four-stanza *décima*

golpe

"Hit," (1) Venezuelan dance music genre; (2) *golpes*, Brazilian *capoeira* dance figures

gozos

Argentine "praises" or unaccompanied religious songs

guaguancó

Cuban couple-dance genre belonging to the *rumba* family

guaiá

Brazilian rattle

guajira

"Rural peasant," (1) Cuban genre belonging to the *canción cubana* family; (2) *guajira-son*, Cuban genre which combines elements of the *guajira* and the *son*

gualambau

Guaraní term for a musical bow similar to the Brazilian *berimbau*

guamo

Conch-shell lip-concussion aerophone used by the pre-Columbian inhabitants of Cuba and Puerto Rico

guaracha

Cuban genre belonging to the *son* family

guaránia

National song genre tradition of Paraguay, created in 1925 by José Asunción Flores

guarura

Venezuelan conch-shell trumpet

guayo

"Grater," Cuban and Dominican metal rasp like the gourd *güiro*, played with a metal scraper (also *güira*)

guía

"Guide," lead singer of Venezuelan *tonos* ensemble

güiro

"Gourd," perhaps of native or Afro-Cuban or Puerto Rican origin; (1) a scraped gourd idiophone with inscribed grooves or notches, found throughout the Caribbean, Central America, and parts of Mexico; (2) in Cuba, also a shaken gourd rattle with a net of beads outside the gourd

guitarra

"Guitar," Spanish term for six-stringed (usually nylon, but also metal in some rural areas of Latin America) plucked or strummed lute chordophone with hourglass shape (*violão* in Brazil); numerous variants exist with the same name; see index under chordophones

guitarrilla (also tiple)

"Little guitar," (1) Guatemalan rare five-stringed guitar with gourd as resonator; (2) Bolivian deep-bodied guitar tuned in five courses

guitarrón
"Large guitar," (1) Mexican bass lute with rounded back, used in mariachi; (2) guitar in Peru, used for bass lines; (3) very large guitar in rural Chile, with up to 25 strings

gunyei
Guatemalan courting songs

guyrambau (also *lambau, mbarimbau*)
Large mouth bow found among the Mbyá

habanera
"From Havana," (1) Cuban genre belonging to the *canción cubana* family; (2) Brazilian dance form featuring dotted rhythm

habi-sanuka
Small Warao container rattle of calabash with wooden spiked handle

Hallelujah
Guyanese syncretic religion of some native Americans living in the savannah

"Hanacpachap Cussicuinin"
Four-part polyphonic piece published in Quechua by the Franciscan Juan Pérez Bocanegra in Lima, 1631

harawi (also *haraui*)
Pre-Columbian Incan nostalgic monophonic love song from which the Peruvian *yaraví* is possibly derived

harawiq
Group of Andean elder women who sing *harawi* in high-pitched, nasal voices

haylli
Call-and-response harvest song in ancient Peru

hebu
Warao ancestor spirit which can cause illness

hebu mataro
Large Warao container rattle made from a calabash with a wooden spiked handle

hekunukabe
Warao ductless vertical flute made from plant stalk

heresemoi
Warao conch-shell end-blown lip-concussion aerophone

herranza
Marking of animals in the Andes, a context for ritual music making

hoa
Warao prayerful song for curing illnesses

hoarotu
"Owner of hoa," Warao shaman in charge of the western cosmic realm

hocket
Borrowed European term meaning "interlocking parts," often referring to the alternating manner of playing panpipe halves in the Andes or *vaksin* trumpets in Haiti

hornada
"Batch" or "ovenful," medley of Venezuelan revueltas or pasajes

huancar
Inca drum

huapango
Mexican variety of the *son*

huapanguera (also *guitarra quinta*)
deep-bodied Mexican guitar with eight strings in five single and double courses

huaylas
Harvest ritual song genre of the central Andes of Peru

huayno (also *wayno*), (1) central Andean dance in fast duple meter with free choreography consisting of two musical phrases in periodic form (aabb); (2) native American–derived (Quechua) Peruvian fast duple-meter song and dance form featuring long-short-short rhythmical pattern; (3) the most popular highland Peruvian song form, used to transmit narrative texts; (4) *huayño*, Bolivian (Aymara) orthography for dance in duple meter

huéhuetl
Nahua large, single-headed, cylindrical, hollowed-out log drum, also used by the Maya

huilacapiztli
Nahua ceramic globular aerophone

ialorixá
Brazilian female temple leader in Candomblé

iamuricuma
Ceremony in the Xingú region of Brazil

idiophone
"Self-sounder," a musical instrument whose sound is produced by the vibration of the hard qualities of the entire instrument itself

ijexá
Afro-Bahian culture associated with Candomblé

ilê
Yoruba "house" or "temple" in Cuban Santería

illacu
Guatemalan shell rattles strung around calves of dancers

ingá
Afro-Peruvian novelty circle dance

ipála
Bolivian special wedding feast song

ira
"Leader" in Aymara, one of the halves (male) of the *siku* (and several other) double-unit panpipe in the central Andes (counterpart of *arca* female half, "follower")

irki
Bolivian animal-horn single-reed-concussion aerophone

isimoi
Sacred Warao heteroglottal single-reed-concussion aerophone without finger holes

iúna
Afro-Brazilian rhythmic pattern

jantarka
Bolivian two-tone pipe played by women during Carnaval

jarabe
Mexican *son* intended especially for dancing

jarana
(1) Mexican guitar (also *guitarra de golpe*) in a variety of

shapes, sizes, courses, and strings; (2) Mexican couple dance resembling the Spanish jota in choreography and meter of its music; (3) Afro-Peruvian musical duel related to the *marinera* of Lima (*marinera limeña*) and which functions as a competition (*contrapunto*) between singers (referred to as *canto de jarana* or *just jarana*)

jarocho
   Mestizo culture of Veracruz, Mexico

jhañjh
   Trinidadian cymbals in the *tassa* ensemble

jíbaros
   "Country folk" of Puerto Rico

jineteada (also *jineteada y doma*)
   Argentine spectacle organized by traditionalist societies, local municipal authorities, or merchants, featuring traditional music and dance

jitarrón
   Flat-backed *charango*-like instrument played during rainy season in southern Peru and northern Bolivia

jongo
   Afro-Brazilian social dance

Jopará
   The widespread language mixture of Guaraní and Spanish in Paraguay

Jordanites
   Members of an African-, Catholic-, and Protestant-derived syncretic religion of Guyana

jota
   Spanish song and dance form using compound duple meter and *hemiola* or *sesquiáltera* (6/8 + 3/4), from which the *cueca* and other American forms may have developed

Jovem Guarda
   (1) Originally a São Paulo television program 1965–1969; (2) *jovem guarda*, a generic term for *iê-iê-iê* (from the Beatles' "Yeah! Yeah! Yeah!"), early Brazilian rock and roll

juey
   Puerto Rican "crab" dance choreography

julajula
   Large panpipes of La Paz and northern Potosí departments, Bolivia

kalenda (also *calenda*)
   Caribbean variations on West African stick fight–dance with musical accompaniment

karaoke
   "Empty orchestra," in Japanese; recorded pop and folk music minus the singer, a type of "sing-along" to cassette tapes and videos, introduced by Japanese immigrants and popular in South America

kasamintu
   Bolivian special tuning

kashwa (also *cachiua*)
   Cheerful song–circle dance genre of pre-Columbian Andean origins, performed by young, single men and women and usually associated with nocturnal harvest rituals

k'epa
   Inca trumpet

kepu
   Conch-shell trumpet in Andes

k'illpa
   Bolivian animal fertility ritual

k'ojom
   Guatemalan cylindrical, double-headed drum

kokyu
   Bowed shamisen-type lute played by people of Japanese ancestry in South America

koten
   Okinawan classical music, performed by musicians of Okinawan heritage in Argentina, Brazil, and Peru

koto
   Thirteen-stringed Japanese zither, played by musicians of Japanese heritage in Argentina, Brazil, and Peru (*kutu* in romanized Okinawan orthography)

krywá
   Cane tube, open on both ends, into which the player hums, played exclusively by women among the Aché-Guayakí of Paraguay

kultrún
   Mapuche single-headed, kettle-shaped membranophone played with one stick by the *machi* shaman

kuraqkuna
   Bolivian community authority who may sponsor fiestas

la batalla
   "The battle," a Venezuelan stick dance

ladainhas
   "Litanies," a *capoeira* song repertoire in Brazil

Ladinos
   (1) Guatemalan urbanites whose primary language is Spanish; (2) sixteenth-century Spanish-speaking Christians of African descent brought from Spain to the Dominican Republic

lambada
   Brazilian adaptation of *carimbó* popular dance form

lancers
   English social dance derived from the quadrille

landó
   Afro-Peruvian song and dance form with a syncopated accompaniment and an underlying (4 + 2)/4 time, said to have come from the Brazilian *lundú*

laud
   "The lute," Cuban Spanish-derived (*la'ud*) twelve-stringed chordophone

laures
   Venezuelan sticks (also *palos*) beaten on the side of the wooden-bodied *mina* drum

lawatu
   Bolivian duct flute

lê
   Afro-Brazilian smallest *atabaque* drum

lemesidi
Guatemalan Christian songs for liturgical use at Mass or prayer services

lichiwayu (also *lechewayo*, *lichiguayo*)
Bolivian notched end-blown flute

liku
soprano-register *siku*

loncomeo (also *lonkomeo*)
Mapuche rhea imitation dance by young boys

lundu
Early Brazilian song type derived from Afro-Brazilian folk dance

lunfardo
Dialect used by the social classes among which the Argentine *tango* originated

llamada
Clarín call in northern Peru that tells the workers at a *mita* to begin working

llamado
Guatemalan rhythm-establishing introduction

machi
Mapuche shaman

machitún
Mapuche shamanic ceremony involving treatment for physical and spiritual illnesses

maculelê
Afro-Brazilian fighting dance

Macumba
Afro-Brazilian syncretic religion in Rio de Janeiro

mãe de santo
Female temple leader in Brazilian *Candomblé*

maestro del coro
Guatemalan maestro cantor or sacristan specialist in ritual music

malembe
"Softly," "slowly," or "take it easy," a Venezuelan rhythm and song

mambo
Cuban genre of the 1950s belonging to the *danzón* family and created by Orestes López

mampulorios
Alternative Venezuelan name for children's wakes (*velorios de angelito*)

mañanitas
"Early morning," nearly synonymous with *serenata*, it includes a range of songs that vary greatly according to local custom in Mexico

mandolina
"Mandolin," either flat-backed Latin type or round-backed West Asian–type plucked chordophone of the lute family, found throughout Spanish-speaking America

mangulina
Dance of the southwest Dominican Republic

maraca
Gourd or calabash container rattle in Cuba, Mexico, Puerto Rico, Venezuela, and many regions of the Americas; usually played in pairs (*maracas*)

mare-hoa
Warao prayerful song sung by a man to entice a woman

maremare
"Happy-happy," a panpipe played by Venezuelan creoles

mariachi
The most nationally prominent folk-derived Mexican musical ensemble since the 1930s, usually consisting of guitars, *vihuela*, *guitarrón*, violins, trumpets, and singers

Marian antiphon
Antiphonal song in praise of the Virgin Mary

marimba
(1) African-derived term for a xylophone found in Central America, Colombia, Mexico, and Venezuela; (2) African-derived lamellophone in Dominican Republic (see also *marímbola*)

marímbola (also *marímbula*)
African-derived lamellophone consisting of a large wooden box with tuned metal strips or tongues that are plucked, presently from Cuba, Dominican Republic, and Puerto Rico, and rarely in Colombia, Venezuela, and other Caribbean regions

marinera
Peruvian dance and song genre in composite 6/8 and 3/4 *sesquiáltera*/*hemiola* meter, related to the *cueca* (see *zamacueca*) and given its name in honor of seamen who died in the War of the Pacific (1879–1883)

marujada
Dramatic Afro-Brazilian dance

matraca
(1) Argentine *criollo* gourd rattle; (2) Bolivian cog ratchet; (3) Brazilian rattle; (4) in El Salvador, Guatemala, and Honduras, a long-handled wooden ratchet of Arab origin that is swung above the head

maxixe (also **maxixi**)
Brazilian fast syncopated dance music form from the late nineteenth century until today

mayohuacán
Wooden slit drum in ancient Caribbean

mayura
Bolivian minor fiesta sponsor

mbaraká
(1) Guaraní large spiked shamanic rattle with stones or seeds inside; (2) Guaraní term for guitar

Mbyá (*also Mbiá*)
Native American culture of Misiones Province, Argentina, and parts of Paraguay (Mbiá is Argentine orthography; Mbyá is Paraguayan orthography)

melê
Afro-Brazilian friction rattle used primarily in the southern region; also *afoxé* and *cabaça*

membranophone
"Skin sounder," a musical instrument whose sound comes from the vibrations of a stretched membrane

membrillo
Guatemalan branch hoop around which skin is wrapped for drums

merengue
(1) Dominican Republic music and dance genre that has become a symbol of national identity; (2) *merengue redondo*, "round *merengue*," based on circular movements of the dancing couple; (3) *meringue*, a song and dance genre in Haiti

mesa
"Table," Spanish term in Peru for a shaman's altar on which ritual objects are placed, including musical instruments

mestizo
Spanish term for an individual of Iberian and native American cultural heritage

mestre capoeira
Brazilian "*capoeira* master"

milonga
Argentine song form and possible inspiration for the *tango*

mimby´ (also *mimb'y*)
Generic Guaraní term for flute

mina
(1) Venezuelan (Barlovento region) set of two single-headed drums; (2) the longer drum of the set paired with the shorter *curbata*; the *mina* is the membranophone that plays improvisations

minuete
Instrumental genre practiced by the Mexican Chichimec and the Pame and unrelated to the European minuet

minyō
Japanese "folk song"; a popular genre among people of Japanese ancestry in South America

mita (also *minka, minga*)
Communal work effort in the Andes, often accompanied by music

moçambique
Brazilian dramatic dance ensemble similar to the *congada*

moda
Generic term for a secular song genre both in Brazil and Portugal

moda-de-viola
"Manner of the viola," traditional song form of rural south-central Brazil, sung as a duet to the accompaniment of two violas

modinha
Brazilian sentimental song genre, originating in late colonial period

montuno
Final section of a Cuban *son*, featuring improvisation

moráo
Ten-tubed panpipe of the lowland Moré of Bolivia

morenada
Bolivian black slave Carnaval dance

moros y cristianos
"Moors and Christians," dance reenactment of Moorish and Spanish battles, popular throughout Hispanic America

mpintín
Puerto Rican rhythmic pattern derived from the Ghanaian Akan

Muharram
Muslim festival that is also celebrated by Hindus in Surinam

muhusemoi
Warao deer-bone vertical flute with slightly notched mouthpiece and three finger holes

mukululu (also *mullu*)
End-blown notched flute with four finger holes from the department of La Paz, Bolivia

murga
Urban Carnaval song genre in Argentina

música caipira
Brazilian "country music"

música criolla
"Creole music," in Venezuela, music of Venezuelan peasants of mixed ancestry

música cuartetera (also *música de cuarteto*)
Popular Argentine dance music genre from Córdoba

música de proyección folklórica
Argentine style based on urbanization of traditional rural repertoires

música regional
"Regional music"

música tropical
"Tropical music," Afro-Caribbean dance-musics, particularly *salsa, cumbia*, and *merengue*, popular throughout the Americas

musiñu (also *mohoceño*)
Bolivian vertical (small one) and transverse (large one) duct flute

musiqueada
Long Paraguayan *serenata*

mutirães
Brazilian voluntary work parties

Nago
A variety of Brazilian Candomblé

nahanamu
Warao harvest festival

ngere
Suyá word that refers to "ceremony," "song-dance,", and a specific genre of singing in unison

nimaj k'ojom
Guatemalan large cylindrical, double-headed drum

Niño Alcalde
Argentine "Child Mayor," theatrical veneration of baby Jesus

novena
Brazilian Catholic religious ritual in honor of a saint or religious figure

novenaria (also *última novena*)

"Novenary," (1) a Colombian and Guatemalan adult wake; (2) *novenario de difuntos*, Puerto Rican nine-day period of prayer for the dead

nquillatún (also *nillipún, nguillatún*)

Mapuche annual fertility/harvest rite, a seasonal ritual during which the *trutruka* is played)

nueva canción

"New song," (1) generic name for pan-Latin American neofolk-protest music that began in Chile in the 1960s and spread throughout the Americas (also *nueva canción chilena*); (2) Dominican Republic counterpart of the Cuban *nueva trova*; (3) *nueva canción latinoamericana*, "new Latin American song," 1970s movement that influenced politically conscious university students

nueva trova

"New song," name given in 1972 to the *canción protesta* "protest song" created in 1967 and which began in Cuba

ñemongaraí

Mbyá annual ceremony related to the ripening of fruits

omichicahuaztli

Náhuatl name for rasp made from the bone of a deer or deerlike animal

oratorio

Profane musical performance given by blacks during religious festivities in colonial Mexico

orisha

"Deity" in Yoruba (Cuban spelling), in Cuban Santería

orixá

"Deity" in Yoruba (Brazilian spelling), in Brazilian Candomblé

orocoveño

Puerto Rican *seis* from Orocovis

orquesta típica

"Typical orchestra," (1) Argentine tango ensemble of 1920s; (2) ensemble in the central Peruvian highlands consisting of saxophones, clarinets, violins, and harp; (3) Mexican ensemble in which musicians clad in folkloric garb played regional melodies on a conglomeration of (primarily stringed) instruments; (4) instrumental ensemble characteristic of Cuban music

orum

The supernatural world in Yoruba cosmovision

Ox Tum

Modern-day Guatemalan version of *Baile del Tun*

Pachamama

"Mother earth" in the ancient Andes

pagoda

A 1980s variety of Brazilian samba song form with racial and political overtones

pa'í

Mbyá religious leader

pai de santo

Brazilian male temple leader in Candomblé

paichochi

Bolivian seed pod rattles worn on the ankles

pailas

Cuban paired membranophones with cylindrical metal bodies

Pajelança

Brazilian religion in Amazon region

pala (also *mano*)

Puerto Rican pegbox

Palchasqa (also *Palcha*)

Q'ero alpaca fertility ritual in February or March

palo

"Stick" or "log," (1) a long drum and its music, associated with saints' festivals in Dominican Republic; (2) *palos*, Venezuelan stick idiophone played on the side of wooden-bodied drums

pampa corneta

In Huancavelica, Peru, a vertical wooden trumpet three to four meters long and made of wood

panalivio (also *penalivio*)

Afro-Peruvian sarcastic song of lament about slavery

pandeiro

Brazilian frame drum like a tambourine with jingles

pandero

Puerto Rican and Dominican round frame drum, like a tambourine but without jingles

pañuelo

"Handkerchief," Puerto Rican and Chilean dance choreography that includes swinging a handkerchief

parang

In Grenada and Trinidad and Tobago, a Venezuelan-inspired Christmas caroling tradition accompanied by a *cuatro* guitar; the term is a corruption of *parranda*

parranda (also *zarabanda*)

(1) Christmas caroling and strolling musical tradition in Spanish-speaking America; (2) Guatemalan music used for celebrating in the streets

parrilladas

Paraguayan steakhouses that feature folk music

partido-alto

Afro-Brazilian folklike dance of primarily black connoisseurs

pasada (see *zapateo criollo*)

pasaje

Venezuelan dance music genre

pasante

Bolivian festival ritual sponsor

patronal festivals

Saint's-day celebrations (see index under festivals)

payador

Usually plural, *payadores*, Argentine challenge singers and vocal ensembles

pelota tatá

Activity of the Paraguayan fiesta de San Juan in which a tar- and kerosene-soaked ball of rags is set afire and kicked through the crowd

peña
(1) Private gathering place or touristic nightclub where folk musicians perform in certain Andean cities where tourism is common; (2) in Argentina, a regionally oriented meeting place for dance and food celebrations; (3) *peñas folklóricas*, restaurants featuring neofolkloric music

perico ripiao
Nickname of small *merengue típico* "typical merengue" dance music group in Dominican Republic, from the name of a 1930s brothel

Petro
Creole deities of Vodou in Haiti, possibly with some Taíno influence

phalahuita
Transverse flute of Peru

phutu wankara
Bolivian long double-headed cylindrical drum

picong
Verbal duels or "wars" between calypsonians in Trinidad and Tobago

pie forzado
"Forced foot," style of *décima* in which the tenth line is always the same

pífano (also *pifano*)
Bolivian cane transverse flute with six finger holes

pifülka (also *pifilka*)
Mapuche single- and double-tubed ductless flute (panpipe type), usually made from wood but also from cane

pinkullu (also *pincollo, pinculu, pincullo, pincullu, pingollo, pinkillo, pinkuyllo, pinquillo*)
(1) Central Andean end-blown duct flute of Quechua origin with three to eight finger holes; (2) *pinculu*, Q'ero vertical, notched, six-note edge aerophone

pirkansa
Ceremonial communal construction music in the Peruvian Andes

pito (also *pitu*)
"Pipe," in Spanish, cane or wooden transverse flute with six finger holes in southern Peru and Panama

plena
(1) Puerto Rican dance-music genre of the twentieth century, featuring commentary about work and events; (2) work song in Dominican Republic; (3) rap in Panama

polca
European-derived social dance, from "polka"

Popol Vuh
"Book of Counsel," manuscript from shortly after the Spanish Encounter from the Quiché region of central Guatemala

porfia
Brazilian musical duel

porteños
Argentine "people of the port" or Buenos Aires residents

posadas
(1) Guatemalan pre-Christmas singing, mainly a Ladino custom; (2) Mexican musical reenactment of Mary and Joseph's journey to Bethlehem

prato-e-faca
Brazilian "plate-and-knife" idiophone

programas folklóricos
"Folk programs," on several commercial radio stations in Lima, Peru)

promeseros
Paraguayan festival pilgrims, both children and adults, often dressed as the patron saint

proximal
In organology, the portion of the musical instrument closest to the mouthpiece

pulilitu
Bolivian animal-horn trumpet

pululu
Bolivian cane and gourd trumpet

punta
(1) Social-commentary song-and-dance form, the most popular and best-liked Garifuna genre; (2) *punta* rock, Guatemalan fusion of traditional *punta* and rock rhythms

punteado
Spanish term for a picking technique on guitar and other lute-type stringed instruments

punto
(1) Cuban instrumental accompaniment related to the *punto campesino*; (2) *punto campesino* (also *punto guajiro*), Cuban song genre associated with the rural population, usually based on the *décima* and its many variants

purahéi as´y
"Mournful polka," song on the subject of the Passion

purrum
Mapuche *nquillatún* song of supplication by women

pututu
Small Andean valveless trumpet made from a single cow horn, conch shell, or piece of tin

qawachan
In Peru, contrasting theme in a faster tempo

q'ayma
"Insipid," referring to old Bolivian Carnaval melodies

qia
"Leader" in the *julajula* Bolivian double-unit panpipe tradition

qina, qina-qina (also *kena, quena*)
End-blown notched flute of the Aymara

quadrilha
Brazilian social dance or square dance generally associated with festivals in honor of Saint John during the June celebrations in the northeast

quena
Spanish orthography of an Aymara name for a notched, end-blown edge aerophone of the central Andes (see also *kena, qina*)

quijada (also *charrasga*)

African-derived scraped or struck idiophone made from the defleshed, dried jawbone of an ass, mule, or horse

quinceaños

"Fifteen years old," *quinceañera*, girl's fifteenth birthday celebration in Paraguay, a time for music making

quinjengue

Afro-Brazilian drum

quintillas

Five-line *copla*

quinto

Smallest and highest pitched of the Cuban *tumbadora* membranophones

quioscos

Bandstands set up in town plazas across Mexico in the late 1800s

quipa (also *qquepa*)

Conch-shell trumpet in Ecuador and Peru

quirquincho (also *charango*)

"Armadillo," small guitar made from the shell of an armadillo

quitiplás

Venezuelan bamboo stamping tubes

rabeca

Brazilian three- or four-stringed bowed lute

rabel

Also *violín*, European-derived stringed instrument originating in the Renaissance period, usually with three strings, played with a bow like a violin

Rabinal Achí

"Hero of Rabinal," modern-day version of Guatemalan *Baile del Tun*)

Radio Fantástica

Argentine FM radio station dedicated exclusively to *música tropical*

Radio Tropical

Argentine FM radio station dedicated exclusively to *música tropical*

rama

Advent tradition in Mexico that involves groups of adults and/or children going from home to home asking for gifts

ranchera

(1) Mexican song genre; (2) Argentine social dance performed during a *jineteada*; (3) Uruguayan name for the European *mazurca* dance; (4) *rancherías*, slums in Venezuela

rap

Consciência Afro-Brazilian "consciousness rap," an alternative to hip-hop

rapá

Hunting bow that the Aché-Guayakí use as a musical instrument by placing it over a resonating container

rasgueado

Spanish term for chordal strumming with fingernails on guitar and lute-type stringed instruments

rasguido doble

Argentine polka-derived social dance

rêco-rêco

Brazilian percussive gourd, metal, or door-spring scraper used in a wide variety of musical traditions

redoblante

Venezuelan side drum

redondo

Venezuelan double-headed drum with internal hourglass shape

reducciones

"Reductions," mission towns established by the Jesuits in Paraguay that were important for music teaching and performance by native Americans

reggae resistência

Brazilian 'resistance' synthesis in reggae form

repicador

Puerto Rican first *bomba* drum

repique

Brazilian high-pitched snare drum

requinto

(1) Small acoustic lead-guitar type of El Salvador and Paraguay; (2) a four-stringed, narrow-bodied Mexican guitar, plucked with plectrum fashioned from cow horn or a plastic comb; (3) a Bolivian duct flute

resbalosa

Amorous Peruvian song and dance with syncopated rhythm, choreography based on *escobillada*

responsero

Singer of funeral songs in Peru

retreta

Sunday performances by municipal, paramilitary, or military bands in Costa Rica, the Dominican Republic, and Uruguay

revuelta

Alternate name for Venezuelan *joropo* music

reyes (Span.); *reis* (Port.)

"Kings," Christmas music tradition about the Magi or Three Kings throughout Latin America

rezadores

Folk priests in the Dominican Republic

rock en español

Rock sung in Spanish

romance

Spanish colonial narrative song form or ballad, usually sung solo or with guitar accompaniment

roncadora

"Snorer," a cane or wooden duct flute played in pipe-and-tabor fashion in Ancash Department, Peru

ronda

Circular children's game of Mexico

rosario

"Rosary," (1) *rosario a la Santa Cruz*, Puerto Rican sung rosary to the Holy Cross; (2) *rosario cantado* (also *rosario cantao*), sung version of the rosary (3) *rosario de promesas*, Puerto Rican sung "rosary of promises"

rosario para los muertos
Puerto Rican sung rosary ritual for "good living" or "dying"

rum
Largest Brazilian *atabaque* drum

rumba
(1) Nineteenth-century origin suburban Cuban musical genre at popular secular festivals); (2) Cuban-derived couple-dance genre

rumpi
Middle-sized Brazilian *atabaque* drum

salsa
Afro-Hispanic Caribbean song and dance form rooted in the Cuban *son* that is today an internationalized form no longer associated with any one country

salsódromos
Nightclubs for dancing *salsa* in Peru

salve
(1) Unaccompanied song with religious texts diffused by missionaries since colonial times, sung at *velorios*; (2) *Salve con versos*, in the Dominican Republic a *salve* with added text in an Africanized musical style; (3) *Salve Regina*, "Hail, Holy Queen," Spanish translation of a Marian antiphon

samba
Brazilian generic term designating a wide variety of secular musical and dance styles of African origin

sambay
Guatemalan erotic dance

San Blás/Saint Blaise
Patron saint of Paraguay, whose feast is celebrated on 3 February

San Juan/Saint John
Patron saint throughout the southern Americas, whose feast is celebrated on 24 June

sanshin
Three-stringed plucked Okinawan lute, similar to the shamisen but covered with snakeskin, played by people of Okinawan heritage in Argentina, Brazil, Paraguay, and Peru

Santa Maria
Afro-Brazilian rhythmic pattern

São Bento grande
Brazilian *berimbau* rhythmic pattern in *capoeira*

São Bento pequeno
Brazilian *berimbau* rhythmic pattern in *capoeira*

sarambo
Velación genre based on the *zapateo* in the Dominican Republic

saya
Afro-Bolivian tropical syncretic music style, formerly a praise song)

seguidilla
(1) Cuban genre belonging to the *punto campesino* family; (2) Chilean genre with seven-line *cueca* stanzas of five and seven syllables with fourth line repeated

seis
(1) Puerto Rican lively genre for dancing; (2) Puerto Rican

slow genre for singing; (3) small Venezuelan guitar with six strings

sekeseke
Warao rustic violin played for entertainment

señalada
Mapuche annual animal-branding gathering)

sencilla
Chiapas *marimba*

serenata
"Serenade," song genre frequently performed at Paraguayan *quinceañeras*; a courting, congratulatory, or devotional serenade

sesquiáltera
Spanish-derived dual meter consisting of superimposed 3/4 and 6/8, often with alternation or hemiola

seti
Guatemalan square dance

sewei
Sacred Warao strung rattle

sextilla
Six-line *copla*

shak-shak
Common *maracas* in Guyana

shakuhachi
A Japanese notched vertical bamboo flute with four finger holes and one thumb hole, played by some people of Japanese descent in Brazil

shamisen
Three-stringed plucked Japanese lute played by people of Japanese heritage in Brazil and Peru

siku (also *sico*, pl. *sikuri* in Bolivia)
Double-unit panpipe consisting of six to eight (or more, seventeen tubes in Bolivia) closed cane tubes per half, requiring two people to play one instrument by interlocking the music; see also *arca*, *ira*

sikuri
Sets or groups of *siku* or *siku* performers

sinsiru
Bolivian bronze llama bells

sirínus
"Sirens," Andean supernatural beings, often carved into the necks of *charangos* and harps

sísira
Container rattle of the main Garifuna shaman in Belize (also *magara*) and Guatemala (also *chíchira*)

soca
Modern, danceable Trinidadian calypso form, short for soul *calypso*

socabón (also *socavón*)
Simple Peruvian guitar accompaniment to the *décima*

son
Pl. *sones*, diminutive *sonecito*, possibly from sonar "to sound," (1) Mexican genre at the core of most regional musical styles oriented toward accompanying social dance, with vigorous, marked rhythm and fast tempo

(2) Cuban song tradition forming a type of *son* complex of genres

sonador
Second Puerto Rican *bomba* drum

sonaja
"Timbrel" in Spanish, in Honduras and Guatemala, a spiked vessel rattle made from a gourd or calabash and filled with tiny stones or dried seeds

suila jut'as
Bolivian heavy metal spurs attached to wooden sandals

surdo
Brazilian double-headed drum used in many genres of Brazilian music, especially *samba* and its derivatives

taieira
Dramatic Afro-Brazilian dance

takipayanaku
Bolivian insult songs sung by in-laws at weddings

takuapú
Indigenous Paraguayan bamboo stamping tube that may have strings of rattles attached, played by women

tambor
Generic Spanish masculine term for a membranophone that exists in a variety of forms, either single- or double-headed, the latter often with a snare (see index under membranophones)

tambora
(1) Generic Spanish feminine term for membranophone (see index under membranophones); (2) small, double-headed drum in *merengue* ensembles in Dominican Republic; (3) long, tubular Afro-Venezuelan membranophone made from a log with two skin heads, played with one stick while held between the knees

tamborazos zacatecanos
Zacatecas-style Mexican pop bands

tamborero
In Peru, a person who beats on the box of the harp as a percussion instrument while a harpist plucks the strings (see *golpeador*)

tambores
Ensemble music of the Brotherhood of San Juan Bautista of Baní, Dominican Republic

tamborim
Brazilian membranophone consisting of a small metal or plastic frame covered with a tight skin, played with a stick

tamborita
Small, double-headed drum of Mexico, played on the head and rim with two drumsticks

tambú (also *barí, tambu*)
Brazilian large conical single-headed membranophone

tamunangue
Venezuelan suite of dances and music

tango
(1) Argentine music and dance of nostalgia and melancholy that originated and is centered around Buenos Aires;

(2) *tango canción*, Argentine sung *tango* genre; (3) *tango característico*, Argentine characteristic sung *tango* genre; (4) *tango romanza*, Argentine instrumental *tango* genre

tanguería
"*Tango* place," in Argentina and Uruguay, a recent Argentine name for *tango* dance club or locale where live *tango* performers can be heard

tanpura (also *tambura*)
Among East Indian communities in Guyana, Surinam, Trinidad and elsewhere, a plucked lute that provides a drone

taquirari
Bolivian tropical syncretic song style from the lowlands

tara
Bolivian broad flute timbre dense with harmonics

tarka
In Bolivia, northern Chile, and southern Peru, a square or slightly hexagonal-shaped (cross-section) wooden duct flute with a hoarse sound

tarkeada
Music played by a *tarka* ensemble

tassa
Kettle-type drum played with a stick at Muslim festivals and weddings in Guyana and Trinidad and Tobago

tayil
Mapuche women's ritual/healing/lineage song

tekeyë (also *tekeya, wanna*)
Yekuana ritual bamboo idioglottal clarinet with internal reed (*suruídey*), played in pairs, one male and the other female

temple
"Tuning," (1) *temple arpa*, Peruvian guitar tuning pattern (E–B–F#–D–A–F#), used to play a *huayno* or *carnaval* in B minor; (2) *temple diablo*, Peruvian guitar tuning pattern (E–C–G–D–BB–G), used to play a *yaraví* in G minor

tenor (also *tenorete*)
Low voice part in Venezuelan *tonos* ensemble

teponaztli (also *teponaztle*)
In Mexico, a Nahua hollowed-out log slit drum or gong with H-shaped incision on its top

tepuzquiquiztli
Náhuatl name for a wooden or metal trumpet

tequina
Taíno responsorial song leader

terno
Brazilian generic term for dramatic dance groups that perform during patron saint festivals

terokará
Board zither with five to seven strings played by the Aché-Guayakí of Paraguay

terreiro
"Temple" in Afro-Brazilian syncretic religious worship in Brazil, Paraguay, and Uruguay

timbalada
Afro-Bahian popular genre featuring timbre of the *timbal*

timbales

Cuban membranophones constructed from metal semi-spherical containers

tinka

Carnival season celebration in Peru in which a llama is sacrificed and ritual offerings are buried for the deities

tinku

"Encounter," Bolivian ritual fighting

tinquy

Q'ero intercommunity popular social dance

tinya

Small Quechua handheld double-skin frame drum in Peru

tiple

"Treble," a medium-sized twelve-stringed, four-course guitar from Colombia

tlapitzalli

Náhuatl name for an end-blown clay or bone tubular duct flute with four holes

toá

Bolivian beeswax friction idiophone

toada

"Tune," Brazilian generic term for song, often associated with popular Catholicism (analogous to Spanish *tonada*)

Todos Santos

"All Saints" or "All Souls" celebration in Americas

tonada

Spanish for "tune," (1) 1990s Chilean song performed by one or two singers in parallel thirds in nasal style; (2) characteristic Cuban melody in the *punto guajiro*; (3) *tonada de toros* "song of the bulls," improvisatory verbal genre associated with ritualized alms collection in the Dominican Republic

tonadillas escénicas

In Mexico, short, simple dramas, replete with new *sones* and other local melodies

tondero

Amorous dance and song of northern coastal Peru, related to *marinera* and *zamacueca*

tono

"Tune" or "tone," European-derived polyphonic song of Venezuela

topamiento de comadres

Argentine female funeral dramatization ceremony of Carnaval

toque

"Hit" in Spanish and Portuguese, Brazilian rhythmic pattern played on *berimbau* and other struck instruments in Latin America

toro

"Bull," *toro candil*, costume in Paraguay in which one or two men play the part of a fighting bull

tortuga

"Turtle," in Guatemala and elsewhere, a tortoiseshell gong struck on its ventral side with a bone, stick, or antler)

totuma

The fruit of a calabash tree used to make rattles, trumpets, and other implements among the Kogi, Warao, and other northern South American cultures

trabajo

"Work," in northern Peru, the working period signified by the music of a *clarín*

tres

"Three," Cuban six-stringed, double-coursed chordophone of the guitar family

tres-dos

Cuban medium-sized tumbadora membranophone

triste

Term in Bolivia and Chile for a nostalgic song musically analogous to the Peruvian *yaraví*

trompa

Venezuelan jaw's harp (Jew's harp), a plucked lamellophone

trompeta de caracol

Spanish term for conch-shell trumpet

tropa

"Troop," Andean group of musicians who play a single type of instrument, such as a *tropa de sikuri*

tropical

"Tropical," *tropicália*, Brazilian avant-garde music movement

trova

"Tune," any song of late nineteenth-century to present, performed by Cuban singers called *trovadores*

trutruka

Mapuche long end-blast cane trumpet with oblique mouthpiece and attached cow-horn bell

tumba

(1) *tumba dominicana*, a *velación* of the northern part of the Dominican Republic; (2) *tumba francesa*, former ballroom dance of Santiago de Cuba, now performed only by national troupes

tumbadora

Cuban membranophone (basically a *conga* drum) that originated in the context of the *rumba*

tun

(1) In Guatemala, a Quiché Maya hollowed-out log slit drum with H-shaped incision on its top (see *teponaztli*, *tunkul*); (2) also *tum*, "cylinder," a long Guatemalan wooden or metal valveless trumpet

tunkul

In Guatemala, a Yucatec Mayan hollowed-out log slit drum with H-shaped incision on its top; see *teponaztli*, *tun*

turas

Venezuelan vertical male-female flute pair

uaricza araui

Pre-Columbian antiphonal dance of men and women sung by the Inca and a choir of young virgins

ukuku

Q'ero costumed representation of a bear during Corpus Christi

Umbanda

Twentieth-century Afro-Brazilian syncretic religion that borrows from aspects of Candomblé, Macumba, and spiritism

umbigada

"Navel," choreographic stomach bump of many Afro-Brazilian circle dances)

ungá (see *ingá*)

vallenato

(1) Rural musical and dance genre from northern Colombia, featuring accordion, drum, and scraper; (2) urban musical and dance genre derived from its rural counterpart of northern Colombia, adding bass, guitar, conga, and cowbell to the rural accordion, drum, and scraper

valona

Décima-based genre in several parts found in the *tierra caliente* (hotlands), the western part of the state of Michoacán, Mexico

vals

"Waltz," (1) romantic vocal music genre in triple meter found throughout Spanish-speaking America; (2) Argentine social dance performed during *jineteada*; (3) *vals criollo*, "creole waltz," most popular national music form in coastal Peru with origins in the mid-eighteenth century Viennese waltz)

valseao (also *valseado*)

"Waltzed" choreography

velación

Individually sponsored, annually recurring saint's celebration in the Dominican Republic

veladas

Evening performances among some members of the African-descended population in the Dominican Republic

velorio

(1) Nightlong celebration or night watch to honor a saint or the Holy Cross in many Spanish-speaking countries; (2) *velorio de angelito*, Paraguayan wake of a young child); (3) *velorio de cruz* "wake of the Cross" in Venezuela

verso

"Verse," Dominican Republic ritual song genre for saints in folk Catholicism

viola

Brazilian plucked and strummed chordophone of Iberian origin (from *viola de mão*, "of the hand"), with five double courses of ten or twelve metal strings

violão

"Guitar" in Portuguese, the common Iberian six-stringed guitar

virgen

"Virgin," (1) a Roman Catholic icon symbolizing the Virgin Mary, but under different names, the object of devotion in many patronal festivals in the Americas; (2) Virgen de Guadalupe, religious festivity for all the Mixtec; (3) Virgen de Punta Corral, Argentine procession attracting largest number of faithful in province of Jujuy

Vodou

Haitian religion of African heritage characterized by spirit possession

vodú

Dominican Republic ceremony of African heritage characterized by spirit possession; Spanish for Vodou

waka pinkillu

Bolivian "bull flute," three-holed duct flute played in pipe-and-tabor fashion

waka tokori

Bolivian dance that caricatures a Spanish bullfight

wak'rapuku (also *wakrapuku*)

Quechua Peruvian circular or spiral valveless trumpet made of cattle-horn sections or pieces of tin, often played in pairs of *primera* and *segunda*

walina

Fixed song genre exclusively associated with the ceremonial cleaning of irrigation channels in Peru

Wancay

Bolivian mythical singer who has the mouth of a toad

wandora

Warao *cuatro*, small, four-stringed chordophone

wanka (also *uanca*)

Bolivian love song

wankara

(1) Bolivian small handheld single-headed cylindrical drum with snare; (2) Bolivian large cylindrical double-headed drum

warime

Ceremony among the Venezuelan Pairoa

wayno (also *huayno*)

In Quechua, *huayño* in Aymara, central Andean fast dance in duple meter, featuring a long-short-short rhythmic pattern

wisiratu

"Owner of pains," Warao priest-shaman in charge of upper cosmic realm

xácara

Brazilian ballad of Iberian origin

Xangô

Portuguese orthography of Shango, a religion in Pernambuco, Brazil

xul

(1) Guatemalan vertical duct flute, open at the distal end; (2) Maya transverse cane flute with beeswax diaphragm and membrane mirliton

yankunu

Probably from "John Canoe," Guatemalan masked warrior dance

yaraví

From Quechua *hawarí*, in Peru a slow, lyrical and often emotional song section

zabumba
  Brazilian large, double-headed bass drum
zamacueca (also *zambacueca*)
  Amorous pantomime dance of courtship in nineteenth-century Peru, a predecessor of the *marinera*
zambomba (also *zambudia*)
  Guatemalan small friction drum
zampoña
  A Spanish term principally used in Chile for the panpipe, especially the double-unit panpipe or *siku* played in northern Chile; see *siku*
zampoñero
  Bolivian large stone statue of panpipe player of c. A.D. 1000

zapateado (see *zapateo*)
zapateo
  From Spanish *zapateado* "foot stamping," (1) dance technique involving rhythmic striking of heels and toes against the floor or each other; (2) Bolivian energetic stamping dance; (3) rural Cuban dance associated with the *punto campesino*; (4) *zapateo criollo*, Peruvian dance genre based on foot stamping
zarabanda
  Popular music in highland Guatemala
zubac
  Guatemalan bone flute

A Guide to Publications

REFERENCE WORKS

Beaudet, Jean-Michel. 1982. "Musiques d'Amérique Tropicale. Discographie analytique et critique des Amérindiens des basses terres." *Journal de la Société des Américanistes* 68:149–203. Paris: Musée de l'Homme.

Béhague, Gérard. 1975. "Latin American Music: An Annotated Bibliography of Recent Publications." *Yearbook for Inter-American Musical Research* 11:190–218.

———. 1993. "Latin America." In *Ethnomusicology: Historical and Regional Studies*, ed. Helen Myers, 472–494. New York: Norton.

Black Music Research Journal. Chicago: Colombia College.

Chase, Gilbert. 1972 [1962]. *A Guide to the Music of Latin America.* 2nd ed. Washington, D.C.: Pan American Union.

Ethnomusicology (*Journal of the Society for Ethnomusicology*). "Current Bibliography," "Discography," and "Filmography" listed under "Americas." Three issues per year.

Fairley, Jan. 1985. "Annotated Bibliography of Latin-American Popular Music with Particular Reference to Chile and to Nueva Canción." In *Popular Music*, Vol. 5, "Continuity and Change," 305–356. Cambridge: Cambridge University Press.

Figueroa, Rafael, comp. 1992. *Salsa and Related Genres: A Bibliographical Guide.* Westport, Conn.: Greenwood.

Lotis, Howard, comp. 1981. *Latin American Music Materials Available at the University of Pittsburgh and at Carnegie Library of Pittsburgh.* Pittsburgh: Center for Latin American Studies.

Kuss, Malena. 1984. "Current State of Bibliographic Research in Latin American Music." *Fontes Artis Musicae* 31(4):206–228.

Latin American Music Review. Austin: University of Texas Press.

Myers, Helen. 1993. "The West Indies." In *Ethnomusicology: Historical and Regional Studies,* ed. Helen Myers, 461–471. New York: Norton.

Nava, Teresa. 1994. "Dance Research in Mexico." *Dance Research Journal* 26(2): 73–78.

The New Grove Dictionary of Music and Musicians, ed. Stanley Sadie. 20 vols. London: Macmillan.

Rodríguez, David J., et al. 1993. *Puerto Rico Recordings in the Archive of Folk Culture.* Washington, D.C.: Archive of Folk Culture, American Folklife Center.

Schaeffer, Nancy. 1995. "Directory of Latin American Films and Videos: Music, Dance, Mask, and Ritual." *Latin American Music Review* 16(2): 221–241.

Schechter, John M. 1987a. "A Selected Bibliography on Latin American Urban Popular Music." In *Latin American Masses and Minorities: Their Images and Realities*, Vol. 2, ed. Dan C. Hazen, 679–682. Madison: Seminar on the Acquisition of Latin American Library Materials (SALALM), Memorial Library, University of Wisconsin.

———. 1987b. "Doctoral Dissertations in Latin American Ethnomusicology: 1965–1984." In *Latin American Masses and Minorities: Their Images and Realities*, Vol. 2, ed. Dan C. Hazen, 673–678. Madison: Seminar on the Acquisition of Latin American Library Materials (SALALM), Memorial Library, University of Wisconsin.

———. 1987c. "Selected Bibliographic Sources in Latin American Ethnomusicology." In *Latin American Masses and Minorities: Their Images and Realities*, Vol. 2, ed. Dan C. Hazen, 664–672. Madison: Seminar on the Acquisition of Latin American Library Materials (SALALM), Memorial Library, University of Wisconsin.

Smith, Ronald R. 1972. "Latin American Ethnomusicology: A Discussion of Central America and Northern South America." *Latin American Music Review* 3(1):8–14.

Stevenson, Robert. 1975. *A Guide to Caribbean Music History*. Lima: Ediciones CULTURA.

Steward, Julian H., ed. 1949. *Handbook of South American Indians*. 5 vols. New York: Cooper Square Publishers.

Thomas, Jeffrey Ross. 1992. *Forty Years of Steel: An Annotated Discography of Steel Band and Pan Recordings, 1951–1991*. Westport, Conn.: Greenwood Press.

Thompson, Donald. 1982. *Music Research in Puerto Rico*. San Juan: Office of the Governor of Puerto, La Fortaleza, Office of Cultural Affairs.

Thompson, Donald, and Annie F. Thompson. 1991. *Music and Dance in Puerto Rico from the Age of Columbus to Modern Times: An Annotated Bibliography*. Metuchen, N.J.: Scarecrow Press.

GENERAL

Aretz, Isabel. 1977. *América Latina en su música*. México, D.F.: Siglo XXI.

———. 1991. *Historia de la etnomusicología en América Latina: Desde la época precolombina hasta nuestros dias*. Caracas: Ediciones FUNDEF-CONAC-OEA.

Aretz, Isabel, Gérard Béhague, and Robert Stevenson. 1980. "Latin America." In *The New Grove Dictionary of Music and Musicians*, ed. Stanley Sadie. London: Macmillan.

Béhague, Gérard. 1973. "Latin American Folk Music." In *Folk and Traditional Music of the Western Continents*, ed. Bruno Nettl, 2nd ed., 179–206. Englewood Cliffs, N.J. Prentice-Hall.

———. 1979. *Music in Latin America: An Introduction*. Englewood Cliffs, N.J.: Prentice-Hall.

———, ed. 1994. *Music and Black Ethnicity: The Caribbean and South America*. Miami: University of Miami North-South Center.

Béhague, Gérard, and Bruno Nettl. "Afro-American Folk Music in North and Latin America." In *Folk and Traditional Music of the Western Continents*, ed. Bruno Nettl, 2nd ed., 207–234. Englewood Cliffs, N.J.: Prentice-Hall.

Bergman, Billy. 1985. *Hot Sauces: Latin and Caribbean Pop*. New York: Quarto Books.

Boiles, Charles Lafayette. 1978. *Man, Magic and Musical Occasions*. Columbus, Ohio: Collegiate Publishing, Inc.

Card, Caroline, et al. 1978. *Discourse in Ethnomusicology: Essays in Honor of George List*. Bloomington: Indiana University Archives of Traditional Music (Ethnomusicology Publications Group).

Courlander, Harold. 1976. *A Treasury of Afro-American Folklore*. New York: Crown Publishers.

den Otter, Elisabeth. 1994. *Pre-Colombian Musical Instruments: Silenced Sounds in the Tropenmuseum Collection*. Amsterdam: KIT/Tropenmuseum.

Díaz Roig, Mercedes. 1990. *Romancero tradicional de América*. Serie Estudios de linguística y literatura, 19. México, D. F.: Colegio de México.

Escobar, Luís Antonio. 1985. *La Música Precolombina*. Bogotá: Universidad Central.

Figueroa, Frank M. 1994. *Encyclopedia of Latin American Music in New York*. St. Petersburg, Fla.: Pillar Publications.

Garofalo, Reebee. 1992. *Rockin' the Boat: Mass Music and Mass Movements*. Boston: South End Press.

Greenberg, Joseph. 1987. Language in the Americas. Stanford: Stanford University Press.

Hernández, Clara, ed. 1982. Ensayos de Música Latinoamericana. Havana: Casa de las Americas.

Heth, Charlotte, ed. 1992. *Native American Dance: Ceremonies and Social Traditions*. Washington, D.C.: National Museum of the American Indian.

Jackson, Irene V., ed. 1985. *More than Drumming: Essays on African and Afro-Latin Music and Musicians*. Prepared under the auspices of the Center for Ethnic Music, Howard University. Contributions in Afro-American and African Studies, 80. Westport, Conn.: Greenwood Press.

Kuss, Malena, ed. 2004. *Music in Latin America and the Caribbean, An Encyclopedic History, Vol. 1, Performing Beliefs: Indigenous Peoples of South America, Central America, and Mexico*. Austin: University Press of Texas.

———. 2006. *Music in Latin America and the Caribbean, An Encyclopedic History, Vol. 3, Latin America—Islands of History: From Precontact Civilizations to 20th-Century Composition*. Austin: University Press of Texas.

———. Forthcoming. *Music in Latin America and the Caribbean, An Encyclopedic History, Vol. 4, Urban Popular Musics of the New World*. Austin: University Press of Texas.

List, George, and Juan Orrego-Salas, eds. 1967. *Music in the Americas. Inter-American Music Monograph Series*, Vol. 1. Bloomington: Indiana University Research Center in Anthropology, Folklore, and Linguistics.

Loukotka, Cestmír. 1968. *Classification of South American Indian Languages*. Reference Series, Vol. 7. Los Angeles: Latin American Center, University of California, Los Angeles.

Manuel, Peter. 1988. *Popular Musics of the Non-Western World: An Introductory Survey*. New York: Oxford University Press.

Marre, Jeremy, and Hannah Charlton. 1985. *Beats of the Heart: Popular Music of the World.* New York: Pantheon.

Moreno Fraginals, Manuel, ed. 1984 [1977]. *Africa in Latin America: Essays on History, Culture, and Socialization,* trans. by Leonor Blum. New York: Holms and Meier.

Mukuna, Kazadi wa. 1990–1991. "The Study of African Musical Contributions to Latin America and the Caribbean: A Methodological Guideline." *Bulletin of the International Committee on Urgent Anthropological Research* 32–33:47–49.

Murphy, Joseph M. 1994. *Working the Spirit: Ceremonies of the African Diaspora.* Boston: Beacon Press.

Olsen, Dale A., Daniel E. Sheehy, and Charles A. Perrone, eds. 1987. "Music of Latin America: Mexico, Ecuador, Brazil." In *Sounds of the World.* Washington, D.C.: Music Educators National Conference. Three audio cassettes and study guide.

Olsen, Dale A., and Selwyn Ahyoung. 1995 [1989]. "Latin American and the Caribbean." In *Multicultural Perspectives in Music Education,* ed. William M. Anderson and Patricia Shehan Campbell, 2nd ed., 124–177. Reston, Va.: Music Educators National Conference.

Olsen, Dale A., and Daniel E. Sheehy. 1998. *South America, Mexico, Central America, and the Caribbean. Vol. 2. The Garland Encyclopedia of World Music.* New York: Garland.

Pineda de Valle, César, comp. 1994. *Antología de la marimba en América.* Guatemala: Librería Artemis-Edinter.

Primera Conferencia Interamericana de Etnomusicología. Unión Panamericana, Washington, D.C., February 1963.

Roberts, John Storm. 1979. *The Latin Tinge: The Impact of Latin American Music on the United States.* New York and Oxford: Oxford University Press.

———. 1998. *Black Music of Two Worlds,* 2nd ed. New York: Schirmer Books.

Robertson, Carol E., ed. 1992. *Musical Repercussions of 1492: Encounters in Text and Performance.* Washington, D.C., and London: Smithsonian Institution Press.

Schechter, John M. 1996. "Latin America/Ecuador." In *Worlds of Music: An Introduction to the Music of the World's Peoples,* ed. Jeff Todd Titon, 3d ed., 428–494. New York: Schirmer Books.

Slonimsky, Nicholas. 1945. *Music of Latin America.* New York: Thomas Y. Crowell.

Stevenson, Robert. 1968a. *Music in Aztec and Inca Territory.* Berkeley: University of California Press.

———. 1968b. "The African Legacy to 1800." *Musical Quarterly* 54/4: 475–502.

———. 1991. "Latin American Music Bibliography." In *Libraries History, Diplomacy, and the Performing Arts: Essays in Honor of Carleton Sprague Smith,* ed. I. J. Katz, 85–99. Stuyvesant, N.Y.: Pendragon Press.

Turino, Thomas. 1992. "Music in Latin America." In *Excursions in World Music,* ed. Bruno Nettl, 232–259. Englewood Cliffs, N.J.: Prentice Hall.

Whitten, Jr., Norman E., and John F. Szwed, eds. 1970. *Afro-American Anthropology: Contemporary Perspectives.* New York: Free Press.

SOUTH AMERICA

Abadía Morales, Guillermo. 1973. *La Música Folklórica Colombiana.* Bogotá: Universidad Nacional de Colombia.

———. 1991. *Instrumentos Musicales: Folklore Colombiano.* Bogotá: Banco Popular.

Alencar, Edigar de. 1965. *O carnaval carioca através da música.* 2 vols. Rio de Janeiro: Livraria Freitas Bastos.

———. 1968. *Nosso Sinhô do samba.* Rio de Janeiro: Civilização Brasileira Editora.

Almeida, Bira (Mestre Acordeon). 1986. *Capoeira–A Brazilian Art Form: History, Philosophy, and Practice.* Berkeley: North Atlantic Books.

Almeida, Raimundo Cesar Alves de. 1993. *Bibliografia crítica da capoeira.* Brasília: DEFER/GDF, Centro de Documentação e Informação Sobre a Capoeira.

Almeida, Renato. 1942. *História da Música Brasileira,* 2nd ed. Rio de Janeiro: F. Briguiet.

Alvarenga, Oneyda. 1982. *Música Popular Brasileira,* 2nd ed. São Paulo: Duas Cidades.

Alves, Henrique L. 1968. *Sua excelência o samba.* Palermo, Brazil: A. Palma.

Andrade, Mário de. 1928. *Ensaio sobre a Música Brasileira.* São Paulo: Martins.

———. 1933. *Compêndio de História da Música,* 2nd ed. São Paulo: Miranda.

———. 1963. *Música, Doce Música,* 2nd ed. São Paulo: Martins.

———. 1975. *Aspectos da Música Brasileira,* 2nd ed. São Paulo: Martins.

———. 1982. *Danças Dramáticas do Brasil,* 2nd ed., 3 vols. Belo Horizonte: Ed. Itatiaia.

———. 1989. *Dicionário Musical Brasileiro.* São Paulo: Editora da Universidade de São Paulo.

Añez, Jorge. 1968. *Canciones y Recuerdos,* rev. ed. Bogotá: Ediciones Mundial.

Appleby, David P. 1983. *The Music of Brazil.* Austin: University of Texas Press.

Araújo, Alceu Maynard. 1964. *Folclore Nacional.* 3 vols. São Paulo: Melhoramentos.

Araújo, Mozart de. 1963. A Modinha e o Lundu no Século XVIII. São Paulo: Ricordi Brasileira.

Archivo de Música Tradicional Andina. 1995. *Catálogo del Archivo de Música Tradicional Andina.* Lima: Pontificia Universidad Católica del Perú, Instituto Riva Agüero.

Aretz, Isabel. 1954. *Costumbres tradicionales argentinas.* Buenos Aires: Huemul.

———. 1967. *Instrumentos musicales de Venezuela.* Cumaná: Editorial Universitaria de Oriente.

————. 1970. *El Tamunangue*. Barquisimeto: Universidad Centro Occidental.

————. 1991. *Música de Los Aborígenes de Venezuela*. Caracas: Fundación de Etnomusicología y Folklore.

Aretz-Thiele, Isabel. 1946. *Música tradicional argentina*: Tucumán, historia y folklore. Buenos Aires: Universidad Nacional de Tucumán.

Arguedas, José María. 1957. *Singing Mountaineers: Songs and Tales of the Quechua People*. Austin: University of Texas Press.

————. 1975. *Formación de una Cultura Nacional Indoamericana*. México: Siglo XXI.

————. 1977. *Nuestra Música Popular y sus Intérpretes*. Lima: Mosca Azul y Horizonte.

————. 1989. *Canto Kechua*, rev. ed. Lima: Horizonte.

Arvelo Ramos, Alberto. 1992. *El cuatro*. Caracas: J. J. Castro Fotografía Infrarroja.

Ayala, María Ignez Novais. 1988. *No Arranco do Grito: Aspectos da Cantoria Nordestina*. São Paulo: Atica.

Ayestarán, Lauro. 1953. *La música en el Uruguay*, vol. 1. Montevideo: Servicio Oficial de Difusión Radioeléctrica.

————. 1967. *El folklore musical uruguayo*. Montevideo: Arca.

————. 1968. *Teoría y práctica del folklore*. Montevideo: Arca.

————. 1994. *Las músicas primitivas en el Uruguay*. Montevideo: Arca.

Aytai, Desiderio. 1985. *O Mundo Sonoro Xavante. Coleção Museu Paulista, Ethnologia*, Vol. 5. São Paulo: Universidade de São Paulo.

Bahiana, Ana Maria. 1980. *Nada Será Como Antes: A MPB dos Anos 70*. São Paulo: Perspectiva.

Barral, P. Basilio María de. 1964. *Los Indios Guaraunos y su Cancionero*. Madrid: Consejo Superior de Investigaciones Científicas, Departamento de Misionología Española.

Basso, Ellen B. 1985. *A Musical View of the Universe*. Philadelphia: University of Pennsylvania Press.

Bastien, Joseph W. 1978. *Mountain of the Condor. Metaphor and Ritual in an Andean Ayllu*. St. Paul, Minn.: West.

Bastos, Rafael Jose de Menezes. 1978. *A Musicológica Kamayurá*. Brasília: Fundação Nacional do Indio.

Baumann, Max Peter, ed. 1992. *Cosmología y música en los Andes*. Berlin: IITM.

Beaudet, Jean-Michel. 1983. "Les Orchestres de Clarinettes Tule des Wayãpi du Haut Oyapock (Guyane Française)." Ph.D. dissertation, Université de Paris X–Nanterre.

Becerra Casanovas, Rogers. 1990. *Reliquias de Moxos*. La Paz: PROINSA.

Béhague, Gerard. 1971. *The Beginnings of Musical Nationalism in Brazil*. Detroit Monographs in Musicology, 1. Detroit: Information Coordinators, Inc.

————. 1979. *Music in Latin America: An Introduction*. Englewood Cliffs, N.J.: Prentice-Hall, Inc.

Bermúdez, Egberto. 1985. *Los Instrumentos Musicales en Colombia*. Bogotá: Universidad Nacional de Colombia.

Biocca, Ettore. 1966. *Viaggi tra gli indi: Alto Rio Negro–Alto Orinoco. Appunti de un Biologo*, 4 vols. Rome: Consiglio Nazionale delle Ricerche.

Blérald-Ndagamo, Monique. 1996. *Musiques et danses Créoles au tambour de la Guyane Française*. Cayenne: Ibis Roque Editions.

Boettner, Juan Max. n.d. (ca. 1956). *Música y músicos del Paraguay*. Asunción: Autores Paraguayos Asociados.

Bolaños, César. 1981. *Música y Danza en el Antiguo Perú*. Lima: Museo Nacional de Antropología y Arqueología, Instituto Nacional de Cultura.

————. 1988. *Las Antaras Nasca*. Lima: Instituto Andino de Estudios Arqueológicos.

————. 1995. *La Música Nacional en los Medios de Comunicación Electrónicos de Lima Metropolitana*. Lima: Universidad de Lima, Facultad de Ciencias de la Comunicación (Cuadernos CICOSUL).

Borges, Bia. 1990. *Música popular do Brasil: Brazilian Popular Music*. São Paulo: B. Borges.

Brandão, Carlos Rodrigues. 1981. *Sacerdotes da Viola*. Petrópolis, Brazil: Vozes.

Browning, Barbara. 1995. *Samba: Resistance in Motion*. Bloomington: Indiana University Press.

Bureau du Patrimoine Ethnologique, ed. 1989. *Musiques en Guyane*. Cayenne: Conseil Régional de la Guyane.

Bustillos Vallejo, Freddy. 1982. *Bibliografía Boliviana de Etnomusicología*. La Paz: Instituto Nacional de Antropología.

————. 1989. *Instrumentos musicales de Tiwanaku*. La Paz: Museo Nacional de Etnografía y Folklore.

Caldas, Waldenyr. 1979. *Acorde na Aurora: Música Sertaneja e Indústria Cultural*, 2nd ed. São Paulo: Nacional.

————. 1985. *Introdução à Música Popular Brasileira*. São Paulo: Atica.

Cameu, Helza. 1977. *Introdução ao Estudo da Música Indígena Brasileira*. Rio de Janeiro: Conselho Federal de Cultura.

Campos, Augusto de. 1974. Balanço da Bossa e Outras Bossas. São Paulo: Perspectiva.

Cardozo Ocampo, Mauricio. *Mundo folklorico paraguayo*, 3 vols. Asunción: Editorial Cuadernos Republicanos.

Carpio Muñoz, Juan. 1976. *El Yaraví Arequipeño*. Arequipa: La Colmena.

Carvalho, José Jorge de. 1994. *The Multiplicity of Black Identities in Brazilian Popular Music*. Brasilia: Universidade de Brasilia.

Carvallo-Neto, Pablo de. 1964. *Diccionario del Folklore Ecuatoriano*. Quito: Editorial Casa de la Cultura Ecuatoriana.

————. 1971. *Estudios afros: Brasil, Paraguay, Uruguay, Ecuador*. Serie de Folklore–Instituto de Antropología e Historia, Universidad Central de Venezuela. Caracas: Instituto de Antropología e Historia, Facultad de Humanidades y Educación, Universidad Central de Venezuela.

Cascudo, Luís da Câmara. 1979. *Dicionário do Folclore Brasileiro*, 5th ed. São Paulo: Melhoramentos.

Castro, Donald S. 1991. *The Argentine Tango as Social History, 1880–1955: The Soul of the People*. Lewiston, N.Y.: E. Mellen Press.

Castro, Ruy. 1990. *Chega de saudade: A história e as histórias da Bossa Nova*. São Paulo: Companhia das Letras.

Céspedes, Gilka Wara. 1993. "Huayno, Saya, and Chuntunqui:

Bolivian Identity in the Music of 'Los Kjarkas.'" *Latin American Music Review* 14(1): 52–101.

Claro, Samuel, et al. 1994. *Chilena o cueca tradicional: De acuerdo con las enseñazas de Fernando González Maraboli.* Santiago: Ediciones Universidad Católica de Chile.

Coba Andrade, Carlos Alberto. 1981. *Instrumentos Musicales Populares Registrados en el Ecuador. Cultura Popular,* vol. 1. Otavalo, Ecuador: Instituto Otavaleño de Antropología.

———. 1985. *Danzas y Bailes en el Ecuador.* Quito: Ediciones Abya-yala.

———. 1992. *Instrumentos Musicales Populares Registrados en el Ecuador,* vol. 2. Quito: Ediciones del Banco Central del Ecuador, and Instituto Otavaleño de Antropología.

Collier, Simon. 1990. *The Life, Music, and Times of Carlos Gardel.* Pittsburgh: University of Pittsburgh Press.

Corrêa, Roberto Nunes. 1989. *Viola Caipira.* Brasília: Viola Corrêa.

Costa, Reginaldo de Silveira. 1993. *O caminho do berimbau: Arte, filosofia e crescimento na capoeira.* Brasília: Thesaurus Editora.

Crook, Larry Norman. 1991. "Zabumba music from Caruaru, Pernambuco: Musical style, gender and the interpenetration of rural and urban worlds." Ph.D. dissertation, University of Texas.

Dark, Philip. 1970. *Bush Negro Art.* London: Alec Tiranti.

Davidson, Harry C. 1970. *Diccionario Folklórico de Colombia. Música, Instrumentos y Danzas,* 3 vols. Bogotá: Banco de la República.

Delfino, Jean Paul. 1988. *Brasil Bossa Nova.* Aix-en-Provence: Édisud.

den Otter, Elisabeth. 1985. *Music and Dance of Indians and Mestizos in an Andean Valley of Peru.* Delft: Eburon.

Díaz Gainza, José. 1962. *Historia Musical de Bolivia.* Potosí: Universidad Tomás Frias.

Dicks, Ted, ed. 1976. *Victor Jara: His Life and Songs.* London: Elm Tree Books.

Dolabela, Marcelo. 1987. *ABZ do Rock Brasileiro.* São Paulo: Estrela do Sul.

Dolphin, Lynette, comp. 1991. *National Songs of Guyana.* Georgetown, Guyana: Department of Culture.

Domínguez, Luis Arturo. 1992. *Fiestas y danzas folklóricas en Venezuela.* 2nd ed. Caracas: Monte Avila Editores.

Efegê, Jota. 1978/79. *Figuras e coisas da música popular brasileira.* 2 vols. Rio de Janeiro: FUNARTE.

Fernaud, Alvaro. 1984. *El Golpe Larense.* Caracas: Fundación de Etnomusicología y Folklore.

Ferrer, Horacio. 1977. *El libro del tango.* 2 vols. Buenos Aires: Galerna.

Flores, Hilda Agnes Hübner. 1983. *Canção dos Imigrantes.* Porto Alegrel: Escola Superior de Teologia São Lourenço de Brindes, Universidade de Caxias do Sul.

Fuks, Victor. 1989. "Demonstration of Multiple Relationships between Music and Culture of the Waiãpi Indians of Brazil." Ph.D. dissertation, Indiana University.

Gallardo, Jorge Emilio. 1986. *Presencia africana en la Cultura de América Latina: Vigencia de los cultos afroamericanos.* Buenos Aires: Fernando García Cambeiro.

Garcilaso de la Vega, El Inca. 1961. *The Royal Commentaries of the Inca,* ed. Alain Gheerbrant. New York: Orion Press/Avon.

Garrido, Pablo. 1943. *Biografía de la Cueca.* Santiago: Ediciones Ercilla.

Godoy Aguirre, Mario. n.d. *Florilegio de la Música Ecuatoriana: La Música Popular en el Ecuador.* Vol. l. No city: Editorial del Pacífico.

Góes, Fred de. 1982. *O país do carnaval elétrico.* São Paulo: Editora Corrupio Comércio Ltda.

Goldfeder, Miriam. 1981. *Por Trás das Ondas da Rádio Nacional.* São Paulo: Paz e Terra.

González, Juan-Pablo. 1991. "Hegemony and Counter-Hegemony of Music in Latin America: The Chilean Pop." *Popular Music and Society* 15(2): 63–78.

González Torres, Dionisio M. 1991. *Folklore del Paraguay.* Asunción: Editora Litocolor.

Gradante, William J. 1991. "'¡Viva el San Pedro en La Plata!': Tradition, Creativity, and Folk Musical Performance in a Southern Colombian Festival." Ph.D. dissertation, University of Texas.

Gruszcynska-Ziólkowska, Anna. 1995. *El poder del sonido: El papel de las crónicas españolas en la etnomusicología andina.* Cayambe, Ecuador: Ediciones Abya-Yala.

Grebe, María Ester. 1980. "Generative Models, Symbolic Structures, and Acculturation in the Panpipe Music of the Aimara of Tarapaca, Chile." Ph.D. dissertation, Queen's University of Belfast.

Guardia Crespo, Marcelo. 1994. *Música popular y comunicación en Bolivia: Las interpretaciones y conflictos.* Cochabamba: U.C.B.

Guillermoprieto, Alma. 1990. *Samba.* New York: Knopf.

Guss, David M. 1989. *To Weave and Sing: Art, Symbol, and Narrative in the South American Rain Forest.* Berkeley: University of California Press.

d'Harcourt, Raoul, and Marguerite. d'Harcourt. 1925. *La Musique des Incas et ses Survivances.* Paris: Librairie Orientaliste Paul Geuthner.

———. 1959. *La musique des Aymaras sur les hauts plateaux Boliviens d'après enregistrements sonores de Louis Girault.* Paris: Societé des Americanistes, Musée de l'Homme.

d'Harcourt, Raoul, and Marguerite d'Harcourt. 1990. *La Música de los Incas y sus Supervivencias.* General translation from the French by Roberto Miro Quesada. Lima: Occidental Petroleum Corporation of Peru.

Harrison, Regina. 1989. *Signs, Songs, and Memory in the Andes: Translating Quichua Language and Culture.* Austin: University of Texas Press.

Herskovits, Melville J., and Frances S. Herskovits. 1969 [1936]. Suriname Folk-Lore. Columbia Contributions to Anthropology, Vol. 27, Part III. New York: AMS Press, Inc.

Hickmann, Ellen. 1990. *Musik aus dem Altertum der Neuen Welt: Archäologische Dokumente des Musizierens in präkolumbischen Kulturen Perus, Ekuadors und Kolumbiens.* Frankfurt am Main: Peter Lang.

Hill, Jonathan D. 1993. *Keepers of the Sacred Chants: The Poetics of Ritual Power in an Amazonian Society.* Tucson: University of Arizona Press.

Holzmann, Rodolfo, and José María Arguedas. 1966. *Panorama de la Música Tradicional del Perú.* Lima: Ministerio de Educación Pública, Escuela Nacional de Música y Danzas Folklóricas (Servicio Musicológico), y la Casa Mozart.

Holzmann, Rodolfo. 1986. *Q'ero, pueblo y música.* Lima: Patronata Popular y Porvenir, Pro Música Clásica.

Hurtado Suárez, Wilfredo. 1995. *Chicha Peruana: Música de los Nuevos Migrantes.* Lima: Eco-Grupo de Investigaciones Económicas.

Instituto Nacional de Musicología "Carlos Vega." 1988. *Instrumentos musicales etnográficos y folklóricos de la Argentina: Síntesis de los datos obtenidos en investigación de campo (1931–1988).* Buenos Aires: Instituto Nacional de Musicología "Carlos Vega."

Izikowitz, Karl Gustav. 1970. *Musical and Other Sound Instruments of the South American Indians: A Comparative Ethnographical Study*, rev. ed. East Ardsley, Wakefield, Yorks: S.R. Publishers Ltd..

Jara, Joan. 1984. *An Unfinished Song: The Life of Victor Jara.* New York: Ticknor and Fields.

Jijón, Inés. 1971. *Museo de Instrumentos Musicales "Pedro Pablo Traversari."* Quito: Casa de la Cultura Ecuatoriana.

Jiménez Borja, Arturo. 1951. *Instrumentos musicales del Perú.* Lima: Museo de la Cultura.

Koorn, Dirk. 1977. "Folk Music of the Colombian Andes." Ph.D. dissertation, University of Washington.

Labraña, Luis, and Ana Sebastián. 1992. *Tango, una historia.* Buenos Aires: Ediciones Corregidor.

Lange, Francisco Curt. 1966. *A Organização Musical durante o Período Colonial.* Actas do V Coloquio Internacional de Estudos Luso-Brasileiros, Separata do Vol. IV.

Lewis, J. Lowell. 1992. *Ring of Liberation: Deceptive Discourse in Brazilian Capoeira.* Chicago: University of Chicago Press.

Lisboa Júnior, Luiz Américo. 1990. *A presença da Bahia na música popular brasileira.* Brasília: MusiMed.

Liscano, Juan. 1973. *La Fiesta de San Juan El Bautista.* Caracas: Monte Avila Editores.

List, George. 1983. *Music and Poetry in a Colombian Village.* Bloomington: Indiana University Press.

Lopes, Nei. 1992. *O Negro no Rio de Janeiro e sua Tradição Musical: Partido-Alto, Calango, Chula e Outras Cantorias.* Rio de Janeiro: Pallas.

Lloréns, José Antonio. 1983. *Música popular en Lima: Criollos y andinos.* Lima: Instituto de Estudios Peruanos.

Mamani P., Mauricio. 1987. *Los Instrumentos Musicales en los Andes Bolivianos.* La Paz: Museo Nacional de Etnografía y Folklore.

Marcondes, Marcos Antonio, ed. 1977. *Enciclopédia da Música Brasileira: Erudita, Folclórica, Popular.* São Paulo: Editora Arte.

Margullo Osvaldo-Muñz, Pancho. 1986. *El rock en la Argentina.* Buenos Aires: Galerna.

Mariz, Vasco. 1983. *História da Música no Brasil*, 2nd ed. Rio de Janeiro: Civilização Brasileira.

Martín, Miguel Angel. 1991. *Del folclor llanero*, 2nd ed. Sante Fé de Bogotá: ECOE Ediciones.

Martins, Carlos A. 1986. *Música popular uruguaya 1973–1982: Un fenómeno de comunicación alternativa.* Montevideo: Ediciones de la Banda Oriental.

Máximo, Joao, and Carlos Didier. 1990. *Noel Rosa: Una biografía.* Brasília: Editora Universidade de Brasília.

McGowan, Chris, and Ricardo Pessanha. 1991. *The Brazilian Sound: Samba, Bossa Nova, and the Popular Music of Brazil.* New York: Billboard Books.

Mendonça, Belkiss S. Carneiro de. 1981. *A Música em Goiás*, 2nd ed. Goiânia: Editora da Universidade Federal de Goiás.

Menezes Bastos, R. J. de. 1978. *A Musicológica Kamayura: Para Uma Antropologia da Comunicação No Alto Xingu.* Brasília: FUNAI.

Meyer, Augusto. 1958. *Cancioneiro Gaúcho.* Porto Alegre: Globo.

Montoya, Rodrigo, Edwin Montoya, and Luís Montoya. 1987. *La Sangre de los Cerros: Antologia de la poesía quechua que se canta en el Perú.* Lima: CEPES, Mosca Azul Editores y UNMSM.

Moreno Andrade, Segundo Luis. 1923. *La Música en la Provincia de Imbabura.* Quito: Tipografía y Encuadernación Salesianas.

———. 1949. *Música y Danzas Autóctonas del Ecuador* (Indigenous music and dances of Ecuador). Quito: Editorial "Fray Jacobo Ricke."

———. 1972. *Historia de la Música en el Ecuador. Vol. 1: Prehistoria.* Quito: Editorial Casa de la Cultura Ecuatoriana.

Moura, Roberto M. 1986. *Carnaval: Da Redentora a Praça do Apocalipse.* Rio de Janeiro: Jorge Zahar.

Mukuna, Kazadi wa. 1979. *Contribuição bantu na música popular brasileira.* São Paulo: Global Editora.

Núñez Rebaza, Lucy. 1990. *Los Dansaq.* Lima: Instituto Nacional de Cultura, Museo Nacional de la Cultura Peruana.

Nyberg, John L. 1974. "An Examination of Vessel Flutes from Pre-Hispanic Cultures of Ecuador." Ph.D. dissertation, University of Minnesota.

Oliveira, Valdemar de. 1971. *Frevo, capoeira, e "passo."* Recife: Companhia Editora de Pernambuco.

Oliveira Pinto, Tiago de. 1991. *Capoeira, Samba, Candomblé: Afro-Brasilianische Musik im Recôncavo, Bahio.* Berlin: Museum für Völkerkunde Berlin.

Olsen, Dale A. 1980a. "Folk Music of South America–A Musical Mosaic." In *Musics of Many Cultures: An Introduction*, ed. Elizabeth May, 386–425. Berkeley: University of California Press.

———. 1980b. "Symbol and Function in South American Indian Music." In *Musics of Many Cultures: An Introduction*, ed. Elizabeth May, 363–385. Berkeley: University of California Press.

———. 1989. "The Magic Flutes of El Dorado: A Model for Research in Archaeomusicology as Applied to the Sinú of Ancient Colombia." In *Early Music Cultures, Selected Papers from the Third International Meeting of the ICTM Study Group on*

Music Archaeology, ed. Ellen Hickman and David Hughes, 305–328. Bonn: N. p.

———. 1996. *Music of the Warao of Venezuela: Song People of the Rain Forest*. Gainesville: University Press of Florida. Book and compact disc.

———. 2002. *Music of El Dorado: The Ethnomusicology of Ancient South American Cultures*. Gainesville: The University Press of Florida (paperback 2004).

———. 2004. *The Chrysanthemum and the Song: Music, Memory, and Identity in the Japanese Diaspora to South America*. Gainesville: The University Press of Florida.

Ortiz, Alfredo Rolando. 1984 [1979]. *Latin American Harp Music and Techniques for Pedal and Non-Pedal Harpists*, 2nd ed. Corona, Calif.: Alfredo Rolando Ortíz.

Pallavicino, María L. 1987. *Umbanda: Religiosidad afro-brasileña en Montevideo*. Montevideo: Pettirossi Hnos.

Pardo Tovar, Andrés. 1966. *La Cultural Musical en Colombia*. Bogotá: Ediciones Lerner.

———. 1976. *El Archivo Musical de la Catedral de Bogotá*. Bogotá: Publicaciones del Instituto Caro y Cuervo.

Paredes Candia, Antonio. 1980. *Folklore de Potosí*. La Paz: Ediciones ISLA.

Parra, Violeta. 1970. *Décimas: Autobiografía en versos chilenos*. Santiago: Ediciones Nueva Universidad, Universidad Católica de Chile.

———. 1979. *Cantos Folklóricos Chilenos*. Santiago: Editorial Nascimento.

Perdomo Escobar, José Ignacio. 1963. *Historia de la Música en Colombia*, 3rd ed. Bogotá: Editorial ABC.

Pereira-Salas, Eugenio. 1941. *Los orígenes del arte musical en Chile*. Santiago: Publicaciones de la Universidad de Chile.

Pérez Bugallo, Rubén. 1993. *Catálogo ilustrado de instrumentos musicales argentinos. Biblioteca de cultura popular, 19*. Buenos Aires: Ediciones de Sol.

Perrone, Charles A. 1989. *Masters of Contemporary Brazilian Song: MPB 1965–1985*. Austin: University of Texas Press.

Pinnell, Richard. 1993. *The Rioplatense Guitar: The Early Guitar and Its Content in Argentina and Uruguay*. Westport, Conn.: The Bold Strummer.

Pinto, Tiago de Oliveira, ed. 1986. *Welt Musik: Brazilien*. Mainz: Schott.

———. 1991. *Capoeira, Samba, Candomblé. Afro-brasilianische Musik im Recôncavo, Bahia*. Berlin: Staatliche Museen Preussischer Kulturbesitz.

Pinto, Tiago de Oliveira, and Dudu Tucci. 1992. *Samba und Sambistas in Brasilien*. Wihelmshavaen: F. Noetzel.

Plath, Oreste. 1979. *Folklore Chileno*. Santiago: Editorial Nascimento.

Pollak-Eltz, Angelina. 1972. *Cultos Afroamericanos*. Caracas: Universidad Católica "Andres Bello."

Pombo Hernández, Gerardo. 1995. *Kumbia, legado cultural de los indígenas del Caribe colombiano*. Barranquilla: Editorial Antillas.

Preiss, Jorge Hirt. 1988. *A Música nas Missões Jesuíticas nos Séculos XVII e XVIII*. Porto Alegre: Martins Livreiro Editor.

Price, Richard, and Sally Price. 1980. *Afro-American Arts of the Surinam Rain Forest*. Los Angeles: Museum of Cultural History and University of California Press.

———. 1991. *Two Evenings in Saramaka*. Chicago: University of Chicago Press.

Price, Sally. 1984. *Co-wives and Calabashes*. Ann Arbor: University of Michigan Press.

Primera Conferencia Interamericana de Etnomusicología. 1963. *Trabajos Presentados*, 131–151. Washington, D.C.: Unión Panamericana, Secretaría General de la OEA.

Puerta Zuluaga, David. 1988. *Los Caminos del Tiple*. Bogotá: Damel Publishers.

Ramón y Rivera, Luís Felipe. 1953. *El joropo, baile nacional de Venezuela*. Caracas: Ediciones del Ministerio de Educación.

———. 1967. *Música Indígena, Folklórica y Popular de Venezuela*. Buenos Aires: Ricordi Americana.

———. 1969. *La Música Folklórica de Venezuela*. Caracas: Monte Avila Editores C.A.

———. 1971. *La Música Afrovenezolana*. Caracas: Universidad Central de Venezuela.

———. 1992. *La Música de la Décima*. Caracas: Fundación de Etnomusicología y Folklore.

Real, Katarina. 1990. *O folclore no carnaval do Recife*. 2nd ed. Recife: Editora Massangana (Fundação Joaquim Nabuco).

Rephann, Richard. l978. *A Catalogue of the Pedro Traversari Collection of Musical Instrument /Catálogo de la Colección de Instrumentos Musicales Pedro Traversari*. Organization of American States and Yale University Collection of Musical Instruments. Quito: Casa de la Cultura Ecuatoriana.

Rodríguez de Ayestarán, Flor de María. 1994. *La danza popular en el Uruguay: Desde sus orígenes a 1900*. Montevideo: Cal y Canto.

Roel Pineda, Josafáto. 1990. *El wayno del Cusco*. Qosqo, Peru: Municipalidad del Qosqo.

Roel Pineda, Josafáto, et al. 1978. *Mapa de los Instrumentos Musicales de Uso Popular en el Perú*. Lima: Instituto Nacional de Cultura, Oficina de Música y Danza.

Romero, Raúl R. 1985. "La Música Tradicional y Popular." In *La Música en el Perú*, 215–283. Lima: Patronato Popular y Porvenir Pro Música Clásica.

———. 1993. *Música, Danzas y Máscaras en los Andes*. Lima: Pontífica Universidad Católica del Perú.

Roth, Walter E. 1924. "An Introductory Study of the Arts, Crafts, and Customs of the Guiana Indians." *Thirty-eighth Annual Report of the Bureau of American Ethnology to the Secretary of the Smithsonian Institution*, 1916–1917. Washington, D.C.: U.S. Government Printing Office.

Salazar, Briseida. 1990. *San Benito: Canta y Baila Con Sus Chimbangueleros*. Caracas: Fundación Bigott.

Sant'anna, Affonso Romano de. 1986. *Música Popular e Moderna Poesia Brasileira*, 3rd ed. Petrópolis: Vozes.

Santa Cruz, César. 1977. *El Waltz y el Vals Criollo*. Lima: Instituto Nacional de Cultura.

Savigliano, Marta E. 1995. *Tango and the Political Economy of Passion*. Boulder, Colo.: Westview Press.

Schechter, John M. 1992. *The Indispensable Harp: Historical Development, Modern Roles, Configurations, and Performance Practices in Ecuador and Latin America*. Kent, Ohio: Kent State University Press.

Schneider, Jens. 1993. "The Nolkin: A Chilean Sucked Trumpet." *Galpin Society Journal* 46:69–82.

Seeger, Anthony 1987. *Why Suyá Sing: A Musical Anthropology of an Amazonian People*. Cambridge: Cambridge University Press. Book and audio cassette.

Setti, Kilza. 1985. *Ubatuba nos Cantos das Praias: Estudo do Caiçara Paulista e de sua Produção Musical*. São Paulo: Atica.

Sherzer, Joel, and Greg Urban, eds. 1986. *Native South American Discourse*. Berlin: Mouton de Gruyter.

Shreiner, Claus. 1993. *Musica Brasileira: A History of Popular Music and the People of Brazil*. New York: M. Boyars.

Sigueira, Batista. 1979. *Modinhas do Passado*, 2nd ed. Rio de Janeiro: Folha Carioca.

Silva Sifuentes, Jorge E. 1978. *Instrumentos Musicales Pre-Colombinos. Serie Investigaciones No 2*. Lima: Universidad Nacional Mayor de San Marcos, Gabinete de Arqueología, Colegio Real.

Smith, Robert J. 1975. *The Art of the Festival*. Publications in Anthropology, Number 6. Lawrence: University of Kansas Press.

Sodré, Muniz. 1979. *Samba: O Dono do Corpo*. Rio de Janeiro: Codecri.

Souza, Tárik de, et al. 1988. *Brazil Musical*. Rio de Janeiro: Art Bureau Representações e Edições de Arte.

Stevenson, Robert. 1960. *The Music of Peru: Aboriginal and Viceroyal Epochs*. Washington, D.C.: Organization of American States.

Stobart, Henry. 1987. *Primeros Datos sobre la música campesina del norte de Potosí*. La Paz: Museo Nacional de Etnografia y Folklore.

———. 1994. "Flourishing Horns and Enchanted Tubers: Music and Potatoes in Highland Bolivia." *British Journal of Ethnomusicology* 3: 35–48.

Suzigan, Geraldo. 1990. *Bossa Nova: Música, Política e Educação no Brasil*. São Paulo: Clam-Zimbo.

Tayler, Donald. 1972. *The Music of Some Indian Tribes of Colombia*. London: British Institute of Recorded Sound. Book and 3 LP disks.

Tinhorão, José Ramos. 1974. *Pequena História da Música Popular: Da Modinha a Canção de Protesto*. Petrópolis: Vozes.

———. 1981. *Música Popular–Do Gramofone ao Rádio e TV*. São Paulo: Atica.

———. 1986. *Pequena história da música popularóda modinha ao tropicalismo*, 5th ed. São Paulo: Art Editora.

———. 1988. *Os Sons dos Negros no Brasil*. São Paulo: Arte Editora.

———. 1990. *História Social da Música Popular Brasileira*. Lison: Caminho da Música.

———. 1992. *A música popular no romance brasileiro. Vol. I: Século XVIII–século XIX*. Belo Horizonte: Oficina de Livros.

———. 1994. *Fado, dança do Brasil, cantar de Lisboa: O fim de um mito*. Lisboa: Editorial Caminho.

Traversari Salazar, Pedro Pablo, ed. 1961. *Catálogo General del Museo de Instrumentos Musicales*. Quito: Editorial Casa de la Cultura Ecuatoriana.

Turino, Thomas.1993. *Moving away from Silence: Music of the Peruvian Altiplano and the Experience of Urban Migration*. Chicago: University of Chicago Press.

Ulloa, Alejandro. 1992. *La Salsa en Cali*. Cali, Colombia: Ediciones Universidad del Valle.

Valencia Chacón, Américo. 1983. *El Siku Bipolar Altiplánico*. Lima: Artex Editores.

———. 1989. *El Siku o Zampoña. The Altiplano Bipolar Siku: Study and Projection of Peruvian Panpipe Orchestras*. Lima: Artex Editores.

Vasconcellos, Gilberto. 1977. *Música Popular: De Olho na Festa*. Rio de Janeiro: Graal.

Vasconcelos, Ary. 1991. *Raízes da Música Popular Brasileira*, rev. ed. Rio de Janeiro: Rio Fundo Editora.

Vásquez Rodríguez, Rosa Elena. 1982. *La Práctica Musical de la Población Negra en el Perú: La Danza de Negritos de El Carmen*. Havana: Casa de las Américas/Ediciones Vitral.

Vásquez, Rosa Elena, and Abilio Vergara Figueroa. 1988. *¡Chayraq!: Carnaval Ayacuchano*. Lima: Centro de Desarrollo Agropecuario.

Vega, Carlos. 1944. *Panorama de la música popular argentina, con un ensayo sobre la ciencia del folklore*. Buenos Aires: Losada.

———. 1946. *Los Instrumentos Musicales Aborígenes y Criollos de la Argentina*. Buenos Aires: Ediciones Centurión.

———. 1952. *Las danzas populares argentinas*. 2nd ed. Buenos Aires: Instituto Nacional de Musicología "Carlos Vega."

———. 1953. *La Zamacueca (Cueca, Zamba, Chilena, Marinera)*. Buenos Aires: Ed. Julio Korn.

———. 1956. *El origen de las danzas folklóricas*. Buenos Aires: Ricordi Americana.

———. 1965. *Las canciones folklóricas de la Argentina*. Buenos Aires: Instituto Nacional de Musicología.

Verger, Pierre, ed. *Fiestas y Danzas en el Cuzco y en los Andes*. Buenos Aires: Editorial Sudamericana.

Vianna, Hermanno. 1995.. Rio de Janeiro: Jorge Zahar/UFRJ.

Vilcapoma I., José Carlos. 1995. *Waylarsh: Amor y violencia de carnaval*. Lima: Pakarina Ediciones.

Whitten, Norman E., Jr. 1965. *Class, Kinship and Power in an Ecuadorian Town: The Negroes of San Lorenzo*. Stanford: Stanford University Press.

———. 1974a. *Black Frontiersman: A South American Case*. Cambridge, Mass.: Shenkman.

———. 1974b. *Black Frontiersmen. Afro-Hispanic Culture of Ecuador and Colombia*. Prospect Heights, Ill.: Waveland Press.

MIDDLE AMERICA

Acevedo Vargas, Jorge Luís. 1986. *La Música en Guanacaste*, 2nd ed. San José: Editorial Universidad de Costa Rica.

—————. 1986. *La Música en las Reservas Indígenas de Costa Rica*. San José: Editorial de la Universidad de Costa Rica.

Andrews V., and E. Wyllys. 1972. *Flautas Precolombinas procedentes de Quelepa, El Salvador*. San Salvador: Ministerio de Educación, Dirección de Cultura, Dirección de Publicaciones.

Anguiano, Marina, and Guido Munch. 1979. *La Danza de Malinche*. Mexico: Culturas Populares, Secretaría de Educación Pública.

Beezley, William H. et al. 1994. *Rituals of Rule, Rituals of Resistance: Public Celebrations and Popular Culture in Mexico*. Wilmington, Del.: Scholarly Resources.

Cardenal Argüello, Salvador. 1977. *Nicaragua: Música y canto*. Managua: Banco de América. Liner notes.

Cargalv, H. (Héctor C. Gálvez). 1983. *Historia de la música de Honduras y sus símbolos nacionales*. Tegucigalpa: N. p.

Carmona Maya, Sergio Iván. 1989. *La Música, un fenomeno cosmogónico en la cultura kuna*. Medellin: Editorial Universidad de Antioquia.

Chamorro, Arturo. 1994. *Sones de la Guerra: Rivalidad y emoción en la práctica de la música P'urhépecha*. Zamora: El Colegio de Michoacán.

Chenoweth, Vida. 1964. *Marimbas of Guatemala*. Lexington: University of Kentucky Press.

Cheville, Lila R., and Richard A. Cheville. 1977. *Festivals and Dances of Panama*. Panama: Lila and Richard Cheville.

Crossley-Holland, Peter. 1980. *Musical Artifacts of Pre-Hispanic West Mexico: Towards an Interdisciplinary Approach*. Los Angeles: Program in Ethnomusicology, Department of Music, University of California, Los Angeles.

Cuadra, Pablo Antonio, and Francisco Pérez Estrada. 1978. *Muestrario del folklore nicaragüense*. Managua: Banco de América.

Densmore, Frances. 1926. *Music of the Tule Indians of Panama*. Smithsonian Miscellaneous Collections 77(11): 1–39. Publication No. 2864. Washington, D.C.: Smithsonian Institution.

—————. 1932. *Yuman and Yaqui Music*. Bulletin 110. Washington, D.C.: Bureau of American Ethnology.

Drolet, Patricia Lund. 1980. "The Congo Ritual of Northeastern Panama: An Afro-American Expressive Structure of Cultural Adaptation." Ph.D. dissertation, University of Illinois at Urbana-Champaign.

Evers, Laurence J., and Felipe Molina. 1987. *Yaqui Deer Songs/Maso Bwikam: A Native American Poetry*. Tucson: University of Arizona Press.

Flores, Bernal. 1978. *La música en Costa Rica*. San José: Editorial Costa Rica.

Florers y Escalanate, Jesús, and Pablo Dueñas Herrera. 1994. *Cirilo Marmolejo: Historia del mariachi en la Ciudad de México*. México, D.F.: Asociación Mexicana de Estudios Fonográficas.

Franco Arce, Samuel. 1991. *Music of the Maya*. Guatemala: Casa K'ojom.

Garay, Narciso. 1930. *Tradiciones y cantares de Panamá, ensayo folklórico*. Brussels: Presses de l'Expansion belge.

García Flores, Raúl. 1993. *¡Pure mitote!: La música, el canto y la danza entre los chichimecas del Noreste*. Monterrey: Fondo Editorial Nuevo León.

González Sol, Rafael. 1940. *Datos históricos sobre el arte de la música en El Salvador*. San Salvador: Imprenta Mercurio.

Hayans, Guillermo. 1963. *Dos cantos shamanísticos de los índios cunas*. Translated by Nils M. Holmer and S. Henry Wassen. Göteborg: Etnografiska Museet.

Holmer, Nils M., and S. H. Wassén. 1963. *Dos Cantos Shamanísticos de los Indios Cunas*. Etnologiska Studier, No. 27. Göteborgs Etnografiska Museum. Göteborg: Elanders Boktryckeri Aktiebolag.

Jáuregui, Jesús. 1990. *El mariachi: Símbolo musical de México*. Mexico: Banpaís.

Joly, Luz Graciela. 1981. *The Ritual "Play of the Congos" of North-Central Panama: Its Sociolinguistic Implications*. Sociolinguistic working paper no. 85. Austin: Southwest Educational Development Laboratory.

Kaptain, Laurence. 1992. *The Wood That Sings: The Marimba in Chiapas, Mexico*. Everett, Pa.: HoneyRock.

Mace, Carroll E. 1970. *Two Spanish-Quiché Dance Dramas of Rabinal*. Tulane Studies in Romance Languages and Literature, Publication No. 3. New Orleans: Tulane University Press.

Manzanares Aguilar, Rafael. 1960. *Canciones de Honduras/Songs of Honduras*. Washington, D. C.: Secretaría General, Unión Panamericana, Organización de los Estados Americanos.

—————. 1972. *La danza folklórica hondureña*. Tegucigalpa: Talleres del Partido Nacional.

Martí, Samuel. 1955. *Instrumentos musicales precortesianos*. México, D. F.: Instituto Nacional de Antropología

—————. 1961. *Canto, Danza y Música Precortesianos*. México, D. F.: Fondo de Cultura Económica.

—————. 1968. *Instrumentos Musicales Precortesianos*, 1st and 2nd eds. México, D. F.: Instituto Nacional de Antropología e Historia.

Mayer-Serra, Otto. 1941. *Panorama de la música mexicana desde la independencia hasta la actualidad*. México, D. F.: El Colegio de México.

McCosker, Sandra Smith. 1974. *The Lullabies of the San Blas Cuna Indians of Panama*. Etnologiska Studier, No. 33. Göteborgs Etnografiska Museum. Göteborg: Elanders Boktryckeri Aktiebolag.

Mendoza, Vicente T. 1939. *El romance español y el corrido mexicano: Estudio comparativo*. México, D. F.: Ediciones de la Universidad Nacional Autónoma de México.

—————. 1984 [1956]. *Panorama de la Música Tradicional de México*. México, D. F.: Universidad Nacional Autónoma de México, Instituto de Investigaciones Estéticas.

Moreno Rivas, Yolanda. 1989. *Historia de la música popular mexicana*, 2nd ed. México, D. F.: Consejo Nacional para la Cultura y las Artes, Alianza Editorial Mexicana.

Muñoz Tábora, Jesús. 1988. *Organología del Folklore Hondureño*. Tegucigalpa: Ministerio de Educación

Navarette Pellicer, Sergio. 2005. *Maya Achi Marimba Music in Guatamala*. Philadelphia: Temple University Press.

Núñez, Evangelina de. 1956. *Costa Rica y su folklore.* San José: Imprenta Nacional.

Peña Hernández, Enrique. 1968. *Folklore de Nicaragua.* Masaya: Editorial Unión, Cardoza y Cia. Ltd.

Pérez Fernández, Rolando Antonio. 1990. *La música afromestiza mexicana.* Xalapa: Biblioteca Universidad Veracruzana.

Pineda del Valle, César. 1990. *Fogarada: Antología de la marimba.* Tuxtla Gutiérrez: Gobierno del Estado de Chiapas, Instituto Chiapaneco de Cultura.

Prado Quesada, Alcides, ed. 1962. *Costa Rica: Su música típica y sus autores.* San José: Editorial Antonio Lehmann.

Reuter, Jas. 1992 [1985]. *La música popular de México: Orígen e historia de la música que canta y toca el pueblo mexicano.* México, D. F.: Panorama Editoria.

Rivera y Rivera, Roberto. 1977. *Los Instrumentos Musicales de los Mayas.* México, D. F.: Instituto Nacional de Antropología e Historia.

Salazar Salvatierra, Rodrigo. 1985. *La música popular afrolimonense.* San José: Organización de los Estados Americanos, Ministerio de Cultura, Juventud y Deportes.

———. 1988. *La marimba: Empleo, diseño y construcción.* San José: Editorial Universidad de Costa Rica.

———. 1992. *Los instrumentos de la música folclórica costarricense.* Cartago: Editorial Instituto Tecnológico de Costa Rica.

Saldívar, Gabriel. 1934. *Historia de la música en México: Epocas Precortesiana y Colonial.* México, D. F.: Editorial "Cultura."

———. 1937. *El Jarabe, baile popular mexicano.* México: Talleres gráficos de la nación.

Scruggs, T. M. 1998a. "Cultural Capital, Appropriate Transformations and Transfer by Appropriation in Western Nicaragua: El baile de la marimba." *Latin American Music Review* 19(1).

———. 1998b. Review essay on publications from Central America. Salvador Cardenal Argüello, comp., Nicaragua: Música y canto; Alcaldía de Managua; Jesús Muñoz Tábora, Organología del Folklore Hondureño; Rodrigo Salazar Salvatierra, Instrumentos musicales del folclor costarricense. *Latin American Music Review* 19(1).

———. 1999a. "'Let's Enjoy as Nicaraguans': The Use of Music in the Construction of a Nicaraguan National Consciousness." *Ethnomusicology* 43(2).

———. 1999b. "Nicaraguan State Cultural Initiative and 'the Unseen Made Manifest'." *Yearbook for Traditional Music* 31.

Sheehy, Daniel Edward. 1979. "The 'Son Jarocho': The History, Style, and Repertory of a Changing Mexican Musical Tradition." Ph.D. dissertation, University of California at Los Angeles.

———. 2005. *Mariachi Music in America: Experiencing Music, Expressing Culture.* Global Music Series. New York: Oxford University Press.

Sherzer, Joel. 1983. *Kuna Ways of Speaking: An Ethnographic Perspective.* Texas Linguistics Sseries. Austin: University of Texas Press.

Smith, Ronald R. 1985. "They Sing with the Voice of the Drum: Afro-Panamanian Musical Traditions." In *More Than Drumming: Essays on African and Afro-Latin American Music,* ed.

Irene Jackson-Brown, 163–198. Westport, Conn.: Greenwood Press.

Smith, Sandra. 1984. "Panpipes for Power, Panpipes for Play: The Social Management of Cultural Expression in Kuna Society." Ph.D. dissertation, University of California, Berkeley.

Stevenson, Robert. 1952. *Music in Mexico: A Historical Survey.* New York: Thomas Y. Crowell.

———. 1968. *Music in Aztec and Inca Territory.* Berkeley: University of California Press.

Suco Campos, Idalberto. 1987. *La música en el complejo cultural del Walagallo en Nicaragua.* La Habana: Casa de las Américas.

Tello Solís, Eduardo. 1993. *Semblanza de la canción yucateca.* Mérida: Universidad Autónoma de Yucatán.

Varela, Leticia. 1986. *La Música en la Vida de los Yaquis.* Hermosillo: El Gobierno del Estado de Sonora, Secretaría de Fomento Educativo y Cultura.

Zárate, Dora Pérez de. 1971. *Textos del tamborito panameño: Un estudio folklórico-literario de los textos del tamborito en Panamá.* Panamá: Dora Pérez de Zárate.

———. 1996. *Sobre nuestra musica típica.* Panama: Editorial Universitaria.

Zárate, Manuel F., and Dora Pérez de Zárate. 1968. *Tambor y socavón: Un estudio comprensivo de dos temas del folklore panameño, y de sus implicaciones históricas y culturales.* Panamá: Ediciones del Ministerio de Educación, Dirección Nacional de Cultura.

CARIBBEAN

Alén Rodríguez, Olavo. 1986. *La música de las sociedades de tumba francesa en Cuba.* Havana: Casa de La Américas.

———. 1994. *De los afrocubano a la salsa,* 2nd ed. Havana: Artex S. A. Editions.

Aparicio, Frances. R. 1998. *Listening to Salsa: Gender, Latin Popular Music, and Puerto Rican Cultures.* Hanover, N.H.: University Press of New England.

Bigott, Luís Antonio. 1993. *Historia del bolero cubano, 1883–1950.* Caracas: Ediciones Los Heraldos Negros.

Bilby, Kenneth. 1985. *The Caribbean as a Musical Region.* Washington, D.C.: Woodrow Wilson International Center for Scholars.

Boggs, Vernon W., ed. 1992. *Salsiology: Afro-Cuban Music and the Evolution of Salsa in New York City.* New York: Excelsior Music Publishing.

Carpentier, Alejo. 1946. *La música en Cuba.* México, D.F.: Fondo de Cultura Económica.

Coopersmith, J. M. 1949. *Music and Musicians of the Dominican Republic, ed. Charles Seeger.* Music Series No. 15. Washington, D.C.: Pan American Union.

Courlander, Harold. 1973. *The Drum and the Hoe: Life and Lore of the Haitian People.* Berkeley: University of California Press.

Daniel, Yvonne. 1995. *Rumba: Dance and Social Change in Contemporary Cuba.* Bloomington: Indiana University Press.

Davis, Martha Ellen. 1976. "Afro-Dominican Religious Brotherhoods: Structure, Ritual, and Music." Ph.D. dissertation, University of Illinois at Urbana-Champaign.

———. 1981. Voces del Purgatorio: *Estudio de la Salve dominicana*, Santo Domingo: Museo del Hombre Dominicano

Deren, Maya. 1984 [1953]. *Divine Horsemen: The Living Gods of Haiti.* London and New York: Thames and Hudson. New Paltz, N.Y.: McPherson & Co.

Díaz Ayala, Cristobóbal. 1994. *Cuba canta ya baila: Discografia de la música cubana, Vol. 1, 1898–1925.* San Juan, P.R.: Fundación Musicalia.

García, David F. 2006. *Arsenio Rodríguez and the Transnational Flows of Latin Popular Music.* Philadelphia: Temple University Press.

Gerard, Charlie, and Marty Sheller. 1989. *Salsa: The Rhythm of Latin Music.* Crown Point, Ind.: White Cliffs Media

Hebdige, Dick. 1987. *Cut 'n' Mix: Culture, Identity, and Carribean Music.* London: Methuen.

Hernández, Julio Alberto. 1969. *Música tradicional dominicana.* Santo Domingo: Julio D. Postigo.

———. 1992. *Música dominicana.* Santo Domingo: Universidad Autonóma de Santo Domingo.

Incháustegui, Arístides. 1988. *El disco en la República Dominicana.* Santo Domingo: Amigo del Hogar

Kuss, Malena, ed. 2008?. *Music in Latin America and the Caribbean, An Encyclopedic History, Vol.2, Performing the Caribbean Experience.* Austin: University Press of Texas.

Lent, John A., ed. 1990. *Caribbean Popular Culture.* Bowling Green, Ohio: Bowling Green State University Popular Press.

Leon, Algeliers. 1984. *Del canto y el tiempo.* Havana: Letras Cubanas Editorial.

Linares, Maria Teresa. *La música y el pueblo.* Havana: Pueblo y Educación Editorial, 1974.

López Cruz, Francisco. 1991 [1967]. *La Música Folklórica de Puerto Rico.* 9th ed. Sharon, Conn.: Troutman Press.

Malavet Vega, Pedro. 1992. *Historia de la canción popular en Puerto Rico (1493–1898).* Ponce: Pedro Malavet Vega.

Manuel, Peter, ed. 1991. *Essays on Cuban Music—North American and Cuban Perspectives.* Lanham, Md.: University Press of America.

———. 2006. *Caribbean Currents.* Revised and expanded edition, with Kenneth Bilby and Michael Largey. Philadelphia: Temple University Press.

McCoy, James A. 1968. "The Bomba and Aguinaldo of Puerto Rico as They Have Evolved from Indigenous, African and European Cultures." Ph.D. dissertation, Florida State University.

Moldes, Rhyna. 1975. *Música folklórica cubana.* Miami: Ediciones Universal.

Moore, Robin D. 1997. *Nationalizing Blackness. Afrocubanismo and Artistic Revolution in Havana, 1920–1940.* Pittsburgh: University of Pittsburgh Press.

Nolasco, Flérida de. 1939. *La música en Santo Domingo y otros ensayos.* Ciudad Trujillo: Montalvo.

Núñez, María Virtudes, and Ramón Guntín. 1992. *Salsa caribe y otras músicas antillanas.* Madrid: Ediciones Cúbicas.

Ortiz, Fernando. 1954. *Los instrumentos de la música afrocubana.* Havana: Cárdenas y Cia Editorial.

———. 1965. *Africanía de la música en Cuba*, 2nd ed. Havana: N. p.

Ortiz Ramos, Pablo Marcial. 1991. *A tres voces y guitarras: Los tríos en Puerto Rico.* San Juan: N. p.

Quintero-Rivera, A. G. 1989. *Music, Social Classes, and the National Question of Puerto Rico.* Washington, D.C.: Woodrow Wilson International Center for Scholars.

Rodríguez Demorizi, Emilio. 1971. *Música y baile en Santo Domingo.* Santo Domingo: Librería Hispaniola.

Rohlehr, Gordon. 1990. *Calypso and Society in Pre-Independence Trinidad.* Port of Spain: G. Rohlehr.

Rosa-Nieves, Cesarro. 1991 [1967]. *Voz Folklórica de Puerto Rico.* Sharon, Conn.: Troutman Press.

Simpson, George. 1965. *The Shango Cult in Trinidad.* Río Piedras: Institute of Caribbean Sudies, University of Puerto Rico.

Vega Drouet, Héctor. 1979. "Historical and Ethnological Survey on Probable African Origins of the Puerto Rico Bomba, Including a Description of Santiago Apostol Festivities at Loiza Aldea." Ph.D. dissertation, Wesleyan University.

Wallis, Roger, and Krister Malm. 1984. *Big Sounds from Small Peoples: The Music Industry in Small Countries.* London: Constable and Co. (New York: Pendragon Press).

A Guide to Recordings

GENERAL

Música de la Tierra: Instrumental and Vocal Music–Vol. II. 1992. Produced by Bob Haddad. Music of the World CDC-207. Compact disc.

Shaman, Jhankri & Néle: Music Healers of Indigenous Cultures. 1997. Written and produced by Pat Moffitt Cook. Roslyn, N.Y.: Ellipsis Arts. CD3550. Compact disc and book.

The Spirit Cries: Music from the Rainforests of South America and the Caribbean. 1993. Produced by Mickey Hart and Alan Jabbour. Notes by Kenneth Bilby. Rykodisc RCD 10250. Compact disc.

SOUTH AMERICA

A bailar la bomba, con los Hermanos Congo. 1985. Quito: FAMOSA-FADISA, 700211. LP disk.

A bailar la bomba. con los Hermanos Congo. 1986. Vol. 2. Guayaquil: Producciones Maldonado-IFESA 339-588l. LP disk.

Aboios/Ceará. 1983. Documentário Sonoro do Folclore Brasileiro INF-039. LP disk.

ACONCAGUA. 1995 [1982]. *Los Jaivas* [Chile]. Colombia CNIA-2-461823. Compact disc.

Afro-Hispanic Music from Western Colombia and Ecuador. 1967. Recorded and edited by Norman E. Whitten. Ethnic Folkways Library FE 4376. LP disk.

Afro-Peruvian Classics: The Soul of Black Peru. 1995. Compiled by David Byrne and Yale Evelev. Luaka Bop 9 45878-2. Compact disc.

Alma del Sur. 1993. Liner essay ("A Celebration of South American Music") by Dale A. Olsen. Narada Collection Series ND-63908. Compact disc.

Amazonia: Cult Music of Northern Brazil. N. d. Produced by Morton Marks. New York: Lyrichord LLST 7300. LP disk.

Amerique du Sud: Musiques Hispaniques. 1993. Auvidis-Ethnic B 6782. Compact disc.

Amerindian Songs from Surinam, the Maroni River Caribs. 1975. Produced by Peter Kloos. Amsterdam: Royal Tropical Institute. LP disk.

Andean Legacy. 1996. Liner essay ("Music of the Central Andes") by Dale A. Olsen. Narada Collection Series ND-63927. Compact disc.

Astor Piazzolla: Octeto Buenos Aires. 1995. Astor Piazzolla [Argentina]. ANS Records ANS 15276-2. Compact disc.

Banda Cabaçal/Ceará. 1978. Documentário Sonoro do Folclore Brasileiro CDFB-023. LP disk.

Bandoneón Pure: Dances of Uruguay. 1993. René Marino Rivero, bandoneón. Recorded by Tiago de Oliveira Pinto. Notes by Maria Dunkel. Smithson/Folkways CD SF 40431.

Basta. 1995. Quilapayún. Disco Alerce CDAL 0223. Compact disc.

Baú dos oito baixos: Bucho com bucho. 1982. Sebastiáo Moraes. Som da Gente SDG-011. LP disk.

Bolivia: Calendar Music in the Central Valleys. 1992. Recorded by Bruno Flety and Rosalia Martínez. Notes by Rosalia Martínez. Le Chant du Monde LDX 274938 CM 251. Compact disc.

Bolivia Panpipes/Syrinx de Bolivie. Recorded by Louis Giraullt. Notes by Xavier Bellenger. UNESCO Collection, AUVIDIS D 8009. Compact disc.

Bororo Vive. 1990. Federal University of Mato Grosso and Museu Rondon. Idéia Livre 19 521.404.030. LP disk.

Bossa Nova: Sua história, sua gente. 1991. Notes by Aloyso de Oliveira. Philips/Polygram 848 302-2. 2 compact discs.

Brazil Classics 3: Forró, etc. 1991. Luaka Bop/Warner Bros. 9 26323-2. Compact Disc.

Brazil: The Bororo World of Sound. 1989. Produced by Ricardo Canzio. UNESCO/ AUVDIS D 8201. Compact disc.

Brésil: Amérindiens d'Amazonie—Asurini et Arara/Brazil: American Indians of the Amazon—Asurini and Arara. 1995. Jean-Pierre Estival. Ocora C 560084. Compact disc.

Brésil Central: Chants et danses des Indiens Kaiapo. 1989. Recorded by René Fuerst, George Love, Pascal Rosseels, and Gustaaf Verswijver. Archives Internationales de *Musique Populaire*. AIMP & VDE-GALLO CD-554/555. 2 compact discs.

Brésil—Musiques du Haut Xingu. 1992. Produced by Pierre Toureille. OCORA Radio France, Harmonia Mundi, C 580022. Compact disc.

¡Cantando! 1992. Diomedes Díaz and Nicholas «Colacho» Mendoza [Colombia]. GlobeStyle ORB 055. Compact disc.

Cantos Costeós: Folksongs of the Atlantic Coastal Region of Colombia. 1973. Produced by George List with Delia Zapata Olivella, Manuel Zapata Olivella, and Winston Caballero Salguedo. Ethnosound EST 8003. LP disk.

Capoeira Angola from Salvador, Brazil. 1996. Grupo de Capoeira Angola Pelourinho. Smithsonian/Folkways SF CD 40465. Compact disc.

Capoeira, Samba, Candomblé, Bahia, Brasil. 1990. Recordings and notes by Tiago de Oliveira Pinto. Berlin: Museum Collection. Compact disc.

Chants et rythmes du Chile: Violeta Parra, Los Calhakis, Isabel et Angel Parra. 1991. Arion ARN 64142. Compact disc.

Charango Cuzqueño. 1985. Julio Benavente Díaz, charango. Recorded by Xavier Bellenger. Notes by Thomas Turino. GREM G 1504.

Chocolate: Peru's Master Percussionist. 1992. Lyrichord LYRCD 7417.

Colombia 92. 1992. Sony CD80804/Globo Records. Compact disc.

Cuando el indio llora: Los Huayanay. 1989. Quito: FAMOSO LDF-l040. LP disk.

Cumbia/Cumbia 2: La Epoca Dorada de Cumbias Colombias. 1993. Produced by Nick Gold. World Circuit WCD 033. Compact disc.

Dance Music from the Countryside. 1992. Pé de Serra Forró Band, Brazil. Haus der Kulturen der Welt SM 1509-2. LP disk.

Danzas y Cantos Afrovenezolanos. 1978. Caracas: Oswaldo Lares. LP disk.

Danzas y Canciones Para Los Niños. 1981. Caracas: Ediciones Fredy Reyna. LP disk.

Do jeito que a gente gosta. 1984. Elba Ramalho. Barclay 823 030-1. LP disk.

Documental Folklórico de la Provincia de La Pampa. 1973. Produced by Ercilia Moreno *Chá*. Buenos Aires: Instituto Nacional de Antropología—Dirección de Cultura de La Pampa. Qualiton QF 3015/16. 2 LP disks.

El Charango. 1988. Ernesto Cavour. La Paz: CIMA. LP disk.

Équateur: Le monde sonore des Shuar/Ecuador: The Shuar World of Sound. 1995. Buda 92638-2. Compact disc.

Flutes and Strings of the Andes: Native Musicians from the Altiplano. 1990. Produced by Bob Haddad. Music of the World CDT-106. Compact disc.

Folklore de mi tierra: Conjunto indígena "Peguche." 1977. Industria Fonográfica Ecuatoriana S.A. (IFESA). ORION 330-0063. Guayaquil, Ecuador, Dist. by Emporio Musical S.A., Guayaquil and Psje. Amador, Quito. LP disk.

Folklore de Venezuela, Vols. 1–8. 1971. Caracas: Sonido Laffer. 8 LP disks.

Folklore Musical y Música Folklórica Argentina. 1966. Buenos Aires: Fondo Nacional de las Artes. Qualiton QF 3000/5. 6 LP disks.

From Slavery to Freedom: Music of the Saramaka Maroons of Suriname. 1977. Lyrichord LLST 7354. LP disk.

Fuego. 1993. Joe Arroyo y La Verdad. Sony CDZ 81063. Compact disc.

Grandes éxitos, Vol. 2. 1993. Joe Arroyo y La Verdad. Vedisco 1017—2. Compact disc.

Hekura: Yanomamö Shamanism from Southern Venezuela. 1980. Recorded by David Toop and Nestor Figueras. Quartz Publications 004. LP disk.

Huaynos and Huaylas: The Real Music of Peru. 1991. Compiled by Ben Mandelson, notes by Lucy Duran. GlobeStyle Records GDORBD 064. Compact disc.

Indian Music of Brazil. Musique Indienne Brésil. 1972. Recorded with notes by Simone Dreyfus. Ed. Gilbert Rouget. Collection Musée de l'Homme. Vogue VG 403 LDM 30112. LP disk.

Indiens d'Amazonie. N. d. Recorded by Richard Chapelle. Le Chant du Monde LDX 74501. LP disk.

Inti-Illimani 2: La Nueva Canción Chilena. 1991. Monitor MCD 71794.

Jarishimi Kichuapi (La Voz del Hombre en Kichua). 1984. Enrique Males. Teen Internacional LP-4l586. Guayaquil: Fediscos. LP disk.

¡¡Jatari!! 4. 1978. Quito: Fábrica de Discos S.A. (FADISA) 710129. LP disk.

Javanese Music from Suriname. 1977. Lyrichord LLST 7317. LP disk.

La América de Bolívar Canta. N. d. Caracas: Colección INIDEF. V.D. 82-033. LP disk.

La candela vida. 1993. Totó la Momposina y Sus Tambores. Carol/ Real World CD 2337-2. Compact disc.

Las canciones folklóricas de la Argentina. Antología. 1984. Buenos Aires: Instituto Nacional de Musicología "Carlos Vega." 3 LP disks.

L.H. Correa de Azevedo: Music of Ceara and Minas Gerais. N. d. Rykodisc-10404. Compact disc.

Lowland Tribes of Ecuador. 1986. Recorded by David Blair Stiffler. Ethnic Folkways Records FE 4375. LP disk.

Lo mejor de la Cumbia Soledeña. 1977. Polydor 2404041. LP disk.

Los Grandes de la Bomba, con Fabián Congo y Milton Tadeo. l989. Ecuador: Novedades, LP323102. LP disk.

Los Masis: El Corazón del Pueblo. 1996. Los Masis. Tumi CD 062. Compact disc.

Marimba Cayapas: Típica Marimba Esmeraldeña. 1979. Guayaquil: ONIX-Fediscos, LP-5003l. LP disk.

Mountain Music of Peru. 1991 [1964]. Produced by John Cohen. Smithsonian Folkways SF 40020 and 40021. 2 compact discs.

Mushuc Huaira Huacamujun. 1979. Conjunto Indigena "Peguche." Guayaquil: IFESA, RUNA CAUSAY 339-065l. LP disk.

Music from Saramaka. 1977. Produced by Richard Price and Sally Price. Ethnic Folkways Records FE 4225. LP disk.

Music of Colombia. 1961. Recorded by A.H. Whiteford. Folkways Records, FW 6804. LP disk.

Music of the Andes. Illapa, Inti-Illimani, Kollahuara, Quilapayun, and Victor Jara. Hemisphere 7243 8 28190 28. Compact disc.

Music of the Haut Oyopok: Oyampi and Emerillon Indian Tribes, French Guiana, South America. 1981. Recorded with notes by David Blair Stiffler. Ethnic Folkways Records FE 4235.

Music of the Jívaro of Ecuador. 1973. Recorded by Michael J. Harner, Ethnic Folkways FE 4386. LP disk.

The Music of Some Indian Tribes of Colombia. 1972. Produced by Donald Tayler. London: British Institute of Recorded Sound. 3 LP disks.

Music of the Tukano and Cuna Peoples of Colombia. 1987. Recorded by Brian Moser and Donald Tayler. Rogue Records, FMS/ NSA 002. LP disk.

The Music of Venezuela. 1990. Memphis: Memphis State University. High Water Recording Company, LP1013. LP disk.

Music of the Venezuelan Yekuana Indians. 1975. Produced by Walter Coppens and Isaías Rodríguez V. Folkways Records Album FE 4104. LP disk.

Music of the Warao. Song People of the Rain Forest. 1996. Recorded and produced by Dale A. Olsen. Gainesville: University Press of Florida. Book and compact disc.

Música Andina de Bolivia. IV festival folklórico "Luz Mila Patiño." 1979. Produced by Max Peter Baumann. Cochabamba: Centro Portales y Lauro y Cía. LP disk.

Música Andina del Perú. 1987. Produced by Raúl Romero. Lima: Archivo de Música Tradicional, Pontífica Universidad Católica del Perú, Instituto Riva Agüero. LP disk.

Música autóctona del Norte de Potosí. VII Festival Folklórico "Luz Mila Patiño." 1991. Produced by Luz Maria Calvo and Walter Sánchez C. Cochabamba: Centro Portales y Lauro y Cia. LP disk.

Música de Venezuela: Cantos y Danzas e La Costa Central. N. d. Caracas: Oswaldo Laress. LP disk.

Música de Venezuela: Indio Figueredo (Homenaje al Indio Figueredo). 1969. Caracas: Oswaldo Lares. LP disk.

Música etnográfica y folklórica del Ecuador. Culturas: Shuar, Chachi, Quichua, Afro, Mestizo. 1990. Recorded by José Peñín, Ronny Velásquez, and Carlos Alberto Coba Andrade. Otavalo: Instituto Otavaleño de Antropología. 2 LP disks.

Música Indígena Guahibo. ca. 1978. Caracas: Fundación La Salle/ Instituto Interamericano de Etnomusicología e Folklore. LP disk.

Música Indigena: A Arte Vocal dos Suyá. 1982. Recorded and produced by Anthony Seeger. Sáo Joáo del Rei: Tacape 007. LP disk.

Música Popular Tradicional de Venezuela. 1983. Caracas: Instituto Nacional del Folklore. LP disk.

Música tradicional de Bolivia. VI festival folklórico nacional "Luz Mila Patiño." 1984. Produced by Luz María Calvo and Roberto Guzmán. Cochabamba: Centro Portales y Lauro y Cía. LP disk.

Música Tradicional de Cajamarca. 1988. Produced by Gisela Canepa Koch and Raul R. Romero. Lima: Archivo de Música Tradicional, Pontífica Universidad Católica del Perú, Instituto Riva-Agüero. AMTA-3. LP disk, cassette [1997].

Música Tradicional de Lambayeque. 1992. Edited by Raúl R. Romero. Lima: Archivo de Música Tradicional, Pontífica Universidad Católica del Perú, Instituto Riva-Agüero. AMTA-6. LP disk, cassette [1997].

Música Tradicional de Piura. 1997. Edited by Manuel Ráez Retamozo and Ana Teresa Lecaros. Lima: Archivo de Música Tradicional, Pontífica Universidad Católica del Perú, Instituto Riva-Agüero. AMTA-9. Cassette.

Música Tradional de la Sierra de Lima. 1997. Edited by Manuel Ráez Retamozo and Ana Teresa Lecaros. Lima: Archivo de Música Tradicional, Pontífica Universidad Católica del Perú, Instituto Riva-Agüero. AMTA-8. Cassette.

Música Tradional del Callejón de Huaylas. 1997. Edited by Manuel Ráez Retamozo. Lima: Archivo de Música Tradicional, Pontífica Universidad Católica del Perú, Instituto Riva-Agüero. AMTA-7. Cassette.

Música Tradicional del Cusco. 1992. Edited by Raúl R. Romero. Lima: Archivo de Música Tradicional, Pontífica Universidad Católica del Perú, Instituto Riva-Agüero. AMTA-5. LP disk, cassette [1997].

Música Tradicional del Valle de Colca. 1989. Edited by Manuel Ráez Retamozo and Leonidas Casas Roque. Lima: Archivo de Música Tradicional, Pontífica Universidad Católica del Perú, Instituto Riva-Agüero. AMTA-4. LP disk, cassette [1997].

Música Tradicional del Valle del Mantaro. 1986. Edited by Raúl R. Romero. Lima: Archivo de Música Tradicional, Pontífica Universidad Católica del Perú, Instituto Riva-Agüero. AMTA-1. LP disk, cassette [1997].

Musik im Andenhochland/Bolivien (Music in the Andean highlands/Bolivia.) 1982. Recording and notes by Max Peter Baumann. Edited by Artur Simon. Museum Collection Berlin MC 14. LP disk.

Musique Boni et Wayana de Guyana. 1968. Produced by Jean-Marcel Hurault. Paris: Collection Musee de l'Homme. Disque Vogue LVLX 290. LP disk.

Musique des Indiens Bora et Witoto d'Amazonie colombienne. 1976. Recorded by Mireille Guyot and Jürg Gasche. Paris: Musée de l'Homme. AEM 01. LP disk.

Musique instrumentale des Wayana du Litani (The Wayana of the Litani River). N. d. Buda 92637-2. Compact disc.

The Noble Songbook of Colombia. N. d. Produced by Joaquín Piñeros Corpos. Bogotá: Universidad de los Andes, LP 501–03. LP disks.

Ñanda mañachi 1 (Préstame el camino). 1977. Produced by Jean Chopin Thermes-Ibarra. Guayaquil: LLAQUICLLA—IFESA. LP disk.

Ñanda mañachi 1 and 2 (Préstame el camino). 1977, 1979. Produced by Jean Chopin Thermes-Ibarra. Guayaquil: LLAQUICLLA - IFESA 339-0502. 2 LP disks.

Ñanda mañachi: ¡Churay, Churay! 1983. Guayaquil: LLAQUICLLA. ONIX-Fediscos LP-59003. LP disk.

Ñuca llacta. 1975. Conjunto "Los Tucumbes." Auténtico Conjunto Folklórico interpretando música autóctona de nuestro país. Ritmos indígenas. Quito: Sibelius, S-4256-SIB-12. LP-12501. LP disk.

O bom do carnaval. 1980. Claudionor Germano. RCA/Cadmen 107.0317. LP disk.

O Melhor de Luiz Gonzaga. 1989. Luiz Gonzaga. RCA CDM 10032. LP disk.

Paiter Merewá: Cantam os Suruis de Rondônia. 1984. Sáo Paulo: Discos Memoria 803.146. LP disk.

Pelas ruas do Recife. 1979. Banda de Pau e Corda. RCA 103.0319. LP disk.

Percussions d'Amérique latine (tracks 3, 7, 12, 14, 17). 1986. Arion CD64023. Compact disc.

Percussions d'amérique latine. N. d. Produced by Gérard Krémer. Arion CD64023. LP disk.

Perou: Huayno, Valse Créole et Marinera. 1994. Playasound PS 65133. Compact disc.

Pérou: Taquile, Île du Ciel: Musique Quechua du Lac Titicaca. 1992. Ocora C580 015. Compact disc.

Peru: Ayarachi and Chiriguano. 1983. Xavier Bellenger. UNESCO MTC 1. LP disk.

Perú: Máximo Damián: El Violín de Ishua. 1992. A.S.P.I.C. X55514. Compact disc.

Perú: Música Negra. 1992. A.S.P.I.C. X55515. Compact disc.

Quechua. Margarita Alvear. 1976. Guayaquil: ONIX. Fediscos, LP-50154. LP disk.

Rebellión. 1992. Joe Arroyo y La Verdad. World Circuit WCD 012. Compact disc.

Reisado do Piauí. 1977. Documentário Sonoro do Folclore Brasileiro CDFB-019. LP disk.

Relevamiento etnomusicológico de Salta, Argentina. 1984. Selección de textos: Rubén Pérez Bugallo. Buenos Aires: Instituto Nacional de Musicología "Carlos Vega." 2 LP disks.

Repentes e emboladas. 1986. Manoel Batista and Zé Batista. Phonodisc LP 0-34-405-215. LP disk.

Ritmos e danças: Frevo. N. d. Fundáçao Nacional de Arte SCDP-PF-01-PE. LP disk.

Ritual Music of the Kayapó-Xikrin, Brazil. 1995. Recorded by Max Peter Baumann. Notes by Lux Boelitz Vidal and Isabelle Vidal Giannini. Smithsonian/Folkways CD SF 40433. Compact disc and booklet.

The Rough Guide to the Music of the Andes. 1996. Produced by Phil Stanton. World Music Network. RGNET 1009. Compact disc.

Selk'nam chants of Tierra del Fuego, Argentina. 1972. Notes and translations of texts by Anne Chapman. Ethnic Folkways FE 4176. 2 LP disks.

Selk'nam chants of Tierra del Fuego, Argentina. 1978. Notes and transcriptions by Anne Chapman. Ethnic Folkways Records FE 4179. 2 LP disks.

Songs of Paraguay: Papi Basaldua and Grupo Cantares. 1994. JVC VICG 5341-2. Compact disc.

Soul Vine Shaman. 1979. Produced by Neelon Crawford and Norman E. Whitten, Jr., with Julian Santi Vargas, María Aguinda Mamallacta, and William Belzner. New York: Neelon Crawford. LP disk.

Surinam: Javanese Music. 1977. Produced by Annemarie de Waal Malefijt and Verna Gillis. Lyrichord LLST 7317. LP disk.

Tango: Zero Hour. 1986. Astor Piazzolla and the New Tango Quintet. Produced by Kip Hanrahan. American Clave. MCA Records. PAND-42138. Compact disc.

Todos os Sons. 1995. Marlui Miranda. São Paulo, Brazil: Associação IHU, Pró Musica e Arte Indigenas. Pau Brasil Som Imagem e Editora, CGC 65.012l.478/0001-87. Compact disc.

Trio elétrico/carnaval de Bahia. 1990. RGE 3 GLO 121. LP disk.

Tropicalísimo. 1989. Peregoyo y Su Combo Vacana [Colombia]. World Circuit WCD 015.

Txai! 1990. Milton Nascimento. Brazil: Discos C.B.S. 177.228/1-464138. Cassette.

Typiquement D.O.M. Compilation 89 Antilles-Guyane. 1989. Produced by Dany Play. Cayenne: TDM production. LP disk.

Vallenato Dynamos! 1990. Meriño Brothers [Colombia]. Globe-Style ORB 049. Compact disc.

Victor Jara: Canto Libre. 1993. Victor Jara [Chile]. Monitor MCD 71799.

Violas da minha terra. 1978. Moacir Laurentino and Sebastião da Silva. Chantecler: 2-04-405-075. LP disk.

Yanoama: Tecniche Vocali Sciamanismo. 1979. Recorded by Ettore Biocca. Produced by Diego Carpitella. Suoni CETRA SU 5003. LP disc.

Wayãpi Guyane. 1980. Produced by Jean-Michel Beaudet. Paris: Musee de l'Homme, SELAF-ORSTOM CETO 792. LP disk.

Zabumba/SE. 1979. Documentário Sonoro do Folclore Brasileiro CDFB-031(1979). LP disk.

MEXICO AND CENTRAL AMERICA

Amando en Tiempo de Guerra (Loving in Times of War). 1988. Luis Enrique Mejía Godoy and Mancotal. Redwood Records 8805. LP disk.

Antología del Son de México. 1985. Produced by Baruj Lieberman, Eduardo Llerenas, and Enrique Ramírez de Arellano. México, D. F.: Corason. Distributed by Rounder Records Corp., Cambridge, Mass. 3 compact discs.

Berry Wine Days. 1996. Peter's Boom and Chime. Produced by Gina Scott. Stonetree Records. LP disk.

The Black Caribs of Honduras. 1953. Produced by Doris Stone. Folkways FE 4435. LP disk.

Black History/Black Culture. 1991. Soul Vibrations. Aural Tradition ATRCD 118 and Redwood Records. LP disk.

Calypsos of Costa Rica. N. d. Produced by Walter Ferguson. Folkways Records, FTS 31309. LP disk.

Cantos de Tierra Adentro. 1980. Los Soñadores de Sarawaska. Ocarina MC-004. LP disk.

Chatuye: Heartbeat in the Music. 1992. Produced by G. Simeon Pillich. Arhoolie Productions, CD-383. Compact disc.

"Chicken Scratch"—Popular Dance Music of the Indians of Southern Arizona. 1972. Canyon C-6085 and C-6162. 2 LP disks.

Cinco siglos de bandas en México. N. d. Vols. 2–4. México, D. F.: Archivo Etnográfico del Instituto Nacional Indigenista FONAPAS. 3 LP disks.

Dabuyabarugu: Inside the Temple: Sacred Music of the Garifuna of Belize. 1982. Produced by Carol Jenkins and Travis Jenkins. Smithsonian Folkways Records, FE4032. LP disk.

Deer Dancer: Jessita Reyes and Grupo Yaqui. 1991. Talking Taco Records TT 110. Compact disc.

El Conjunto Murrietta Tocando Norteño. 1978. Canyon C–6162. LP disk.

El Mariachi Tepalcatepec de Michoacán: El Michoacano. 1994. Discos Dos Coronas DDC 9401. Compact disc.

El Triunfo: Los Camperos de Valles—Sones de la Huasteca. 1992. Los Camperos de Valles. Produced by Eduardo Llerenas. Música Tradicional MTCD 007. Cassette disc.

En Busca de la Música Maya: Canción de la Selva Lacandona. 1976. Produced by Yuichi Matsumura and Mabuchi Usaburo. Japan: King Records GXH (k) 5001-3. LP disk.

Fiesta de Palo de Mayo. 1986. Dimensión Costeña. ENIGRAC CE-6009. LP disk.

Fiesta Tropical. 1991. Banda Blanca. Sonotone Music POW 6017. LP disk.

Flautas Indígenas de México. 1995. México, D. F.: Departamento de Etnomusicología del Instituto Nacional Indigenista, serie VII: Organología Indígena, vol.1, INI-VII-0. Compact disc.

Guaymi—Térraba. Antología de Música Indígena Costarricense. N. d. Asociación Indígena de Costa Rica, Pablo Presbere. Onda Nueva. LP disk.

Guitarra Armada. 1988. Carlos Mejía Godoy and Luis Enrique Mejía Godoy. Rounder Records 4022. Originally released on INDICA, S.A. (Costa Rica) MC-1147, 1979, re-issued on ENIGRAC MC-015 and MC 1147, 1980. LP disk.

Honduras—Música Folklórica. N. d. [1988]. Tegucigalpa: Secretaría del Turismo y Cultura. LP disk.

Indian Music of Mexico. 1952. Recorded and produced by Henrietta Yurchenko. Folkways FE-4413. LP disk.

Indian Music of Mexico. 1957. Recorded and produced by Laura Boulton. Folkways FW-8851. LP disk.

Indian Music of Northwest Mexico. 1977. Canyon C-8001. LP disk.

Indian Music of Northwest Mexico. 1978. Canyon C-8001. LP disk.

Instrumental Folk Music of Panama. 1994. Danzas Panama. JVC VICG-5338. Compact disc.

Kunda erer ma-ir ranto niuff/Aguilas que no se olvidan. 1996. Grupo indígena chichimeca de San Luis de la Paz, Guanajuato. México, D. F.: Departamento de Etnomusicología del Instituto Nacional Indigenista. INI-VI-05. Compact disc.

La Misa Campesina. N. d. [1980]. Carlos Mejía Godoy and El Taller de Sonido Popular. ENIGRAC NCLP—5012. LP disk.

La música en la Mixteca. 1994. México, D. F.: Subdirección de Radio del Instituto Nacional Indigenista and Secretaría de Desarrollo Social, serie "Sonidos del México Profundo," núm.7, INI-RAD-II-7; XETLA. Compact disc.

La música en la Montaña de Guerrero. 1994. México, D. F.: Subdirección de Radio del Instituto Nacional Indigenista and Secretaría de Desarrollo Social; serie "Sonidos del México Profundo," núm.10, INI-RAD-II- 10; XEZV. Compact disc.

La Sierra Gorda que Canta: A lo Divino y a lo Humano. 1995. Recorded and produced by María Isabel Flores Solano et al. Guanajuato: Instituto de la Cultura del Estado de Guanajuato, Dirección General de Culturas Populares y Discos Corazón. Compact disc.

La Voz de la Costa Chica. 1994. Instituto Nacional Indigenista. Subdirección de Radio Difusora XEJAM, "La voz de la Costa Chica," Jamiltepec, Oaxaca, and Secretaría de Desarrollo Social, INI-RAD-I- 3. Compact disc.

La Voz de las Huastecas. 1994. Instituto Nacional Indigenista. México, D. F.: Subdirección de Radio Difusora XEANT, "La voz de las Huastecas," and Secretaría de Desarrollo Social, INI-RAD-I- 2. Compact disc.

La Voz de la Sierra: Segundo Aniversario. 1994. Instituto Nacional Indigenista. México, D. F.: Subdirección de Radio Difusora XEGLO "La voz de la Sierra," and Secretaría de Desarrollo Social, INI-RAD-I- 4. Compact disc.

"Lanlaya"—Canciones de Amor Miskito [Nicaragua]. 1987. Grupo Lanlaya. ENIGRAC CE-021. LP disk.

Malekú—Guatuso. Antología de Música Indígena Costarricense. N. d. Asociación Indígena de Costa Rica, Pablo Presbere. Onda Nueva. LP disk.

"Mama Let Me Go." 1989. Dimensión Costeña. ENIGRAC CE-6028. LP disk.

Mariachi Coculense "Rodríguez" de Cirilo Marmolejo 1926–1936. 1993. Reissue produced by Chris Strachwitz. Arhoolie/Folklyric CD 7011. Compact disc.

MAYAPAX: Música tradicional maya de Tixcacal Guardia, Quintana Roo. 1993. Instituto Nacional Indigenista. México, D. F.: XEPET "La voz de los mayas," INI-RAD I-1 (XEPET). Compact disc.

Sones from Jalisco. 1994. Mariachi Reyes del Aserradero. Produced by Eduardo Llerenas. Corason COCD 108. Distributed by Rounder Records, Cambridge, Mass. Compact disc.

Mariachi Tapatío de José Marmolejo. 1994. Reissue produced by Chris Strachwitz. Arhoolie/Folklyric CD 7012. Compact disc.

Maya K'ekchi Strings. 1996. Produced by Gina Scott. Stonetree Records. LP disk.

Mexico: Fiestas of Chiapas and Oaxaca. 1991. Recorded by David Lewiston. Notes by Walter F. Morris, Jr., and David Lewiston. Elektra/Nonesuch 9 72070-2. Compact disc.

Mexico's Pioneer Mariachis. 1993. Mariachi Coculense de Cirilo Marmolejo and Cuarteto Coculense. Vol. 1. Produced by Chris Strachwitz. El Cerrito, Calif.: Arhoolie-Folklyric CD7011. Compact disc.

Mexico's Pioneer Mariachis, Vol. 3.1992. Produced by Chris Strachwitz. Mariachi Vargas de Tecalitlán. El Cerrito, Calif.: Arhoolie-Folklyric CD7015. Compact disc.

Mixtecos y triquis en la frontera norte. 1994. México, D. F.: Subdirección de Radio del Instituto Nacional Indigenista and Secretaría de Desarrollo Social, serie "Sonidos del México Profundo," núm. 5, INI-RAD-II-5 (XEQIN). Compact disc.

Modern Maya: The Indian Music of Chiapas, Mexico. 1975. Produced by Richard Anderson. Folkways FE 4377. LP disk.

Música Afroantillana de Mexico: Combo Ninguno, "Traigo este son." N. d. Combo Ninguno. Discos Pentagrama PCD-070. Compact disc.

Música de la Costa Chica de Guerrero y Oaxaca. 1977. Produced by Thomas Stanford. México, D. F.: Instituto Nacional de Antropología e Historia, Serie de Discos INAH 21. LP disk.

Música Indígena de México, Vol. 5—Música Indígena del Noroeste. 1976. Produced by Arturo Warman. México, D. F.: Instituto Nacional de Antropología e Historia. LP disk.

Music of Mexico, Vol.1. 1994. Conjunto Alma Jarocha, "Sones Jarochos" [Veracruz]. Produced by Daniel E. Sheehy and Chris Strachwitz. El Cerrito, Calif.: Arhoolie CD354. Compact disc.

Music of Mexico, Vol. 2. 1994. Ignacio Montes de Oca H. Conjunto Alma de Apatzingán, "Arriba Tierra Caliente" [Michoacán]. El Cerrito, Calif.: Arhoolie CD426. Compact disc.

Music of Mexico, Vol. 3. 1995. La Huasteca; Huapangos y Sones Huastecos; Los Caimanes (1995) and Los Caporales de Pá-nuco (1978). Produced by Chris Strachwitz. El Cerrito, Calif.: Arhoolie 431. Compact disc.

Music of the Indians of Panama the Cuna (Tule) and Chocoe (Embera) tribes. 1983. Recorded and produced by David Blair Stiffler. Folkways Records, FE 4326. LP disk.

Music of the Miskito Indians of Honduras and Nicaragua. 1981. Recorded and produced by David Blair Stiffler. Smithsonian Folkways Cassette Series 4237. Cassette with liner notes.

Music of the Tarascan Indians of Mexico: Music of Michoacan and nearby mestizo country. 1970. Recorded and produced by Henrietta Yurchenko. New York: Folkways 4217. LP disk.

Music of Veracruz: The Sones Jarochos of Los Pregoneros del Puerto. 1990. Produced by Dan Sheehy and Joe Wilson. Rounder Records CD 5048. Compact disc.

Música Popular Mexicana: Sones Huastecos. 1990. Trío Xoxocapa. Discos Pentagrama PCD 117. Compact disc.

Música Popular Poblana: Homenaje a don Vicente T. Mendoza. 1995. Produced by Garza Marcue and Rosa María. México, D. F.: Fonoteca del Instituto Nacional de Antropología e Historia, INAH 032. LP disk.

Música y canciones de Honduras. 1975. Produced by Rafael Manzanares. ELIA 01—03. 3 LP disks.

Musiques des Communautes indigènes du Mexique. 1969–1970. Produced by Francois Jouffa, Maurice Morea, and Serge Roterdam. Vogue LDM 30103. LP disk.

Nicaragua—música y canto. 1992 (1977). Produced by Salvador Cardenal Argüello. Managua: Radio Güegüence (Banco de América LP). 7 compact discs.

¡Nicaragua...Presente!—Music from Nicaragua Libre. 1989. Produced by John McCutcheon. Rounder Records 4020/4021. LP disk.

Nicaraguan folk music from Masaya: Música Folklórica de Masaya. 1988. Recorded and produced by T. M. Scruggs. Flying Fish FF474. LP disk.

Palo de Mayo. N. d. [1976]. Los Bárbaros del ritmo. Andino 010. LP disk.

Panamá: Tamboritos y mejoranas. 1987. Produced by Eduardo Llerenas and Enrique Ramírez de Arellano. Música Tradicional MT10. LP disk.

Panamanian Folk Music and Dance. 1971 (1968). Produced by Lila Cheville. LP disk.

Qué resuene la tarima. 1990. Grupo Tacoteno. Produced by Modesto López and Juan Meléndez. Discos Pentagrama PCD-146. Compact disc.

Quinto Festival de Música y Danza Indígena. 1994. México: Departamento de Etnomusicología del Instituto Nacional Indigenista, serie VIII. Archivo sonoro digital de la música indígena INI-ETM-VIII-01. Compact disc.

Saumuk Raya—Semilla Nueva. N. d. [1986, Nicaragua]. ENIGRAC 018. LP disk.

Serie de discos. 1967–1979. Irene Vázquez Valle, general editor. México, D. F.: Instituto Nacional de Antropología. 24 LP disks of Mexican regional and indigenous music with descriptive notes.

Sewere. 1996. Scott, Gina. The Original Turtle Shell Band. Produced by Gina Scott. Stonetree Records. LP disk.

Sistema de Radiodifusoras Culturales Indigenistas. 1995. Testimonio musical del trabajo radiofónico. México, D. F.: Subdirección de Radio del Instituto Nacional Indigenista and Secretaría de Desarrollo Social, INI-RAD-I-5. 2 compact discs.

¡Son Tus Perfumenes Mujer! N. d. [mid-1970s]. Los Bisturices Harmónicos. Banco Nicaraguense. LP disk.

Songs and Dances of Honduras. 1955. Produced by Doris Stone. Folkways 6834. LP disk.

Songs of the Garifuna. 1994. Produced by Lita Ariran. JVC VICG-5337. Compact disc.

Street Music of Panama. 1985. Produced by Michel Blaise. Original Music, OML 401. LP disk.

Tarahumara Matachin Music/Matachines Tarahumaras. 1979. Canyon C-8000.

Tradiciones Populares de Costa Rica. N. d. Grupo Curime. San José: Indica S.A., PP-17-83. LP disk.

Traditional Music of the Garifuna (Black Carib) of Belize. 1982. Produced by Carol Jenkins and Travis Jenkins. Smithsonian Folkways Records, FE4031. LP disk.

The Vanishing Indians: Costa Rica and Panama, Tribes of the Talamanca Division. N. d. Lyrichord Stereo LLST 7378. LP disk.

Yaqui Dances—the Pascola Music of the Yaqui Indians of Sonora, Mexico. 1957. Produced by Samuel Charters. Folkways FW-957. LP disk.

Yaqui Festive and Ritual Music. 1972. Canyon C-6140. LP disk.

Yaqui Fiesta and Religious Music—Historic Recordings from Old Pascua Village. 1980. Produced by Edward H. Spicer. Canyon CR-7999. LP disk.

Yaqui Pascola Music of Arizona. 1980. Canyon CR-7998. LP disk.

Yaqui Ritual and Festive Music. 1976. Produced by Robert Nuss. Canyon C-6140. LP disk.

Yaqui—Music of the Pascola and Deer Dance. 1976. Canyon C-6099. LP disk.

Ye Stsöke: Breve Antología de la Música Indígena de Talamanca. N. d. Indica S.A., PP- 470-A. LP disk.

CARIBBEAN

A Carnival of Cuban Music. 1990. Routes of Rhythm, vol. 1. Produced by Howard Dratch et al. Rounder CD 5049. Compact disc.

Afro-Cuba: A Musical Anthology. 1994. Produced by Morton Marks. Rounder CD 1088. Compact disc.

Afro-Dominican Music from San Cristóbal, Dominican Republic. 1983. Produced by Morton Marks. Folkways FE 4285. LP disk.

Aires Tropicales. Tropical Breeze. 1996–1997. Various artists. Sony CD 82363/2-469889. Compact disc.

Cantar Maravilloso: Los Muñequitos de Matanzas. 1990. Compiled by Ben Mandelson. Notes by Lucy Duran. GlobeStyle CDORB 053. Compact disc.

Caribbean Carnivals/Carnavals des Caraïbes. 1991. Seeds Records SRC 119. Compact disc.

Caribbean Island Music: Songs and Dances of Haiti, the Dominican Republic and Jamaica. 1972. Produced by John Storm Roberts. Nonesuch H-72047. LP disk.

Caribbean Revels: Haitian Rara and Dominican Gaga. 1991. Recorded by Verna Gillis. Notes by Gage Averill and Verna Gillis. Smithsonian Folkways CD SF 40402. Compact disc.

Cien por ciento puertorriqueño. 1997(?). Edwin Colón Zayas y su Taller Campesino [Puerto Rico]. Disco Hit Productions DHCD-8034.

Con un Poco de Songo. 1989. Batacumbelé [Puerto Rico]. Disco Hit Productions DHLP-008-CD.

Cradle of the New World. 1976. Recorded by Verna Gillis. Folkways FE 4283. LP disk.

Cuban Counterpoint: History of the Son Montuno. 1992. Rounder CD 1078. Compact disc.

Cuban Dance Party. 1990. Routes of Rhythm, vol. 2. Produced by Howard Dratch et al. Rounder CD 5050. Compact disc.

Drums of Defiance: Maroon Music from the Earliest Free Black Communities of Jamaica. 1992. Recorded and Compiled by Kenneth Bilby. Smithsonian/Folkways CD SF 40412. Compact Disc.

El Rey y La Reina del Merengue. 1996. Johnny Ventura y Milly [Dominican Republic]. Sony PROD-7060. Compact disc.

En jíbaro y tropical. 1997. Taller Musical Retablo [Puerto Rico]. TMR02CD. Compact disc.

The Golden Age of Calypso: Dances of the Caribbean Islands. 1996. Compiled by Philippe Zani. EPM Musique 995772. Compact disc.

The Island of Española. 1976. Recorded by Verna Gillis. Folkways FE 4282. LP disk.

The Island of Quisqueya. 1976. Recorded by Verna Gillis. Folkways FE 4281. LP disk.

Los Muñequitos de Matanzas: Vacunao. 1995. Qbadisc QB 9017. Compact disc.

Los Pleneros de la 21 and Conjunto Melodía Tropical: Puerto Rico, Puerto Rico Mi Tierra Natal. 1990. Notes by Howard Weiss, Morton Marks, and Ethel Raim. Shanachie SH 65001. Compact disc.

Maroon Music from the Earliest Free Black Communities of Jamaica. 1992. Produced by Kenneth Bilby. Washington, D.C.: Smithsonian/Folkways Recordings CD ST 40412. Compact disc.

Music from Oriente de Cuba: The Estudiantina Tradition. 1995. Estudiantina Invasora. Nimbus NI 5448. Compact disc.

The Music of Santería: The Oru del Igbodu. 1994. Produced by John Amira. Companion book by John Amira and Steven Cornelius. White Cliffs Media WCM 9346. Compact disc.

The Original Mambo Kings: An Introduction to Afro-Cubop 1948–1954. 1993. Notes by Max Salazar. Verve 3214-513-876-2. Compact disc.

Orquesta Aragon: The Heart of Havana, vol. 2. 1993. RCA 3488-2-RL. Compact disc.

Pa' Que Suene el Pandero . . . ¡PLENEALO! [Puerto Rico]. 1997(?). Disco Hit Productions DHCD-8102. Compact disc.

Paracumbé tambó. 1997. Produced by Emanuel Dufrasne González and Nelie Lebón Robles [Puerto Rico]. Distributed by Rounder Records. Ashé CD 2005. Compact disc.

Rhythms of Rapture: Sacred Musics of Haitian Vodou. 1995. Produced by Elizabeth McAlister. Smithsonian/Folkways SF CD 49464. Compact disc.

Sacred Rhythms of Cuban Santería/Ritmos sagrados de la santería cubana. 1995. Centro de Investigación y Desarollo de la Música Cubana. Smithsonian/Folkways SF CD 40419. Compact disc.

Septetos Cubanos: Sones de Cuba. 1990. Produced by Eduardo Llerenas. Música Tradicional MTCD 113/4. Distributed by Rounder. 2 compact discs.

Sones Cubanos: Sextetos Cubanos, vol. 1: Sones 1930. 1991. Produced by Chris Strachwitz and Michael Iván Avalos. Arhoolie CD 7003. Compact disc.

Songs from the North. 1978. Recorded by Verna Gillis. Folkways FE 4284. LP disk.

Spirit Rhythms: Sacred Drumming and Chants from Cuba. N. d. Nueva Generación. Latitudes LT 50603. Compact disc.

West Indies: An Island Carnival. 1991. Produced by Krister Malm. Notes by Daniel Sheehy and Krister Malm. Compact disc.

A Guide to Films and Videos

GENERAL

The Americas II. The JVC Video Anthology of World Music and Dance, vol. 28. 1990. Edited by Fujii, Tomoaki. (VTMV-58). Videocassette.

The JVC/Smithsonian Folkways Video Anthology of World Music and Dance of the Americas, vols. 4–6. 1995. Directed by Okada, Yuki. Montpelier, Vt.: Multicultural Media, ML3410.C362 1999 VD4 (3 videocassettes, from a set of 6).

"Teaching the Music of Hispanic Americans." 1991. Organized by Dale A. Olsen, Linda O'Brien-Rothe, and Daniel E. Sheehy for *Teaching Music with a Multicultural Approach*, MENC Preconference Symposium of the Music Educators National Conference Annual Meeting, Washington, D.C., 1990. Reston, Va.: Music Educators National Conference. Videocassette and book.

SOUTH AMERICA

A Festa de Moça (The Girl's Celebration). 1987. Directed by Vincent Carelli. Distributed by Video Data Bank, Chicago, Ill. Videocassette.

Apu Condor (The Condor God). 1992. Directed by Gianfranco Norelli. Distributed by Documentary Educational Resouces, Watertown, Mass. Videocassette.

Bossa Nova: Music and Reminiscences. 1993. Directed by Walter Saslles. Barre, Vt.: Multicultural Media, Videocassette.

Carnival Bahia. 1982. Produced by Carlo Pasini and Peter Fry. Films Incorporated Video, Chicago. Videocassette.

Carnival in Q'eros: Where the Mountains Meet the Jungle. 1990. Written and filmed by John Cohen. Distrubuted by University of California Extension Media Center, Berkeley. Videocassette, 16 mm.

Caxiri or Manioc Beer. 1987. Victor Fuks. Distributed by Indiana University Audio/Visual Center, Bloomington. Videocassette.

Central and South America: Belize, Brazil, Chile, Colombia, Guatemala, Guyana. The JVC/Smithsonian Folkways Video Anthology of World Music and Dance of the Americas, vol. 5 1995. Directed by Yuki Okada. Montpelier, Vt.: Multicultural Media, ML3410.C362 1999 VD5 (1 videocassette).

Central and South America: Mexico, Nicaragua, Peru, Venezuela. The JVC/Smithsonian Folkways Video Anthology of World Music and Dance of the Americas, vol. 6 1995. Directed by Yuki Okada. Montpelier, Vt.: Multicultural Media, ML3410.C362 1999 VD6 (1 videocassette).

Corpus Christi en Cusco. 1996. Directed by Luis Figueroa. Produced by Juan Ossio [festival in Cusco, Peru]. Archive of Traditional Andean Music, Pontífica Universidad Católica del Perú. VAMTA-7. Videocassette.

Demonstration of Multiple Relationships between Music and Culture of the Waiápi. 1989. Victor Fuks. Distributed by Indiana University Audio/Visual Center, Bloomington. Videocassette.

El Charanguero: Jaime Torres, the Charango Player. 1996. Produced by Simona and Jeffrey Briggs. Multicultural Media 1007E. Videocassette.

Fiesta de la Virgen del Carmen de Paucartambo. 1994. Directed by Gisela Cánepa Koch [festival in Paucartambo, Peru]. Archive of Traditional Andean Music, Pontífica Universidad Católica del Perú. VAMTA-2. Videocassette.

Gaiteros: The Music of Northern Colombia. N. d. Produced by Egberto Bermúdez. 3/4-inch videocassette.

Instrumentos y Géneros Musicales de Lamayeque. 1994. Directed by Gisela Cánepa Koch [northern Peru]. Archive of Traditional Andean Music, Pontífica Universidad Católica del Perú. VAMT-3. Videocassette.

José Carlos and His Spirits: The Ritual Initiation of Zelador Dos Orixas in a Brazilian Umbanda Center. 1989. Produced by Sidney M. Greenfield. Department of Anthropology, University of Wisconsin-Milwaukee. Videocassette.

La Fiesta del Agua. 1995. Diected by Gisela Cánepa Koch [festival in Huarochirí, Lima, Peru]. Archive of Traditional Andean Music, Pontífica Universidad Católica del Perú. VAMTA-5. Videocassette.

Las Cruces de Porcón. 1997. Directed by Gisela Cánepa Koch [festival in Cajamarca, Peru]. Archive of Traditional Andean Music, Pontífica Universidad Católica del Perú. VAMTA-6. Videocassette.

Mamita Candelaria. 1996. Directed by Luis Figueroa. Produced by Juan Ossio [festival in Puno, Peru]. Archive of Traditional Andean Music, Pontífica Universidad Católica del Perú. VAMTA-8. Videocassette.

Mountain Music of Peru. 1984. John Cohen. New York: Cinema Guild. Videocassette, 16 mm.

Music, Dance and Festival. 1987. Victor Fuks. Bloomington: Indiana University Audio/Visual Center. Videocassette.

Palenque: Un Canto. 1992. Produced and directed by María Raquel Bozzi [about San Basilio de Palenque, Colombia]. Distributed by María Raquel Bozzi, Los Angeles, Calif. Videocasssette.

Peruvian Weaving: A Continuous Warp. 1980. John Cohen. New York: Cinema Guild. Videocassette, 16 mm.

Q'eros, the Shape of Survival. 1979. John Cohen. New York: Cinema Guild. Videocassette, 16 mm.

Shotguns and Accordions: Music of the Marijuana Regions of Colombia. 1983. Beats of the Heart Series. Produced and directed by Jeremy Marre. Shanachie SH-1205. Videocassette.

The Spirit of Samba: Black Music of Brazil. 1983. Beats of the Heart Series. Produced and directed by Jeremy Marre. Shanachie SH-1207. Videocassette.

Survivors of the Rainforest. 1993. Directed by Andy Jillings. Distributed by Channel 4, London. Videocassette.

Tinka de Alpaca. 1994. Directed by Gisela Cánepa Koch [festival in Arequipa, Peru]. Archive of Traditional Andean Music, Pontífica Universidad Católica del Perú. VAMTA-12. Videocassette.

Toro Pucllay: El Juego del Toro. 1997. Directed by Luis Figueroa. Produced by Juan Ossio [festival in Apurímac, Peru]. Archive of Traditional Andean Music, Pontífica Universidad Católica del Perú. VAMTA-9. Videocassette.

Umbanda: The Problem Solver. Produced by Steven Cross and Peter Fry. Films Incorporated Video, Chicago. Videocassette.

Waiampi Instrumental Music. 1987. Victor Fuks. Distributed by Indiana University Audio/Visual Center, Bloomington. Videocassette.

Waiápi Instrumental Music. 1988. Victor Fuks. Distributed by Indiana University Audio/Visual Center, Bloomington. Videocassette.

Warao. 1975. Jorge Preloran. University of California, Los Angeles. Videocassette, 16 mm.

Wylancha. 1991. Directed by Gisela Cánepa Koch. Archive of Traditional Andean Music, Pontífica Universidad Católica del Perú. VAMTA-4. Videocassette.Videocassette.

Yanomamö. 1975. Napoleon A. Chagnon and Timothy Asch. Distributed by University of Pennsylvania. Videocassette, 16 mm.

MIDDLE LATIN AMERICA

Central and South America: Belize, Brazil, Chile, Colombia, Guatemala, Guyana. The JVC/Smithsonian Folkways Video Anthology of World Music and Dance of the Americas, vol. 5 1995. Directed by Yuki Okada. Montpelier, Vt.: Multicultural Media, ML3410.C362 1999 VD5 (1 videocassette).

Central and South America: Mexico, Nicaragua, Peru, Venezuela. The JVC/Smithsonian Folkways Video Anthology of World Music and Dance of the Americas, vol. 6 1995. Directed by Yuki Okada. Montpelier, Vt.: Multicultural Media, ML3410.C362 1999 VD6 (1 videocassette).

The Devil's Dream. 1992. Mary Ellen Davis [about Guatemalan music]. The Cinema Guild, New York. 16 mm.

Enemies of Silence. 1991. Produced by Jeremy Marre [about two mariachi musicians in Mexico]. Harcourt Films, London. Videocassette, 16 mm.

Gimme Punta Rock . . . Belizean Music. 1994. Produced by Peter and Suzanne Coonradt. Available from Partners in Video, 3762 Elizabeth St., Riverside, Calif. 92506. Videocassette.

Huichol Sacred Pilgrimage to Wirikuta. 1991. Produced by Larain Boyll. University of California Extension Center for Media and Independent Learning, Berkeley. Videocassette.

Maya Fiesta. 1988. Produced by Allan F. Burns and Alan Saperstein [about the San Miguel festival of Guatemalan migrants in Florida]. Indiantown, Fla.: Corn-Maya. Videocassette.

Tex-Mex: Music of the Texas-Mexican Borderlands. Beats of the Heart Series. Produced and directed by Jeremy Marre. Shanachie SH-1206. Videocassette.

CARIBBEAN

The Caribbean [Barbados, Cuba, Curaçao and Bonaire, Dominica, Haiti, Jamaica, Martinique, Puerto Rico, St. Lucia, Trinidad and Tobago] *The JVC/Smithsonian Folkways Video Anthology of World Music and Dance of the Americas,* vol. 4 1995. Directed by Yuki Okada. Montpelier, Vt.: Multicultural Media, ML3410.C362 1999 VD4 (1 videocassette).

Caribbean Crucible. 1984. Directed by Dennis Marks [about African background, Dominican Republic, and Jamaica]. Repercussions: A Celebration of African-American Music (series). Videocassette.

Divine Horsemen: The Living Gods of Haiti. 1985. Filmed by Maya Deren. Mystic Fire M101. Videocassette.

En el País de los Orichas. 1993. Conjunto Folklórico Nacional de Cuba. Distributed by Blackmind Book Boutique, Brooklyn, N.Y. Videocassette.

The King Does Not Lie: The Initiation of a Shango Priest. 1992. Produced by Judith Gleason and Elisa Mereghette. New York: Filmakers Library. Videocassette.

Legacy of the Spirits. 1985. Filmed by Karen Kramer. New York: Erzulie Films. 16 mm.

Los Muñequitos de Matanzas. 1993. Produced by E. Natatcha Estebanez [about Cuban music]. Distributed by WGBH Educational Foundation, Boston. Videocassette.

Oggun. 1993. Conjunto Folklórico Nacional de Cuba. Distributed by Blackmind Book Boutique, Brooklyn, N.Y. Videocassette.

Routes of Rhythm. ca. 1993. Narrated by Harry Belafonte [Cuban music and dance]. Distributed by Multicultural Media. 3 videocassettes and study guide.

*Rumbas y comparsas de C*uba. 1993. Distributed by Blackmind Book Boutique, Brooklyn, N.Y. Videocassette.

*Salsa: Latin Pop in the Cities.*1983. Beats of the Heart Series. Produced and directed by Jeremy Marre. Shanachie SH-1201. Videocassette.

Sworn to the Drum: A Tribute to Francisco Aguabella. 1995. Directed by Les Blank. Distributed by Flower Films, El Cerrito, Calif. Videocassette, 16mm.

Voices of the Orishas. 1994. Produced and directed by Alvaro Pérez Betancourt. Berkeley: University of California Extension Center for Media and Independent Learning. Videocassette.

Notes on the CD / Audio Examples

1. Yanomamö male shaman's curing song, excerpt (1:32)
   Performed by the headman Iyäwei, who is chanting to *hekura* under the influence of *ebena*
   Recorded by Pitts (from Coppens Collection, Caracas) on 20 May 1969 in Iyäweiteri, a Yanomamö village, Boca del Ocamo, Amazonas, Venezuela

2. Yekuana male shaman's curing song, excerpt (1:02)
   Performed near a Yekuana village, Amazonas, Venezuela
   Recorded by Walter Coppens

3. Warao male *wisiratu* shaman's curing song, excerpt (1:33)
   Performed by Bernardo Tobal, accompanying himself with his *hebu mataro* rattle
   Recorded by Dale A. Olsen on 25 August 1972 in Yaruara Akoho, Delta Amacura Federal Territory, Venezuela

4. Warao male *hoarotu* shaman's curing song, excerpt (0:49)
   Performed by José Antonio Páez
   Recorded by Dale A. Olsen on 1 August 1972 in Yaruara Akoho, Delta Amacura Federal Territory, Venezuela

5. *Sikuriada* (music for *siku* panpipes) (1:30)
   Performed by musicians from Jachakalla, Charkas, Potosí, Bolivia
   Six *siku* (*zampoña*), including one *sanka* (eight tubes plus seven tubes); two *ch'ilis* (small, one octave higher: eight tubes plus seven tubes); and *bombo* (bass drum)
   Recorded by Henry Stobart in November 1986 in Charkas Province, northern Potosí Department, Bolivia

6. "Kulwa" (*kupla, cobla*) (1:19)
   Approximately forty male musicians from Wapaka community kneel while playing their *julajula* panpipes (five sizes, tuned in octaves)
   Recorded by Henry Stobart in October 1986 in Charka Province, northern Potosí Department, Bolivia

7. *Lichiwayu* notch flutes (1:36)
   Notch flutes of two sizes: *jatunta* (big) and *juch'uycito* (small), a fifth apart, and *caja* drum (played with two hard beaters)
   Recorded by Henry Stobart in August 1987 in Alonso de Ibáñez Province, northern Potosí Department, Bolivia

8. "Walata Grande" ('Great Walata') *huayño* (1:21)
   Performed by the Tocamarka tropa (ensemble) from Walata Grande
   Eighteen *musiñu* duct flutes (four sizes playing in parallel fifths, octaves, and dissonant intervals); two *clarinetos* (wooden clarinets); *clarín* (with clarinet mouthpiece); and four *tamboras* (military side drums)
   Recorded by Henry Stobart in December 1986 in Lahuachaka, Aroma Province, La Paz Department, Bolivia

9. *Tarkeada* (music for *tarka* flutes) (2:17)

Performed by musicians from Zona Sud. Twenty-six *tarka* duct flutes (two sizes tuned in parallel fifths), three *tamboras* (military side drums), and one *bombo* (bass drum)

Recorded by Henry Stobart in March 1987 in Lahuachaka, Cercado Province, Oruro Department, Bolivia

10. "Lunesta, martesta" ('Mondays, Tuesdays') (2:02)

Performers from Ayllu Sikuya, Chayanta Province, Potosí Department, Bolivia

Two female singers accompanied by *charango*

Recorded by Henry Stobart in May 1987 in Chayanta Province, northern Potosí Department, Bolivia

11. *Folia de reis* (*folia* of the Magi) (1:52)

Performed by members of the Folias de Reis Unidos dos Marinheiros, from Itaú, Minas Gerais, Brazil. Accordion, three *pandeiros* (tambourines), *violão* (guitar), *viola* (small guitar), male singer, and chorus

Recorded by Welson A. Tremura on 16 August 1997 in Olimpia, São Paulo, Brazil, during the Thirty-third Folkloric Festival of Olimpia

12. Moçambique (1:19)

Performed by members of the Moçambique de Nossa Senhora do Rosário, from Uberlândia, Minas Gerais, Brazil

Five *bumbos* (bass drums), three *chocalhos tipo prato* (plate-shaped shakers), *apito* (whistle), *grupo de figurantes* (dancers)

Recorded by Welson A. Tremura on 17 August 1997 in Olimpia, São Paulo, Brazil, during the Thirty-third Folkloric Festival of Olimpia

13. "É bonito cantar" ("Singing Is Beautiful"), *cantoria* of the *embolada* genre (1:30)

Performed by Carlito de Arapiraca and Furió on a street corner in Alagoas, Brazil. Two *pandeiros* played by the singers

Recorded by Larry Crook on 13 July 1984 in Arapiraca, Alagoas, Brazil

14. *Forró do pife* (*forró* for *banda de pífanos*) (1:53)

Performed by the Bandinha Cultural de Caruaru Severino: Pedro da Silva and João Manuel da Silva, *pífanos* (cane fifes); Antônio do Nascimento, *tarol* (thin snare drum); Manuel dos Santos, *zabumba* (bass drum); Maurício Antônio da Silva, *surdo* (tenor drum); and João Alfredo dos Santos, *pratos* (hand cymbals)

Recorded by Larry Crook on 19 April 1987 in Caruaru, Pernambuco, Brazil

15. *Forró de sanfona* (*forró* for accordion) (1:26)

Performed by Toninho de Calderão, keyboard accordion, and unknown musicians playing *zabumba*, *tarol*, *pratos*, and triangle

Recorded by Larry Crook on 19 September 1987 in Caruaru, Pernambuco, Brazil

16. "Boa noite todo povo" ("Good Night Everyone"), a *maracatú rural* (rural *maracatú*) (1:46)

Performed by the group Maracatú Leão Brasileiro, featuring a *mestre de toadas* (lead singer) and other anonymous musicians, at a street performance during carnival celebrations

Trumpet, *tarol*, *congué* (iron bell), *onça* (large friction drum), and *ganzá* (metal shaker); one microphone shared by the lead singer and the trumpeter
Recorded by Larry Crook on 27 February 1988 in Recife, Pernambuco, Brazil

17. *Canto a lo pueta* ("song of the poet"), also called *décima* (1:47)
Performed by Santos Rubio, a blind musician who accompanies himself on the *guitarrón*.
Recorded by Daniel E. Sheehy in 1973 in Pirque, Puente Alto, Santiago Province, Chile

18. "Tengo que hacer un barquito" ("I Have to Make a Little Boat"), *cueca* dance-song (1:43)
Sung by Eufrasia Ugarte, who accompanies herself on button accordion. She is also accompanied by Benito Aranda, who strikes carefully loosened slats of a wooden box with his fingers
Recorded by Daniel E. Sheehy in 1973 in San José, Algarrobo, Valparaíso Province, Chile

19..Song by blind *rondador* (panpipe) player (0:59)
Performed by a beggar-musician in the Ibarra market
Recorded by Charles Sigmund in 1975 in Ibarra, Ecuador

20. Song in Quechua about a young man, alone in the world, looking for a wife (2:14)
Performed by Pedro Tasiguano, who accompanies himself on the harp
Recorded by Charles Sigmund in 1975 in Llano Grande, 24 kilometers north of Quito, Ecuador

21. *Huayno* (Andean dance-song) (2:35)
Performed by Narciso Morales Romero on *roncador y caja* (pipe and tabor)
Recorded by Dale A. Olsen on 1 September 1979 in Huaylas, Ancash Department, Peru

22. Festival de la Virgen del Carmen (patronal festival dedicated to the Virgin of Carmen) (1:30)
Performed by local musicians and people from Alto Otuzco, Cajamarca, Peru
Female vocalists, *flauta y caja* (pipe and tabor), two *clarines* (*clarín* trumpets)
Recorded by Dale A. Olsen on 16 July 1979 in Alto Otuzco, Cajamarca, Peru

23. "No lo cuentes a nadie" ("Don't Tell Anyone"), *huayno* (2:42)
Performed by the *orquesta típica* Selección del Centro, directed by Julio Rosales Huatuco. Harp, two violins, clarinets, alto and tenor saxophones
Recorded by Dale A. Olsen on Sunday, 24 June 1979 in Acolla, Junín, Peru, during a private party for the festival of San Juan Bautista (Saint John the Baptist)

24. "Quien ha visto aquel volcán" ('Whoever Has Seen this Volcano' [El Misti]), *yaraví* from Puquina, Arequipa (2:44)
Performed by Nicanor Abarca Puma on *charango*
Recorded by Dale A. Olsen on 12 August 1979 in Arequipa, Peru

25. "Zancudito," *hatajo de negritos* (2:02)
Performed by Amador Vallumbrosio, *caporal* (director), and José Lurita, violin

Recorded by William David Tompkins in 1976 in El Carmen, Chincha Province, Peru

26. "La Catira" ("The Light-Haired Woman") (2:42)

Performed by José León (Venezuela), *bandola*, and musicians playing *cuatro* (small guitar), *maracas*, and string bass

Recorded by Dale A. Olsen on 17 March 1982 at the School of Music, Florida State University, Tallahassee

27. Festival de San Juan (patronal festival of Saint John) (1:41)

Private performance during a party on Sunday afternoon with *mina* (large drum), *curbata* (small drum), and *laures* (sticks struck on sides of *mina* drum)

Recorded by Dale A. Olsen on 24 June 1974 in Curiepe, Barlovento, Venezuela

28. "Cuaulleros" (1:47)

Performed by Nicandro Aquino, harp; José María Isidro and Teódulo Isidro, violins; and Eleazar Arrollo, *jarana*, with *uaultl* (*palos* or sticks) and *xauanillsll* (*sonajas* or bells)

Recorded by Arturo Chamorro on 1 October 1984 in Pómaro, Michoacán, Mexico

29. *Danza de corpus* (Corpus Christi dance) (1:22)

Recorded by Arturo Chamorro on 2 October 1984, in Pómaro, Michoacán, Mexico

30. "Siquisirí," *son jarocho* (3:31)

Performed by a trio of *jarocho* musicians: Isidoro Gutiérrez, *jarana* and *pregonero* (lead singer); Luis "Huicho" Delfín, *requinto jarocho*; and Gregorio (last name unknown), harp

Recorded by Daniel E. Sheehy on 22 February 1978 in the *cantina Las Palomas* (The Doves) in Alvarado, Veracruz, Mexico.

31. "Ámalihaní," the central rite of ancestor placation in a Garifuna family *dügü* ceremony (2:16)

Performed in the *dabuyaba* (ancestral temple) in Dangriga, Belize, by the shaman (*buyei*) John Mariano (playing *sísara*), three drummers (playing three *garawoun segunda* drums), a song leader, and singing family members and relatives

Text: "My grandmother, we are quieting you down. My grandmother, the cock is crowing. It is silent now. I am for you; you are for me. Grandmother, water."

Recorded by Oliver Greene on 16 July 1996 in Dangriga, Belize

32. "El Corredizo" (refers to running, moving) (1:34)

Music to accompany *chinegros* performance; the second of several *sones* played between the ritual duels of pairs of dancers.

Pito (vertical, wooden flute) and two *tambores* (small, double-headed drums).

Recorded by T. M. Scruggs in July 1987 in Nindirí, Nicaragua

33. "Los Novios" ("The Sweethearts") (2:27).

This is one of the approximately thirty-six pieces in the Nicaraguan folklore repertoire that accompany the series of dances generically known as el *baile de la marimba* ("the dance of the marimba").

Marimba de arco trio: Marco Martínes, *marimba de arco*; Angel Martínes, *guitar-rilla*; and Omar "Bigote" Martínes, *guitarra*.

Recorded by T. M. Scruggs on 9 March 1989 outside Masatepe, Nicaragua

34. "Los Coros de San Miguel" ('The Choruses of Saint Michael'), *salve* with drums in the style of the southwest Dominican Republic (0:53)

One *palo mayor* (master drum) and two *alcahuetes* (accompanying drums)

Recorded by Martha E. Davis in 1979 in Azua, Dominican Republic

35. "Dice Desidera Arias" ("According to Desidera Arias"), *merengue* (2:30)

Performed by a variant of a typical *merengue* ensemble: male vocalist accompanying himself on *tres* (Cuban small guitar), *güira* (metal scraper), *marimba* (large lamell-lophone), and *tambor* (drum), and chorus (the other musicians).

Recorded by Dale A. Olsen on 17 December 1979 in a hotel courtyard in Boca Chica, Dominican Republic

36. Song for Legba, dance for Ogoun (2:02)

Performed at the *ounfò* (temple) "Kay Nicole"

Recorded by Lois Wilcken on 31 July 1985 in La Plaine, Haiti

37. *Rara* instrumental music (1:41)

Performed by Rara Sanbout

Recorded by Gage Averill on 19 February 1991 in Les Salines, Port-au-Prince, Haiti

38. Afro-Martinican street music (2:16)

One male singer (*chacha* player), two *boula* drums, one *suru* drum, one *bambú* idiophone, one *chacha* rattle, and male chorus (the other musicians)

Recorded by Dale A. Olsen on 21 December 1977 in La Savane Park, Fort-de-France, Martinique

39. "Koumen non k'alé fè," *koutoumba* music (1:30)

Recorded by Jocelyne Guilbault on 25 June 1981 in St. Lucia

Notes on the CD 2 Audio examples

1. "Ibarabo Ago Mo Juba" (Song for Eleguá), *orú cantado* (2:45)

From *Havana, Cuba c. 1957: Rhythms and Songs for the Orishas from the Historic Recordings of Lydia Cabrera and Josefina Tarafa*. Produced, compiled, and annotated by Morton Marks. Smithsonian Folkways SFW CD 40489, Track 6. *Orú cantado* with *batá* drums, performed by Cándido Martínez and Antonio Alberiche, song leaders, and chorus and *batá* trio led by Miguel Santa Cruz and Juan González.

2. "Las Leyendas de Grecia" ("The Legends of Greece"), *guaguancó* (7:20)

Performed by Grupo Afrocuba de Matanzas at the 1989 Smithsonian Folklife Festival. From *Cuba in Washington*. Produced by René López, annotated by René López, Juan Flores, Dr. Danilo Orozco González, Andrew Schloss, and Michael Spiro. Smithsonian Folkways Recordings SFW CD 40461. Track 2, 7:20.

3. "Así es el Changüí" ("That's How Changüí Is"), *changüí* (3:20)

Performed by Grupo Changüí de Guantánamo at the 1989 Smithsonian Folklife Festival. From *Cuba in Washington,* Track 5. Produced by René López, annotated by René López, Juan Flores, Dr. Danilo Orozco González, Andrew Schloss, and Michael Spiro. Smithsonian Folkways Recordings SFW CD 40461.

4. "Yo Canto en el Llano" ("I Sing on the Plain"), *son* (4:51)

Performed by Cuarteto Patria and Compay Segundo at the 1989 Smithsonian Folklife Festival. From *Cuba in Washington*, Track 9. Produced by René López, annotated by René López, Juan Flores, Dr. Danilo Orozco González, Andrew Schloss, and Michael Spiro. Smithsonian Folkways Recordings SFW CD 40461.

5. "En un Eterno Poema" ("In an Eternal Poem"), *seis villarán* (3:53)

Sung by Miguel Santiago Díaz, accompanied by the group Ecos de Borinquen. From *Jíbaro Hasta el Hueso: Puerto Rican Mountain Music by Ecos de Borinquen*, Track 14. Smithsonian Folkways Recordings SFW CD 40506, 2003. Produced by Héctor Vega Druet and Daniel Sheehy, annotated by Daniel Sheehy.

6. "Los Gallos Cantaron" ("The Roosters Sang"), *aguinaldo jíbaro* (5:31)

Sung by Karol Aurora De Jesús, accompanied by the group Ecos de Borinquen. From *Jíbaro Hasta el Hueso: Puerto Rican Mountain Music by Ecos de Borinquen*, Track 13. Smithsonian Folkways Recordings SFW CD 40506, 2003. Produced by Héctor Vega Druet and Daniel Sheehy, annotated by Daniel Sheehy.

7. "El León" ("The Lion"), *plena* (2:49)

Performed by Viento de Agua Unplugged, Héctor "Tito" Matos, lead vocal. From *Viento de Agua Unplugged: Materia Prima*, Track 2. Smithsonian Folkways Recordings SFW CD 40513, 2004. Produced by Héctor "Tito" Matos and Daniel Sheehy, annotated by Juan Flores, Héctor "Tito" Matos, and Daniel Sheehy.

8. "Se Oye Una Voz" ('A Voice Is Heard'), *bomba* (3:30)

Performed by Marcial Reyes y sus Pleneros de Bayamón at the 1989 Smithsonian Folklife Festival. From *Puerto Rico in Washington*, Track 6. Smithsonian Folkways Recordings SFW CD 40460, 1996.

9. "El Cihualteco" ("The Man from Cihuatlán"), *son jalisciense* (2:45)

Performed by Mariachi Los Camperos de Nati Cano. From *¡Viva el Mariachi! Nati Cano's Mariachi Los Camperos*, Track 17. Smithsonian Folkways Recordings SFW CD 40459, 2002. Produced, compiled, and annotated by Daniel Sheehy.

10. "El Perro" ("The Dog"), *son calenteño* (2:14)

Performed by Grupo Arpex. From *¡Tierra Caliente! Music from the Hotlands of Michoacán by Conjunto de Arpa Grande Arpex,* Track 3. Smithsonian Folkways Recordings SFW CD 40536, 2006.

11. "El Aguanieve" ("The Mist"), *son huasteco* (3:13)

Performed by the Huastecan trio, Los Camperos de Valles, Marcos Hernández Rosales (*huapanguera* and vocals), Joel Monroy Martínez (violin and vocals), and Gregorio Solano Medrano (*jarana huasteca* and vocals). From *El Ave de Mi Soñar: Mexican Sones Huastecos*, Track 1. Smithsonian Folkways Recordings SFW

CD 40512, 2005. Produced by Artemio Posadas and Daniel Sheehy, annotated by Daniel Sheehy.

12. "La Bamba," *son jarocho* (3:09)
Performed by José Gutiérrez, Felipe Ochoa, and Marcos Ochoa of Veracruz, Veracruz, Mexico. From *La Bamba: Sones Jarochos from Veracruz*, Track 1. Smithsonian Folkways Recordings SFW CD 40505, 2003.

13. "La Llorona" ("The Weeping Woman") (2:47)
Performed by an unidentified marimba ensemble from Oaxaca, Mexico. From *Marimba Band*, Track 3, Cook Records Cook 05007, n.d. Available at http://www.smithsonianglobalsound.org/containerdetail.aspx?itemid=2196.

14. "Los Trece" ("The Thirteen"), *guarimba* or *seis por ocho* (2:48)
Performed by Marimba Chapinlandia from Guatemala City. From *Chapinlandia: Marimba Music from Guatemala*, Track 6. Smithsonian Folkways Recordings SFW CD 40542, 2007.

15. "Brincando na Roda" ("Playing in the Ring") (3:40)
Performed by Grupo de Capoeira Angola Pelourinho, from Salvador, Bahia, Brazil. From *Capoeira Angola 2: Brincando na Roda*, Track 1. Smithsonian Folkways Recordings SFW CD 40488, 2003.

16. "Sueño de Barrilete" ("Kite Dream"), *tango* (3:03)
Performed by Suni Paz, written by Eladia Blázquez. From *Bandera Mía: Songs of Argentina*, Track 10. Smithsonian Folkways Recordings SFW CD 40532, 2006.

17. "Pájaro Chogüí" ("Chogüí Bird"), *polka paraguaya* (2:03)
Performed by Los Tres Paraguayos. From *Guantanamera! Latin American Hits*, Track 7. Monitor Records MON61490. Available at http://www.smithsonianglobalsound.org.

18. "China Uha Taki" or "Female Sheep Song" (pertaining to the Q'eros Sinalay or marking festival, also called Santos). Recorded 27 October 2005 by Holly Wissler, in the annex of Yanaruma (community of Hapu, one of the eight communities of the Q'eros). The principal female singer is Berta Apasa Machacca, who is accompanied by panpipes.

19. "Pantilla T'ika," or "My Sacred Phallcha Flower." Recorded by John Cohen in 1984 in the community of Hatun Q'eros, one of the eight communities of the Q'eros. The principal female singer is Monica Apasa Vargas. From *Mountain Music of Peru*, Volume 1, Track 38, labeled "Palcha ritual in the corral" (3:36). Smithsonian Folkways Recordings SFW CD 40020, 1991.

INDEX

Candomblé. *See* African heritage in Latin America, Afro-Brazil; religious belief systems, African-derived, Brazil)

Carnival (*Carnaval*), 1, 498, 500
  in Argentina, 392, 507, 513
  in Bolivia, 423, 427, 437, 501, 504, 507, 509, 512
  in Brazil
    Bahia, 367, 369, 495, 497, 502
    Rio de Janeiro, 58, 74, 333, 363, 501
    tropical-forest region, 287
  in the Caribbean, 104
  in Cuba, 121
  in Dominican Republic, 104, 111, 149, 155
  in Haiti, 132–35, 137, 140–41
  in Mexico, 28, 58
  in Panama, 237–38
  in Peru, 451, 476
  in Q'eros culture, 464–66, 469–70, 472
  in Trinidad and Tobago,

cassettes. *See* mass media and music industry, sound recordings

censorship. *See* politics, censorship

cha-cha-chá, 103
  in Cuba, 112, 114, 118, 120, 499
  in Mexico, 204
  in Peru, 459

chant, 41. *See also* myths and narratives; vocal music
  in Bolivia
    enchanting voices, 418
  in Guatemala
    plainchant, 218
    shamanic, 218
  in Haiti, 131
    priyì ginen, 131
    ragga, 138
  in Inca culture
    saynata, 440
    uaricza araui, 440
  in Kuna culture, 251–52, 257–62
    for female puberty ritual, 253, 258
    through flutes (*gormaked*), 254
    for funeral, 257
    medicinal, 258
  in Mapuche culture, 411–14
  in Paraguay, shamanistic, 376
  in Selk'nam culture, 69, 386, 406
  in Tarahumara culture, 212
  in tropical forest, 276
  in Tupinambá culture, 327

chicha music. *See* popular music, rock music, peru

children's games and songs, 54, 69, 81, 91, 132, 496
  in Brazil, 357, 499
  in Dominican Republic, 146
  in Mexico, 196–97, 199–200, 510
  in Venezuela, 306

choral music. *See* vocal music

chordophones, classification of, 39–40
  bows (musical), 182, 206, 210, 475
    berimbau, 357, 497, 499, 503, 511, 513
    cajuavé, 374, 498
    cunculcahue, 387, 501
    gayumba, 153, 502
    gualambau (also *guyrambau*; *lambau, mbarimbau*), 372, 503
    rapá, 374–75, 510
    tambour maringouin, 153
  lutes, bowed (violin-types)
    cello, 118, 120, 330
    kokyu, 96, 505
    one-stringed, 375
    rabeca, 335–36, 509
    rabel, 388, 509
    rebec, 335, 419
    sarangi, 93
    sekeseke, 316, 318–19, 511
    tanpura, 93, 512
    violin (*violin*), 40, 226–27, 232, 319, 335, 373, 375, 390, 419, 471, 478, 481, 499, 506–07, 509–10
      in shamanism, 28
      as introduced by missionaries and other Europeans, 46, 210, 223, 330, 372, 375, 387, 419, 446–48, 450
      as Amerindian instrument, 28, 46–47, 214, 316, 318, 387–88
      for parties, 60
      in ensembles, 118–22, 189, 191, 194–95, 203, 210, 224, 226–27, 237, 241–42, 286, 310, 330, 373, 395–96, 419, 423, 442, 453, 455
      folklore of, 319
      teaching of, 122
      playing style of, 199, 300, 424
      construction of, 210, 223, 375
      accompanying dancers, 214, 424, 453
      accompanying singers, 224
      ritual use of, 227, 389
      one-stringed, 375
  lutes, plucked (guitar–types)
    bandola (*bandola andina, bandola llanera, bandola oriental*) 224, 300, 309–10, 492
    bajo sexto, 196, 496
    bandolim, 335, 497
    bandolín, 224, 300, 310
    bandurria, 106, 119, 224, 373, 445, 447, 464, 474, 497
    banjo, 121, 448, 454, 497
    bordonúa, 166–67, 171, 497
    cavaquinho, 272, 333, 335, 362, 498
    charango (also *quirquincho*; *chillador*), 272, 499, 502, 509
      aesthetic of high–pitched tuning, 44, 432, 445
      amplifiers for, 50

in Argentina, 387, 393
in Bolivia, 419, 424–28, 430–32, 434–36
in *nueva canción* ensembles, 42, 98
in Peru, 445, 447, 458, 462, 464
ritual use of, 424, 451, 504, 511
tuning of, 445

cinco, 300, 304, 310, 499
cinco de seis cuerdas, 300, 304, 499
cinco y medio, 300, 499
cuatro, 40
  in Dominican Republic, 147
  in Puerto Rico, 40, 147, 166–68, 171–72
in Venezuela, 147, 241, 272, 286, 294, 298–300, 302, 304, 306, 309–12, 316, 318, 500
cuatro con cinco cuerdas, 300, 304
cuatro de cinco cuerdas, 300
cuatro y medio, 300
discante, 299
electric bass, 49, 66, 85, 120, 137, 196, 219, 365, 401, 455
electric guitar, 41, 137, 219, 365, 396, 425, 434, 455,
guitar (*guitarra*), 40, 148, 224, 237, 265, 272, 286, 299, 445, 503
  as accompanying instrument, 114, 116–17, 157–58, 160, 172, 189, 191, 193, 195, 202, 214, 245
  amplification for, 41, 50, 219
  in Argentina, 97
  in Bolivia, 419, 424, 430, 434,
  compositions for, 231
  construction of, 113, 210
  in Cuba, 118–21, 123
  in Dominican Republic, 148, 155, 157–58, 160
  in ensembles, 49, 116, 119–21, 137, 168, 194, 203, 227, 238
  ethnicity and playing of, 185, 219
  in Haiti, 137
  in Mexico, 185, 189, 193–94
  in *nueva canción*, 98,
  in Panama, 238–40
  in Peru, 442, 445–48, 450, 454, 458, 462, 479–81, 483–84, 500
  player also taps rhythms on harp, 194
  in Puerto Rico, 164, 168, 171–72
  ritual and shamanistic use of, 227–28
  secular use of, 46
    in Spanish colonial period, 106, 210
  teaching of, 123
  tuning of, 228, 445, 462
  used by Amerindian cultures,
    among Garífuna, 219
    among Maya, 221, 223–24, 226–28
    among Tarahumara, 210, 214
  in Venezuela, 306, 310
guitarra de golpe (also *vihuela*), 194–95, 203, 504

in Mexico, 196, 200
in Paraguay, 377, 381, 511
sesquiáltera. See rhythms and meters
sexuality
  appeal of pop stars, 50
  bars and brothels, 60
  in Bolivia, courtship songs, 418
  in Afro-Brazilian popular genres, 367
  dancing and, 72
  homosexuality, 69
  and identity, 68
  taboos related to, 69
  transvestites, 69
sexual symbolism of musical instruments
  shape of
    in Bolivia, 433
    in Peru, 45
  sound of
    in Bolivia, 433
    in Tukano culture, 43, 52
shamanism. See religious belief systems,
    shamanistic
shawms. *See* aerophones, reed concussion,
    double reeds
singing. *See* vocal music
soca, 88, 93, 103
  in Garífuna culture, 220
societies and social organizations. *See* African
    heritage in Latin America,
    religions (secret societies)
son
  in Argentina, 401
  in Cuba, 111–21
    changüí, 114–15
    son montuno, 115, 173
  in Dominican Republic, 158, 160
  in Guatemala, 224, 226, 230–32
  in Haiti, 137
  in Mexico, 184–86, 203–05, 208
    regional genres of, 188–96
  in Peru, 441, 459, 476, 478, 480
  in Puerto Rico, 173
song. *See* vocal music
song duels
  amor fino, 479
  in Argentina, 398
  in Aymara cultulre, 44
  in Brazil, 74, 336, 498, 501, 509
  cantoria, 336, 498
  in Chile, 41
  cifra, 398
  canto a lo pueta, 41
  controversia, 114, 244
  in Cuba, 114
  cururu paulista, 336
  décima, 479
  desafío, 336, 498, 501
  embolada, 501
  gato, 399
  jarana, 483–84, 487

milonga, 398
  in Nicaragua, 74
  in Panama, 244–45,
  payada, 398, 479
  in Peru, 479, 483–84, 487
  picong, 93, 508
  porfía, 33
  repentistas, 346
  in Trinidad and Tobago, 93, 508
song texts. *See* poetry
spiritual metamorphosis and transformation.
    See also religious belief systems,
    shamanistic
  in Bolivia, 418
  in Kuna culture, 257
  in Mapuche culture, 387
  shamanism and, 56, 278, 320
  in tropical-forest ceremonies, 278, 281
  in Warao culture, 29, 320, 323
Stevenson, Robert M., 16, 23, 35, 183,
    206–08, 233, 462, 485
storytelling. *See* myths and narratives
structure. *See* form and structure
syncretism, 11, 57, 354, 491. *See also* religious
    belief systems, African–derived
taboos, 26,
  in Paraguay, 374.
  in Bolivia, 418
Tambor de Mina. *See* religious belief systems,
    African-derived, Brazil
tango, 64, 83, 97–98, 272, 274, 385, 405–07,
    457, 497, 502, 505, 507, 512
  association with bars and brothels, 60–61
  association with nightclubs (*tanguerías*), 61, 395
  Astor Piazzola, 395–97
  the *bandoneón* (accordion) in, 97, 395
  Carlos Gardel, *274*, 395
  ethnicity of, 98
  fusion with folk, jazz, and rock, 397, 402–04
  and internationalism, 64, 88, 397
  history of, 395–97
  musical forms influenced by, 171
  and politics, 4
  prototypes of, 398
  prominent choreographers of, 397
  prominent musicians of, 395–97
  and social events, 394
  typical orchestras of, 396–97, 405
tempo. *See* rhythm and meter
Tenrikyô. See religious belief systems, Asian
texture (musical). *See* melody, design (structure)
tourism and touring, 20, 53–54, 61–62,
    74–76, 87–89, 98, 103
  in Argentina, 396
  in Bolivia, 417, 428, 434–35
  in Brazil, 276, 288–89, 358, 366–67
  in Dominican Republic, 143, 158–59
  in Guatemala, 231
    Maya culture, 228
  in Haiti, 126, 128, 136–37, 140–41

in Mexico, 184, 204–05, 211
  in Panama, 234–36, 247–48
    Kuna culture, 259, 261
  in Paraguay, 380
  peñas, 61, 159, 400–01, 435, 458, 485, 508
  in Peru, 438, 456, 458, 486
  in Venezuela, 299
    Warao culture, 316, 318
trance. *See* ceremonies; religion; shamanism
transculturation, 7, 37, 79, 272, 490–91 (*see
    also* globalization)
travelers' and missionaries' accounts. *See*
    chroniclers
tuning and temperament. *See also* melody
    (design [structure] of, modes)
  modes and/or scales
    diatonic, 121, 192, 194, 224, 226,
      229–31, 299–01, 375, 378, 421,
      442, 446
    hexatonic, 354
    pentatonic, 421,
  musical instruments
    bordonúa, 167
    charango, 44, 424, 427–28, 430, 432,
      445, 499
    cuatro, 40, 147, 500
      in Dominican Republic, 147
      in Puerto Rico, 167
      in Venezuela, 300
    guitar, 224, 228, 445–46, 500
    harp, in Peru, 446
    mejorana, 241
    requinto, 167
    tiple, 167
    tres, 147
    viola caipira, 335
Turkish people. *See* immigrants to Latin
    America

Umbanda. *See* religious belief systems, African-
    derived, Brazil

vallenato, 49, 514
vals, 514
  in Argentina, 397
  in Dominican Republic, 154, 157
  in Guatemala, 231
  in Mapuche culture, 412–13
  in Mexico, 186
  in Panama, 238
  in Peru (*See also* vals criollo), 453, 484
vals criollo, 97, 447, 453, 462, 484, 514
Vega, Carlos, 41, 52, 386, 439–40, 462, 485,
    487
velorio, 145, 168, 298, 302–03, 381, 505, 510,
    514
Viceroyalty
  of Brazil, 32, 268
  of La Plata, 32, 268
  of New Granada, 32, 47, 268

Viceroyalty (*continued*)
  of New Spain, 31–32, 47, 318, 268
  of Peru, 32, 47, 268, 440
video recordings. *See* mass media and recording
  industry
villancicos, 4, 122, 218, 376, 478, 481
vocal music (*see also* chant; *décima*; hymns;
    laments; lullabies; myths and
    narratives; popular music;
    serenades; *son*; song duels;
    villancicos; work music)
  in Argentina
    alabanza, 391–92, 495
    baguala, 389, 396, 496
    cifra, 397–98, 499
    copla, 392, 399, 500
    estilo, 397, 399, 501
    gloria, 391
    gozo, 391
    milonga, 171, 395, 397–98, 412, 506
    murga, 392, 394, 507
    protest songs, 399
    ranchera, 397, 457, 498, 510
    salve, 391–92
    secular, 394–401
    Tierra del Fuego, 69, 386, 406
  in Bolivia
    ipala, 428
    saya, 431, 434, 511
    takipayanaku, 428, 511
  in Brazil
    aboio, 358, 495
    brão, 328, 336
    canções praieiras, 363, 498
    Candomblé ritual songs, 354–55, 364
    cantoria, 336, 350, 495, 498
    ciranda, 357, 499
    décima, 361
    desafio, 361, 498
    dupla, 337, 346–47
    embolada, 336, 361, 500–01
    folia de reis, toadas of, 338
    ladainha, 357, 505
    lundu, 331–32, 361, 505
    moda, 336
    modinha, 272, 331–32 , 348, 351,
      361–62, 506
    pagode, 263, 508
    porfia, 336, 509
    samba–lenço, 341, 360
  in Chile
    nueva canción, 4, 11, 42, 72, 98, 158, 399,
      434, 458, 507
  in Cuba
    canción, 114–119,
    changüí, 114–15
    claves, 117
    criolla, 117, 119
    guajira, 117, 119–20
    nueva trova, 113, 158, 458, 507

punto guajiro (also *punto cubano*), 113–14,
    509
romance, 106
seguidilla, 114
son, 111–21
tonada, 114
  in Dominican Republic
    anthem, 156, 158–59, 162
    bachata, 160, 162
    balada, 160
    bolero, 157, 160
    criolla, 157
    desafío, 146–47
    mediatuna, 146, 149, 153
    merengue, 148, 152–55, 157–61
    plena, 146, 148
    romance, 146, 153, 162
    salve, 145–46, 148–50, 152–55, 162
    salve de pandero, 155
    Salve Regina, 145, 510
    sung rosary, 145–46, 149, 154
    tonada de toros, 146, 154, 513
    vals, 154, 157
    verso, 146, 154
  Garífuna (Garífuna) culture
    jungujugu de Chugu, 219–20
    lemesidi, 220, 505
    parranda (also *paranda*; *zarabanda*),
      219–20
    punta, 219–20
  in Guatemala, 228
    posada, 222, 509
  in Haiti
    priyè ginen, 131
    secular songs, 131–32
    Vodou songs, 130
  of Indian people
    bhajan, 93, 497
  in Kuna culture
    chanting, 251–52, 257–59
    lullabies, 249, 259–61, 263
  in Mapuche culture
    kantún, 412
    öl, 412–13
    purrum, 509
    tayil, 411–13, 416
  in Maya culture
    bix rxin nawal, 228, 497
    ritual songs, 226–28
  in Mexico
    balada, 205
    bambuco, 195, 202, 496
    canción ranchera, 201–02, 498
    canción romántica, 201–02, 205, 498
    chilena, 190, 193
    copla, 185, 189–92, 194–95, 198–99
    corrido, 4, 187, 195–96, 198–99, 208, 500
    gusto, 194
    son, 190
    son guerrerense (*son calentano*), 190, 194

son huasteco, 190–91
son istmeño (*son oaxaqueño*), 190, 192–93
son jalisciense, 190, 195
son jarocho, 190–91
son michoacano (*son calenteño*), 190, 194
valona, 190, 194, 514
  in Panama, 235, 244–45
    congos, 235, 244
    controversia, 244
    décima, 244
    gritos, 245
    saloma, 245
  in Paraguay
    alabanza, 376
    corito, 378
    gozo, 376
    guaránia, 379, 381–82, 503
    musiqueada, 381, 507
    purahéi asy, 377
    purahéi jahe'ó, 377
    villancico, 376
  in Peru
    amor fino, 479
    carnaval, 449
    coplas, 453, 500
    cumanana, 479
    décima, 479, 501
    harawi (also *haraui*), 440, 448–49, 503
    haylli, 440, 449
    huaylas, 449, 503
    huayno, 449, 451, 455, 458, 464, 467,
      471, 478, 490, 499, 503
    jarana, 483–84
    kashwa (also *cachua*), 440, 449
    marinera, 454
    marinera limeña, 483
    muliza, 449
    santiago, 449
    triste, 449, 479
    walina, 450, 514
    wanka (also *uanca*), 440
    yaraví, 449, 479
  in Puerto Rico
    décima, 168, 170, 498, 501
    rosario cantao, 168–69, 174
    seis, 170–72
  in Q'eros culture, 463–73
    choqewanka, 464
    Pukllay taki, 465
  in Selk'nam culture, 69, 386, 406
  in Taíno culture
    areito (*areyto*), 21, 30, 105, 127, 144,
      164, 496
  in Tarahumara culture
    matachín, 211
    tutuguri, 212–13
  in Venezuela
    aguinaldo, 299, 306, 495
    corrido, 308
    fulia, 298, 302